Subsistence Agriculture & Economic Development

Subsistence Agriculture & Economic Development

edited by

Clifton R. Wharton, Jr.

ALDINETRANSACTION
A Division of Transaction Publishers
New Brunswick (U.S.A.) and London (U.K.)

First paperback printing 2008
Copyright (C) 1969 by Transaction Publishers, New Brunswick, NJ

This book is printed on acid-free paper that meets the American National Standard for Permanence of Paper for Printed Library Materials.

Library of Congress Catalog Number: 2008002640
ISBN: 978-0-202-36225-0
Printed in the United States of America

Library of Congress Cataloging-in-Publication Data

Subsistence agriculture and economic development / [edited by]
    Clifton R. Wharton, Jr.
            p. cm.
    Reprint. Originally published in 1969.
    Includes bibliographical references and index.
    ISBN 978-0-202-36225-0 (alk. paper)
    1. Peasantry—Congresses. 2. Agriculture—Economic aspects—
Developing countries—Congresses. I. Wharton, Clifton R., 1926-
II. Conference on Subsistence and Peasant Economics (1965 :
University of Hawaii) III. Agricultural Development Council.
    IV. East-West Center. Institute of Advanced Projects.

HD1417.W47   2008
338.109172'4—dc22   2008002640

Preface

SUBSISTENCE FARMS cover some 40 per cent of the cultivated land of the world and support 50 to 60 per cent of mankind. Yet theories and facts about subsistence agriculture are meager. Policies and programs for the development of subsistence agriculture are even more scarce.

The reasons for this neglect in attention are not difficult to understand. Research concerning subsistence and peasant farmers is particularly difficult because their market participation is limited. In turn, action programs designed to stimulate development among subsistence farmers have frequently failed because of limited knowledge about them.

The degree of attention to subsistence agriculture among social scientists has been uneven among the relevant disciplines—perhaps greatest among the social and economic anthropologists and least among the economists and agricultural economists. One explanation for the relative dearth of attention by economists is that the science of economics and its techniques of analysis over the past several generations have been based upon market participation—buying and selling. For a long time it was generally true that economists considered as their province only that part of human behavior involving participation in the market, and even then under certain assumptions about the nature of man's behavior and his institutions—assumptions which some social scientists viewed as highly restrictive and ethnocentric. Economists

labeled as "noneconomic" and "given" or assumed a range of factors, motives, and cultural and institutional conditions which caused farm operators to engage in behavior different from that predicted by economic theory. The validity of these assumptions and even the empirical findings derived from analysis employing these assumptions have been subject to various attacks, especially in the case of peasant farmers and subsistence agriculture.

Many noneconomists and some economists have often pointed out that, at early stages of agricultural technology, much of production is for home consumption, much of production activity is done by family members, and the nature of human relationships affects the conduct of economic relationships. Under these conditions some have believed that considerations of the market do not always apply, and that this is one reason why farm operations in such agricultural societies do not always behave in the way that the principles or theories of economics would indicate. Others maintain that, even in cases of pure subsistence production, economic principles are valid and that so-called peasant farmers are both economically rational and economically efficient in production.

For many years the majority of the evidence which assessed the economic behavior of subsistence and semisubsistence farmers came from the anthropologists. European peasants fell to the lot of economic historians. Today's subsistence farmers in the developing regions of Asia, Africa, and Latin America were largely ignored by most social scientists, especially economists and agricultural economists.

In recent years this pattern has changed. Now a number of economists are beginning quite seriously to analyze the behavior of peasant farmers with respect to production and consumption and to assess the extent to which "economic" decisions of farmers are made on the basis of considerations which are market and nonmarket. Unfortunately a great deal of the recent work is being carried out in scattered locations around the world and is being published in journals, sometimes even in foreign languages.

Since so much of agriculture in the developing world is subsistence and semisubsistence, the Board of Trustees of the Agricultural Development Council decided that it would be appropriate to bring together and stimulate the work of those persons already interested in working on this topic. The Council trustees felt that it might be worthwhile to gather together such persons from the different disciplines to pool their thinking, exchange ideas, criticize each other's analyses, and stimulate more widespread study of this important topic.

The conference was held for a week, February 28 to March 6, 1965, at the Center for Cultural and Technical Interchange Between East and West (East–West Center), University of Hawaii. Finances for the conference were provided by the Agricultural Development Council and the Institute of Advanced Projects, East–West Center.

The conference became a major multidisciplinary confrontation of social scientists interested in and working on the problem of developing subsistence agriculture. Forty leading social scientists from eleven different countries participated—economists, agricultural economists, sociologists, rural sociologists, anthropologists, social psychologists, and political scientists.

The increasing interest of economists and agricultural economists in the problems of developing subsistence agriculture is to be welcomed, for the successful transition from subsistence to commercial agriculture requires considerably more knowledge. It is axiomatic that one of the major changes that must take place in the developing world as part of the

process of agricultural development is the increasing commercialization and modification of agricultural production. Farm operators must make more and more purchases of equipment and supplies to be used in the production process, and they must produce more and more crops for sale in the market. Yet before this process can take place, much greater understanding is required about subsistence agriculture and the peasant farmer —the focus of the effort.

The Editor regrets the length of time which has elapsed between the conference and the issuing of the book. Despite this lapse a majority of the papers still retain their currency and required only minor updating or the inclusion of a few new references. Therefore, the papers included in this volume represent the latest theoretical, historical, and empirical work in this rapidly burgeoning field. In a few cases additional chapters or supplementary material not presented at the conference but considered germane for rounding out the topic have been written and included.

Part I concentrates upon three topics— social structure of peasant societies, the institutional aspects of agrarian economies, and the motivational characteristics of subsistence farmers.

Part II presents the microeconomics of peasant production—the theoretical aspects, the policy implications of those theories, and selected empirical evidence of their economic behavior.

Part III is devoted to the theories of change and growth in subsistence agriculture and to the role of agriculture in economic development.

Part IV offers materials on how to modernize traditional agriculture and the execution of agricultural development—concentrating upon the theoretical and policy aspects and presenting four case studies of programs of planned change.

Part V consists of a "research agenda" which presents the major issues which arose in the conference and the priority areas where additional research is needed.

The chapter by Fisk and Shand is a compilation of their three articles which previously appeared in the Australian Economic Record. The two case studies by Professors Behrman and Bateman are original papers which were not presented at the Conference but which fit the format of the book and therefore merit inclusion. The chapter by Professor Nicholls is a reprint of his article which appeared in the *Journal of Political Economy*. Although Professor M. L. Dantwala and Dr. Selo Soemardjan were unable to attend the meeting, their papers have been included.

Throughout the volume every effort has been made to introduce a high degree of disciplinary cross-fertilization. The author of a major paper will usually represent a different discipline from his commentators, thereby adding further insight to the presentation as well as providing an alternate view of the same topic. In addition many chapters include a case study containing materials or empirical data designed to illuminate or to supplement the other presentations.

Thus, the book constitutes a multidisciplinary summary—theories, facts, and policies —on the problems of developing subsistence agriculture. The summary is, of course, not exhaustive, since not everything could be covered in such a short compass, but it is hoped that this selective compilation will provide the stimulus and basis for future research in this important field.

CLIFTON R. WHARTON, JR.

Contributors

Milton L. Barnett, Associate, Agricultural Development Council, Inc.

Merrill J. Bateman, Associate Professor of Economics, Brigham Young University, U.S.A.

Jere R. Behrman, Associate Professor of Economics, Wharton School of Finance and Commerce, University of Pennsylvania, U.S.A.

Gelia T. Castillo, Associate Professor of Rural Sociology, University of the Philippines, Philippines

V. M. Dandekar, Professor of Economics, Gokhale Institute of Politics and Economics, India

M. L. Dantwala, Professor of Economics, University of Bombay, India

Henry F. Dobyns, Chairman, Department of Anthropology, University of Kentucky, U.S.A.

Leonard W. Doob, Professor of Psychology, Yale University, U.S.A.

Carl K. Eicher, Associate Professor of Agricultural Economics, Michigan State University, U.S.A.; formerly Director, Economic Development Institute, University of Nigeria

Raymond W. Firth, Professor of Anthropology, London School of Economics and Political Science, United Kingdom

E. K. Fisk, Professorial Fellow, Research School of Pacific Studies, Australian National University, Australia

Nicholas Georgescu-Roegen, Harvie Branscomb Distinguished Professor, Department of Economics, Vanderbilt University, U.S.A.

Allan R. Holmberg, Late Professor of Anthropology, Cornell University, U.S.A.

Bruce F. Johnston, Professor and Economist, Food Research Institute, Stanford University, U.S.A.

William O. Jones, Professor and Director, Food Research Institute, Standford University, U.S.A.

Dale W. Jorgenson, Professor of Economics, University of California (Berkeley), U.S.A.

J. Leonard Joy, Professorial Fellow in Agricultural Development, Institute of Development Studies, University of Sussex; formerly Senior Lecturer in Economics, London School of Economics and Political Science, United Kingdom

Raj Krishna, Professor of Economics, University of Rajasthan; formerly Senior Research Fellow, Institute of Economic Growth, University of Delhi, India

John W. Mellor, Professor of Agricultural Economics, Cornell University, U.S.A.

Arthur T. Mosher, President, Agricultural Development Council, Inc., U.S.A.

Hla Myint, Professor of Economics, London School of Economics and Political Science; formerly Lecturer in Economics, Oxford University, United Kingdom

Delbert T. Myren, Head, Communications Department, International Maize and Wheat Improvement Center, Mexico

Chihiro Nakajima, Professor of Agricultural Economics, Kyoto University, Japan

William H. Nicholls, Professor of Economics and Director, Graduate Center for Latin American Studies, Vanderbilt University, U.S.A.

Jin Hwan Park, Professor of Agricultural Economics, Seoul National University, Korea

David H. Penny, Fellow, Research School of Pacific Studies, Australian National University, Australia; formerly, Agricultural Development Council, Inc., Visiting Professor, University of North Sumatra, Indonesia

David E. Pfanner, Program Associate, International Division, Ford Foundation, U.S.A.

Syed A. Rahim, Research Specialist, Pakistan Academy for Rural Development, Comilla, Pakistan

José Paulo Ribeiro, Director, Rural Credit Branch, Caixa Economica do Estado de Minas Gerais; formerly Executive Director, Associacao de Credito e Assistencia Rural, Minas Gerais, Brazil

Everett M. Rogers, Professor of Communication, Michigan State University, U.S.A.

Vernon W. Ruttan, Professor and Head of Department of Agricultural Economics, University of Minnesota, U.S.A.; formerly, Agricultural Economist, International Rice Research Institute, Philippines

Theodore W. Schultz, Professor of Economics, University of Chicago, U.S.A.

Richard T. Shand, Fellow, Research School of Pacific Studies, Australian National University, Australia

Selo Soemardjan, Professor of Economics, University of Indonesia, Indonesia

Anthony W. Tang, Professor of Economics, Vanderbilt University, U.S.A.

Daniel Thorner, Director of Studies, École des Hautes Etudes (Sorbonne), France

Abraham M. Weisblat, Associate, Agricultural Development Council, Inc., U.S.A.

Clifton R. Wharton, Jr., Vice President, Agricultural Development Council, Inc., U.S.A.

With an Introduction by John D. Rockefeller 3rd

Contents

Preface   v

Contributors   ix

INTRODUCTION

The Challenge of Population and Food, JOHN D. ROCKEFELLER 3RD   3

1. The Development Problems of Subsistence Farmers: A Preliminary Review, ARTHUR T. MOSHER   6

2. Subsistence Agriculture: Concepts and Scope, CLIFTON R. WHARTON, JR.   12

PART I   The Subsistence Farmer, Agrarian Cultures, and Peasant Societies

3. Social Structure and Peasant Economy: The Influence of Social Structure Upon Peasant Economies, RAYMOND FIRTH   23

    Comment: An Economist's View of Social Structure Interaction with the Subsistence Economy, ABRAHAM M. WEISBLAT   37

    Comment: The Influence of Social Structure on the Javanese Peasant Economy, SELO SOEMARDJAN   41

    Case Study: A Semisubsistence Village Economy in Lower Burma, DAVID E. PFANNER   47

4. The Institutional Aspects of Peasant Communities: An Analytical View, NICHOLAS GEORGESCU-ROEGEN   61

    Comment: Old and New Approaches to Peasant Economies, DANIEL THORNER   94

    Comment: The Peasant Economies of Today's Underdeveloped Areas, H. MYINT   99

    Case Study: New Evidence on Farmer Responses to Economic Opportunities from the Early Agrarian History of Western Europe, T. W. SCHULTZ   105

5. Motivations, Values, and Attitudes of Subsistence Farmers: Toward a Subculture of Peasantry, EVERETT M. ROGERS   111

Comment: A Critical View of a Subculture of Peasantry, GELIA
CASTILLO 136
Comment: Testing Theories Concerning a Subculture of Peasantry,
LEONARD W. DOOB 142
Case Study: Growth of "Economic Mindedness" Among Small
Farmers in North Sumatra, Indonesia, D. H. PENNY 152

PART II The Economic Behavior of Subsistence Farmers

6. Subsistence and Commercial Family Farms: Some Theoretical
   Models of Subjective Equilibrium, CHIHIRO NAKAJIMA 165
   Comment: Models of the Family Farm, RAJ KRISHNA 185
   Comment: On Subjective Equilibrium of the Subsistence Farmer,
   ANTHONY M. TANG 190
   Case Study: Effects of Increasing Commercialization on Resource
   Use in Semi-Subsistence Farms in South Korea, JIN H. PARK .. 196
7. The Subsistence Farmer in Traditional Economies, JOHN W. MELLOR ... 209
   Comment: The Subsistence Farmer in Traditional Economies,
   CARL K. EICHER 227
8. Supply Relationships in Peasant Agriculture: Editor's Introduction ... 229
   Case Study: Supply Response and the Modernization of Peasant
   Agriculture: A Study of Four Major Annual Crops in
   Thailand, JERE R. BEHRMAN 232
   Case Study: Supply Relations for Perennial Crops in the Less-
   Developed Areas, MERRILL J. BATEMAN 243

PART III Theories of Change and Growth

9. The Early Stages of Development in a Primitive Economy: The
   Evolution from Subsistence to Trade and Specialization,
   E. K. FISK and R. T. SHAND 257
   Comment: The Demand for Food, Leisure, and Economic Sur-
   pluses, WILLIAM O. JONES 275
   Case Study: Subsistence and Transition among the Ibaloi in the
   Philippines, MILTON L. BARNETT 284
10. Development in Agrarian Economies: The Role of Agricultural
    Surplus, Population Pressures, and Systems of Land Tenure,
    WILLIAM H. NICHOLLS 296
11. The Role of Agriculture in Economic Development: Classical
    versus Neoclassical Models of Growth, DALE W. JORGENSON 320
    Comment: Sectoral Interdependence, Structural Transformation,
    and Agricultural Growth, BRUCE F. JOHNSTON 348
    Comment: Two Sector Models and Development Policy, VERNON
    W. RUTTAN 353

PART IV Developing Subsistence Agriculture

12. Transforming Traditional Agriculture: Editor's Introduction 363
    Comment: Questions of Economic Analysis and the Consequences
    of Population Growth, V. M. DANDEKAR 366
    Comment: Diagnosis, Prediction, and Policy Formulation,
    J. LEONARD JOY 376
    Case Study: The Problems of a Subsistence Farm Economy: The
    Indian Case, M. L. DANTWALA 382

13. The Execution of Agricultural Development: Case Studies of
     Planned Change: Editor's Introduction   387
     Case Study: The Cornell Program in Vicos, Peru, ALLAN R.
     HOLMBERG and HENRY F. DOBYNS   392
     Case Study: The Comilla Program in East Pakistan, SYED A. RAHIM   415
     Case Study: The ACAR Program in Minas Gerais, Brazil, JOSÉ
     PAULO RIBEIRO and CLIFTON R. WHARTON, JR.   424
     Case Study: The Rockefeller Foundation Program in Corn and
     Wheat in Mexico, DELBERT T. MYREN   438

PART V   Research Priorities on Subsistence Agriculture

14. The Issues and a Research Agenda, CLIFTON R. WHARTON, JR.   455

     Index   469

Introduction

Introduction

The Challenge of Population
and Food[1]

JOHN D. ROCKEFELLER 3RD
Chairman, Board of Trustees
Agricultural Development Council, Inc.

YOU ARE GATHERED HERE, from several continents and many disciplines, to share and deepen your insights into the problems of increasing the output of subsistence farming. Both the difficulty and the importance of your task become evident when we realize that today more than half of humanity depends largely upon this type of agriculture; when we realize that large numbers of the people alive today will die before their time because of malnutrition.

In this conference you will analyze subsistence farming from several aspects: economic, sociological, cultural, motivational, and historical. Never before, I am told, has it had the concentrated attention of authorities from so many fields and from both East and West. I hope you share the excitement, the sense of opportunity, that I feel.

I should like to place the subject of this conference in perspective with the problem of world population growth.

My considered belief is that unchecked population growth is as critical as any problem facing mankind today. Until recently I believed the control of nuclear weapons to be even graver. However, we can hope that the use of these weapons can be prevented, but the world cannot hope to escape a tremendous increase in its population. The well-being of mankind depends upon both weapons control and population. Should we fail to restrain the use of nuclear weapons, our civilization is in danger of sudden and violent death. If we cannot control population growth, life as we know it or—more important perhaps—life as we want it to be, shall surely, slowly waste away. It becomes, therefore, a paramount task of our time that man work to stabilize population growth—and soon enough to escape the smothering consequences.

I am returning from a trip to Asia, one of a number in recent years. There I had the opportunity to observe, close at hand, the effects of unchecked population growth. My belief in its seriousness was confirmed as I saw again the terrible tolls that it exacts in both human and national terms.

1. Opening address given on February 28, 1965, to the Conference on Subsistence and Peasant Economics, Honolulu, Hawaii.

3

Somber though the outlook may be, I still find reason for hope. The work of population stabilization, after all, is very new. Recognition of the problem is steadily increasing where it was hardly mentioned—or even thought about—a generation ago. Now, more and more, concern is mounting and population is being discussed by public officials, religious leaders, and private citizens in many parts of the world.

Also there is emerging an improved technology for contraception, not only refinements of oral contraceptives, but the development of intrauterine devices which offer great promise for widespread use. We can hope that these tiny pieces of plastic may symbolize the beginning of the ultimate solution of the population problem.

At the same time key pilot projects in several countries are amassing new knowledge about how large populations can be effectively stabilized.

The immediate problem before us is to increase the food supply to meet rising population even while stabilization programs are being developed. The extent and urgency of this task are indicated by the Third World Food Survey of the F.A.O. which projected that, in just ten years, food supplies must increase by a full third merely to sustain the world's population at its present unsatisfactory level of diet.

There is no question that the clock of history is moving swiftly. Already a tragic and growing imbalance exists between the world's agricultural output and its population. Until population is stabilized, every increase in food production is an important holding action. In effect, we are "buying time" until the scales of survival can be brought into lasting balance.

How then can we best increase food production? I believe an important key to the answer is the subsistence farmer.

We define him, as you know, as the farmer who uses most of what he grows to meet the needs of his own family. He is found wherever land is arable, from the Amazon to Appalachia, from Southern Italy to India. He may grow rice in Southeast Asia or corn (maize) in the southeastern United States. He almost always works close to the edge of poverty, eking out a living as best he knows how, with implements that are often primitive. His number is beyond accurate count but would appear to be growing.

Since an estimated 40 per cent of the land under cultivation is subsistence rather than commercially farmed, an increase in the output of subsistence farms would have an important effect on the overall agriculture yield. And the unrealized potential of subsistence farming may be even greater than from commercial farming, which is already relatively efficient.

The stakes, therefore, are indeed high. Not only can we help improve the lot of the individual farmer and his immediate family, but we can add new resources to his community and nation with potentially far-reaching effects upon the total economic stability of the developing world. Therefore, the challenge of this conference, as I see it, involves not only the cold realities of economics, but also the warm humanitarian impulses we feel toward these millions of farmers whose labors gain them hardly more than survival.

Despite the importance of the subsistence farmer, little is known about him. I understand that there is substantial literature on the subject but that past work has suffered from a number of deficiencies, one of which is that there has been little coordination and exchange between disciplines. Anthropologists have studied the primitive tribes of Borneo and Congo while economists have tended to focus on the more commercialized farmers. It is fundamental to the concept of this conference that the subsistence farmer is not merely an economic man; he has a psychological side, a social side, and a cultural side. Too little is known of his motivations and human responses, of his sociocultural environment, and of his ability to change the age-old patterns of his life. We lack knowledge of his economic behavior and the full significance of how his sector of the national economy relates to the whole.

The list of questions that need answers is long. For example, how can a poor farmer, barely able to grow enough for his own survival, afford even the simplest investment in seed, insecticides, and machines that may produce a better crop? How can his struggling government afford to give him the subsidies, the technical assistance, the extension programs that it seems he must have? Then there are all the questions of individual motivation: How can he be induced to put aside centuries-old methods to experiment with the new and the foreign when he is experimenting, literally, with the food his family must have to survive? How can one persuade an individual, self-reliant by nature, to work in intelligent concert with others, who are sometimes total strangers?

Each of you, a specialist in his field, knows these questions well. In the next few days we hope you will become familiar with how your knowledge can contribute to the findings of other disciplines in seeking the answers.

The long-range objective of our conference is that the publication of its papers and the establishment of research priorities will serve to stimulate and guide action in this vitally important area.

I trust that you will take pride in what your work here may accomplish because each achievement of this conference will bring closer the day when all men will be free from hunger. Those now struggling just to stay alive will have at least a chance to achieve more than mere survival, to lead lives of satisfaction and purpose—in short, an opportunity to live as well as to survive.

I

The Development Problems of Subsistence Farmers:

A Preliminary Review

A. T. MOSHER

I HAVE ALWAYS HAD great admiration for Woodrow Wilson. Nevertheless, I would like to begin by quoting from a critical essay about him. There may be a useful lesson for us in some remarks made about President Wilson by Walter Weyl in his essay "Prophet and Politician."

This faith of Mr. Wilson in his Fourteen Points, unexplained and unelaborated, was due to the invincible abstractness of his mind. He seems to see the world in abstractions. To him railroad cars are not railroad cars but a gray, generalized thing called Transportation; people are not men and women, corporeal, gross, very *human* beings, but Humanity—Humanity very much in the abstract.

"Subsistence economics" is a combination of two abstractions. Most of the prepared papers we have in hand, from which to launch our discussion, carry assigned titles phrased largely in abstract nouns. These abstractions are useful, but the purpose of the Agricultural Development Council in calling this conference will not be achieved unless we can get behind them to the people whom they both represent and tend to conceal.

The Agricultural Development Council is concerned primarily about the economic and human problems of agricultural development in Asia. Most of the farmers of Asia among whom this agricultural development would have to take place are subsistence farmers. Their farming is carried on more to provide food for the family, or for the village community or tribe, than it is for sale to an outside market. If this situation continues, very little agricultural development can occur, and the levels of living of the people on these farms cannot rise. For agricultural development to take place, it is essential, among several other necessities, that farms become less and less subsistence and more and more commercial, producing increasingly for the market. In order that we or others can help that to happen, it is essential that we learn more about what motivates subsistence farmers at the present time and what new influences can be brought to bear to help them move toward greater commercialization of their farming.

Who, specifically, is it that we have in mind when we speak of the subsistence farmer?

He is the farmer just north of Lake Victoria in Uganda who has the use of all the land he may want to cultivate, whose staple food is bananas, who cultivates an area about twice the size that is necessary to feed his family in a year of favorable weather as protection against the occasional poor harvest. If the weather is good and the harvest plentiful, he leaves half of the crop to rot in the field because he has no market for it.

He is the elderly college professor in the Philippines who all of his life has grown rice on his home farm, utilizing hired labor, to meet his own family's needs for their staple food and to supply the families of his married children living in towns and cities, so that they need not be dependent for food on an uncertain market.

He is the farmer on the Ganges Plain of India who grows food primarily for his own family and to exchange in kind for the services of the village carpenter, potter, barber, and other artisans. He sells any surplus that may remain after these needs have been met for cash, to meet the costs of basic living necessities not produced in the locality, perhaps to pay rent, and hopefully to make a payment on his indebtedness.

He is the farmer in the northern part of the state of Minas Gerais in Brazil who operates a self-sufficient farm much like those of early Colonial America, growing his own food, cutting his own timber, making his own implements, building his own house, and selling each year a few pigs that have their own built-in transportation for the twenty-mile trip to the nearest market.

In New Guinea he is a member of an isolated tribe, cutting the trees and the brush from a few plots of land in order to cultivate a crop for a few years and then moving on to clear another site as the fertility of the plots he has been cultivating gradually diminishes.

Obviously subsistence farmers are not a homogeneous group. They differ widely in the amount and fertility of the land they have available. They differ as to the economic setting in which they live. What they have in common is that they think of their farming operations largely in terms of providing for family needs through their own production.

This is not to say that they do not think of costs and returns. But in addition to, or perhaps in some cases instead of, cash costs, they may have a different kind of costs in mind. To them, a "cost" may be arduous work, or leisure or ceremonial foregone, or the pain of appearing to be different in a community of static traditions, or the ridicule that the failure of a new technique would bring down upon them. The certainty of having rice, or wheat, or corn, when the family needs it is frequently a part of the "returns" that subsistence farmers take into account. One of the tasks of our conference will be to examine the nature of these "perceived" costs and returns for subsistence farmers.

If we classify as subsistence farmers those who sell for cash or barter less than 50 per cent of the production of their farms, no one really knows with precision just how many such farmers there are in the world. In 1936, Whittlesey estimated that subsistence farming, together with hunting and fishing, supported about 60 per cent of mankind, or 1.6 billion people [Whittlesey, 1936]. In 1948 the Woytinskys estimated that 55 per cent of mankind lived in economies in which subsistence farmers predominated [Woytinsky and Woytinsky, 1953, p. 419]. This would be 1.4 billion people. To that number would have been added subsistence farmers in economies where they are a minority of the total population. To this must also be added the effect of the rapid rate of population growth in recent years.

What is the problem with which we are trying to grapple? Simply stated it is this: How can subsistence farmers be encouraged and helped in making their farms less and less subsistence farms and more and more commercial?

This does not always involve making small farms larger.

Small subsistence farms vary all the way from those that sell practically nothing to those that sell almost 50 per cent of their products. A farmer can progress along this line, continuously selling more and more of his products as he increases the productivity of his farm. Many farmers in Japan and Taiwan have moved out of the subsistence category entirely and have become highly commercial without any appreciable increase in the size of their farms.

If additional arable land, not now in farms, is available, or if some farmers leave for employment in the towns, the farms of the remaining farmers can increase in size. However, there are many localities and even large regions where this cannot happen. A rapid rate of population growth and lack of industrialization will keep as many people as are now in agriculture on farms for a long time to come, and farms will remain small.

What can happen is that farms, large or small, can increase in productivity, becoming more and more commercial. It is this process of moving into greater productivity that we are to discuss in this conference.

Why are we concerned?

There are some among us who are concerned about this problem because of the plight of the hundreds of millions of people dependent on subsistence agriculture. They did not choose to be born where they were. They are not responsible for the resource endowment, or lack of it, of their countries. They did not create the existing population pressure, although they may be contributing to it. Some of them are reaching out for a better level of living than they now have. The rest of them are being squeezed into tighter and tighter corners by the more productive and more advantaged persons. They deserve a better break. They deserve to participate in any economic advance their societies may achieve.

There are others among us who say, "Not so fast. One does not wish greater productivity into existence. Resources are scarce. They must be applied where they will do the most good, and that is not in subsistence agriculture. Economic growth must come first and should be stimulated at the points at which it can come most easily. It may be regrettable, but it is true, that the greatest returns per dollar spent are achieved by expanding the opportunities of commercial farmers. Gradually the growth of the whole economy will raise the level of living of those who are now subsistence farmers more than will any attempt to help them directly."

True, economic growth is basic. Without it no amount of income redistribution, no sentimental concern for the underdog, can have much effect. Even agricultural development itself is dependent on the availability of industrial products such as fertilizers, implements, pesticides, and new sources of power.

But the converse is also true. The health of industries is dependent on a productive agriculture, partly to feed the cities and partly as a market for manufactured goods. The faster those now engaged in subsistence agriculture increase their productivity and move more and more into commercial operation of their farms, the greater the demand for industrial goods will be and the faster the total economy can grow.

So there are these two quite different bases of interest, one growing out of immediate concern for the welfare of the people involved, and the other emphasis on total economic growth and the optimum allocation of resources to that end.

Each approach has its value; each can serve the other.

The revolutionary days through which we are living certainly demonstrate that the human spirit cannot be wholly contained; second-class citizens don't stay put; the time lag between rising levels of living in one part of a society and those in another cannot be too long without an explosion.

Next, what are our tools for the work of the conference?

Most prominently they will be the tools of analysis of our several academic disciplines. They will be the tools of the economist, to probe man's activities in producing, exchanging, and consuming goods and services. They will be the tools of the anthropologist, to help uncover and explain the fabric of the total way of life of a particular group of people. They will be the tools of the sociologist, to reveal the ways in which special groups of people organize themselves and interact with other groups within the society.

At the same time, as we use these tools, we shall be reexamining their relevance to the problem before us. There may be some question as to how far different ones of the economist's tools of analysis are relevant to the problem of achieving those *changes* in the life of a people that first bring them into the market out of a largely self-sufficient mode of economic life. To the extent that anthropology seeks to encompass the whole life of a people and to stress the interdependence among all of its facets, there may be some lack of complete fit between its dominant preoccupations and the issues of what most wholesomely, or least disastrously, rends this fabric and introduces some of the disharmonies and conflicts that are an inevitable part of economic growth and progress. The tools of sociology may not be adequate to help us discover how new organized groups of people coalesce around new interests. And for all of us, schooled increasingly to expect and to honor statistical distributions of phenomena, how do we catch the important impact of deviant behavior at the end of a distribution in the direction of commercialization, or of innovation, or of invention?

I don't want to deprecate our tools. They are powerful instruments, and we can use many of them. But is it not true that each of them is like a powerful searchlight, gaining much of its focus by abstracting many features of the everyday workaday world of the complex human beings and societies we need to understand? And can we be sure that in the process of using such sharply focused searchlights we are not in danger of leaving unilluminated quite significant parts of that common life in between, or underneath, the aspects that our searchlights reach?

Our several tools of analysis may be too narrowly pertinent to a particular point and not sufficiently cognizant of the total humanity of the man—what we need may be something including, but beyond, what we normally call an "interdisciplinary approach." For it is not at all certain that, taken collectively, these formal tools of our several disciplines reveal the configuration of the whole problem. There may be interrelated aspects of what we need to understand for which the only integrator available to us is the human mind, as suffused by empathy and intuition as it is informed by insights from scientific observation.

It is for this reason that I hope that, while we use our conventional analytical tools for all they are worth, we not exaggerate their value and not shirk from tackling this problem in our capacity as the whole persons we are.

Finally, what can we hope to accomplish as a result of our conference? This is hard to predict.

I do hope we will have two questions in mind as we proceed. First, are the measures required to help subsistence farmers increase their productivity different in kind from those needed by commercial farmers, or is a difference in relative emphasis all that is required? Second, can we distinguish between those characteristics of subsistence farmers that are critical, from the standpoint of causality, to movement into greater productivity and more commercial operation of their farms, on the one hand, and those characteristics that are merely associated with subsistence agriculture or with movement out of it, on the other?

As for the first question, we know that there are five essentials for growth in agricultural productivity anywhere [Mosher, 1966].

One is transportation. Agriculture basically depends on utilizing solar energy, through the process of photosynthesis in the leaves of plants. It must always remain "spread out" to utilize sunlight where it falls. Unlike most other industries, agriculture cannot be concentrated near its ultimate customers or near existing transportation facilities; you can't just choose to locate all farms where there already are railway sidings. Transportation facilities of one kind or another must reach to each farm.

The second essential is markets for farm products and a marketing system to get them where they are wanted. Farmers must be able to sell to others, at home or abroad. To this end three things are necessary: someone, somewhere, who wants to use the farmer's product; a marketing system to get the product from the farmer to the consumer; and confidence of the farmer in this marketing system.

Third, agricultural development requires the discovery, or invention, or development, largely through formal research, of more efficient techniques for utilizing solar energy through the life processes of plants and of plant products through the life processes of livestock. This involves developing new fertilizers, evolving effective means of controlling pests and diseases, developing new implements and power sources to accomplish improved techniques of cultivation and husbandry, and putting each of these new techniques to the test of comparative costs and returns from the standpoint of the farm business as a whole.

Fourth, the farmer must have access to the supplies and equipment needed to put these new techniques into operation on his farm. These fertilizers, improved seeds, pesticides, and implements must be sound technically and priced so that they are profitable to use, dependable in quality, and available precisely when needed.

Finally, the farmer must have adequate incentives to cause him to adopt the new practice or practices. Foremost among these is remunerative price relationships—relationships between the prices he can count on getting for his products and the prices he must pay for the supplies and equipment he must buy and use in order to get the increased production. Another powerful incentive is the share of the harvest that the farm operator can himself retain. This is where the prevailing system of land ownership and terms of tenancy have an important effect. Still another is the size of the increment in production that a new technique, or group of techniques, can promise.

No matter whether agriculture is subsistence or commercial, there are several additional activities or services that can accelerate the process of development: general education, the training of agricultural technicians, and education of the urban elite (who influence governmental policies affecting agriculture) about the need and the requirements for agricultural development.

Another important accelerator is facilities for providing production credit to farmers—credit to purchase the additional inputs that could substantially increase agricultural production.

A third accelerator of agricultural development is voluntary farmer associations of various types: cooperative societies, 4-H clubs, farmers clubs, and community construction projects. These have two advantages. One is that they can get tasks accomplished which individual farmers, operating alone, cannot achieve. And by involving group discussion of new ideas and ad hoc organization around a specific interest, they can affect the local climate of public opinion within which the individual farmer must live and work. In addition, they can shift the social organization of the locality away from groups based largely on birth, or on the needs of a largely static society, toward groups and prestige based on developmental activities.

A question I hope we can keep in mind is: can we distinguish between those characteristics of subsistence farmers that are crucial, in a causative sense, to the move toward greater productivity and those that are associated with subsistence farming but not really critical, either positively or negatively, from the standpoint of economic growth?

We could spend an interesting week together sharing each other's insights about subsistence farmers and come out of the exercise each with a more comprehensive

catalog of factors *associated with* subsistence farming, but without making the distinction I am asking for here. I hope we shall not stop there but go on trying to determine which characteristics of subsistence farmers, or changes in which characteristics of, or influences on, them could make the critical difference in moving into more commercial farming.

It is also possible that among those factors that are *responsible* for change some can be influenced directly, while others may emerge indirectly or unobtrusively within a matrix we do not completely understand.

In Edward Arlington Robinson's poem, *Tristram,* her father says to Isolt of Brittany:

Wisdom was never learned at any knee,
Not even a father's.
Wisdom is like a dawn that comes up slowly
Out of an unknown ocean.

Some of the operative factors in moving farmers from subsistence to economic-mindedness may be like that. It may not be possible to influence them directly, nor may it be important to try to do so. They may emerge of themselves out of the flux that can be created by influencing other factors. It would be immensely helpful if we could distinguish among factors that need to be manipulated, those that are operative but derivative, and those that are merely resultant.

I think we may each reasonably expect to come out of this conference with a far better map of the world of subsistence agriculture, subsistence economics, subsistence behavior than we have had before. But let us also try to come out of it with some more effective operational tools for helping subsistence farmers move into greater productivity, into more commercially oriented production.

Subsistence farmers and their families, commercial farmers and theirs, are much more than cultivators. They are not a gray abstraction called Humanity; they are men and women with hopes and fears, capacities and creativity. What we can aspire to contribute to, through our efforts here, is the improvement of their opportunities, through greater agricultural productivity, to do some of the many, many different things they may choose to want to do. Let us hope that the outcome of the conference may be such that some of the millions of those who today are subsistence farmers around the world will sooner or later have reason to be glad.

References

MOSHER, 1966.   Arthur T. Mosher, *Getting Agriculture Moving* (New York: Praeger, 1966).

WHITTLESEY, 1936.   Derwent Whittlesey, "Major Agricultural Regions of the Earth," *Annals of the Association of American Geographers*, Vol. 26, No. 4 (December, 1936), 199–240.

WOYTINSKY and WOYTINSKY, 1953.   W. S. Woytinsky and E. S. Woytinsky, *World Population and Production* (New York: Twentieth Century Fund, 1953).

2

Subsistence Agriculture:
Concepts and Scope

CLIFTON R. WHARTON, Jr.

Some Basic Concepts

The problem of modernizing subsistence agriculture cuts across disciplinary boundaries. Only an integrated approach which recognizes and takes account of the major interrelationships among a wider range of variables than those traditionally the concern of a single discipline can provide an appropriate framework for studying the dynamics of change.

There are a number of approaches which might be employed to integrate the various social sciences [Easton, 1965, pp. 14–15]. In the present case, no attempt was made to accomplish a genuine integration of the disciplines, conceptually or theoretically; instead, the focus of the effort was to bring together relevant findings and insights from the different disciplines for a greater understanding of the problem of developing subsistence agriculture.

Despite the need for interdisciplinary approaches to development and the growing awareness of its importance, communication between disciplines is still fraught with pitfalls. Perhaps the greatest problems in any multidisciplinary confrontation of social scientists are those which revolve around concepts and tools of analysis. Conceptual schemes and

analytic methodologies tend to differ, since each discipline is as a rule restricted to a rather particular limited segment of human behavior. The experience of the conference was no exception.

On the whole, members of the conference showed a genuine appreciation of the value of such interdisciplinary exchanges and of the contribution which each discipline could make to the others. No monolithic synthesis or a fully generalized social sciences model was developed, but there was a recognition of the interaction of significant variables across disciplines and an approval of the search for greater awareness of such interactions.

Among the major conceptual difficulties which recurred throughout the meeting, the most frequent concerned the various notions of "subsistence" and different levels of analysis or aggregation. "Subsistence production" and "subsistence levels of living" provided less difficulty than "subsistence agriculture," "subsistence economy," and "subsistence farmer." Of all these concepts, the definition of "subsistence farmer" and/or "peasant" created the greatest recurring disagreements. The particular concepts selected for summarization in the sections which follow are those which seemed to create the greatest difficulty. They are presented here to alert the reader to the significant differences which underlie apparent but misleading terminological uniformities as one moves from author to author (and at times even within the same paper).

SUBSISTENCE PRODUCTION AND SUBSISTENCE LIVING[1]

The term "subsistence" has become ambiguous by its imprecise use. The confusion arises because the term is defined and used both to describe the minimum of food and shelter necessary to support life as well as the source or means of obtaining that minimum of the necessities of life. Thus, the dictionary definition of the term allows "subsistence" to be used to describe "subsistence production" or "subsistence living" or both. Though both "subsistence production" and "subsistence living" frequently coincide, they are not necessarily synonymous. Rather than use the term "subsistence" loosely, one should specify in each case whether one is referring to "subsistence production" or to a "subsistence level of living."

Pure "subsistence production" refers to a self-contained and self-sufficient unit where all production is consumed and none is sold and where no consumer or producer goods and services from sources external to the unit are purchased. Pure subsistence production is characterized by the total absence of commercialization and monetization. The interesting feature of a pure subsistence unit is the close relationship between farm and home or production and consumption; they are inherently a unified process.

Admittedly, the farmer characterized by pure subsistence production is rarely found in the real world. The more common cases are farmers whose average production may be characterized by various degrees of subsistence or various degrees of commercialization. What is involved is a continuum or spectrum from pure subsistence at one extreme to pure commercialization at the other (Fig. 2.1). The term "subsistence and semisubsistence" can be used to describe situations falling to the left of the 50 per cent

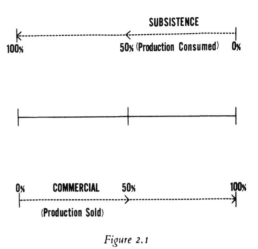

Figure 2.1

midpoint, and situations falling to the right of the midpoint can be classified as "semicommercial and commercial." Thus, "subsistence production" can be used to describe a situation where the fruits of an individual or group productive effort are directed more toward meeting immediate consumption needs out of production, without any or few intermediaries or exchange (barter or monetary). It must be emphasized, however, that focusing upon the percentage of total production sold or consumed describes only one characteristic of any farm, a point which will be amplified below.

The term "subsistence" has also come to be associated with low levels of living. But "subsistence living" must be distinguished from "subsistence production," even though the two often go together. While it is true that subsistence production usually results in levels of living which are best described as abysmal poverty by most standards, it is possible, though rare, to find cases where the associated level of living is reasonably adequate.

One difficulty with notions of subsistence living is determining what is in fact the absolute minimum level or the content of such a minimum. As Zweig [1948, p. 46] points out, "It is easier to speak of poverty than to define it."[2] Malthus and Ricardo recognized this problem in determining the

---

1. This presentation draws mainly from Wharton [1963].

2. Zweig uses three standards to measure poverty: personal or individual standards, social standards, and scientific standards.

"standard of life" line for their population analysis. What is the absolute minimum for human survival? One answer is the medical-nutritional one similar to Zweig's scientific standard of poverty. In this case the subsistence minimum is that below which incidence of nutritional deficiency diseases becomes higher than some arbitrarily stipulated level—such as the occurrence of hunger edema. Or the minimum could be that below which physical exertion is reduced (again below some arbitrary standard) or below which physical deterioration takes place. Nutritionists can stipulate minimum levels of dietary intake taking into account differences in height, weight, temperature, physical activity, and the like. But having stipulated the minimum level of various nutritional constituents, we are still faced with the need to take account of man's taste and socialized preferences. A minimum nutritional diet for least cost can easily be prepared, as shown by Stigler [1945].[3] But subsistence or minimum cost diets invariably have a subjective element, and Stigler's article helped to emphasize the arbitrary and subjective elements in any minimum food standard. Standards as to minimum subsistence, poverty lines, and so forth, are bound to be relative and arbitrary and reflect prevailing social and economic values.[4]

THE SUBSISTENCE FARMER

The cultivation of agriculture throughout the world varies not only as to the crops grown and basic ecologic settings, but also as to the individuals or groups of individuals who direct the process. When one focuses upon the farmer as the central decision-maker, the agent which intervenes in the original

rhythm of nature, one finds an extremely heterogeneous group. The group as a whole may be described as "agricultural cultivators," but the term would then embrace primitive tribes in the innermost recesses of the Amazon as well as the modern, commercial corn farmers of Iowa.

Several distinctive labels are employed by each discipline to characterize different types of agricultural cultivators. As would be expected, there are differences in the specification of these labels between disciplines and within disciplines. The critical difficulties lie in determining the variables or criteria which may be used to delineate each type and, for those criteria which involve discrete variation, in specifying the degrees or cutoff points which will separate the types.

The definition of "primitive cultivators" usually involves the least difficulty and disagreement. Among the general class of "primitives" two groups are distinguished: (a) those who rely wholly upon hunting, fishing, and gathering of fruits, nuts, and roots for their subsistence and who do not engage in acts of cultivation of plants or domestication of animals for food; and (b) those who usually engage in some "swidden" or "slash and burn" or "shifting" agriculture to provide their subsistence. Thus one has "primitive hunters or gatherers" and "primitive cultivators."

The definitional problems begin when one moves to the sedentary agriculturists. Two terms are commonly used to describe the next group of agricultural cultivators—"subsistence farmers" and "peasants."[5] For the sake of convenience, we will use the two terms interchangeably in the discussion which follows, though it must be emphasized that the term "peasant" tends to have specialized meanings in each discipline.[6]

The most common starting point for a definition of a "subsistence farmer" or "peasant" is that the farm family's goal of production is for family food rather than for commercial sale. There is a direct and close interrelationship between production and consumption. The goal of productive activity

---

3. Stigler's food budget in 1944 was US $60 for an entire year; the diet, however, consisted of 53 lbs. of wheat; 107 lbs. of cabbage; 13 lbs. of spinach; 134 lbs. of pancake flour; and 25 lbs. of pork liver. The diet was nutritionally balanced, but no one would willingly follow such a monstrously dull diet.

4. Rowntree made a famous study of poverty in York, England, at the turn of the century. Using certain absolute levels of diet, housing, and the like, he found that one-third of the inhabitants were below standard. When the study was redone in 1935 and again in 1950 using the same 1899 absolute standards, "poverty" was practically nonexistent [Rowntree, 1901, 1941, 1951]. For a more recent model explaining how minimum standards of subsistence living are determined at any point in time and how they change through time for subsistence producers, see Wharton [1963].

5. The term "peasant" has a pejorative connotation among certain national groups but is used extensively in the literature, especially by anthropologists, without any deprecatory meaning.

6. For sociology, see Sanders [1945] and for anthropology, see Wolf [1966] and Nash [1966].

in cultivation is family survival. Such farmers are therefore "subsistence producers" working for a "subsistence living."

Such a definition, however, is inadequate because it concentrates merely upon one facet or characteristic of the peasant or subsistence farm family. Any definition of a subsistence farmer which is based upon the predominance of meeting family needs through their own farm production includes a heterogeneous group of agriculturists whose ecologic, social, political, cultural, and economic settings were quite varied. Some farmers who would be classed as "commercial" because they sell 99 per cent of what they produce may still secure a sizable fraction of their food from "own farm production" or "farm family privileges." Farmers who produce inedible crops, such as cotton, oil palm, rubber, or jute, may still use a portion of their land to produce all the foodstuffs required for home consumption. At the other extreme, one finds farmers who consume all that they produce and sell nothing and are virtually indistinguishable from the "primitive cultivators" engaged in shifting agriculture. How to distinguish among such agriculturists is extremely difficult.

Throughout the conference several criteria were advanced to distinguish "subsistence farmers" and "peasants" or to develop subclasses. Some of these definitions will be found in the chapters and comments which follow. However, it may prove useful to set out some of the major criteria which were advocated in a somewhat systematic fashion, so that the reader may be alerted to the differences.

One of the interesting features of the criteria which are preferred by the various disciplines is the preponderance of those which reflect the *degree of integration* of the subsistence farmer or peasant family with the wider outside world. Many of the criteria seek to measure the extent of interaction and interdependence of the subsistence farm family with nearby villagers and distant cities. Such externalities are seen as an important index of exposure to and acceptance of the modernizing influences associated with economic development.

With each measure of external involvement, the *nature* of the involvement is often fully as important as the *degree* of involvement. The freedom with which the peasant producer can seek out marketing outlets in search of a higher price is fully as important as the percentage of crop sold. The extent to which societal or cultural forces dictate when certain steps in the production process are to be taken is just as significant as the percentage of hired labor used. Thus, many of the measures selected must be seen, not only from the standpoint of the integration of the peasant farmer into the larger economic, social, and cultural networks, but also from the standpoint of the nature of this integration.

Economic Criteria

The Sale of Farm Products Ratio. This criterion employs the production/consumption or commercial/subsistence spectrum described above. According to this criterion, the subsistence farmer is best described as one who consumes a majority of his production. The ratio of production sold to total production can be used to determine his degree of subsistence orientation. This fact makes him a "dual" farmer, one whose decisions simultaneously must take account of both farm and home considerations. Consumption and production decisions are intertwined, and the degree of dependence upon own farm production makes consumption/survival considerations overrule or dominate the commercial ones thereby affecting decision-making and economic behavior.

Hired Labor or Purchased Factor Inputs Ratio. Another criterion suggested was the ratio of hired labor to total labor used in production and the ratio of purchased factor inputs to all inputs used in production. Both of these were considered to be useful indexes of farmer involvement and integration into the wider economy, since modernization of the agricultural process necessarily requires increased purchase of factor inputs produced outside the farm. In the same fashion that the sale/consumption ratio measures his degree of involvement in the wider economy on the consumption side, the labor or factor input ratio would be a measure of his involvement on the production side. There was some feeling that the increases in the consumption ratios would lag behind the production ratios, i.e. as modernization proceeds, the fraction of total product sold on the market would be likely to increase faster, in the early stages, than the fraction of inputs bought.

Level of Technology. The level of technology employed was also suggested as a useful criterion for distinguishing subsistence farmers, the implication being that they use less productive or simpler techniques. Sometimes this technological variable was seen as reflected in the farm implements employed for specific tasks, viz. digging stick, hoe, plow, tractor; at other times in the farm practices used. Related to this, of course, are the various relative measures of productivity.

Income and Levels of Living. Some persons felt that the basic group to be discussed invariably constituted the low-income end of any distribution of farm people within any political unit, and that its universal characteristic was poverty. According to this criterion, peasant or subsistence farmers are cultivators who are poor. But to employ such a criterion requires the determination of some absolute minimum-income standard or a minimum level of living, whose content is admittedly difficult to specify either in absolute or in relative terms.

Decision-Making Freedom. Some felt that an important distinguishing characteristic of subsistence or peasant farmers was the lesser or narrower limits on decision-making. The subsistence farmer was seen as one who had a more limited number of choices; his degrees of freedom both on the farm and in the home were severely restricted. For some, the important restraints upon freedom of choice were of an economic institutional nature, such as serfdom or tenancy imposed by the agrarian structure. For others, the limits were seen as those imposed by the limited number of alternative opportunities faced by the farmer and his family.

Sociocultural Criteria

Noneconomic Factors in Decision-Making. According to this criterion, the most distinctive feature of subsistence or peasant farmers is the strong influence, if not dominance, of sociocultural considerations in the process of production and labor use and in the distribution or exchange of agricultural output. For example, the particular crops chosen may reflect the need to meet certain anticipated kinship obligations, and the subsequent distribution of the product is made along societally or culturally determined lines rather than on purely economic ones. The whole economic decision-making and action complex is thus affected significantly by noneconomic forces. Such forces include more than just cultural and social obligations; they include institutional factors as well.

Degree of "Outside" Contact. Sociologists employ several measures to assess the degree of external contact which farmers have beyond the boundaries of the farm or of the immediate village. These measures, both spatial and mental, have been found useful in measuring receptivity to new ideas and in predicting the rate of adoption of new practices. According to this criterion, those farmers with less external contact or who have a high "localite" focus constitute the peasant or subsistence farmers.

Nature of Interpersonal Relations. Another suggested distinction concerns the extent to which economic behavior is affected by the strength of interpersonal relations, with peasants or subsistence farmers having stronger interpersonal relations than modern or commercial farmers. This criterion also tends to distinguish those persons who preferred "familism" from those who are more individualistic in outlook and to correspond to Hoselitz' [1960, Ch. 2, 3] contrasts of achievement vs. ascription, particularism vs. universalism, and diffuseness vs. specificity.

Psychological Differences. A few participants felt that peasants had distinctive psychological characteristics which affected their goals and goal-implementing actions. The entire motivational and attitudinal complex was seen as primary in its effect upon economic decisions and behavior. The choice of concepts and measures ranged from McClelland's [1961] "achievement motivation" to Penny's "subsistence-mindedness" (see case study in Chapter 5 below).

Developmental Criteria

Some pointed out that the most universal characteristic of subsistence or peasant farmers is their unchanging adherence to established patterns of production. Although most peasant farmers have experienced and are experiencing *some* change, the rate of change is very slow or almost imperceptible. Thus, the dynamic/static distinction is an appropriate one. Again, it is not an either/or dichotomy, but one where relative degrees of variation are found. Among the measures of change which might be used with respect to this criterion, the most frequent suggestions were changes in output and various single-factor and multiple-factor productivity measures.

In summation, the application of particular criteria were rarely seen in purist or either/or terms. Where the criterion involves discrete variation along a spectrum, the critical issue is in determining the cutoff point. Most participants felt that several criteria were not mutually exclusive. In fact, the most interesting aspect of the exercise was the similarity of conclusions regardless of the criteria employed. No matter which criterion is used, there is a strong tendency to end up with the same basic set of cultivators as would be selected by any of the other criteria. As a rule, the application of these criteria, singly or all together, tended to describe the same universe.

SUBSISTENCE ECONOMIES AND SUBSISTENCE AGRICULTURE

An economy may be defined as the total of all economic organizations and economic activities that are carried out within a specified spatial area or political unit.[7] The economy is one part of the institutional framework of society concerned with the material wants of man, both goods and services. Most economies tend to be thought of in terms of large political units, such as nations or states. However, such groupings of economic units and activities along politically determined spatial lines are unsatisfactory for certain conceptual

and analytical purposes. Not only are the political and geographic boundaries arbitrary, but the characteristics of the economic units contained within an administrative division are frequently nonhomogeneous. (The specification of what constitutes an "economic" organization and activity is an equally important problem, especially in subsistence agriculture; but we will not attempt to explore this difficulty at this point.)

Moreover, the categorization of economic activity is just as important as the level of aggregation or the extent of the spatial/political unit being considered. For example, a "rural economy" does not embrace the same set of economic units and economic functions as an "agricultural economy." Similarly, a "national economy" does not necessarily embrace the same set of economic units and economic functions as a *particular* "state economy."

Thus, when discussing sectoral breakdowns of a national economy for the purposes of viewing agriculture, three dichotomous categories are commonly employed: (a) rural/urban; (b) agriculture/nonagriculture; and (c) subsistence/commercial (or monetized/nonmonetized).[8]

The application of each criterion results in a distinct grouping of individual economic units and economic activities. The rural/urban split is one which strictly relies upon a location/spatial delineation involving a population/areal measure; the density of population within the delineated area is the crucial element in the classification. The agriculture/nonagriculture division relies upon the basic difference in the nature of the production process; agriculture involves a deliberate manipulation of biologic processes, as on farms, whereas nonagriculture involves mechanical or chemical transformation of materials in shops or factories, or the largely "nonmaterial" provision of "services."[9]

---

7. Wagner defines an economy as: "a particular social unit bound together by explicit or implicit rules for making decisions, and prevailing over a definite territory" [1960, p. 52].

8. For a good summary of geographic taxonomies, see Henshall [1967]. Nash [1966] devotes a good deal of his book to disentangling these issues from the standpoint of economic anthropology. The problem of classification has been further compounded by attempts to develop historical schema reflecting some "natural" evolutionary trend in the development pattern of economic systems. (See Thorner [1962].)

9. The classification "agriculture" is narrower than the "primary" sector, usually employed in the primary, secondary, tertiary classifications [Kuznets, 1957, p. 5].

Neither of the first two sectoral delineations are entirely satisfactory for our purposes. For example, within any rural area or agricultural sector one can find pure subsistence farmers, commercial farmers, and all the "in-betweens." In the United States one can find commercial farmers in New Jersey, and yet, not too many miles away in the Appalachian hills, there are almost pure subsistence farmers. In Filipino agriculture one can find highly commercial sugar-cane or coconut plantations, while nearby there are rice producers who sell only when they have a surplus. Thus, whether one uses a demographic density/spatial unit or an industry classification, one finds included an amalgam of farming types. "Subsistence agriculture" and "subsistence economy" can be physically coexistent and contiguous with commercial agriculture and a modernized or monetized economy within the same geographic/political location. In fact, there are situations where there is some degree, even though minor, of interaction between elements of the two; flows of product or service move between elements of the subsistence economy and elements of the commercial economy. Hence, these two criteria or rural/urban and agriculture/nonagriculture do not segregate the particular group which is the subject of our inquiry.

The third breakdown of "subsistence/commercial" is perhaps the most meaningful and useful one for our purposes, especially if we ascribe these terms to agriculture and/or a part of the economy.[10] Thus, "subsistence agriculture" becomes that part of the agricultural sector made up of those farms and farm families characterized as subsistence on the basis of any or all the criteria advanced above. Similarly, the "subsistence agricultural economy" becomes the economic activities carried out by these individuals in the production, consumption, distribution, and exchange of goods and services for the satisfaction of human wants.

Much conceptual confusion has resulted from a failure to clarify the use of these terms, especially when applied to larger collectivities. The result has often been disputes over whether the political entity of

"Urugana" is or is not a "subsistence economy." In most cases the classification of the larger political entity or economic system as being *predominantly* "subsistence" requires the selection of a criterion to determine the *degree* of predominance and the selection of an arbitrary level to segregate types.

Having gone through this exercise in conceptualization and taxonomy, a few concluding remarks are in order. As explained above, the term "subsistence farmer" or "peasant farmer" was generally seen to delineate virtually the same universe of farmers regardless of the criterion employed. Much of the dispute as to criterion is in reality a dispute, not as to the individuals who would be embraced by the criterion, but rather the particular characteristics which the analyst or researcher would like to emphasize. The "label" which he applies and the content which he gives to the term is thus largely a reflection of his analytical predisposition or biases.

By the same token, the use of the terms "subsistence agriculture" and "subsistence economy" have been described above as being primarily a reflection of the previous choices in delineating "subsistence farmers." Hence, "subsistence agriculture" is essentially the kind of industry in which subsistence farmers are engaged, while the "subsistence agricultural economy" is the activities which they carry out through societally determined patterns of economic organization.

It must be emphasized that none of these definitions or concepts will be found adhered to uniformly in the papers below. In fact, the reader should be alert to determine for himself in each case exactly how the particular writer is using these terms.

The Scope and Magnitude of the Problem

Various estimates of the number of subsistence farmers in the world have been attempted. None of them is completely satisfactory. Some thirty years ago Whittlesey [1936] estimated that subsistence farming, hunting, and fishing involved about 60 per cent of mankind. This meant that 1.6 billion persons were dependent upon a subsistence agriculture.

Using a "subsistence economy" approach

10. This division is somewhat similar to Wagner's [1960] who uses a "subsistence economy" and "exchange economy" (both "closed" and "open").

(those economies where subsistence farmers predominate), Woytinsky and Woytinsky [1953, p. 419] estimated that in 1948 about 55 per cent of mankind (about 1.4 billion persons) was involved in a subsistence economy.

I have not found any more recent attempts to estimate the number of subsistence farmers or persons dependent upon subsistence production on a world basis, but I doubt if there has been very much reduction in the number of persons involved. In fact, there are logical reasons why one might expect there to have been a net increase in the percentage of the world's population involved in subsistence agriculture in the twenty years from 1948 to 1968: the population growth rate in the very largest political entities in the world (China, India, Pakistan, Indonesia) has far exceeded the ability of those countries to absorb the increasing population in nonagricultural occupations. Hence, one would logically expect an even larger number of persons being forced to gain a livelihood from subsistence agricultural pursuits.

How important is the persistence of subsistence farming in the world, and on what basis is that importance to be gauged? First, one can obviously use the humanitarian index of number of human beings: what percentage of all people in the world are engaged in or dependent upon subsistence agriculture? (Or, what percentage of all farmers are subsistence farmers?) There is little question that, measured in these terms, the problem is overwhelming. At least one-half of humanity is engaged in or dependent upon subsistence agriculture.[11]

Alternatively, one could determine importance in terms of the role of subsistence farmers in the agricultural productive process: what fraction of all agricultural output is produced by subsistence farmers? (Or what fraction of the marketed agricultural output is produced by such farmers?) I do not know of any attempts to estimate such a fraction, but my guess is that the output of such farms is less than the percentage which such farmers are of all farmers, i.e. if 60 per cent of all farmers are subsistence producers, then I would guess that they account for less than

40 per cent of all agricultural output. If we limited the percentage calculation to agricultural production which is marketed, the percentage would be even lower, perhaps around 20 per cent. (Woytinsky and Woytinsky did attempt to estimate how much of the world's income is generated in the subsistence-economy area in 1948 and arrived at a figure of 15 per cent of the world's income of $549 billion [Woytinsky and Woytinsky, 1953, p. 420].)

A third index of importance would be the command which such subsistence farmers have over agricultural resources: viz., what fraction of total cultivated land is controlled by subsistence farmers? Again I do not know of any recent estimates. My guess is that here the percentages would be the same as for the second alternative concerning amount of farm products produced.

One can readily appreciate that as a human problem the subsistence farmer and subsistence agriculture is without peer. Yet at first one can think that it does not constitute a positive opportunity for development or even a desirable avenue for development, given the insignificant resources involved and the limited role currently performed in production. However, as the following papers reveal, there are significant, unexploited developmental opportunities, and the subsistence farmer constitutes a major beneficiary from *and* contributor to the process of agricultural development.

References

CLARK and HASWELL, 1964. Colin Clark and M. R. Haswell, *The Economics of Subsistence Agriculture* (London: Macmillan, 1964).

EASTON, 1965. David Easton, *A Framework for Political Analysis* (Englewood Cliffs, N.J.: Prentice-Hall, 1965).

HENSHALL, 1967. Janet D. Henshall, "Models of Agricultural Activity," in *Models in Geography*, Richard J. Chorely and Peter Haggett, eds. (London: Methuen, 1967).

HOSELITZ, 1960. B. F. Hoselitz, *Sociological Aspects of Economic Growth* (Glencoe, Ill.: Free Press, 1960).

KUZNETS, 1957. Simon F. Kuznets, *Quantitative Aspects of the Economic Growth of Nations*, "II. Industrial Distribution of National Product and Labor Force," in *Economic Development and*

---

11. For another view of the problem with considerable emphasis on the nutritional element, see Clark and Haswell [1964, esp. Ch. 1].

Cultural Change, supplement to Vol. V, No. 4 (July 1957).

McClelland, 1961. David C. McClelland, *The Achieving Society* (Princeton, N.J.: Van Nostrand, 1961).

Nash, 1966. Manning Nash, *Primitive and Peasant Economic Systems* (San Francisco: Chandler, 1966).

Rowntree, 1901. B. Seebohm Rowntree, *Poverty, A Study of Town Life* (London: Macmillan, 1901).

Rowntree, 1941. B. Seebohm Rowntree, *Poverty and Progress* (London: Longmans, 1941).

Rowntree, 1951. B. Seebohm Rowntree, *Poverty and the Welfare State* (London: Longmans, 1951).

Sanders, 1945. Irwin T. Sanders, "Characteristics of Peasant Societies," in *Farmers of the World*, Edmund de S. Brunner *et al.*, eds. (New York: Columbia University Press, 1945).

Simon, 1957. Herbert A. Simon, *Models of Man: Social and Rational* (New York: Wiley, 1957).

Stigler, 1945. George J. Stigler, "The Cost of Subsistence," *Journal of Farm Economics*, Vol. 27, No. 2 (May 1945), 303–14.

Thorner, 1962. D. Thorner, "Peasant Economy as a Category in Economic History," Paper at Second International Economic History Conference, August 29–September 4, 1962. Reprinted in *Economic Weekly* (Bombay), Special Number (July 1963).

Wagner, 1960. Philip L. Wagner, "On Classifying Economies," in Norton Ginsburg, ed., *Essays on Geography and Economic Development* (Chicago: Department of Geography, Research Paper No. 62, University of Chicago, 1960).

Wharton, 1963. Clifton R. Wharton, Jr., "The Economic Meaning of 'Subsistence,'" *Malayan Economic Review*, Vol. 8, No. 2 (October 1963), 46–58.

Whittlesey, 1936. Derwent Whittlesey, "Major Agricultural Regions of the Earth," *Annals of the Association of American Geographers*, Vol. 26, No. 4 (December 1936), 199–240.

Wolf, 1966. Eric R. Wolf, *Peasants* (Englewood Cliffs, N.J.: Prentice-Hall, 1966).

Woytinsky and Woytinsky, 1953. W. S. Woytinsky and E. S. Woytinsky, *World Population and Production* (New York: Twentieth Century Fund, 1953).

Zweig, 1948. Ferdynand Zweig, *Life, Labour and Poverty* (London: Gollancz, 1948).

I

The Subsistence Farmer, Agrarian Cultures, and Peasant Societies

CHAPTER

3

Social Structure and Peasant Economy:
The Influence of Social Structure
Upon Peasant Economies[1]

RAYMOND FIRTH

THE ASSIGNMENT of this paper raises some basic questions of cooperation between social anthropologists and economists. What do economists know of the work of anthropologists in the study of peasant economics, and what do they think they really need from anthropologists? In making a model of a subsistence farm economy, an economist needs no anthropological help in drawing his inferences. Whereas formerly economists were not much interested in peasant societies, nowadays both economists and anthropologists share much experience of Asian, African, and Latin American cultures, and it is therefore hard for an anthropologist to see exactly where he can contribute something that his economist colleague does not already know. Moreover, anthropologists themselves have their own major task—the construction of a comparative theory of society, partly for general interest and partly as a help to understand how our own societies work. So it is not easy to detach anthropologists to act as

handmaids to economists—who are not always certain they want anthropologists anyway. Yet there are many anthropologists, of whom I am one, who think that there is a job of anthropological collaboration to be done, as in describing the institutional matrix of economic decision-making and in estimating the relative strength of incentive factors.

How does such a view mesh with an economist's approach? One significant question for development of a peasant economy is the weight to be put on stimulating aspiration as against economic opportunity. With some other anthropologists, I am definitely on the side of those who think that lack of opportunity rather than failure of aspiration is a major retarding influence. I have seen how the provision of an assured market for produce or for labor can promote development of the economy. This means, of course, not simply the provision of better communication and transport facilities, but also of a regular demand for the commodity or service which the peasant economy can supply. Aspirations may need to be encouraged, as when the peasant thinks that certain benefits—e.g. of

1. I am much indebted to Professor Alice Dewey and to J. L. Joy for most helpful critical comment on an earlier draft of this paper, and to Dr. Abraham M. Weisblat and other colleagues at Honolulu for very useful further discussion.

modern education—are beyond his grasp. But very often it is not so much a problem of stimulating aspirations as of the choices involved between competing aspirations. Nowadays a Malay adolescent and his parents may not need to be shown that literacy is a valuable asset and leads to a good job; they may have to make the painful choice between the boy's immediate earnings as a farmer or a fisherman and the delay in income due to his pursuit of further education. To an anthropologist, "aspirations" have to be interpreted both in personal and in institutional terms, and the issues are often complex. They involve a rational choice between alternatives offering different kinds of satisfactions, and these satisfactions may embody social as well as economic factors in the more limited sense. These social factors may not be hindrances, "frictions" in the old-fashioned terminology; they often supply important incentives, as when the desire for improved social status leads to economic initiative and competitive production. I am not implying that all economic opportunities are utilized. Institutional factors may often be significant in impeding use of a resource. Malays, as good Muslims, do not rear pigs, though if they followed the example of the Chinese farmers who live in the same environment, they could blend the extraction of tapioca flour and the feeding of the waste to pigs with great advantage. Understanding, not only of the nature, but also of the strength of such institutional or ideological elements is essential if economic development policy is to be realistic.

An area where anthropologists can be of assistance to economists working in the peasant field is in helping to translate the results of model analysis into real-life situations. A model is a heuristic instrument; it is designed for analytical purposes, in order to try to discover significant relationships between variables. To complain that a model of, say, a subsistence farmer's decisions does not portray actual conditions is to misunderstand the aim of model construction. But where the results of analysis of the model are to be applied to actual economic conditions in a peasant community, the abstract assumptions of the model must be given empirical content. A convenient assumption for model-building purposes may be that a household labor force is internally homogeneous, and of the same quality also as labor which can be hired from outside. An anthropologist may be able to demonstrate that this assumption is incorrect in practice and may point out significant differences between input in respect of kin and nonkin labor. It may be convenient also in setting up a model to assume that household assets are under unified control. But in practice, when questions of security, convertibility, or other use of assets are concerned, it may be necessary to distinguish different kinds of assets—those brought by husband into the marriage, those brought by wife, and those jointly acquired during the tenure of the marriage. In such contexts, a social anthropologist may be able to demonstrate the validity of his analysis in relation to the understanding of how a peasant economic system operates and changes.

The title of this paper sets some problems of definition. For the purpose of our discussions, peasants have been initially defined as farmers who sell or exchange only a minor part of their total farm production or, if they sell a major part, still do so at a level which leaves them in the lowest income group of the farmers in their country. Such a definition, if intended to be rigorous, could create considerable difficulty for anyone attempting to classify a farming population on the ground. The emphasis on exchange as the criterion of definition is clearly intended to cover the category of subsistence farming. This probably accords reasonably well with definitions of peasantry which focus upon relatively simple technology and low productivity. W. W. Rostow's conception [1960, p. 4] of the traditional society, having as its central feature a technological ceiling on the level of attainable output per head, does, in its agricultural sector, fit this well enough. So does T. W. Schultz's stress [1964, pp. 28, 106, *passim*] on the crucial feature of traditional agriculture being the low rate of return on investment in customary agricultural factors. But whereas "subsistence farming" is an almost pure economic concept, "peasantry" or even "peasant economy" is not. Any economic system presupposes a social structure. But the notion of a peasant economy usually links intimately together the economic system and a particular *kind* of social structure.

PEASANT SOCIETY AND ECONOMY

But what kind of social structure? The simplest formulation is probably the one which defines peasant farming as that which relies primarily or completely on family labor.[2] Family labor is a quasi-economic concept—only quasi because the ties which hold the members of the family together in co-operative work cannot be subsumed solely in terms of their common economic interest in production and its reward. As Nash [1961, p. 189] has pointed out, in peasant and primitive societies the context of economic choice, the family or household, is a multi-purposed social organization. Unlike a firm, it cannot liquidate itself if it makes poor calculations.

More elaborate definitions speak, not only of peasant economy, but also of peasant society and introduce two major criteria for delimitation. One is that peasants are agriculturalists whose occupation is a livelihood and a way of life, not a business for profit [Redfield, 1956, p. 27]. In its negative term this definition is suspect. As Schultz argues, in agreement with many anthropologists, traditional agriculture is niggardly but this niggardliness is not necessarily a function of unique preferences—especially those concerning work and thrift [Firth, 1946, pp. 82, 126–128, 140–144]. Putting it bluntly, peasants on the whole would probably prefer to make a profit rather than not, and to go into business for profit if they could see a clear way to do so. But in its positive form the definition has more meaning. A peasant economy is one which links purchasers and consumers, resource allocation and product allocation, in a network of ties which are more personal, more directly perceptible, than in a more developed, complex economy [Firth, 1946, pp. 22–26; 1961, Ch. IV].[3]

The important second feature in the concept of a peasant society along these lines is the relation of the peasant to the town. This can be viewed primarily in a technological frame, as Soviet policy has done. Joseph Stalin, in discussing problems of agrarian

2. E.g. in discussions of European peasantry, as by S. Bulgakov and Hertz, cited by V. I. Lenin [1939, p. 134]. See also chapter by N. Georgescu-Roegen in this volume.

3. For an example of a peasant economy where villagers "continually seek to turn the impersonal single-stranded tie into a multiple personal loyalty" see Stirling [1964, p. 81].

policy in the U.S.S.R., pointed out that as the peasant began to receive from the town machines, trucks, agronomists, and other assistance, "the old type of peasant with his savage mistrust of the town which he regarded as a plunderer is passing into the background" [1947, p. 313]. But for anthropologists such as Kroeber or Redfield, the relation of the peasant to the town is on a much broader social base. Kroeber has stressed the point that peasants form a rural class segment of a larger population which usually contains urban, sometimes metropolitan, centers. Redfield has spoken of peasants as "the rural dimensions of old civilizations." In such a concept the social structure of the town may be a most important influence on the economic and social structure of the peasant.

I have mentioned these matters, if only in passing, because they raise a most significant point of perspective—that one cannot adequately discuss peasant economy without consideration of the wider economy and of the wider society of which peasant society forms only a part. Who can hope to understand the peasant economy of Russia without consideration of the history of feudalism and serfdom in that country, and the whole conceptualization of social status and social stratification to which the social life and the productivity of the peasant were closely related?

There is a further point of even more direct influence on the peasant economy. Any broad connotation of "social structure" must include the political and legal structure of the society, and by this the economic position of the peasantry may be most powerfully affected. Historically, one has only to cite the successive measures of the government of India, both before and after the attainment of independence, to deal with the position of *zamindars* vis-à-vis that of the *ryotwari* in the matter of land revenue, or of the Tokugawa Bakufu to regulate the economy and life of the Japanese peasantry in the interest of the samurai and their own feudal rule, to acknowledge the significance of such wider complex structural factors on the level of peasant productivity and peasant incomes. In a more revolutionary situation, the changing politicolegal structure of the Soviet Union and of the Chinese Peoples' Republic has resulted in far-reaching modifications in the general character and daily operations of the economy of their peasantry. As Lord Hailey has pointed out [1952], "There must inevitably arise in the life of all advancing societies a stage when the State has to intervene to regulate the formation of systems of land tenure." But he added this cautionary note: unless this is done with a full awareness of the consequences likely to ensue, the result may gravely prejudice the welfare of the agrarian population. Moreover, as he also indicated, the problem of what changes are needed in the land tenure system will be viewed not merely as economic issues but as political issues as well. Hence the structure of the political system is a highly significant element in the set of structural forces brought to bear upon the peasant economy. There is no need to labor this point. I do not think that my task in this paper is conceived as including the analysis of such complex situations. But I would not wish to be thought to have totally ignored this sector of the problem.

By social structure in this particular context I understand, then, primarily not the structure of the wider society, but the internal local structure of peasant communities themselves—supported or opposed as may be by the overall politicolegal framework. Here is the first important point to stress—that these local social structures show a great diversity [Firth, 1961, Chs. III and IV; Wolf, 1955]. It may be simple, though I would doubt it, to aggregate peasant economies in a single type; it certainly is not so with peasant societies. The major problem of this paper is presumably to consider to what extent peasant social structures facilitate or hinder the development of their economies. I must say at once, then, that any reader who is expecting crisp generalizations of broad scope will be disappointed. It is not that economic anthropology lacks a macrosector;[4] but there is still so much work to be done on the relation of social forms to economic processes that our generalizations remain as yet very imperfect and uncertain, hardly more than hypotheses to be tested over a range of instances. In order to understand adequately what is the relation between social structure and economic action in peasant conditions, it is necessary to

4. For an example of a macroframework, to which anthropologists contributed together with sociologists and economists, see UNESCO [1964].

study each specific peasant society under consideration. And if practical results are wanted to change the level of the economy, such study may be needed in great detail, so complex are the linkages between some of the factors.

Here we become concerned with the most difficult of the three terms in the title of this paper, the notion of "influence." The idea that the operations of a peasant economic system are facilitated or hindered by the nature of the peasant social structure or by some significant factors in it is not new. But in this respect anthropological orthodoxy has recently tended to reverse its position. For many years some social anthropologists, and I include myself among them, devoted considerable energy to demonstrating the importance of economic concepts and economic institutions in the simpler societies. We also tried to show how economic operations in these societies were conditioned to a significant degree by the particular social structures. Hence we argued that an analysis which limited itself to the economist's then conventional treatment of market operations was inadequate to explain all peasant economic behavior. This issue has since been taken up so enthusiastically by some of our colleagues [e.g. Polanyi, et al., 1957] that they have argued, not for the inclusion of a wider range of factors in the economist's analysis, but for a rejection of the ordinary economic principles. The grounds for this view are said to be that in the marketless economies the individual has no specific institutional framework to guide him into rational economic activity with recognition of scarcity, nor into an optimum allocation of his resources. Personally I do not accept this view. But in its focus upon the social significance of widespread systems of redistribution and exchange in nonmarket, nonprice conditions, such analyses do provide powerful support to the standard anthropological position that social structures are primary to much economic activity.

At the same time a movement of another kind has developed, emphasizing how much social institutions, such as unilineal descent groups and types of family, described by many anthropologists as if they were autonomous structures, have been conditioned by economic circumstances and a competitive economic rationality. Worsley's critique of Meyer Fortes's study of Tallensi kinship structure demonstrated how land hunger seemed to be more important than filial piety in stimulating a man to return from his bush farm to his patrimonial land. He pointed out also how the Tallensi emphasis on amity and cooperation of father and son was in conflict with the facts of economic necessity, if indeed it was not an ideal formulation to mitigate struggles arising from such necessity. Worsley's formulation that the particular forms which kinship roles will take corporate unilineal descent groups, agnatic systems without lineages, and the like—are largely determined by economic and "historical" forces [Worsley, 1956, pp. 37–75] has a familiar ring. But in a viewpoint that goes back to L. H. Morgan, both E. R. Leach and J. Goody stress the significance of property roles as correlates to variations in the kinship system. "The concepts of descent and of affinity are expressions of property relations which endure through time"; "the constraints of economics are prior to the constraints of morality and law" [Leach, 1961, pp. 11, 9].

This stress upon the significance, if not the primacy, of economic factors in the social field of what may be regarded as a peasantry is partly a response, within the theoretical system of social anthropology itself, to a growing interest in studies of social process as opposed to more purely structural studies. But I think it is also due in some degree to the pervasive effect of increasing contact between social anthropologists and economists.[5] There has been a growing realization by social anthropologists of the possibilities of more subtle analysis of their own material in economic terms [e.g. Tax, 1953; Nash, 1958, 1961; Epstein, 1962; Salisbury, 1962; Pospisil, 1963; Belshaw, 1964]. The upshot of this is that now few social anthropologists would look upon the influence of social structure on the economic system of a peasant community as simply a one-way relationship. If elements of the social structure are to be isolated as parameters in examining varia-

tions of economic behavior, this can only be for heuristic purposes. It is from this point of view, then, that I approach the present theme.

The problem is not just to demonstrate that a peasant economy is directly related to the present peasant social structure. It is, rather, to assume this and to ask in what economic sectors what elements of the social structure are most relevant and to what degree.

SOME RELEVANT ELEMENTS OF PEASANT SOCIAL STRUCTURE

What are the elements of the social structure most likely to be implicated in economic action? So varied is the field that one cannot be dogmatic. But broadly, among the structural features of a peasant society ordinarily apt to affect economic choices are: neighborhood ties; family and household ties; ties of kinship; ties of ritualized friendship and of quasi-kinship such as godparenthood; status and class differences; relations of patronage and clientship; leadership conferred by ascribed criteria such as seniority of residence or ritual office; local political roles; patterns of religious offering.

I obviously can deal with only a few factors and begin with a consideration of some of the relations between kinship ties, status differences, and land allocation.

KINSHIP, STATUS, AND LAND ALLOCATION

Conventionally a peasant economy is an agricultural one. Some other producers at the same general level of income, such as fishermen and rural craftsmen, sharing the same community life and values, are interrelated by kinship with peasant agriculturalists and on occasion join their ranks. There is a case for including these in the general peasant category [Firth, 1946, p. 22; 1961, p. 87]. But while I think this usage is convenient, there is one significant difference between the agriculturalists and the others. A focus on land as a primary factor of production allows the possibility of the acquisition of relatively permanent transferable rights over it—rights which are not paralleled in the control of the less durable resources used in either fishing or craftwork. It is a matter of observation that

5. See Bohannan and Dalton [1962] and Firth and Yamey [1964] for examples of such collaboration. Preparation of the latter volume was greatly aided by a Symposium on Economics and Anthropology at Burg Wartenstein, Austria, August 1960, attended by anthropologists, economists, and economic historians, under the auspices of the Wenner-Gren Foundation for Anthropological Research. See also UNESCO [1964].

those who control such relatively permanent land rights acquire also social status in the community. If the use rights over land are temporarily transferred to others, then not merely is economic reciprocity involved, but so is some degree of social subordination. The person working the land tends to be regarded socially as inferior to him who exercises the more permanent nonworking rights over it; rent receiving and status tend to coincide. In this sense, then, a peasant agricultural community tends, in a rather different way from a community of fishermen, to create and maintain a more durable and more rigid social structure.

The existence of this status structure in turn tends to affect the system of economic choices in regard to land. Renting land is common enough, especially in the more developed peasant economies. But purchase rather than lease tends to be a long-term aim, with the result that, if a peasant has accumulated capital, he may well tend to invest it by buying a piece of land rather than by improving his equipment and working a larger area more efficiently on leasehold. The landless peasant in particular tends to be at the bottom of not only the economic but also the social ladder. In economic terms this status interest means an added factor in the purchase demand for land and consequently a tendency to enhance its price.

Transmission of land rights from one generation to another is normally deeply involved with the structure of a peasant society. A vivid illustration of this is given by Nadel [1946], who describes how the possession of land enters as a paramount factor into distinctions of social status and forms of social unity in Eritrean society. *Resti* ownership, derived from first occupation of land by a family, gives a hereditary social status which is permanent and inalienable and entails valued prerogatives. These include some bizarre entitlements, such as the right to be presented with the tongues of all oxen slaughtered at wedding or funeral feasts. But they also include more substantial economic benefits, such as the right to supervise and organize communal labor; to receive fines from trespassers when guarding pasture lands or a share of the crops when guarding village fields; to be eligible for election to the office of village chief, which carries with it some

income from legal fees. Now a significant point is that in this society such "fringe benefits" from ancestral landholding do not necessarily cease when the land itself is given up. One can understand that status in the sense of public esteem might continue to attach to a person who had owned land or whose ancestors had owned land by original title. But in this case the material evidences of status also continue to accrue. Even a sale of his ancestral land does not lose a person either his social status or his associated privileges, if he takes the precaution to retain a token plot. Hence not only may a *resti* lose his land and retain his status; the notional concept of him as a (former) landholder allows him to alter his investment pattern as regards land yet continues to provide him with some income therefrom. So, a structural concept of the continuing validity of an original possession of an asset gives a perpetual title to certain distributive shares, not from the yield of that asset as such, but from the general community income.

This is only one type of income which may accrue in a peasant economy though based upon no tangible asset. Analogies to it are characteristic of many peasant economic systems where status differentiations, such as chieftainship, are built into the social structure. One way of looking at this is to consider social status itself as an economic asset. A question which then arises is how far can one differentiate systems of different kinds here: those, such as the Eritrean, where this status asset is transferable but only by hereditary means; those where such a status asset can be transferred for a consideration but is not hereditary; and those where it is not transferable at all but is a purely personal endowment. Again, while such an intangible asset may give rise to a tangible income, how far does the possessor of the status asset contribute, as by qualities of leadership or administrative judgment, toward the production from which his income is drawn? On the basis of existing information, these questions can be answered only imperfectly; much more research is needed still.

I now turn to some other aspects of the relation of social structure to the allocation of land. The term peasant on Redfield's definition, as in other contexts also, does not necessarily imply the existence of landlords.

But the general structure of the society as regards land ownership may deeply affect the specific resource allocation.[6] The relations of persons to land in any economy and society are complex, involving rights of a number of different kinds. What is commonly known as individual "ownership" of land is really the ability of one person, backed by the sanctions of the society, to exercise what are in the last resort only a limited set of rights—primarily those of unique status in regard to the land, special share of the produce and of freedom to transfer it to some other person. In a Western industrial type of society, rights of use, of income, and even of transfer may be heavily restricted by overt or implied counterrights on the part of other persons or of the community at large; for example, as by the kind of building he is legally allowed to erect thereon, or by the land being subject to requisition for highway construction in the interests of the community.

So also in a peasant society land ownership is a parcel of rights over pieces of land, but the items in the parcel are differently arranged and constituted. One of these in many peasant societies is the set of rights of the kin group of which the individual is a member. When expressed in terms of the inheritance pattern and of the management pattern, these kin group rights make for considerable variation in allocation and use of land. In one major type of group rights there is individual occupancy, use, and transmission right, subject to the overriding interest of the group, which debars alienation of the land to anyone outside the group. In another major type the members of the group share an undivided estate, in which they all have occupancy and use rights on a kind of first-come-first-served basis but no right of transmission to other group members, even to their own children, of anything more than the produce of their annual crop. Commonly in such circumstances standing timber and the fruit of perennial trees are treated as communal group property, to be equally shared or to be drawn upon by individual members as need appears to dictate. Economically the system in its

traditional form tends to allow land assets to be available to those who can make most use of them, in terms of personal energy and skill and command of household or other client labor. Sanctions of the group, by public disapproval or withdrawal of cooperation, prevent a man from using more land than local views of equity allow. But conversely, when circumstances change, as by the development of a new commercial market for crops, productivity may be adversely affected. Since the application of extra energy, skill, and labor outside the normal run, if it is put into permanent improvements, goes to the benefit of all, including members of the group who may have done no work, an especially energetic man may be inhibited from trying to better his position. Transitional conditions of improving technology and expanding markets outside the community emphasize this effect, since at the same time other external social forces tend to weaken the traditional sanctions for encouraging hard individual and communal work by other members of the community. Social benefit and private benefit thus first coincide, then diverge, and only much later may converge again, after a substantial rearrangement of the structure of the society has taken place, often under pressure.

One of the significant economic functions of the overriding rights of kin groups, especially descent groups of a corporate kind, such as the many African patrilineage systems, the Malayo-Indonesian systems, such as the matrilineages of Minangkabau and Negri Sembilan, or the "ambilateral" groups of the Maori of New Zealand, has been to restrict the free market in land.[7] As Schneider [Schneider and Gough, 1961, p. 5] have pointed out, a descent group is a decision-making group, involved in the mobilization and conservation of its resources. Alienation of their land rights by individuals has been prevented, not only in the interests of the other living members of the group, but also with the idea of preserving the rights in the land for future generations. This concept of the wider social good to be conserved by limitation of the individual peasant's rights of transfer of land has taken many forms and

6. "Among institutional arrangements for the control and distribution of resources, systems of land tenure and land use stand out in peasant agricultural societies as major determinants of productive efficiency and flexibility, and hence of economic growth" [Belshaw, 1964, p. 181].

7. [Swift, 1965; Firth, 1959, pp. 469–70]. Maretin [1961] shows how the introduction of a market for rubber has tended to break up the Minangkabau system of group landholding.

presents one of the more difficult practical problems when set alongside the need to insure or stimulate the most effective economic use of the land. Again, the problem seems to have become especially acute with the development of contact with an external market, more modern forms of technology, and competing uses for the land, including operations by nonmembers of the community. In general, as far as central governments have been concerned, the trend on the time scale seems to have been, first, to ignore the local group interest of the peasantry and allow, even encourage, individual alienation of land, often by people who in the eyes of the community had no right to offer it. Later, governments tended to perceive the rationale of the system and give it some legal backing, however imperfectly, in the new system of sanctions. Hence the widespread recognition of systems of "reserves" "customary lands" "tribal lands" in which local attempts at conservation, for political as well as for economic reasons, received the backing of Western legal enactments. But what emerged as time went on was a double process of attrition. This was quite apart from the not disinterested efforts of Western businessmen and others to breach the barriers which impeded their own profit seeking. On the one hand, the need for interpretation of the enactments in formal legal procedures, as they affected the rights of individual members of the groups concerned, imperceptibly led to modifications, especially through the judgments in court cases, of traditional rules about rights over the land.[8] On the other hand, the legal safeguards for the common interest came to be perceived as too rigid as individuals within the group saw themselves hampered in their economic enterprises by the inability to raise capital on their rights in the group lands. In its turn, this led in many cases to new procedures. Among the most interesting of these, from the economic point of view, has been the use of traditional group alignments as corporate holders of assets. This has occurred with some New Zealand Maori and with the Menomini, Navaho, and some other American Indian tribes. They have converted their traditional tribal group structures into forms of modern legal corporations to control the

revenues obtained from using their group lands for agriculture, pastoralism, or exploitation of the timber, oil, or other resources discovered in them.[9] The overt use of a principle of traditional social structure to serve as a foundation for modern productive organization and sharing of income is as yet fairly rare; but it is a subject worth further exploration.

The older conventional anthropological view was that the kinship structures of primary interest in production as corporate groups were unilineal units of the clan or lineage order. But more recently it has been realized that there is a continuum from these strictly demarcated descent units using only one type of parent consistently for the transmission of land rights to much more amorphous kin units using a wide range of cognatic and affinal ties. From an economic viewpoint, what these more latitudinarian groups represent is more opportunity for individuals to exercise personal choice in selection of their resources for agriculture. This gives an enterprising man more chance to take advantage of differentials in land fertility, to use his agricultural initiative and technical skill to more productive effect. In my view, a unilineal descent group offers more advantage for a consistent retention of a valuable asset; a cognatic descent group offers more opportunity for individuals to seek out economic advantage in use of resources.

The general significance of descent group and other kin rights in the allocation of resources is that, while they may compress individual initiative, they do tend to cater more widely to the interests of all individuals in the community. In particular, the interests of the more vulnerable sectors—children, widows, old people—tend to be protected and economic viability allowed them, since in effect their kinship ties are a form of intangible asset which can be mobilized on occasion to yield a tangible return.

WOMAN'S ROLE IN MANAGEMENT OF ASSETS

THE ideology of economic relations between the sexes, especially in family terms—between

---

8. See Taylor [1937] for data on Malay rights in land so affected.

9. For a detailed examination of the Menomini case, see Keesing [1939, esp. Chs. VI and VII, pp. 235–6]; and of the Maori case, Firth [1959, p. 470].

brother and sister and between husband and wife—is very relevant for the handling of land assets. A marked instance of this is in societies organized into matrilineal descent groups. The idea that in a peasant society land is owned mostly by men is probably fairly widespread. Yet Swift [1965, p. 36] points out how his survey of the land register in 1955 in a matrilineal area he was studying in Negri Sembilan, Malaya, revealed that of 157 rice land titles, only 7 were held by men. A man may buy rice land, but in bargaining about land sales, the question of kinship is continually raised, and people other than the seller discuss whether the buyer is a proper person to receive the land. So strong is the principle of female ownership of rice land that a man buying some will ordinarily register it in the name of his wife or daughter. He cannot register it in his own name without seeming to be planning to divorce his wife!

On the other hand, the elementary family is the prime economic unit, and formally at least, the husband is the entrepreneur for that unit. Schneider has pointed out elegantly [Schneider and Gough, 1961, pp. 7–8] how, by reason of the fact that, in general, administration of assets is an economic role of men, a matrilineal lineage system is not a simple mirror image of a partilineal one. In the latter case the allocation of land and other major property follows the same rules as the allocation of personnel to descent groups—the title goes through men. In the former case the allocation of land and other major property goes through men, but the allocation of personnel to descent groups—"group placement"—goes through women. In both cases it is men who have the primary responsibility as managers of the descent-group assets.

But just as the arrangement of economic control in descent groups may be conceived to spread out along a continuum from strict unilineal to broad bilateral transmission and acquisition of rights and administration of resources, so also economic control as between the sexes. Anthropologists are very familiar with a sex division of labor by which men perform the harder tasks, demanding not only more energy but also more skill and excitement, whereas women do those which demand less of these qualities but more drudgery. This is in part a division based on differences of physical capacity and biological

endowment—while a man can procreate, he cannot conceive and bear a child, nor does he have the task of suckling it. But it is also a conventional social division, based in any particular case on what is thought to be right and proper for the sexes to do. Some social systems promote productivity by women, others inhibit it. Status and class differentials are often important here, but the structure of kin groups appears much less so. Some societies allow that only men can act as managers of either personal or group assets. The Malays of Negri Sembilan, with their matrilineal descent group system, say that women "cannot understand affairs." In some other Malay areas on the East Coast, lacking such corporate descent groups, women act very efficiently as entrepreneurs in fish or vegetable marketing. Yet this entrepreneurship is not a simple correlate of the absence of descent groups;[10] traditionally built-in concepts of the respective roles of the sexes are also important.

Most anthropologists and economists have probably consistently underrated the role of women as managers in the economic process. But an interesting instance of women as managers of resources in a field where patrilineal descent groups are important is that of the Nsaw people of the Cameroons described by Kaberry [1950, pp. 313–322]. Women in this society do most of the farming and from an early age begin to cultivate some millet, maize, or sweet potatoes on tiny plots. Later, a woman farms her own plots on her own lineage land and even after marriage will retain her interest in them, though as a rule she will then make most of her farming plots on her husband's lineage land. Normally, once a woman has been granted a plot of land, she continues to farm it for the rest of her life. She regards such a plot as her own, safeguards her boundaries, and by convention can rest secure in the knowledge that without due cause she will not be dispossessed during her lifetime. She also may transmit her cultivation rights to a son or daughter.

But the Nsaw also provide an example of how complex land rights in a peasant economy may be, and how modern innovations tend

10. Dewey [1962] brings out how cultural tradition gives women in Java great freedom of movement as compared with restrictions upon them in, say, the Middle East.

to put new pressures on the economic system. Nsaw express one important feature of their position in the saying, "Men own the land, women own the crops," or alternatively, "A woman owns only a farm, she does not own the earth." The significance of this is that no woman in this society has any legal claim to the disposal of land. Such right lies in the hands of a male head of the lineage, whose role it is to administer lineage property. He has the responsibility for making allocations of plots of land among more distant relatives, friends, and strangers who approach him with requests for land. In making these allocations, he is responsible for safeguarding the patrimony of the lineage for the next generation; e.g. kola trees and raffia plantations may be sold or pledged only after other male members of the lineage have been consulted and then only in cases of emergency and on a small scale. These are "things of the lineage"—that is, they are its capital, the "source of salt and oil," the means by which money is obtained to buy necessaries. Hence the statement that a woman does not own the land, she only owns the crops, must be understood in the context of the Nsaw conception of the difference between quasi-permanent occupation for cultivating purposes, with receipt of the income, and a permanent right to disposal of the land, including the right to recall it with due reason. Such a system gives implicit assurance of security of tenure and rights of usufruct to a woman as to a man for her economic effort.

But this example also illustrates how a long-established element in the social structure may tend to change under modern economic pressures. As Kaberry points out, for an economy based largely on subsistence agriculture the traditional land rights system seemed adequate. But with the development of new sources of income through livestock, fruit, and coffee plantations, there is pressure for assets on which a large and increasing amount of effort has been expended by a cultivator to be more completely at his or her own disposal. Hence, tendencies for more individualization of permanent land rights, for women as well as for men, have emerged. Significantly, too, as against the traditional implicit assumption of inheritance by customary rule, a case is beginning to be made for

inheriting land by will. In many other societies hitherto governed by customary rules of land inheritance, introduction of such verbal or written testamentary disposition has also begun.

The significance of different modes of inheritance is well-known. We may contrast systems in which only one child receives the land with other systems in which the land—or its worth—is divided among all the children. On small peasant holdings inheritance by one child, in form of primogeniture or (sometimes) ultimogeniture, means that the other children go out to seek a living elsewhere. The community may be drained of a large fraction of its labor supply, but the holdings are conserved. With equal division of assets, there may be less pressure on members of the family to migrate in search of employment. On the other hand, grave pressure on land may arise, and in the bilateral system of inheritance fragmentation of farms is likely.[11] Small holdings created by fragmentation are often relatively uneconomical, but as Pitt-Rivers [1954, p. 46] has pointed out for the peasants of Andalusia, the custom of dividing all inheritance equally among the children of both sexes is usually in harmony with the general values of family life and therefore has sanctions to support it which economic arguments alone may be insufficient to alter.

USE OF LABOR RESOURCES

So far I have considered mainly the effect of different social structures on the mobilization of land resources. To some extent the significance of descent group and allied kin units is parallel as regards mobilization of labor resources. In most peasant economic systems the primary production unit is a household—not merely a family, if that term is used fairly strictly in an anthropological sense to apply to an immediate domestic unit of parents and children. The peasant household is not a simple monolithic unit, as economists' models may assume. Not infrequently it

11. E.g. in Cyprus, Switzerland, and among the New Zealand Maori, problems of fragmentation, which have been of great concern to governments, have been tackled by various consolidation measures. The difficulty is that without a radical alteration in farming technology or in the inheritance system, the consolidation process must assume a continuing form to cope with the division made in successive generations.

includes kin of wider genealogical connection, who help to provide labor in return for their keep but who do not have full managerial or other rights in household assets and activities. Nash [1961] has pointed out how in the Mexican peasant Indian community he studied, the household unit, with its recruitment on a kinship basis, sets the size of the labor force available for the local specialist craft of pottery-making. Wealthier households can attract sons-in-law or daughters-in-law to live with them and so have a slightly larger labor-force potential. But the absence of any practice of payment of wages in this type of household production system limits the unit's ability to expand pottery activities.

Yet a peasant economy does not necessarily mean absence of wage labor. A strong contrast has sometimes been drawn between the peasant who works his own land and the peasant who hires out his labor to work the land of others. In the history of land reform and peasant revolution, the significance of the category of landless wage-laboring peasantry in opposition to land holding labor-employing peasantry has been very great. But in many peasant economies the distinction in individual terms is by no means clear-cut. Pitt-Rivers [1954, p. 41] points out how in Andalusia the small irrigated farm is a family concern, and the family may employ a man for a few weeks at a time when extra help is needed; or equally, at a time when there is spare labor, a member of the family may go out to work for a daily wage. Family members are at different times both employer and employee. The issue is often complicated, however, by the existence of a status evaluation. He who hires out his labor is regarded as subordinate to him who hires it, and this factor can impede the mobility of labor and its availability for new enterprise. Moreover, in situations of economic change, if wage labor is not a norm in the society, the social objections to it may act as a constraint in inhibiting the potential employer as well as the potential labor. One objection to wage labor, which commonly demands regular hours and consistency over a period, is that engagement in it tends to break up the network of economic and social obligations in the community; whether by going out to work or by hiring others to work, a man

reduces the time and energy available for more general community demands.[12]

In even relatively developed economies of the "subsistence" type an important mechanism for mobilization of labor has been traditionally the recognition of communal interest and the sanction of public opinion. I myself saw in 1940 two cases of construction of brushwood dams by Malay peasants in Negri Sembilan, using communal labor and supervision, unpaid. In structural terms the significant element in this creation of a public asset by such communal effort is the recognition of the people concerned that they are members of a social unit, sharing in economic as well as social benefits, hence rationally motivated to participate in the communal job, whatever sacrifices of time, energy and alternative earnings may be entailed. But other more intangible social appreciations are also involved. One of the most difficult tasks of development officers has been precisely to identify and tap the sources of such social appreciations as community pride. Historically, as the personal observations of many people must have indicated about 1945, the work of road-making and building construction inspired by Chadwick at Udi in Eastern Nigeria[13] gave a striking example of how communal productive activity can be so mobilized with the aid of an external stimulus.

SOCIAL STATUS AND PRODUCT ALLOCATION

I have been discussing mainly the ways in which some of the major elements of peasant social structure have provided conventions for the allocation of resources. Under this head one could also consider the effects of specific status structures in a society. Many peasant communities in the African and Oriental field have an elaborate status structure of a political and economic kind which provides a framework for the use of assets, in particular land and labor. The Baganda are an outstanding example of an African society where the control of land in customary tenure lay ultimately in the political authority

12. To take another example of a common type of situation, Dewey [1962, pp. 24–6] shows how wage relations of Javanese peasants are determined by a network of social relations between employer and employed.

13. The film *Daybreak at Udi* illustrated some of the results of this community development scheme.

exercised by the ruler, the Kabaka, and those chiefs whom he deputed to administer the lands in his name. The peasantry in this case tended to be traditional retainers of chiefs. Though normally they had fair security of tenure, perhaps occupying the same site for several generations, they were tenants at the chief's discretion, and the main sanction against their exploitation was the necessity of the chief to have as many retainers as possible occupying his land [Mair, 1933]. With the introduction of modern crops, land registration, and freehold tenure, as well as great immigration of labor, the situation has become much more complex. Land has come to be regarded as a trading commodity, and its availability has increased. But the reinforcement of economic disparity by status differentials seems to be still an important feature of the economy [Richards, 1954, pp. 126–140].

In many situations the control of rulers, chiefs and other people of high status in a peasant society has been titular rather than economic in the sense that not they but the peasant cultivators received the income from the land. As Kaberry [1950, p. 312] has observed of the claim of the Fon to the overlordship of Nsaw land, its implications are political rather than economic. One need not accept all the strictures of Potekhin [1956, p. 13] that the real relations of chief to tribe in an African society are those of exploitation based on his right to dispose of the land. Nevertheless, it does seem true that in the structure of even a small-scale peasant society it is necessary to understand the system of recognition of intangible assets to understand the distribution of income. In return for a tangible income from the produce of the land, the services performed by a chief or other leader are often of a kind which, if not intangible, e.g. ritual performances for fertility, at least are very difficult to measure. Here should be distinguished clearly the role of a chief as controller of land allocation from his position as owner, i.e. major rightholder over any portion of land. What he receives as income in the former case is not an economic rent for the land but an acknowledgment (sometimes called "tribute") for his controlling services. This material acknowledgment may represent a compensation for the costs of his performance of administrative duties

in regard to the land, or of more general duties as keeper of public order and initiator of public works. It may be also a recognition of his political authority. But with change of economic and legal circumstances a chief may find himself in a position to preempt rights of ownership, i.e. of sole control, formerly not his or only shared with his people. He may also insist on his traditional income without performing all the traditional services to merit it. The widespread resentment that has been shown against the economic control over "stool" lands exercised by chiefs in, say, Ghana, when compared with the respect accorded their social and ritual functions, illustrates some aspects of the problem. The difficulty has been exacerbated by Western governments, who have often implicated chiefs in their administrative and revenue-collecting systems, so bringing upon them a double charge of alienation from their people. It is interesting to note here that the lack of involvement of chiefs of the Maori in a governmental administrative system seems to have saved them from this resentment on economic and political grounds. So that, while deprived of authority, they have been able to exercise influence toward social and economic betterment side by side with other members of the community often more technically qualified.

ECONOMIC EFFECTS OF CEREMONIAL AND RITUAL INSTITUTIONS

IN the relation of the social structure of a peasant community to its economy, the effects of engagement in ceremonial and ritual institutions may be very important. In common with most other anthropologists, I think that the deleterious effects of such institutions have often been exaggerated. It is true that by setting standards of consumption at certain periods of a person's life, they do on occasion tempt him to an engagement of his resources which leads, not to further productivity, but to the incurrment of debt. The effects of this are particularly manifest in a peasant community which makes fairly full use of monetary facilities and are particularly marked where the moneylenders belong to a different cultural or ethnic community than that of the borrowers. But for the most part I think it can be argued that what happens when a feast or other large display takes place at a marriage or a funeral is a series of transfer payments among kinfolk and other members of the community. In some cases, as those noted by myself in Kelantan, Malaya, some of these transfer payments may be aggregated and used for investment in productive equipment, such as a fishing boat or net [Firth, 1946, pp. 176–182]. There may be some postponement of production as a result, but not infrequently there is also some stimulus to production. Nash [1961, p. 187] has pointed out how, in the Mexican community he studied, the level and rhythm of output were in no small measure the consequences of the ceremonial cycle. In many of the much more primitive societies of New Guinea, their economic system hinges to an important degree on the periodic accumulation and slaughter of pigs in large numbers. Social status as a leader of widespread reputation is in these societies linked very closely with energy, initiative, and skill, both in personal labor in vegetable cultivation and pig rearing and also in expert lending out of resources in such a way as to be able to mobilize them with an appropriate increment when the occasion arises. Here undoubtedly in this socioeconomic system large-scale pig slaughter in the context of the acquisition of status is one of the major elements in the provision of an incentive pattern in the economy as a whole.

A difference can be drawn, however, between those elements of a ceremonial cycle which are a matter of personal choice and those which are dictated serially by the general canons of the society. It is the latter in particular which can be a drain upon resources. In some cases they seem to be viewed in this light by the members of the society concerned. Nash has pointed out how in the Mexican community he observed there are series of offices in which a man who is a representative of a family must serve. These civil and religious offices are arranged in a hierarchy, they are unpaid, and a man must serve in a dozen of them before he is relieved of communal service. They are a drain on his working time and use up some of the household resources. They are therefore a continuing cost all through a person's adult productive life. Moreover, certain special

offices are extremely costly to hold, involving more than the annual income of even the richest member of the community in feasting neighbors, relatives, and officers of the hierarchy and in renting the special costumes needed for the procession. When a man undertakes such a post, this involves his whole family and leaves them with much depleted assets. Selection of the officeholder is done fairly strictly by ability to pay—which is fairly conspicuous in such a close-knit community—and refusal to serve would be liable to invoke a charge of witchcraft. Hence, there is in operation a continuous social mechanism for leveling out inequalities of wealth—for insuring that wealth does not adhere simply to family alliance [Nash, 1961, p. 190]. Among economists, Dusenberry [1959] has been one who has emphasized the social character of consumption patterns and the interdependence of the consumption behavior of individuals in a community. This is well borne out by anthropological findings over a wide range of peasant economic systems.

SUMMARY

No very novel conclusions can be made to emerge from a general survey of this kind, but it may be worthwhile reemphasizing certain general themes. The first is that in the microeconomic sphere peasants are well aware of the possibilities of rational economic actions and make strong endeavors to better their economic position. In their own traditional economy they watch margins most carefully and switch their productive efforts accordingly. In conditions of development they have shown themselves very apt to take advantage of the benefits to be obtained from new crops, such as rubber or cocoa, and it has been often the operators in the Western market or an alien government who have attempted to restrict their production. In the macroeconomic field they have not shown the same perspective, primarily because of lack of an understanding of how large-scale commodity markets work and the existence of external competitors with differential advantages.

Considering that another paper in this series (Rogers, Chapter 5) deals with motivation, values and attitudes of subsistence farmers, I have not thought it proper to discuss questions of incentive in peasant economies in any detail. But much of what I have examined could be put in such a frame. Clearly the objectives of the peasant in his economic activity are governed in a very large degree by the uses to which he can put his income. The consumption demands of his family for clothing and ornaments, as well as for food, are important as stimuli to his effort. These are dictated in turn by the general standards of the peasant society, which are tending to alter more and more rapidly as a wider range of consumption goods opens up. But peasant production still often tends to be target production. Expenditure on clothing and jewelry, weddings and funerals, tends to be set at a conventional level by a combination of social and economic criteria—the critical or approving behavior of friends, neighbors, and kin and the amount of reciprocity which they are prepared to give according to what they themselves have received. The rewards for economic effort may lie to a great degree in the fulfillment of social obligations and social roles, and patterns of decision are regulated accordingly. On the other hand, membership in a community implies constraints upon resource use as well as stimuli. Attitudes toward what is "proper" for women or kinsfolk to do can inhibit the use of resources.

The point to be borne in mind is that it is rare for us to be able to identify and isolate with generality any single feature of a social structure as being in itself either an economic stimulus or an economic constraint. The complex interrelation of social elements means that in order to understand the relation of any element to the economic process, a specific analysis of the particular society and economy must be made. This is particularly so when any attempt is made to identify suitable points for economic development and to change the society in the interests of economic growth.

References

BELSHAW, 1964. C. S. Belshaw, *Under the Ivi Tree: Society and Economic Growth in Rural Fiji* (London: Routledge & Kegan Paul, 1964).

BOHANNAN and DALTON, 1962. Paul Bohannan and George Dalton, *African Markets* (Evanston, Ill.: Northwestern University Press, 1962).

DEWEY, 1962. Alice G. Dewey, *Peasant Marketing in Java* (Glencoe, Ill.: Free Press, 1962).

DUSENBERRY, 1959. James S. Dusenberry, *Income, Saving and the Theory of Consumer Behavior* (Cambridge: Harvard University Press, 1959).

EPSTEIN, 1962. T. Scarlett Epstein, *Economic Development and Social Change in South India* (Manchester: Manchester University Press, 1962).

FIRTH, 1946. Raymond Firth, *Malay Fishermen: Their Peasant Economy* (London: Routledge & Kegan Paul, 1946).

FIRTH, 1959. Raymond Firth, *Economics of the New Zealand Maori* (Wellington: R. E. Owen, Government Printer, 1959).

FIRTH, 1961. Raymond Firth, *Elements of Social Organization* (3rd ed., London: Watts, 1961).

FIRTH and YAMEY, 1964. Raymond Firth and B. S. Yamey, eds., *Capital Saving and Credit in Peasant Societies* (Chicago: Aldine Publishing Company, 1964).

HAILEY, 1952. Lord Malcolm Hailey, "The Land Tenure Problem in Africa," In Land Tenure supplement to *Journal of African Administration*, Vol. 4, No. 4 (October 1952), 3–7.

KABERRY, 1950. P. Kaberry, "Land Tenure Among the Nsaw of the British Cameroons," *Africa*, Vol. XX, No. 4 (1950), 307–23.

KEESING, 1939. F. M. Keesing, *The Menomini Indians of Wisconsin*, Memoirs of the American Philosophical Society, Vol. X (Philadelphia: American Philosophical Society, 1939).

LEACH, 1961. E. R. Leach, *Pul Eliya, A Village in Ceylon: A Study of Land Tenure and Kinship* (Cambridge: Cambridge University Press, 1961).

LENIN, 1939. V. I. Lenin, *Theory of the Agrarian Question*, Selected Works, Vol. 12 (London: Lawrence and Wishart, 1939).

MAIR, 1933. Lucy P. Mair, "Baganda Land Tenure," *Africa*, Vol. VI, No. 2 (1933), 187–205.

MARETIN, 1961. J. V. Maretin, "Disappearance of Matriclan Survivals in Minangkabau Family and Marriage Relations," *Bidragen tot de Taal,—Land,—en Volkenkunde* (The Hague: Martinus Nijhoff), Vol. 117, No. 1 (1961), 168–95.

NADEL, 1946. S. F. Nadel, "Land Tenure on the Eritrean Plateau," *Africa*, Vol. XVI, No. 1 & 2 (1946), 1–22, 99–108.

NASH, 1958. Manning Nash, *Machine Age Maya: The Industrialization of a Guatemalan Community* (Glencoe, Ill.: Free Press, 1958).

NASH, 1961. Manning Nash, "The Social Context of Economic Choice in a Small Society," *Man*, Vol. LXI, No. 219 (1961), 186–191.

PITT-RIVERS, 1954. J. Pitt-Rivers, *People of the Sierra* (London: Weidenfeld and Nicholson, 1954).

POLANYI, ARENSBERG and PEARSON, 1957. K. Polanyi, C. M. Arensberg and H. W. Pearson, *Trade and Market in the Early Empires* (Glencoe, Ill.: Free Press, 1957).

POSPISIL, 1963. L. Pospisil, *Kapauku Papuan Economy* (New Haven, Conn.: Yale University, Publications in Anthropology No. 67, 1963).

POTEKHIN, 1956. I. I. Potekhin, "Clan Relations in the System of Social Relations in the Present Day African Village," Paper presented by the Soviet Delegation at the International Congress of Anthropological and Ethnological Sciences, Moscow, 1956.

REDFIELD, 1956. Robert Redfield, *Peasant Society and Culture* (Chicago: University of Chicago Press, 1956).

RICHARDS, 1954. Audrey I. Richards, *Economic Development and Tribal Change* (Cambridge: Heffer, 1954).

ROSTOW, 1960. W. W. Rostow, *The Stages of Economic Growth* (London: Cambridge University Press, 1960).

SALISBURY, 1962. R. F. Salisbury, *From Stone to Steel: Economic Consequences of a Technological Change in New Guinea* (Melbourne: Melbourne University Press, 1962).

SCHNEIDER, and GOUGH, 1961. D. M. Schneider and Kathleen Gough, eds., *Matrilineal Kinship* (Berkeley and Los Angeles: University of California Press, 1961).

SCHULTZ, 1964. Theodore W. Schultz, *Trans-forming Traditional Agriculture* (New Haven, Conn.: Yale University Press, 1964).

STALIN, 1947. Joseph Stalin, *Problems of Leninism* (Moscow: Foreign Languages Publishing House, 1947).

STIRLING, 1964. P. Stirling, *Turkish Village* (London: Weidenfeld and Nicholson, 1964).

SWIFT, 1965. M. G. Swift, *A Malay Peasant Economy in Jelebu* (London School of Economics Monographs of Social Anthropology No. 29), (London: Athlone, 1963).

TAX, 1953. Sol Tax, *Penny Capitalism: A Guatemalan Indian Economy* (Washington: Smithsonian Institute, Publication No. 16, 1953). First Published 1937.

TAYLOR, 1937. E. N. Taylor, "Malay Family Law," *Malayan Branch Royal Asiatic Society*, Vol. XV, Part 1 (1937), 1–78.

UNESCO, 1964. *Social Prerequisites to Economic Growth* (Paris: UNESCO, 1964).

WOLF, 1955. Eric R. Wolf, "Types of Latin American Peasantry: A Preliminary Discussion," *American Anthropologist*, Vol. LVII, No. 3, Part 1 (1955), 452–71.

WORSLEY, 1956. P. M. Worsley, "The Kinship System of the Tallensi: A Revaluation," *Journal of Royal Anthropological Institute*, Vol. 86, Part 1 (1956), 37–75.

COMMENT

An Economist's View
of Social Structure Interaction
with the Subsistence Economy

ABRAHAM M. WEISBLAT

CURRENT PROBLEMS of economic and social change have made social scientists aware of the necessity of learning more about each other's work, particularly as it relates to specific problems they are all trying to solve. The bearing of economic conditions on the character of a social system and the relevance of social factors to economic decision is becoming more apparent to social scientists concerned with the problem of developing economies.

Professor Firth's paper is concerned with the interaction between social and economic factors in a peasant society. He attempts to identify some of the salient characteristics of the peasant social structure that can act as stimuli or restraints in the process of economic development and warns of the complexity of trying to change the social structure in the interests of economic growth.

Professor Firth points out that the traditional anthropological view that "operations of a peasant economic system are facilitated or hindered by the nature of the peasant social structure" has shifted greatly. "Few social anthropologists would look upon the influence of social structure on the economic system of a peasant community as simply a one-way relationship." The result is that anthropologists now assume that a peasant economy is directly related to the peasant structure and concentrate on asking, "in what economic sectors what elements of the social structure are most relevant and to what degree."

What about the economist? I do not think the economist has questioned the fact that economic growth depends on social as well as economic conditions, nor has he questioned the relevance of social factors to economic decisions. The difference in emphasis stems not only from the subject-matter discipline, but from the fact that until recently the majority of today's economists have worked on problems relating to developed, commercial, and industrial economies rather than the underdeveloped, subsistence, and agricultural ones. Nevertheless, the economist has been aware and even accepts as a basic principle in economic analysis that the values of the individual, the community, or the society are the criteria by which goals, ends, or objectives are selected or which determine what is done with time and energy and how conduct is organized.

If we look at the work of the early political economists, we can see how the social structure did play a role in economic development and that the early economists were aware of this. The important factor in Western development which we tend to forget was that the majority of "values" held by people, communities, and societies were positive factors for encouraging economic growth. For example, Max Weber and others have written extensively on the positive role of Protestantism in Western economic development. The economist can be criticized where he tends to forget or ignore the fact that he does take values into consideration. The term *ceteris paribus*, "all other things being equal," used and accepted as a basic part of the economist's theoretical framework, is clear evidence of the importance of the noneconomic dimension, for among the assumed constants are noneconomic as well as economic variables. It was not until the economist became concerned with underdeveloped economies, having different sets of values from those in the advanced commercial countries, and where the workings of the socioeconomic system were different from the developed commercial and industrial economies, that the economist was reminded of the role of values. The problem became even more acute when it began to look as

though some of these values result in social structures which are deterrents to economic development.

The economist's current dilemma in dealing with the role of social structure in economic development has another dimension. The value that was relevant to economic decision-making in the Western industrial and developed economies could be generalized into a set of principles. One did not have to study each country separately to arrive at a general theoretical framework for development. When we begin to deal with the developing society which has a variety of systems, from simple to complex, the significant relations between social factors and economic decisions are different, represent a far greater range, and are much more varied in their positive and negative impact on economic growth.

The contribution of anthropology to the problems of economic growth in the underdeveloped countries is to help the economist see and identify more clearly the relevance of social factors to economic decision. Professor Firth's paper shows how the anthropologist can contribute to the knowledge of the working of socioeconomic systems different from the developed commercial and industrial economies, particularly in identifying significant social relationships in peasant society that affect economic growth. Professor Firth carefully limits the subject of the paper "to consider to what extent peasant social structures facilitate or hinder the development of their economies." Before examining these relationships, it would be useful to summarize briefly Firth's definition of the peasant economy. The peasant economy is *not* subsistence farming, which Firth indicates is an almost pure economic concept focusing upon relatively simple technology and low productivity. The notion of a peasant economy usually links intimately together the economic system and a particular kind of social structure. "A peasant economy is one which links purchasers and consumers, resource allocation and product allocation, in a network of ties which are more personal, more directly perceptible, than in a more developed, complex economy." Firth notes that individual peasants are rational in their economic behavior and tend to maximize the use of their resources wherever possible within the social structure in which they operate.

Finally, Firth points out that one cannot adequately discuss the peasant economy without considering the wider economy and the wider society of which peasant society forms only a part. This would have to include the political and legal structure of the society—significant elements in the set of structural forces brought to bear upon the peasant economy. In his paper, however, the social structure being examined is *not* the structure of the wider society, but the peasant communities themselves—supported or opposed as may be by the overall politicolegal framework.

What are the elements of the social structure most likely to be basic to economic action? Professor Firth identifies a number he considers critical and discusses and analyzes a few significant relationships in detail. They are: the ways in which different type of rights holding in land affect its use; what kind of choices are involved in the assembly of a labor force; what sanctions maintain its operations; how far ceremonial and ritual procedures affect the allocation of productive effort.

Professor Firth presents some very impressive evidence as to the significance of these particular interrelationships—how in one instance social status can be transformed into an economic asset and how individual rights may be submerged to the good of the group. The difficult problem is noting and differentiating the interaction of the economic and the social, and the way it occurs. Clearly, what the peasant does with his income is determined by the general standards of the peasant society. But his products are limited from too much divergence by a combination of social and economic criteria:

The critical or approving behavior of friends, neighbors, and kin and the amount of reciprocity which they are prepared to give according to what they themselves have received. The rewards for economic effort may lie to a great degree in the fulfillment of social obligations and social roles, and patterns of decision are regulated accordingly. On the other hand, membership in a community implies constraints upon resource use as well as stimuli.

Professor Firth's conclusion is that in order to understand the relation between social structure and economic action, it is necessary to study each specific peasant society under consideration. So complex are the linkages between some of the factors that if practical results are wanted in order to change the level of the economy, great detail is needed.

As an economist, I find Professor Firth's paper exciting and helpful, and at the same time I am left with a great sense of frustration. He certainly has made the case for the economist's turning to anthropology, at least to a social anthropologist of Professor Firth's caliber, for help in considering the economics of underdeveloped countries. Professor Firth concludes by emphasizing that the complex interrelation of social elements requires that any attempts to change the society in the interests of economic growth must rest upon adequate analysis—"a specific analysis of the particular society and economy." But for an economist this is a question rather than a conclusion: what is adequate analysis? If, in order to understand the relationship between social structure and economic action, it is necessary to study each specific peasant society, then is there really any such general classification as the "peasant society"?

In his introductory essay in the recent volume *Capital, Savings and Credit in Peasant Societies* [Firth and Yamey, 1964], Professor Firth points out that anthropologists are beginning to consider this interrelationship in a systematic way. The weakness in their analysis is that examinations have been selective rather than systematic in the past, and it is systematic analysis that the economist wants. To quote Professor Firth:

What are the actual processes of decision making at various levels of economic enterprise and for various categories of groups and individuals, and what is the relation to political power? How is the distribution process likely to facilitate the social aims of the community or the functional or individual aims of certain sectors of it only? Is the economy under scrutiny a stationary one, or is it a progressive one with increased net assets, and what are the effects in either case upon the structure of the society? What framework of ideas is required in order to tackle such questions?

Capital, Savings and Credit in Peasant Societies, indicates that the interaction of the social and economic structure of a society can be systematically analyzed. What is clearly needed are further detailed studies of the interaction between social and economic relationships that will give us some basis for a clear formulation of *theory* in the socio-economic field in which men like Yamey and Firth are pioneering.

Economists might help develop this field by raising some of the questions which they feel are relevant and important. Let us start with the three basic propositions Professor Firth and economists accept:

1. Peasants are as rational or irrational in their behavior as any other group in the world.
2. Economic and noneconomic factors are interrelated.
3. The interrelationships between economic and noneconomic factors are complex and operate *both* ways.

Surely we need more knowledge than that. If this knowledge is mere description, it has very limited value. The aim should be to get stable relations which are causal and general.

Now for some critical questions. Assuming that a peasant economy is directly related to the peasant structure, would the social and economic goals for which such a society is striving be maximized by maximizing economic change while at the same time minimizing social change? This hypothesis permits a number of interesting questions:

What economic changes can be made with a minimum of social change?

What economic changes will be the ones resulting in the greatest social change; the least social change?

Are there societies where the real desire is maximizing social change regardless of economic consequences or minimizing social *and* economic change?

Where can economic changes be made *only* as a result of substantial social change? And where can economic changes be made *without* social change?

Even within the framework of underdeveloped economies, we can note two different types, both in need of help. One is stagnating in near static equilibrium. People can be near starvation and going without elementary requirements in "penny capitalistic" economies which are in equilibrium. Here the problem is how to bring about change in the social structure. How do you introduce the variety of factors needed to bring abuot change which will destroy the old equilibrium, whose existence paralyzes

economic and social growth, without destroying the useful elements of social structure while simultaneously providing the material components for a better life? What are the various concepts and the strategic variables that will bring about desired change?

The other type of underdeveloped economy, and perhaps more typical of developing countries today, are those in which traditional social structures are disintegrating under the impact of postcolonial modernization to the point where we cannot be sure what the interaction between the social and economic either is or even was. Here the critical problem is to identify those variables out of the past that will promote social, economic and political stability. I hope the anthropologists can help us in this area, and indeed Professor Firth's paper cites a number of cases where the advent of outside forces has modified the social and economic structure. Let us, if we can, move from descriptive case studies to a point where we can develop some systematic picture of the impact of external forces, regardless of origin or source. Certainly, a careful examination of colonialism and its introduction of legal, political, and economic change is one area of research. We must begin to look at societies, not only in terms of how and what they are, but how and what has changed them, if we are to move ahead in helping the newly developing areas.

Finally, I would like to suggest three possible causal relations that are worth testing.

1. Introducing economic change itself will bring about drastic social change, and the deliberate "operation" on both the social and economic variables will be more efficacious than on one alone.
2. In both traditional and dynamic societies there are innovators. In the traditional society it is, of course, a minority group. If one wants to bring about change in both economic and social structure, we should support, encourage, and help this innovative group until it is in a position to put the traditional majority on the defensive and induce them to change their basic concepts. This should result in a change in the social structure helpful to the alteration of the economic structure.
3. There is a wide spectrum of economic factors that can affect social change. I

would argue that three—transport, communication, and monetization—are the most explosive for changing a society. It is these three that have the greatest impact on developing and creating new ideas—ideas which lead to modernization and "take-off" development.

I hope that some time soon we can begin to test some of these suggested hypotheses and begin seriously considering others that will help determine the several causal relationships between the economic and noneconomic factors in peasant societies.

Reference

FIRTH and YAMEY, 1964. Raymond W. Firth and B. S. Yamey, eds., *Capital, Saving and Credit in Peasant Societies* (Chicago: Aldine, 1964).

COMMENT

The Influence of Social Structure
on the Javanese Peasant Economy

SELO SOEMARDJAN

PROFESSOR FIRTH'S paper excels in scholarly quality. In its compact size the paper has clearly shown the significance of relating social anthropology and economics on the theoretical level; and in doing so it has added a new stimulus for scientists in both fields to maintain a better mutual understanding for a more penetrating and revealing analysis of peasant economies and peasant societies.

The two concepts of peasant economies and peasant societies are in fact inseparable, as Professor Firth correctly remarks. One cannot just talk about peasant economies without considering relevant features of peasant societies, because not merely have peasant societies made peasant economies a system of allocating scarce goods and services, but they have made it a way of life, a peasant culture so to say, which permeates every aspect of their daily doing and thinking and which is inextricably interwoven in their social structure. It is therefore hard to write on this assigned subject, the title of which assumes a one-way influence from social structure to peasant economies because of the fact that (in a peasant society) influence is mutual and equally strong in both directions between the two factors.

In discussing Professor Firth's paper, I do not wish to enter the theoretical field, which is well covered by the author, who has extensively drawn from the works of many other competent scholars, but to focus on several perhaps more useful points and relate them to empirical data gained by observing peasant communities and by interviewing a sizable number of their members in Java, Indonesia, in the second quarter of 1964.

THE JAVANESE PEASANT ECONOMY

First a few words about the definition of peasants. Professor Firth has defined peasants as farmers who sell or exchange only a minor part of their total farm production or, if they sell a major part, still do so at a level which leaves them in the lowest income group of the farmers in their country. As an anthropologist, however, he does not want to confine himself to such an exclusively economic definition of what is usually called a subsistence farmer. Professor Firth prefers to see the peasant as an individual exposed both to peasant economy and to a particular kind of social structure.

The Javanese peasant, while a member of the lowest income group of the farmers in Java, is not so by "necessity." The Javanese peasant economy, nonpriced, marketless, and consumption-oriented, has come about mainly because of *a deficiency in communication* between peasants' production and the market. The deficiency, if not the absence, of this communication can be attributed to three different factors.

The first is that the peasant's agricultural

undertaking simply does not produce enough to establish a continuous link between his farm and the market. This phenomenon is common in Java, the world's most over-populated agricultural island, where there are 1,477 people per square kilometer (and up to 1,707 in the most fertile areas of Central Java) and where only an average of 0.135 hectares[1] of arable land is available per person, or less than one third of the minimum size of landholding per peasant family as set by the Agrarian Law. It is not worthwhile for the Javanese peasant, on his tiny plot of land, to produce for the market, and the best he can do is produce for his own household needs. But however poor his household, he needs other things than those which his land can provide him. He is forced to sell part of his products on the market to purchase salt, kerosene for his lamp, and clothing. He also has to pay his tax to the government, who no longer want to receive it in kind but demand payment in cash. If he can sell his labor for cash somewhere and in a way which does not arouse the disapproval of the community, the Javanese peasant is most likely to do so in preference to selling part of his farm produce. But if forced to, he or his wife will bring some of the products of the land to the nearest marketplace, as Clifford Geertz says, not for the purpose of trading, but only to convert it into cash to acquire additional household funds [Geertz, 1963]. After having sold his products for a price which may not have any bearing on the prevailing interplay of supply and demand, but which is very often determined by the farmer's need for nonagricultural commodities, he will purchase in the same marketplace whatever he can buy with his money, so that he comes home with things and without or with only little cash in his pocket.

The second factor which accounts for the lack of communication between farm and market is geographical in nature. A farm may be located at such a distant physical isolation from any market that products of the land have no other channels of disposal than to the peasant's own household and extended family in the village. In this case a farmer may have surplus of land and crops, more than he and his family can con-sume, but he sees no chance to transfer his surplus products to the market. The less well-developed road and transport system in some parts of Java, and in many other islands of Indonesia, leaves no other alternative for the peasant than to produce for his own limited needs. By standards of the farmers' community, a peasant who is in this way forced to a subsistence production system may be considered wealthy. The limited consumption possibilities in his isolated village, however, do not allow him to go beyond the general consumption ceiling to enjoy his wealth. He may once in a while carry parts of his farm products on foot or horseback to distant markets to sell, but here again he sells only to acquire and come home with nonagricultural commodities to use in his household. There is not much of a commercial motive in his act of selling and buying.

The third factor responsible for the poor connection between farm and market exists in a situation in which the peasant has plenty of land and physical facilities are available to take his products to the market, as is the case in the newly opened agricultural transmigration areas in Sumatra. Yet such a peasant sometimes fails to develop the ability to enter the world of commerce for three reasons: (a) There seems to be no incentive to rise above the level of subsistence farming to which he was accustomed while still living in overcrowded Java. (b) Because of poorly developed farming technology and lack of managerial and entrepreneurial skills, the peasant cannot produce beyond the capacities of his family, which amounts to only little above the needs of his household. (c) There is only a small marginal profit to gain if the peasant goes to the market to sell his products, and it is easier to stay at home and wait for the collecting merchant to come and purchase whatever the peasant will not miss. Being cut off from the market by the middleman (the collecting merchant), the peasant has little occasion to react to or profit from price fluctuations. It is a well-known complaint of the civil administration, in newly opened farming areas in Sumatra or elsewhere, that Javanese peasants who have been moved from Java to those areas where they can get land free always remain poor, whereas the collecting merchants become wealthy in a relatively short time.

1. Central Bureau of Statistics, *Statistical Pocketbook, 1963* (Djakarta, Indonesia).

LAND

Professor Firth mentions that in many agricultural communities there is a tendency of peasant groups to exercise sanctions to prevent a man from using more land than local views of equity allow. Such limitative group rules are understandable if there is a scarcity of land in proportion to the population. And yet in the many villages in Central and West Java that I have personally visited I have not found any norm, either formal or informal, which inhibits a peasant from acquiring and using as much land as he is able to work upon. It is only very recently that the Republic of Indonesia, not the village communities themselves, decided by the Basic Agrarian Act of 1960 that no peasant family should own more than a maximum of 5 hectares of land, or 7.5 hectares in some of the dry and less fertile areas of Java. There is, however, very often a rule made by village councils—the village administration and all landowners in a village community—that, in any transaction concerning land, first priority for the use or acquisition of land be given to the owner's blood relatives residing in the village, second priority to other members of the village community, and the last priority to people outside the village. This rule is clearly intended to bar absentee landowners, who might disturb the social and economic interests of the local peasant community. But it does not put a limit on the size of land one can possibly own or work upon. Whatever limitations a peasant experiences in his agricultural activities come mainly from the low level of farming technology. The mere use of nonmechanized tools understandably confines the peasant to a relatively small size of land in his undertaking, even if he gets the help of his neighbors and other friends in the hectic seasons of the year.

A peasant economy which does not make much use of money, either as a price index or medium of exchange, usually does not know or understand the system of landlease at a prefixed price or rent. Excess land owned by a peasant is given to another—most often landless—member of the village community to work on a sharecropping basis. The shares of the product for landowner and tenant are fixed by tradition based upon the availability of irrigation water. Wet farming, which requires relatively less human labor and gives a higher yield, entitles the tenant to half of the harvest, and dry farming to one-third. But here again the relationship between landowner and tenant is not purely economic, but it is to a considerable extent social in character. The landowner is expected to extend material or financial aid whenever the tenant needs it, and on the other hand the tenant is supposed to be available any time his labor is needed to help the landowner. It may be due to the custom of having the family act as an agricultural working unit that in most cases an owner-tenant contract develops into a kinshiplike relationship between an older and a younger member of one family. This may also be the reason why the Sharecropping Act, issued simultaneously with the Basic Agrarian Act and meant to protect with rational and administrative rules the supposedly economically weaker tenant against the dominant landowner, does not find much support from either party in its implementation.

The general idea in Java's peasant communities is not that a peasant should be limited in the ownership and use of land, but that a successful member of the community should share his wealth with the community and let other members of the community share in the enjoyment of his wealth.[2] This notion was explicitly expressed by both peasant and non-peasant members of some villages when I raised the question of the limits an individual has to consider when striving for personal prosperity. It was generally agreed that an individual was allowed—the word "encouraged" was not used—to acquire as much "worldly" wealth as he possibly can, provided he does not forget his religious obligations and his community. Being in a community with an overwhelmingly Islamic membership, an individual was supposed to pay his prescribed *zakat* and *fitrah* contributions for the poor and to contribute for the building and maintenance of mosques, religious schools, and other Islamic institutions in his community. The non-religious obligations to the community could be realized by contributions for the building of roads, school buildings, village hall, and other works for public use and also by being

2. See also the discussion by Rogers in Chapter 5 of the present volume.

ready to help whenever another member of the community knocks at one's door.

In discussing women's role in management and in assets, Professor Firth mentions the fairly widespread custom that land in a peasant society is owned mostly by men. This applies also to the peasant communities in Java, but there are many landholdings registered under the name of women. Deliberate purchase of land is usually done by men, since the actual management of the farm is generally exercised by men; either he is husband or the oldest son of the woman owner. But many women secure title to land as an inheritance from their parents. Customary inheritance law rules that each child should receive a legitimate share of the inheritance, a son getting twice the share of a daughter. Either partner of a married couple can legally hold a title to land, but the products go into the family pot called *gana-gini*. This is in contrast with the women's position in the Nsaw, where "men own the land, women own the crops," or alternatively, "a woman owns only a farm, she does not own the earth." A woman in Java can own the land, but the family owns the crops. As a formal landowner, a woman has the same rights and obligations as a man in the village community, but in exercising them, a woman landowner is usually represented by either her husband or her eldest son. She has, however, an undisputed dominant position in the family household. It is the wife who keeps the family purse and who has the decisive word in the family economy.

Referring to Kaberry, Professor Firth agrees that tendencies have emerged for more individualization of permanent land rights, for women as well as for men. Evidence shows that this trend is also observable in peasant communities in Java. It is well known that at the time of the forced system of agriculture in the second half of the past century, and continuing into the second decade of this century, the Dutch colonial administration encouraged and facilitated the establishment of communal land rights in Java. The idea was that when land rights were held in the hands of a village community, it was easier for the administration to control land use through it and to force the population to grow commercial crops for the foreign market. After the abolishment of the forced

agricultural system, a process of individualization of land rights developed in almost all parts of Java. First, all land owned by the village community was distributed in rotating usufruct among its members—resident heads of nuclear families. Then the peasants were allowed to hold their share of land for life. Subsequently each peasant could pass his share to his heirs after death, and finally he was permitted to sell his land, but only with the approval of the village council. The present situation in most villages is such that each peasant can have the exclusive and inheritable rights of ownership on his land, but in disposing of it he is subject to the approval of the village council or of the village administration, who have the duty of guarding the welfare of the community as a whole. This trend toward individualization is to a large extent due to the growing desire of the individual peasant to enjoy the results of his efforts to improve the land and to acquire a higher yield. But in spite of this distinct individualizing trend in holding one's rights to land, the peasant is not entirely free from communal pressures in his agricultural activities. In particular when farming requires the use of irrigation water, each peasant is forced to follow the decisions of the village council in terms of the choice of his crops and the time of plowing and planting, because it is the village council who decides upon water distribution. In areas where farming is dependent on rainfall for lack of irrigation, all farmers as under command from heaven start working on their land almost simultaneously as soon as the first rains start to fall. The concentration of labor in the field during short periods of time, the simultaneous need for water and other farming facilities for all peasants in the same locality, and again the low level of farming technology that leaves little room for variation in the peasants' activities, are all forces which drive the peasants to stringent conformities in his actions which go beyond the technical aspects of agriculture and into the peasant's everyday life in his community.

COMMUNITY CONFORMITY

For purposes of economic development, economists are unapprovingly concerned with overpopulation and consequent small and scattered landholdings, together with the material poverty of the peasant. But more resistant to progress and development is the peasant's strong attitude of conformity toward his community, and particularly so is his mental set, which is entirely wrapped up in his traditional techniques of agriculture. His strong submission to the community prevents the peasant from accepting new systems of farming and technical or economic innovations to better his material living unless approved and justified by his community. An individual may carry out better techniques of farming, using better implements and better seeds which guarantee a higher yield, but he will stand alone as long as his innovations fail to complete the process of institutionalization in the community.

In a village in West Java I saw a striking evidence of stubborn resistance to innovation. There were two plots of wet rice land, adjacently located and both of the same quality. One was owned and worked upon by a peasant who received his land as an inheritance from his deceased father. The other piece was owned by a well-educated man who had, in economic and social terms, outgrown his community by owning and running a weaving factory in the village and by maintaining continuous communication with the faraway city. He also had received his land as an inheritance from his father. But this man, being too busy with his factory and other nonagricultural activities, could not work on his land personally and hence had hired his neighbor to do the farming for him for cash payment. As a paid farmhand, his neighbor was under orders to carry out new techniques and to use locally made new implements. In spite of the higher and better yields of the nontraditionally farmed land as compared to the surrounding rice fields of the peasants, there was no one who tried to adopt the new farming techniques and new implements. Neither did the paid farmhand who continued to farm on his own land while working for three years on his neighbor's field, despite the opportunity given to him to borrow and use the new tools on his own land.

My inquiries disclosed that the factory owner, though born and partly brought up in the village, was no longer considered a genuine member of the community because of his nonconforming habits, because of the wealth he was able to accumulate outside agriculture without involving other members of the community and thus without giving them the chance to share in its enjoyment, and finally because he hired his neighbor for cash payment instead of letting him do the farming on his land under a traditional share-cropping agreement. He was a nonconformist in the extreme, and for this reason nobody considered it appropriate to follow or adopt his farming techniques, even though people were convinced that they worked better than the old methods in the village. If it is difficult to change traditionally established farming habits, it is equally hard, perhaps even harder, to instill in the peasant a desire for more income and better economic position.

How hard such an effort is might be indicated by the ideal state of individual prosperity, which was in the minds of both peasants and nonpeasants in a few villages in Central and West Java. Their ideal state of prosperity is when a man has a decent house to shelter him and his family from rain and sunshine; enough clothing to wear in the rice fields, at home, and on formal occasions; and enough food to overcome the period extending from the last harvest to the next. Those who have seen villages in Java know that this level of prosperity is beyond the reach of millions of peasants on that island, but it gives a clear evidence that the peasant's world of desires is narrowly confined to what in other, economically more advanced, societies would be labeled as the minimum level of living for a family. In other words, the peasant's goals in his activities, firmly based on his needs for housing and *sandang-pangan* (food and clothing), do not go beyond the limits of subsistence and hence cannot pull him above the level of subsistence farming. The discouraging feature is that nonfarmers in the community cherish the same ideas of prosperity. This is an indication that their departure from agriculture was done by necessity and not by deliberate choice, so that if their is any chance, they will gladly return to the world of subsistence farming.

This farming-oriented attitude can hardly be justified with economic reasoning, since the economic income of the subsistence peasant may be less than his total minimum wants. The deeper reasons may be more sociological than economic. The non-landowner does not enjoy as much prestige and as many social privileges as does the landowner. In fact, only landowners enjoyed political rights in the village. At the time of communal landownership, only recognized resident heads of families could share in the use of land, and in exercising its duties the village administration was almost exclusively concerned with them while paying a minimum of attention to others. When landholdings became more permanent and individualized, the former landusers who were made landowners attained an even stronger and more prestigeful status in the community.

With land playing such a prominent role in the economic and social life of the people, it is no wonder to see land as the major yardstick for the measurement of social and even economic prestige. Land, and not any other kind of material wealth, counts supreme in the Javanese village. If a man is successful in accumulating wealth without himself being a landowner and farmer, the community will recognize his economic success, but it will not recognize him as a member. He is considered an outsider, perhaps a stranger, socially and culturally.

In this context we may mention the tax system in the villages, which has some bearing on the existing social structure. Congruent with the land-based social structure, the principal taxes levied in the village were head taxes, abolished in 1946, and land rent, until 1954. Head tax, evenly levied upon every landholder irrespective of the quality and size of his land, was based upon public recognition of one's position as landowner. From an economic and rational viewpoint, the head tax could be considered unfair because it placed a proportionally heavier burden on those with small landholdings than it did on the large landholders.

The peasants, however, looking at it from the social side, considered the tax quite justified and fair. The head tax put every landowner in the same category as the privileged landowners, so all enjoyed the same prestige and the same privileges without regard to anything else.

The head tax was abolished by law all over the country in 1946 as feudalistic and inconsistent with new democratic ideas introduced by the national revolution. Political rights were then spread over all citizens, disregarding their relationship to land. Socially, the law failed everywhere to establish any significant change from an agrarian to a nonagrarian rural community. In almost all cases village communities have retained their land-based social structure.

In a second fiscal measure to weaken the ties that keep the peasants strangled with their small plots of land, the government changed the land rent, which varied in amount according to quality and size of the landholding, into an income tax. Land is no longer made the basis of the tax system but is replaced by financial income, from whatever sources it may be derived. In this way it was hoped that peasants through their income could place themselves on the same level as other nonpeasant members of the community. If that goal could be accomplished, it would be less difficult to channel the excess peasant population into other sectors of the economy outside agriculture. For this purpose the measure has, so far at least, not yet attained much success because of the scarcity of nonagricultural employment in Java's rural areas.

THE YOUNGER GENERATION

A factor that may open new vistas of economic development in Java's rural areas is the changing attitudes toward life in general among the younger generation. The national revolution, which has drastically destroyed the inferiority complex that hampered the social-psychological development of peasant communities in the past; the rapidly expanding system of education which supplies the means for vertical mobility to everybody who wants it; and the growing trend toward urbanization and industrialization have their dynamizing impact on the younger generation. They realize that there is no room in agriculture for those who want to get ahead in the world, and they do want to attain more and better achievements than their peasant parents. Young people in the rural areas are now more attracted to industries, the armed forces, and the administration than they are to agriculture. Hence many of them have left their village of origin, leaving the less ambitious brothers home to continue the work of their parents on the ever shrinking land. There are even peasant parents now who deviate from the established tradition and wish to educate their children to become anything but peasants. This gives a valuable clue for economic and social development in peasant communities: do not spend too much energy trying to change the old generation of peasants, but rather start educating the younger generation for planned development.

Reference

GEERTZ, 1963. Clifford Geertz, *Peddlers and Princes: Social Development and Economic Change in Two Indonesian Towns* (Chicago: University of Chicago Press, 1963).

CASE STUDY

A Semisubsistence Village Economy in Lower Burma

DAVID E. PFANNER

THE AGRICULTURAL ECONOMY of Burma supports over three-quarters of its population, furnishes most of its food, and provides the government with the majority of its revenue through the export and sale of rice. Rice production is largely based on small, peasant holdings, found most extensively in the valleys and deltas of Burma's major river systems, particularly the Irrawaddy. The following paper examines the Burmese peasant as both producer and consumer, the community in which he lives, its history, and some of the economic and social factors which influence his economic behavior. The profile of the community is typical of that of Lower Burma, illustrating a type of peasant agriculture midway between subsistence production and production for national and international markets. The study also points to critical factors involved in growth in agricultural production in such a community.

DEVELOPMENT OF THE ECONOMY IN LOWER BURMA

In the years following the conquest and pacification of Lower Burma in the early nineteenth century, a phenomenal expansion in agricultural production took place as a result of improved security conditions, availability of fertile land, an assured rainfall, and a government policy encouraging immigration and migration. Increased world demand for rice and new markets associated with the opening of the Suez Canal in 1869 spurred development even further. The settling of the delta of Lower Burma and the expansion of rice production there constitutes the most spectacular development of Burma's economic history, transforming an entire area of jungle and waste the size of New Jersey into ten million acres of paddy land and one of the world's major rice exporting areas.

The history of this development [Furnivall, 1931; Andrus, 1948] reveals much about the Burmese, their adaptability to new conditions, responsiveness to economic incentives, and the social reaction to the British colonial administration and the agrarian structure which developed under it. Although the area under cultivation and production grew rapidly, it was a one-sided development, since the Burmese cultivator shared little in the rewards and prosperity which it brought to foreign elements in the population; the strains that developed in Burmese society during those years of contact with the West are visible today in the virulent economic nationalism under the Ne Win regime which is dedicated to insuring economic gains for the Burmese alone, whatever the cost.

The development of a market agriculture in Lower Burma was accomplished largely by Burmese colonists who migrated south from the parched fields of Upper Burma. The task of clearing and planting the land was enormous, forcing the British to pay tribute to the early pioneers exposed to such continuing discomforts as the boiling hot sun and malaria. The Annual Report of Burma for 1916–1917 contains the following passage: "The Burman, although reputed to be easy going and improvident, has shown considerable readiness in adapting himself to the rapidly changing conditions and the greatest achievements in the history of the province, namely the colonization of Lower Burma, has been almost entirely the work of the Burmans."

During the century between 1830 and 1930 the area in Lower Burma under paddy increased from 66,000 to 9,911,000 acres [Government of Burma, 1932, p. 1]. The greatest increase in acreage occurred between 1860 and 1905, the period after the opening of the Suez Canal until most of the cultivable land had been settled. During these years, the area planted to rice in the Irrawaddy and Lower Salween and Sittang Valleys alone increased by 5.5 million acres [Andrus 1948, 43].

The Pegu District of Lower Burma was one of the chief rice producers where the improvement of communications contributed greatly to development. Eager to settle the district, the British took measures to encourage immigration and improve transport. The bunding of the Sittang River to prevent its overflow into the western plains, the construction of the Rangoon–Toungoo Road, and the Pegu Canal were three such early projects. The Rangoon–Toungoo link of the Rangoon–Mandalay Railway, completed in 1848, opened up the plain of Pegu to immigration of Mons from Thaton and Burmese from Upper Burma, as well as Shans, Karens, Taungthus, and, to a minor extent, Indians.

The human cost of clearing the land in Pegu District was high, as much heavy jungle cutting had to be done and the local malaria of a particularly virulent type took a heavy toll of the pioneers [Government of India, 1917]. The area under cultivation extended rapidly, however, and by 1911 it was estimated that over nine-tenths of the cultivable land was occupied, and just prior to the Japanese invasion, 99 per cent of cultivable land was planted to rice [Government of Burma, 1955, pp. 18, 19]. In 1908 the rice-milling industry in the district was almost nonexistent, yet the number of mills rose to 66 by 1934, despite the nearness of the Rangoon mills [Government of Burma, 1936, pp. 63, 66].

The population of Lower Burma was at an extremely low level prior to and following the British annexation in 1824. Following the reestablishment of peace and a stable government, however, population rose rapidly. After the 1858 war exiles began to return to their homes and were joined by a steady flow of immigrants from the north. Laborers from the central basin who migrated to cultivate or harvest in the south soon heard of opportunities and became landowners themselves. Indian moneylenders were present to help finance their efforts by advancing capital or a land mortgage on occupied land. In this way the large virgin tracts of Lower Burma were rapidly colonized. Despite the increase in population, however, the proportion of Burmese residing in urban areas actually declined, reflecting not only traditional Burmese social and economic preferences and capabilities, but also the influx of foreign immigrants that settled in the towns.

Indian immigration to Burma was encouraged and assisted in the late nineteenth century to relieve population congestion in certain Indian districts and to introduce new crops, methods, and labor into the relatively underpopulated Burma. Indian immigrants never formed a large part of the agricultural population, for Burmese immigrants from Upper Burma filled manpower needs in the delta, but Indians were very significant in urban occupations dealing with preparation of rice for export and in financing the crop. The significance of the Indian population stemmed not from numerical strength, but from its occupational distribution, the successful competition with Burmese in moneylending and in certain low-paying positions, and in the control Indians came to have on Burmese agriculture.

It was the Indian *chettyars* (businessman and moneylenders) who provided the cash required for clearing and cultivating land in Lower Burma. Much of this land eventually came under the direct control of these moneylenders when mortgages were defaulted because of imprudent consumption, cattle deaths, falling crop prices, or illness on the part of the cultivator. Another laborer would take over and the process would be repeated. Although Indians did not always want to hold the land, it was acquired in later years in order to insure a supply of paddy for their mills. During the depression of the 1930's land values fell so low it was worth less than the outstanding debts, and many peasants lost their land at this time to the *chettyars*. From 1930 to 1937 the area occupied by nonagriculturalists in Lower Burma rose by 60 per cent, while the total area occupied rose by only 3 per cent. By 1941, nearly 50 per cent of the land in Lower Burma was held by nonagriculturalists: in the thirteen principal rice growing districts, *chettyars* occupied 25 per cent of the total occupied land and 50 per cent of the area occupied by nonagriculturalists.

Associated with the problem of land alienation was that of land tenancy, which was characterized by ruinous rents, indebtedness, and lack of security in tenure that combined to produce a large floating population of tenants who moved from holding to holding. Large-scale commercial agriculture never developed in Lower Burma, and although some landlords owned thousands of acres, the typical unit rented to a tenant was from fifteen to thirty acres. The landlord, Indian or Burmese, had little interest in the land, and tenants were locked in permanent debt and barely subsisting because of the high rents. Prior to the Japanese invasion, almost 60 per cent of the land was rented to tenants; and of this, 48 per cent of the area was held by tenants who had been in possession of the land for only one year.

The extent and depth of this agrarian problem and the subsequent social disorganization have been widely commented upon since and was well known to the colonial administration. No solution was found, however, and reform measures came too late to be effective. Despite the enormous increase in production of rice in Lower Burma, most Burmese peasants did not share in this prosperity. The living levels of the cultivator improved little during the decades prior to World War II, with some evidence indicating his welfare actually declined after the 1930's.

Whether because of a preference for agriculture or because entrance to urban industrial and commercial occupations was denied, the occupational and social structure that developed confined the Burmese to rural agricultural pursuits with little contact with modern economic life. Agriculture came to be characterized by increasingly impoverished tenants, who produced an ever-increasing number of political rebels and criminals. The breakdown of the discipline of the monastic order and the inability of local government to cope with the social disorder were associated with a number of serious outbreaks against the British during the decade of the 1930's.

The traditional social structure of Upper Burma never really developed in the south, which was characterized by an anomie related in large part to a land-tenure system which carried few rewards or incentives for the cultivator, who had few alternatives outside agriculture. In the plural society which developed, an alien British and Indian minority controlled the economic, political, administrative, military, and legal institutions, while the rural Burmese, through their customary law, exercised control only over local community matters. No aristocracy could develop based on the monarchy, and no large middle class or social elite emerged based on wealth or territorial loyalty. Burmese participation in government and its share in the economy was thus minimal. The frustration of seeing foreigners reap economic benefits, while the Burmese standard actually declined, caused widespread feelings of deprivation and provided a fertile ground for political agitation and ethnic hostility. In this environment it is not surprising that the Burmese did not readily accept Western concepts, values, and innovations, which had worked largely to their disadvantage during the colonial period.

Before wider Burmese political participation could affect the political climate following the separation from India in 1937, war struck, and the Japanese launched the Burmese on the road to independence outside the Commonwealth. During the process, however, Burma suffered enormous destruction of her industrial, transportation, communications, agricultural, and productive capacity. Millions of acres of fertile paddy land were overrun by jungle, with the area under cultivation dropping by half between 1940 and 1945. Production of rice dropped from 8 million tons in 1940 to 2.8 million tons in the early postwar years. War damage was only partially responsible for the slow economic growth after independence, however—a second and equally important factor was the outbreak of civil war in 1948, which continued to disrupt rural patterns of production until 1951.

It is against this background that agriculture in postwar independent Burma must be interpreted.

During the two decades that have elapsed since Burmese independence, her governments have set about to correct what they have regarded as serious defects in the economic, social, and political structure that developed under the British colonial administration. Government economic policy and programs under the leadership of Prime Minister U Nu included commitments to end foreign economic control, land nationalization, and access to cheap credit facilities for the peasant. The regime of General Ne Win has pursued economic nationalism even more vigorously, nationalizing all banks and retail trade, forcing the repatriation of hundreds of thousands of Indian businessmen and middlemen.

Agricultural policy in independent Burma has ranged from almost total neglect, during the years U Nu attempted to industrialize the country, to recent efforts at rural development by the military government. Agricultural production and productivity have generally remained unaffected and in a depressed state, however. The year 1965 saw the unbelievable phenomenon of rice rationing in some Burmese cities, a situation growing out of the chaos following the faulty purchasing and distribution program of the Revolutionary Council's "Burmese Way To Socialism" policy, which abolished all private trading in rice.

Mayin Village[1]

The Pegu District of Lower Burma shares many of the agronomic characteristics of the deltaic plains so well suited to rice culture: warm temperature throughout most of the year; ample rainfall well distributed throughout the monsoon; and flat land of relatively fertile soil. During the monsoon the district gets about 127 inches of rain a year, from mid-May to mid-October. Its soils are of the heavy clay or clay-loam type, overlaid with lighter surface soils, making them difficult to work except when soaked.

1. Unless otherwise indicated, the data on Mayin village was collected by the author during his field research in 1959 and 1960 [Pfanner, 1962].

The Ngasein and Medon groups of rice include the varieties most commonly grown. They are relatively long-lived, taking about 170 days or more to mature. The government has been encouraging the cultivation of early-maturing varieties, which permit the early planting of groundnuts. The normal yield of paddy has been estimated at 1,650 pounds per acre for the district, a figure very close to the all-Burma average of 1,516 pouhds in 1959–1960.

The district is divided into distinct natural tracts, with the Pegu Yomas and their foothills to the west coming down to the Rangoon–Mandalay Railroad and motor road, with an eastern tract comprising a large plain containing the Pegu and Sittang Rivers.

The Mayin Village Tract lies in this eastern plain of the Sittang, sixty miles northeast of Rangoon and eight miles north of the district capital of Pegu. To the west about seven miles is a dense forest covering the southern end of the low-lying Pegu Yomas; the area between this forest and the Sittang eighteen miles to the east, composed almost entirely of paddy fields. Mayin village is one of four villages in the Mayin tract, each having a distinct social and geographic identity but populated entirely by culturally similar ethnic Burmese. They were founded a hundred years ago by settlers from the Minbu and Meiktila districts of Upper Burma who migrated south seeking opportunities following British annexation of the territory.

Mayinywama, the largest of the four villages of the Mayin Village Tract, contains 152 houses, a population of 700, and is generally typical of the rural villages of the Lower Burmese districts. The village, often referred to simply as Mayin, depends almost entirely on rice cultivation for its subsistence and income; 92 per cent of all household heads are working as paddy farmers. Groundnuts are grown as a second crop.

The soil of Mayin is of average fertility, rainfall is adequate, but the arrival and departure dates of the southwest monsoon can be a critical factor in rice agriculture here as elsewhere. In 1960 most Mayin cultivators (92 per cent) were technically tenants on government land, the distribution having been made by a village committee under the Land Nationalization Act of 1953 (as amended). Under this Act, up to 50 acres owned by cultivators was exempted from nationalization, while the rest of the land held by nonresident owners (largely Indian) was distributed to resident cultivators by the committee. The work of the village committee was subsequently suspended because of disagreements that arose in its implementation of the Act, but its initial distribution of land formed the basis for tenancy applications cultivators were required to file under previous existing legislation in order to work the land.

Compared with the district as a whole, size of holdings are more uniform in Mayin. There are no farms under 6 acres, and 88 per cent of the farmers fall in the range from 6 to 20 acres.

THE FACTORS OF PRODUCTION AND THEIR COMBINATIONS

The 113 farms of Mayin are peasant proprietorships, employing family labor for the most part and utilizing a technology which has remained unchanged for generations. One of the outstanding characteristics of Lower Burmese agriculture is the remarkable uniformity and similarity of farm units which produce the same crop in the same way year after year. Differences in productivity do not depend on any basic or novel rearrangement of the traditional factors of production, nor upon differences in technology or type of seed stock.

The 113 farmers of Mayin planted 1700 acres of their land to paddy in 1959–1960. The average size farm in Mayin is 15.15 acres, the average production being 32 baskets of paddy, or 1,472 pounds per acre. This figure is slightly above the district and all-Burma average of 1,380 pounds in 1955 [Union of Burma, Department of Agriculture, 1955, n.p.], and below the 1959–1960 Burma average of 1,517 pounds reported by the FAO during this period. This yield compares with 5,307 pounds for Australia; 4,237 pounds in Japan; 1,240 pounds in Thailand and 981 pounds in the Philippines [FAO, 1960, Table 18, p. 50].

Following the paddy harvest, a total of 300 acres was double-cropped and planted to groundnuts by 94 per cent of the farmers, adding at least 26 per cent to total gross incomes in 1959–1960. The rapid acceptance

of this crop by the Burmese peasants is a clear indication of their response to economic incentives. The success of this innovation, which dates from 1956, can be attributed to an assured market and transport facilities to get the crop to market, the utilization of existing land, family labor, and a simple technology and crop management requiring little capital outlay on a crop that provided an important, inexpensive contribution to the diet, i.e. cooking oil, and a significant source of cash income from its sale.

The cycle of agricultural operations and the implements used in the production of rice are not essentially different from those used during the prewar years. In March and April, Mayin farmers burn over their fields to destroy insects and cut wood, bamboo, and roofing material in nearby forests; houses, field huts, and cowsheds together with farm implements are built and repaired during May, and late in this month and into the next, fields are plowed and harrowed, rice seed beds prepared, and seed sown. Transplanting takes place in July, and until November fields are tended and grass cut for cattle. The threshing floor is prepared in November, and in this month and the next, paddy is cut and transported to the threshing area. Harvesting, threshing, and winnowing occur mostly during January and February, which also see the sale of the crop and transport of a portion of it from the fields to home-storage facilities.

Before the recent nationalization of the rice trade by the military government, the great bulk of the Mayin rice crop was sold to merchants (largely Chinese), brokers, or mill owners who came to the village from nearby towns in trucks and purchased the paddy direct from the threshing floor. A 1960 survey of a representative sample of Pegu District farmers revealed that 68 per cent of the rice crop which was sold was disposed of in this manner, while 32 per cent was taken to the depots of the State Agricultural Marketing Board [Hla Than, 1960]. The farmers got less for their crop from the merchants and millers, but they avoided problems of transportation to the point of sale and received payment immediately, which was not the case when the government was buyer.

Approximately 56 per cent of the total rice production of Mayin is sold, while 44

Table 3.1. Disposition of Paddy Production among High, Medium,
and Low Productivity Groups, Mayinywama, 1959–1960.

	High productivity group	Medium productivity group	Low productivity group	All groups
Total Production (in baskets)	3,100	2,190	1,170	6,470
Proportion Total Production Sold	66%	66%	10%	56%
Proportion Total Production Retained	34%	34%	90%	44%
Disposition of Retained Production:				
Proportion Used for: (in per cent)				
Seed rice	8	10	5	7
Home consumption	35	39	15	29
Labor payments	52	44	13	36
Interest and repayment of loans	5	7	67	28
	100% (1,051 baskets)	100% (748 baskets)	100% (1,045 baskets)	100% (2,844 baskets)

SOURCE: Pfanner, 1962, Table 15, p. 203.

per cent is retained for: home consumption; payment to agricultural laborers by the farmer-producer; repayment and interest on loans involving repayment in kind; and seed rice for the next year's crop. The disposition of the rice crop among three groups of 15 farmers, differing according to their productivity of rice yields, is seen in Table 3.1. The significance of these figures will be referred to in later pages.

Agricultural occupations accounted for 92 per cent of all household heads in 1960, and of these, 83 per cent worked their own land and 17 per cent worked as agricultural laborers. There are few occupational roles outside of agriculture, the only others being native doctor, shopkeeper, and seamstress. Nine farmers had multiple occupational roles: two were also carpenters, one a blacksmith, and five were petty traders and one a native doctor. Apart from the important religious roles (not included in the above, since Buddhist monks reside in village monasteries and not in homes) occupational role distinctions are vague and ill-defined. There is little division of labor or occupational specialization associated with distinctive social status. The Burmese social system in the villages is characterized by a uniform social structure which lacks major distinctions of wealth, occupation, or status, with the single important exception of the Buddhist clergy.

With the exception of rice transplanting, members of the nuclear family provide most of the labor for the farms. Compared with some villages in the area, Mayin contains a relatively high proportion of farmers to farm laborers with no land of their own. Out of a total of 152 household heads in the village, 76 per cent are farm operators, and of the 17 per cent which are farm laborers, about a third are women. Laborers are employed for periods ranging from two months to the entire agricultural cycle. For the whole eight-month season, they receive 125 baskets of paddy plus their food and tobacco; for a five-month period, the rate is 65 to 70 baskets.

Large labor inputs are required during the relatively short period when rice seedlings must be transplanted. At this time family labor is usually insufficient, and outside resources are called upon in the form of one of the seven formally organized groups of female transplanters from the village. Each of these groups, usually under the leadership of an older spinster, contracts with individual farmers to work his fields for a specified number of days during a certain period. For her management and supervisory services the group leader receives an additional daily K1/50 ($.30; the Burmese Kyat is worth approximately $.21). Generally speaking, these neighborhood groups are made up of women and girls from a particular section of the village who work the fields belonging to farmers living in that neighborhood. The groups average 12 members each, ranging in size from 8 to 16 women, each of whom works a total of about 60 days during the agricultural cycle. The fields worked are not necessarily those nearest their own home, for holdings are rarely geographically contiguous.

The distribution of land under the land-nationalization legislation assigned fields in different areas, the total holding thus being made up of a number of individual dispersed fields.

This local form of labor organization is extremely efficient and has in it a remarkable degree of flexibility which makes it adaptable to a variety of needs. There are two forms of payment to group members; one is a flat daily rate of K1/50; more often, however, the labor is performed on an exchange basis by which a woman performs a day of work in the fields of a family who has in the past, or will in the future, provide a day of work in her own family's fields. Under this arrangement no money changes hands, but careful records are kept. If a laborer works more days than is returned in the form of labor, she is paid K1/50 for each such day.

The basis of agricultural labor and co-operation is both contractual and reciprocal and does not depend upon the mutual obligations among a group of extended kin. Insofar as the kin group is concentrated in a particular neighborhood, there may be an element of kinship in the arrangement, but it is neither obligatory or necessary. In a similar fashion, if a farmer needs a helping hand in the fields, as in the construction of a field hut, he calls upon his neighbors in nearby fields and not upon his kin group.

Labor expenses form the greatest single cost of production in Mayin, particularly the cost of transplanting, which gives higher production than broadcasting the seed. The labor-exchange gang described above is one means by which labor cash costs can be reduced. It also illustrates how significant the contribution of women is to the successful operation of the farm. Sickness on the part of a farmer's wife can be economically disastrous, as it can mean the equivalent of 60 man-days of cash costs which could otherwise be avoided by exchange labor. Unmarried men considering the choice of a future mate take strength and health into account as well as beauty.

In summary, while the basic unit of production is the individual nuclear family, increased efficiency and higher productivity demand a larger group for the transplanting operation. The supply of such labor through contracts with labor gangs is based on ter-ritorial and economic considerations rather than obligations of kinship or friendship.

The basic equipment required for the operation of a farm of the size most frequently encountered in Lower Burma requires a considerable capital investment: two bullocks and/or buffalo; a bullock cart; steel-tipped plow; rotary harrow and six-toothed harrow; hoe; rake; sickle; rope; a cowshed and field hut; seed rice and groundnut seed. Artificial and natural fertilizer are used to only a very minor extent and then usually on seed beds. It has been estimated that a farmer in the Pegu District requires an initial capital outlay of K1560 ($328) to work 10 acres of land, exclusive of any consumption expenses after the crop has been planted. The three basic items the peasant cannot fashion for himself are the cattle (K450 per pair); bullock cart (K450) and rotary harrow (K75) for a total of K975.

CREDIT AND SAVINGS

IN order to finance their production, and in many cases their current consumption, nearly all farmers find it necessary to borrow at the beginning of the agricultural cycle. The loans taken out at this time are usually repaid at harvest time, so that interest normally accrues over a period of seven to eight months. The average cultivator in the Pegu District requires an annual loan of K561 to finance his paddy crop, according to a 1960 survey of Pegu farmers by the District Department of Agriculture. In the village of Mayin the writer estimated that the average farmer took out annual loans totaling K528 to finance both paddy and groundnut production, the average paddy loan amounting to K435. It is difficult to separate the "production" aspects of these loans from "consumption," but for practical purposes the loans can be considered production loans, since the farmer and his family must eat during the production process.

It is unlikely that Mayin farmers have substantial savings, or they would not find it necessary to finance their crops at high rates of interest year after year. Those who do have liquid assets do not keep them in the form of cash, but as gold jewelry that can be used as collateral on secured loans from moneylenders in Payagyi or Pegu.

The relatively inexpensive loans from

government sources form only a small part of the total loan requirements in Burma [Aye Hlaing, 1958b, pp. 7–8, 21]. Among a sample of Mayin farmers only about 10 per cent of total loans came from government agencies, despite the presence of a village branch of the State Agricultural Bank. This bank is one of two government outlets for loans for agricultural purposes, the other being General Administration loans disbursed by the Township Officer through a village loan committee. The GA loans were only K5 per acre and formed an insignificant part of agricultural credit, as disbursements totaled only K650 in 1959–1960.

The excellently managed State Agricultural Bank branch in Mayin distributed paddy loans of K30 per acre to 71 villagers, who took out an average loan of K300. This must be compared with credit needs of approximately K56 per acre, the average paid-out costs of paddy production. Not all farmers are members of the Bank, however, and total government credit in the village is estimated at about 23 per cent of total need. The significance of this lies in the high cost of nongovernment credit and the consequent continuing indebtedness in the village. Government loans carry an interest rate of only 12 per cent per annum, of which half is retained by the village SAB branch for a reserve fund to be used eventually as its own revolving source of capital from which to make loans. The other half is absorbed by the parent bank for operating expenses.

There are four common forms of borrowing from private sources: the unsecured cash loan; the secured cash loan; the borrowing of cash with repayment in paddy; and the borrowing of paddy with repayment in paddy. Cultivators without collateral who borrow cash pay K5, or more frequently K6, per month for every K100 borrowed, an annual interest rate of 72 per cent. Most loans are taken out at planting time and repaid as soon as the rice has been harvested, being held about eight or nine months. The effective annual interest rate on secured loans, i.e. loans on which gold is pawned, is 36 per cent. The most ruinous form of loan is the *sabapay* loan, or repayment of K150 cash with 100 baskets of paddy at harvest time, which are worth K285, which is the fixed price for which paddy sells and implies an annual interest rate of 90 per cent or more on this form of loan. Another rather common practice is to borrow paddy (usually for consumption purposes) and return twice the amount borrowed, an indication that many farmers operate very close to the margin. The source and cost of credit in Mayin is summarized in Table 3.2.

INCOME AND EXPENDITURE

Total gross agricultural production for the entire village in 1959–1960 had a value of K244,350, or $51,400, of which 73 per cent was derived from paddy, 27 per cent from groundnuts. The average farm family

Table 3.2. Source and Cost of Credit in Mayinywama by Productivity Groups[a]

SOURCE OF CREDIT	HIGH PRODUCTIVITY GROUP		MEDIUM PRODUCTIVITY GROUP		LOW PRODUCTIVITY GROUP		ALL GROUPS	
	Interest in Kyats	% Total loans	Interest in Kyats	% Total loans	Interest in Kyats	% Total loans	Interest in Kyats	% Total loans
State Agricultural Bank (annual rate: 12%)	172	24	104	18	15	1	291	10
Secured Loans (annual rate: 36%)	205	28	93	16	110	8	408	15
Unsecured Loans (annual rate: 72%)	264	37	380	66	288	21	932	35
Sabapay (annual rate: 90%+)	80	11	—	—	974	70	1,054	40
Total Interest Paid	721	100	577	100	1,387	100	2,685	100
Average Interest Paid	144		115		277		179	

[a] Interest paid in kind has been converted to cash value at the rate of K2/85 per basket.
SOURCE: Pfanner, 1962, Table 19, p. 220.

income was thus $445, or $345 per family for the village as a whole. Increments to income from working as an agricultural laborer, selling fish, and the like, are insignificant, adding only 1–2 per cent to agricultural income. The distribution of gross farm income is seen in Table 3.3, and average farm income in Table 3.4. (The selection of the three productivity groups will be described in later paragraphs.)

Table 3.3. Distribution of Gross Farm Income in Mayinywama, 1959–1960.

Income Group	Number of farmers	Per Cent
Under K750	5	4
750–1199	8	7
1200–1649	25	22
1650–2099	30	26
2100–2549	20	18
2550–2999	11	10
3000–3449	4	4
3450–3899	6	5
3900 and over	4	4
	113	100

Median gross family farm income: K1984 ($420).
SOURCE: Pfanner, 1962, Table 7, p. 142.

It is estimated on the basis of a carefully detailed study of the production costs and consumption of 15 farm families that net agricultural income averages 47 per cent of gross income. This means an average agricultural family net income of K977 ($206) and a per capita net income of K288 ($48). These figures would rise to $245 and $57 respectively if the value of home-produced, home-consumed rice is added.

Apart from rice and groundnuts, there is no agricultural production of commercial significance. Livestock is raised as a source of draft power, but not for slaughter or for sale for slaughter. Chickens are semidomesticated and occasionally slaughtered or sold for slaughter to local merchants who market them in Pegu. Three families keep a half-dozen pigs among them. There is no commercial truck gardening, and few fruits or vegetables are grown for home consumption. Wood and thatch are cut in nearby forests for building and firewood. The other main dietary staple in addition to rice is a fish paste (*ngapi*) and is made by most families from fish caught locally.

Burmese peasants are very much a part of the money economy but could subsist fairly well without it. Rice and groundnuts are produced for both home consumption and for the market, so the great bulk of food needs as well as housing and many of the farm implements are obtained independently of the market. Mayin villagers are dependent upon the proceeds from crop sales for a number of consumer goods they no longer produce themselves, however, such as cloth and cooking and drinking utensils, and for repayment of some loans and services.

The disposition of net disposable income among 15 representative farm families in 1960 was as follows:

Item	Per Cent of Income
Food	32
Tobacco and betel	12
Clothing	7
Housing (mainly roofing)	9
Medicine	2
Religion	24
Social	9
Other	5
	100

These figures require a word of explanation, since they would not be representative of any

Table 3.4. Average Farm Income among Three Productivity Groups, Mayinywama (All Figures in Kyats)

	High productivity group	Medium productivity group	Low productivity group	All groups
Average Gross Agricultural Income	2,478	1,842	1,084	1,801
Average Production Costs	1,002	785	777	855
Average Net Agricultural Income	1,476	1,057	307	947
Average Net Nonagricultural Income	15	24	53	30
Average Total Net Income	1,489	1,081	360	977

SOURCE: Pfanner, 1962, Table 21, p. 223.

one family. The "Religion" category reflects mainly the cash contributions to initiation ceremonies for Buddhist novices (*shinbyu*) and the annual offering of robes and alms at each of the monasteries (*kahtein*). About 85 per cent of total expenditures on religion by this group was contributed by two families sponsoring a *shinbyu*, an event which takes place each time a family celebrates the entrance of a son into the monkhood. Every male in the village is a novice for some period of his life, but it is not an event which every family supports each year. It is estimated that about 6.5 per cent of average net family income is devoted to religious purposes if the family is not sponsoring a *shinbyu*.

PROBLEMS OF VILLAGE DEVELOPMENT

Agricultural production in Burma has remained at generally low levels during the period since independence in 1948. The reasons for this are varied and complex, but generally reflect the low productivity associated with: political instability and insurgents in many rural areas, which have disrupted transportation, marketing, and distribution and have terrorized and robbed villagers; seed varieties and crop management practices that have limited yields which could be raised under more optimal conditions; an inefficient marketing system incorporating such low prices paid to the farmer or merchant by the government that they did not provide sufficient incentive to improve yields; lack of sufficient credit at reasonable rates of interest with which to finance the crop; and finally, while the Burmese family and kinship system is sufficiently flexible to adapt as well as any to whatever demands are put upon it by economic development, certain aspects of religious life and values have had at least a dampening influence on economic growth. The accumulation of goods is not socially valued; the most respected members of society, the Buddhist monks, lead extremely austere lives; and religious expenditures tend to absorb increases in income, which in most cases does not show much surplus above the cost of living and production costs. Religion must be regarded within a generally closed and traditional economic and social system, however, and compared with some

of the other factors described above, it cannot be assigned major economic significance.

Given the limiting constants of land, seed varieties, prices paid, and a uniform technology, what accounts for differences of productivity among Burmese farmers, and what are the social implications of these differences? To answer these questions, a cross section of 15 farmers was selected that differed greatly among themselves in terms of their productivity but which as a group resembled the Mayin cultivators as a whole. The size of their farms, fertility of the land, average size of family, and so on, were not significantly different from the village as a whole. The data accumulated about this group of 15, divided into three groups of high, medium, and low productivity, is useful in understanding the reasons behind differences in productivity and in the identification of agrarian problems in Burma, particularly those associated with the costs of production.

Labor input is the critical factor in Mayin, as it has been shown to be for other areas of Burma [Aye Hlaing 1958a; 6–7]. The reason is the higher yields that can be obtained from transplanting compared with broadcasting the seed, but transplanting takes a larger labor input. The utilization and cost of labor cannot be considered apart from the general problem of the cost of credit, for one depends on the other to a certain degree. It can be shown that productivity, income, and ultimately welfare are partly a function of the cost of credit.

Interest charges paid on loans taken out by the high-productivity group form a smaller proportion of the costs of production than interest on loans taken out by other groups, even though the total amount of the loans is greater. In Table 3.5 we see the high-productivity group borrows an average K656, compared with an average K498 for the medium-productivity group and an average K431 for the low-productivity group. The interest paid on these loans is K144, K115, and K277 for the high-, medium- and low-productivity groups respectively, or 16 per cent, 16 per cent, and 44 per cent of the total production costs of each of the respective groups (Table 3.6). In Table 3.2 we can see why the costs of credit are such a high proportion of total costs for the low-productivity group. In all, 70 per cent of all

Table 3.5. Cost of Credit Loans and Interest on Loans Paid by Three Productivity Groups
(in Kyats)

	High productivity group	Medium productivity group	Low productivity group	All groups
Total Loans:				
Paddy	2,725	2,050	1,760	6,535
Groundnut	555	440	396	1,391
Total	3,280	2,490	2,156	7,926
Total Interest Paid[a]	721	577	1,387	2,685
Average Size of Loan	656	498	431	528
Average Interest Paid	144	115	277	179
Interest as Per Cent of Principal	22	23	64	34

[a] Interest and principal paid in kind in the *sabapay* type of loan has been converted to its cash value at the rate of K2/85 per basket.
SOURCE: Pfanner, 1962, Table 18, p. 216.

loans made to this group were of the *sabapay* variety, which receives the highest rate of interest of all types. Only 11 per cent of the loans taken out by the high-productivity group were of this costly variety. Among the high-productivity group, 24 per cent of total loans come through the State Agricultural Bank, but these loans account for only 1 per cent of loans made to members of the low-productivity group.

The relationship of labor costs to the cost of credit is apparent. Without capital, cultivators cannot hire transplanters; without transplanters, productivity is low; and low productivity means low income. If the cost of credit is high, there is less money available for hiring transplanters, and the analysis of the three productivity groups indicates that this is precisely the situation. The high-productivity farmers are those who have taken out the largest loans but at the lowest rates of interest, and who have the highest production costs because of their high labor costs. Their productivity is so great that their greater production absorbs the high costs, and they are thus also characterized by relatively high incomes.

It has been shown that despite its successes, the State Agricultural Bank provides but a partial solution to the credit problem and may even contribute to an ever widening economic gap between members and nonmembers. This is especially likely if village bank branches come to resemble exclusive clubs and do not encourage and support new membership. The bank has an important

Table 3.6. Comparison of Paddy Costs of High, Medium,
and Low Productivity Groups in Mayinywama

	HIGH PRODUCTIVITY GROUP		MEDIUM PRODUCTIVITY GROUP		LOW PRODUCTIVITY GROUP		ALL GROUPS	
	Average costs in Kyats	% Total costs	Average costs in Kyats	% Total costs	Average costs in Kyats	% Total costs	Average costs in Kyats	% Total costs
Depreciation on Equipment and Livestock	193	22	227	33	178	28	199	27
Labor	509	58	317	46	146	23	323	44
Interest on Loans	139	16	113	16	277	44	176	24
Land Tax and Rent	32	4	37	5	35	5	35	5
Total	873	100	694	100	636	100	733	100
Average Cost per Acre	68		51		50		56	

SOURCE: Pfanner, 1962, Table 24, p. 231.

educational function to perform for its present membership and for those who may one day fulfill the requisites for membership.

The most prominent village moneylenders are without exception also members of the State Agricultural Bank branch, so that in a sense the government is helping to finance their moneylenders and thus to promote their profits at the expense of cultivators who, for whatever reason, are not bank members. With the single exception of an elderly shopkeeper, the other four moneylenders investigated are vigorous farmers in the prime of life who take an active role in village affairs but avoid any position of official responsibility. None are assistant headmen, none are on the executive committee of the Village Council, the State Agricultural Bank, the Village Loan Committee, or the Village Land Tenancy Disposal Committee. Information collected during interviews with three of these four revealed that they were among a group of four bank members who relied exclusively on this form of credit. All other members and cultivators who were not members resorted to private sources as well, the single exception being a relatively wealthy shopkeeper.

The conclusion is inescapable that these men not only do not need to borrow to finance their crops, but that they borrow at cheap rates from the government and reloan at higher rates. In so doing they undoubtedly perform a service to those ineligible for membership in the SAB who need credit, but the effect is that those most in need of credit are often denied it and are forced to borrow from those who have access to it but do not need it, profiting handsomely from loans made possible by their membership in the bank.

Moneylending is an extremely profitable economic investment, and as long as it remains so, it will continue to absorb some surplus assets of farmers who might otherwise make more productive investments. With the land tenancy laws in effect in 1960, there was little investment possible in additional land, another reason why funds are being channeled into moneylending, since one of the traditional alternatives was closed.

Burmese moneylenders are replacing the *chettyars* as the source of private credit of the most expensive kind: the unsecured cash loan and the *sabapay*, or repayment-in-kind

type. Their position in the social structure of Burma could not be more different from that of *chettyars*, however. The *chettyars* were an alien, ethnic, linguistic, and religious minority against whom great hostility had been directed in Burma during the colonial administration. Burmese moneylenders are local residents who are not only neighbors, but among the main supporters of village religious institutions and activities and in this sense are responsible for a certain degree of redistribution of income. It is unlikely, however, that their generosity will affect the growing gap between the haves and have-nots within the village.

The point in the economy where religion becomes most significant is the effect of religious values on economic behavior, the role of the Buddhist monk, and the disposition of family income in merit-making. As a highly visible living example of meritful and exemplary conduct, as the embodiment of the highest cultural values, the sponsorship and continued support of the monk is considered one of the highest forms of merit-making. The monks of Lower Burma are well supported and, compared with the population at large, are well-fed and housed.

An average of from 6 to 8 per cent of net disposable cash income available after production costs was spent for religious purposes in Mayin in 1959–1960. On the surface this figure may not seem to represent a large proportion of income of expenditures, but it does become significant when compared with the proportion of income saved or invested in economically advanced countries or with the allocation of surplus income beyond subsistence. The proportion devoted to religion may increase significantly if a son is initiated into the monkhood, the average outlay being about $75.

The extent to which income is devoted to these religious purposes is the extent to which alternative consumption or investment choices are rejected, and it is here that the economic effects of such expenditure are seen. The social benefit and psychological satisfaction derived from these ceremonies is enormous, but there is a tendency for increments to income to be absorbed in this fashion. Increases in productivity, increased income through higher prices paid for the product, or through the growing of a second crop as groundnuts, is often nullified. Thus, the growing of groundnuts and the 25 per cent addition to incomes has not resulted in significantly less indebtedness in the village. The process is being accentuated by the increasing tendency on the part of the laity to adopt the urban pattern of cash contributions to the monastery, or offerings which require an expenditure in cash rather than in kind.

The effect of these expenditures is to inhibit the accumulation or concentration of wealth despite additions to income and also to diminish or level differences in income, since the wealthier villagers are expected to be and are, in fact, more generous in their contributions than the less wealthy. The differences in income that do exist are generally not reflected in a significantly higher standard of living or consumption and are not devoted to a higher farm investment but may provide increased leisure through the use of hired labor in place of family members. Needless to say, this may also mean keeping a child in school longer, or a son in the monkhood rather than in the fields.

The Buddhist monk, in the pivotal role in the institutionalized form of the Burmese religion, is segregated from economic activity and institutions that govern this activity. This is another way of saying that the economy is highly secular, with a sharp line drawn between religious and economic roles and activities. This is not a recent phenomenon and must be attributed in part to characteristics of the role norms which tend to isolate the monk from contemporary affairs. These norms can be seen as a continuation of the monastic tradition in Burma which has, until recent years, always stressed doctrinal orthodoxy and monastic discipline. The great reforms which have occurred in the history of Burmese Buddhism have been concerned with the preservation of orthodoxy, consolidation, and the Vinaya rules of monastic discipline. There is little evidence that the Sangha has made an attempt to interpret or adapt Buddhist philosophy to changing conditions. At the village level the monk appears as neither an obstacle to nor promoter of economic development as far as his activities or attitudes are concerned, the exception being the prohibition on the taking of life in any

form. Within certain limits the monk neither advances nor impedes economic innovations that have been introduced and, in keeping with the traditional performance expected of his role, generally remains neutral and indifferent to the activities involving agricultural extension or community development.

Seen within the context of the Burmese social system, however, there are characteristics of the monk role which could be considered as a potential obstacle to economic growth—features which, though functional for the religious system, are negative or dysfunctional for the economy. A characteristic of the present social structure is that the distribution of highest social honor, if not always the greatest economic rewards, is to those roles which are associated with religious values. Secular roles generally have not ranked as high in the status hierarchy as have religious roles, specifically that of the monk. Thus, there are incentives or rewards adhering to religious roles, including lay roles such as pagoda builder or monastery builder, which do not exist to the same extent in occupational or professional secular roles. Insofar as role activities functional for economic growth are not appropriately encouraged or rewarded, economic growth will be delayed, for one requirement for development is sufficient encouragement in the social system to stimulate innovation and other economic behavior leading to growth.

CONCLUSIONS

This brief sketch of a Burmese rice-growing community has described a traditional peasantry which is essentially self-sufficient but at the same time well integrated into the national economy through the marketing of its agricultural food surplus. The rural economy and village communities of Lower Burma are not basically different now from prewar years, which perhaps speaks well for the resilience of the Burmese social system, which has had to withstand severe shocks in recent years. One thing that emerges clearly from this study is the importance of an examination of history for an understanding of any particular group of peasants and its present condition. History is also useful, as we have seen, in examining generalizations about the economic responsiveness and drive of peasants.

The peasants of Lower Burma are more closely identified with their traditional cultural values than they are with external forces which are directly or indirectly working toward change. "Modernizing" change is often generated from urban areas, but up to the present there has been little in the towns to attract the peasants except their relative security during this period of political instability and rebellion. Towns have often become overcrowded with refugees, and there have been few opportunities for employment by the unskilled famers. We have also seen that there have been only limited opportunities to achieve wealth through agriculture since there has been restriction on the amount of land that could be owned, technical limits on yields, and an economic pricing policy that has provided little incentive to bring more land into production or make the investment required to increase yields. The government has been more concerned with economic nationalism and Burmanization than it has with providing alternatives or opportunities outside agriculture. The government has forced the departure of many Indian landlords and moneylenders, but this in itself has not led to increased productivity, and the government has taxed agricultural production heavily as its main source of revenue through its price policy.

The adherence of the Burmese to Buddhist values as guides to conduct cannot be considered simply as conservatism or an unwillingness to modernize, because the means to modernize have not been generally available. When new economic opportunities are recognized as such, the Burmese will not be slow to take advantage of them as they have in the past. As we have seen, one recent innovation, the growing of groundnuts, was adopted very quickly. But the additional income generated by the sale of his crop was insufficient to ease the credit problem or the burden of indebtedness, because the extra income was diverted to meet religiously determined patterns of expenditure. Thus the case study of Mayin illustrates a community where the economic gain from an innovation has gone largely to promote achievement within the traditional social system, rather than to support those activities upon which the community's production depends.

References

ANDRUS, 1948. J. Russell Andrus, *Burmese Economic Life* (Stanford, Calif.: Stanford University Press, 1948).

AYE HLAING, 1958a. Aye Hlaing, *Some Aspects of Seasonal Agricultural Loans in Burma*, Economics Research Project, Economic Paper No. 14, Departments of Economics, Statistics, and Commerce, University of Rangoon, 1958.

AYE HLAING, 1958b. Aye Hlaing, *Agro-Economic Problems in Burma*, Economics Research Project, Economic Paper No. 21, Departments of Economics, Statistics, and Commerce, University of Rangoon, 1958.

BURMA, GOVERNMENT OF, 1932. Government of Burma, *The Rice Crop in Burma*, Agricultural Survey No. 17 (Rangoon: Department of Agriculture, 1932).

BURMA, GOVERNMENT OF, 1936. Government of Burma, *Rice*, Department of Agriculture, Markets Section Survey No. 9 (Rangoon: Department of Agriculture, 1936; reprint, 1958).

BURMA, GOVERNMENT OF, 1955. Government of Burma, *Notes on Agriculture in Burma* (Rangoon: Government of Burma, reprint, 1955).

BURMA, UNION OF, 1955. Union of Burma, "A Note on the Pilot Crop-Cutting and Fertilizer Experiment in Paddy Conducted in Cultivators' Fields in Pegu District, 1954–1955." By R. S. Koshal, FAO Agricultural Statistician, ETAP, Burma, and Maung Maung Khin, Statistician, Department of Agriculture, Burma, 1955. (Mimeographed.)

FAO, 1960. Food and Agriculture Organization, *Production Yearbook 1960* (Rome: FAO, 1960).

FURNIVALL, 1931. J. S. Furnivall, *An Introduction to the Political Economy of Burma* (Rangoon: Peoples' Literature Committee and House, 1931; 3rd. ed., 1957).

INDIA, GOVERNMENT OF, 1917. Government of India, *Burma Gazeteer*, Pegu District, Vol. A. Compiled by Mr. A. J. Page, I.C.S., Settlement Officer (Rangoon: Superintendent of Government Printing and Stationery, 1917).

PFANNER, 1962. David E. Pfanner, "Rice and Religion in a Burmese Village." Unpublished Ph.D. dissertation, Department of Anthropology, Cornell University, Ithaca, New York, 1962.

HLA THAN, 1960. Hla Than, "Sample Survey of Productivity and Consumption in Pegu District, 1959–60." Unpublished manuscript, Department of Agriculture, Pegu District, 1960.

4

The Institutional Aspects of Peasant Communities: An Analytical View[1]

NICHOLAS GEORGESCU-ROEGEN

OVER THE LAST 20 years especially, evidence of the failure of policies founded upon orthodox or Marxian economics to solve the difficulties of the underdeveloped agricultural economies—whether within the Communist world or outside it—has been continuously mounting. As a result, a reaction against the received doctrine has begun to spread slowly but persistently among traditional economists. This very volume is one relevant symptom of the new orientation which has already produced a fast-growing literature on peasant economies and communities.

Peasant communities, we now begin to realize, constitute a social category distinct from the urban, bourgeois societies upon which both orthodox and Marxist theories were molded. Consequently, in order to understand the problems that beset the peasant class in many parts of the world and to increase our chances of improving the lot of the vast masses of the unfortunate, it is absolutely necessary to arrive at some understanding of the peculiar institutions by which most peasant communities still live. Like all understandings, this one too requires more than a mere recital of facts; it calls for discovering a rationale behind the facts, which in the case of institutions means to discover their internal logic. This paper is offered as a modest contribution toward this particular end.

The historical side of peasant institutions with particular emphasis on Europe has been covered elsewhere [Georgescu-Roegen, 1969]. Therefore the primary focus in the present paper will be upon peasant institutions at the community or village level, examined with a substantial amount of pure economic analysis so that these "strange" institutions may become more intelligible to students formed at the school of traditional economic theory. For in the ultimate analysis, as the oldest philosophers taught, everything must rise from a cause or a reason. In the light of this

1. The version published here differs from that presented at the A/D/C Seminar: some sections of the original version have been left out, others have been shortened. The version presented at the seminar, amplified and completed with some closely related topics, will appear as a separate monograph by this author, *The Peasant Economy: A Historical and Analytical Essay* (Bloomington: Indiana University Press, 1969). The author's research on this subject is part of the activity of the Graduate Program in Economic Development of Vanderbilt University. The program is supported by a Ford Foundation grant.

reason, nothing, whether the "irrationality" of traditional economists or of the peasant institutions, is irrational.

THE PEASANT ECONOMY AND TRADITIONAL ECONOMICS

Since interest in the study of peasant economies and village communities is most likely to emerge in a country with an overwhelming peasant population, it is normal that the pioneering in this direction should have been done by European economists. But why should the economists of a nation like the United States, which is the most urbanized and industrialized in the world and which moreover has never possessed a peasantry, suddenly become interested in the economy of peasant societies? What are the factors responsible for the tardy discovery of peasant economics and sociology?

Bridgman, a Nobel laureate for physics famous also for his writings on the philosophy of science, argued that the major handicap of economics is the characteristic intellectual opportunism of its servants [1950, pp. 303–305]. Now, no one can deny that, economic historians being excepted, every economist who has won a place in the history of thought —from Cantillon and Quesnay to Schumpeter and Keynes—has been intellectually opportunistic in the sense that each has been exclusively preoccupied with the contemporary economic problems of the society in which he happened to live. And the same is true of all those numerous Eastern economists who are little, if at all, known in the West precisely because they were interested only in the peasant economy.

But, I submit, the economic profession should take pride in being opportunistic in the above sense. Surely it would have been everybody's loss and nobody's gain if, for instance, Keynes had applied his talent to studying the problems of a country with an agriculture ravaged by prolonged wars—as was the case of France in Quesnay's time— instead of those posed for a modern government by periodic spells of high industrial unemployment. And, as we can now appreciate, it would have been uneconomical and even absurd if the social scientists in nineteenth-century Russia had been preoccupied with the industrial working class

instead of Russia's peasantry. By the same token, we cannot but applaud the fact that the economists of the countries with an advanced economy have shifted their main interest to the problem of how to speed up the development of the underdeveloped economies as soon as this problem became vital for their own countries.

On the other hand, there is no denying that the intellectual opportunism of the economic profession has had some undesirable and unnecessary consequences. In contrast to natural scientists, students of human society have been prone to theorize about any social form without a direct, material knowledge of it, by merely extrapolating the laws they have established for the society known to them immediately. Some even claim a merit for doing so. But no other profession has committed the sin of theorizing in a vacuum as often and with as complete an ingenuousness as the economist of the Classical and, especially, the Neo-Classical tradition. The circumstances speak for themselves: the more he learned about the pasticular economy in which he lived, the more absorbed he became in its study. Needless to add, the sin became even more stubborn as economic science developed along Ricardian lines in becoming more quantitative and less institutional, hence less historical. For although numbers possess some unique powers, they also have a hidden vice: they tend to lure us into ignoring form and qualitative factors.

Surprisingly enough, denunciations of the sin came primarily from the ranks of economists themselves. The celebrated *Methodenstreit*—the strife of methods during the last decades of the nineteenth century among German economists—comes naturally to mind. Unfortunately, it turned out to be mainly a denunciation of theory in general, which was tantamount to blaming the soda for the intoxicating power of a mixed drink. That is why the *Methodenstreit* seems to us so frustrating. Only later on do we find the real root of the difficulty touched upon occasionally. For an illustrious example, the lament that "Ricardo and his followers . . . work[ed] out their theories on the tacit supposition that the world was made up of city men" ran through all editions of the modern bible of traditional economics, Marshall's

Principles [1949, p. 62]. Yet the lament, or rather the denunciation, has caused no stir.

The situation is most intriguing: although the fact that life can take on an infinite variety of biological forms is unanimously recognized, there is appreciable disagreement concerning the qualitative variability of social forms. In fact, traditional thought in economics is characterized by the position that the economy of every society is only a particular instance of a unique pattern, that of the civil society. The phenomenon can best be explained by the attraction economists have felt, many still feel, for urban society and town life, perhaps because the towns display greater institutional uniformities than any other communal organization.

From the earliest times towns have tended to become increasingly alike to each other; contact between distant settlements, whether within the same or different cultural groups, has always been achieved through the exchange of commodities and ideas, i.e. through media attached to urban life. The result is that by now towns all over the world present an almost identical spectrum of institutions. This was already the case for the urban centers of Western Europe at the time of the founders of Classical economics. And since the picture an observer can draw of the world or of the universe cannot possibly include elements other than those perceived through the particular window from which he happens to contemplate the outside, no Classical economist can be indicted for not having discovered the variability of social and, hence, economic forms. As Marshall [1949, p. 62] correctly explained, "the people whom they [the Classical economists] knew most intimately were city men." One may feel pretty sure that Adam Smith's confidence in his own economics must have become stronger after his visit to France. This applies with even greater force to Marx's orientation, since he had occasion to verify directly the uniformity of the bourgeois society in more urban centers than any other nineteenth-century economist. Along the same line of thought, one should also find it natural in retrospect that the first impulse to economic anthropology should have come from Lewis H. Morgan, who "spent a great part of his life among the Iroquois Indians ... and was adopted into one of their tribes."[2] Had the English peasantry survived as a *significant* social stratum for England's productive capacity or had there been a peasantry in the United States, the science of economics would have, most probably, developed on broader tracks than those of the Classical school.[3]

In connection with the preceding remarks, the case of Marx deserves a special note at this juncture. For Marx, unlike all other Classical economists of his time, was fully aware (through Hegel's influence) of the importance of institutional differences for economic science. He thought of economists as strange creatures precisely because for them "the institutions of feudalism are artificial institutions, those of the bourgeoisie are natural institutions" [Marx, 1900, p. 120f]. Another spelled-out example is found in one of his earliest writings, where Marx takes Ricardo to task for his "bourgeois horizon" in making the primitive hunter and fisher "consult the annuity tables [of] the London Exchange" [Marx, 1904, p. 69f].[4] Yet no Classical economist has had so decisive a role as Marx in spreading among both the orthodox and the unorthodox chapters of traditional economics the tenet that peasants do not even constitute a social class and, hence, it is senseless to speak of a peasant economy as a distinct analytical category.[5]

We should not fail to note another, equally significant, case. The important place of agriculture in the economy of the United States has created an intense interest in agricultural economics among American students and policy-makers alike. The symptoms are seen in such government initiatives as those of Theodore Roosevelt, who in 1908

2. For which see Engels [1884, p. 25]. Professor Raymond Firth drew my attention to the fact that Morgan's living among the Indians is a mere legend. However, Morgan's lengthy contacts with the Indian tribes as well as his adoption by the Senecas are historical facts.

3. Tradition, however, is a powerful master. Quite recently the majority of British economists received with immense satisfaction Walter Eucken's attempt—perhaps the ablest of all—to justify the Classical position in his *Foundations of Economics* [1940].

4. See also Marx's emphatic remarks on the institutional differences bearing upon the writings of British and French economists [1904, p. 56n].

5. David Mitrany [1951] offers a most complete and able analysis of the impact of this article of Marxist faith upon the ideology, strategy, and policy of the Communist Party in Russia and other East European countries. Some additional thoughts on the struggle between Communists and Agrarians are found in the author's essay [1960, pp. 1–40].

created the Country Life Commission, and of Woodrow Wilson, who in 1919 established the Division of Farm Population and Rural Life. However, the most interesting outcome is the American school of agricultural economics, whose admirable scientific achievements stand above all others in the same domain. That this domain has been confined to *farm economics* is averred by the very title of the foremost periodical of the school.[6] To point out that there is an immense difference between a *farmer* economy—regulated by cash profits and resting on a granular texture of individual interests—and a *peasant* economy is not to belittle in the least the merits of that school, but only to note a relevant fact for our topic: because of its particular objective, the American school of agricultural economics has been the staunchest preserver of the traditional viewpoint concerning the universal validity of Classical and Neo-Classical theory.[7]

As we observed earlier, a sustained interest in a study of the village community is most likely to emerge in a country with an overwhelming peasant population. And since any sociological study—be it of the industrial worker or of the peasant—can be undertaken only by a prepared mind, a second necessary condition for the formation of such an interest is the existence of a sufficiently sophisticated intelligentsia. The economic conflict, which in such a setting is apt to germinate around the condition of the peasant, would then easily provide the necessary intellectual motive. These conditions suffice to identify Russia during the early decades of the last century and to account for the dominant concern with the condition of the Russian peasants among the leading intellectuals from the mid-nineteenth century on —Herzen, Chuprov, and Chaianov, to mention a few among the best known.[8] (For

further details see Georgescu-Roegen [1969].)

First the Slavophiles and then the Narodniki set their hope for the economic salvation of Russia on the resilient qualities of the Russian peasant villages. In fact, it was the Narodniki who, in reaction to the extreme romanticism of the Slavophiles, proclaimed—a strange idea for that time—that no adequate agrarian policy can be devised without a *direct* study and understanding of the peasants' social conditions. Their outspoken scorn for "theory" was the ultimate consequence of this excessive positivism. But whatever one may think about this characteristic bent of the Narodniki or about their platform, the fact remains that it was their ideology and determination that opened the field of peasant sociology.

The Narodniki as well as their ideological heirs, the agrarians, used to accuse their political adversaries of viewing the peasant problem not as a problem concerning people but as one of land. The same accusation applies equally well to the long line of students who, for decades after Haxthausen's work [1847–1852], reduced the sociology of peasant communities to the problem of the origin of landed property. The basic problem, that of the institutions peculiar to the peasant communities, was thus set aside immediately after Haxthausen revealed its importance. A long time elapsed before the tide turned. British functionaries in India, like Haxthausen in Russia, were in a position to observe closely the life in the native villages. Some were greatly surprised by the contrast between life in the Indian villages and what they had thought to be the normal, the rational. The result was a series of most interesting studies, which not only aroused the interest of other European scholars but also set village sociology again on its natural track [Maine, 1861, pp. 252–261; Baden-Powell, 1892, 1896, 1899]. They inspired at least one British scholar, F. Seebohm [1896], to turn to the living villages of Great Britain and their documented history with the idea of searching for some relevant vestiges of the unknown past.

Thus, although the peasant community as a distinct social category was discovered by the intellectuals of a peasant nation, the Narodniki, the inspiration source of the method now considered the most appropriate

---

6. A parallel orientation is observed in sociology. Witness the standpoint adopted by numerous writers such as D. Sanderson [1917], C. R. Hoffer [1926], and W. Gee [1929].

7. Perhaps the only interlude worth mentioning was marked by the interest J. D. Black and M. L. Wilson, in particular, manifested in the late 1930's for problems closely related to the economy of peasant societies [Black, 1939a, 1939b; Wilson, 1939a, 1939b].

8. It is instructive to observe that the situation of the peasant class developed into a conflict for the first time in the West, to wit the *jacqueries* and the peasant wars of the earlier ages. But the intelligentsia of that time lacked adequate sophistication.

for village sociology has been provided by British scholars. Given Great Britain's interest in *and* also her peculiarly sophisticated attitude toward her colonies, there is nothing paradoxical about this mutation.

Village Typology and Taxonomy

The greatest predicament of the student of the peasant community was incisively formulated by the Rumanian sociologist Stahl [1946, 40]: "There is no 'Rumanian' village, but only 'Rumanian villages.'" What that scholar, who had spent long years of observation among the Rumanian peasants, wanted to impress upon us is that village communities do not form a homogeneous universe even if we confine our attention to a region with a fairly uniform history. On the other hand, we must admit that there are differential aspects— perhaps more important for the policy-maker than for the analytical student—justifying a division of peasant villages along their ethnical origins: the Russian *mir*, the Swiss *allmend*, the Scandinavian *allmenning*, the Saxon *tun*, the English *vill*, the Irish *tuath*, the German *Dorf*, the Rumanian *sat*, the French *communal*, the Indonesian *ndesa*, the Indian *pueblo*, and the like. Some sort of classification, be it for the sake of exposition alone, is indispensable for any further morphological study of the villages within each of these broad classes. One of the criteria frequently adopted in the literature is the topographical location: plain village, hill village, mountain village. Another criterion distinguishes between the compact and spread-out villages, still another between villages with irregular fields and villages with strip fields. At times villages are divided into wheat-growing, rice-growing, potato-growing, and so on. Nothing is basically wrong with these and other similar classifications. But they come very close to classifying mammals, for instance, into black-haired, brown-haired, and so forth. In other words, they are mere catalogs. Whatever its practical use, a mere catalog does not satisfy the urge of the understanding any more than that of a mail-order house does.

To be revealing, a classification must be taxonomic—that is, it must reflect some force function, as does the Mendeleev table or biological taxonomy, for example. It is natural, then, for one to think that because village institutions are subject to evolution, it should be possible to arrive at a taxonomy of village communities which, like biological taxonomy, would map out, however imperfectly their evolution. Unfortunately, criteria for such a taxonomy seem so far unavailable. In all probability, even a new Linnaeus could not change the situation.

The reason for the immense variability of forms is the same in the social and biological domains. It only works more powerfully in the former than in the latter. With the first living cells that emerged from *inorganic* (viz. inert) matter, a new phenomenal domain, the *organic*, came into being. Thereafter life could propagate itself through an entirely different process than the original one—that is, life begot life. That is why life has assumed forms without number which could not arise directly from a calm sea of warm mud, as the first living cells presumably did. Moreover, in their evolutionary process life-bearing forms have not followed a unilinear direction, nor even a treelike pattern. Often lines which branched out at one point came to meet again in another form.

The story repeated itself as the first social forms emerged among the herds of men living until that time as any other animals do. The *superorganic* domain—to use the well-chosen term of Kroeber [1917]—came into being at that moment. Social forms, like biological forms, have ever since evolved from other social forms with a flexibility far greater than that of organic evolution. Whatever might be the reason for it, the fact is that the necessity of the laws indisputably weakens as we pass from the inorganic to the organic and from the latter to the superorganic level.

Diffusion of mutations in the organic world cannot go beyond the limits set by sexual reproduction: no mutation of drosophila, for example, can pass on to the mammal class. On the other hand, once some form of individual property in land emerged in one community, it propagated itself easily to other communities. Clearly, individual landed property among the contemporary Iroquois or Incas has not come about in direct line from the institutions of the old Indian tribes. As Maitland [1897, p. 345] nicely put it, the Anglo-Saxons did not arrive at the alphabet or the Nicene Creed by following all the initial stages; they got them from others. Everything points to the fact that mutations, in both directions, not only occur more easily at the superorganic than at the organic level, but also represent greater discontinuities. There is no question that revolutions and counterrevolutions are phenomena specific to the superorganic domain.

Some authors—like Stahl, for instance [1946, pp. 48, 156]—have classified village communities according to the degree that the land of the village is held in individual property. Yet such a classification can hardly represent a relevant taxonomy for all village forms. At most, it may serve as a convenient device for analyzing the social transformations over a relatively short historical span and within some definite area. To use an analogy, the classification in point is comparable to that of a biological species according to its varieties.

Property rights in land have been advocated so frequently as the best classification for a taxonomy of peasant villages that a brief digression to buttress my objections is in order. There is more than one reason why the degree of individual property cannot provide a force function for a general taxonomy of villages. To begin with, the change from individual to communal property has not been a rare phenomenon—Communist revolutions apart. Engels himself had to admit [1884, pp. 133–143] that this "back mutation" occurred on a large scale after the collapse of the Roman empire under the barbarian invasions. In France, the same change has been noticed as late as the eighteenth century [Lafargue, 1901, p. 70]. According to some authorities, the Russian *mir* itself, far from being a direct continuation of the primitive communism of the Slavs—as the Narodniki and the Marxists believe—is a relatively recent back mutation imposed from above for the purpose of insuring better collection of taxes and providing stricter control of the agricultural manpower.[9]

As Vinogradoff observed [1920, p. 42],

during the expansion of the Roman Empire "the Romanisation of outlying provinces [was] at the same time the barbarisation of Rome." How many times land thus passed from one regime to another and then back to the first during the long periods about which we know very little is a moot question. What is certain is that the extensive anthropological studies undertaken recently show that some definite form of personally inheritable property in land is rather common among extant societies that are far less evolved than were the village communities of Tsarist Russia or sixteenth-century England.[10] Moreover, some of these "primitive" societies are still practicing polygyny, a fact that does not fit into Engels' thesis.

The earliest human settlements may have differed little from an animal herd, but authorities on this difficult subject assure us that each one deserving the name of *social community* was established by a "successful brigand" of some sort or other. Indeed, it seems impossible to think of a tribe or clan, however primitive, without a chief. But the connection between a leader and a settlement is found long after individual property emerged. Documents attest that the "successful brigand" who founded Rome endowed every settler with individual landed property —of the Roman type, to be sure. Throughout the Middle Ages, and even much later, numerous villages or domains were founded on the same basis by "enterprising barons" and even by "rich, bourgeois-like entrepreneurs," not to mention kings and princes.[11]

9. The original author of this thesis is B. N. Chicherin, who advanced it in two articles (1852) not available in translation. Chicherin summarized his argument in his article "Leibeigenschaft in Russland" [1861]. But see also the works cited in Robinson [1949, p. 274n24]. Robinson is right in observing that "in the whole range of Russian history, there is perhaps no subject so obscure and so highly controversial as that of the *mir's* origin."

10. See the summarizing conclusions of a survey covering some two hundred societies hardly touched by outside civilization in Murdock [1949, p. 82]. Also the monographs on the aborigines of Vietnam, Luzon, Borneo, Java, Ceylon, Formosa in Murdock [1960]. One should also note the observation made by Baden-Powell [1896, pp. 7ff, 131, 402; 1899] concerning the absence of communal lands in the village communities of Dravidian tradition in South and Central India and among the Tibeto-Burman (Kolarian) settlers in Eastern India. The point that all these instances pertain to non-Aryan populations may have some significance.

11. Bloch [1952, pp. 3–20]; Orwin and Orwin [1954, p. 19]. The phenomenon was not confined to the nations with a nobility organized after the Germanic tradition. Villages known to have had a "lord" as far back as one can go or founded by a princely grant as a reward for some military feat were not uncommon in the history of Rumania [Stahl, 1946, p. 49]. After the forced exodus of the Tartars under Catherine II, the vast area of Southern Russia thus emptied was populated among others by German and Serbian immigrants to whom land was given—as is true for all colonists—in complete individual property.

Numerous also are the villages in the southern half of Europe that descend from a Roman *castrum* or *vicus*, where only the Roman form of property once existed. Consequently it would be absurd to contend, as Marx did, that in every extant rural or urban agglomeration the Iroquois "shows through unmistakably" [Engels, 1884, p. 90].

No doubt it would be equally absurd to maintain that every extant village in Southern and Western Europe began as a *villa nova* founded on the principle of individual property, just as Rome or Boston was. Of course, if one trusts only the written evidence, one can never discover the existence of villages having no birth certificates. "I have read *all* these documents, not once, but several times, not in extracts, but all through from beginning to end", declares Fustel de Coulanges [1885, pp. 172f, 171 n1], but "one cannot find there one single word, before the tenth century, meaning community." To proceed otherwise, he insists, is not good history.[12] Yet history—especially, the history of peasant communities—is not always recorded or faithfully recorded by documents.

For this very reason most students of village communities have abandoned the old methods for reconstructing the past either by extrapolating the Iroquois or by trusting the written testimony. Nowadays they first search for the concrete traces of the past in the institutions of our own era, even in the landscape of the countryside, and interpret the written sources or accept anthropological parallelisms only in the light of such contemporary remains—in some of which, luckily, the past is often very much alive. They thus aim at a reconstruction of the past by a method akin to paleontology.

THE ANATOMY OF THE PEASANT VILLAGE

A general principle of scientific procedure is that each special science should build its analytical framework on those elements which represent atomic units within its particular domain. They are the elements that, if divided further, cease to reflect the

very phenomena in which the corresponding discipline is interested. In chemistry, for example, the atomic unit is the molecule, not the atom or the intraatomic particle, because chemical properties are borne by the former, not by the latter. There are incontrovertible reasons, I submit, why the village community constitutes the analytical atom in the phenomenal domain of peasant sociology.

To begin with, the village, next to the human individual, is the most clearly delimited social entity. Like the human individual, it is a perfectly natural, atomic, social unit. As history shows, kingdoms, provinces, counties, and even cities, can be split into several other kingdoms, provinces, and the like. The same is true of tribes and clans. But a peasant village, as long as it remains peasant, is indivisible. Whole clans or parts of them have often left their home village and founded a new village elsewhere, but this does not mean that the latter is a part cut from the former. Nor can this swarming be taken as proof that the peasant village is not an organic unit in the strictest sense of the term: all biological organisms multiply by the same process as peasant communities—that is, through internal growth.

Secondly, a study of peasant institutions must focus its attention first of all on that social entity which is certain to display their entire spectrum. Villages within a geographical region may have identical institutions and, moreover, be connected with each other in different ways so as to form a social entity, some *terra*, as its name goes in medieval tradition (for which, see Stahl [1939]). Its study is of no little value. But if one would decide to exclude the village altogether from the picture, the analysis of this higher social organization will bring the village back in full force. A simple formalization of the structure will show this without difficulty. Let $A_1, A_2 \ldots$ be the individuals belonging to such a *terra* and $R_1, R_2 \ldots$ be all institutional relations that may exist between an A_i and an A_j. The analytical map of the true relations $A_i R_k A_j$ will immediately separate the whole structure into several distinct nuclei, each corresponding to one of the villages. The analytical separation results from the fact that the number of relations true for any pair A_i, A_j of the same nucleus exceeds by a significant magnitude the number of

---

12. It should be noted, however, that Fustel de Coulanges had the better of those of his opponents who also invoked written testimonies. See, for instance Fustel de Coulanges [1885, chapter V] and E. D. Glasson [1890].

relations applicable to internuclear pairs. Of course a whole group of villages may be related so as to form a tribe; or the families of the same village may be associated in clans which in turn may cut across a number of villages. Yet the relations applicable to families belonging to the same village outnumber by far those between the families of the same clan but of different villages.

Thirdly—a reason that should carry great weight with the student of peasant economies —the economic activity of the village forms a unit of production as close-knit as a simple workshop. A peasant household can perform practically no economic activity independently of those of others. On the contrary, as has been repeatedly emphasized, all must move in step, whether it is for cultivating the fields, mowing the meadows, cutting wood from the forest, or depasturizing the animals.

In all economic respects, not only in respect to production, the village is not a granular mass of households, much less of individuals, loosely connected through anonymous markets, factories, banks, or other similar urban institutions. Above all, it is not a civil society. On the contrary, it is an indivisible social and economic whole, "an organized and self-acting unit"—as Sumner Maine, among many, characterized it [Maine, 1871, p. 125; Vinogradoff, 1920, p. 325].

Some of the preceding thoughts are easily recognizable in almost any definition proposed for the traditional (nondegenerate) village community. Such a community, says Baden-Powell [1896, p. 9], rests upon

the connection which a group of cultivators must have when located in one place, bound by certain customs, with certain interests in common, and possessing within the circle of the village the means of local government, and of satisfying the wants of life without much reference to neighboring villages.

Similarly, Chuprov [1902, p. 4], whose attention was fixed on the Russian *mir*, describes it as

a totality of households disposing of a territory and connected by traditional relationships characterized by the principle that the totality has the right of interfering in the economic activity of every household.

More recently, Ruopp [1953, p. 4], while recognizing the analytical difficulties raised

by the concept of community, admits—a very significant fact—that these difficulties do not exist for the village, which alone constitutes a definite whole cemented by multiple integrative forces.

To gain, however, a greater insight into these definitions, two questions should be considered in some detail: What is the primary basis of the oneness of the traditional village community? By what means has it preserved this specific quality over a period reaching far back into prehistory?

THE UNITY OF PEASANT VILLAGES

No observer, however casual, of the life in a peasant village has failed to be strongly impressed by the exceptional feeling of unity binding all members together. Most systematic students of the problem, however, have been content with describing the outward manifestations of this spirit, i.e. the rules of conduct which the village community itself developed over time. Some have suggested either that there is nothing behind these manifestations or that the spirit of unity has grown out of the conduct rules. A few, however, have tried to find the cause of this spirit.

As previously mentioned, the most popular thesis is that of Maine [1861, p. 64ff] and Engels [1884]: the universal bond uniting the members of a village community derives from their blood relationships, i.e. from an evolutionary residual of the primitive family group or human herd. An idea which Ruopp [1953, p. 3] notes goes back to Aristotle. The thesis is plausible enough for villages descending directly from a group family or a clan. But how many actual villages, past or present, fall into this category? Besides, kinship on a large scale does not seem to be a *necessary* condition for the typical bond among village members. If it were, we could not explain this bond in numerous villages founded in Europe during the early Middle Ages by settlers we positively know to have been Christian, hence monogamous. Some authorities maintain that even the early village community of the Germans was not a *gens* [Maitland, 1897, p. 349]. Still more perplexing would be the case of those villages which initially were Roman settlements and later were invaded by barbarian people, or vice versa. Maine, no doubt, realized that the kinship thesis fails to explain the universal bond of the village communities which no longer form a group family or a clan. In his own time, that was the case for every village in Europe, if not in India as well. For these, Maine [1875, p. 87] turned to another principle: they are "bodies of men held together by the land they cultivated [together]."

Maine's thesis raises several questions. In the case of a village consisting of a single group family, we are especially certain that its land was cultivated in common. Yet why should the sociologist then choose kinship rather than communal cultivation as the explanatory principle of the village bond for this particular situation? Communal cultivation would certainly suffice to cover both the tribal and the familial (but communalistic) village. However, it still could not account for another salient phenomenon, which seems to have escaped Maine's attention. Even after all land in a village came under individual property and, as a consequence, came to be cultivated in severalty—as had happened in England by Maine's time—the village community more often than not continued to function as a social and economic whole. Equally significant, villages newly created by various colonization plans or land reforms, though amorphous and anarchic at first, in time acquired all the qualities of an organic structure little different from that of older communities. There is an obvious danger in elevating any temporal form of society to a universal working principle. If either kinship or land communalism were such a principle, then in the absence of exogeneous cataclasmic forces we should expect every tribal village to remain tribal and every *mir*-like organization to preserve its communalism forever.

Since manifestations of a community bond are found as far back in time as any meaningful evidence is available, the primary cause of this bond must be sought in some very primitive phase of human evolution. The answer then seems inescapable: the tap root of the village spirit of unity must be that instinct which man shares with many other living creatures, the cooperative or, as Veblen preferred to call it, the gregarious instinct. Needless to add, this instinct in turn is the product of natural selection through the Darwinian advantage of group action, first in defense and second in livelihood.[13]

VILLAGE TERRITORY AND OPTIMUM SIZE

The fact that in the traditional village (meaning the peasant village) habitations are clustered densely in one place—the village hearth, as it is known in many a peasant vernacular—may very well be explained by the gregarious instinct. But the same instinct would equally well explain the nomad horde, which had neither the net individuality of the village community nor its peculiar cohesion. The gregarious instinct, therefore, does not suffice by itself to produce these qualities. They are qualities that cannot be divorced from the problem of size (of unit size, not of quantum size).

A bond as inclusive and as staunch as that of the traditional village community cannot be a phenomenon indifferent to size. Not even the physical bonds of inert matter, we should note, are indifferent to this variable. As I have argued in a paper already cited, towns, cities, and metropolises did not turn into civil societies because the institution of the universal bond had proved intrinsically deleterious or because the *Weltanschauung* of the townee had come about by a biological mutation. For purely physical reasons alone, the old bond could not remain operative at the large size of urban agglomerations [Georgescu-Rogen, 1960]. But there is also another element of the problem to which biologists who have studied the influence of population density upon the behavior of many species would invite our attention: cooperation is a Darwinian fitness when the group living on a given territory is small but intraspecies competition appears with the growth of the population [Allee, 1940]. What then kept the village community from outgrowing that size at which the bond would be operative or constitute a Darwinian fitness? For the answer to this question we must take a second look at the role played by land.

Land has indeed played from primeval times the most decisive role in the development and preservation of the unity of the village community, but not as *mere land*. It is only recently, after repeated studies of the

13. Cf. J. B. S. Haldane [1935, p. 131]: "altruistic behavior is a kind of Darwinian fitness, and may be expected to spread as the result of natural selection."

village *in vivo*, that we have come to notice that no peasant village is settled on just a slice of land. The village territory is in relation to the village hearth as a complete garden in relation to its homestead. Perhaps that is why villages in Western Europe came to be known by such names as *villa* or *tun*, *tuin*, which originally all meant "garden." In addition to the house lots (each with its own courtyard) and to a well-planned net of roads, the village territory comprises not only the cultivable acreage, but also some woodland, some grazing land, and, most vital of all, a body of water—a creek or a river, a pond or a lake. Not infrequently, it includes some orchards or vineyards.[14]

This structure clearly reflects the gamut of the basic, perennial needs of human life. The fact that a village territory has such a splendidly balanced composition of all vital land resources may seem simple and ultraobvious. But it has caused many a thoughtful student to marvel at the wisdom of the original settlers who could not possibly be guided by any scientific knowledge proper [Orwin and Orwin, 1954, p. 27; Denman, 1958, p. 61]. Their intuition may appear all the more incredible if one takes into account the fact that what we see now on the map of almost any village is the work of numberless generations on a site which initially was nothing but thick forest or thicket. It thus seems that Oswald Spengler's likening the peasant to a plant with its roots deeply spread into the right kind of soil is not, after all, mystical nonsense [1929, p. 89f]. For nowhere does the biological intertwine with the economic so intimately as in that activity by which man confronts directly the living sector of his environment.

A site suitable for a permanent settlement of cultivators must fulfill some very restrictive conditions. It must contain all the land resources enumerated above; in addition, these resources must be roughly balanced in the same proportions as the basic and, hence, nonsubstitutable needs they severally satisfy. That is not all. Since at no time before the turn of the last century was transportation a relatively easy task, the various resources

had to be conveniently located around some suitable spot for the village hearth to be settled. These conditions together greatly limit the choice of a suitable site. The third condition limits also the optimum size of the village territory and, as a consequence, the optimum size of the village community for any past state of the arts.[15]

We need no sophisticated theory of location to understand why—given that the gregarious instinct moved the first settlers to build their habitations in a cluster—the optimum size of the village territory could not exceed some relatively small area (especially in the earliest times). The textbook illustration of the gardener who must walk an increasingly greater distance after each refilling of the spray can suffices. Also, its nature is so elemental that we need not wonder why its principle was immediately felt even by the earliest cultivators.

These, then, are the reasons why village communities are neither so small as to include only a couple of households nor larger than a few thousand people.[16] The problem now is to see what helped them to remain at the optimum size in spite of the continuous growth of population. For as population increased, a point was inevitably reached where an additional individual could no longer be supported by the village resources at the prevailing state of husbandry arts. From what has been said earlier, it should be clear why expanding the village territory could not be a definite remedy, *even if there still was "free" land beyond*. The solution is

14. For maps of villages from different regions of Europe, see Seebohm [1896, passim]; Bloch [1952, p. 267ff]; Orwin and Orwin [1954, passim]; Robinson [1949, p. 217]; Stahl [1946, p. 289ff].

15. The relation between the state of the arts and the optimum size—well known to the economist—finds an indirect confirmation in the variability of village size according to the main activity practiced by the village. Murdock [1949, p. 81] reports that for the communities surveyed the fishing and hunting villages had on the average 50 people, those practicing agriculture and husbandry, about 450 people.

16. In connection with the above point, it is instructive to mention an idea applied by the Czarist government shortly before World War I and which later found many champions among Danish agricultural economists. It consists of consolidating the open land of the village and resettling every family on one single lot, house and all, as in the pattern of American farms. See Robinson [1949, p. 217]. Since an alternative and, moreover, much simpler operation is to consolidate only the field strips, the idea is totally inept, unless one can prove that the optimum size of a "village" is always that of a single household. For our own thesis, it suffices to note that for this last proposition to be true, transport facilities have to be so well developed that very few countries besides the U.S.A. would meet the condition.

spelled out by the numerous instances of several neighboring villages having the same basic "last name" and a different "first name" —Altdorf, Neudorf, Hochdorf, Niederdorf, or something of the sort. As population pressure approached the critical level, one group of the village community migrated and founded a new village on a nearby site [Vinogradoff, 1920, p. 146f].

One point, however, needs to be sufficiently stressed: migration has at all times constituted the last resort of the village community in avoiding overpopulation. The bond uniting the various members of such a community—which must have been the stronger the farther back we go in time— should have made the thought of migration repelling even to a barbarian—nay, especially to a barbarian. So, the peasant communities first bent their efforts to discover means by which the village resources could be made more productive so that people may not have to migrate. This technological development, about which I shall say more later on, gradually increased the optimum size of the village communities, but the increase was very slow. In any case, it did not keep pace with the increase in population. Thus, even though it was the last resort, migration had to go on, and it did so as long as suitable sites were available over the hill or even farther. Thereafter, the peasants had to assault the cities—as they are still doing in many parts of the world. For the village must preserve its optimum size one way or the other, lest it perish: the agrarian problem, as Chayanov first observed [1923, p. 131], is primarily a population problem. (See also Georgescu-Roegen [1960].)

To sum up: it is the economic optimum size of the material basis—the village territory —that accounts for the individuality of the village community. And it is the peculiar, almost invariable structure which this material basis must possess in order to sustain the basic needs of its occupants that has held the people of the same village together in one economic and social unit. Migration, as long as there were new sites available, helped the village communities in preserving their optimum size with respect to the state of the arts and the conditions of each locality.

As I have hinted earlier, the relative smallness of its optimum size made it possible for the village community to acquire an organic structure—that is, a structure in which every individual part is subservient to the activity of the whole. And, like any organism, the village community could not survive without a pronounced tendency to stability. Oral tradition has served as the most important element in this respect. But we should not fail to note the important fact that even this tradition—the only means available until quite recently for preserving the conduct rules from one village generation to another— could not have fulfilled this role as well as it has done if the size of the village community could have grown beyond a certain limit. For as I shall argue later, the stability of village institutional matrices derives primarily from the fact that, the village population being small, an oral tradition can be imparted to all.

PROPERTY RIGHTS IN LAND AND THE PEASANTRY

A careful review of the literature would show that property rights have been and still are regarded as the main pivot of the institutions of peasant communities. Students of peasant communities repeatedly emphasize the relationship between the peasant and the land. The institutional patterns of control over land—collective, communal, individual—are frequently cited as the most basic factor affecting the economic process in a peasant economy. Yet this accepted doctrine regarding the influence of property rights upon economic behavior and economic development is spurious. In my view, the doctrine ignores a fundamental fact, namely that the institutions of peasant communities have never sought to control the "fund" factors of the economy (land) but the "flows" factors (the incomes from land). Since the alternative view has prevailed in the literature so long, the root of this error in the sociological analysis of peasant communities must first be exposed before we can proceed to describe the economic physiology of peasant communities.

In retrospect, one fact in the development of village sociology appears clear. It was the intellectual forcefulness of Maine's work that impressed a long line of writers to reduce village sociology to one proposition: "The historical passage from collective to individual property," as Kovalevskii formulated it most clearly in the title of one of his works [1896].

I have already cited some factual evidence which casts great doubt upon Maine's theory of unilinear and uniform evolution of village institutions and, all the more, upon the sweeping generalization of the same idea by Lavelye, Engels, Kovalevskii, and many others. To speak against all these, there are the back mutations mentioned earlier.

There is the Chicherin-Seebohm argument that in most parts of Europe, at least, land communalism is the original shell of the serfdom imposed upon an earlier community of free landholders.[17] The very evidence adduced by the advocates of the thesis that every instance of communal administration of land in any civilization is a direct survival of primitive agrarian communism, often lends support to this argument. For example, Laveleye's analysis of land tenure in Egypt traces the Moslem tradition of a single land proprietor uninterruptedly to the Pharaohs' era [Laveleye, 1878, pp. 44, 327]. Clearly, then, if some sort of land communalism was still observed in Egypt at the end of the nineteenth century, it could not have been the direct descendant of "natural communism."[18] The problem of what was before the first pharaoh, emir, or satrap therefore cries for an answer. And the answer cannot be given by simply visualizing what we would do if we, modern *Homines sapientes*, had to live in a primitive era.

A different way of answering the problem, though not wholly free from a somewhat cognate sin, is the interpretation of archeological remains of vanished settlements. Some of these tend to show that long before man turned to settled agriculture, the cemetery was the first fixed site to which man felt attached. The landmarks around these early cemeteries support the hypothesis that land

was then divided in lots, each one cultivated separately by a "family" [Denman, 1958, p. 7f]. And if one also accepts Toynbee's argument that some loose attachment of man to land (as a swidden cultivator) was a necessary prerequisite for nomadism proper to develop [Toynbee, 1956, pp. 167–169], then separate "possession of land in use" must be a very old practice. This does not necessarily mean that either then or later on such a practice conformed to some innate human instinct. Laveleye, in arguing that land communalism is the natural state because it embodies "the juristic instinct of people" [Laveleye, 1878, p. 23] simply forgets that the juristic instinct of the primeval man was, if anything, the law of the jungle.

It must be admitted that the search for the historical passage from "agrarian communism" to individual property has brought to the surface a wealth of sociological facts which otherwise might be still unknown. Yet the searchers have failed to bring back what they set out to discover because their vision was marred by the purely juristic perspective that, with unparalleled talent, Maine blended into it from the outset. In one place Maine did argue that such terms as "*command, sovereign, obligation, sanction, right,*" become empty of empirical content if applied to the traditional village communities of India [Maine, 1871, pp. 67–70, 164]; but when it came to "property," he did not hesitate to use the term in describing the institutional setup of the same communities or in comparing it with the British system of property rights. Under Maine's influence, the study of the peasant communities became for many a study of land laws with the accent only on "property."

Today, anyone who says "property," whether collective or not, ordinarily means an almost irrevocable and easily transferable *title* of juridic value to a *fund* coordinate of the economic process—to a slave, to a field acreage, to a piece of technical equipment, to a house and so on. But the very *raison d'etre* of such a title, which is the existence of at least two parties potentially opposed to each other, seems to be glossed over. No doubt, to speak of the "collective property" of mankind over our planet would constitute what Alfred North Whitehead denounced as "the fallacy of misplaced concreteness." It is

---

17. "The Russian land community is the outcome of serfdom," [Chicherin, 1861]. See also Seebohm [1896, pp. 78, 368ff]. Baden-Powell [1896, pp. 184, 433; 1899, p. 51f], too, attributed the origin of the joint ownership of land in the North Indian village to the submission of the older agricultural communities by Aryans.

18. The case of the Javanese *ndesa* constitutes an excellent example of the difficulty in determining the evolution of village institutions. Little is known about the life of the Javanese communities before the Dutch administration. All subsequent accounts come from Dutch government officials, occasionally from Dutch scholars. They were the only source for Laveleye's analysis, which differs essentially from that of R. M. Koentjaraningrat in Murdock [1960].

some time now since Maitland pointed out the muddle in saying that the public land is the "collective property" of the nation [Maitland, 1897, 342f]. The same applies to using the term "property" in describing that village institution typified by the *mir*. To rationalize such an institution by saying that "the soil still remains the collective property of the clan, to whom it returns from time to time, that a new partition may be effected" [Laveleye, 1878, p. 4; Kovalevskii, 1891, p. 92], is not only a perplexing use of terms but also results in a loss of essence. On the other hand, we do not have to go farther back in history than the last century to see that "individual property" could not apply even to the fief of a landlord in many parts of Europe; there, landlords and former serfs got their titles to land at the same time, through one agrarian reform or another. In Hungary some landlords never became *landowners*; they ceased to be landlords with the advent of the Communist regime (1945).

THE ECONOMIC PHYSIOLOGY OF PEASANT COMMUNITIES

The considerations of the preceding sections suggest two guide lines for any attempt at delineating the physiology of the peasant economies.

First, we must reexamine the wealth of available information on past and present village institutions without any preconceived thesis and, especially, without any prepared etching traced by the property meshes of civil society. Secondly, we should not insist upon reaching a vast evolutionary synthesis embracing all village communities. This does not mean to renounce all analysis. For even though it does not seem possible to fit all village institutional matrices into a finite number of taxonomically relevant boxes, we can discern in the multitude of their forms some features which appear with striking frequency both in time and space. An analytical sifting of these features reveals, as I hope to prove next, that the economic physiology of the traditional village community, in general, is governed by a few principles of extreme simplicity.

Before proceeding, one word of caution is necessary in relation to these principles: it would be a great mistake to attribute their

genesis to constitutional preoccupations in all cases. The more relevant ones, indeed, came into being either as a result of the struggle of the village community with its natural environment or because some indifferent feature happened to last a long time during the history of the village. However, it would be equally wrong to deny that once such a principle becomes part of a tradition, it generally turns into an independent sociological agent. As such, it may serve not only as a guiding light for constitutional preoccupations but also as an influential factor of economic evolution (see below).

We may begin with those principles, two in number, that are more transparent. The first principle is that only labor creates value, and hence, labor must constitute the primordial criterion in the sharing of the community's income. Its tradition goes back to the margin of the economic (exosomatic is the right term) evolution of mankind. For only on that margin did labor alone matter: land was not limitatively scarce, and tools were so simple and of such short life that they were not yet capital.[19]

The second guiding principle is that of equal *opportunity* for all, and—we should insist—not equal *income* for all. The Narodniki and the Marxists notwithstanding, nothing would distort more the general picture of the village than a background of thoroughgoing communism with equal shares for all. That would mean that personal merits and toil come last if at all, or as Rousseau indirectly put it, "the fruits go to all, the land belongs to no one" [Baden-Powell, 1896, p. 401]. A close examination of the factual evidence will reveal that the opposite is true of village philosophy. *Equal opportunity to toil should be open to all, but the fruits go to him who has applied his labor and industry;*[20]

19. It is instructive to note that every argument by which Marx [1932, p. 46ff] justifies his fundamental tenet that "as values, all commodities are only definite masses of congealed labor-time" implies either conditions prevailing on that historical margin—where "coats" were produced without any constant capital—or a cumulative regress to the same margin. Marx, therefore, was as much of a "marginalist" as his famous predecessor, Ricardo.

20. A most eloquent illustration is provided by a peasant custom in eighteenth century Switzerland. All men would line up, as in a race, on the village meadow; at a signal, they all would start to mow, each over an equal track. The race ended, each takes home the hay he mowed; the meadow is then opened to the cattle of all [Lafargue, 1901, p. 54]. Similar customs have been noticed elsewhere, even as far as the Urals [Laveleye, 1878, p. 24].

"a fair start in life" for all, as Vinogradoff suggested [1920. pp. 30, 326], with freedom for everyone to shoot ahead in proportion to his own efforts. Needless to say, with the passage of time the last part of this principle must ultimately breed loopholes tending to weaken the power of the first clause. The interesting fact is that the leading thought of the principle survived nevertheless in social attitudes even after the village community had lost part of its faculty for self-government. We can recognize it plainly in the custom of periodic reallocation of the land use— the battle horse of those who read "primitive communism" into every village institution—as well as in several other institutions. For even though the principle, just like the "unseen hand" of Adam Smith, seems to have guided the common life of the village, circumstances varying with time and place molded it into a wide range of efficacious institutions.

There is hardly any doubt that the primeval man, with no fixed abode, lived on the forest. Even after he became a cultivator, the forest continued to support man in his economic struggle. For a very long time man raised pigs and cattle only on pannage and leaf fodder, a practice which has survived in some areas down to our own time [Stahl 1946, p. 100ff]. But the most important thing man has wrung from the forest is land itself. Almost the entire area now under cultivation in Europe was initially woodland, which man gradually cleared. We know of vast operations of *défrichement* which were undertaken systematically in France from the beginning of the eleventh to the end of the fourteenth century and in England during the reigns of the two Charles. Rumania's present fertile plains were covered with thick, forbidding forests until the second half of the last century [Bloch, 1952, p. 3ff; Orwin and Orwin, 1954, p. 15; Stahl, 1946, pp. 91, 111]. But man's war against the forest began with the first cultivators and became more intensive with every season. It had to go on even in the absence of any increase in population; the achievable yield per acre is limited at any time by the state of the arts and, moreover, *inevitably decreases if this state does not advance*.

At the time when the only agricultural implement was a hard stick, only virgin land could yield some surplus over the seed.[21] New land had to be cleared continually, cultivated for one or perhaps two seasons, and then abandoned to the wild weeds and brush. How many people labored together in one complete enterprise from land clearing to harvesting is hard to say. The answer depends on how large was then the optimum size of such an enterprise, which in turn depends on many factors impossible to assess in retrospect. One thing, however, seems certain: as long as a settlement consisted of relatively few people, they all worked together, whether they lived as a group family or in several large families bound by multiple kinship ties. But in the case of large settlements—and almost any settlement ultimately became large as population increased—people sooner or later came unwittingly to associate in squads of optimum size. After all, it may be this economic cleavage that led to the social cleavage into clans and further into households, not vice versa.

Be that as it may, as long as land clearing was to be repeated every year, or almost so, and woodland was still plentiful, there was no need for submitting the use of land, cleared or not, to any restrictive rules. The crop alone mattered. As to this matter, there was a most natural solution in those circumstances: the crop belongs to those who have labored for it. Its distribution among co-workers raised no difficulty, any more than the distribution of the family income does nowadays in the overwhelming majority of families. No doubt, the people most likely to be associated together in one primitive economic enterprise were already related to each other by family ties.

With the gradual improvement of the "plowing" stick and the discovery of the advantage of burning the brush between crops, it became possible for a piece of newly cleared land to bear crops for an increasing number of years before it had to be abandoned.[22] A question now comes

21. Bloch [1952, p. 26] reports that even in seventeenth-century France the average harvest was only three to six times the seed.
22. Because of the extraordinary fertility of virgin land, the practice described above has survived to this century in some parts of Europe where forests are still plentiful, e.g. in the French provinces of Ardennes and Vosges [Bloch, 1952, p. 27] and in Rumania [Stahl, 1946, pp. 104, 129].

immediately to the mind of the theoretical economist: in these circumstances, who had the right to use a piece of land after the first crop? For a modern economist is apt to think that any economic clan, after exhausting the powers of the land it had itself cleared, would have sought to cultivate next the land cleared by others. It is more plausible, however, that no clan thought of this possibility. The tradition that anybody who has cleared a piece of land is entitled to use it undisturbed by others must have acquired through its long life such a grip on the minds of those early peasants that none could even think of a different arrangement in life. Besides, there was no extraneous force to compel those peasant communities to cast away the old tradition: forests were then still plentiful and remained so for a very long time to come.

As numerous written documents of relatively recent times attest, the principle just discussed continued as a pillar of tradition in village communities for an amazingly long time, long after forests became scarce. We also find it very much alive in the living fossils of village sociology, the village communities that have preserved many of their archaic institutions [Laveleye, 1878, p. 21; Baden-Powell, 1896, pp. 205–207; Baden-Powell, 1889, pp. 129; Kovalevskii, 1898, p. 143; Kovalevskii, 1896, p. 183f; Stahl, 1946, p. 163]. The significance of this survival can hardly be overemphasized. In the survival of this principle—in all probability the oldest of all economic rules—we have a striking illustration of how a rule of conduct may originate from economic practices, not by necessity, and how, once it becomes a part of tradition, it may acquire immunity to economic change and thus become a sociological factor of a new nature.

Nothing could be more erroneous than to see any trace of "property" in the principle that he who clears a piece of land has the exclusive right to use it for crops. The point may be related to the fact that the oldest written law of India, the Manu Law, says that each *works* his land, not that each *owns* his land [Kovaleskii, 1896, p. 186].

As mentioned above, in early times cultivators abandoned of their own will a piece of land as soon as its powers were exhausted. Even to a mind accustomed to

the idea of individual property it would appear nonsensical to think of ownership of a valueless thing. Thus, once a piece of land was abandoned, anyone else could later "vivify it"—to borrow the Koran's expression—and use it again for crops [Kovalevskii, 1898, pp. 143, 320; Kovalevskii, 1896, p. 186f]. The principle was so sternly followed from generation to generation that it gave rise to many local proverbs: "You occupy land by the plow, not by the hatchet," one runs.

The idea that sprang up from the early art of tillage is now clear; since he who cleared a piece of land in those times knew that the result of his labor did not go beyond a couple of harvests, he could not be entitled to any other benefit than that toward which he had labored. The principle is embodied in many written laws, not too old, which stipulate that he who clears or vivifies a piece of land can have the exclusive use of it for only a small number of years, usually three [Kovalevskii, 1898, p. 164].[23] We find it also at the basis of many peasant institutions.

One such institution is the free use of the natural pastures, woodlands, and fishing waters by all members of the community. Since such natural gifts were not the creation of anybody's labor, no one was entitled to the exclusive use of them for any period of time. This institutional setup is not only one that has survived longest, but is found in lands as far apart as England, Russia, and India [Nasse, 1871, O'Curry, 1873; Laveleye, 1878, p. 116ff; Kovalevskii, 1891, pp. 76, 106ff; Baden-Powell, 1899, pp. 18, 129; Stahl, 1946, p. 161]. Even the successive agrarian reforms in Russia and Rumania, for example, though intended to establish a new order on the principle of individual landed property, refrained from completely abolishing the communal use of pastures, woodlands, and fishing waters.

Another institution sets in even stronger light the idea that land is to be used, not to be owned by exclusion. It is the custom called "open field pasture" in England, *vaine pâture* in France, and *Gemenglade der Felder* in Germany. According to it, after harvest all fields are opened for pasture to everyone's

23. It is most interesting to note that in Colombia, a country where land is still plentiful in proportion to the population, a 1946 law stated that any person can become the owner of up to 2,500 hectares of *baldios* (virgin land) provided he vivifies it and actually uses it.

cattle and remain so until the next tilling.[24] Once the practice was common to all European countries; it survived in many parts of Western Europe until the nineteenth century and all over Eastern Europe well into our own time [Nasse, 1871, p. 15; Seebohm, 1896, p. 12; Bloch, 1952, pp. 40–49; Kovalevskii, 1896, p. 193; Stahl, 1946, p. 131]. There is no need to insist in detail on its economic rationale. Old meadows were gradually brought under the plow and new ones torn from the forest. As the limit was reached where no further expansion of meadows could be made at the expense of the forest, the stubble became the only additional means by which the animals of a growing community could be supported. Open field pasture may have also been induced by the discovery of the advantage of manuring. In any case, it came about as a natural extension of the depasturing of animals in common on the undivided grazing land or in woods. But its survival comes from the fact that it fitted so well with the old principle concerning the use of land.

Even after land came to be held as individual property in severalty, the right to keep a field closed remained restricted to the period during which the field was bearing a crop. Once the crop was harvested, the field became "land" again. In the judgement of Maine [1871, p. 86], the institution of open field pasture had such deep roots that in his time the courts would not have dared to rule against that right. Also, the right of gleaning after harvest remained open to all; as the French saying went, "the corn ear belongs to him who sowed, the stubble to all" [Bloch, 1952, p. 48]. This admirably expresses the traditional principle that one has an inviolable right only to what he sought at the outset to obtain by his labor; the *windfalls of any sort belong to all*. But splendid though this principle appears from an ethical viewpoint, its application met with increasing difficulties

24. "Open field" is occasionally used to denote open field pasture. In its discriminate use, however, it denotes a setup of which open field pasture is only a part. It includes, in addition, the separation of the arable land into two or three rotation fields, the distribution of each field in intermixed strips for each household, the compulsory cultivation of the fields according to some general rules, and the communal use of the woods, grazing land, and waters. Arable land may or may not be subject to periodic reallocation [Vinogradoff, 1920, p. 165f].

as the progress of technology lengthened the period between the investment of labor and its ultimate reward.

As population increased, additional plow land was needed. It was obtained by occasional campaigns in which the entire village took part in clearing a large track at a time, as the lasting prints left by each such track on the village territory now reveal. As a result of these successive clearing operations, the plow land cultivated by each household came to be distributed in several strips—as a rule one strip in each field cleared in one campaign. This is, no doubt, the real origin of the intermixed strips that have characterized the distribution of arable land in almost all peasant villages. True, since land quality generally varied from one area cleared in one campaign to another, strip mixing represented an equalitarian distribution as well. But, as we have just seen, its origin had no connection with constitutional preoccupations; these came only later.

With population continuing to grow, the limit was ultimately reached where further clearing of woodland would have upset the balance of necessary resources within the village territory. Each household had to go on cultivating the same land that its ancestors had cleared. On the surface, the continuous use of the same land strips by the same family may look to the modern mind as if they were held as individual property. The village community, however, did not think so. The proof lies in the fact that at a later date the community was able without much ado to introduce the periodic redistribution of plow land.

The picture is clear. As some families branched out more than others, the traditional distribution of the plow land ceased to represent a balance between earned income and the size of the household. In a small community of people living close to each other, so that everyone knows exactly what everyone else does and has, inequality cannot be ignored for long, especially if property in land is an unknown idea and the tradition is that all should have a fair start in life. One may remain indifferent to a starving family but hardly so if the family is his next-door neighbor.

To repeat, as long as it was still possible to clear land from the forest, there was no reason for any constitutional preoccupations with equality—whether we have in mind a primeval village or one founded anew in later times. The point is that "agrarian communism," as some writers label the institution of periodic and equalitarian distribution of land, is a feature of an evolved type of village community, not of the most primitive one. Moreover, it emerged from constitutional preoccupations alone, the aim of which was to preserve a principle of long tradition—equal opportunity for all. Once can hardly think of a better example to show that the social philosophy embodied in tradition may be an effective factor of social evolution.

That a periodic redistribution of plow land may have also come about because of the increasing economic demands of a "lord" who had become the master of the village, as Chicherin and Seebohm argued, cannot be denied. Doubtless, heavy taxation by the lord, or by the state too, could kindle the peasants' preoccupations with equality. But it seems far more probable that even a conqueror of a village, for political expediency, only copied the form other villages had already developed. For it is difficult to believe that a master of land tracts large enough to form a village had any economic reason to think of dividing them in intermixed strips. But the best proof that the system of intermixed strips is not necessarily connected with a period of servility are those villages where a land distribution *per stirpes* (i.e. in proportion to some ancestral quotas) survived to our own time—as happened in thousands of cases in Rumania.[25]

We should also note that at the time when periodic redistribution was introduced, the village community must have already reached a strong control over not only the plow land but also over almost all farming activities. What had been learned through a very long practice, namely that the powers of the soil are rejuvenated by letting it lie fallow for a

while, had already led to the division of the entire plow land into rotation tracts. This institution in turn gradually led to that of the compulsory cultivation, i.e. to the *Flurzwang*, by which to eliminate the possibility that a prepared strip should be damaged during the tilling of the adjacent ones. Therefore, the village community as a whole had already achieved a substantial degree of authority in farming matters before the advent of land communalism; we do not need to assume that only the personal power of a master enforced the complicated practice of rotation and *Flurzwang*.

The institution of periodic redistribution of land, once believed to be a specific feature of the Russian *mir*, existed all over Europe, though its form varied greatly from one place to another. In the highlands of Scotland, in some parts of France, not to mention Eastern Europe, it survived into the last century [Haxthausen, Vol. I, 1847, p. 52, p. 34; O'Curry, 1873; Maine, 1875, p. 101; Seebohm, 1896, p. 15; Bloch, 1952, p. 47].[26] Among the Anglo-Saxons it was known as *run-rig* or *rundale*. In some cases, which seem to be correlated with a hilly or mountaineous location, it was made *per stirpes*. In others, the redistribution was made on a more equalitarian basis, in equal shares per family or in proportion to family size [Maine, 1875, p. 195; Laveleye, 1878, p. 21; Stahl, 1946, p. 36]. A highly significant fact is that, whatever the distributive criterion, in most regions each family was assigned, not a particular lot, but an abstract coefficient, as it were, which only determined the area of all strips for each family. The location of each strip was determined by lottery, held now and then or even every tillage season. This procedure, together with the fact that in all cases each family was attributed one strip in every land tract of different quality, obviously reflects some eager equalitarian preoccupations. Intermixed strips equalize not only the average soil quality, but also the distance one has to travel to his fields.[27]

Since crop rotation with fallow in between

25. In 1852 in some mountainous districts of Rumania two-thirds of the village communities were still *free* villages, with a *per stirpes* organization. A 1912 census reveals that in all regions their number had hardly diminished in the meantime. These communities were reputed for their stubborn resistance to any attempt to encroach on their traditional rights and freedom of self-government by the old or the modern state authority. An eminent chronicler of the early eighteenth century describes the *terrae* formed by these villages as "republics" [Stahl, 1938].

26. Periodic repartition was occasionally practiced in India as well [Baden-Powell, 1899, pp. 67f, 104; Kovalevskii, 1896, p. 188].

27. Both the lottery drawing and the allocation of strips in various locations were practiced in East as well as in West Europe [O'Curry, 1873; Maine, 1875, p. 101; Stahl, 1946, p. 118].

reduced the productive capacity of a village to one-half or at best to two-thirds of the arable land, increased population pressure and decreasing availability of new sites for swarming compelled the peasants to seek new ways of increasing the fertility of land.[28] Frequent manuring removed the necessity of periodic fallow. Irrigation in dry-climate regions assured a higher average and more stable yield. Earthworks sheltered the fields from floods, soil erosion, or landslides. Operations such as these made it possible for him who undertook them to justify and obtain the right to a prolonged use of the piece of land improved by his own effort and industry. Thus, the very principle that everyone is entitled to the fruits of his labour, and only to these, prepared the stage for landed property in severalty.[29] Yet the principle itself did not disappear altogether from the social matrix, even after the institution of property crept into the life of the village. There still remained the tradition formed during millenia around that principle as a backbone.

Before stopping to have a look at this tradition, let us point out one extraordinary object lesson of the long history of the village community. Brief though the analysis of this section had to be, it shows the village always intent on winning the arduous battle with an exacting nature and concomitantly on keeping a balance of economic shares among its members. But the point deserving special emphasis is that the traditional village community has never been concerned with the distribution of titles to economic *funds*. Instead, as its economic institutions show, it has constantly been concerned with the distribution of the *flow of comprehensive income*—that is, with the distribution of both the fruits and the burden of labor. And since the village constitutes thus far the social organization with the longest life in human evolution, the conclusion, in my opinion, is inescapable: the economic conflict at bottom turns upon the distribution of the *income flow*, not upon the distribution of *funds*. Equally significant is the amazing diversity of the institutions through which the village has sought to direct the income flow during its long history. All this proves that the institution of property is neither the first nor the last artifact man has devised and will devise in order to rationalize this or that pattern of distributing the income flow. Current trends in many parts of the world suggest that it is worth pondering on this object lesson of village economic physiology.

PEASANT TRADITIONS AND ATTITUDES

Nowadays not only town people but also many social scientists think of the peasant as a rock of irrational traditions. That an optical illusion, so to speak, is responsible to a great extent for this opinion is beyond doubt. Whenever the observer belongs to another tradition than the observed, an optical illusion is inevitable. The fact that even a Londoner, say, finds the tradition of a Parisian unintelligible—and vice versa!—is part of a very general phenomenon. And we can be sure that the peasant, too, thinks of the townee as a slave of a tradition he cannot understand. We usually consider it utterly inept, for instance, that in many village communities living on the verge of starvation a great deal of food is wasted at the numerous festivals held with punctual regularity throughout the year. On the other hand, the peasant—were he sufficiently sophisticated—would certainly decry, for instance, the even more numerous feasts in town at which much food is wasted while there are still many hungry mouths around. Actually, he could cite many other instances of the same sort; for the

28. Incidentally, Bloch [1952, p. 64ff] finds that there is some correlation between the type of plow used and that of crop rotation. A two-crop rotation prevailed mostly in the southern regions of Europe, the French *midi* in particular, where also the Roman plow (i.e. the swing plow) was predominant. On the other hand, a three-crop rotation was practiced almost exclusively where the wheel plow—probably an invention of the people living in Northern Europe—was the current implement. Very likely this regional distribution had something to do with the soil being lighter in the south and heavier in the north. Ordinarily the swing plow had to be pulled by eight oxen on the fields of England. Orwin and Orwin [1954, pp. 30–33] give a very useful description of all plowing implements, but their argument [1954, p. 12] that the swing and the wheel are equally efficient is faulty: they say that the swing plow cuts as deeply and as uniformly as the other provided the plowman constantly steadies it and controls the depth "by throwing his weight upon the stilts."

29. Naturally it was much easier for man to discover the advantage of irrigating than of systematic manuring, so that the earliest instances of individual property rights some from dry-climate areas. See Baden-Powell [1896, pp. 180, 400, 408; 1899, p. 105]. They are found at an early date also in the areas of North Germany, where the technique of marling eliminated the need for crop rotation [Seebohm, 1896, p. 372].

town, too, has its own tradition—a tradition which is not as free from strange peculiarities as one may think. No human society could survive without a tradition, any more than it can live without a common and, for all practical purposes, stable vocabulary.

THE RESILIENCY AND POWER OF PEASANT TRADITIONS

THE tradition of a peasant community stands out in two important respects: first, it has an extraordinary resiliency, and second, it encompasses almost every action and reaction of every member of the community.

There are two factors one may immediately think of in explaining the first characteristic of village tradition. As explained above, because of the small size of the village community, a tradition preserved by word of mouth was known in detail by every adult person. Everyone learned it gradually as he grew up and took part in various village activities. In addition, the communalist and equalitarian essence of the principles discussed in the preceding section could hardly allow a system of authority in which the voices of some members would not be heard. True, in a later phase of development we find some village communities where authority is exercised only by a council of elders within which, exceptionally, a headman may have had a preponderant role. But for a long time before this aristocratic form of government came about, the same villages knew only the authority of the village assembly. In most parts, however, the village assembly never lost its constitutional power completely.

In a political setup, where every member of the village community knows in detail the received tradition and also has a full voice in the debates, tradition has almost as many defenders as there are people in the assembly. Proposals for changing an old rule have little chance of being accepted.How strong the resistance to change may be in this situation is illustrated by the fact that on certain matters a single "nay" used to be sufficient to defeat such a proposal [Gomme, 1890, p. 262]. In later periods, the village elders merely proclaimed what had been from old [Maine, 1871, p. 68].

Tradition, whether in a peasant village or in any modern society, has a distinctive property to which not enough attention has been paid in the literature. Tradition not only embodies the rules of conduct for one individual in relation to others but also dictates the attitude of the individual towards tradition itself. It is this reflexive property of tradition that accounts for the individual of modern society being less attached to tradition than the peasant. Also, the fact that in modern societies the written part of tradition, i.e. that embodied in the system of laws, has a greater force than that carried orally, is a dictate of tradition. The same is true of the fact that in a peasant society only oral tradition has value.

No species, social or biological, could survive for long if it could mutate each second: natural selection would not have the time required for separating advantageous from deleterious mutations. The peculiar chemical stability of the biological gene—a property at which natural scientists still marvel—prevents chaos at the organic level; the reflexive property of tradition prevents it at the superorganic level. That is why, as I stated earlier, no society can live without tradition, or more exactly, without some traditional attachment to its institutions.

Nor can an organism survive if it is unable to adapt itself to the inevitable changes in its material environment. Now, tradition seems to be an impediment in this respect. From all we know, the longer an institutional matrix has been in use, the stronger becomes the traditional attachment to it. However, this law of cumulative inertia must not be interpreted rigidly. It only explains why principles of a very long tradition never give in completely under the pressure of material changes and why even some institutions that have no connection with the material basis of human activity seem to have an extraordinary tendency to survival. Principles of long tradition always restrict the extent of a necessary adaptation because, as we have seen in the preceding section, every new institution must fit into the traditional *Weltanschauung*.

Why peasant institutions have always had "a tendency to a more lasting duration than other human institutions" [Nasse, 1871, 13]— as many students have noted—should now be clear. During its long history up to recent times, the village community was seldom under pressure to change its mode of life. Migration over the hills, a short average life of the individual, as well as the fact that basic human needs have a low saturation limit, took the sting out of population increase. Technical innovations, highly significant though they were, came at distant intervals of time. Attachment to tradition could thus grow to the point that one can hardly discern any changes in the history of a given village community or in those forming a *terra*. It is this fact, one may guess, that led Oswald Spengler [1929, p. 26] to argue that the peasants form the most durable—eternal, he said—class.

The resiliency of the institutional matrix of a peasant community, it should be stressed, does not prove that all institutions spring up with a rigid necessity from material conditions. As the example of handshaking shows, institutions may have diverse origins. The point is that an institutional matrix has the peculiar power of transforming into an institution some rather indifferent event that has by accident occurred with some regularity over a period of time. The evidence of this peculiar power lies in the extreme variability of numerous institutions from one area to another. As we know, some village communities are exogamous, others endogamous;[30] in some the bride is expected to bring a dowry into the new family, in others it is the groom who must pay a nuptial price to the bride's family [Kovalevskii, 1891, p. 28]; in some, immediate relatives keep and work their lands jointly, in others every new family gets possession of its share(s); land redistribution is made at times per head, at others per household, at still others *per stirpes*.

Most students have also remarked that the institutional matrix of a village community is far from being as sharply defined as the rules embodied in a written system of law. It would be, however, a mistake to think that, because of this imprecision, village institutional matrices are as soft with regard to change as urban institutions that do not have a legal status. We must not confuse the softness with which institutional principles are applied in each concrete instance with lack

of resiliency. It is incorrect to argue that, in countries where nonstatutory law serves as a basis for court decisions, the common law is an easily mutable body of principles because of the flexibility with which the courts interpret them. And if the principles of village institutions are applied with even greater flexibility, it is because the bond between the people of a village makes them more fully aware of the fact that genuine justice is incompatible with an interpretation of the law as rigid as that of mathematical theorems. Authority on law though he was, Maitland [1897, p. 349] was greatly mistaken in arguing that the village community lacked social cohesion on the ground that "there was no form of speech or thought in which [the communal feeling] could find an apt expression [because] *it evaded the grasp of the law*," or that the village assembly had no jurisdiction because it "would be comparable rather to the meetings of shareholders than to sessions of a tribunal." To be sure, *some* institutions of a village community are so differently interpreted by various villagers that an observer may easily be confused about their reality. Such institutions are on the verge of becoming obsolete or, having become so, are merely part of the village folklore. But in regard to vital economic or constitutional matters, village tradition has at all times contained a core as hard in its force and sanctions as British common law.

Little remains to be said about other factors that have something to do with the power of tradition in peasant communities. One may mention, first, the human proclivity to conformity—an evolved manifestation of the primitive instinct of imitation—which accounts for the survival of spontaneous attachment to unwritten tradition everywhere. However, in the case of village communities, conformity was further enhanced by the fact that from the outset all people had to conform to an economic activity the rhythm of which is dictated by the solar system, and later on to an even stricter schedule, that of the *Flurzwang*. Because every household had to produce the entire gamut of life's necessities for itself, all were engaged in almost the same activities. Nor was there any room for a differentiation of techniques within the small and closed community of one village. Whatever the prevailing state of the arts, in the

---

30. As a rule, the traditional Rumanian village was endogamous [Stahl, 1946, p. 35]; while the neighboring southern Slav communities were strongly exogamous [Maine, 1886, p. 254]. The same applies to India's tradition [Baden-Powell, 1899, p. 26].

same village everyone used the same technique for plowing, harvesting, spinning, weaving, building, and the like. It is understandable that this uniformity bred conformism in every other respect, beginning with how one gets a bride and ending with how high the fences around the house should be. Lack of contact between villages lying in different *terrae* helped conformism to grow such deep roots that even when, in time, contact between adjoining *terrae* became more intense, this could not affect the proclivity to conformity. The only outcome was that institutions, especially those of an indifferent nature, became uniform over increasingly large areas.

As I have said earlier, the variability and diversity of peasant institutional matrices are so wide and irregular that the thought of covering it by a relevant taxonomy seems utterly hopeless. Agrarians have argued, in the Narodniki tradition, that the only way to disentangle some general picture from such a complex of individual forms is to focus one's attention upon the *Weltanschauung* of the peasant. For peasant institutions, though greatly different, may have a common substratum of rationalizations and attitudes. The Agrarians have been right, I think, in their claim that the discovery of this special substratum calls for another method than that of the so-called objective sciences. What one needs is delicate touch in interpreting opaque facts. A sympathetic attitude is not enough: what is needed is a trained faculty of empathic understanding. Contrary to current thought in many quarters, this position is far from being silly. Indeed, if we deny man's faculty of empathy, there really is no game we can play at all, whether in philosophy, literature, science, or the family [Georgescu-Roegen, 1966, p. 129]. On the contrary, it is an absurd asymmetry to maintain, on the one hand, that matter can be studied only by instruments of the same essence—material, that is—and, on the other hand, to deny that mind is a legitimate, in fact the most essential, instrument for studying mind.

No one denies that only analysis can bring into full light the various connections between the elements of a problem. But some may go a step further and contend that, since we can discover what lies deep below the polychromic surface of institutional details by an analysis such as above (pp. 00–00), we should dismiss empathic interpretation from our thoughts completely. Let me then hasten to disclaim that I could have built that analysis without knowing the empathic interpretations of peasant institutions at which numerous earlier authors had arrived after observing life in villages directly. The reader should have no difficulty in seeing that there is an intimate connection between the principles set forth by my analysis and the attitudes which, according to the interpretative school of thought, constitute the distinctive characteristic of the peasant's *Weltanschauung*.

EQUALITY OF OPPORTUNITY WITH DIFFERENTIAL REWARDS

Most students of peasant communities agree that the traditional peasant village is a little world complete in itself. For the peasants living in such a world generation after generation, it is natural that the world beyond, i.e. that of the town, should be a strange unknown [Baden-Powell, 1899, p. 14]. The converse is not less true. As Kautsky [1900, p. 3] once admitted, for the earliest Socialists —and we may note, for Marx as well—who were all town people, "the peasant was a strange and mysterious, nigh disquieting, creature." One would expect then some important differences between the peasant's and the townee's ideas about the purpose of society. But the reason why the two visions are directly opposed, as they indeed are, is not so immediately apparent.

The most important difference between the two visions hinges on the opportunity one has to earn a livelihood through his own efforts and industry. According to his notion of social justice, the peasant generally does not mind earning a bare minimum of subsistence, but a world in which the opportunity to labor for it does not exist for everyone is completely unintelligible to him. In the preceding section I have insisted on this point, in order that we may now see where the root of the conflict between the economic philosophies of the village and of the civil society lies.

The allocation and the employment of human resources in the urban society is governed by the principle of marginal productivity, which we consider to be the normal criterion because "it is the foundation of the businessman's policy in buying productive power" [Knight, 1933, p. 104; Schumpeter, 1934, p. 77]. Now, this "icy water of egotistical calculation . . . has resolved personal worth into mere exchange value," as Schumpeter noted [1951, p. 293]. And the individualistic peasant—as we shall find him to be—may resent this degradation. But this resentment, like all resentments, is only relative and, hence, of secondary importance for our problem. The real evil—the greatest of all, in fact—is that calculation on the margin is incompatible with equal opportunity to work for all, because it results in a smaller employment of labor than any formula found in the history of the village. As an analytical proposition, this is elementary if one pauses to consider the two alternatives. But there is also the convincing evidence that as landlords in the peasant countries of Eastern Europe turned into capitalistic calculators, *genuine* unemployment made its first appearance in the countryside [Georgescu-Roegen, 1960].

The town strives to satisfy the *effective* demand for consumer goods by employing as few men as possible. As Carl Menger [1950, p. 170] bluntly admitted, "labor services do not have value as a matter of necessity." Moreover, individual merit comes first in determining who is to be employed. The traditional village, on the contrary, wants to enable as many of its people as possible, preferably all, to labor for a livelihood within its ecological niche without primary consideration of individual merit. Merit determines not who can labor but only how much one's earnings shall be. The peasant knows only that he has a *real* demand for the necessities of life and that he is eager to toil for them; he cannot make any sense of a principle according to which someone else's effective demand should decide whether or not he can earn a living.

Some 40 years after Engels and Marx in the Communist Manifesto denounced the "idiocy" of the peasant, Engels [1884, p. 121] had to admit in so many words that when the Irish peasants "find themselves in one of the big English or American towns among a population with completely different ideas of morality and justice, they easily become confused about both morality and justice."

Surprisingly enough, that is precisely what the Agrarians have preached at all times: the soul of the village is solidarity and social justice, that of the town is treachery, shrewdness, and "every man for himself" [Mitrany, 1951, p. 40]. In this connection it is highly significant that one of the earlier Marxist deviationists, completely unaware of the coincidence, took exactly the same stand as the Narodniki: "To the village, not to the town, we must turn for the elucidation of the notion of association in the sense of the Socialist program" [Sorel, 1901, p. 35]. The line between the Agrarian ideology and Marx's ideas about peasantry could not be more sharply drawn. And one should not treat lightly the thought that the great similarity between the socialist principle "from each according to his ability, to each according to his needs" and the economic philosophy of the village is responsible for the rather puzzling fact that Marxism sold its first ticket to a peasant, not to an industrial, society. Craft and wile alone could not have achieved this tour de force.

However, we must not commit the error of believing that the village community is the paradigm of economic equality or the very expression of the much lauded "natural communism." That the social organization of the traditional village is communalistic—a term coined precisely for avoiding the verbal source of confusion—does not mean that the majority of such villages about which we have some reliable evidence did not possess their "aristocracies" [Baden-Powell, 1896, p. 335; Baden-Powell, 1899, p. 16; Bloch, 1952, p. 49]. In the villages practicing distribution of land *per stirpes*, a "landed aristocracy" emerged as a natural process. In many others we find a "cattle aristocracy," which established itself with even greater ease because chattels seem to have been always personally owned.[31] Nor should we overlook the economic differentiation resulting from owning slaves when slavery existed. Orchards and vineyards, because they did not come under the rule of the plow, also constituted a basis for wealth differentiation. But, to repeat, what the village has striven to offer to its people, including the landless immigrant, is not undifferentiated equality,

31. For the Bo-Aires, the cattle nobility of the ancient Irish, see O'Curry [1873, p. ci.].

nor even the guarantee of a continuous minimum of fair subsistence, but security in the long run for all who are willing to toil.

The peasant has also been described by some as strongly individualistic. There is great truth in this opinion, provided the term "individualistic" is properly qualified for the occasion. Living in a society where no one needs a name badge when people meet, the peasant naturally has a total respect for the individual person. In a village *anyone*, even the poorest fellow, is *someone*, not a mere name or a number. Nothing could be more resented by a peasant than one's failure to recognize the individuality of each member of the village. The peasants would immediately volunteer to help the field worker learn to know each villager by his own individual traits, good or bad. There is, then, no need to insist on the reaction of the immigrant peasant to the general anonymity of large agglomerations. But we should note that this feeling of being *someone* does not speak against the peasant's identifying his interest with those of the community as a whole, i.e. against the bond of which I have spoken in earlier sections. As Maine had occasion to note in connection with India's peasant communities, a peasant would not even voice a grievance unless he could express it as a wrong for the entire village [Maine, 1871, p. 68]. Nor has the "individualistic" peasant been unwilling to associate and even march in perfect step with others. The practices related to the *Flurzwang* reflect a willingness to cooperate equal, at least, to that required by any industrial plant. Besides, in western Europe, where the traditional village first began to disintegrate, the practice of compulsory cultivation survived for a long time thereafter.

On the other hand, the spontaneous association of several independent households for cultivating their fields in common has not been so general a phenomenon in settled agriculture as the theorists of "natural communism" claim [Baden-Powell, 1899, p. 16; Kovalevskii, 1891, p. 182; Bloch, 1952, p. 156]. Coaration alone seems to be a fairly common institution at some stages. By the Brehon Laws, for example, it was mandatory for the whole village. In many places it would not have been possible to plow all fields within the short period imposed by

climate without bringing out all draft animals. These were the cases where the soil was unusually heavy for the plow then used, so that a large team of oxen was needed to pull it. The real reason for coaration, therefore, was the relative shortage of animals and, perhaps, plows, not—as Kovalevskii [1898, p. 131] liked to argue—some special love for work in common.[32] The same economic necessity led the poorer peasants to pool their plowing chattels together even if the whole village did not [O'Curry, 1873; Seebohm, 1896, p. 121; Denman, 1958, pp. 126, 131; Arensberg and Kimball, 1940, p. 73]. The individualistic peasant has always shown a marked preference for being alone responsible for what he does and earns. But as concerns other forms of aiding the less fortunate, he seldom failed to respond to the call [Kovalevskii, 1898, p. 132; Arensberg and Kimball, 1940, p. 75; Murdock, 1960, p. 94].

To sum up the broad lines of the general picture: village life is dominated by a strong feeling of unity, reflected in an oral tradition which varies from one case to another and is in some respects very specific, in others highly diffused. But in spite of this unity, the village community is not an undifferentiated association of people within which the individual loses his own personal worth and entertains no ambition for personal affirmation.

There are several specific attitudes which should be of great interest to the economist, especially to the economist concerned with the economic development of underdeveloped economies with a numerous and suffering peasantry. The first group of these attitudes pertain to the economic behavior of the peasant. Two other attitudes should be discussed because of their particular relevance for a sound, feasible policy for solving the difficulties of the economies of the sort just mentioned. They are, first, the love peasants have for raising a large family and, second, their deep distrust of every idea that the town tries to sell them.

PEASANT ECONOMIC BEHAVIOR

Private enterprisers and public policy advisers alike have repeatedly expressed their exas-

---

32. Bloch [1952, p. 61] mentions the case of the peasants in Brittany who rejected the idea of constituting a single sheep flock for the whole village.

peration with the peasantry because, as they have generally explained, the peasants are "proverbially indolent" and also have no desire whatsoever beyond securing a bare subsistence. Briefly, they are economically inert [McCulloch, 1825, p. 353; Starcs, 1939].[33] But if the peasant had generally been inherently indolent and economically inert, instead of hard-working, frugal, and thrifty, there would have been no basis from which urban civilization could develop. Before anyone could even think of devoting his time and talent to observing the stars, or building temples and palaces, or producing other works of art and gadgets for comfort and amusement, or even teaching, he had to be fed by others. The point, which goes back at least to Xenophon, is that there can be no nonagricultural activity before agriculture has reached the stage where the work of one can feed two [United Nations, 1951, p. 58]. And there can be no doubt that the initial relation between towns and villages was not that of symbiosis but of parasitism. Moreover, a great deal of this parasitism has subsisted almost everywhere; the town has maintained its hold on the countryside through the fiscal power and military authority of the state, a hold which even the progress of democratic institutions has not eliminated entirely [Kautsky, 1900, p. 314ff].

The apparent indolence of the peasant—as I have argued elsewhere—may after all be only unwanted leisure imposed by the limitativeness first of land and later, as a consequence, of capital equipment [Georgescu-Roegen, 1960]. There are, however, obvious differences between the eagerness to work of peasantries which are equally overcrowded but have a different political history. The explanation of these differences must be sought in this history. Where the villages happened to be exploited for long periods by the state to the limit of mercilessness, the peasant first tried to appear poor to the tax collectors. Continuous exploitation made him really poor. Ultimately he discovered that working just enough to stay poor was the best strategy for making the most of his life in the struggle with his exploiters. The cumulative inertia of tradition did the rest.

But where his fate had not been so harsh,

we find the peasant holding toil in the highest esteem. That this represents an old, normal tradition with cultivators of the soil is seen in the fact that some primitive communities used to produce more than they usually needed and destroy the surplus during a festival just before the next harvest [Bancroft, 1886, p. 192; Thurnwald, 1932, p. 209]. This custom may seem utterly antieconomical. Let us note that the freakish nature of the weather in most parts of the globe must have impressed upon many cultivators the fact that one is never safe in toiling just what would suffice for an average year.

Concerning the peasant's economic decisions we find two opposing opinions. Many of those who have watched closely the peasant maintain that most of these decisions are entirely determined by traditional, hence inflexible, rules, and consequently the village economy more often than not violates the economic principle of product or utility maximization.[34] On the other hand, traditional economists as a rule maintain that, whatever friction may exist in a village economy, this economy must conform to the general principles embodied in the analytical apparatus of the standard theory. For example, Schumpeter [1934, p. 80], who was not speaking out of complete ignorance of the peasant, insisted that "the peasant sells his calf just as cunningly and egotistically as the stock exchange member his portfolio of shares."

We must admit that this was true of all peasants of the Hapsburg Empire in Schumpeter's time and also of any peasant who nowadays trades produce and wares in an urban market. Yet what matters for village sociology is how the peasant behaves, not outside, but within his own community. We could not commit a greater enormity than to assume that in his own community the peasant behaves just as the stock exchange dealer. To the peasant it does matter whether it is a poor widow who must sell a calf under the pressure of necessity. The stock exchange dealer, on the other hand, does not care whom he corners when he buys cheap; to

33. But see, by contrast, the insight of Marshall [1949, p. 226].

34. One of the earliest allusions to this economic "backwardness" is found in Gomme [1890, p. 18], who mentions the repeated complaints of the British economic reformers about "the unreasoning folly of the peasant farmers, who love to do only what their fathers had done."

repeat an earlier thought, he has no means of knowing from whom he buys and, hence, whether the latter needs the money badly or is actually a smarter dealer.

As a touchstone example of the difference between the two patterns of economic behavior, let us mention a feature of American Indian life reported by a famous scholar as clear evidence of the spirit of solidarity in a peasant community. Any villager, he observed, "may help himself to his neighbor's store *when needy*" [Bancroft, 1886, p. 191]. Now, the last qualification is significant. For obviously no society could last long if *anyone* had free access to his neighbor's store. The condition that one must be *needy* to deserve help raises no difficulty in principle. The town, too, seems to recognize that the needy should be helped by the more fortunate. But the difference between town and village is that the latter is in a position to know who really is needy in every particular instance. Circumstances vary greatly, and only the intimate knowledge everyone in a village has about everyone else makes it possible to apply a moral principle with the necessary flexibility. In proportion to the means at its disposal, the village seems indeed far more efficient in taking care of the poor, in preventing crimes, in assessing penalties, and at the same time making everyone respect the oldest of all commandments—to earn one's bread by the sweat of one's brow.[35] To recall an earlier remark, it is the small size of the village community that both imposes and maintains an ethical temper which Hegel would have regarded as the only genuine one: the individual is actual only in the identity of all its interests with the total.

The preceding observations bring to mind an important issue of methodology (rather, of epistemology) over which the Agrarians and their critics fought in vain. Agrarian ideologists insisted that theory is the surest way for an economist to commit scientific suicide. But, as I have pointed out earlier, this was a wrong conclusion from a correct datum. The datum, for which they could vouch better than the economists of the orthodox school, is that the theoretical

apparatus constructed by that school is useless, even disastrous, for the study of village economy. This economy having the characters of an organic whole, the use of the standard analytical tools, which have been designed for handling the isolated parts of the civil society, can only result in the destruction of the very phenomenon one wants to study. As Whitehead [1919] once pointedly remarked, murder is the prerequisite for using the test tube of physicochemistry in biology. In fact, at present nothing justifies the hope of constructing a strictly quantitative model of the traditional type for the village economy. The ultrarationalist dogma according to which every phenomenal domain can be exhaustively described by such a model has long since suffered blow after blow from none other than the science of physics. Much less can it then be upheld or even nursed in the domains where social or biological life takes more forms than there are numbers or, in contrast to numbers, interpenetrate each other. These caveats do not imply that one should neglect the possibility of representing some of the general aspects of the village economy by a quantitative *simile*. For a simile is helpful in many ways; above all, it may detect errors in our reasoning, just as the rule of casting out nines may signal arithmetical mistakes.[36]

One can, as the author once did [Georgescu-Roegen, 1960], represent the choice-function of a peasant by $\psi(Y; Y_s)$, where Y_s merely marks the fact that village institutions work their way through the behavior of every village member. But it would be foolhardy to think that such a formula quantifies this behavior. Since we have no means to denote a concept other than using a symbol, one must guard against thinking that a symbol necessarily represents an arithmomorphic concept.

The problem of quantifying behavior is far more complex than is generally thought. The received doctrine notwithstanding, the Paretoan ophelimity, $\psi(Y)$, does not tell the complete story, even for an individual of a civil society, precisely because its formula pays attention only to the quantitative elements of the problem.

35. Baden-Powell [1899, p. 141] also thinks that the Indian village is more efficient even as sanitation is concerned. Most likely, this was the case in his own time. But in some parts of the world even nowadays there are urban slums far more pestiferous than the poorest villages.

36. For a more elaborate discussion of the points of methodology touched above, see Georgescu-Roegen [1966, pp. 114–129].

It is indisputable that the *outcome* of any economic choice is expressible as a vector Y, the coordinates of which represent quantities of commodities. But in actuality the choice itself is not between two such vectors, Y_1 and Y_2, but between a set of complex pairs (Y_1, α_i) and (Y_2, β_j), where α_i and β_j denote the various actions by which Y_1 and Y_2 are obtainable. One may beg for a dollar, or pinch the cash register, or ask his brother to give him a dollar for keeps. What one would most likely do depends upon the institutional matrix of the community to which he belongs. The point is that whether the outcome of choice is Y_1 or Y_2 is not independent of the cultural *value* which the actions α_i and β_j have according to the institutional matrix of the particular economic agent. To leave an employer with whom one has been for some long years only because another would pay better or, conversely, to let out an old employee because business is slack is not compatible with every cultural tradition.

Even in urban societies there are cases where an individual's choice is determined not only by the purely economic coordinates Y_1 and Y_2, but also by the cultural values of α_i and β_j. Such instances are, however, rare. The contrary is true of a peasant community; more often than not it is the cultural value that weighs more in the peasant's decision if this decision concerns other village members. Consequently, when one asserts that the peasant's economic behavior is irrational, the assertion implies that a choice is rational if and only if it is made on the basis of commodity quanta alone.

SIZE OF FAMILY

Of all the attitudes prevailing among peasant societies, one alone poses a really difficult problem of which we are becoming increasingly aware: it is the desire of the peasant to raise a family as large as it might come.[37] But as any geneticist would tell us, the mere desire for a large family does not suffice to produce it. Large families can exist only

where there is also a high fertility. The point I wish to stress is that the desire for a large family by itself could not explain why the peasant population has grown and is still growing faster than the urban one, in spite of its enormously greater tribute to wars and pestilence.

One may be tempted to argue that high fertility must always prevail over low fertility and in the long run eliminate it completely, and hence, the present high fertility of peasant populations is self-explanatory. But a biologist again would instruct us that high fertility alone does not represent a Darwinian fitness. It may be associated with multiple disadvantages which would make the individuals possessing that gene less fit to survive than those who do not possess it. The most instructive illustration pertinent to our topic is the fact that in urban societies, especially in an urban society with the institution of private property, high fertility represents an appreciable economic disadvantage [Fisher, 1930, pp. 228–255].

The question of why the gene of high fertility has eliminated that of low fertility within peasant populations—instead of merely continuing to survive alongside the other, as is the case for urban populations—has hardly been entertained. No doubt it is a difficult question because of the lack of sufficient data, but one can at least offer some plausible speculations. Of all the writers on the village community, Laveleye [1878, p. 31] alone saw some connection between a peasant economic institution and population growth. He argued that the Russian *mir*, by distributing the plow land equally per capita, "removes every obstacle to the increase of population, and even offers a premium for the multiplying of offspring." But after he thus almost touched the core of the problem, he went off on a wrong track.[38]

Simple arithmetic suffices to show that if *at all times each individual shares an equal opportunity with all others and in all respects*, the relative frequency of the high fertility gene must tend toward 100 per cent. This is the intrinsic advantage of that gene. Even though the village community has never been a

37. This particular bent is by now a commonplace. Yet the reader may find it interesting to peruse the detailed evidence in Arensberg-Kimball [1940, p. 136f]. This evidence is all the more revealing since the Irish peasant is the only one to have adopted a custom aimed at controlling the increase in population: the custom of refraining from marriage when the land owned is small.

38. Laveleye immediately turned to proving that, on the contrary, peasant nations (Russia and France) cannot grow as fast as the others (England and Prussia). It should be noted that his data, first, are incomplete and, second, do not bear on fertility alone.

model of the absolute equality required by the preceding theorem, it has approximated it closely enough for us to explain the present high fertility of peasant populations by the equalitarian structure of the traditional village. However, other factors may have increased the relative advantage which high fertility has under conditions of equal opportunity for all.

One such factor is the cunning role of the laws of returns in a community which continuously redistributes its land so as to maintain some equality between all households with respect to the man-land ratio. From the viewpoint of the village, land had become scarce long before the institution of equalitarian redistribution of land came about. Consequently, in the villages practicing this sort of redistribution the size of the economic unit of every household must have been well below the optimum scale, i.e. every economic unit was operated at a size where the returns to an additional dose of land and labor were increasing. In addition, all units were operated with practically the same man-land ratio. In these circumstances, the result of an increase in some family was twofold. First, the income per head in that family *increased* because of the increasing returns to the additional dose of land and labor. Second, the same income *decreased* in every family that did not grow, because land was taken away from it to be given to the other. What was on the surface an equalitarian system actually represented a systematic discrimination against the gene of low fertility.

A similar discrimination, perhaps even more potent, has its roots in the special nature of the agricultural process which, except in some very rare spots of the earth, follows a very unequal rhythm. For long periods during the year labor power and implements find no use; during some phases of the vegetation cycle one needs all the draft animals one can get hold of and during others all the hands. In particular, harvesting by hand is an operation that requires the mobilization of the whole family, including children, for it must be performed by every household within a very short time at the same critical moment for the entire village [Arensberg and Kimball, 1940, pp. 46, 74]. To bring in all the grain safely and as quickly as possible necessitates a multiple division of labor. This requirement is all the more pressing for a bumper crop. Let us also note that, at least on the Eurasian continent, climate conditions seem to lead to a skew distribution of crop yields such that the most frequent yield is far smaller than the average. In these circumstances a small family cannot take full advantage of a bumper crop because it cannot provide the required division of labor. The economic loss thus incurred places such a family in a disadvantageous position in comparison with the large family. No wonder, then, that the peasant's thoughts have been continuously focused on the best years and on how to take full advantage of them. For a very long period, which ended only recently as villages no longer had any safety valve against the pressure of population, the peasant had a ground for thinking that "if you don't have [many] children, you are no good," as the Irish say [Arensberg and Kimball, 1940, p. 136f]. The rationale behind the peasant's desire for a large family—as I have suggested in a paper read before the Agricultural Economics Society of Thailand (February 1963)—does not differ in essence from that of the modern industrialist who also wants an excess capacity so as to be able to take advantage of any increase in demand when it comes.

Undoubtedly the problem is more complicated than the preceding analysis might suggest. But this analysis at least points out the sort of factors that are responsible for the present situation in which the attribute of high fertility has come to be associated with the peasant's traditional desire to raise as large a family as may come.

DISTRUST OF THE TOWN

The peasant views any idea or anyone coming from town with suspicion, and rightly so. Political history tells of numberless stratagems, one more ingenious than another, by which the town has repeatedly inveigled the village into accepting a losing deal. Over the years the peasant has thus learned by his own misfortunes to distrust the voice that comes from town. He has even preferred to align himself with his direct masters, the landlords, against the forces of the bourgeoisie, not because he is reactionary (as some have charged), but because the landlords opposed the encroaching by the town. A townee, too, ultimately comes to distrust anyone who has tried constantly to deceive him. It is natural that at present in most parts of the world the peasant is "unwilling to accept advice" from the urban authority [Starcs, 1939]. And it is highly significant that the poorer the peasantry in a country, the stronger is this unwillingness.

It does not matter to the peasant whether the urban authority comes to him with some taxation scheme or with some technical advice. As far as that authority is concerned, the peasant wants "to be left alone"—a conclusion at which even as casual an observer as Carlo Levi, physician and painter, arrived in his sociological novel *Christ Stopped at Eboli*. For even "honest" advice has often proved disastrous for the peasant. Doreen Warriner, for instance, reports [1939, p. 160] that in Hungary during the 1930's she saw much mechanized equipment abandoned though hardly used. During a field study I once came across the same situation in Rumania. Many middle-income peasants had followed the counsel of enthusiastic experts concerning the superiority of tractors over draft animals. But the buyers soon discovered, first, that to pay for fuel, parts, and repairs they had to sell more produce than the animals would eat and, second, that they still had to keep the animals for the indispensable task of transportation.

THE PRESENT IMPASSE

The contrast between the economic situation of the peasants in the overpopulated areas of the globe and that of the farmers in the thinly populated countries—the United States, Canada, Australia, and even Argentina—has led some to believe that overpopulation is the disease of peasant farming [Wilson, 1939b, p. 55]. The analysis presented in this essay sets this belief on a deeper basis: the world is now confronted with a vast peasant population which possesses both the biological potential and the strong wish to raise families of unlimited size. The obvious impasse is that this situation may ultimately endanger the food supply of the cities before resolving itself into a Malthusian holocaust at the source.

From the plans now aired or carried out,

we seem to think that the cure of the disease is extremely simple: just tell the peasants to practice birth control. Unfortunately, for the reasons explained above, the peasant will hardly listen—at least not in sufficient number for the solution to work in time. In any case, the solution exceeds the power of economic science. So, the economist can do nothing more than attend to the most urgent problems of a short-run nature. But even for this narrower task the standard methods with which he is ordinarily acquainted are not of much help.

First, the economist must take into consideration also the constraints deriving from the traditional economic institutions of the particular peasant society with which he happens to deal. The point that "man is not a passive instrument, with a movement determined by a simple law: one must therefore know how man [in each society] adapts himself to his task"—as Sorel [1901, p. 8] put it—is not new.[39] Maine repeatedly denounced the tremendous loss resulting from the fact that the British wanted to superimpose on India's tradition an administrative and fiscal system imported from Britain [Maine, 1861, p. 252; Maine, 1871, p. 115; Marshall, 1949, p. 762]. An interesting counterproof is supplied by the Austrian legislation of the last century which, after some groping, was adapted to fit the southern Slavs' institution of *zadruga* (a patriarchal household economic unit) [Stahl, 1946, p. 151].

Second, in the impasse reached by the peasant economies the biological has burst through its economic shell and now demands recognition by whoever approaches the problem. And this demand cannot possibly be satisfied with the aid of standard economic analysis alone. For some reason or other this analysis views the economic process as a mechanical analog, i.e. as a circular motion between production and consumption. A biological process, on the contrary, is irreversible, not circular. Moreover, if instead of artificially reducing the economic process to a closed mechanical system, as we have done ever since Jevons and Walras, we carefully consider all its material aspects, we must arrive at the con-

39. A. G. Richey, too, insisted that "the good and evil effects of any law depend upon its being applicable or inapplicable to the social condition of the society into which it is introduced."

clusion that this process is only an extension of the biological evolution of the human species. Like any biological process, the economic process, too, cannot create or destroy energy matter. Both are irreversible processes because both are only consumption processes as far as their material nature is concerned.

Any material process associated with life consumes low entropy—the term by which thermodynamics covers free (usable) energy and material structures arranged in some regular patterns. It transforms the input of low entropy into an output of high entropy, i.e. into dissipated (unusable) energy and valueless waste. The important point is that the real product of such a process is not material, but a pure *flux*—the enjoyment of life by the corresponding life-bearing entity. Moreover, the material transformation of low entropy into high entropy is irrevocable. Actually, the Second Law of Thermodynamics states that low entropy, even if left to itself, continuously turns into high entropy.

For the economist the moral is twofold. First, no scrap campaign can be completely successful; in other words, it is infinitely more profitable (in terms of entropy) to obtain gold from a mine than to gather it from the sands of the seas. Second, the economic process is sustained only if it includes a continuous tapping of the environment for low entropy.[40]

There are two distinct types of activities by which this tapping is mainly done. In mining, man simply helps himself, as it were, to low entropy from the *stocks* existing in the earth's crust. In husbandry, he mainly catches the low entropy which reaches us as a *flow* of solar energy. In this activity, land plays a role completely analogous to that of the fisherman's net. If the globe were bigger, we could catch a greater amount of solar energy. But given the size of our planet, the maximum amount of this energy that can be caught annually is rigidly determined. This is the real reason why we feel that land is scarce in a

different way than other factors. To be sure, the total amount of coal-in-the-ground, for example, is also limited. The important difference is that it lies in our power to decide how much of it we may consume in any given year.

There is an equally vital difference between husbandry and mining: husbandry must slavishly follow the unequal seasonal rhythm in which the energy radiated by the sun determines the climatic conditions in each spot of the earth. The difference is even more conspicuous if we compare husbandry with manufacturing. In manufacturing, a process can, in principle, go on uninterruptedly at our will as long as the other two sectors supply the necessary inputs of low entropy. It is precisely because of this latitude that man has been able to shorten radically the time necessary to weave an ell of cloth but hardly at all the time needed to grow corn or raise a domestic animal. The same freedom of choice is responsible for the factory system, an *economic* invention of an importance which has not been sufficiently appreciated. Indeed, only in the factory system is it possible to eliminate completely the periods of idleness imposed on practically every agent by the elementary process which transforms the input(s) into products [Georgescu-Roegen, 1965; 1967]. The point is that, contrary to Marx's claim that we can transform the entire agricultural sector into "open-air factories," husbandry will, in all probability, remain a discontinuous sequence of annual activities.[41]

We may now understand why the work of the Entropy Law, although the very root of man's struggle for life, has been ignored by an economic science interested almost exclusively in the economy of the town. The peasant, on the other hand, has never lost sight of the problem. "Whoever could make two blades of grass to grow . . . where only one grew before, would deserve better of

40. I am aware of the fact that these ideas as well as some of the subsequent paragraphs may seem esoteric to many an economist. Yet it is impossible for me to elaborate them within the space or the scope of this essay. I have attempted to do this in Georgescu-Roegen [1965; 1966, Part I, Chapters 2–5; 1967], to which I refer the reader desirous of greater detail.

41. I can think of two counterexamples; however, in the ultimate analysis they strengthen the above argument. First, there are spots on the globe—Bali Island is one—where, because of the small seasonal variations of the climate, crops could be raised in an assembly-line fashion; but such spots are highly exceptional. Second, chickens are now produced in the United States by chicken "factories." The spectacular decrease in the real cost of production brought about by this innovation needs no complicated argumentation: the famous "chicken war" suffices as a proof.

mankind," observed Jonathan Swift.[42] This is precisely what the peasant communities have succeeded in doing in their long history to our own times. The basic principles of modern agriculture have been laid out by none other than the peasant [Orwin and Orwin, 1954, p. 32]. Not even the principles by which the plow is nowadays constructed have another origin. It would therefore be foolish to believe that the peasants have not accumulated any economic wisdom during their long struggle with the hardest of all economic problems. The reality is that the peasant communities in an overwhelming number have ultimately reached a point when the problem has no longer a solution within their own reach, even if they would stop growing at the same rate as in the past.

From across the fence there comes the widely supported idea of absorbing the agricultural labor surplus through industrialization and of concomitantly preventing those remaining on the land from increasing their average consumption of food [Nurkse, 1953, pp. 37, 43]. It should be obvious to every economist that this scheme solves neither the present food scarcity nor the marasmus of the village: it merely proposes to implement an old idea that the peasant is only a special kind of draft animal entitled to a subsistence ration of food and nothing else. This is not the proper place to dwell on the contradictions inherent in all policies of industrialization and only industrialization, but I cannot refrain from inviting the reader to ponder over the case of India and also over the picture of a world in which all underdeveloped countries will have completely achieved their present dreams of economic development through industrialization alone.

Of course, the "industrialization" of agriculture is an idea entirely different from and largely independent of that of the industrialization of the entire economy. And, as I shall explain presently, it is the only rational economic solution for the impasse. But in connection with its application we hear the objection (or the complaint) that the peasant

stubbornly clings to his old techniques. This is undoubtedly true. We would err, however, in believing that the peasant needs to be instructed on the advantage of mechanization. However vaguely, he is aware of the fact that the mechanization of agriculture originated within his own society with the substitution of the foot plow for the swidden stick. Nor can there be any doubt in his mind about the fact that land yields more if one uses the plow instead of the caschrom (the foot plow). His opposition to the new changes derives from an internal logic that looks at the net rather than at the gross advantage. According to this logic, he knows perfectly well that if pastures are not freely available from a still unconquered forest, then one has to share the gross product with his draft animals, and his net product may not be much greater. Wherever land reached the limit of absolute scarcity, feeding the animals became one of the most agonizing problems of the village community. "The horse eats people" is an adage in which the Rumanian peasant has crystalized a substantial dose of economic "analysis." We must rest assured that if the antiquated caschrom has survived until this century in parts of the British Isles—as reported by Orwin and Orwin [1954, pp. 30, 153]—it is a sign of economic wisdom for the circumstances, not a symptom of "rural idiocy." And if the wooden plow, similarly, has survived in many East European villages, the reason is only that, in exchange for the iron plow, the town demanded a share of the crop larger than the difference made by such a plow.

Other implications of the mechanization of agriculture beyond the present level are apt to make the peasant apprehensive. He finds it very strange that, grain being so scarce, one should wish to use machines which often result in a greater loss of grain than if the same task is performed by the old methods (harvesting and threshing are good examples). Nor can he make good sense of using machines while the village has so many free but idle hands. Thoughts such as these and a long history of poor deals with the town explain why the peasant fears that the proposal for increased mechanization is only another crafty device by which the town seeks to increase its share of agricultural produce at the expense of the toiler of land.

42. The Entropy Law of Thermodynamics in fact says that even one single blade of grass cannot grow on the same spot year after year on end. Yet the heresy, inherited from William Petty and James Anderson through Marx and Engels, that agricultural production "can keep pace with human population whatever that might be," lingers in many minds at this late hour.

The situation calls for some sober, down-to-earth rethinking that would, for once, recognize the distorting screen raised by any criterion of profitability between us and the most important economic issues. One point is beyond the shadow of a doubt: mechanization must go on, for the simple reason that man shall no longer share the crop with the draft animals. There also are elementarily obvious reasons why we must definitely stop equating mechanization with the introduction of giant combines and huge tractors and, implicitly, advocating kolkhozation of one kind or another. The contrast between the achievements of Japan with the garden tractor and the family farm and those of the Socialist regimes speaks loud enough. The increased use of artificial fertilizers must also go on, not only because of the deficit of manure created by the elimination of the draft animals, but also because the soil has long since been impoverished by the work of the Entropy Law within the closed entropic process of peasant farming over millennia. In a nutshell, the "buffaloes," their "fodder," and the "manure" must now be supplied by the town, but not at the prices based upon the present living comfort of the townees. Otherwise we dodge the issue and, implicitly, vindicate the traditional mistrust of the peasant for whatever the town proposes. The town has the choice between two alternatives, both involving a sacrifice in personal welfare for some time to come. One alternative is to allocate part of the industrial capacity, now used to produce goods of urban comfort, to the production of tractors, fuel, and fertilizers. The other is to increase the working day and redistribute resources so as to produce these goods while preserving the present level of *real* income.[43]

No doubt the peasants, too, will have to be induced to cooperate in the proper manner with this new relationship between the town and the countryside. To win the confidence of the peasant, a task which is the hardest of all, may require the mobilization not only of our knowledge, but also of an army of educated people capable of educating the peasant—a Peace Army instead of a Peace Corps. The author, however, is unwilling to air his view concerning another problem, namely whether the town is capable of educating itself so as to raise such an army and accept the sacrifices that go with the whole scheme.

References

ALLEE, 1940. W. C. Allee, "Concerning the Origin of Sociality in Animals," *Scientia*, Vol. LXVII (1940), 154-160.

ARENSBERG and KIMBALL, 1940. C. M. Arensberg and S. T. Kimball, *Family and Community in Ireland* (Cambridge, Mass.: Harvard University Press, 1940).

BADEN-POWELL, 1892. B. H. Baden-Powell, *The Land Systems of British India* (3 vols.; Oxford: Clarendon Press, 1892).

BADEN-POWELL, 1896. B. H. Baden-Powell, *The Indian Village Community* (London: Longmans, Green, 1896).

BADEN-POWELL, 1899. B. H. Baden-Powell, *The Origin and Growth of Village Communities in India* (New York: Scribner's, 1899).

BANCROFT, 1886. A. L. Bancroft, *The Works of Hubert Howe Bancroft*, Vol. I (San Francisco: A. L. Bancroft, 1886).

BLACK, 1939a. J. D. Black, "The Problem of Surplus Agricultural Population," *International Journal of Agrarian Affairs*, Vol. I (1939), 7-24.

BLACK, 1939b. J. D. Black, "Discussion," *Proceedings of the Fifth International Conference of Agricultural Economists*, (London: Oxford University Press, 1939), 86-87.

BLOCH, 1952. Marc Bloch, *Les Caractères originaux de l'histoire rurale francaise* ("French Rural History; An Essay on Its Basic Characteristics"), (Paris: Librarie Armand Colin, 1952), English translation by J. Sondheimer (Berkeley: University of California Press, 1966). First published in Oslo: H. Aschehoug, 1931.

BRIDGMAN, 1950. P. W. Bridgman, *Reflections of a Physicist* (New York: Philosophical Library, 1950).

CHAYANOV, 1923. A. V. Tschajanow (Chayanov), *Die Lehre von der bauerlichen Wirtschaft* (Berlin: P. Parey, 1923).

CHICHERIN, 1861. B. N. Chicherin, "Leibeigenschaft in Russland" in Bluntschli and Brater, eds., *Deutsches Staats-Wörterbuch*, VI, Stuttgart: Expedition des Staats-Wörterbuchs, 1861), 393-411.

Chuprov, 1902. A. A. Tschuprow, *Die Feldgemeinschaft: Eine morphologische Untersuchung* (Strasbourg: K. J. Trübner, 1902; quotations translated by Georgescu-Roegen). For a brief information on Chuprov see J. M. Keynes,

43. The point recalls the concept of the working day upon which Marx alone insisted. But even Marx did not realize the full importance of it as a coordinate of the economic process.

"Professor A. A. Tschuprow," *Economic Journal*, Vol. XXXVI (1926).

DENMAN, 1958.   D. R. Denman, *Origins of Ownership: A Brief History of Land Ownership and Tenure in England from Earliest Times to the Modern Era* (London: Allen and Unwin, 1958).

ENGELS, 1884.   Frederick Engels, *The Origin of the Family, Private Property and State in the Light of the Researches of Lewis H. Morgan* (New York: International Publishers, 1942).

EUCKEN, 1950.   Walter Eucken, *The Foundations of Economics* (London: William Hodge, 1950). The original, in German, published in 1940.

FISHER, 1930.   R. A. Fisher, *The Genetical Theory of Natural Selection* (Oxford: Clarendon Press, 1930).

FUSTEL DE COULANGES, 1885.   N. D. Fustel de Coulanges, *Recherches sur quelques problèmes d'histoire* (Paris: Hachette, 1885).

GEE, 1929.   W. Gee, "Rural Sociology as a Field of Research in the Agricultural Experimental Stations," *American Journal of Sociology*, Vol. XXXIV (1929), 832–46.

GEORGESCU-ROEGEN, 1960.   Nicholas Georgescu-Roegen, "Economics Theory and Agrarian Economics, "*Oxford Economic Papers*, Vol. XII, No. 1 (February 1960) 1–40.

GEORGESCU-ROEGEN, 1965.   Nicholas Georgescu-Roegen, "Process in Farming vs. Process in Manufacturing: A Problem of Balanced Development," *Proceedings of Economic Problems of Agriculture in Industrial Society and Repercussions in Developing Countries*, International Economic Association, Rome, 1965.

GEORGESCU-ROEGEN, 1966.   Nicholas Georgescu-Roegen, *Analytical Economics: Problems and Issues* (Cambridge, Mass.: Harvard University Press, 1966).

GEORGESCU-ROEGEN, 1967.   Nicholas Georgescu-Roegen, "Chamberlin's New Economics and the Unit of Production," in R. E. Kuenne, ed., *Monopolistic Competition Theory* (New York: Wiley, 1967), 31–62.

GEORGESCU-ROEGEN, 1969.   Nicholas Georgescu-Roegen, *The Peasant Economy: A Historical and Analytical Essay* (Bloomington, Ind.: Indiana University Press, forthcoming 1969).

GLASSON, 1890.   E. D. Glasson, *Le Communaux et le domaine rural à l'époque franque: Réponse à Mr. Fustel de Coulanges* (Paris: F. Pichon, 1890).

GOMME, 1890.   G. L. Gomme, *The Village Community* (London: W. Scott, 1890).

HALDANE, 1935.   J. B. S. Haldane, *The Causes of Evolution* (Ithaca, N.Y.: Cornell University Press, 1935).

HAXTHAUSEN-ABBENBURG, 1847–1852.   August F. L. M. von Haxthausen-Abbenburg, *Studien über die innern Zustände, das Volksleben und insbesondere die ländlichen Einrichtungen Russlands* (3 vols., Hanover: Hahn, 1847–1852).

HOFFER, 1926.   C. R. Hoffer, "The Development of Rural Sociology," *American Journal of Sociology*, Vol. XXXII (1926), 95–104.

KAUTSKY, 1900.   Karl Kautsky, *La Question agraire* (Paris: V. Giard and E. Brière, 1900). The original, in German, published in 1899.

KNIGHT, 1933.   F. H. Knight, *The Economic Organization* (Chicago: University of Chicago Press, 1933).

KOVALEVSKII, 1891.   M. Kovalevsky, *Modern Customs and Ancient Laws of Russia* (London: D. Nutt, 1891).

KOVALEVSKII, 1896.   M. Kovalevski, "Le Passage historique de la propriété collective à la propriété individuelle," *Annales de l'Institut International de Sociologie*, Vol. II (1896), 175–230.

KOVALEVSKII, 1898.   M. Kovalewsky, *Le régime économique de la Russie* (Paris: V. Giard et E. Brière, 1898).

KROEBER, 1917.   A. L. Kroeber, "The Superorganic," *American Anthropologist*, Vol. XIX (1917), 163–213.

LAFARGUE, 1901.   P. Lafargue, *The Evolution of Property from Savagery to Civilization* (London: S. Sonnenschein, 1901). Originally published as a series of articles in *Nouvelle Revue*. The first English translation published in 1891.

LAVELEYE, 1878.   Emile L. V. De Laveleye, *Primitive Property* (London: Macmillan, 1878). The original, in French, published in 1874.

McCULLOCH, 1825.   J. R. McCulloch, *Principles of Political Economy* (Edinburgh: W. and C. Tait, 1825).

MAINE, 1861.   H. J. Sumner Maine, *Ancient Law, Its Connection with the Early History of Society, and Its Relation to Modern Ideas* (London: Dent, 1861).

MAINE, 1871.   H. J. Sumner Maine, *Village Communities in the East and West* (London: J. Murray, 1871).

MAINE, 1875.   H. J. Sumner Maine, *Lectures on the Early History of Institutions* (London: Holt, 1875).

MAINE, 1886.   H. J. Sumner Maine, *Dissertations on Early Law and Custom* (New York: Holt, 1886).

MAITLAND, 1897.   F. W. Maitland, *The Domesday Book and Beyond* (Cambridge: Cambridge University Press, 1897).

MARSHALL, 1949.   Alfred Marshall, *Principles of Economics* (8th ed., New York: Macmillan, 1949). First edition published in 1890.

MARX, 1900.   Karl Marx, *The Poverty of Philosophy* (London: Twentieth Century Press, 1900). The original, in French, published in 1847.

MARX, 1904.   Karl Marx, *A Contribution to the Critique of Political Economy* (Chicago: C. H. Kerr, 1904). The original, in German, published in 1859.

MARX, 1932.   Karl Marx, *Capital*, Vol. I (Chicago: C. H. Kerr, 1932). The original, in German, published in 1867.

MENGER, 1950. Carl Menger, *Principles of Economics* (Glencoe, Ill.: Free Press, 1950). The original, in German, published in 1871.

MITRANY, 1951. David Mitrany, *Marx Against the Peasant* (Chapel Hill, N.C.: University of North Carolina Press, 1951).

MURDOCK, 1949. G. P. Murdock, *Social Structure* (New York: Macmillan, 1949).

MURDOCK, 1960. G. P. Murdock, ed., *Social Structure in Southeast Asia* (Chicago: Quadrangle Books, 1960).

NASSE, 1871. E. Nasse, *On the Agricultural Community of the Middle Ages and the Enclosures of the Sixteenth Century in England* (London: Macmillan, 1871). The original, in German, published in 1869.

NURKSE, 1953. Ragnar Nurkse, *Problems of Capital Formulation in Underdeveloped Countries* (New York: Oxford University Press, 1953).

O'CURRY, 1873. E. O'Curry, *On the Manners and Customs of the Ancient Irish* (London: Williams and Norgate, 1873).

ORWIN and ORWIN, 1954. C. S. Orwin and C. S. Orwin, *Open Fields* (2nd ed., Oxford: Clarendon Press, 1954). First edition published in 1938.

ROBINSON, 1949. G. T. Robinson, *Rural Russia Under the Old Regime* (New York: Macmillan, 1949).

RUOPP, 1953. Phillips Ruopp, ed., *Approaches to Community Development* (The Hague: W. Van Hoeve, 1953).

SANDERSON, 1917. D. Sanderson "The Teaching of Rural Sociology," *American Journal of Sociology*, Vol. XXII (1917), 433–60.

SCHUMPETER, 1934. J. A. Schumpeter, *The Theory of Economic Development* (Cambridge, Mass.: Harvard University Press, 1934). The original, in German, published in 1911.

SCHUMPETER, 1951. J. A. Schumpeter, *Essays*, R. V. Clemence, ed., (Reading, Mass.: Addison-Wesley, 1951).

SEEBOHM, 1896. F. Seebohm, *The English Village Community* (4th edition, London: Longmans, 1896). First edition published in 1883.

SOREL, 1901. G. Sorel, Introduction to G. Gatti, *Le Socialisme et l'agriculture* (Paris: V. Giard et E. Brière, 1901; quotations translated by Georgescu-Roegen).

SPENGLER, 1929. Oswald Spengler, *The Decline of the West*, Vol. II (New York: Knopf, 1929).

STAHL, 1938. H. H. Stahl, "Organizarea socială a ţărănimii" (Social organization of the peasantry), *Enciclopedia României*, Vol. I (Bucharest: Enciclopedia României, 1938), 559–576.

STAHL, 1939. H. H. Stahl, *Nerej: Un Village d'une region archaïque, Monographie sociologique dirigée par H. H. Stahl* (3 vols., Bucharest: Institut des Sciences Sociales de Roumânie, 1939).

STAHL, 1946. H. H. Stahl, *Sociologia satului devălmaş românesc*. Vol. I: *Organizarea economică şi juridică a trupurilor de mosie* (Bucharest: Institutul de Stiinţe Sociale al României, 1946).

STARCS, 1939. P. Starcs, "The Problem of Surplus Agricultural Population," *International Journal of Agrarian Affairs*, Vol. I (1939), 79–90.

THURNWALD, 1932. R. Thurnwald, *Economics in Primitive Communities* (London: Oxford University Press, 1932).

TOYNBEE, 1956. Arnold Toynbee, *A Study of History*, abr. D. C. Somervell (New York: Oxford University Press, 1956).

UNITED NATIONS, 1951. United Nations, *Measures for the Economic Development of Underdeveloped Countries* (New York: United Nations Publications, 1951).

VINOGRADOFF, 1920. Paul Vinogradoff, *The Growth of the Manor*, (3rd ed., London: Sunnenschein, 1920). The first edition published in 1904).

WARRINER, 1939. Doreen Warriner, *Economics of Peasant Farming*, (London: Oxford University Press, 1939).

WHITEHEAD, 1919. Alfred North Whitehead, "Time, Space, and Material," *Problems of Science and Philosophy*, Aristotelian Society, Supplement, Vol. II (1919), 44–58.

WILSON, 1939a. M. L. Wilson, "The Problem of Surplus Agricultural Population," *International Journal of Agrarian Affairs*, Vol. I (1939), 37–48.

WILSON, 1939b. M. L. Wilson, "The Social Implications of Economic Progress in Present Day Agriculture," *Proceedings of the Fifth International Conference of Agricultural Economists* (London: Oxford University Press, 1939), 41–56.

COMMENT

Old and New Approaches
to Peasant Economies

DANIEL THORNER

THE SUBJECT of this conference, according to some of the papers, is peasant and subsistence economies; according to others, it is peasant and subsistence economics. In the remarks which follow, I shall assume it to be both—that is, economies *and* economics.

The paper which I have to discuss is long and bears a formidable title: "The Institutional Aspects of Peasant Economies: A Historical and Analytical Review." The last and largest section of Professor Georgescu-Roegen's paper—amounting, in fact, to two-fifths of the total—is devoted to "Peasant Tradition and Attitudes." Since this subject is being treated in other sessions, I propose to confine my remarks to the opening 40 pages of Dr. Georgescu-Roegen's paper.[1]

CONCEPT AND COVERAGE

At the outset I must share with you a misgiving or two. Although I have read with care what he has written, I am by no means sure how Dr. Georgescu-Roegen is using the expression "peasant economy." When is a society a peasant economy, and when is it not? Under what conditions, or in the presence of what institutions or cluster of institutions, does a society become a peasant economy, and when does it cease to be one?

I trust it will be apparent that I am not quibbling over a definition but expressing regret over the absence of any delimitation of the terrain, of the field of coverage. Whose behavior are we trying to analyze when we speak of peasant economies or economics of the peasantry? What peasants? When? Where? How many?

Similar questions present themselves when we refer to peasant economies, when we take a historical approach to the institutions of peasant economies. What are these peasant economies? Where did they prevail? What was their size? When did they exist? How long did they last? What were their essential, irreducible elements?

To answer these questions we would have to be explicit about the level or levels of abstraction or generalization that are involved: individual cultivators, patriarchal families, entire villages, districts, regions, sectors, whole national economies, or entire economic systems. Unless we specify the problems to which we are addressing ourselves and the degree (or degrees) of abstraction at which we are working, we are likely to wander around among sectors, levels, and lines of analysis the way visitors to Washington used to get lost in the Pentagon when it was first opened.

VILLAGE LEVEL

Dr. Georgescu-Roegen's discussion of the institutional aspects of peasant economies is pitched at the level of the village. He reviews the long debate about the nature of the village community that raged from the middle of the nineteenth century to the era of World War I. He takes us through the controversy about property in land, the disputed passage from collective or group property to individual private property in land; and he rings the changes in position or emphasis associated with the names of Haxthausen, Maurer, Maine, Laveleye, Fustel de Coulanges, and

1. My comments on Dr. Georgescu-Roegen's paper are given here as they were presented to the conference in Honolulu in 1965. Evidently they refer to the original version which Dr. Georgescu-Roegen prepared for the conference. He has subsequently altered the order of treatment, the form, and the content. A number of the points and passages to which I directed my comments have been modified or suppressed. At this date, I make no effort to criticize the recast version of Dr. Georgescu-Roegen's paper. Instead, for the record, I have left my comments in exactly the form in which they were made in March 1965, in Honolulu.

Baden-Powell, all of whom flourished before 1900.

Dr. Georgescu-Roegen's point of departure, then, is a nineteenth-century dispute about village structure and associated rights in land. The opposing positions duly found their place in the textbooks and manuals published 40 or more years ago. The best brief account of the whole discussion known to me is that by Josef Kulischer. He did the volume on Russian economic history for the classic series of handbooks in economic history edited in the interwar period from Leipzig by Georg Brodnitz. What is more, Kulischer, a professor at the University of Leningrad, had the signal honor of being invited to do the two volumes on the general economic history of Europe for the most distinguished series of historical manuals then being issued in Germany, that edited by von Below and Meinecke.

Kulischer goes over the debate about village structure, group property, and individual property. He is remarkably clear and concise (*Allgemeine Wirtschaftsgeschichte*, Vol. I, Part I). Yet one gets up from reading it with a feeling of doubt or uneasiness as to whether the basic question at issue has been soundly posed. When Marc Bloch, the best-known French economic historian of the twentieth century, reviewed Kulischer's book, he praised it in the highest terms. But on this question of the village and rights in land, Bloch was reserved. Putting his finger on the soft point, he observed: "Le mot 'propriété,' c'est bien un trompeur" [Bloch, 1929]. I have the impression that Kulischer is far from the last person to have been decieved by that tricky word, property, especially private property, or individual private property in land.

Thanks to the work of historians, economists, sociologists, and anthropologists, we know that the bundle of legal and customary rights labeled "property" is exceedingly, almost unbelievably, complex. The contents of that bundle have varied from society to society. So does the way in which the contents may be split up among different social groups. Within a given society the nature of the bundle and its social division may change through time. The subject is too shifty and too intricate to be treated under such blanket heads as "group property" and "private property." As C. Reinold Noyes has pointed

out in his comprehensive study, we require a much more subtle and sophisticated framework for grappling with the subject.

This is presumably what Marc Bloch had in mind when he labelled "*propriété*" a "*trompeur*." The search for it in the older framework of analysis may be time-consuming and misleading. Dr. Georgescu-Roegen has referred in strong, almost embarrassing, terms to my little article entitled, "Peasant Economy as a Category in Economic history" [1963]. In that article the word "property" does not occur once. I am of the opinion that we can analyze the history and institutions of peasant economies more fruitfully with other terms that bring out the varying patterns of rights in land and rights to the fruits of the land.

It may be that, in the final analysis, Dr. Georgescu-Roegen shares this view, at least *grosso modo*. If so, perhaps it would have been preferable to have indicated this explicitly at the outset of his paper. After all, the limitations and oversimplifications of nineteenth-century analysis of "property" and its evolution are by now something of a commonplace in history and the social sciences. There are many aspects of agrarian institutions and agrarian evolution whose study in recent generations has been more rewarding than that of "group property" and "private property" in village communities. It may be worthwhile to allude here to one or two of these other topics and approaches.

RECENT STUDIES OF THE AGRARIAN FRAMEWORK

One such fruitful line of historical research has been the study of rights in land and the process of agricultural production in a much broader context of the social composition of villages, the patterns of land settlement and habitation, the nature of the labor supply, the position of bond servants or other unfree laborers. With this broad framework in mind, the investigator studies the field systems, crop patterns, farming practices, implements, yokes, harness, draft power, and fodder supply. If he is fortunate or gifted, or both, he is able to work out interrelations among these elements and the factors previously listed. Nowadays he may utilize historical archaeology—immense strides forward have been recorded in recent decades in this discipline—aerial photography, or ingenious cartography.

This type of research in agrarian history got much of its impetus from the journal founded in Paris in 1929 by Marc Bloch and Lucien Febvre under the title *Annales d'histoire sociale et economique*. It is carried forward there and in other professional journals, particularly in economic and agricultural history and geography, in England, on the Continent, in the United States and elsewhere.   ·

In fact, an even more specialized journal *Études Rurales*, was set up four years ago in France precisely for these studies. It is a striking success.

The study of the institutional framework in the countryside and of social differentiation and social classes among the peasantry, then, has become a highly exciting field and has attracted personnel qualified in many disciplines. Besides Bloch and Lefebvre one thinks, for example, of such names as Gourou, Faucher, Weulersse, Postan, Kosminsky, B. H. Farmer, Sautter, Chevalier, R. E. F. Smith, Kula, Gieyzstor, Duby, Dumont, and Labouret. They and their coworkers have greatly enriched our understanding of the social setting in which agricultural production is carried on. To none of these authors and to none of the journals in which they have written do we find a reference in Dr. Georgescu-Roegen's original paper.

A FALSE DICHOTOMY: SUBSISTENCE VS.
MARKET ORIENTATION

From the economic point of view, were the households of classical antiquity or the manors of medieval times closed in on themselves—i.e. self-subsistent—or were they market oriented? For several generations historians and economists have been discussing and trying to clarify this question. They have left us a large and instructive literature, some of which may be useful for an understanding of the institutions of peasant economies. I refer in particular to certain of the issues raised in regard to markets and trade in the ancient world [Polanyi et al., 1957]; and to the debate (associated with the names of Pirenne and Dopsch) about the relative importance of "natural" economy and money economy in medieval Europe,

particularly from the eighth to the tenth centuries.

As I know you would not want me to be prolix, let me ask the very bald question: what is the upshot of this debate? Any pat, brief answer must necessarily be exceedingly oversimplified; nonetheless, here goes. To a large extent the debates turn out to have centered on an issue that was formulated with insufficient precision. Any large economic structure containing some towns and numerous villages is practically certain to have elements of both "natural" economy and "money" economy. Far from expecting to find one to the exclusion of the other, we ought to expect to find both, since they normally coexist. (I shall not try to deal here with some of the complex points posed by Professor Polanyi.)

Before proceeding, may I remind you that by definition [Thorner, 1963], I understand the term "peasant economy" to require the presence of towns and a division or break between these towns and the countryside that is simultaneously political, economic, social, and cultural. (Cf. the writings of Sir James Steuart, Karl Marx, Alfred Kroeber, Robert Redfield, Raymond Firth, et al.)

No peasant economy so defined can be called a pure subsistence economy. The towns are there, and the townspeople must be fed. In one way or another, food must go from, or be taken from, the peasants to feed the town dwellers. No peasant economy can thus be oriented only toward the subsistence of the peasants. Rather, all peasant economies must to a certain extent be market oriented or, at the very least, town oriented. After all, the backs of the peasants must bend to support and feed the towns.

In other words, when you have a case of a *pure* subsistence economy, then you may be sure that it is not a peasant economy, as here defined. There may be such pure cases on the upper Amazon or deep in the interior of New Guinea, but they do not fall within our category of peasant economy.

Seen in this perspective, the analysis of peasant economies requires a frame of reference capable of treating the towns and the countryside together, to bring out their interrelationships. The level of treatment or degree of abstraction must be higher than that of the village, even of the villages taken as a whole. Elsewhere I have suggested that the most suitable level of analysis would be the state, nation, country as a whole, or empire [Thorner, 1963].

Dr. Georgescu-Roegen's paper, as I indicated earlier, is pitched at the village level. The conceptual framework of his paper is not explicitly designed to encompass the structural relations of village and town. Hence there are basic institutional aspects of peasant economies which in his historical and analytical review are left by the wayside.

LIFE OF THE VILLAGE

The village has the central place in Dr. Georgescu-Roegen's thought, and he attributes special values to it. To him the village is a single, indivisible whole, characterized by harmony and equality of opportunity. The land furnishes the material basis of life, and the traditional institutions maintain a universal bond linking each village member to all the others. At bottom this togetherness rests on the gregarious instinct which, if one may liven the argument a bit, spills over into organic unity and results in unparalleled fecundity of the rural population.

The village community is presented as undisturbed by a struggle for land. Rather, the village acts to direct income flows, to balance economic shares in income among its members. Thus, unlike quarrelsome urban people, the villagers are not marred by class antagonisms. Instead, the peasants constitute one single social class. The dictum is quoted approvingly from Oswald Spengler that the peasants form the most durable social class. Thus the argument, taking us away from rural realities, lands us in the realm of myth and idealogy.

TOWN ECONOMISTS AND THE VILLAGE

Dr. Georgescu-Roegen argues that the peasant living in his little village world finds the town a strange unknown. Conversely, a town person (a "townee," as he is termed) finds the peasant irrational. Among the town persons least qualified to understand the behavior of the peasantry were the classical economists, particularly Ricardo and his followers. They assumed the world was made up of city men. Perhaps the classical economists would have been more comprehending if the *English* peasantry had survived, but it did not.

In presenting this line of argument, Dr. Georgescu-Roegen does not mention Ireland and is wary about Scotland and famous Scottish economists, for he is aware that the peasant crofters survived in the Scottish Highlands into the twentieth century.

Unfortunately for Dr. Georgescu-Roegen, this argument does not even hold for England. He has completely overlooked Dr. Richard Jones, the successor of Malthus as Professor of Political Economy at Haileybury, the college set up not far from London by the East India Company to train its young recruits before they were sent out to rule India. Jones published in the 1830's a devastating critique of the Ricardian theory of rent, under the title *An Essay on the Distribution of Wealth and on the Sources of Taxation: Book One, Rent*. It was reprinted first in 1896 in Ashley's series of Economic Classics. Kelley reprinted it in New York in 1956 and has announced still another reprint for 1965. The central point of Jones' critique of Ricardo turns on his insistence that the institutions of *peasant* societies are quite different from those of capitalist societies and hence require a different theoretical explanation. Walter Bagehot, by the way, as Editor of the *Economist*, thoroughly endorsed Jones' position.

Dr. Georgescu-Roegen quite rightly treats Karl Marx as a classical economist but criticizes him as never having had the opportunity to observe a peasant economy or to study a noncapitalist agriculture. Let us leave aside Ireland as well as the case of the Scottish crofters, both of which Marx had followed closely. Similarly with Marx's treatment of Richard Jones, to whom he devoted a chapter in his history of theories of surplus value. The fact is that Marx was fascinated by the agrarian changes in Russia in the 1860's and 1870's. He learned Russian in order to read the zemstvo reports and other agrarian inquiries. Three volumes of Marx's notes on these Russian reports have been published, and a fourth has been announced. (I might add that Marx served as the representative of the Russian Section on the General Council of the First International, founded in 1864.)

AGRARIANS, NARODNIKS, POPULISTS OF RUSSIA

For a century from the 1840's onward in Russia there were intellectuals sympathetic to the peasantry to whom Dr. Georgescu-Roegen refers as Populists or Narodniks. He terms economists associated with them the Agrarians, and he calls their doctrine Agrarianism, or the Agrarian doctrine or ideology.

As it happens, we have had for some years now a magnificent study of the origins and growth of the Narodnik or Populist movement. This is by Professor Franco Venturi of Turin, translated into English in 1961 under the title, *Roots of Revolution*, the original Italian title was simply *Il populismo russo*, i.e. Russian Populism. Venturi breaks off his treatment in 1881, the year of the assassination of the Czar, because he feels that event and the severe, shattering repression which followed constitute a fundamental divide in the nature, the thought, and the action of the movement. If one were to try to periodize the years after 1881, one would doubtless have another break at the revolution of 1905, and surely a still greater one in 1917. It is doubtful whether the term should be applied at all after 1917, though one sometimes does come across the terms Neo-Populists and Neo-Populism.

Of all this Dr. Georgescu-Roegen says nothing. Further, for some unexplained reason he has completely failed to refer to the most distinguished figure of the movement in mid-nineteenth century Russia, N. G. Chernyshevsky.

So far as concerns the economic doctrine or doctrines of this Russian movement, Dr. Georgescu-Roegen refers almost exclusively to twentieth-century works and to works available in languages other than Russian. He tells us that by agrarian economics he means "the economics of an overpopulated agricultural economy" [Georgescu-Roegen, 1960, p. 1 ff]. The principal, practically the only, so-called Agrarian economist he cites in support of this is A. V. Chayanov. He declares that Chayanov held that the agrarian problem is primarily a population problem.

As it happens, I have been associated for the past few years with a project to make two of Chayanov's principal works available in

English. In this connection I have recently published a note on Chayanov [Thorner, 1965]. My colleague, Professor Basile Kerblay of the Ecole des Hautes Etudes of the Sorbonne, has prepared a comprehensive and authoritative presentation of Chayanov's position [Kerblay, 1964]. On these bases I am prepared to say that Dr. Georgescu-Roegen has fallen into serious error.

Chayanov considered Russia of the period 1911–1930 to have many agrarian problems but did not believe it was overpopulated. A moment's reflection will remind us that Russia had Central Asia and Siberia. Actually Chayanov wrote that his theory of peasant economy applied to Russia because it was *not* overpopulated, whereas his theory could not be applied to India and China without modification, because they *were* overpopulated.

Dr. Georgescu-Roegen tells us that the Agrarians were pronounced positivists who were dead opposed to theory. I quote: "Agrarian idealogists simply asserted (and insisted) that theory is the surest way for an economist to commit suicide." I do not know of anything in the writings of Chayanov to justify such an assertion. Chayanov and his colleagues were constantly putting forward and revising theories on many subjects. He was himself under continual attack in the Russia of the 1920's for being too much of an Austrian marginal theorist!

Dr. Georgescu-Roegen tells us, finally, that the Agrarians had an overt scorn for quantitative theoretical analysis. This is the exact reverse of the position. Chayanov and his school had a positive passion for quantitative data and took great pains in reworking and refining these data so as to fit them into neat equations, models, and illustrative diagrams. There is no need to argue the point further, since this will be clear to all who consult the translation of Chayanov's book, *The Theory of Peasant Economy*, issued by the American Economic Association [Thorner et al., 1966].

References

BLOCH, 1929. Marc Bloch, Review of book by Josef Kulischer, *Revue Historique* (1929).

GEORGESCU-ROEGEN, 1960. Nicholas Georgescu-Roegen, "Economic Theory and Agrarian Economics," *Oxford Economic Papers*, Vol. XII No. 1 (February 1960), 1–40.

KERBLAY, 1964. Basile Kerblay, "A. V. Čajanov: Un Carrefour dans l'Evolution de la Pensée Agraire en Russie de 1908 à 1930," *Cahiers du Monde Russe et Soviétique* (Paris), Vol. V, No. 4 (October–December 1964), 411–60. For an English translation of this study, see Thorner *et al.* (1966, xxv–lxxv).

POLANYI, ARENSBERG and PEARSON, 1957. Karl Polanyi, Conrad M. Arensberg and Harry W. Pearson, eds., *Trade and Market in Early Empires* (Glencoe, Ill.: Free Press, 1957).

THORNER, 1963. Daniel Thorner, "Peasant Economy as a Category in Economic History," *The Economic Weekly* (Bombay), Special Num-

ber, Vol. XV (July 1963), 1243–52. See alternately the same article in the proceedings, *Second International Conference of Economic History, Aix-en-Provence, 1962* (Paris and the Hague: Mouton and Co., 1965), Vol. II, 287–300.

THORNER, 1965. Daniel Thorner, "A Post-Marxian Theory of Peasant Economy: The School of A. V. Chayanov," *The Economic Weekly* (Bombay), Vol. XVII (1965), 227–36.

THORNER, KERBLAY and SMITH, 1966. D. Thorner, B. Kerblay, and R. E. F. Smith, eds., *A. V. Chayanov on The Theory of Peasant Economy* (Homewood, Illinois: Richard D. Irwin, for the American Economic Association, 1966).

COMMENT

The Peasant Economies
of Today's Underdeveloped Areas

H. MYINT

I SHOULD LIKE to discuss Professor Georgescu-Roegen's paper from the standpoint of the present-day peasant economies of the underdeveloped countries. As you know, these economies differ a great deal from each other. There are some which may still hope for a considerable increase in agricultural production through improvements in transport and communications, marketing, and the like, making it possible to extend the area under cultivation. There are others which are "overpopulated" in the sense that there is little further elbow room of unused land. Here expansion in output must come mainly through improvements in techniques and organization. Again, the peasant economies of the underdeveloped countries are at different stages of transition from the "subsistence" to the "money" economy, and the scope and intensity of "monetization" vary considerably, not only between different countries, but also between the different parts of the same country. At one extreme we may have peasant societies which approximate to the "pure subsistence economy," selling very occasionally or selling only a small proportion of their products for cash. At the other extreme we may have full commercial specialization, where peasant producers devote the whole of their resources to the production of cash crops, either for the export market or for the domestic market. Again, even with the full spread of the exchange economy in the markets for products, there may be considerable variations in the spread of the money economy to the markets for factors of production. Some peasant producers may "specialize" in the production of cash crops while employing only their family labor. Others may use a considerable amount of wage labor (sometimes paid in kind) on a fairly regular basis. Again, in most countries the free market in the sale and renting of land may be restricted by communal ownership, tribal laws, feudal systems, and government regulation. But there have also been examples, e.g. Burma under the British, where agricultural land was bought and sold like stocks and shares. Finally, depending on their stage of "monetization," peasant producers may be in varying stages of self-sufficiency or complete dependence on the moneylender or the landlord for their capital requirements.

This brief sketch[1] is sufficient to show that all over the underdeveloped world the peasant economies are in different stages of disinte-

1. See my book [Myint, 1964, Chs. 2–4].

gration under the dual impact of the pressure of population and the spread of the exchange economy, particularly so when this is spearheaded by the expansion of peasant exports such as those to be observed in Southeast Asia or West Africa. In fact, it is not unfair to say that it is only in a few remote and dwindling parts of the underdeveloped world that we can hope to find village communities studied by the nineteenth-century European sociologists. How far, then, do their studies into the historical origins and the quintessential features of the village community help us to understand the present-day problems of the peasant economies in the underdeveloped countries? I must confess that I find them rather less relevant and illuminating than is suggested in Professor Georgescu-Roegen's paper.

Even if we accept that the peasant economies in the underdeveloped countries might have originated in the way described by Professor Georgescu-Roegen, the brute fact remains that they are everywhere in the process of rapid change. Thus, in order to say something useful or relevant about these peasant economies, we are perforce obliged to concentrate on the dynamic process of disintegration and transition, instead of studying them in a static or *in situ* way, trying to distill the eternal verities of village life.

Next I would question whether the model of the traditional village based on European historical experience has much relevance for the understanding of the present-day peasant economies in many parts of Asia and Africa. To be sure, we may be able to find the counterpart of the European traditional village in long-settled regions, e.g. in many parts of India, Java, or Northern Burma. But when we consider the broad perspective of the history of peasant economies in Asia and Africa, and even in parts of Latin America in the later nineteenth and early twentieth centuries, another model immediately suggests itself to us: the model, not of the traditional European village, but of the "opening-up process" of the American West and the "moving frontier." Thus Furnivall [1956] speaks of the "epic of bravery and endurance" of the Burmese peasants clearing 10 million acres of swamp and jungle of the Irrawaddy Delta for the expansion of rice cultivation

after the opening of the Suez Canal. A similar expansion of cultivation can be observed in Siam and Indochina. The West Africa peasant producers of cocoa and palm oil also went through a similar process of pioneering expansion in the early decades of the twentieth century. Sir Keith Hancock speaks about the movement of different frontiers, "the traders' frontier" and the "missionaries' frontier" in shaping the history of the British Commonwealth. Even in Latin America, which is characterized by the movement of the "big man's frontier" and of the "hollow frontier" (as in the internal migration in Brazil), it is possible to find instances of the small man's "homesteading frontier" (as in the Antioqueno Colonization in Western Colombia) [Furnivall, 1956, pp. 85–116; Ingram, 1955, pp. 43–46; Hancock, 1942; Hirschman, 1963, pp. 98–99; Bauer, 1954, Ch. 15].

Now this process of expansion of peasant economies in the underdeveloped countries in entirely different from the process of the mother village giving birth to a daughter village through the slow accretion of population, as in Europe. On the contrary, the expansion of cultivation was very rapid and spectacular: both the Southeast Asian and the West African peasant export production followed a typical S-shaped growth curve, maintaining an average growth rate of about 5 per cent per annum for two to three decades, and this without any significant reduction in the production of their food crops. This "export explosion" was brought about by improvements in transport and communications and in law and order, making it possible to open up for cultivation a widening circle of the unused hinterland. Above all, it was triggered by the world demand for their exports. Here, in contrast to the conventional picture of the peasants with limited wants, it was the growth of new wants and the introduction of the new imported consumers' goods which was the prime inducement to the peasants to undertake the rapid and arduous process of clearing the jungle.

It may also be noted that the "export explosion" in the peasant economies of Southeast Asia and West Africa preceded the population explosion, and for many decades the rate of expansion in production was well above any possible natural rate of population growth. Since peasant production, in contrast to mines and plantations, did not depend on immigrant labor, this meant that the labor required for expansion in output was supplied by internal migration or by drawing on the "disguised unemployment" which must have initially existed in these economies before they were opened up to foreign trade. To those who are used to associating "disguised unemployment" with overpopulated countries and shortage of land, it may at first sight appear surprising that I should postulate "disguised unemployment" in a situation where there was plenty of unused land available for the labor of clearing. The cause of disguised unemployment here was the lack of demand and marketing facilities. Before Burma was opened up to foreign trade, the Burmese peasant with his available techniques, supply of cattle and land, and his family labor could have produced a much greater quantity of rice than he actually did produce for his requirements. But he chose not to do so. And the reason is simple: every other peasant family could do the same and, given the poor transport and communications, there was no one to buy this potential surplus production of rice. It is no wonder, then, that the Burmese peasants, like most other peasants in a similar situation, chose "leisure" instead of working hard to produce things which no one would buy. Some Western sociologists seem to have deduced that this "preference for leisure" and "limited wants" for material goods were inherent and permanent characteristics of the peasants or of the Orient. But as soon as the opportunity and incentive for increasing output was provided by foreign trade, both the Southeast Asian and the West African peasants responded in a dramatic way to economic incentives and the lure of new goods, as shown by the recorded figures of their export production.

Where there was a free market in land and where a very large amount of land passed into the hands of absentee landlords and moneylenders, bent on extracting the maximum rent out of tenants without giving them security of tenure, as was the case in Lower Burma in the 1920's and 1930's, the resulting "village" was indeed at the opposite pole from the traditional village described

by Professor Georgescu-Roegen. Here, instead of a close-knit group of families with long taproots stretching into remote history, many of the Lower Burmese villages were no more than a random collection of poor immigrants from Upper Burma who were there because they had offered the highest bid for their tenancy (sometimes out of sheer lack of alternatives) and who might part from each other after a season or two if they were evicted for nonpayment of rent or for debt. (See also Pfanner case study, above.)

Turning now very briefly to Latin America, I can see that the concept of the traditional village may have some relevance for the Indian pueblo in the remoter heights of the Andes or the depths of the Amazon. But it seems to be quite inadequate for understanding one of the major social and economic upheavals affecting the larger proportion of the rural population in Latin America: viz, their tendency to rush in large numbers to the big towns. The population of Cali in Colombia is supposed to be increasing at 8 per cent per annum, mainly through the inflow of people from the surrounding country, and any casual visitor to any of the big cities in Latin America cannot avoid being impressed by the dimension of the problem by the size of their shantytowns. In some cases this may be impelled by land hunger or by the breakdown of law and order; but in other cases it also seems to be in large part due to the "pull" of the city lights and the expectation of high wages to be earned in cities. Here again we have the reverse of the traditional idea of the peasants as those who just want to be left alone.

When tested against the broad perspective of the peasant economies of the underdeveloped countries, there is only one feature, although a very important feature, which can be salvaged from the traditional model of the village described by Professor Georgescu-Roegen: that is the constancy of the agricultural techniques in most peasant economies. The Southeast Asian expansion in rice production was carried out with little or no change in techniques of production, simply by bringing more land under cultivation. Even where a new crop was introduced, as in the case of cocoa in West Africa, the secret of its success as a peasant export crop seems to be that it requires fairly simple methods of cultivation which can be readily incorporated into the existing agricultural techniques of the region. In fact, in the first few years of cocoa production, it seems to be complementary with the production of food crops such as yams, as the two can be interplanted. While I accept this and am in fact anxious to characterize technical backwardness as the key problem of the peasant economies of the under-developed countries, I feel that this well-recognized phenomenon can be stated simply and directly without bringing in the nineteenth-century sociological theorizings about the traditional village community in Europe. Indeed, the crux of my quarrel with Professor Georgescu-Roegen's paper is that he has permitted these sociological theorizings to obscure the analysis of the causes, and perhaps also the cure, of the technical backwardness of peasant agriculture in the underdeveloped countries.

The obscurity springs from Professor Georgescu-Roegen's belief that because of its sociological and institutional peculiarities, peasant economy is fundamentally different from what he calls the Civil Society, to which conventional economic analysis applies, and that the failure to recognize this fundamental difference has led to "the failure of the economic policies based on the Classical-Marxist viewpoint to solve the problems of underdeveloped agricultural economies." Professor Georgescu-Roegen directs his attack against both the Marxist economists and the conventional Western liberal economists. He attacks the Marxists for attempting to impose a sort of primitive communism on the village, insisting on "equal shares for all," which goes against the fundamental village philosophy of "equal opportunity to toil for all, but the fruits to go to him who has applied labor and industry." He attacks the Classical and bourgeois economists for treating the peasants as though they were city businessmen and for applying the marginal productivity principle to the allocation of human resources which rewards men according to efficiency and individual merits. This, he believes, goes against the fundamental philosophy of the traditional village which holds that "as many of its

people, preferably all, should be able to labor for a livelihood within its ecological niche without consideration for individual merits."

Now, one would have said that the failure of the Communist approach to solve the problem of expanding agricultural output was due to the failure to offer adequate incentives to the peasants. This may happen either through very heavy agricultural taxation implicit in many forms of "collective farming" (as Ragnar Nurkse once remarked, this meant that the state was to "collect" everything) or by supplying only the capital inputs, such as farm machinery, fertilizer, and the like, without expanding the supply of the incentive consumers' goods. I believe that this diagnosis is coming to be increasingly accepted in Soviet Russia and many other Communist countries in Europe.

If this is correct, I should have thought that this was the most remarkable independent support for the ordinary bourgeois Western economist's approach to the peasants: through a system of providing economic incentives. I should also have thought that the important issue we should be discussing is not the question whether peasants respond to economic incentives, but how to organize the institutional and marketing structures to provide the maximum incentives a country can afford to induce the peasants to expand output and to adopt improved methods of cultivation. I entirely agree with Professor Georgescu-Roegen that when agricultural experts in the underdeveloped countries complain that the peasants are too "conservative" to adopt modern scientific methods, it is usually the experts who are making the mistake of trying to introduce the so-called modern techniques, which are not economically advantageous to the peasants in terms of the actual extra costs and the extra money returns and that peasants are merely proving themselves better economists by refusing to adopt them. But if this is so, then the real difference between the peasant from the underdeveloped countries and the American farmer is not that the former behaves less like the "economic man" than the latter, but merely that the scientific and agricultural advice which the latter receives (being based on research and experimentation tailor-made for the American farming conditions) is of a much superior quality. This is an argument for improving the quality of agricultural research based on the special problems of the peasants in the underdeveloped countries, and not for not using economic incentives.

Professor Georgescu-Roegen quotes with relish Marx's jibe against Ricardo's "bourgeois horizon," which makes the primitive hunter and fisher "consult the annuity tables of the London Exchange." I need not remind him that the hypothesis that each producer maximizes his money profits is a very crude approximation, which is not applicable even to American businessmen, with their firmly rooted notions about "business ethics," "fair trade practice," and so on, or British businessmen who, beyond a certain point, are more interested in undertaking "prestige" work or in buying knighthoods than in straining after the last penny of extra profit. Surely any sensible economist must realize that what producers normally try to do is to maximize their satisfaction as determined by their tastes and temperaments, social and moral values, institutional setting, and so forth, and even elementary textbooks recognize the principle of equalizing the net advantages or counting the "fringe benefits," as we should say nowadays. Any sensible economist studying the peasants must therefore take into account these nonmonetary considerations and the way in which their social and institutional environments affect them. Here one may also add that as the same investors in the stock market may prefer the lower returns on gilt-edged securities to the higher but riskier returns on equities, it is quite rational for peasants in "overpopulated" countries with very little margin for taking risks above their subsistence level to be content with a lower return from subsistence production rather than choose the higher but riskier returns from cash production.[2]

To say that it is necessary to take into account all the economic and sociological complexities in applying the profit maximization principle to the peasants is rather different from saying that peasants are fundamentally different from townspeople and that they do not respond to economic incentives in the same way as townspeople or the farmers in the advanced countries do. The real question is whether we can understand and help the peasants of the underdeveloped countries better by starting from the broad hypothesis that they tend to maximize their money returns like anybody in the advanced countries than by using an entirely different set of sociological principles of the sort proposed by Professor Georgescu-Roegen.

I have said enough in support of the ordinary bourgeois Western economists' approach to peasants in terms of effective economic incentives. Now let me turn briefly to Professor Georgescu-Roegen's statement of the philosophy of the traditional village which he proposes to use as an alternative framework of analysis. According to him, this consists of two simple principles: equal opportunity of work to all members of the village and the sharing of the global income according to the amount of labor performed by each. On reflection, it will be seen that, far from being a universally valid principle of village life, it is merely a reflection or a survival from the days when there was plenty of surplus land which insured everyone who wished to work the opportunity for work. In an increasing part of the underdeveloped world, the population explosion has destroyed the possibility of fulfilling these conditions. Whatever our sympathies with this older way of life, it seems to be beyond recall, and the best we can do is to help the peasants to adjust successfully to the present day realities of life. To say as Professor Georgescu-Roegen appears to say that "the theoretical framework of traditional economies is useless, and dangerous for a student of peasant societies," because "it can only result in the destruction of the very phenomenon one plans to study," seems to be carrying nostalgia to the point of obscurantism.

In conclusion, may I say that I have ventured to state my differences with Professor Georgescu-Roegen rather sharply because ultimately we are united in our sympathy for the peasant as the eternal underdog, continually being exploited by the townsman,

2. The peasant producers of Southeast Asia and West Africa, starting from a situation of abundant surplus land, were able to take to production of cash crops for the export market without reducing their subsistence output. In this way their risks were much lower than those for peasants in overpopulated countries, with little surplus land, who would have to reduce their food output to reallocate land for cash production.

the tax collector, the moneylender, and the landlord. He has tried to protect the peasants by erecting a special sociological theory around them. In contrast, I believe that the best way to protect the peasants is to emphasize that in their basic economic behavior they are not fundamentally different from anybody else, so that they should not be discriminated against. In the history of the peasants in the colonial era, special sociological theories, such as the "backward sloping supply curve of labor," the peasant's supposed preference for leisure as against work and material reward, the oriental peasant's supposed otherworldliness, and other such theories have been (with or without their authors' consent) used to justify the exploitation of the peasants, for the adoption of negative pressures instead of positive economic incentives, the imposition of heavy taxation and forced labor. Political independence has not lessened these dangers to the peasants, for they are now faced with governments anxious to promote economic development through rapid industrialization, using peasant agriculture as the milch cow to subsidize the industrial sector. In these circumstances, it is still important to stress that the expansion of the manufacturing sector cannot be sustained for long without a "balanced-growth" development of the agricultural output and that, to achieve this, the peasants must be given the maximum economic incentives their countries can afford, to induce them to expand output and adopt improved methods. Some of the poorer underdeveloped countries with acute population pressure may decide, after taking into account their local circumstances and their time preference for present and future consumption, that they cannot afford the resources to produce a sufficient amount of incentive consumers' goods to induce the expansion of agricultural output by relying purely on positive incentives. But this political decision not to rely purely on economic incentives should be clearly distinguished from the sociological theory that economic incentives, even if they can be given, will not work on the peasants.

References

BAUER, 1954. P. T. Bauer, *West African Trade* (Cambridge: Cambridge University Press, 1954).

FURNIVALL, 1956. J. S. Furnivall, *Colonial Policy and Practice* (New York: New York University Press, 1956).

HANCOCK, 1942. W. K. Hancock, *Survey of British Commonwealth Affairs*, Vol. II, Part I (Oxford: Oxford University Press, 1942).

HIRSCHMAN, 1963. Albert O. Hirschman, *Journeys Towards Progress* (New York: Twentieth Century Fund, 1963).

INGRAM, 1955. James C. Ingram, *Economic Change in Thailand Since 1850* (Stanford, Calif.: Stanford University Press, 1955).

MYINT, 1964. H. Myint, *The Economics of the Developing Countries* (London: Hutchinson, 1964).

CASE STUDY

New Evidence on Farmer Responses
to Economic Opportunities
From the Early Agrarian History of Western Europe[1]

T. W. SCHULTZ

THE EVIDENCE TO WHICH I turn is from the recent monumental study by B. H. Slicher Van Bath, *The Agrarian History of Western Europe A.D. 500 to 1850* [1963].[2] Although the evidence does not consist of an abundance of data that can be tested empirically by modern econometric techniques, it nevertheless provides us with a considerable body of proof bearing on these matters.

There is the widely held belief that farmers during ages past were bound by cultural factors so formidable that there was little or no room for economic progress. What support is there for this belief? One can readily identify the appearance of a number of new farm products and new agricultural inputs (techniques). What is the evidence on the time it took for farmers to accept them? In view of the advantages and profitability of these new products and inputs, was the lag such that strong cultural factors are the only plausible explanation? A basic question must be faced with respect to the response of the early European farmers to economic incentives more generally. What about the centuries when subsistence agriculture predominated? When agriculture became market oriented, did relative prices of products and factors change from time to time enough so that large adjustments in agricultural production were called for? Did agriculture expand or contract accordingly? Did agriculture tend toward the type of long-run stationary equilibrium attributed to traditional agriculture?

1. I am indebted to Earl J. Hamilton for his clarifying comments and encouragement and to Arcadius Kahan for his data on early Russia which support parts of the analysis here set forth.
2. Slicher Van Bath builds on the rich, accumulated work of historical scholarship. The list of his sources requires 20 pages (see pp. 337–357).

ACCEPTING WHAT IS NEW

Let me begin with new farm products and new inputs. The products that qualify are potato, sugar beet, maize, flax, and madder—not an exhaustive list. The new inputs include the scythe (replacing the sickle), the horse (replacing the ox), plow, churn, threshing machine, and many more. The general view is that farmers during these many decades were unbelievably slow in taking advantage of the economic opportunity afforded them by such new products or new inputs. The usual explanation is that they were so slow because of strong cultural factors that bound them and kept them from acting otherwise. But what this interpretation of their responses fails to see is the fact that most of these new products or new inputs *were not necessarily profitable at the time when they became available*. This fact is clear and cogent for a long list of such products and inputs in the study by Slicher Van Bath. To show why it was true, a short review of several of these developments will be helpful.

The Potato Picture

Although it had been long known that in many parts of Europe an acre of potatoes would produce much more food than an acre of cereals, and although potatoes were destined to play a large role in European history, farmers were very slow in producing them either for home consumption or for sale. There were two reasons why farmers were so slow: the market developed very slowly, and they were up against some special costs in producing potatoes. To make it worthwhile, there had to be a demand for potatoes. As cattle fodder they were accepted, but for many decades not for human consumption. Once they became acceptable as food, particular costs hung heavily over the supply; thus, as the demand expanded, the profitability of potato production was held down by the high perishability of this product (compared to cereals), the high transport costs, the high farmyard manure requirement, and the fact that after a couple of years producers had to purchase their seed potatoes from another district. In responding to the demand once potatoes were accepted as food, these special costs adversely affected the profitability of this crop even before the potato blight became so serious [Slicher, 1963, pp. 266–271].

Sugar Beet Failures

As a source of sugar, the real comparative advantage still belongs to sugar cane, the production of which is concentrated between the temperate and tropic zones. Despite this advantage, sugar beets have taken over an increasing share of the market in countries located in the temperate zone, notably so in Western Europe. But this expansion would have been impossible except for the high level of protection that has been accorded to sugar beets. The question at hand is, why were European farmers so slow in increasing the production of sugar beets even after they were subsidized and protected? In this case there obviously was a market for sugar, but even so, decades elapsed before sugar beets became a large and established crop.

Credit for being the first to extract sugar from beets is attributed to Professor Andreas Marggraf (1747); Franz Carl Achard continued these experiments, and in 1799 induced the King of Prussia to support his enterprise, but these ventures in Silesia soon went bankrupt [Slicher, 1963, p. 277]. The Napoleonic government soon after this offered a subsidy, but it too was unsuccessful. "In 1811 Napoleon decreed the planting of 32,000 hectares of sugar beet" in his empire, and to attract capital for the construction of a beet-processing plant, a 100 per cent profit per annum was allowed [Slicher, 1963, p. 277]. But this enterprise was a complete failure. The seed was inadequate, the soil requirements were unknown, weeding of beets was un-

satisfactory until farmers could distinguish between the young beet plants and the weeds, transport facilities were wholly insufficient, for many farmers could not deliver their beets before they were rotten. The sugar yield was unbelievably low—only 2 per cent —and the taste of the sugar was disagreeable. The Netherlands also tried and found that this new venture was exceedingly costly. Thus, although a protected market for sugar was assured, the production of sugar beets was confronted by many serious technical problems which took upwards of half a century to solve.

The Sickle-Scythe Story

The scythe story begins in the late Middle Ages, and yet the sickle was still being used in some parts of Western Europe well into the modern period. It is ever so plausible to believe that the much more efficient scythe could easily have replaced the inefficient sickle, for surely use of the scythe did not require any hard-to-come-by skills and much learning from experience on the part of farmers. The productivity gains from adopting the scythe were large and presumably obvious, yet these farmers stubbornly continued to use the traditional sickle. Thus, the presumption has been that economic incentives were to little avail, leading to the inference that cultural factors thwarted the adoption of the profitable scythe. But what is here considered to be obvious turns out on close examination to be contrary to fact.

The critical facts [Slicher, 1963, pp. 186–187] are that the sickle had marked advantages in reducing the costs of transporting the harvested grain from the field to the farmstead; for the straw was left in the field and only the heads (ears) were carried to the storage sheds. The straw had little value until farm animals became important and the gathering of leaves from wooded areas for bedding was restricted, thereby increasing the value for straw for feed and for bedding. Moreover, the amount of storage space required was much less when the crop was harvested with a sickle. Then, too, when using the sickle, the grain was freer of weeds because the heads were as a rule above the undergrowth of weeds. When farmers acquired more draft animals and carts, transport costs declined. When straw became valuable for feed and bedding, new larger sheds were built in which to store the sheaves. As a consequence of these developments, it became economical to replace the sickle with the scythe. Thus the adoption of the scythe was not a simple matter; on the contrary, it required major readjustments in farming, which in turn were dependent upon far-reaching developments in transportation, animals for draft and food, a demand for straw and storage facilities, all of which occurred very slowly. Accordingly, the way the sickle-scythe story has long been told seriously maligns the calculating capacity and the response to profitable productivity gains of these early European farmers.[3]

Introduction of New Industrial Crops

Although the number of industrial crops is fairly large, the production of flax and madder will suffice to show that, when there is a strong demand and when the technology is at hand, even though it is both different and more complicated than that used in producing the established crops, the response of farmers to the profitability of such crops come through clearly. As raw material for the linen industry, flax became the most important of the industrial crops. Since flax requires much labor, flax growing was profitable only in densely populated regions [Slicher, 1963, p. 271]. Since flax exhausted the soil rapidly, farmers found it necessary to purchase manure in order to continue growing flax. Thus, "with the beginning of flax culture the trade in manure sprang up." Then too, the areas that specialized in flax, reduced their production of food grains, and this shift meant that some food grains had to be imported. But in spite of these impressive adjustments, the production of flax became important. The logical inference is that flax production was possible technically, it was profitable, and farmers responded.

Among the dye plants, madder required a rich and friable soil, a complex use of row plants on beds, and propagation in which suckers were taken from the rootstock of the parent plants. Despite these new practices and the special kilns required for drying, production increased markedly in response to the growing market for the red dye made from madder.

The conclusion from these brief accounts is of course far from conclusive, for admittedly the records do not provide the data that would be required to estimate precisely the profitability of the new products or of the inputs and the annual rate at which they were introduced or accepted. These accounts, however, support the judgment that these early European farmers were not immobilized by cultural factors; on the contrary, they appear to have been calculating entrepreneurs who could and did act intelligently in responding to new economic opportunities from these sources or in resisting those which did not offer genuine gains.

PRICES, WAGES, AND SUPPLY
RESPONSE

The history of Western Europe which is under consideration for our purpose may be divided into two parts, namely up to 1150 and since then. Agriculture was predominantly for subsistence during the first part, leaving aside early Italy. Nevertheless, there were times when it expanded and others when it contracted. Although the population estimates are admittedly tenuous, the apparent growth and decline is so large that there would seem to be little room for doubt that agriculture expanded much and then contracted greatly. For example, during this first part, from A.D. 1 to the year 200, the population of Europe is thought to have increased by four-fifths. It then declined and by 700 was less than one half of what it had been in 200.[4] The Middle Ages, 700 to 1150, which belong to the first part of this history, can be divided

---

3. Similarly the case of Indian corn (maize), which is acceptable as food and excellent as cattle fodder, but which has been grown by so few farmers in Western Europe, is also cited to show how they have lagged in introducing nontraditional crops; meanwhile the Soviet Union has taken the lead in growing corn. But this interpretation of the corn-growing possibilities in Western Europe is patently wrong. Corn simply cannot compete with the established crops throughout most of Western Europe because of climate. The climatic requirements of corn restricted it to the Mediterranean area. Here it prospered on particular soils. Yields were much higher than those of wheat; it was used for food and as cattle fodder. It too required heavy manuring.

4. M. K. Bennett [1954] places the population of Europe for A.D. 1, A.D. 200, and A.D. 700 at 37 million, 67 million, and 27 million, respectively.

into three subperiods, beginning with a century and a half that was prosperous, followed by an equally long period of contraction and then another of expansion.

The classification proposed by Slicher [1963, p. 133] is as follows:

Part I. Direct Agricultural Consumption (Mainly Subsistence Agriculture)
  A. 500–700   Antiquity to Middle Ages
  B. 700–1150   Early Middle Ages
    (1) 700–850   Prosperous period
    (2) 850–1000   Declining period
    (3) 1000–1150 Recovery period
Part II. Indirect Agricultural Consumption (Market-Oriented Agriculture)
  A. 1150–1550   Late Middle Ages
    (1) 1150–1300   Prices strongly favorable to agriculture
    (2) 1300–1450   Prices very adverse to agriculture
    (3) 1450–1550   Recovery of prices favored agriculture
  B. 1550–1850   Modern Times
    (1) 1550–1650   Prices strongly favorable to agriculture
    (2) 1650–1750   Prices somewhat adverse to agriculture
    (3) 1750–1850   Prices favorable to agriculture

Subsistence Agriculture

The period from 500 to 1150, which was so largely subsistence, should be of special interest. Some historians have applied the concept of a *natural economy* in examining it. In general the economy was administered under the manorial system, but it is hard to see what inferences can be drawn for our purposes. Obviously no hypothesis that requires microdata can be tested. Farm people produced little more than was needed for their own consumption; and as far as is now known, there were no market prices. What is known is that there was little division of labor. "Men had to do many other kinds of work besides farming. It was a *society with full employment*, where everyone was occupied; yet in spite of all this activity, the standard of living remained sadly low" [Slicher, 1963, p. 37; italics added]. Prosperous periods and declining periods were closely linked to population growth and decline. But changes in the demand for and

supply of the sources of agricultural production, as it rose and fell, are not traceable.

The supply response to prices is clearly evident after the late Middle Ages. To show this response, I have selected two periods for comment. The first period, from 1300 to 1450, is one of prolonged and marked agricultural contraction, during which relative prices had turned very adverse to agriculture. The second period, from 1450 to 1650,[5] is one of agricultural expansion in response to changes in prices highly favorable to agriculture.

Supply Contraction

The pattern of changes in relative prices associated with the period from 1300 to 1450 and with later periods of agricultural contraction are as follows: the price of cereals declines most, that of livestock products somewhat less, and that of industrial products still less. Meanwhile the wages of skilled workers fell even less than any of the three classes of agricultural products (real wages rose) and that of unskilled workers least (their real wages rose more than that of skilled workers) [Slicher, 1963, p. 115].[6] The key to this change in the pattern of prices is the decline in the population. Bennett's[7] estimates show a drop in the population of Europe from 73 million in 1300 to 45 million in 1400 (the big drop came in 1348–1351). The combined population of France, Germany, and England appears to have declined by as much as 45 per cent between 1300 and 1450.[8] What happened as a consequence of the related movements of relative prices is stated succinctly by Slicher.

When . . . low cereal prices are combined with high real wages owing to a declining population

5. I have combined Slicher's recovery period from 1450 to 1550 of the late Middle Ages with his very-favorable-to-agriculture period between 1550 and 1650 of modern times because, for the purpose at hand, they are of one piece with respect to supply responses.
6. In England, for example, on the estate of the Bishop of Winchester wages more than doubled relative to wheat prices. When wages and wheat prices are expressed in grams of silver, and when these are made equal to 100 for the period 1300–1390, wheat prices fell to 65 and wages rose to 151 by 1380–1399; thus wages rose 132 per cent relative to wheat prices [Slicher, 1963, 138].
7. From data cited by Slicher [1963, p. 78].
8. Calculated from estimates appearing in Slicher [1963, p. 81], which indicate that the population of these three countries fell from 39 million to 27 millions during this century and a half.

causing a serious labor shortage, the farmer loses both ways, since cereal prices fall especially low, while wages for unskilled labor become practically unpayable. In this situation a changeover from cereal-growing to animal husbandry is very attractive, since the latter requires much less labor and gives a better return on capital. In this branch of farming wages form a less important part of the costs. Prices remain high [relative to the price of cereals] because of the more elastic demand for livestock products. A transition to horticulture and growing industrial crops has a special appeal for the working owner of a small farm, because there need be no wages to pay [Slicher, 1963, pp. 127–128].[9]

There is an abundance of evidence to support the proposition that the response of farmers was not only consistent with these changes in relative prices and wages but also of many parts. The acreage devoted to cereals was reduced, and more land was used for livestock farming. Fodder crops were expanded. More specifically, reclamation stopped. Marginal land was abandoned, and rents, of course, fell.

In France the expansion of farmland in Picardy had ceased from the middle of the thirteenth century, in Artois after 1270, and in Brie from 1300; in the fourteenth century the cultivated lands were left to grow wild and turned back to woodland. East German colonization had passed its zenith by 1330. No further reclamation was undertaken by the monasteries in Scotland after 1350. The cultivated area shrank in almost all the countries of Europe; in many parts farms, and even whole villages, were abandoned. In England these were known as "lost villages," in Germany as "Wüstungen" [Slicher, 1963, p. 142; see also Ecole, 1965].

Supply Expansion

Turning next to the pattern of prices that brought forth a large expansion in agriculture, characteristic of the period from 1450 to 1650, the shifts in relative prices and wages were the opposite of those leading to contraction. Cereal prices rose most, livestock products somewhat less, and industrial crops still less; while wages of skilled workers rose less than the price of agricultural products (real wages fell), and wages of the unskilled

9. I have added the phrase appearing in brackets. The text makes it clear that it is the difference in the income elasticity of the demand for cereals and for livestock products that is relevant here.

rose least (real wages of unskilled labor declined even more than that of the skilled). The supply response consisted of an expansion in arable farming. While measures were taken to improve the land by applying marl, lime, and seaweeds and by purchasing manure from the villages, yet less farmyard manure was available because the numbers of livestock were reduced. Meadows were turned into arable land and marginal (waste) land was reclaimed for cultivation because the growing of cereals paid better than livestock farming.

A closer look at prices is instructive. In France from the end of the fifteenth century to the beginning of the seventeenth, the price of grain rose ten times and that of cattle eight times. Food prices rose much more than wages or prices of industrial products. The following prices (indices) in 1620 show the increase that occurred from 1451–1475 to 1620 in France and also in England and Alsace [Slicher, 1963, p. 197]:

	England	France	Alsace
	(1451–1475 = 100)		
Food	555	729	517
Industrial products	265	335	294
Builders' wages	200	268	150

In France the real wages of farmhands, without board, had fallen by 1578 to one-half of what it had been in 1470 [Slicher, 1963, p. 199].

The most convincing evidence of the supply response of farmers is the expansion of cultivated area through reclamation, drainage, and polders. Expansion from these sources as a rule took some years to complete; moreover, the investment component was large by the financial standard of that period. There is no doubt that the "sixteenth century saw great activity in the reclamation of land" [Slicher, 1963, p. 200]. The rice fields in the Po Valley were laid down. Throughout many parts of France, England, and the Netherlands much drainage was undertaken. The tables and charts showing the movement in wheat prices and the amount of land gained in the Netherlands by polders is impressively strong evidence [Slicher, 1963, pp. 200–206]. (See especially the two tables and two charts.) As one would expect, there was a lag, but the observable lagged response was strong and large.

The number of new products and inputs that became available were only a few small drops in a large bucket when they are seen over the centuries during which they appeared. The large movements in relative prices and wages that have been considered, of course, conceal many periods when the changes in these prices and wages were of minor importance. There are many clues that during these more stable periods the allocative efficiency and the rates of return to investment in agriculture conformed to the type of long-run stationary equilibrium characteristic of traditional agriculture.

References

BENNETT, 1954. M. K. Bennett, *The World's Food* (New York: Harper, 1954).

ÉCOLE, 1965. École des Hautes Etudes, Centre des Recherches Historique, *Villages desertes de histoire economique XI–XVIII siècle, les hommes et la terre* (Paris: S.E.V.P.E.N., 1965).

SLICHER, 1963. B. H. Slicher Van Bath, *The Agrarian History of Western Europe, A.D. 500 to 1850* (New York: St. Martin's, 1963).

5

Motivations, Values, and Attitudes

of Subsistence Farmers:

Toward a Subculture of Peasantry[1]

EVERETT M. ROGERS

THE PRESENT ESSAY attempts to synthesize what is presently known about the motivations, values, and attitudes of subsistence farmers. As Oscar Lewis [1964, p. xxix] observes,

Although peasantry is as old as civilization itself and constitutes the bulk of the population in the underdeveloped countries and in the world, we still have much to learn about peasants, their values, problems and aspirations, the intimate details of family living, the effects upon their lives of Western technology and culture and their potential for participation and leadership in the modern world.

Understanding this dimension of subsistence farmers is central to the process of change for social man is the basic catalyst in all economic development. Programs of directed social change designed to reach peasants are likely to fail unless based upon understandings of

the values, attitudes, and motivations of this audience.

A central principle of effective communication is that one must know his audience. This principle is especially important in programs of directed change.

A particularly ineffective communication attempt helps illustrate this point. Along a well-traveled highway in an Asian nation I once observed a "before-after" type of signboard designed to promote the adoption of birth-control methods among villagers. On the left-hand portion of the billboard was a sad-faced villager, his wife, and ten children, standing before a mud-walled hut. In contrast, on the right-hand portion was shown a smiling peasant, his happy wife, three children, and his smart *pucca* house. Over these two scenes was the caption: "The Way to Happiness and Security." But the passing villagers mistook this title to mean that if one had many children, they would care for one in his old age. This bit of selective perception was not as serious as it might otherwise have been, however, as the caption was in foot-high *English* letters, and an investigation in a

1. The author wishes to acknowledge the assistance of H. Stuart Hawkins, Research Assistant in Communication, in the preparation of this paper, and the valuable suggestions of Lawrence Witt, Professor of Agricultural Economics at Michigan State University. The central notion of subculture of peasantry is discussed in a much-expanded form in Rogers with Svenning [1968].

nearby village disclosed that only 12 per cent of the residents were literate in Hindi, and none in English. Unless planners of such programs recognize and attempt to improve their understandings of their peasant audiences, their efforts will continue to be unsuccessful.

My review of the literature reveals an essentially negative picture of peasants, and the reader should be forewarned lest he assume that the author's review implies a wholehearted endorsement of such a stereotype. There are several reasons why the word picture which emerges is that of a strong antidevelopment posture among peasants. First, describing the motivations, values, and attitudes of subsistence farmers is necessarily static—the way they are today, not yesterday or tomorrow. Consequently any description of traditional peasantry tends to be highly negative, emphasizing those characteristics which inhibit the forces of change.[2] Second, the failures and obstacles to efforts at directed change seem to have attracted far more attention of researchers than those instances where positive changes have taken place. Whether this is due to the greater drama of the failures is hard to say. Nevertheless, it must be continually borne in mind that subsistence farmers *do* change and *have* changed—imperceptibly at times, dramatically at others. In fact, there are probably very few peasant villages in the world today that have not yet felt at least a breath of the winds of change.

This essay is divided into three main sections. I will define such concepts as attitudes, values, motivation, and then proceed to outline a subculture of peasantry, as well as provide some evidence for the central elements of this subculture, and conclude with some implications for programs of change and for future research.

INTRODUCTION: DEFINITIONS AND CONCEPTS

Given the number of concepts and terms which abound in the literature in this field

and the equally wide differences in their definition and content among social researchers, it will be necessary to digress briefly and offer my specification on these terms as they will be used.

Social Change

Social change will be used to describe the process by which alterations in the structure and function of a social system occur [Rogers, 1967]. The social structure of a system consists of the various social statuses (such as divisions made on the basis of age, sex, or power classifications) and the interrelationships among these statuses. The fundamental unit of social function is role, the actual behavior of an individual in a social status. Thus, social change consists of alterations in the statuses and roles in a social system.

Social change may be classified as:

1. *Immanent change*, in the sense that it originates from within the system, with little or no external initiative. An example is a new idea invented by a peasant and then imitated by his village peers.

2. *Contact change*, because it is introduced from sources external to the social system under analysis. There are two types of contact change:

(a) *Selective contact change* occurs when outsiders unintentionally or spontaneously communicate new ideas to members of a social system. The receptors of these innovations are left to their own choice and interpretation of these innovations. While the new idea comes from outside the social system, the initiative for learning about the innovation comes from within the system. An illustration is the adoption of fertilizers and sprayers by peasants in a Colombian village, who first observed these innovations in other villages and eventually copied their use.

(b) *Directed contact change* is brought about by outsiders to the social system who, on their own or more usually as representatives of programs of change, seek to introduce new ideas in order to achieve definite goals. An example of

2. Foster [1967] argues that this negative stereotype of peasants is because their values and attitudes, conditioned by centuries of tradition, have changed more slowly than the contemporary social environment. As a result they are to some degree out of touch with reality in comparison to development planners and change agents, who thus view peasants negatively.

directed social change was the introduction of Catholicism in Latin
American and other countries by
Spanish and Portugese conquerors.
In the present era, government-
sponsored programs to secure the
adoption of technological innovations in agriculture, health, education, and industry provide many
examples of contemporary directed
social change.

These three types of social change may be
categorized on the basis of the *initiative* for
change and the *source* of the change. Immanent change or invention consists of a new
idea initiated from inside of the social system.
In contact change the new idea comes from
outside of the social system. If the initiative
for the change comes from within the system,
it is a case of selective contact change. Directed
contact change occurs if the new idea originates externally and the initiative for adopting
the change also comes from external sources.

Members of a social system often do not
place credibility in the agents of directed
change, in part because their motives are
doubted and in part because the program of
directed change may not be based upon
existing *needs* of the system's members. Thus,
one tactic of change often utilized by change
agents is to convince their clients to perceive
that a directed contact change is really selective
contact change. This fundamental stratagem
underlies many specific change-agent methods,
ranging from farmer demonstrations of new
fertilizer practices to the free samples given
physicians by medical-company detailmen.
The purpose of any demonstration is to
establish credibility for the innovation within
the social system by having a respected
member of the system adopt the innovation,
with technical assistance from the change
agent. This tactic of making directed contact
change appear to be selective contact change
through use of demonstrations may backfire.
Hardin [1951] cited an example in the
United States, where Soil Conservation
Service demonstrators were suspected by
their neighbor farmers because the demonstrators were perceived as "too friendly" with
the change agents.

Economic development is thus a type of
social change usually involving all three types
of change—immanent, selective, and directed.

Since World War II, however, economic
development has increasingly consisted of
directed social change—one in which new
ideas are introduced into a social system in
order to attain higher per capita incomes and
levels of living. Immanent and selective
change are simply too slow in an era of
rising frustrations in undeveloped countries.
New technologies, production techniques,
farm requisites, and products have been
introduced in an attempt to alter traditional
production methods and social organization.
New varieties, improved seeds, pesticides,
fertilizers, and at times even new crops have
been involved. Even the institutions and
methods for the transfer and introduction of
these changes have been the object of
research and experimentation.

Culture and the Subculture of Peasantry

One of the most important lessons that we
have learned from anthropologists and
sociologists is that village life in different
countries is tremendously varied in cultural
and historic background, in language and
leadership, and in the methods by which
change is accomplished. A typical statement
of this "principle of diversity" is that made by
the anthropologist Tax [1963, p. ix]: "Each
continent and each region has its own kinds
[of peasant communities], and in the end, of
course, every one is unique.... The first
advice one offers the administrator of a
program is to know the place and the people
and the character of the culture."

Despite the great diversity of peasant
peoples, the central assumption of the present
paper is that meaningful generalizations *can*
be made about peasants, as distinct from
commercial farmers or urbanities, which will
generally hold true in most cultural settings.

Taken to ridiculous extreme, the principle
of diversity implies that every peasant is
somehow different from every other peasant.
A converse, which should also be recognized,
is that peasants have certain subcultural
similarities in common which seem to hold
true across villages in the same country and
across countries. My argument for recognition
of a subculture of peasantry in this paper in no
way implies that further studies on a village-
by-village basis are unnecessary, especially if
these village investigations are then com-

bined into searches for common generalizations *across* villages.

A *culture* consists of material and nonmaterial aspects of a way of life, shared and transmitted among the members of a society, and constantly changing over time.

A *subculture* contains many elements of the broader culture of which it is a part but has special aspects not shared by the broader culture or by other members of the particular society. For example, Colombian peasants are Colombians and share most aspects of their national culture, but in addition they have certain elements of a "peasant culture." Subcultures are possessed by subsocieties within broader societies. There are many types of subcultures; examples are those of juvenile delinquents, college students, steam fitters, used-car salesmen. Within each of these subcultures, the members have certain attitudes, values, and other elements in common.

The idea of a peasant subculture has been suggested by others but has not previously been systematically synthesized in terms of its central elements. For instance, Foster [1962, p. 45] argued for the universality of a peasant subculture: "The similarities in peasant life the world around are so marked that we are justified in sketching an 'average' community to serve as a guide to what characteristics we may reasonably expect to find when attempting to introduce innovation."

The notion of a subculture of peasantry comes most directly from Lewis [1959], who has pictured what he considers the central elements in a culture of *poverty*, which he insists is *not* synonymous with peasantry.

Lewis' culture of poverty consists of such universal elements as a provincial orientation, a lack of integration into national institutions, low formal participation, a constant struggle for survival, and many others. Lewis emphasized that these elements were functionally interrelated and the total configuration of poverty was more than just the sum of the parts.

Somewhat similarly, we shall describe a subculture of peasantry whose elements are functionally interrelated in consistent harmony. A few of these elements of peasantry are similar to Lewis' elements in the culture of poverty, but most are different because not all peasants are necessarily in the poverty class, and the culture of poverty is shared by urban poor as well as by peasants. The descriptions of the two subcultures also differ in method of construction; Lewis seems to have induced his culture of poverty from empirical observations of Mexican poor, while the present subculture of peasantry is abstracted from a variety of analyses about subsistence farmers in a number of national settings.

Motivations, Values, and Attitudes

Motivations, values, and attitudes are important elements in the subculture of peasantry, even though all of our subcultural elements are not quite identical with any of these three concepts.

An *attitude* is a predisposition to act—a mental stance that provides clues regarding the action that an individual is inclined to take at some future time. In fact, the terms "attitude" and "opinion" are used synonymously by most social scientists. An example of an attitude is a subsistence farmer's suspicious feelings toward strangers from the city.

Social *values* are abstract and often unconscious assumptions of central importance as to what is right or of moral worth. While attitudes vary widely from individual to individual in the same social system, values are more likely to be similar among the members of a system. Values are more general, more abstract, than are attitudes. While they serve as very general guides to social behavior, they are often too abstract to specifically predict an individual's future action. Examples of values are the high concern with masculinity of Latin American males and the emphasis upon achievement among modern North Americans.

Motivations are often, and partly incorrectly, considered to be synonymous with motives. Motives are needs or desires for certain types of activity; they represent states of individual disequilibrium or dissatisfaction in regard to some object or end-state. In contrast, motivations are impellers of action at a specific point in time. They are more transitory in nature than motives but are similar in the sense they are states of desire.

All these terms—motivations, attitudes, and values—are guides to the understanding of behavior, but they vary in degree of specificity versus generality. Most elements in the subculture of peasantry are probably closer to values than to motivations or attitudes.

Methodology

The data for the present paper come largely from a synthesis of the available literature about subsistence farmers whether they are called peasants, *peones, fellahs, muzhiks, cafoni, fazendeiros,* or *campesinos.* Most of these studies were completed by anthropologists or sociologists in single communities, without intention of providing the basis for constructing a subculture of peasantry. Hillery [1961] synthesized ten peasant village descriptions to construct his model of the main elements of the "folk village." Hillery shares the viewpoint of the present author when he stated:

Perhaps most unsung among sociological and anthropological works are the painstaking and detailed descriptions of identifiable social systems [peasant villages] which have been accumulating, especially over the past few decades. These descriptions are in reality sources of data, sources which have greater value if they are taken in concert than if examined singly.

The studies included in the present synthesis were drawn in an attempt to secure coverage of the world's major continents. Unfortunately, many more descriptions of Latin American peasants are available than are those of their African, Asian, or Middle Eastern counterparts [Wagley, 1964a, p. 22].

TEN ELEMENTS IN THE
SUBCULTURE OF PEASANTRY

There are ten central elements in our subculture of peasantry:
1. Mutual distrust in interpersonal relations.
2. A lack of innovativeness.
3. Fatalism.
4. Low aspirational levels.
5. A lack of deferred gratification.
6. Limited time perspective.
7. Familism.
8. Dependency upon government authority.
9. Localiteness.
10. A lack of empathy.
One danger in focusing our attention upon

these ten elements is overconcentration; I would urge, however, a search for an eleventh, a twelfth, and so on.

I. MUTUAL DISTRUST IN
INTERPERSONAL RELATIONS

Peasant communities are characterized by mutual distrust, suspiciousness, and evasiveness in interpersonal relations. There are few exceptions to this statement in the research literature; one exception was found by Redfield [1930, p. 124], who described Tepoztlan, a small Mexican town, as "A relatively homogeneous, isolated, smoothly functioning and well-integrated society made up of a contented and well adjusted people."

Fifteen years later, Lewis' findings in the same village [1951, pp. 428–429] "Emphasize the underlying individualism of Tepoztlan institutions and character, the lack of cooperation, the tensions between villages within the *municipio,* the schisms within the village, and the pervading quality of fear, envy, and distrust in interpersonal relations." Lewis [1960] found the typical peasant an individualist, withdrawn, self-reliant, reluctant to seek or give economic aid, or to cooperate with others.

Redfield [1955, p. 134] sought to explain these differences by saying, "The hidden question behind my book is 'What do these people enjoy?' The hidden question behind Lewis' book is 'What do these people suffer from?' " Foster [1960][3] reviews these works, considers various other writings about peasant societies, adds some of his own impressions gained in another Mexican village, and concludes that Lewis' non-Rousseauan view is more correct than is Redfield's.

Lobreato [1962] concluded that his data from a farm village in South Italy supported Lewis' view of the peasant as suspicious and noncooperative in his interpersonal relations with peers.

Similarly, Reichel-Dolmatoff and Reichel-Dolmatoff [1961] found the people in Aritama, a Colombian peasant community they studied,

controlled and taciturn, evasive and monosyllabic. They are always afraid of giving themselves away

---

3. See also the comments following the Foster article by Oscar Lewis, by Julian Pitt-Rivers, and Foster's rejoinder.

somehow, of being ridiculed because of the things they say or do, or of being taken advantage of by persons of authority. This reserve, however, is not only displayed towards strangers but characterizes their own interpersonal contacts as well.

An identical pattern of interpersonal relations was found in India by Carstairs [1958]. The Hindu peasants in his study were characterized by paranoid reactions of mutual distrust, displays of goodwill and flattery followed by dubious afterthoughts, and an apparent lack of empathy regarding others' feelings, so that their fellows' motives always seemed arbitrary, inscrutable, and suspect.

A Middle East fable illustrates the mutual distrust found in peasant human relationships and is itself an important way in which this value is taught to children. It seems there was a monkey and a scorpion on the bank of a flood-swollen river. The scorpion suggested to the monkey that they cooperate in solving their transportation problem. If the monkey would swim the river, the scorpion would perch on his head and give directions. In midstream the scorpion stung the monkey, and they both drowned.

This fable is not completely representative of the peasant mentality of mutual distrust. Were the monkey and the scorpion true peasants, they would never have joined their pact of mutual advantage in the first place. Both would still be waiting to cross the river.

The nature of interpersonal relations among peasants serves as a powerful block to co-operative organizations and to most community development programs, based on the notion that people, with the help of some professional technical advice, can cooperatively solve their social and economic problems. The basic community-development assumption of peasant cooperation is seldom found and is one reason for the lack of success of many community-development self-help programs in peasant settings.

Hickey [1964, pp. 279–280] analyzed the social career of a credit cooperative in a South Vietnamese peasant community. He concluded, "The lack at village level of communal personal association was manifest in the unsuccessful village cooperative. . . . The trust and cooperation needed to make a success of the organization clearly was lacking." The economist Hendry [1964, p. 244] studied this same village and con-

cluded, "There is a relatively weak sense of communal identification or community interest . . . without vigorous leadership, communal activities in Khanh Hau do not seem to go very far."

The lack of concern with community affairs was explained by Banfield in term of the rule by which Italian peasants seemed to play their game of life: maximize the material, short-run advantages for oneself; assume that all others will do likewise. From this basic rule flow various consequences for the peasant:

1. The claim of any person to be inspired by public interest should be regarded as fraud.

2. Not only is public-spiritedness lacking, but most peasants want to prevent others from getting ahead. [Banfield, 1958, p. 18]. The peasant "will vote against measures which help the community without helping him because, even though his position is unchanged in absolute terms, he considers himself worse off if his neighbors' position changes for the better" [Banfield, 1958, p. 101].

Banfield [1958, p. 163] regarded his respondents as prisoners of their own ethos. Their inability to act concertedly in the common good was a fundamental impediment to their economic progress.

A generally similar ethic of distrust toward mutual self-help has been termed the "ego-focused image of change" by Hirschman [1958, pp. 14–20] and "zero-sum entrepreneurship" by Leibenstein [1957, pp. 112–119] both apt terms when applied to peasants as well as to some developing nations.

Perceived Limited Good

Why are peasant subsocieties characterized by mutual distrust in interpersonal relations? Part of the answer probably lies in what Foster[4] calls the "image of limited good," the peasant notion that all desirables in life (including land, wealth, health, friendship, love, power, security, and safety) exist in finite quantity, are always in short supply, and the available quantity cannot be increased by

4. The clearest statement of the image of limited good is George M. Foster [1967]; but the basic notion appeared earlier in Foster [1962].

means within the peasant's power. If good exists in limited amounts in a village, and if the system is relatively closed (as are most peasant villages as a result of geographical isolation and other factors), it logically follows that one can get ahead only at the expense of others. This type of cognitive orientation—that the pie is limited by an unexpandable pie tin—leads the peasant to be suspicious of his always hungry neighbors. For if one man tries to eat a larger slice, the division of the pie for his peers is upset. Foster utilizes the image of limited good to explain why Mexican peasants dislike giving blood transfusions and why they even like to hoard their perceived "limited" supply of semen.

The basic notion of perceived limited good has been noted by other analysts of the peasant subculture. Leslie [1960, p. 71] stated, "For the most part they [the Mitla Mexican peasants] assumed that one man's gains were another man's losses." Mandelbaum [1963, p. x] stated that Indian villagers hold "the idea that the good things of the village are forever fixed in amount, and each person must manipulate constantly to garner a larger slice for his own."

Thus we see that the image of limited good may be one reason for the peasant's mutual distrust in interpersonal relations. One consequence of this pervasive mutual distrust is that most peasant villages remain unmoved on the banks of the river of economic development.

2. LACK OF INNOVATIVENESS

Peasants generally lack innovativeness in their reaction to new ideas. To say that peasants are oriented to tradition is to state a truism rather than to offer an explanation of their behavior. Peasants often follow a course of action established by their ancestors; in many cases they may not have full knowledge of alternatives. But even when innovations in agricultural production, in sanitation, health and nutrition, and in marketing are presented to subsistence farmers, their record of adoption has seldom been enthusiastic. This lack of innovativeness may be due in part to the inappropriateness of the innovations.

Some evidence of the lower innovativeness of peasants as compared to commercial

farmers[5] living in the same Colombian villages is available from a reanalysis of data which I gathered.[6] In each of four different villages, peasants were much less innovative than commercial farmers in adopting both agricultural and home ideas.[7]

One reason why peasants are not more innovative is because their way of life has conditioned them to avoid the risky, the novel, the uncertain [Myren, 1964]. If one does not gamble,[8] he can never win, but he can never lose, either. Sharks, they relate, are only dangerous to those who go swimming [Strassman, 1964, p. 161]. This unfavorable orientation to change is partially a result of generations of cultural conditioning.

It is often said that the lack of peasant innovativeness is a function of scarce economic resources. Peasants *are* poor, and a lack of ready capital undoubtedly serves to discourage the adoption of new practices which require cash outlay. This type of reasoning, however, does not explain why peasants are also reluctant to adopt innovations which are economically costless but potentially profitable.

Some question has been raised in the literature as to the degree of economic orientation of subsistence farmers. Some authors prefer to think of peasants as miniature economic men, dealing in small change to be sure, but quite within the bounds of economic rationality. Such a view is expounded in

5. The categorization of respondents as subsistence vs. commercial was made on the basis of whether they operated five hectares or less (subsistence) or more than five hectares (commercial). This measure leaves much to be desired but is a common rule of thumb classification used widely by Colombian government agencies to differentiate between subsistence and commercial farmers. In terms of the crops grown and the type of agriculture prevalent in the Andean regions of Colombia, a farmer with more than five hectares probably is oriented mainly to commercial sale of his production (which is heavily potatoes, and barley for beer manufacture).

6. A total of 214 farmers were interviewed in the four villages, of whom 156 were classified as peasants and 56 as commercial farmers.

7. An agricultural innovativeness score was constructed for each respondent, based on his relative time of adoption of 16 farm practices; the home innovativeness scale was constructed similarly for homemaking and health practices.

8. It might seem inconsistent that peasants dislike "gambling" on farm production innovations, yet they will purchase lottery tickets, bet on fighting cocks, and so on. Foster [1964] suggests this may be due to the peasants' view of the world; lottery betting, for example, is viewed as gaining at the expense of the external world rather than of one's fellow villagers. This does not explain cock-fight bets, however.

Tax's analysis of a Guatemalan village, which he has entitled "Penny Capitalism."[9] Tax states: "The Indian is perhaps above all else an entrepreneur, a business man, always looking for new means of turning a penny. If he has land enough to earn a good living by agriculture as such, he is on the lookout for new and better seeds, fertilizers, ways of planting; and always new markets" [Tax, 1963, p. 12]. I tend to doubt the generality of Tax's word picture of penny capitalists; in fact, Tax himself points out that the community he studied is an exception in terms of economic behavior.

Lewis [1960, p. 90] emphasizes a lack of production efficiency considerations among his Mexican subsistence farmers. "So long as a man devotes himself to work, he feels secure and blameless, regardless of how little he produces."

An analysis by Jimenez [1964] of an *ejido* (cooperative farm) in Mexico, where about half of the farm production was self-consumed, generally indicated a lack of economic rationality in farmer decision-making.

They usually think in terms of "amount" of "carretas" or "canastos" [baskets] in their total land. They do not think in terms of how many hours they need for a specific practice. But usually they say it depends on "weather," if weather permits to do this, or to do that, then they will do it. They basically plant their crops not because those are the most profitable in money, but because they need to plant what they need and like to eat.

In general the available evidence tends to indicate that peasant behavior is far from completely oriented to rational, economic considerations. Undoubtedly, however, the degree to which peasants are efficiency-minded, market-oriented, and economically rational depends in large part on the degree of modernization of the village. Our earlier definition of peasants implied that their villages are somewhere on a continuum from pure folklike isolation to modern urbanism. Just where a specific peasant community is on this continuum at a certain point in time may

have much to say about the type of economic behavior exhibited. Nevertheless, it seems quite dangerous to assume that subsistence farmers will be promptly motivated to adopt agricultural innovations once only the pecuniary advantages of this acceptance have been pointed out.

In summary, the norms of most peasant communities are negative toward change as a result of past generations of generally unfavorable conditioning toward innovations. These norms against innovativeness are firmly enforced by various means of social control in the village. Deviation from such norms will be gradually encouraged as village isolation breaks down and villagers gain new reference groups outside of the village.

3. FATALISM

Fatalism, a passive feeling that an individual's efforts cannot determine his future,[10] has been widely reported as characteristic of peasant peoples. For example, Banfield [1958, p. 109] found that 90 per cent of the TAT stories told by his Italian respondents had themes of calamity and misfortune; only two or three of 320 protocols were happy in tone. Levi [1947, p. 77] characterized his peasant respondents as possessed by "passive brotherliness" and "fatalistic, comradely, old-age patience."

Fals Borda [1955, p. 245] reported his Colombian peasants had developed "An ethos of passivity—that quality of moving only when acted upon by an outside force, or of receiving and enduring with little or no reaction."[11] The religious attitudes of Fals Borda's respondents were of complete resignation, "The Lord giveth and the Lord taketh away" [1955, pp. 219–226]. These spiritually fatalistic peasants were "anesthetized by religion" to be content with their physical distress. But their occupation, not their church, was felt to be the basic cause of fatalism; their deteriorating agriculture permeated their lives [Fals Borda, 1955, p. 129]. Other

9. Schultz [1964] draws heavily on Tax's analysis, and also on a study of one Indian village, to support a view of subsistence farmers as economically rational in adopting farm innovations and otherwise behaving, in terms of their limited resources, as economic men in diminutive scale but, i.e., ignores a wealth of contradictory evidence from other peasant analyses.

10. Thus, fatalism is essentially similar to the powerlessness dimension of alienation, as delineated by Melvin Seeman [1959].

11. Hendry [1964, p. 112] rather similarly described the fatalism with which farmers in a Vietnamese village reacted to disease among their chickens. "Some villagers ascribe the pestilence to bad luck or regard it as a punishment by heaven for unspecified misdeeds; others just accept it as a fact of life to which they must adjust."

analysts—for example, Lewis [1960, p. 77]—feel that peasant fatalism is due to authoritarian family structure, which produces youngsters who are passive and dependent. In contrast, Carstairs [1958, pp. 54, 106] traced his respondents' fatalistic orientations to an all-pervading uncertainty, a feeling that "nothing and nobody can be relied on, not even one's own self." Levi [1947, p. 78] credited his respondents' high degree of fatalism to their ignorance of cause-effect relationships; all happenings were explained as due to an adverse fate.

Somewhat similarly, Reichel-Dolmatoff, and Reichel-Dolmatoff [1961, p. 259] stated:

The villager's fatalistic outlook on life results in failure to see a relationship between work and one's economic condition. Having enough is thought to be almost entirely due to "luck" (suerte) and is never believed to be brought about or furthered by personal effort and initiative. This "lucky" accumulation of wealth is suspected of being the result of shrewd, if not immoral, practices in business transactions, but work, in the sense of persistent individual effort, is never recognized as the reason back of success.

So just as an omnipresent fate is blamed for misfortune by peasants, so is it credited for success. Because a subsistence farmer has always found it difficult through his struggles with nature to raise his level of living, when he or one of his neighbors achieves progress, it is reasonable for him to credit this success to supernatural intervention (the often encountered Latin American notion of a successful individual's "pact with the Devil"), his finding of buried treasure,[12] or some other fatalistic explanation.

The dysfunctional consequences of peasant fatalism seriously impede programs of directed social change. How can change agents convince peasants of the utility of self-help efforts when these subsistence farmers believe that the determinant of their relative well-being is a supernatural fate? Thus, while the fatalistic orientation of peasants perhaps arose as a functional explanatory rationalization for their relatively deprived state, this fatalism, once imbued, serves dysfunctionally to discourage efforts at self-help. As Rao [1963, p. 58] aptly observed, "An almost fatalistic tendency prevents people from being in a state of healthy discontent." This brings us to a consideration of aspirations.

4. LOW ASPIRATIONAL LEVELS

Social aspirations are desired future states of being, such as levels of living, social status, education, and occupation. A common observation by most students of peasantry is that their respondents have relatively low levels of aspiration. For example, Lewis [1960, p. 90] noted that "the majority of Tepoztecans seem to lack strong drive or ambition for self-achievement. They tend to be satisfied if they have enough food and clothing from harvest to harvest." Foster [1965] pointed out that: "The Anglo-Saxon virtues of hard work and thrift seen as leading to economic success are meaningless in peasant society. Horatio Alger not only is not praiseworthy, but he emerges as a positive fool, a clod who not knowing the score labors blindly against hopeless conditions."

One evidence of the low aspirational levels in one Latin American village studied by a sociologist is that there was no word commonly used for "future." A sense of fatalism, the image of limited good, and the reality of blocked opportunities have conditioned the peasant to live without aspirations for advancement. Niehoff [1964] suggested that blocked opportunities are one reason for low aspirational levels in certain Southeast Asian countries. "The Lao, Thai, Burmese and Cambodian peasant has been exploited and used by authoritarian rulers for so long, in conditions where true economic expansion was next to impossible, that he has developed an attitude of resignation and acceptance."

Rogers (see above) found that peasants in four Colombian villages had much lower educational and occupational aspirations for their children than did commercial farmers (living in the same villages). In fact, the average commercial farmer desired about twice as many years of education for his children as did the average subsistence farmer. These sharp differences are some evidence of the lower aspirations of peasant farmers.

---

12. Both Foster [1967, pp. 145–150] in Mexico and Carstairs [1958, p. 90] in India report that respondents utilized treasure tales, which were unfounded in fact, to explain the success of certain peasants in their village. I encountered the same phenomena in Colombian peasant villages.

Achievement Motivation

A peasant's life situation, with its limited resources, blocked opportunities, authoritarian child rearing, and long history of exploitation by others, tends to produce individuals with low levels of achievement motivation.[13] Low levels of aspiration, a lack of achievement motivation, and a sense of fatalism may be highly functional for peasants whose opportunities have historically been severely limited. Rosen [1964] stated this viewpoint clearly, although he was not writing specifically about peasants, when he said, "Where poverty is widespread and opportunity for advancement very limited, where only a few enjoy power and independence while most are powerless and dependent, the belief that the individual has little control over his environment is perhaps inevitable—and probably psychologically functional."

It is a widespread notion in many developing countries that the rare individual with higher levels of achievement motivation who is produced in a peasant village is likely to migrate cityward where there may be greater opportunities to express his achievement values. One result of this selective farm–city migration is a draining off of those individuals with higher levels of achievement motivation. Left are peasant pools of low aspiration.

Furthermore, Rogers (see above) found that the subsistence farmers living in each of four Colombian villages had lower levels of achievement motivation than did commercial farmers (who lived in the same villages). Although the differences in levels of achievement motivation were not great, their consistency in all four of the villages is rather convincing.

Aspirations for Level of Living

Although the goal of most local, national, and international programs of directed social change is to raise levels of living, there are very few research studies which seek to determine the correlates of levels of living among

peasants in a developing country or, more importantly for present purposes, the variables related to aspirational levels for a higher *standard* of living.[14] The strength of these aspirations depends upon a comparison of an individual's standard of living with his actual level of living. Economists often assume that an individual's standard of living always exceeds his level of living and that this disequilibrium provides a motivation for change.[15] Perhaps if this gap between "wants" and "gets" is too wide, levels of frustration rise to the point where revolution or social disorganization occurs [Rogers with Svenning, 1968].

This dissatisfaction probably arises, at least in part, from invidious comparisons with others who have higher levels of living. Thus, we would expect peasant contact with urban centers through trips and mass-media exposure to lead to higher aspirations.

Stickley *et al.* [1967], using data from families in three Colombian peasant villages, found that level of living scores (composed of possession of such items as a flashlight, sewing machine, and an enclosed latrine) were positively correlated with farm size, literacy, mass-media exposure, and number of trips per year to Bogotá. However, satisfaction with level of living was also positively related to these variables, contrary to our previously stated expectation. Those peasants who were most satisfied with their level of living had most communication with the world outside of their village. Evidently this cosmopolite communication led directly to higher levels of living (or vice versa) and indirectly to greater satisfaction with levels of living.

Undoubtedly there is need for further investigation of the determinants of various aspirational levels among subsistence farmers.

Inconspicuous Consumption

Not only are peasant aspirations low in relation to nonpeasants, but when a subsistence

---

13. *Achievement motivation* is a social value which emphasizes a desire for excellence in order to attain a sense of personal accomplishment. This definition comes directly from Rogers and Neill [1966]. The meaning, however, is based upon McClelland [1961, 1963]. So defined, achievement motivation (in spite of its "surname") is a generalized type of value orientation.

14. The *level of living* of an individual is the actual degree to which a person's basic needs of nutrition, clothing, housing, health, and sanitation are met over a period of time. A *standard of living* is the desired degree to which a person's basic needs are met (hence, it is a specific type of aspiration), while the level of living is the actualities that exist.

15. This standard differs from Wharton's [1963] "minimum subsistence standard of living" both in location and direction, though it also has significance for economic behavior.

farmer achieves a higher level of living than his peers, he consumes his material gains in a non-Veblenian style. Wiser and Wiser [1963, p. 157] emphasize this point with the title of their study, *Behind Mud Walls*. In the words of their respondents, "Our walls which conceal all that we treasure, are a necessary part of our defense . . . our fathers built them . . . of earth so that they might be inconspicuous . . . Old walls tell no tales." Similar evidence of a "mud-walls complex" was reported by Lewis [1960, p. 36] and Foster [1964] in Mexico. The latter suggested that the reason for the mud walls is that "People who threaten the community by acquiring or appearing to acquire more than their traditional share are discouraged from persisting in this action by gossip, slander, backbiting, fear of witchcraft, and physical violence or the threat of bodily harm."

But the net result of the mud-walls complex (or the "principle of equivalence" as Foster [1965] prefers to term it) is that it probably tends to limit the development of stronger aspirations for material possessions among fellow peasants.[16]

A recent U.S. State Department policy is for the development of a "national market" in developing nations. The logic is that, as household consumer goods are made available for purchase by villagers in these countries, aspirations for more consumer goods will be developed and motivation for higher farm production will be created among peasants.[17] The national-market scheme, one might think, will be limited by the tendency for inconspicuous consumption among subsistence farmers.

Furthermore, Wagley [1964b, p. 214] pessimistically commented on the national market strategy of change. "Material improvements such as radios, electric fixtures, mechanical farm tools, cheaper clothing, and imported foods, are generally not available to the Amazon rural worker, or are beyond the scope of his earning power; therefore such material improvements provide little incentive."

A perceptive journalist, Nair [1962, p. 192]

questioned the aspirational assumption of the national community development program in India.

Planning in India is framed on the assumption—which in view of the extreme poverty of the people would seem logical—that the desire for higher levels of living is inherent and more or less universal among the masses being planned for. . . . From what I have seen and experienced, however, it would seem that a great majority of the rural communities do not share this concept of an ever-rising standard of living. . . . Whatever the level, it tends to be static, with a ceiling rather than a floor. . . . Generally, the lower the level, the more static the aspirations tend to be.

5. A LACK OF DEFERRED GRATIFICATION

Deferred gratification is the postponement of immediate satisfaction in anticipation of future rewards.[18] In many life decisions an individual may choose between immediate or short-range rewards on the one hand or more long-range goals and their resulting satisfaction on the other hand. Deferred gratificaition is often referred to as a "pattern" because it involves a consistent set of connected behaviors. The pattern is evidently largely acquired through personality socialization in early life.

The evidence indicates that peasants are typified by impulse gratification rather than the deferred gratification pattern; they opt for spending vs. saving money, early sexual initiation vs. virginity until marriage, and for other immediate alternatives. The proportionately high expenditures of peasant incomes that go for alcoholic consumption are sometimes cited as evidence of impulse gratification. Fals Borda [1955, pp. 145-146] reported that 20 per cent of his respondents' expenditures went for drinks and tobacco (rising to 40 per cent during fiestas), in comparison to 40 per cent for food, 20 per cent for clothing, and 10 per cent on farm inputs. Tax [1963, p. 177] noted that "The alcoholic-intoxicants budget is far greater than the housing budget, and the amount of money spent on liquor is about a fourth of that spent on clothing; it is more than that for any item of food excepting corn and meat; and it is

16. A somewhat similar view is taken by Mellor in Chapter 7. For a theoretical variant of this point developed by an economist, see Nakajima's, Chapter 6.

17. A statement on the creation of national markets may be found in Chapter II, "How to Make a National Market," in Rostow [1964, pp. 132-144].

18. This definition is based primarily upon Schneider and Lysgaard [1953].

almost as much as is spent on all tools and household utensils and supplies."

Undoubtedly specific levels of alcoholic consumption are strongly influenced by cultural factors, and high levels of consumption are not universal among all peasants (for example, Hindu farmers are teetotalers); nevertheless, this behavior, where found, at least signifies a lack of capital saving and perhaps suggests a lack of deferred gratification.

Any sifting of the available evidence, [Firth and Yamey, 1964] conveys the general impression that peasants are not noted for their tendency to save. As Hendry [1964, p. 182] commented in regard to a Vietnamese village which he investigated, "Thrift is not particularly valued as a virtue among these people, and few of them make conscious efforts to save for specific goals."

Perhaps the deferred-gratification pattern is a leisure that can only be afforded by those with adequate resources to permit postponement of a share of them, 42 per cent of a national sample of Turkish peasant families reported that in the past year they had gone hungry for a period of several days [MIT, 1964]. Banfield [1958, p. 98] suggested somewhat similarly that Italian peasants will not use their ballot for their long-run interest if their vote thus affects their short-run, material advantage.

For whatever the precise reason, deferred gratification seems uncharacteristic of peasants. Thus, in terms of the Aesop fable, subsistence farmers behave more like the grasshopper than the ant. And this lack of deferred gratification tends to maintain their position of hungry grasshoppers rather than well-provisioned ants. For upward social mobility certainly depends in part on the ability to postpone immediate gratification for the sake of long-range ends.

6. LIMITED TIME PERSPECTIVE

Time orientations are subject to wide culture-to-culture variations, as is well known. Eight o'clock "Colombiano time," for example, is equivalent to nine thirty "Norteamericano time" when speaking of the hour to arrive at a Bogotá party.

But within most societies peasants lack the degree of time consciousness possessed by urbanites or commercial farmers. As Carstairs [1958] pointed out, punctuality and precision are largely foreign to village life.

Tannous [1956] felt that the lack of time perspective was one of the major values of Middle Easterners, especially peasants.

In the Middle East, a highly developed time-consciousness is certainly lacking. This is especially true among the rural people who constitute the large majority. They are bewildered and overwhelmed by our pace. To them life is not to be ticked off by seconds, minutes and hours. They go by the sun and the moon, by the seasons, and by long seemingly endless years.

Pierce [1964, p. 12] described a typical instance of behavior in relation to time in a Turkish village that he studied. An old man in the village was requested to deliver some logs to a new house-construction site. He was always "on time," but being on time meant something quite different to him than what it means to urban Turks. When the old man said he would deliver the logs in the morning, he might appear sometime shortly after sunrise or just before noon. He measured time in terms of the four segments of the day between the five prayers of a good Moslem.

Peasants generally tend to think in terms of cruder time periods, which lack the precision felt to be important by their clock-watching urban cousins. Subsistence farmers tend to place much less emphasis upon the time dimension. In their nature-oriented, fatalistic, and localistic style of life, concern with nine o'clock appointments, May 1 planting dates, and five-year plans is neither necessary nor particularly functional. Not only are his perceptions of time less precise and less important to the peasant, but he is also less future oriented. This tendency to think more in terms of past and present tense than in future, is related to such other elements in the subculture of peasantry as fatalism and lack of deferred gratification.

7. FAMILISM

Familism is the subordination of individual goals to those of the family. The opposite of familism is individualism.

The considerable importance of the family as a reference group to peasants was emphasized by Lewis [1960, p. 54] in his observations of Tepoztlan.

Families in Tepoztlan are strong and cohesive, held together by traditional bonds of loyalty, common economic strivings, mutual dependence, the prospect of inheritance, and, finally, the absence of any other social group to which the individual can turn. Cooperation within the immediate family is essential, for without a family the individual stands unprotected and isolated, a prey to every form of aggression, exploitation, and humiliation known in Tepoztlan.

Individualism, Lewis [1960, p. 88] claimed, was secondary to conformity and submission to the needs of the family. Support for this view of the subordination of the individual to his family was provided by Wiser and Wiser [1963, p. 122], who reported the words of a typical Indian peasant: "Each of us is not thinking of his own self. No villager thinks, of himself apart from his family. He rises or falls with it. . . . Our families are our insurance."

Peasant life is primarily familistic and only secondarily individualistic. This means that the appeals of programs of change to individual achievement are likely to be conditioned strongly by family considerations. Why should a subsistence farmer operate extra land when any gain from his effort is likely to go to his relatives? Success brings the relatives, as also happens with Hollywood stars. Perhaps the nature of familistic orientations in peasant societies helps in part to explain their relatively low levels of aspirations.

Familism is likely to explain in part the relatively lower innovativeness of peasants in comparison to commercial farmers. When decisions to adopt or reject new agricultural ideas are made jointly by the entire family, often dominated by older, authoritarian patriarchs, little innovativeness is likely to result.[19] Perhaps it is significant that as a society modernizes in the direction of urbanization and industrialization, familism generally breaks down. Familism, one of the elements in the subculture of peasantry, thus acts as both a brake to change, and a usual victim of it.

19. Some support for this notion of a negative relationship between familism and innovativeness is supplied by studies in the United States [Fliegel, 1956], but is not very well supported by a study of 80 Indian peasants, where a negative, but very low correlation was found [Bose, 1962].

8. DEPENDENCY UPON GOVERNMENT AUTHORITY

The peasant's attitude toward national and local government appears typically to be a peculiar combination of *hostility* toward and *dependence* upon it.

Hostility Toward Government

Numerous investigators have commented upon the peasant's distrust of his government. For example, it has been noted that "The relations between the common village people and government officials are characterized by considerable distance, reserve, and distrust" [Dube, 1958, p. 82]. Similarly, "The villager has been victimized by persons more knowledgeable than he since the beginning of time" [Foster, 1962, p. 48].

For Italian peasants, Levi [1947, p. 76] says, "The State is more distant than heaven and far more of a scourge, because it is always against them. . . . Their only defense . . . is resignation, the same gloomy resignation, alleviated by no hope of paradise, that bows their shoulders under the scourges of nature."

In some cases it appears that peasant villagers work out devious means to follow governmental edicts at the same time that they circumvent the law. Pierce [1964, p. 84] described a Turkish village in which the local leader (or *muhtar*), was always the oldest male in the village. In recent years the official method of selection was changed. "Under the Republic it is required by law that the *muhtar* be an elective office. From 1923 until the mid-fifties this had little effect, as the villagers simply voted the oldest man back into office at each election."

In modern peasant settings, where the pure subsistence independence of the peasants is gradually giving way to increasing control by the merchants of town and city and by government officials, perhaps it is not surprising that villagers view their government with attitudes of hostility. A long history of exploitation at the hands of outsiders has conditioned the villager to this view. But at the same time, the peasant looks to government for solution to problems beyond his ken.

Dependence Upon Government

Because the subsistence farmer's perception of the possibility of self-help is low, dependence upon government is high [Rao, 1963, p. 60]. A national sample of Turkish peasants [MIT, 1964, p. 9] widely recognized the importance of such village problems as inadequate roads and the lack of water for irrigation. But "Villagers tend to regard most village improvements as the job of the government rather than their own."

This dependence upon governmental authority may in some cases even lead to overreliance of peasants upon suggestions from this source. Deutschmann and Fals Borda [1962a] found that the predominant pattern for peasants in a Colombian village was to adopt farm innovations without trying them out first on a small-scale basis. In comparison, U.S. farmers almost always pass through a trial stage enroute to full use [Rogers, 1962]. The difference in behavior was explained by the Colombian researchers as due to the greater receptivity of peasants to an authoritarian source of information, such as government extension workers. Perhaps it is worth noting that in Saucío, the Colombian village investigated, there was a high degree of disadoption of certain innovations, such as a new potato variety, soon after compliance adoption had occurred. In some cases, peasants had adopted "by the numbers," without really knowing how to correctly use the new practice. The eventual result was failure.

9. LOCALITENESS

The rural and the urban sectors of developing countries still coexist as separate worlds, almost completely unknown to each other. *Localiteness* is the degree to which individuals are oriented within, rather than externally, to their social system. Cosmopoliteness, the opposite of localiteness, is generally much less characteristic of peasants than of urbanites or commercial farmers. There are two main expressions of localiteness in the case of peasant villagers, geographical mobility and mass media exposure.

Geographical Mobility

The composite picture that one gains of the peasant is of an individual severely circum-scribed by his physical surroundings. "Almost everyone born in the valley lived and died there. In [the village] he would marry someone who had also been born and reared there. Hence, such things as international politics or even national politics did not concern him much" [Pierce, 1964, p. vii].

The physical isolation of the peasant was described in the case of one Colombian village [Reichel-Dolmatoff and Reichel-Dolmatoff, 1961, p. 26].

Most people move only between their houses and their fields. Year after year they use only a certain trail and when asked about trails in another direction they are often ignorant or uncertain of them. They may know a few neighboring trails, those used by villagers who have their fields in the same general direction, but a man who owns a field on the slopes west of the village does not necessarily know how the slopes to the east of it can be reached. And there is little interest in knowing.

The exact degree of localiteness in geographical mobility obviously varies in each specific village according to the availability of roads and means of transportation, nearness of cities, and other factors. Thus, data from a national sample of Turkish peasants [MIT, 1964] are particularly valuable because they give us the total picture for at least one developing nation. "The median Turkish villager lives in a village which is about nine kilometers from the nearest road over which regular highway transport passes." Furthermore, almost half of the peasants lived more than three hours' travel time (by usual means) from the nearest small town, and almost half lived in a village isolated by the weather for four months out of the year. About 19 per cent never or almost never left their village yearly, and another 21 per cent left their village only once or twice a year. Only 55 per cent had *ever* been to the nearest city. In fact, 77 per cent had no family members living outside their village, and hence were unlikely to receive letters or visits from individuals living outside the village.

Thus, one gains a picture of the Turkish peasant[20] as having little physical contact with

---

20. Rogers reanalyzed data from four Colombian villages (see footnote 5) to show that subsistence farmers had much less travel to cities than did commercial farmers. In the most traditional village, peasants averaged 0.3 trips to urban centers in the past year, while commercial farmers averaged 7.8 trips.

Table 5.1. Exposure of Peasants to Four Types of Mass Media

Types of Mass Media Exposure	Venezuela[b] Peasants (N=8,000)	Turkish[b] Peasants (N=4,957)	Farmers in Three Relatively Modern Colombian[c] Villages (N=160)	Farmers in Two Relatively Traditional Colombian[c] Villages (N=95)
1. Percentage of respondents reading a newspaper at least once				
a. Per week[a]			60%	20%
b. Per month	35%	36%		
2. Percentage of respondents having seen a film in the past year	38%	26%	68%	11%
3. Percentage of respondents listening to radio at least once a week	85%	43%	60%	44%
4. Percentage of respondents having watched TV at least once in the past year	17%	None Available	13%.	None Available

[a] These percentages also include someone else reading the newspaper to the respondent.
[b] Frey [1964].
[c] Rogers [1966].

nonpeasant life in his country, although the fact that *some* villagers are cosmopolites suggests (perhaps as a result of military or similar experiences) certain implications to which we shall return later.

MASS MEDIA EXPOSURE

As Schramm [1963, p. 38] pointed out, "In the oral, traditional society the provisions for wide-horizon communication are inefficient: the traveler and ballad singer come too seldom and know too little. A modernizing of society requires mass media." A basic proposition is that exposure to mass media on the part of peasants leads them down the road of modernization. One reason is because "Much of the content in all of the media, including advertising, is informational, educational, or propagandistic in nature, designed to inform or persuade people about various kinds of modernization" [McNelly, 1964].

Through exposure to the mass media peasants could overcome the barriers of physical isolation. The data in Table 5.1 from peasant respondents in Venezuela, Turkey,[21]

21. In addition to these data in Table 5.1, Frey found that 56 per cent of his respondents had *never* seen a film and 52 per cent had *never* read a newspaper or heard one read aloud [Frey, 1964].

and Colombia show that many peasants have some minimum level of mass media exposure, but it appears to be much less than in urban areas of developing nations[22] or in media-saturated societies such as the United States or Western Europe. In general it appears that more peasants attend to radio than to the other mass media studied. This might be due partly to cost considerations, and partly due to illiteracy, which acts as a block to peasant exposure to the print media (such as newspapers).

Several investigations[23] sought to determine the role of literacy and of mass-media exposure in causing modernization among peasants. Literacy is certainly a key variable in any long-range attempt to introduce new ideas in developing countries, because until peasants become literate, they can have little print mass-media exposure except, perhaps through literate family members or friends,

22. Studies of urbanites in Latin America have found higher mass media exposure than that shown in Table 5.1 [Carter and Sepulveda, 1964; Deutschmann et al., 1961; McNelly and Deutschmann, 1963; McNelly and Fonseca, 1964]. In four of the five Colombian communities shown in Table 5.1, Rogers found a higher media exposure for commercial farmers than for peasants.

23. One of these analyses was completed in six Middle Eastern countries and is excellently reported by Lerner [1958]. Another investigation was in a Colombian community and is reported in Deutschmann and Fals Borda [1962a, 1962b] and Deutschmann [1963]. Yet a third investigation, conducted in five Colombian villages, is reported by Rogers and Herzog [1966].

Even though radio, films, and TV are channels that have the potential of "getting through" to illiterates, there is evidence from a study in one Colombian peasant community [Deutschmann, 1963] that literates are much more likely than illiterates to be in the radio-listening audience. In that study, about twice as many literate farmers listened to radio as did illiterates (52 per cent as compared to 28 per cent). Perhaps equally significant, and more surprising, was the fact that many of the illiterates purchased newspapers (48 per cent) and had books in their households (62 per cent). Deutschmann explained this rather surprising result by suggesting that perhaps literate family members or friends served as communication links to the printed mass media for illiterate peasants.

Rogers [1966], in an analysis of data from five Colombian villages, found that literacy was most highly related to newspaper readership, somewhat less so to radio listening and magazine readership, and least to film and TV watching. These findings are consistent with our expectations that literacy is more highly related to printed media exposure than to nonprinted media exposure. In fact, it might be considered surprising that literacy is not more highly related to mass media exposure. Nevertheless, Colombian illiterates had much lower mass media exposure of all kinds than did literates. So while mass-media exposure *could* overcome the localiteness of peasants that is due to physical isolation, media exposure is generally fairly low among subsistence farmers, and one reason for this relatively low exposure, as we might expect, is the illiteracy barrier.

In general, however, the Colombian peasants with high mass-media exposure were characterized by higher modernization, whether measured by agricultural innovativeness, educational and occupational aspirations for children, or political knowledge. Furthermore, in each of the five villages studied by Rogers [1966], opinion leaders (those peasants sought by their peers for information and advice) had much higher mass media exposure (to radio, newspapers, and the like) than their followers. This suggests that, at least in these Colombian villages, there may have existed a sort of two-step flow of communication, whereby the leaders received ideas from the mass media and passed these

messages along to their followers via word-of-mouth channels.

On the other hand, Rogers and Meynen [1965] found that *not one* of the respondents in these Colombian villages reported using *any* mass-media communication source at *any* stage (awareness, interest, evaluation, or trial) in the adoption of 2,4-D weed spray.[24] Nevertheless we have just seen that for these same respondents mass-media exposure is highly related to such modernization variables as agricultural innovativeness, political knowledge, and so on. What, then, is the role of mass-media exposure in development and change? It appears that among Colombian peasants mass media create a *generally favorable attitude toward change*, but mass media do not get far in supplying technical facts about new farm ideas.

10. EMPATHY

Lerner [1958, p. 50] defined empathy as the degree to which an individual is able to project himself in the roles of others. He saw empathy as a central *element* in the modernization of peasants, acting as a mediator and lubricant for such other modernization variables as literacy, urbanization, mass-media exposure, political participation, and industrialization. Lerner found peasants in six Middle Eastern countries to have lower empathy than urbanites. His results have largely been confirmed in Turkey [MIT, 1964], Pakistan [Eister, 1962], India [Rao, 1963], and Colombia [Rogers with Svenning, 1968].

The typical measure of empathy is to ask respondents how they would solve a specific problem if they were in such roles as village leader, county manager, and president of the country. There is reason to think that until peasants can empathize with the roles of "moderns," such as those depicted in the mass media, these nonemphatic individuals will themselves have difficulty in taking on more modern roles. An example of low empathy is the Turkish peasant who, when Lerner [1958, p. 3] asked him what he would do if he were President, declared, "My God! How

24. In contrast, mass-media communication channels were found to be of considerable importance, especially at the awareness stage and for earlier adopters, in the adoption of 2,4-D weed spray by Iowa farmers [Rogers and Beal, 1958].

can you ask such a thing? How can I . . . I cannot . . . [be] president of Turkey . . . master of the whole world!"

Little is presently known about how empathy develops among peasants, but it is probably through meaningful interaction with persons in other roles. One reason for relatively low peasant empathy is because personality socialization occurs in a restricted environment, where there are a limited variety of roles to learn. Exposure of non-emphatic individuals to mass media is unlikely to have much impact, and trips to cities probably would not, either. The lack of empathy among peasants thus acts as a sort of "mental isolator," which immunizes the subsistence farmer from cosmopolite influences.

FUNCTIONAL INTERRELATIONSHIP
OF THE ELEMENTS

The previous discussion of the ten main elements in the subculture of peasantry makes plain their functional interdependence. In fact, to separate the subculture, in reality a harmonious whole of mutually reinforcing parts, into ten elements is to perform an analytical injustice which can only be allowed in a conceptual sense.

Actually, we have little empirical evidence of the interrelationship of these subcultural elements, although high intercorrelations must surely be the case. Bose [1962] found six peasant values in India interrelated about as we would expect, although he utilized somewhat different terms for his values (such as innovativeness, rationality, tradition, business, and religion) than we have used here. Strangely, familism was not highly interrelated with the other peasant values.

The notion of the high interrelationship of the subcultural elements of peasantry suggests the difficulty of finding a "handle" with which to prime the pump of planned change. To alter one peasant value is to alter the other nine.

Lewis [1964, p. xxxii] perhaps provides an apt summary of the subculture of peasantry in his description of his chief informant, a Mexican peasant named Pedro Martinez, who "shares many classic peasant values—a love of the land, a reverence for nature, a strong belief in the intrinsic good of agricultural labor, and a restraint on individual

self-seeking in favor of family and community. Like most peasants, he is also authoritarian, fatalistic, suspicious, concrete-minded and ambivalent in his attitudes toward city people." In different terms and with different emphasis, Pedro Martinez emerges as a composite of our subculture of peasantry.

IMPLICATIONS OF THE SUBCULTURE
OF PEASANTRY

FOR PROGRAMS OF PLANNED CHANGE

Many of the complex interrelationships that seem to exist among these elements in the subculture of peasantry remind one of a series of locked boxes, each containing the keys to the other boxes [Hägerstrand, 1965, p. 244]. But the lid to some of these boxes may be a bit ajar, and it is the task of the present section of this paper to suggest where to pry first.

A Communication Approach

Our point of view in this prying process will be a communication approach. We generally agree with Pye [1963, p. 3], except in his choice of verb tense, that "It was the pressure of communications which brought about the downfall of traditional societies." Obviously, until there is communication of ideas from sources external to the peasant village, directed contact change will not occur in peasant values, attitudes, and motivations. And while levels of mass-media exposure and physical travel to urban centers are low among peasants, there are *some* cosmopolite peasants, at least enough to serve as a yeast for further social change.

So while the peasant village is relatively isolated, it does have some relationships with the external world. The marginal men who stand with one foot in the village and the other in a wider sphere are (and will be) a crucial linkage for efforts to introduce social change. Whether these cosmopolites are referred to as "cultural brokers" [Wolf, 1956], "gatekeepers" [Stycos, 1952], or by some other term, they have not been adequately studied. As Wagley [1964a, p. 45] stated,

As yet little is known about this important group, or better, these individuals, for it would seem that they generally operate as individuals. To date, most sociologists and anthropologists who have studied

Latin American peasant societies have concentrated upon the internal structure of the local community, rather than the relationship of the local community to the larger society.

The same statement might be made for other portions of the Third World.

While some breakdown in localiteness can be brought about by improved roads and transportation service, the major lever to pry open the locked box of localiteness is through mass media. There are too many villagers and too many villages in the developing world, and the rate of road-building is relatively too slow; generally the longer lever of mass media is an easier tool.

Yet we know that the mass media, while they *can* be very effective in creating awareness of new ideas, are relatively weaker than interpersonal communication in changing attitudes and stimulating action.[25] Most often, a radio or TV message leads only to passive listening, rather than learning, behavior change, action. As Schramm [1964, p. 123] pointed out, there are certain tasks the mass media can do, and others they cannot do, to introduce planned change. One must conclude that what is needed to introduce planned change among peasants in developing societies is a program of *mass media coupled with interpersonal communication.*

A suitable model is something like the National Farm Radio Forum begun in Canada in 1939, and since widely copied by Japan in 1952; India in 1957; Pakistan and Mali in 1961; Nigeria in 1962; Ghana, Madagascar, and Jordan in 1964; and Brazil and Malawi in 1966. In all these programs, groups of villagers meet at a regular hour (often on a weekly basis) to listen to a radio program (although it could equally well be a television program, except perhaps for cost factors), which is then followed by group, discussion of the ideas presented. For example, the Radio Sutatenza program in Colombia involves local discussion groups (set up by village priests), who listen on relatively low-cost transistor radios to adult literacy and other educational programs and study with the help of prepared printed study materials. About 50,000 radio receivers had been

distributed by 1959 [Torres and Corredor, 1961]. A program in El Salvador and Honduras copied after Radio Sutatenza was investigated by Rhoads and Piper [1963].

The effectiveness of these approaches using mass media *cum* interpersonal communications appears to rest on the following factors:

1. Program content must be relevant to peasant problems (usually new farm, sanitation, or health ideas) and beamed at an appropriate audience level. Visual aids, such as charts and chalkboards, can add to learning effectiveness.

2. The postprogram discussion must emphasize local application of the ideas presented.

3. Feedback of audience reactions, interests, and questions of clarification must be made to the mass media communicator.

4. For other villagers, as well as for the discussion group members, to be affected by the program, village opinion leaders must be included in the discussion group's membership.

One of the relatively few investigations completed to date on the effects of radio forums is a UNESCO-sponsored study in India. Mathur and Neurath [1959] and Neurath [1962] found that in terms of knowledge gained from the programs: listeners who were not members of forums learned little more than nonlisteners to the programs, but forum members showed considerable gains over either nonlisteners or nonforum listeners; and the illiterates among the forum members gained as much knowledge as literate members.

There is much that we do not yet know about the effects of radio or television peasant forums,[26] but this communication approach to change offers potential that is worth exploration.

Existing Social Organization

Another implication for programs of change from the present analysis is that *a system of*

25. This point has been consistently demonstrated by research on communication channels used at stages in the adoption process for farm innovations, both that completed in the United States and in developing countries. For a summary of these studies, see Rogers [1967].

26. Investigations of these effects are currently underway under UNESCO sponsorship in 14 villages in Costa Rica and 8 in India over a two-year period utilizing a before-after treatment with control design. A comparison is being made among radio farm forums, literacy classes and reading forums, and animation in creating knowledge, favorable attitude, and adoption of agricultural and sanitation practices. For a description of the method of animation, see Hapgood [1964].

social organization exists among peasants, and this social structure may be utilized by change agents to introduce innovations.

Let us consider the religious institution, often a particularly important type of social organization in peasant life. There are examples of priests in Latin American peasant villages who effectively block programs of change when the social machinery of the priesthood is not consulted and utilized. A striking illustration comes from an Andean village in Colombia which the author investigated. An influential elementary-school teacher had led villagers to build a new road, form a purchasing and marketing cooperative, set up a community development council, establish experimental plots to test new crop varieties, and otherwise move progressively toward modernism—all in the space of about three years. But the local priest was not properly brought into planning of these activities. In order to remove his perceived rival for village leadership, the priest arranged to have the school teacher fired from his position, using the excuse that the teacher had "desegregated" the elementary school into mixed boy-girl classes. Within a year, without the help of the innovative school teacher, the village lapsed back into its former traditional ways.

Yet in Latin American villages, the priest *can* act as a powerful agent of change, and in some villages this has occurred [Jimenez, 1965]. Most social researchers in Latin American countries soon learn the necessity of securing prior approval from the black-frocked legitimizer before beginning personal interviewing in a peasant village.

A generally similar point is made by Niehoff [1964; Arensberg and Niehoff, 1964, pp. 4–5] in his analysis of the role of Buddhist monks in community-development projects in Laos, where he investigated why 15 of 17 village wells had failed. The construction of these wells had been sponsored by the U.S. AID mission in Laos, the wells were needed by the villagers, and they were used day and night. Yet within a short time after their construction, most of the wells were broken and in disuse because maintenance and repair was almost completely ignored. But there were two exceptions—the wells which had been put on *wat* (church) grounds, which were not only maintained but improved upon. "The

grounds around them were kept neat and dry. The *wat* grounds were fenced off so animals could not wander about. Around one of them a concrete base about 20 feet in diameter had been built so excess water would not accumulate." Niehoff concluded, "The attitude of present [U.S.] technicians that monks are a quaint vestige of the past and should only be ignored is a product of the Westerners' cultural biases. New village projects should be undertaken either with the active participation of the monks or at least their approval."

Fals Borda [1955, p. 230] also provides testament of the importance of working through existing social structure in introducing change in the Colombian community that he studied. "Enlightened teaching by the Church can improve greatly the social and mental condition of the people of Saucío. The Church has all the power and the means at hand to bring about such a healthy change. The result of such teaching might easily be a more alert peasant class, a peasant class eager to strive for a better life, an asset to the nation."

FOR RESEARCH ON PEASANTRY

Improved Methodologies

The steps in the research process as taught in usual social-science methodology course in developed countries may have to be modified considerably when these methods are utilized to study peasants [Havens et al., 1965]. In fact, special methodologies must be worked out for studying sociocultural systems that are strange to the researcher.

Importance should also be attached to training social-research workers in developing countries who are especially equipped to study subsistence farmers. Lewis [1959] claims that when one leaves the poverty class, he can no longer analyze it accurately, whether he is a journalist, teacher, or a social scientist. Probably most social scientists do not come from the peasant class, but some researchers have greater ability at "traditional empathy" (a capacity to put themselves in the roles of peasants), and these individuals, we would think, will be more successful in studying the peasant subculture.

While there is much we presently know

about the attitudes, values, and motivations of peasants, there is a strong need for future research. When one considers the tremendous village-to-village differences in peasant life that exist within any country, one realizes the inadequacy of the data upon which this paper is mainly based. Certainly we need improved sampling designs in studying peasants. One early step is comparative analyses of several peasant communities within the same nation. In our study of five Colombian villages [Rogers and van Es, 1964], we concluded that while a somewhat similar pattern of findings emerged from each of the communities, much was gained by having five replications under varying community conditions. One can place greater confidence in one's results if they are consistent across communities.

What is eventually needed, however, are national samples of peasants, conducted in a method somewhat similar to Frey's [1963; MIT, 1964] national cross-section of Turkish peasants. Then we can speak with authority about *the* Turkish peasant. Until then, academic controversy is likely to continue (for instance, about the degree of economic rationality of peasants) because everyone is looking at data from *their* peasant village.

Unanswered Questions

As we progress from descriptions of single peasant communities to a more difficult and complex kind of investigation involving correlational analyses of mathematically expressed variables, we should seek to answer the following questions about communication and change among peasants.

1. Who are the opinion leaders in peasant villages; how do they differ from their followers in their communication behavior, values and attitudes, and social characteristics?
2. Who are the innovators (the first to adopt new ideas) among peasants; how do they differ from later adopters in their personal and social characteristics and communication behavior? Why?
3. Who are the cosmopolites in peasant villages; what is their physical mobility, mass-media exposure, and opinion leadership?
4. What factors explain the relative success or failure of programs of directed social

change (such as public health, agricultural extension, and the like) in their impact upon subsistence communities?
5. What is the interrelationship among the elements in the subculture of peasantry; are there certain elements which may be altered more easily than others?

Field Experiments

Much can be learned to answer these questions from correlational analyses of data gathered at one point in time. But correlational analyses can tell us little of a cause-effect nature. We can never learn, for example, whether innovativeness causes cosmopoliteness or vice versa, or whether the two variables vary together in an interdependence relationship, where a small change in one causes a small change in the other, which in turn causes a small change again in the other variable, etc. Only field investigations over time, with before-after measures in experimental and control groups, can tell us which direction the causal arrows run.

Examples of some field experiments under way on communication and change among peasants are the following.

1. A UNESCO-sponsored study in India and Costa Rica on the relative effectiveness of radio farm forums, literacy classes and reading forums, and animation in causing knowledge, favorable attitude, and adoption of agricultural and sanitation innovations (see above).
2. An investigation [Spector et al., 1963] of the effect of radio broadcasts and filmed presentations in convincing Ecuadorian peasants to adopt marmalade, latrines, and vaccination.
3. An AID-sponsored study by Michigan State University of the impact of various communication approaches to introducing innovations in three developing countries (Brazil, Nigeria, and India).

Simulating Communication and Change

A recent advance in data handling and conceptualization among quantitative geographers in Sweden and the United States offers great, but yet largely unrealized, advantages for studying communication and change among peasants. This recently developed approach is known as Monte Carlo diffusion simulation. Simulation consists of the following essential steps.

1. A model of the diffusion of new ideas is constructed from past research, theoretical knowledge of communication processes, and observation of reality. This simulation model consists of certain "rules of diffusion" which seek to approximate lifelike conditions and processes. A set of rules for one model are: (a) the simulation begins with one adopter of an innovation in a social system, (b) information about the innovation spreads to other adopters through pairwise tellings, (c) these tellings occur at a certain rate over time periods, which are called "generations," and (d) the destination of each telling is determined randomly (hence the term Monte Carlo), according to a mean information field, which is a probabilistic expression of decreasing interpersonal communication with increasing physical or social distance.

2. This model is then run in a computer (or else by nonmachine methods) by a random, Monte Carlo selection process which acts to make the simulation process lifelike. At the end of each generation, the number and location of adopters and nonadopters are printed out by the computer or recorded on a map.

3. The final generation output is then compared with reality in terms of how many units have adopted and who and where they are. Where the fit of the simulation to reality is not close, the model may be changed until its rules of the game more closely approach reality.

4. Then, the model is applied to other similar social systems so as to predict diffusion in these systems. For example, one might develop a simulation model (through steps 1, 2, and 3 just described) in one peasant village, and then use this model to predict future diffusion in this same village (as time can be compressed or expanded in a simulation), or to predict adoption patterns in other similar villages, or to find optimum strategies for change agencies to maximize the rate change and/or to minimize the cost

and effect of achieving change. Specifically, one could determine for change agencies how many change agents they should have, how many opinion leaders they need to work through, how many innovators must adopt an innovation before further effort at securing change may not be needed, what kinds of economic or communication incentives are most efficient in causing adoption, and so forth. It appears that one could even predict some of the social consequences, desirable or not, of a program of change. And while our example has been for one or more peasant villages, the same simulation procedure appears to be applicable at regional, national, or international levels as well.

This approach to diffusion simulation was begun by a Swedish geographer, Torsten Hägerstrand [1952]. Although his first reports were available in English in 1952, his methodology did not find "adopters" in the United States until about five years later [Hägerstrand, 1960]. Now an enthusiastic coterie of quantitative geographers are carrying Hägerstrand's approach forward. Simulations are available of the diffusion of hybrid seed corn in an Iowa county [Tiedeman and Van Doren, 1964], of the adoption of deep wells in Colorado [Bowden, 1964], and of various farm innovations, milk control organizations, public swimming baths, and a religious movement in Sweden [Hägerstrand, 1965]. A recent attempt has been made to simulate the effects of various shapes of physical and social barriers to diffusion of innovations [Yuill, 1964].

These simulation studies suffer from a heavy emphasis upon spatial variables in communication and change, to the partial exclusion of other social structural and social psychological variables (such as social status, cosmopoliteness, and mass media exposure), which past research tells us is of great importance in affecting the diffusion of innovations. A Swedish sociologist George Karlsson [1958] proposed a number of simulation models which center on nonspatial variables and processes; unfortunately no data are provided us on the use of these models. One of Karlsson's models, modified to apply to conditions in a Latin American peasant community by Deutschmann [1962], is presently being run at Michigan State University and results will be forthcoming shortly [Stanfield et al., 1965]. This work is designed to overcome the previous neglect of structural and social psychological variables in spatial diffusion simulation by quantitative geographers, as well as the complete absence of diffusion simulations among peasants in developing nations (where one might expect the spatial dimension of diffusion to be particularly important).

An important next step in research on peasantry is to attempt Monte Carlo simulation of communication and change processes. Peasant villages provide obvious advantages as locales for Monte Carlo diffusion simulations: the basic, primitive nature of communication behavior as compared to the mass-media-saturated nature of other locales, the localistic tendency of peasants which emphasizes the sharpness of village boundaries and results in relatively few communication channels by which innovations enter the village from external sources, the relatively small number of individuals involved.

An underlying theme of this paper is the importance of knowing one's audience if one is to communicate change to it in a successful manner. Because illiterate peasants are unlikely to write many good books about their subculture, our understanding of their way of life is often incomplete. This essay was designed to improve the accuracy of our image of the peasant subculture.

Perhaps there is a simile to Cervante's Don Quixote, who desired to change and improve a world of his imagination, a world that had not existed for many years, if ever. Quixote, the change agent, paid little heed to the reality-based advice of Sancho Panza, and Quixote's efforts at conquering dragons and damsels ended in failure.

The present essay is thus offered in the spirit of Sancho Panza, toward better understanding of peasants' values, attitudes, and motivations.

References

ARENSBERG and NIEHOFF, 1964. Conrad M. Arensberg and Arthur H. Niehoff, *Introducing*

Social Change: A Manual for Americans Overseas (Chicago: Aldine, 1964).

BANFIELD, 1958. Edward C. Banfield, *The Moral Basis of a Backward Society*, (Glencoe, Ill.: Free Press, 1958).

BOSE, 1962. Santi Priya Bose, "Peasant Values and Innovation in India," *American Journal of Sociology*, Vol. 67, No. 5 (March 1962), 552–60.

BOWDEN, 1964. Leonard W. Bowden, "Simulation and Diffusion of Irrigation Wells in the Colorado Northern High Plains," Paper presented at the Association of American Geographers, Syracuse, New York, 1964).

CARSTAIRS, 1958. Morris G. Carstairs, *The Twice-Born: A Study of a Community of High-Caste Hindus* (Bloomington, Ind.: Indiana University Press, 1958).

CARTER and SEPULVEDA, 1964. Roy E. Carter, Jr., and Orlando Sepulveda, "Some Patterns of Mass Media Use in Santiago de Chile," *Journalism Quarterly*, Vol. 41, No. 2 (Spring 1964), 216–24.

DEUTSCHMANN, 1962. Paul J. Deutschmann, "A Machine Simulation of Information Diffusion in a Small Community," San José, Costa Rica, Programa Interamericano de Información Popular, 1962.

DEUTSCHMANN, 1963. Paul J. Deutschmann, "The Mass Media in an Underdeveloped Village," *Journalism Quarterly*, Vol. 40, No. 1 (Winter 1963), 27–35.

DEUTSCHMANN, et al., 1961. Paul J. Deutschmann, et al., "Mass Media Use by Sub-Elites in 11 Latin American Countries," *Journalism Quarterly*, Vol. 38, No. 4 (Autumn 1961), 460–72.

DEUTSCHMANN and FALS BORDA, 1962a. Paul J. Deutschmann and Orlando Fals Borda, *Communication and Adoption Patterns in an Andean Village* (San José, Costa Rica: Programa Interamericano de Informacion Popular, 1962).

DEUTSCHMANN and FALS BORDA, 1962b. Paul J. Deutschmann and Orlando Fals Borda, *La Communicacion de las Ideas entre los Campesinos Columbianos* (Bogotá: Facultad de Sociologia, Universidad Nacional de Colombia, Monografias Sociologias 14, 1962).

DUBE, 1958. S. C. Dube, *India's Changing Villages: Human Factors in Community Development* (Ithaca N.Y.: Cornell University Press, 1958).

EISTER, 1962. Allen W. Eister, "Critical Factors in the Modernization Process in Western Pakistan," *Yearbook of the American Philosophical Society*, 1962, 362–65.

FALS BORDA, 1955. Orlando Fals Borda, *Peasant Society in the Colombian Andes: A Sociological Study of Saucio* (Gainesville, Fla.: University of Florida Press, 1955).

FIRTH and YAMEY, 1964. Raymond W. Firth, and B. S. Yamey, eds., "Capital, Saving and Credit in Peasant Societies" (Chicago: Aldine, 1964).

FLIEGEL, 1956. Frederick C. Fliegel, "A Multiple Correlation Analysis of Factors Associated with Adoption of Farm Practices," *Rural Sociology,* Vol. 21, No. 3-4 (September–December 1956), 384–92.

FOSTER, 1960–61. George M. Foster, "Interpersonal Relations in Peasant Societies," *Human Organization,* Vol. 19, No. 4 (Winter 1960–61), 174–78.

FOSTER, 1962. George M. Foster, *Traditional Cultures and the Impact of Technological Change* (New York: Harpers, 1962).

FOSTER, 1964. George M. Foster, "Speech Forms and Perception of Social Distance in a Spanish-Speaking Mexican Village," *Southwestern Journal of Anthropology,* Vol. 20, No. 2 (Summer 1964), 107–22.

FOSTER, 1965. George M. Foster, "Peasant Society and the Image of Limited Good," *American Anthropologist,* Vol. 67, No. 2 (April 1965), 293–315.

FOSTER, 1967. George M. Foster, *Tzintzuntzan: Mexican Peasants in a Changing World* (Boston: Little, Brown, 1967).

FREY, 1963. Frederick W. Frey, "Surveying Peasant Attitudes in Turkey," *Public Opinion Quarterly,* Vol. 27, No. 3 (Fall 1963), 335–55.

FREY, 1964. Frederick W. Frey, "The Mass Media and the Peasant," Paper presented at the Association of Education in Journalism, Austin Texas, 1964.

HÄGERSTRAND, 1952. Torsten Hägerstrand, *The Propagation of Innovation Waves* (Lund, Sweden: Royal University of Lund, Lund Studies in Geography, 1952).

HÄGERSTRAND, 1960. Torsten Hägerstrand, "On Monte Carlo-Simulation of Diffusion," Paper presented at the Office of Naval Research-National Research Council Conference, Chicago, 1960.

HÄGERSTRAND, 1965. Torsten Hägerstrand, "Quantitative Techniques for Analysis of the Spread of Information and Technology," in C. A. Anderson and M. J. Bowman, eds., *Education and Economic Development* (Chicago: Aldine, 1965).

HAPGOOD, 1964. David Hapgood, "Rural Animation in Senegal," *International Development Review,* Vol. 6, No. 3 (September 1964), 15–18.

HARDIN, 1951. Charles M. Hardin, " 'Natural Leaders' and the Administration of Conservation Programs," *Rural Sociology,* Vol. 16, No. 3 (September 1951), 279–81.

HAVENS, et al., 1965. Eugene A. Havens, *et al., Medición en Sociología* (Bogotá: Universidad National de Columbia, Facultad de Sociologia, 1965).

HENDRY, 1964. James B. Hendry, *The Small World of Khanh Hau* (Chicago: Aldine, 1964).

HICKEY, 1964. Gerald Cannon Hickey, *Village in Vietnam* (New Haven, Conn.: Yale University Press, 1964).

HILLERY, 1961. George A. Hillery, Jr., "The Folk Village: A Comparative Analysis," *Rural Sociology,* Vol. 26, No. 4 (December 1961), 337–53.

HIRSCHMAN, 1958. Albert O. Hirschman, *The Strategy of Economic Development* (New Haven, Conn.: Yale University Press, 1958).

JIMENEZ, 1965. Gustavo Jimenez, *The Role of the Rural Parish Priest in Introducing Social Change,* Ph.D. dissertation (Madison, Wis.: University of Wisconsin, 1965).

JIMENEZ SANCHEZ, 1964. Leobardo Sanchez Jiminez, "A Bench Mark Study Before Introducing Improved Agricultural Technology in El Mangal, a Tropical Ejido of Mexico," Paper presented at the First Interamerican Research Symposium on the Role of Communications in Agricultural Development, Mexico, 1964.

KARLSSON, 1958. George Karlsson, *Social Mechanisms: Studies in Sociological Theory* (Glencoe, Ill.: Free Press, 1958).

LEIBENSTEIN, 1957. Harvey Leibenstein, *Economic Backwardness and Economic Growth* (New York: Wiley, 1957).

LERNER, 1958. Daniel Lerner, *The Passing of Traditional Society: Modernizing the Middle East* (Glencoe, Ill.: Free Press, 1958).

LESLIE, 1960. Charles M. Leslie, *Now We Are Civilized: A Study of the World View of the Zapotec Indians of Mitla, Oaxaca* (Detroit, Mich.: Wayne State University Press, 1960).

LEVI, 1947. Carlo Levi, *Christ Stopped at Eboli* (New York: Farrer, Straus, 1947).

LEWIS, 1951. Oscar Lewis, *Life in a Mexican Village: Tepoztlán Re-Studied* (Urbana, Ill.: University of Illinois Press, 1951).

LEWIS, 1959. Oscar Lewis, *Five Families: Mexican Case Studies in the Culture of Poverty* (New York: Basic Books, 1959).

LEWIS, 1960. Oscar Lewis, *Tepoztlán: Village in Mexico* (New York: Holt, 1960).

LEWIS, 1964. Oscar Lewis, *Pedro Martinez: A Mexican Peasant and His Family* (New York: Random House, 1964).

LOBREATO, 1962. Joseph Lobreato, "Interpersonal Relations in Peasant Society: The Peasant's View," *Human Organization,* Vol. 21, No. 1 (Spring 1962), 21–24.

MCCLELLAND, 1961. David C. McClelland, *The Achieving Society* (Princeton, N.J.: Van Nostrand, 1961).

MCCLELLAND, 1963. David C. McClelland, "The

Achievement Motive in Economic Growth," in Bert F. Hoselitz and Wilbert E. Moore, eds., *Industrialization and Society* (Paris: UNESCO, 1963).

McNELLY, 1964. John T. McNelly, "Mass Communication and the Climate for Modernization in Latin America," Paper presented at the Association for Education in Journalism, Austin, Texas, 1964.

McNELLY and DEUTSCHMANN, 1963. John T. McNelly and Paul J. Deutschmann, "Media Use and Socioeconomic Status in a Latin American Capital," *Gazette*, Vol. 9, No. 1 (1963), 1–15.

McNELLY and FONSECA, 1964. John T. McNelly and Eugenio Fonseca, "Media Use and Political Interest at the University of Costa Rica," *Journalism Quarterly*, Vol. 41 (1964), 225–31.

MANDELBAUM, 1963. David G. Mandelbaum, "Forward," in William H. Wiser and Charlotte Viall Wiser, *Behind Mud Walls, 1930–1960* (Berkeley, Calif.: University of California Press, 1963).

MATHUR and NEURATH, 1959. J. C. Mathur and Paul M. Neurath, *An Indian Experiment in Farm Radio Forums* (Paris: UNESCO, 1959).

MYREN, 1964. Delbert T. Myren, "Role of Information in Farm Decisions Under Conditions of High Risk and Uncertainty," Paper presented at First Inter-American Research Symposium on Role of Communications in Agricultural Development, Mexico City, Mexico, October 5–13, 1964.

NAIR, 1962. Kusum Nair, *Blossoms in the Dust: The Human Factor in Indian Development* (New York: Frederick A. Praeger, 1962).

NEURATH, 1962. Paul M. Neurath, "Radio Farm Forum as a Tool of Change in Indian Villages,' *Economic Development and Cultural Change*, Vol. 10, No. 2 (April 1962), 275–83.

NIEHOFF, 1964. Arthur Niehoff, "Theravada Buddhism: A Vehicle for Technical Change," *Human Organization*, Vol. 23, No. 2 (Summer 1964), 108–12.

PIERCE, 1964. Joe E. Pierce, *Life in A Turkish Village* (New York: Holt, Rinehart, 1964).

PYE, 1963. Lucien W. Pye, *Communications and Political Development* (Princeton, N.J.: Princeton University Press, 1963).

RAO, 1963. Lakshmana Y. V. Rao, "Communication and Development: A Study of Two Indian Villages," Ph.D. dissertation, (Minneapolis: University of Minnesota, 1963).

REDFIELD, 1930. Robert Redfield, *Tepoztlán: A Mexican Village* (Chicago: University of Chicago Press, 1930).

REDFIELD, 1955. Robert Redfield, *The Little Community* (Chicago: University of Chicago Press, 1955).

REICHEL-DOLMATOFF and REICHEL-DOLMATOFF, 1961. Geraldo Reichel-Dolmatoff, and Alicia Reichel-Dolmatoff, *The People of Aritama: The Cultural Personality of a Colombian Mestizo Village* (Chicago: University of Chicago Press, 1961).

RHOADS and PIPER, 1963. William G. Rhoads and Anson C. Piper, *Use of Radiophonic Teaching in Fundamental Education* (Williamstown, Mass.: Roper Public Opinion Research Center, Williams College, 1963).

ROGERS, 1962. Everett M. Rogers, *Diffusion of Innovations* (Glencoe, Ill.: Free Press, 1962).

ROGERS, 1966. Everett M. Rogers, "Mass Media Exposure and Modernization Among Colombian Peasants," *Public Opinion Quarterly*, Vol. 29, No. 4 (Winter–1965–66), 614–25.

ROGERS, 1967. Everett M. Rogers, *Elementos de Cambio Social: Difusion de Innovaciones* (Bogotá: Facultad de Sociología, Universidad Nacional de Colombia, 1967).

ROGERS and BEAL, 1958. Everett M. Rogers and George M. Beal, "The Importance of Personal Influence in the Adoption of Technological Changes," *Social Forces*, Vol. 36, No. 4 (May 1958), 329–35.

ROGERS and HERZOG, 1966. Everett M. Rogers and William Herzog, "Functional Literacy Among Colombian Peasants" (East Lansing: Department of Communication, Michigan State University, 1966).

ROGERS and MEYNEN, 1965. Everett M. Rogers and Wicky L. Meynen "Communication Sources for 2,4-D Weed Spray Among Colombian Peasants," *Rural Sociology*, Vol. 30, No. 2 (June 1965), 213–19.

ROGERS and NEILL, 1966. Everett M. Rogers and Ralph E. Neill, *Achievement Motivation Among Colombian Farmers* (East Lansing, Mich.: Department of Communication, Michigan State University, Diffusion of Innovation Research Report 3, 1966).

ROGERS with SVENNING, 1968. Everett M. Rogers with Lynne Svenning, *Modernization Among Peasants: The Impact of Communication* (New York: Holt, Rinehart, 1968).

ROGERS and VAN ES, 1964. Everett M. Rogers and C. Johannes van Es, *Opinion Leadership in Traditional and Modern Colombian Peasant Communities* (East Lansing, Mich.: Department of Communication, Michigan State University, Diffusion of Innovations Research Report 2, 1964).

ROSEN, 1964. Bernard C. Rosen, "The Achievement Syndrome and Economic Growth in Brazil," *Social Forces*, Vol. 42, No. 3 (March 1964), 341–54.

ROSTOW, 1964. Walter Rostow, "How to Make a National Market," in *View from the Seventh Floor* (New York: Harper, 1964), Chapter II.

Rural Development Research Report: Preliminary Report, 1964. (Cambridge: Center for International Studies, Massachusetts Institute of Technology, 1964).

SCHNEIDER and LYSGAARD, 1953. Louis Schneider and Sverre Lysgaard, "The Deferred Gratification Pattern: A Preliminary Study," *American Sociological Review*, Vol. 18, No. 2 (April 1953), 142-49.

SCHRAMM, 1963. Wilbur Schramm, "Communication Development and the Development Process," in Lucien W. Pye, ed., *Communications and Political Development* (Princeton, N.J.: Princeton University Press, 1963).

SCHRAMM, 1964. Wilbur Schramm, *Mass Media and National Development: The Role of Information in the Developing Countries* (Stanford, Calif.: Stanford University Press, 1964).

SCHULTZ, 1964. Theodore W. Schultz, *Transforming Traditional Agriculture* (New Haven, Conn.: Yale University Press, 1964).

SEEMAN, 1959. Melvin Seeman, "On the Meaning of Alienation," *American Sociological Review*, Vol. 24, No. 6 (December 1959), 783-91.

SPECTOR, et al., 1963. Paul Spector, et al., *Communication and Motivation in Community Development: An Experiment* (Washington, D.C.: Institute for International Service, 1963).

STANFIELD, ROGERS and LIN, 1965. David J. Stanfield, Everett M. Rogers, and Nan Lin, "Simulation of the Diffusion of Innovations" (East Lansing, Mich.: Department of Communication, Michigan State University, Working Paper 7, 1965).

STICKLEY, et al., 1967. Thomas S. Stickley, et al., *Levels of Living Among Farmers in Three Columbian Neighborhoods* (Columbus, Ohio: Department of Agricultural Economics and Rural Sociology, Ohio State University, Mimeo Bulletin AE 414, 1967).

STRASSMAN, 1964. Paul Strassman, "The Industrialist," in John J. Johnson, ed., *Continuity and Change in Latin America* (Stanford, Calif.: Stanford University Press, 1964).

STYCOS, 1952. Mayone J. Stycos, "Patterns of Communication in a Rural Greek Village," *Public Opinion Quarterly*, Vol. 16, No. 1 (Spring 1952) 59-70.

TANNOUS, 1956. Afif I. Tannous, "Technical Exchange and Cultural Values: Case of the Middle East," *Rural Sociology*, Vol. 21, No. 1 (March 1956), 76-79.

TAX, 1963. Sol Tax, *Penny Capitalism* (Chicago: University of Chicago Press, 1963).

TIEDEMAN and VAN DOREN, 1964. Clifford E. Tiedeman and Carlton S. Van Doren, *The Diffusion of Hybrid Seed Corn in Iowa: A Spatial Simulation Model* (East Lansing, Mich.: Institute for Community Development and Services, Michigan State University, Technical Bulletin B-44, 1964).

TORRES and CORREDOR, 1961. Camilio Torres and Berta Corredor, *Las Escuelas Radiofonicas de Sutatenze, Colombia* (Bogotá: Oficina Internacional de Investigaciones Sociales de FERES, 1961).

WAGLEY, 1964a. Charles Wagley, "The Peasant," in John J. Johnson, ed., *Continuity and Change in Latin America* (Stanford, Calif.: Stanford University Press, 1964).

WAGLEY, 1964b. Charles Wagley, *Amazon Town* (New York: Knopf, 1964).

WHARTON, 1963. Clifton R. Wharton, Jr., "The Economic Meaning of 'Subsistence'," *Malayan Economic Review*, Vol. 8, No. 2 (October 1963), 46-58.

WISER and WISER, 1963. William H. Wiser and Charlotte Viall Wiser, *Behind Mud Walls, 1930-1960* (Berkeley, Calif.: University of California Press, 1963).

WOLF, 1956. Eric R. Wolf, "Aspects of Group Relations in a Complex Society: Mexico," *American Anthropologist*, Vol. 58, No. 6 (December 1956), 1065-1078.

YUILL, 1964. Robert S. Yuill, *A Simulation Study of Barrier Effects in Spatial Diffusion Problems* (Evanston, Ill.: Department of Geography, Northwestern University, Technical Report 1, 1964).

COMMENT

A Critical View of
a Subculture of Peasantry

GELIA CASTILLO

PROFESSOR ROGERS synthesizes what is presently known about the motivations, values, and attitudes of subsistence farmers by outlining a subculture of peasantry and providing some evidence for the central elements of this subculture. He then concludes with some implications for programs of change and for future research. An underlying theme in his message is the importance of *knowing one's audience* in designing programs of directed social change.

My discussion will attempt to examine the usefulness of the subculture of peasantry for the purposes of directed social change, suggest a few elementary research problems, and indicate the need to know, not only one's audience, but also one's communicator and the character and direction of the message if we are to understand the subsistence farmer's response or lack of response to change.

It should be recognized that Professor Rogers' task of presenting a synthesis of what is presently known was not at all an easy one, and therefore his efforts are of great service to us. I consider his ten elements as an excellent take-off point in the beginning of an inquiry on the subsistence farmer.

THE SUBCULTURE OF PEASANTRY

"A subculture" is said to "contain many elements of the broader culture of which it is a part, but has special aspects not shared by most members of a society." The identification of a peasant subculture, then, presupposes that one knows the broader culture of which it is a part and that one is able to isolate special aspects not shared by most members of a society. Therefore a subculture of peasantry outside the context of the broader culture has little meaning because, in order to know what aspects are not shared, one has to know what aspects are shared. (See also Firth in Chapter 3.)

If there is a subculture of peasantry, is there also a subculture of commercial farmers? If there is, what are the possible central elements in such a commercial subculture? In other words, is the subsistence farmer a different breed of farmer or is he simply a greater or a lesser version of a commercial farmer, depending upon the central element at which one is looking? The answer to this question is crucial, because if he is a different breed of farmer, then obviously he will not respond to the same incentives in the same manner as a commercial farmer does.

This is not to say that the concept of peasant subculture be totally discarded because it has absolutely no value. What I am suggesting is that programs of change need more definitive answers to questions on who is the subsistence farmer. For the academician, who is so many steps removed from the realities of the development world, this construct probably does not need to be more specific. It might be sufficient for his purposes. But for the action-oriented social analyst, who has to come up with an identification of the strategic variables which will help the planner or policy-maker, lumping together peasants into one category tends to obscure significant peasant variations[1] which are so essential in outlining programs of change. Current village studies in the Philippines, where extension programs are under way, lends emphasis to the importance of "localness" in determining one's message and strategy for communication.

The social scientist who is called upon to lend his enlightened insights on the strategy of development is constantly faced with the problem of coming up with data which could be useful to administrators and change agents, all of whom consider themselves as experts on village life. If data have to meet the

1. A similar comment was made on the rural-urban dichotomy by Gross [1948].

test of planners, administrators, and village level workers, they have to be more explicit [Lewis, 1958, p. 9]. As Longmore [1948] points out: "Since all generalizations can be only approximations of reality, the rural sociologist constantly strives to clarify the more general social facts in their relationship to specific rural situations."

THE TEN ELEMENTS

The nature of Rogers' ten central elements in the subculture of peasantry makes it extremely difficult to identify the concrete data which are subsumed under each element. Furthermore and most important, these elements were all presented as negative, inhibitory factors to economic development. Are there *no* positive elements in Rogers' subculture of peasantry? If one were to get carried away by this "series of locked boxes, each containing the keys to the other boxes," the subsistence farmer is indeed "locked in."

Fortunately, I do not share this kind of pessimism. R. P. Dore's [1960] and J. M. Saniels' [1963] analyses of Japan's case show how traditional values of familism and authoritarianism were mobilized in the modernization of Japan. The frequently cited reluctance of the farmer to produce more because he has to share with relatives is an extremely one-sided view of familism. Evidence from the Philippines show that extended family obligations are mutual and reciprocal—seldom one-way traffic.[2] If a farmer shares the harvest with his relatives, chances are these relatives helped him in the farming operations one way or another. Even the adoption of farm and homemaking practices tends to be a family affair. Again, as was the case in Japan, even if the authoritarian patriarch were still very much around, he could also decide *for* rather than *against* new agricultural ideas. In addition, the family could and often does function as the individual's support in his efforts to achieve changes and as an insurance or guarantee against loss in situations of high risk associated with any technological change.

The peasants' so-called lack of innovative-

ness has been repeated so often that most of us have accepted it as a self-evident truth. Professor Rogers points out that

it is technically possible to double or even triple agricultural production in developing countries through the widespread adoption of more fertilizer, more irrigation, improved seed varieties, etc. To date most of the increase in national agricultural production that has occurred in developing countries has probably been on the part of large commercial producers who make up a small share of the farm population. Subsistence peasants have benefited little from new technology. [Original version]

Is it possible that the peasants' inability to benefit from new technology is because technology has been geared toward the needs and resources of commercial farmers rather than toward those of subsistence farmers? Moreover, the imperfections of new technology, when transported from the experiment station to the farm where other things are not equal or from developed to developing countries, have far too often been ignored in the analysis of why farmers fail to respond as expected.

The history of Japanese agricultural improvement as described by Dore [1960] reveals a movement from the *state of adoption* of foreign plants, seeds, and farm tools to the *state of domestication*. Although things Western were quickly assimilated, the new methods often proved unsuitable. Hence the Japanese called together intelligent, experimenting farmers for the purpose of exchanging and diffusing information about the best traditional practice of particular regions. They talked about the danger "in leaping ahead to the new and neglecting what is good in the old."

It is possible that present-day experiment stations in developing countries operate on the assumption of a one-way flow of information —from the experiment station to the farm and rarely, if ever, in the other direction? The professional—journal-oriented—scientist probably seldom entertains the thought that he might learn something from so-called traditional farmers. In the Philippines, for example, our extension workers claim that most of the research findings are not practical and economically feasible under barrio conditions [University of the Philippines, 1965]. Hence, in defining the farmer's adoption behavior,

2. Data from an ongoing project on "The Concept of Nuclear-Extended Family: An Analysis of Its Empirical Referents," Social Research Division, College of Agriculture, University of the Philippines.

one should look into the specific reasons for the low adoption score. A concrete instance may serve to illustrate:

In the conduct of field trials to test the performance of a new rice variety, orders for seeds came pouring in from farmers who were very much impressed by the growth of the plants. But when harvest time came and they saw how difficult it is to thresh the new rice variety, all the orders for seeds were withdrawn, for it took twice as much time and effort to thresh the seed as the old variety [Martinez, 1964].

In other instances, farmers are sold the idea of certified seeds and fertilizer application, but fertilizers and seeds are nowhere to be obtained. Or when the seeds are finally obtained even from high-prestige sources, they fail to germinate. Sometimes, too, the different maturing time of a high-yielding rice variety makes it foolish for a farmer to adopt it unless all his field neighbors do so. For if his rice is left alone in the field while all his neighbors have harvested theirs, his particular field becomes the lone host to pests, diseases, and rodents. On the other hand, straight-row planting of rice is gaining acceptance among Filipino farmers in spite of additional labor cost because of its advantages in terms of ease in weeding and cleaning the fields in the interest of higher yields.[3] Farmers could also be persuaded to organize for the purposes of obtaining cheaper feeds and fertilizer at the time needed. They were even willing to repair the road to enable a big truck to bring in the fertilizer. When, due to constant rain, the truck bogged down and additional expenses were incurred in hauling the fertilizer, farmers paid the additional cost involved, because it was still cheaper than getting the fertilizer through retailers [Custodio and Cuento, 1964]. Quite often the extension worker's handicap lies in proving to the farmer that the new technology, with all its additional cost, really pays when applied to his farm.

A more dramatic illustration of how farmers respond to economic incentives is provided by the case of Philippine tobacco growers. The government price support program pushed the country's tobacco production from 3 million kilos in 1954, when the program started to 30.4 million kilos in 1962. This was not just a case of increase in production but also a change from the native to Virginia tobacco [Castillo, 1964].[4] A similar response was cited by Chauhan in India, where the villagers at all levels enthusiastically added tobacco, a paying commercial crop, to their traditional food crop economy, even though no extension agency was present [Chauhan, 1960]. There are many more instances of the "economic man" which could be cited, but this would leave me, a rural sociologist, open to the suicidal charge of allowing economics to explain away sociology!

Let us turn now to the other elements of peasantry, such as low aspirational levels, fatalism, lack of empathy, dependence upon government authority, and perceived limited good. Somehow I find it hard to arrive at a logical point of reference with respect to *how deferred* is deferred gratification. If by impulse gratification we mean the peasant eats three square meals a day instead of setting aside one meal for tomorrow, then he is indeed impulsive. If we consider alcoholic consumption as an indicator of lack of deferred gratification, then I suspect that the Frenchman would be regarded as extremely "impulsive."

If I may be allowed to include some personal observations, I have often thought of the American "Fly now, pay later" styles of consumption and their romantically conspicuous adolescent boy-girl relations as distinct candidates for lack of deferred gratification. I also could not agree that delayed marriage necessarily means delayed gratification and therefore, in this respect, peasants are no more lacking in deferred gratification than "modern man" who gets married later. We also think that the Westerners' practice of working very hard the year around, just to save for a two-week vacation at the Riviera, is as much a predisposition "to spend rather than to save" as the peasants' annual fiesta celebration. But perhaps you would consider the vacation as rational behavior and the fiesta, irrational. Incidentally, in our current study on alterna-

---

3. From Research on Alternative Extension Approaches being undertaken in 40 villages by the College of Agriculture, University of the Philippines.

4. The author acknowledges the assistance of Othaniel A. Coloma, Fabian A. Tiongson, and Vernon W. Ruttan for bringing this matter to her attention.

tive extension approaches, only 1 per cent of those who borrowed money spent their loan for fiestas. A majority of the farmers incurred debts either for subsistence or for productive purposes.

The peasant's aspirational levels have also been problematic to me. In my country farmers' aspirations are so high that they would rather see their children become lawyers, doctors, teachers, and government employees rather than farmers. Even farmer parents of vocational agriculture high-school seniors would rather see their children go to college than go to farming immediately after graduation [Contado et al., 1964]. But perhaps a distinction should be made between aspiration and expectation. Findings[5] from eight Philippine villages show that 49 per cent of the farmers want college education for their children, but when they consider their present circumstances, only 7 per cent expect that this would be realized. Now—is this a case of low aspirational levels, fatalism, or is this just being realistic?

With respect to lack of empathy and Lerner's experience with the Turkish peasant, a similar response was made by a Filipino farmer who was asked, "If you had saved ₱1,000, what would you do with it?" The answer was, "I'd rather not think about it lest I get crazy." Since then, we have been wondering whether it is the farmer or the researcher who lacks empathy. Professor Rogers mentioned that some researchers have greater ability at "traditional empathy" (a capacity to put themselves in the roles of peasants). I wonder how *we* would score if the peasant asked us the following question: "Given the state of the arts and the circumstances I find myself in, if you were in my place, what would you do differently from what I am doing now?" Perhaps if we had more "traditional empathy," we would be asking more meaningful questions of the subsistence farmer.

Regarding dependence upon government authority, the nature of such dependence needs to be examined further. The Filipino farmer, for example, depends upon government authority mainly for material assistance

[Dia, 1964] and perhaps rarely for technological guidance. If government authority is backed up by scholarly authority—for top officials are scholars in their own right, as has been the case with Japan [Dore, 1960]—then dependence upon government authority is an accelerator of innovative behavior. But in countries where government officials are backed up more by political recommendations rather than by technological competence, then perhaps it is fortunate that farmers do not look up to them for technological guidance. In this .connection also the concept of perceived limited good seems to be very much less characteristic of our peasants than it is of our politicians, customs, and revenue collectors at different government levels.

PROGRAMS OF PLANNED CHANGE

In terms of the implications of Rogers' subculture for development planning, I share Oscar Lewis' view [1958, p. 322] "that the concept *peasant society* may be a meaningful or useful classification for comparative research but it is not sufficiently predictive in regard to cultural content and structure to take the place of knowledge of concrete reality situations especially in planning programs of culture change."

The subculture of peasantry also presents a real danger that it might serve as a conceptual "trap," with each element explaining away the other elements, with the likely consequence that change agents no longer need to look for facilitators and inhibitors of change outside of this subculture to explain underdevelopment. These ten "negative" elements of peasantry might even serve as a convenient scapegoat for the scientist who is developing innovation and the extension worker who is introducing new practices since usually no further arguments ensue after they declare that "farmers are simply resistant to change." We do not want them to get off that easily, for they are as much part of the development scheme as any subsistence farmer.

My intention is not to be caustic, but to insure that communicators are aware of the problems involved in using the subculture of peasantry as a frame of reference for designing programs of change. Obviously I do not have all the answers as to what constitutes an adequate conceptual scheme for studying

5. Data were obtained from a current research project on "Social and Political Factors in Barrio Development" being conducted by O. F. Sison, G. D. Feliciano, and G. T. Castillo, College of Agriculture, University of the Philippines.

peasants because, if I did have such answers, I would be busy writing that book which promises to be a best seller. We need to understand the peasant in a manner which will stand the test of change agents, from the director to the village worker, whether it be a health program or a radio farm forum. I suggest that the subculture of peasantry is of limited value for the abovementioned purpose, for it does not enable the communicator to know his audience *well* enough to develop meaningful messages intended to influence behavior.

Finally, there is the perennial problem of the ultimate goals of planned change. Considering everything that will be said in this volume about the subsistence farmer, I would like to quote a character in *Village Japan* [Beardsley et al., 1959, p. 471] who was reacting to those who find the Japanese mysterious, contrary, or paradoxical. "All these questions of yours, Sensei, get me to wondering whether you people think of us as ordinary human beings. What we do . . . —isn't so hard to figure out. True, it's not just like America. But you in America try to leave everyone happy, too, I suppose, even if you do go about it differently. . . . To me, anyhow, our way looks like a reasonable way of fitting human nature to the circumstances. And our way of doing it makes pretty good sense, if only your people would stop to think about it."

In the 1964 International Conference of Agricultural Economists, I chose to join the group discussion on rural development. For two afternoons representatives from developed countries discussed rather seriously their problems, ranging from embarrassing food surpluses, disintegrating rural villages, and labor shortage, to employment dislocations and a host of other pressing problems. On the third day they asked me the reason for my silence. My answer was quite simple: "After listening to all the problems which developed people have, I can't help wondering what in the world we are hurrying to get there for!"

This remark, however, was made only half-facetiously, for I was reminded of a Filipino provincial governor's response to the development worker who indicated the need to change farmers' attitudes: "My question to you is two-fold," said the governor. "What are the farmers' attitudes and what do you

want to change them to?"[6] Yes, do we know what we want to change our farmers to?

SUGGESTED AREAS FOR RESEARCH

Professor Rogers' call for improved methodologies ranges from correlational analyses of mathematically expressed variables to a Monte Carlo diffusion simulation approach. My own methodological frustrations center on the rather elementary problem of getting reliable data in a peasant setting. Published materials very rarely and casually, if ever, mention the difficulties encountered in actual research operations [Wharton, 1960]. I would like to see detailed documentations on the dynamics of interviewing—the whole process of identifying and finding the respondent, motivating him to answer so-called silly questions, and finally concluding the interview in such a way that another researcher may find the respondent more receptive. The interest here is not so much on the senior author's or the project leader's report, but more on the interviewer's or research assistant's experiences and their interpretations of them. For example, in the Philippines we have observed certain advantages in using female interviewers to establish rapport in order to obtain needed information. They have had to "turn on their charm," play innocent, or once in a while masquerade as married women for self-protection. Sharing with our colleagues the operational research problems encountered and concrete solutions worked out would go a long way toward the training of other research workers in developing countries. It would also help assuage uneasy feelings regarding data reliability and validity. Besides the realities of data gathering, we should also inquire about the empirical indicators of motivations, attitudes, and values referred to in various village studies. What techniques were employed in getting at these indicators?

In the substantive area, there are a few studies which have promising implications for policy and action:

1. The economizing behavior of the subsistence farmer. As Petrini [1964] points out: "It is a challenge to rural sociologists to find out if farmers who do not accept innovations really are nonadjust-

6. An incident related to me by Dr. Milton L. Barnett.

ment oriented or if they simply have no other choice when available resources and alternatives are taken into consideration."

2. Familism and its effect on decision-making among subsistence farmers. Under what circumstances does it foster or inhibit economic development?

3. Family size preference of the subsistence farmer and the factors operating for or against family limitation. Suppose fear of God and fear of consequences on health are indicated as objections to the application of technology to population problems, and if one were engaged in such a campaign, the second fear might have more potentialities for conquest. Incidentally, an American drug company in the Philippines has tried to get around the first objection by selling their pills as "cycle regulators" rather than as "conscience violators." On this basis we have been told that permission to use "regulators" may be obtained in order to pave the way for more effective rhythm. This illustrates in a small way the importance of "knowing one's audience."

4. Farmers' acceptance or rejection of agricultural innovations with as much focus on the characteristics of the innovation as on the farmer himself. Hopefully, results of such studies could be fed back to developers of technology.

5. The nature and extent of religion's and/or superstition's effect on receptivity to new agricultural ideas. We have observed in our current studies that if farmers are asked about their superstitious beliefs regarding certain practices, they usually enumerate quite a few, but whether these actually get in the way of accepting a new idea may be another matter. For example, an anthrax epidemic reported by extension workers related that farmers gathered together their carabaos, and each one brought lights to drive the evil spirits away. It is interesting that this ritual was only resorted to during the period when the veterinarian and his vaccine were nowhere in sight. As soon as the vaccine came, the ritual was discontinued, and 80 per cent of the farmers submitted

their animals for vaccination [Ganchorre et al., 1964]. This situation is probably no different from that of plane passengers after take-off. You almost have no choice but the rosary beads.

Finally we need to know and understand the motivations, attitudes, and values of planners, policy-makers, researchers—foreign "experts" included. The values of such people exert more influence in evolving so-called grassroots development programs than we realize or care to admit.

References

BEARDSLEY, HALL and WARD, 1959. Richard K. Beardsley, John W. Hall and Robert E. Ward, *Village Japan* (Chicago: University of Chicago Press, 1959).

CASTILLO, 1964. Andres Castillo, "Problems of the Virginia Tobacco Industry," *Philippine Economic Review*, Vol. 9, Nos. 8–9 (1964), 42–43, 48.

CHAUHAN, 1960. Brij Raj Chauhan, "Rise and Decline of a Cash Crop in an Indian Village," *Journal of Farm Economics*, Vol. 42, No. 3 (August 1960) 663–66.

CONTADO, CASTILLO and JARMIN, 1964. Tito E. Contado, Gelia T. Castillo, and Martin V. Jarmin, "A Search for Trained Young Men in Farming: A Study of Vo-Ag Seniors' Choice of Occupations" (Los Banos: College of Agriculture, University of the Philippines, 1964).

CUSTODIO and CUENTO, 1964. Jaime R. Custodio and Caridad G. Cuento, *The Bunggo–Hurnalan Farmers' Association* (Farm and Home Development Office Report, 1964).

DIA, 1964. Manuel A. Dia, "The Filipino Farmers' Image of Government: A Neglected Area in Developmental Change," Paper presented at the Seminar on Social and Economic Aspects of Agricultural Development, Los Banos, College of Agriculture, University of the Philippines, May 1964.

DORE, 1960. R. P. Dore, "Agricultural Improvement in Japan: 1870–1900," *Economic Development and Cultural Change*, Vol. 9, No. 1, Part II (October 1960), 69–91.

GANCHORRE et al., 1964. Don Ganchorre, et al., "Progress Report on Action Program in Binan, Laguna, April to November 1964" (Los Banos: Farm and Home Development Office, College of Agriculture, University of the Philippines, 1964).

GROSS, 1948. Neal Gross, "Sociological Variation in Contemporary Rural Life," *Rural Sociology*, Vol. 13, No. 3 (September 1948), 256–73.

LEWIS, 1958. Oscar Lewis, *Village Life in Northern India: Studies in a Delhi Village* (Urbana, Ill.: University of Illinois Press, 1958).

LONGMORE, 1948. T. Wilson Longmore, "Discussion" of Neal Gross' "Sociological Variation," *Rural Sociology*, Vol. 13, No. 3 (September 1948), 256–73.

MARTINEZ, 1964. Vicente Martinez, "Progress Report on Action Program in Barrio Pansol, Pila, Laguna, May–November 1964" (Los Banos: Farm and Home Development Office, College of Agriculture, University of the Philippines, 1964).

PETRINI, 1964. Frank Petrini, "Changes in Goals and Values," Paper presented at the First World Congress of Rural Sociology, Dijon, France, August 17–22, 1964.

UNIVERSITY OF THE PHILIPPINES, 1965. University of the Philippines, *Innovator*, Vol. III, No. 2 (Los Banos: A Monthly Newsletter of the Farm and Home Development Office, College of Agriculture, University of the Philippines, February 1965).

SANIEL, 1963. Josefe M. Saniel, "The Mobilization of Traditional Values in the Modernization of Japan," Paper read at the International Conference of the Congress for Cultural Freedom, Diliman, Quezon City, Philippines, June 3–9, 1963.

WHARTON, 1960. Clifton R. Wharton, Jr., "Processing Underdeveloped Data from an Underdeveloped Area," *Journal of the American Statistical Association*, Vol. 55, No. 289 (March 1960), 23–37.

COMMENT

Testing Theories
Concerning a Subculture of Peasantry

LEONARD W. DOOB

IN ORDER TO INFLUENCE people, Professor Rogers reminds us in his paper, it is essential to understand their current attitudes, values, and motives. At the outset, before more specific and more up-to-date information is empirically obtained, a knowledge of their culture provides preliminary clues to those predispositions. For this reason he seeks, through a laudable process of abstraction, to isolate "the central elements in our subculture of peasantry." The evidence he offers comes largely from Latin America, but there are also references to the general literature on social change and to other areas, viz. the Middle East, India, Malaya, Indonesia, and Italy.

The principal question which my discussion would raise concerns the validity of the ten elements outlined by Rogers. One way of appraising that validity is to determine whether or not the same elements characterize peasants with different cultural backgrounds. By a fortunate happenstance I have toiled in a theoretical vineyard similar to Rogers' while seeking to find common elements, not exclusively among peasant, but more generally among nonliterate peoples in

areas to which, undoubtedly fortuitously, he himself makes no reference. Not surprisingly, since both of us reflect the subculture of social science, our independent conclusions are more or less identical. Thus what Rogers calls "a lack of deferred gratification" I have stated as a proposition in the following words: "People changing centrally from old to new ways are likely to become more tolerant of delay in the attainment of goals" [Doob, 1960, p. 88].

Instead of trying to demonstrate further that the two of us are geniuses because we agree with each other in spite of the absence of collusion, it seems more fruitful to examine the kind of evidence gathered in Africa and elsewhere and to rearrange already published and some unpublished data under Rogers' headings. This discussion would simultaneously throw a few chunks into the geographical holes in Rogers' presentation while testing his theories and pointing out various problems arising in connection with both validation and measurement. If citing his own research makes the discussant appear immodest or brash, he can say only that no one knows better than he their limitations The data, moreover, have a salient advantage: they can be displayed most concisely in tabular form and hence may possibly serve as another tempting target for other researchers. Apologies for the indelicate egocentricity, nevertheless, are offered most abjectly, albeit with a confident grin.

THE SAMPLES

The principal materials from Africa were gathered in 1955, those from Jamaica in 1957, and those from the Tyrol in 1961. In Africa and Jamaica, adult samples were carefully selected; each person was interviewed and tested, almost always at a single session lasting about two hours. Two of the societies are in East Africa (Luo and Ganda), the third in South Africa (Zulu). Since the primary interest of the investigation was in acculturation, or culture contact, from a psychological standpoint, each sample was divided into two groups on the basis of the one criterion which seemed most highly correlated with the influence of the West, viz. formal education. In tabulations and in the text, therefore, *low* means no or very little education, *high* considerable education from the Western standpoint. Unless otherwise stated, the figures in all tables are percentages; an asterisk (*) indicates that the difference between a pair is statistically significant (p<.05, two-tail, almost always chi-square, otherwise *t*-test). Some of the important attributes of the three African samples are given in Table 5.2 [Doob, 1960, p. 282]:

THE TEN PROPOSITIONS

Rogers in his paper has really done more than isolate ten elements: as his own exposition shows, he has embodied the elements in sentences which consequently are principles, hypotheses, or at least propositions. He is presenting and defending ten theses. Since it is proposed to test the ten propositions by comparing "low" and "high" subgroups from samples of Africans and Jamaicans, Rogers would certainly be entitled to raise certain objections, which I take the liberty of introducing for him:

1. Not all those persons "low" in education were peasants according to Rogers' definition, although more of them were represented in the "low" than in the "high" groups. Agreed; and if time had permitted, it would indeed have been both better and possible to isolate "peasants" and to compare them with nonpeasants.

2. The samples are too small. Agreed; but at least their number is clearly specified, whereas generally anthropological reports do not indicate the *n*'s and often give the impression that there are no or few deviations from the modes being reported.

3. The measures (direct questions, TAT-type projective tests, performance tests, observations during the interview) are not valid or reliable indicators of attitudes, values, and motives. This charge had best be mooted, since there is no a priori way to decide whether such measures are more or less valid or reliable than the formal and informal ones behind the evidence offered by Rogers.

4. The validity of the ten elements cannot and should not be tested by comparing the "low" groups with the "high" groups, for the assumption must thus be made that those elements characterize peasants and do not characterize nonpeasants. In fact, this assumption is implicit in Rogers' analysis, and seems to me to be quite legitimate; would he agree?

Table 5.2

		LUO		GANDA		ZULU	
		low	*high*	*low*	*high*	*low*	*high*
	n	24	23	63	70	69	37
1. No or almost no knowledge of English		71*	9	74*	23	79*	0
2. Occupation: cultivator or unskilled		42	26	59*	16	82	6
3. Urban residence		0	0	24*	68	50*	92
4. Religion: "pagan"		30*	0	1	3	29*	0
5. Claims a European friend		63*	96	53	65	39*	61
6. Age (mean years)		52	49	44*	35	50	45

The major difficulty here, as Rogers explicitly recognizes, is that few pure peasant communities exist today: the outside world is usually exerting its influence, no matter how slight or ineffective. For this reason, in my own publications I refer to the *unchanged*, the *changing*, and the *changed* in trying to formulate principles; and in Lerner's terminology, most peasants right now either are or are about to become "transitionals" [Lerner, 1958].

5. No critical deliberate test of the ten propositions has been made; rather, in a purely *ex post facto* manner tidbits of evidence have been arranged under Rogers' ten headings. Alas, the charge is correct; but what else can one do with data already collected and collated? The better procedure of course, as Rogers states, is to conduct new research and make predictions in advance.

In the following sections the headings are quoted from Rogers. Then his accompanying definition or salient sentence of exposition is followed by what appears to be relevant evidence. In all tabulations blank spaces signify that the item or test was not or could not be used in the particular society. Statements encased in quotation marks were presented more or less in that verbal form to informants, and the figures represent the

percentages of those *agreeing* with the viewpoint so expressed.

1. *"Mutual Distrust in Interpersonal Relations"*

"Peasant communities are characterized by mutual distrust, suspiciousness, and evasiveness in interpersonal relations."

The first seven rows of Table 5.3 offer data obtained from ambiguous drawings which, it is assumed, tap hostility projectively; the remaining are conscious reactions to direct statements. On the whole, few significant differences appear, and with exceptions here and there, the trend of the differences suggests that *more* of the "high" than the "low" groups revealed the "distrust" postulated by Rogers' proposition which, consequently, is here not verified.

2. *"Lack of Innovativeness"*

"The norms of most peasant communities are negative toward change, as a result of past generations of generally unfavorable conditioning toward innovations." Table 5.4 shows results on various standardized tests; the first three rows indicate the percentage of informants who were not able to grasp the instructions concerning the particular tests;

Table 5.3

	LUO		GANDA		ZULU	
	low	high	low	high	low	high
1. "Chief" in ambiguous drawing "dislikes" the "follower"	17	39	10	16	14	26
2. "Follower" in ambiguous drawing "dislikes" the "chief"	43	52	26	34	17	37
3. "European" in ambiguous drawing "dislikes" the "African"	5	0	6	6	27	22
4. "African" in ambiguous drawing "dislikes" the "European"	18	22	8	20	30	36
5. "Father" in ambiguous drawing "dislikes" the "son"	5	9	9	11	7	14
6. "Son" in ambiguous drawing "dislikes" the "father"	5	9	7	8	6	25
7. Person in ambiguous drawing looks "unhappy"	33	46	9★	32	46	70
8. "World is dangerous, people are evil"	75	87	59	49	70	83
9. "Failure results from secret plots of others"	50	39	53	58	70	69
10. "People should be successful in spite of others' jealousy"	25	22	54	61	36	23
11. "People should speak only well of a rival"	91	91	91	94	66★	20
12. "Cook can use medicine to get wages raised"			25★	0	29	22
13. "People should talk less and work more"	91	100	75	83	81	91
14. "Liars will be punished in the next world"	83	78	64	65	81	74

Table 5.4

	LUO		GANDA		ZULU	
	low	*high*	*low*	*high*	*low*	*high*
1. Visual retention test	63★	22	15★	3	44★	6
2. Embedded figures test	83★	30	30	11	65★	21
3. Sorting test	8	0	18★	4	16★	3
4. No recall of communication			44★	11	42★	18
5. Rorschach: reject first plate	8	0	9	9	27	29
6. Rorschach: reject one or more plates	17	4	32★	19	44	35
7. TAT-type test: reject first card	4	0	22★	4	9	0

the fourth, the percentage unable to recall a communication offered during the interview; and the remaining three, the percentages rejecting (or, from the viewpoint suggested here, unable to respond to) the two projective tests.

If the "low" groups have the "negative" norms toward change postulated by Rogers' proposition, then, either as cause or consequence, it might be anticipated that they would be less able to adapt themselves to the kinds of novel situations required by the Western-type tasks offered these African informants in the above tests. Indeed, all of the statistically significant differences in the above table and almost all of the nonsignificant ones are in the direction which confirm this expectation.

3. "Fatalism"

"A passive view of the world implying the feeling that an individual's efforts cannot determine his future."

The first three items in Table 5.5 seem directly to reflect a "passive view of the world," and the results therefrom largely substantiate the proposition. The fourth may or may not be related to fatalism, and it turns out to be not at all decisive.

4. "Low Aspirational Levels"

"Desired future states of being, such as levels of living, social status, education, and occupation are reported to be relatively low."

Table 5.6 assumes that people's aspirational levels affect their evaluation of the present and the past as well as their anticipations and fantasies concerning the future. With the exception of those in the last row, the findings confirm the proposition.

5. "A Lack of Deferred Gratification"

"Peasants are typified by impulse gratification rather than the deferred gratification pattern" (the postponement of immediate satisfaction in anticipation of future rewards). (See Table 5.7.)

The one significant difference elicited by the first item goes contrary to the proposition; in fact, the "low" group among the Ganda, who were largely cultivators, maintained that they had to plan their crops a year or so ahead, whereas the "high" group, being teachers, government officials, and the like, by and large had occupations with tenure and hence did not have to plan. The second item perhaps taps imagination to a greater degree; and here the proposition is clearly verified.

Table 5.5

	LUO		GANDA		ZULU	
	low	*high*	*low*	*high*	*low*	*high*
1. "A waste of time to plan for future"	42	17	22	16	66★	34
2. "Inability to anticipate life five years hence"	29	17	5	8	60★	35
3. "Ability is more important than luck"			22★	44	8	9
4. "People should talk less and work more"	91	100	75	83	81	91

Table 5.6

	LUO		GANDA		ZULU	
	low	high	low	high	low	high
1. Dislike of present occupation	8	22	9	19	20★	51
2. Anticipated nongratification in occupation	4	5	5	13	32	44
3. Indicates only vague plan for spending windfall of £500	29	17	22	20	43★	17
4. "People were happier in old days"	46	39	46	46		
5. "Life in heaven is better than life on earth"	69	70	33★	57	57	43

Table 5.7

	LUO		GANDA		ZULU	
	low	high	low	high	low	high
1. Claims to plan for a year or more	92	100	65★	44	75	77
2. Prefers to spend £5 now rather than invest or receive £50 in a year	32	14	52★	31	24	11

Table 5.8

	low	high	urban	rural
n	89	23	46	43
Subjective Time				
1. Experiences difference between subjective and objective time	86	100	77★	94
2. Claims time passes slowly when little to do, and vice versa	7★	64	6	8
3. Claims time passes slowly in "bad" times, and vice versa	47★	0	62★	33
4. Claims time passes differently as age increases	97	95	94	100
5. Claims time passes more slowly as age increases	30★	5	36	23
Estimate of Length of Interview				
6. Correct or within 10 minutes	38	59	51★	25
7. Underestimates	11	12	15	7
8. Overestimates	76	48	66	84
Estimate of 15-Second Interval				
9. Literally correct	6	4	7	4
10. Underestimates within 4 seconds	11	9	9	13
11. Underestimates (total)	48★	22	49	49
12. Overestimates within 4 seconds	6	9	5	7
13. Overestimates by more than 1 minute	9	4	12	7
14. Overestimates (total)	44★	74	33	47
Reproduction of 10-Second Interval				
15. Literally correct	4	0	7	0
16. Underestimates within 2 seconds	11	9	9	13
17. Underestimates (total)	58	70	56	61
18. Overestimates within 2 seconds	11	9	7	15
19. Overestimates by more than 30 seconds	5	0	7	2
20. Overestimates (total)	37	30	35	39

The first two items under "Fatalism" above might also have been included here and have thus contributed further validating evidence.

6. "Limited Time Perspective"

"Within most societies, peasants lack the degree of time consciousness possessed by urbanites or commercial farmers." Time consciousness was not adequately investigated in the three African societies, but various measures of time judgments were obtained from samples living in six communities of Jamaica. The results are offered in terms of the usual breakdown based upon education as well as a division of the "low" group into rural and urban subgroups.

Table 5.8 indicates the kind of difficulty involved when a proposition is tested concretely and under controlled conditions; the situation inevitably is somewhat artificial. At any rate, there are few reliable differences between the pairs of groups in terms of actual accuracy of temporal judgments (rows 6, 9, and 15); the one clearcut difference (row 6, rural-urban) is contrary to Rogers' proposition. The urban group in this instance, however, was largely composed of people living in a Kingston slum who were so demoralized that, perhaps, they paid little attention to the time of day or night. Differences in "subjective time" are relatively

numerous and on the whole suggest that more of the "low" and of the rural groups found time passing slowly during adversity and with increasing age.

7. "Familism"

"Peasant life is primarily familistic and only secondarily individual."

The data in Table 5.9 almost without exception indicate that more of those in the "low" group are oriented toward the family as Rogers' proposition suggests. A notable exception is item 17, where the contrary is shown, perhaps because in a period of quickened nationalism better-educated Africans wished to indicate their own responsibility to their fellow citizens—the categorization here was derived from the question, "What would you like to do during your life that would make you happiest and most proud of yourself?" Items 4 to 11, based on crude, direct inquiries, simply suggest the possibility that different attitudes toward the two parents may be associated with education.

8. "Dependency upon Government Authority"

"The peasant's attitude toward national and local government appears typically to be a peculiar combination of hostility toward, and dependence upon." (See Table 5.10.)

Table 5.9

	LUO		GANDA		ZULU	
	low	high	low	high	low	high
1. "Father" in ambiguous drawing "dislikes" "son"	5	9	9	11	7	14
2. "Son" in ambiguous drawing "dislikes" "father"	5	9	7	8	6	25
3. "Son" in ambiguous drawing expresses hostility	4★	26	16	29	11★	39
4. Father judged "kindest"	32	15	20	14	11	13
5. Father "taught" most	41	45	25	22	22	23
6. Father "loved" most	14	29	16	11	13★	0
7. Father "respected" most	36	52	23★	45	40	33
8. Mother judged "kindest"	18	45	20★	38	24★	47
9. Mother "taught" most	5	20	18	28	21★	47
10. Mother "loved" most	23	19	30	45	40★	63
11. Mother "respected" most	9	5	7	5	8	13
12. Recalls no special person for childhood quarrels	63	30	64★	30	44	39
13. "Brothers can never be friends"	13	30	40	30	39	46
14. "Kinship is closer than friendship"			83★	59	59	37
15. "Wife earning money may spend it as she pleases"	13	4	8★	42	39	31
16. "Polygynist can be good Christian"	58	57	38	42	49	66
17. Claims to seek group rather than individual goal	73	83	61★	89	42★	82

Table 5.10

	LUO		GANDA		ZULU	
	low	high	low	high	low	high
1. Dislike of leader A	17	35	13	29	17★	51
2. Dislike of leader B	22	35	17	22	20	54
3. Dislike of leader C	13	36	7★	23		
4. "A chief should always be obeyed"	58★	9	76★	44	94★	80
5. "Leaders are more important than followers"	75	50	87★	64	46	34
6. Stresses leadership qualities of "a good chief"	18	35	19	7	29	23

The leaders referred to in the first three rows were all appointed by the colonial or the central authorities and hence legitimately test the proposition in question—the items, therefore, provide unspectacular verification. Consistent is the finding in rows 4 and 5 that more of the "low" groups showed respect toward the traditional chief. The findings in the last row are equivocal.

9. "Localiteness"

"Cosmopoliteness, the opposite of localiteness [the degree to which individuals are oriented within, rather than externally, to their social system], is generally much less characteristic of peasants than of urbanites or commercial farmers."

Table 5.11 is confined to attitudes toward two of the outgroups existing in all three of the societies, viz. Europeans and Asians· Few of the differences are statistically significant; and the same is true of two other items examined above (rows 3 and 4 of the tabulation accompanying Rogers' first proposition). If anything, the trend seems to be for more of the "high" groups to feel hostile toward these outgroups.

In another part of the world, the North Tyrol in Austria and the South Tyrol in Italy, I have collected from school children, through their regular teachers, spontaneous essays on the open-ended topic of "What do you like and what do you not like about your *Heimat?*" [Doob, 1964, pp. 122–123]. The word *Heimat* is an ambiguous term, whose referents extend from "home" to "fatherland." Deliberately for present purposes, two schools in each region have been compared: one in a rural area, where most parents of the

Table 5.11

	LUO		GANDA		ZULU	
	low	high	low	high	low	high
1. "European" in ambiguous drawing evokes ambivalence	32	48	80	66	42	58
2. "African" in ambiguous drawing evokes ambivalence	64	55	27	13	42	42
3. Ambivalence toward Europeans	22	39	28	41	33	27
4. Dislike of Europeans	4	22	23	23	21	36
5. Ambivalence toward Asians	26	57	25	29	38	31
6. Dislike of Asians	30	44	36	53	35	53
7. Ambivalent admirations of Europeans	29	52	19	33	4★	17
8. Admiration of Europeans	46	22	41	39	52★	29
9. Ambivalence toward receiving admiration of Europeans	26	31	35	35	26	11
10. Seeks admiration of Europeans	24★	0	23	16	32	17
11. Claims a European friend	63★	96	53	65	39★	61
12. Claims an Asian friend	25	22	46	43	16	31
13. "Possible for Africans to have European friend"	46	64	78	81	52	63

children probably satisfy Rogers' definition of peasant, and the other in a prominent city or town (Innsbruck in North Tyrol, Meran in South Tyrol); the ages of the children in North Tyrol ranged from 10 to 16 and in South Tyrol from 8 to 13. Table 5.12 gives the percentages mentioning the indicated themes (as ascertained through a systematic content analysis):

Table 5.12

| | SOUTH TYROL | | NORTH TYROL | |
	rural	urban	rural	urban
n	49	61	267	238
Land				
Landscape	86	80	78	85
Churches	54*	23	44*	31
Buildings	96	91	87*	96
Land and buildings	100	99	98	100
People				
Historical figures	4	3	21*	30
Leaders	2	0	3	2
Family and children	12	2	13	8
Ingroup	48	38	69	65
Italians	20	15	5	10
Outgroup	24	32	33*	50
Human beings	60	62	80	83
Culture				
Symbolic objects	8	10	29*	39
Cultural objects	46	37	59*	70
Cultural products or activity	22	31	30*	53
Miscellaneous				
Weather	30*	48	28*	38
No "dislike"	12*	37	17*	8

Although numerous statistically significant differences appear, especially between the two schools in North Tyrol, it is to be noted that none of them is extremely large. On this basis, then, children in the rural comunities roughly referred to the same referents as those in the cities and hence in their essays showed few distinctive symptoms of localiteness. Fewer in both rural communities, however, mentioned outsiders, a finding perhaps in line with Rogers' proposition.

As ever, a word of caution is needed: the obtained differences may or may not reflect varying conditions confronting peasants (or neopeasants) and urban dwellers, but simply local conditions. Thus in another semiurban community of the South Tyrol, 21 per cent

of the children (n = 113) referred to an outgroup other than the Italians; this figure is lower than both the urban and rural percentages shown above. Obviously the survey technique as such, as Rogers also argues cogently, cannot establish the causal connections postulated by this proposition or any of the others.

10. *"Empathy"*

"Peasants . . . have lower empathy than urbanites."

Table 5.13 was employed [Doob, 1960] to measure, not "empathy," but sensitivity to other people and from that viewpoint offers a reasonably consistent picture: fewer of those in the "low" group possessed that quality as here measured. (Once again, some of the same items have been previously used in the present discussion in connection with other propositions.) The assumption is made that such sensitivity aids empathy; if that be so, then the Rogers' proposition has been tentatively verified.

By and large, the exposition has now shown, data from Africa and elsewhere can be roughly subsumed under, or at a minimum illustrate, the propositions suggested by Rogers. The notable exception has been the first one pertaining to distrust. I would consequently salute Rogers, and I hope he feels quietly elated.

LAG

In appraising the measures we have employed to test Rogers' theories, it is important to remember that beliefs and values linger on even when people's milieu changes or when they change their milieu. Another concrete study from Africa is offered for illustrative purposes. The informants were Zulu women who were interviewed by a Zulu woman [1960, pp. 302–303]. One group was living permanently in the city of Durban, South Africa (labeled "Stable Urban" in the table below); another had only recently arrived in that city ("Urban"); and yet another, temporarily visiting male relatives and friends there, was solidly anchored in the rural reserves ("Rural"). Once again the figures are the percentages agreeing with the indicated statements.

Table 5.13

	LUO		GANDA		ZULU	
	low	high	low	high	low	high
1. One human response to Rorschach Plate II	0	17	23	18	18	23
2. One human response to Rorschach Plate III	55★	83	57	66	37★	71
3. One human response to Rorschach Plate VIII	29	58	28	34	16	29
4. One human response to ambiguous drawing	17	41	35	49	52★	76
5. Immediate "suggestibility" on Rorschach test	83	83	54★	76	70	73
6. Delayed "suggestibility" on Rorschach test	62★	22	20	28	32	23
7. No or ambiguous response to drawing of "chief-follower"	21	4	20	13	54★	22
8. No or ambiguous response to drawing of "European-African"	29★	4	23	19	42	31
9. No or ambiguous response to drawing of "father-son"	22	13	23	13	58★	17
10. Claims preference for group, not individual, goal	73	82	61★	89	42★	82
11. Seeks to avoid unpopularity	0★	35	3	5	3	5

Table 5.14

	Stable Urban	Urban	Rural
n	70	56	36
Family Practices			
1. "Groom's family should offer special gifts"	89	95	100
2. "Wife earning money may spend it as she pleases"	31	7	8
3. "A man may choose wife without his own parent's consent"	56	0	6
4. "A woman should be married by her dead husband's brother"	39	22	81
5. "Second child should not arrive before weaning of the first child"	100	98	100
6. "A husband should never beat his wife"	90	83	86
7. "An unmarried woman should not have a child"	97	100	94
8. "An unmarried son should give father his earnings"	97	96	100
9. "Women should want many children"	67	79	97
10. "A married woman should never have a lover"	89	100	100
11. "A woman should never marry someone from her own clan"	99	96	100
12. "Poor, helpless relatives must be supported"	75	94	92
13. "A woman should respectfully avoid her parents-in-law"	81	93	100
"Facts"			
14. "Chiefs can make it rain"	37	39	49
15. "Native doctors can treat any disease"	29	13	46
16. "Sick may die if seen by 'unclean' persons"	44	54	77
17. "Deceased ancestors can cause child's illness"	60	69	100
18. "Illness may result from intercourse with menstruating woman"	71	93	94
19. "Character eventually depends upon training by older children"	93	91	97
20. "Wealth in money is better than in cattle"	73	61	9
21. "Polygynist can be a good Christian"	21	34	51
22. "A lie is always wrong"	74	86	100
23. "Zulu women should not brew beer for sale"	76	89	97
24. "Stealing is never justified"	99	98	100

In Table 5.14, similarities and differences in the proportions approving the indicated family practices and subscribing to the so-called facts are clearly visible; in general, there was more agreement than disagreement among the three groups. Thus practices and ideas from another era continue to function in the present generation, and even urban dwellers retain peasant proclivities.

THE PROBLEM OF COMMUNICATION

Suppose the ten propositions of Rogers were even more completely verified; how, then, could they be related to communicating with peasants? Rogers has stated that "this social structure" found among peasants—the mighty ten—"may be utilized by change agents to introduce innovations." Naturally; but before this can be done and before approval can be given to a concrete radio program, such as Rogers uses as an illustration, certain guidelines need to be delineated:

1. The relative strengths of the ten components must be determined. It is not enough merely to know that peasants in a given community are likely to be mutually distrustful, to lack innovativeness, and so on. We also need to know how seriously they do in fact oppose the introduction of desired changes. How important is each one of the tendencies in the society and hence in certain individuals? Such information is further required by the fact, as Rogers indicates, that the components interact and the outcome can be grasped only if the elements are carefully assessed.

2. The ten components must be located in specific people. Are they, for example, present in both leaders and followers, among the influential and the noninfluential? Here is simply a concrete way of putting knowledge of the social structure to work.

3. Other variables and principles must be invoked before a successful communications program can be planned. The communicator often comes face to face with another kind of complicated interaction, only two examples of which will be quickly given. First, what media exist, or which ones can be brought into existence? Media must be defined sufficiently broadly to include both the mass media and the informal channels which exist in any society. Then, secondly, for a given purpose what kinds of psychological responses should be evoked? If the peasants in question are distrustful, should they be motivated to action by the arousal of anxiety and, if so, how anxious should they be made? How can anxiety be linked to the goal of the communication through the specified media?

4. After isolating all the complicated variables and formulating magnificent propositions, the content of the communication must eventually be planned, and somehow an audience must be attracted and its attention must be held. Thus, if one is trying ultimately to have peasants utilize more scientific methods of agriculture, where and how does one begin? Does it make sense, for example, to raise a question that is likely to be of universal interest, such as: Why are there clouds? Why does it rain?

5. Both within society and within people a change produced by a communication or by any other source is likely to have additional consequences, not all or even many of which are foreseeable in advance. Thus a pilot study in which small samples of literate and illiterate Hausa peasants in Northern Nigeria were compared [Doob, 1961, pp. 175-179] revealed differences with respect to perceiving novel situations, learning, understanding photographs, knowledge of news, contact with various media, scientific beliefs, and the like. One does not know whether the more alert Hausa joined adult literacy classes or whether those classes made the students more alert, but in either case the teaching as such was associated with innumerable other kinds of behavior besides reading and writing. Similarly, when some official "merely" teaches peasants and their leaders to use fertilizer or plow more efficiently, without wishing to do so, he may set up a chain of responses which in the short or the long run affects their attitude toward, or knowledge of, traditional folklore, modern science, medicine, and religion.

The discussion will now be concluded on a note that may sound dismal but is really meant to be most cheering. We may be following a will-o'-the-wisp when we think that we can ever formulate abstract propositions reducible to the kind of concrete level which must be reached before effective communication can occur. The idiosyncracies are too numerous, the interactions too swirlingly complicated. Each new research project, each new communication, though it be a bold and unique adventure requiring ultimately its own program for a computer, is able to utilize the experience of the past as tentative, sometimes even tenuous, guides to what will be discovered or accomplished. We provide ourselves with a kit of tools as we approach the future, but then only empirical glances allow us to select the particular ones of utility at the moment. It is for this reason that peasants might be better understood and aided if there were clearing houses through which wisdom from the past could be applied, not routinely and dogmatically, but cautiously and creatively.

References

DOOB, 1960.   Leonard W. Doob, *Becoming More Civilized* (New Haven, Conn.: Yale University Press, 1960).

DOOB, 1961.   Leonard W. Doob, *Communication in Africa* (New Haven, Conn.: Yale University Press, 1961).

DOOB, 1964.   Leonard W. Doob, *Patriotism and Nationalism* (New Haven, Conn.: Yale University Press, 1964).

LERNER, 1958.   Daniel Lerner, *The Passing of Traditional Society: Modernizing the Middle East* (Glencoe, Ill.: Free Press, 1958).

CASE STUDY

Growth of "Economic-Mindedness" Among Small Farmers in North Sumatra, Indonesia

D. H. PENNY[1]

IN MY STUDY OF "The Transition from Subsistence to Commercial Family Farming in North Sumatra" [Penny, 1964] I have interrelated technological, economic, and social changes to measure the extent to which farmers have become active participants in the development process. Those that have become active participants are classed as "economic-minded"; those that have not, as "subsistence-minded."[2] An index of economic mindedness was constructed to show the nature and extent of differences in the willingness and ability of farmers to participate in the development process. Eight villages were studied in detail. In some the peasants have already become commercial farmers, in others they have begun to change, while in yet others no aspect of the social system—not farming methods or attitudes to work and to learning or life goals—shows any appreciable sign of change.

These findings, and my interpretation of them, are summarized in this paper. The villages studied and the research method used are discussed first. Then the construction and use of the index of economic-mindedness is explained. The next section discusses the sequence in which changes have occurred, and the reasons for the observed differences in farmer behavior are then given.

THE SURVEY AREA AND METHODS

A total of 180 farmers in eight North Sumatran villages were interviewed by the 36 fourth-year students of the Faculty of Agriculture of the University of North Sumatra in April–May 1962, in the course of their one-month's practical village work. The

1. I am greatly indebted to my wife, Janet, and to M. S. Hutabarat, Achmad Sjofjan, S. B. Simandjuntak, and H. Situmorang, my colleagues at the Faculty of Agriculture of the University of North Sumatra, for their advice and criticism. Herman Southworth, Rainer Schickele, and David Pfanner assisted with the revision. Their help is likewise appreciated.

2. A number of people have asked why "economic-minded" was used instead of "commercial-minded" or "market-minded." From one point of view, either of the two alternatives would have been better than the term actually chosen, since all farmers, including the most subsistence-oriented, make economic decisions (see also below). There are two reasons why I prefer the term economic-minded over the possible alternatives. They are: both alternatives have some possibly undesirable ideological connotations; to reserve the term economic-minded to farmers who are active participants in the development process means that one can distinguish between economic decisions that have limited objectives (e.g. subsistence or subsistence-plus) and those that lead to ever-rising levels of income and are thus economic from a developmental point of view.

Table 5.15. Summary Table Showing Some Key Characteristics of the Eight Survey Villages
8 North Sumatran Villages, Crop Year 1961–1962

	Tiga Nderket	Nagasa-ribu	Namum-belin	Sumbul	"Tamiang"	Pematang Djohar	Lintong ni Huta	Lubuk Tjemara
Rank on Index of Economic-Mindedness	I	II	III	IV	V	VI	VII	VIII
Distance from Medan km	90	100	45	150	130	15	250	35
Rainfall mm	1,800	1,400	3,300	2,150	2,500	1,800	1,800	1,900
Height above sea level m	880	1,400	80	1,050	20	10	1,050	10
Yield wet rice per Ha qu	28	15	19	20	20	22	47	15
Land per farm ha	1.2	2.2	3.1	1.6	1.9	1.8	0.9	1.9
Labor per farm A.M.E.[a]	2.4	2.2	1.8	1.7	2.6	2.2	3.1	2.7
Man-land ratio A.M.E./ha	2.0	1.0	0.5	1.1	1.4	1.2	3.4	1.4
Nonland capital Rp	5,600	8,000	6,000	4,300	8,000	6,800	5,500	7,700
Land in perennials %	12%	13%	66%	34%	59%	24%	2%	11%
Major crops[b]	Veg.	Veg.	Rubber	Rice, Coffee	Rubber	Rice	Rice	Rice
Value added per farm Rp '000	128	54	49	39	59	58	61	44
Farm expenditure Rp '000	24	22	5	6	3	3	7	3
Wages paid Rp '000	30.3	1.7	1.5	0.9	0.8	2.5	3.8	2.4
Rent paid Rp '000	0.4	0.1	0	2.7	0	0	7.5	2.4
Interest paid Rp '000	0.3	0.2	0	0.5	0	0	3.1	0
Major ethnic groups	Batak: Karo	Batak: Simelu-ngun	Karo & Javanese	Batak: Toba etc.	Javanese & Malay	Javan. & Simelu-ngun	Toba	Malay

[a] Adult male equivalent.
[b] More than 40% of total farm receipts.
SOURCES: Penny [1964], Table 2.1, p. 32.

data collected cover resource availability, costs and returns, land use, and farming methods. In addition, each farmer was queried regarding changes in farm size, crops grown, and farming methods that have occurred within his working lifetime. The villages were selected to include the major type of farming areas in the province.[3] They differ in height above sea level (range 10 to 1,400 meters), rainfall (range 1,400 to 3,300 mm) and other physical features. They are also at differing distances from the major market (15 to 250 km.). The farmers are from five distinct ethnic groups: in four villages the farmers are from single ethnic groups; in the remainder, they are from mixed backgrounds. In most villages the farmers interviewed were randomly chosen (See Table 5.15).

3. No proper basis exists yet for choosing a representative sample of villages. Suffice it to say that the eight villages chosen are each similar to other villages in the area (and different from each other).

The agriculture of North Sumatra is diverse. The diversity imposed by natural factors and complicated by ethnic and cultural factors is further complicated by the recent history of the area. The Dutch came to settle, and rule, in the 1860's; in the following 80 years a large and highly profitable plantation industry (mostly rubber) was built up in the lowlands on the east coast. The Dutch also built many roads (mostly for the estates or for military purposes), to which almost all villages in the province, including the eight studied, have access.

Farmers also have relatively free access to land; land prices are often less than the value of one year's production. As they have ready access to markets and to land, the farmers might be said to be operating in the same economic environment. Many unexploited or partly exploited economic opportunities are available in all villages. In two of them the most profitable alternative for some farmers is to migrate to another area, and though no individual farmer faces exactly the same set of development opportunities many have already done so. Thus, even in his home village, there is nothing to prevent any man who so wishes from increasing his income substantially.

AN INDEX OF ECONOMIC-MINDEDNESS

Despite the fact that all the farmers studied are operating in the same economic environment, their responses to opportunities for increasing their incomes have been diverse. The eight villages were ranked on an index of economic-mindedness (see Fig 5.1).

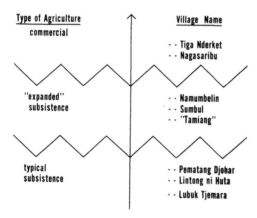

Figure 5.1. Ranking and Classification of Villages

Roughly 50 years ago the farmers in all villages would have fallen into the "typical subsistence" or "pure subsistence" categories. At that time almost no commercial (cash) crops were grown, no artificial fertilizer or insecticides were bought, nor did farmers use any improved seed. Since then some farmers have become commercial farmers, others remain tradition-bound, while yet others are in transition from subsistence to commercial farming. Two matters must be covered before we discuss how the index was constructed and the implications of the observed variations between villages for a theory of agricultural development.

First, some definitions. The farmers have been classified according to their attitude towards economic change; thus my use of the clumsy compound adjectives. My reason for employing new terms is that the words "subsistence" and "commercial" have far too many meanings!

The first agriculture was *pure subsistence agriculture*. It is characterized by primitive methods, little or no surplus, and low cultural development. Long-lasting but necessarily very small and "primitive" civilizations have been built on the basis of this type of agriculture. The farmers must of necessity be subsistence-minded because output is low, there are no markets nor any obvious way of increasing their agricultural productivity.

In many parts of the world pure subsistence agriculture has given way to *typical subsistence agriculture*. The latter is more productive than the former—farmers produce surpluses and live in an exchange economy. Many large and imposing civilizations, the so-called agrarian empires, have been built on the surplus derived from this type of agriculture. Subsistence states or empires may also have a static economy, as the agricultural surplus needed to sustain the nonfarming groups may be maintained for many centuries.

"Expanded" subsistence agriculture is a transitional type and comes into being when the agricultural surplus is used for other than the traditional subsistence purposes of pyramid building, meeting the costs of the Roman Legions or erecting Olympic stadia. In an economy with an "expanded" subsistence agriculture, exchange relations between agriculture and the rest of the economy both become more important and assume different forms. Farmers, from either pure subsistence or typical subsistence backgrounds, begin to produce for wider markets and to produce industrial raw materials. "Expanded" subsistence agriculture may evolve into commercial agriculture, or the economy may retrogress to a typical subsistence situation (at perhaps a different level than previously).

Once economic development is solidly under way, *commercial agriculture* becomes the rule. After a certain point in the development process has been reached, retrogression becomes highly unlikely.

It should be noted that all economies, except the very small and the very primitive, are characterized by exchange relations. Thus one should not seek to differentiate between subsistence and commercial agriculture merely by the existence or absence of exchange relations. The differences lie in the size and composition of the surplus, the uses to which it is put, and the attitudes of both producers and users of agricultural products toward economic activity.

The other matter that should be touched on before describing how the villages were ranked on the index of economic-mindedness is why it was that the village and not the individual farmer was used as the unit of analysis [Penny, 1964, Ch. 2]. The reason is that the within-village differences in economic-mindedness were much narrower than the between-village differences. This observation is particularly true for villages where the farmers are already economic-minded *or* remain subsistence-minded. In villages with rank numbers III, IV, and V—that is, those in the "expanded" subsistence category— interpersonal differences are somewhat greater than in the other five villages studied.

The index is a device to show in a summary, yet convincing, way that farmer behavior and attitudes towards economic activity are indeed different from village to village. It is all too often simply accepted that peasant farmers are either reluctant, because they are tradition-bound, or unable, because of resource limitations, or both, to initiate or otherwise participate actively in the process of agricultural development. It is only after it has been shown that farmers do in fact differ in these regards—as they do in North Sumatra—that it becomes possible to ask why they differ. Only after the realities of the rural situation are understood does it become possible to formulate and execute effective agricultural development policies.

The index was formed by ranking (the farmers in) each village according to an evaluation of management behavior. Ten indicators, each of which permitted inter-village comparisons, were used.[4] They were:

1. the extent to which commercial crops are grown (monotonic relationship with economic-mindedness);[5]

2. the willingness of farmers to give up growing certain crops (have they given up unprofitable crops in the past?);

3. the planting intentions of farmers (do farmers intend to move in the direction of more profitable crops?);

4. the extent to which farmers are willing to rely on off-farm sources of planting materials (monotonic relationship);

5. the pest and disease control methods used (are farmers willing to sacrifice *and* organize in order to control pests and diseases better?);

6. the number of rice-varieties grown (the fewer, the more the economic-mindedness);

7. the use of labor-saving devices (monotonic relationship—adoption of labor-saving devices is often resisted owing to fear of social disruption);

8. the use of purchased production requisites (monotonic relationship);

9. the uses to which borrowed money is put (with the same income, the economic-minded farmer will borrow for production, the "expanded"-subsistence farmer will prefer not to borrow, and the subsistence-minded farmer will borrow for consumption and to finance ceremonies);

10. the dependence of farmers on bought food (monotonic relationship).

A second index, based on an evaluation of farmers' attitudes to economic activity, was used to check the validity of the first.[6] Three items were used to form this second index:

1. the reasons farmers themselves give for growing the crops they do (farmers know that they're economic-minded or subsistence-minded!);

---

4. The coefficient of concordance for the final ranks assigned the villages was 0.785, significant at the 0.001 level. The rank correlation coefficients between each village's rank on one indicator and its final overall rank ranged between 0.75 and 1.00. All but four of these correlation coefficients were significant at the 0.01 level. The remainder were significant at the 0.05 level.

5. Commercial crops are all those grown primarily in response to market demand. Conversely, subsistence crops are those grown primarily to meet the farmer's needs, the surplus, if any, being for sale. Thus rice would be classed as a subsistence crop in both Indonesia and Thailand, even though in the latter country it is the principal agricultural commodity that is traded. On the other hand, corn would be classed as a subsistence crop in Indonesia but not in Thailand. Throughout Asia, including North Sumatra, factor returns to subsistence crops are lower than those for commercial crops. This is a large part of the reason why those well-known profit-making institutions, the estates, rarely if ever grew rice, corn, peanuts, soybeans, or other subsistence crops.

6. The coefficient of concordance in this case was 0.869, significant at the 0.02 level. The correlation between a village's rank on the first (main) index and its rank on the second was 0.95 (significant at 0.01 level).

2. the obstacles to increased production as seen by farmers (are farmers aware of the possibilities for increased production that are within their control, or do they indiscriminately blame external forces?);

3. farmer response to extension (monotonic relationship).

North Sumatran agri-*culture* is diverse; so are the cultures of its people. Part of every culture, or social system, is the economic subsystem. It is not surprising, therefore, that there should be such a high correlation between the "behavior" index and the "attitudes' index. Likewise there is a high correlation between changes on one indicator and changes in *all* others.

The high correlations between rankings on the first and second indexes and between rankings on each indicator suggest that there is no need in practice to use so many indicators. Three indicators are enough to give a good general picture of the way farmers are likely to react in a given situation or to a given policy. The three best would seem to be "the extent to which farmers are willing to rely on off-farm sources of planting materials"; "the use of purchased production requisites"; and "farmer response to extention."

Farmers in some parts of North Sumatra have shown an amazing capacity for making rapid change. Others have made few or no changes in their farming methods or their way of life.

The farmers in all eight villages studied were subsistence-minded at one time: few if any changes had occurred in any villages until 40–50 years ago. (See Tables 5.16 to 5.18).

All change takes time. It took the farmers of Iowa 14 years to adopt hybrid corn [Rogers, 1962, p. 34]; the farmers in Tiga Nderket, the most progressive of the eight villages, adopted fertilizer in 10 years. In the case of fertilizer, too, the Iowa farmers took longer than the farmers in Tiga Nderket. By any standard, economic change in Tiga Nderket has been rapid.

By most commonly used definitions of commercial farming, the farmers in Namumbelin would be classed as commercial, since 71 per cent of all output is sold.[7] In my own

typology, the farmers in Namumbelin fall clearly into the "expanded"-subsistence category. In an excellent essay, Swift [1964] has shown that farmers who sell a large proportion of their output are not necessarily commercial, or economic-minded, farmers.

The commercialization of agriculture involves the development of a two-way tie to the market economy—input and product—so as to take fullest advantage of economic opportunity. In Namumbelin, and in many villages like it in Southeast Asia and elsewhere, the farmers do produce large surpluses and are thus dependent on the market *on the selling side*. Their dependence on the market is negligible when it comes to the purchase of new tools and equipment, other production requisites, or food.

All farmers, whatever the stage of development, make economic choices. It is only the economic-minded who continually use their resources with a view to raising their incomes. All peasants living and working in economies that are monetized to any extent value money and the things that money can buy. It is only the economic-minded who possess a proven ability to use the economic opportunities available to them.

The subsistence-minded farmers in Lubuk Tjemara (village VIII) make economic decisions. These include decisions regarding the area to be sown to rice compared with other crops; decisions relating to the intensity of cultivation; and decisions on where their surplus can best be sold—at the farm or in nearby markets. If present patterns of decision-making remain unchanged, there will be no economic progress in Lubuk Tjemara.

What then of Namumbelin? It has already been shown that farmers in Namumbelin grow quite an amount of commercial crops, principally rubber. It is likewise clear from Tables 5.17 and 5.18 that they have begun to use off-farm sources of planting materials and to buy fertilizers and other production requisites. They are much more likely to become efficient, modern farmers than those in Lubuk Tjemara, but they are either unaware of or reject some very profitable avenues for increasing their incomes. For instance, if selected rubber seeds were used, and no other changes made, per hectare production would double. Improved seeds cost little and have long been available. From

---

7. This figure of 71 per cent is not coterminous with the 61 per cent of total receipts from commercial crops (see Table 5.3). Namumbelin farmers also sell a part of their subsistence crop production.

Table 5.16. Percentage of Total Receipts from Commercial Crops
Three North Sumatran Villages

Village	Rank on index of economic-mindedness	Prechange	Now	Village rank on this indicator
Tiga Nderket	I	0%	86%	1
Namumbelin	III	a	61	3
Lubuk Tjemara	VIII	a	2	8

a Very small, and "accidental" in the sense that some crops which are now commercial were grown on a small scale for home use.
SOURCE: Penny [1964], Table 4.1, p. 128 (abridged).

Table 5.17. Percentage of Farmers Who Have Ever Bought Improved Planting Materials
From Experimental Stations or Commercial Sources
Three North Sumatran Villages

Village	Rank on index of economic-mindedness	Prechange	Now	Village rank on this indicator
Tiga Nderket	I	0%	100%	1.5a
Namumbelin	III	0	64	4
Lubuk Tjemara	VIII	0	0	7.5a

a Tied rank.
SOURCE: Penny [1964], Table 4.5, p. 133 (abridged).

Table 5.18. Expenditure on Production Requisites (Water; all fertilizers; insecticides, etc.; and bought seed)
Three North Sumatran Villages

Village	Rank on index of economic-mindedness	Prechange	Now	Village rank on this indicator
Tiga Nderket	I	Rp. 0	Rp. 15,300	1
Namumbelin	III	0	800	4.5a
Lubuk Tjemara	VIII	0	20	8

a Tied rank.
SOURCE: Penny [1964], Table 3.16, p. 106 (abridged).

an economic point of view, the behavior of the Namumbelin farmers is illogical in this case.

It is still rare indeed in North Sumatra to find farmers who are willing to use rice seed other than their own. There are a number of excellent reasons why this should be so. But with rice, the farmer does select his seed grain carefully, and according to quite acceptable technical criteria [Senosedjati, 1961, p. 11]. With rubber, any old seeds will do. Enough rubber seed of guaranteed quality to plant a hectare costs about $5; the

increase in gross yield is at least $75 per hectare per year for the life of the trees. If a farmer makes a mistake in selecting his rice seed, he can correct his error in the following year; with rubber he bears the burden of his error for 30 years or more. I should add that the Namumbelin farmers acknowledged the lack of logic in their behavior when this discrepancy was pointed out to them.

One further example should be given to show the difference between farmers in Tiga Nderket and Lubuk Tjemara. Above, it was noted that response to extension was one of the indicators used when forming the subsidiary index of economic-mindedness. One of the tasks of the students on their return to the faculty was to develop an extension talk based on an analysis of the farm management data they had collected in each village. Every extension talk prepared noted at least five development opportunities for each of the eight villages. In Tiga Nderket many of the farmers wrote down what the student said in the course of his talk, and in the discussion which followed, many pertinent and detailed questions were asked. It was clear from the questions that the farmers there had analyzed the production problems they faced and that they were stymied only because the necessary technical information was not available (there is no horticultural research station in the area). By contrast the farmers in Lubuk Tjemara could not be persuaded to foregather to hear the extension talk; they remain convinced that their way is the best way. In another village, Pematang Djohar, which ranked VI, the farmers listened politely but asked only a few questions of a very general nature.

Economic behavior and attitudes to economic activity are interrelated, as are all social behavior and attitudes. As development occurs both behavior and attitudes change; in North Sumatra a very wide range in both may be observed despite the sameness of the underlying economic environment.

HISTORICAL PATTERN OF CHANGE

It is understandably difficult to pin down the economic history of each of the villages studied. Nonetheless, it is possible to show in a general way the changes that have occurred in the economic environment facing each farmer.

There has been some trade in agricultural products along both the east and west coasts of Sumatra for many centuries. This trade was limited for the most part to the exchange of surplus food for cloth, household utensils, and agricultural implements.

In almost every case new crops were the first agricultural innovation adopted after the Dutch arrived in force in the area. Rubber came to be grown by the plantations in the first decade of this century; peasants began to grow it some eight years later. Coffee was grown by smallholders even earlier. It is easy to adopt new crops; seeds, and the like are cheap and easily transportable; little or no income is foregone if the new crop is planted on waste land, and few difficult new skills have to be learned in most cases. Farmers in the tropics have long grown a great number of crops, but they are rarely highly skilled at growing any except the major ones, especially rice. Farmers can grow many crops because the soils and climate in the settled parts of the equatorial regions are not restrictive; this also explains their willingness to try new ones.

Almost all the changes in farmer behavior reported here, however, occurred after the villages had reasonable access to roads (the 1920's). The Dutch colonial administration became more "effective" after the roads were made, and there is no doubt that the impact of colonial rule played a big part in shaking up these previously static agricultures (even though this was by no means the professed aim of colonial policy).

North Sumatran peasants, like all subsistence-minded farmers, were accustomed to rely on local knowledge and local resources. Fertilization, with organic or inorganic fertilizers, was not practiced. The arrival of some Chinese farmers—they came, in very small numbers, with the roads—introduced new knowledge into local agricultures in some parts of the province. The Chinese, too, were bound by custom and tradition in their agricultural practices, but using manure, rotten fish, and other organic materials as fertilizer had long been part of their tradition. Some indigenous North Sumatran farmers followed suit.

The Dutch established a not very active extension service in the province in the 1920's. In some villages, notably village VII among the eight studied, the research and extension work done by the Dutch led some peasants to make changes. The roads also made the farmers more mobile; 39 per cent of the farmers interviewed had worked or farmed elsewhere than in their present village. In many cases these men were exposed to farming traditions different from their own. Indeed, the farmer innovators are almost always men who have traveled, perhaps as itinerant merchants or perhaps merely to somewhat more distant markets, where they met and talked with farmers from other areas. There was no spectacular growth in economic-mindedness prior to Indonesia's independence in 1945. Of the eight villages studied, the village now ranked seventh would have been first at that time.

Independence and the nationalist revolution brought many changes. Indigenous business men quickly built up a widespread and efficient distribution system for fertilizer and other production requisites *in some areas.* Colonial restrictions on local (i.e. intra-provincial) migration were lifted, and much land previously barred to peasants became available for settlement. New villages were formed (e.g. village VI) and many old villages expanded (e.g. villages III and V). Where, as in Namumbelin (III), the new settlers were from a completely different tradition than the original people, fruitful interethnic competition led to the adoption of improved farming techniques by both groups.

Perhaps the most important direct result of independence for agricultural development was the immense growth in the education system. In Indonesia, as elsewhere, prestige attaches to the educated man. Farmers in many villages had long wanted a high-school or college education for their children; now they could hope to provide it. To do so, however, they had to produce more, as it costs quite a deal of money to send a child to school away from home. The level of aspirations of farmers for their children's education is also closely correlated with economic-mindedness.

WHY HAS DEVELOPMENT OCCURRED SO UNEVENLY?

To identify causal factors when *all* components of a social system are changing is next to impossible. Nonetheless the attempt is worth making. All these eight micro-economies have been exposed to the same external shocks. All are served by roads, fertilizers and other new production requisites are available, all village people have felt the winds of change generated by the nationalistic revolution, and there are more schools throughout the province. Many opportunities for change exist. Why, then, has the response to these opportunities been so diverse?

There is no final answer to this question. In my dissertation I examined the part played by the following factors as possible "causes": religion; family structure; land tenure; provisions for social welfare; institutional determinants of rental, wage, and interest rates; the composition of the diet; education; and others. None of these factors taken singly explains economic-mindedness.

There are two things that clearly differentiate the villages where farmers are now economic-minded from those where they remain subsistence-minded. The first is the cultural heritage; the second is the nature of the main commercial crop grown. Of the two, the cultural heritage is the more important.

Farmers do not make their economic decisions in a social or cultural vacuum; they are profoundly influenced by the customs, norms, and mores of the society in which they live. All of the eight villages studied felt the impact of colonial rule and of Indonesia's independence, yet the economies of only five of the villages have changed much. Why, then, has the reaction of their formerly stable social systems to the external shocks been so diverse? An explanation must be sought in the nature of the social systems concerned.

The areas where the greatest changes have occurred are those which, up to 50 or so years ago, had the least developed agricultural technology—the Karo and Simelungun highlands. The primitiveness of the Karo and Simelungun agricultural technology was also associated with local religion (animism), lack of political cohesion, little functional differentiation in society, and undeveloped art forms. Their culture was a folk, or pure subsistence, culture. On the other hand, the farmers of Javan, Malay, and Toba origin had, at that time, a rather more productive agricultural technology and a generally "higher" level of culture. It was thus much easier for the Karo and the Simelungun farmers to sacrifice their old methods and old ideas for the new than it was for the Javans, the Malays, and the Toba Batak.[8]

8. The Karo, the Simelungun, and the Toba people are all Batak; they have the same basic social organization and the same *adat* (system of customary law). The Dutch penetrated the Toba area earlier than the other two. There were two outstanding results of this penetration; the Toba people were converted to Christianity, and many missionary schools were set up. Subsequently many Toba Batak left the area to become schoolteachers, clerks, or traders; farming was (and is) looked down upon. Prior to the coming of the Dutch to their area, the Toba Batak had wet-rice agriculture; this is relatively new in the Karo and Simelungun Batak areas.

Further evidence may be provided in support of the hypothesis that farmers practicing pure subsistence agriculture are more likely to respond to *given* economic opportunities that the more advanced typical subsistence farmers. It is commonly believed that no progress is likely in traditional (typical subsistence) agricultures until the pernicious influence of landlords, money-lenders and trading monopolies has been eliminated. There is much to be said for this view, and where such institutional obstacles exist, little progress is likely until they have been removed. Their removal will not, however, guarantee economic progress. For example, many of the smallholders in North Sumatra are ex-plantation laborers of Javan origin. They became farmers during the Japanese occupation of Indonesia (1942-1945). It is extremely rare to find any of these men renting land to or from others. Similarly they are rarely in debt. The "classic" institutional obstacles no longer exist, but these farmers from a typical subsistence background remain subsistence-minded, using only traditional tools in traditional ways to meet their own needs.[9]

The second, and subsidiary, factor is the nature of the commercial crops grown. The farmers in villages I and II were able to grow cool-weather vegetables. Rubber and coffee were the major choices in villages III–V. Cool-weather vegetables are technically demanding, and to grow them well, the adoption of fertilizers, new tools, and more careful management is required. Neither rubber nor coffee make the same demands. See also Sjofjan and Aly [1965] and Swift ([1964].)

CONCLUDING POINTS

North Sumatran smallholder agriculture is diverse. Even though all farmers may be said to be operating in essentially the same economic environment, their response to opportunities for change has ranged from whole-hearted acceptance, as in Tiga Nderket,

through indifference to rejection, as in Lubuk Tjemara. More than anything else, a farmer's willingness to innovate seems to be a function of his cultural heritage.

It is useful for policy-makers to know whether farmers are already economic-minded, are in the process of becoming so, or remain subsistence-minded. An agricultural price policy appropriate to a situation where farmers are subsistence-minded may hinder development once farmers have become more economic-minded. The same is true for tax, agricultural-credit, and land-tenure policy.

There is quite a deal of evidence to show that with research and extension all farmers in North Sumatra could become much more productive than they currently are. This is not true for the whole of Indonesia, however, for over much of Java more drastic (revolutionary) action will be necessary before the way is clear for sustained socioeconomic development. In North Sumatra, too, agricultural development would be quicker and smoother if certain institutional obstacles were mitigated—for example, the marketing system needs further improvement, and government price and exchange-rate policy needs modification. Even so, many North Sumatran farmers have already shown a tremendous capacity for assuming the risks and burdens of economic development. In the process of becoming economic-minded, these farmers have made many changes in the crops they grow and the methods they use. Farmers cannot be described as "progressive" or "modern" until:

1. they have decided that they want to increase their incomes;
2. they are confident that it is possible for them to do so; and, most important of all,
3. they have learned how to do so.

All farmers make economic choices, but only some of them make "choices that are economic." Only those farmers who are able and willing to make "choices that are economic" may be classed as active participants in the process of agricultural development.

Three concluding points need to be made.

First, there are many unexploited development opportunities, even in villages where farmers are already economic-minded. Indonesian farmers, even the economic-minded,

9. The Simelungun farmers in village VI are in the minority there. The reason why these farmers of Simelungun origin are much less economic-minded that the Simelungun farmers in Village II is discussed in Penny [1964, 186–189]. Suffice it to say here that a typical subsistence culture is dominant in the area around village VI and that the economic decisions made by these Simelungun farmers are strongly influenced by it.

find it difficult to cooperate, even though higher incomes for all could be created through cooperative endeavor. This deficiency is very noticeable in erosion control, pest eradication, and the control of livestock overgrazing. Farmers do, however, continue to work well together in traditional ways, for example in house-building, the erection of public buildings (mosques, village halls, and the like), and keeping the irrigation channels clean.

Second, the development that has occurred to date (and will continue) in North Sumatra would have been seriously retarded had not Indonesia achieved its independence from colonial rule.

Third, it would be valuable to know the extent to which the development patterns revealed in North Sumatra are duplicated in other areas, particularly in countries like China, where institutional arrangements are different.

References

PENNY, 1964. D. H. Penny, "The Transition from Subsistence to Commercial Family Farming in North Sumatra," unpublished Ph.D. dissertation, Cornell University, Ithaca, New York, 1964.

ROGERS, 1962. E. M. Rogers, *Diffusion of Innovations* (Glencoe, Ill.: Free Press, 1962).

SENOSEDJATI, 1961. Senosedjati, "A Report Based on Data Collected by Students in the Village of Selesai in January 1960" (in Indonesian), Report No. 2, Student Research Series, Faculty of Agriculture, Medan, 1961.

SJOFJAN and ALY, 1965. Achmad Sjofjan and Ibrahim Aly, "Why Are Farmers in 'Tamiang' Better at Growing Rice than Rubber?" (in Indonesian), Report No. 3, Research Series, Faculty of Agriculture, Medan, 1965.

SWIFT, 1964. M. G. Swift, "Capital, Saving and Credit in a Malay Peasant Economy" in R. Firth and B. S. Yamey, eds., *Capital, Savings and Credit in Peasant Societies* (Chicago: Aldine Publishing Co., 1964).

II

The Economic Behavior

of Subsistence Farmers

6

Subsistence and Commercial Family Farms:

Some Theoretical Models of

Subjective Equilibrium

CHIHIRO NAKAJIMA[1]

THE AIM OF THIS PAPER is to describe the subjective equilibrium of family farms under different situations, with special emphasis on subsistence farms. Therefore, the macroeconomic aspects of the problem will not be discussed in what follows.

All the farms in the world can be classified by the following two criteria: one is the degree of subsistence production (or commercialization), i.e. the proportion of production consumed (or sold); and the other is the degree of being a family farm (or nonfamily farm), i.e. the proportion of family labor (or hired labor) in total labor input on the farm. Thus we have a continuum of two dimensions taking the proportion of production consumed in one dimension and that of family labor in another, as shown in Figure 6.1. Every farm in the world has its own coordinate in the square. We can conceive a farm of pure subsistence production, using only family labor, at one extreme and a farm

of pure commercialization, using only hired labor, at the other. Admittedly the former is rarely found in the real world, and the latter is likely to be very small in percentage.

Let us call a farm which is located in the neighborhood of the left-downward corner in the square "subsistence-production family farm"; a farm in the right-upward corner, "commercial nonfamily farm"; a farm in the left-hand upward corner, "commercial family farm; and a farm in the right-downward

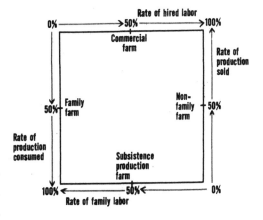

Figure 6.1.

1. This paper has been written under influences of Masao Otsuki [1941], Alexander Tschajanow [1923] and J. R. Hicks [1939]. I am indebted to Osamu Tanaka of Kobe University, Yasukichi Yasuba of Osaka University, and Clifton R. Wharton, Jr., of Agricultural Development Council for many valuable suggestions.

corner, "subsistence-production nonfamily farm." The last one will be seldom found in any society. It follows that all the subsistence-production farms are among the family farms.[2]

Due to ambiguity in the use of the term "subsistence," Wharton [1963] advocated distinguishing between "subsistence production"—as a term describing the degree of production consumed—and "subsistence living," describing the level of living. There will hardly be any objection to regarding the "subsistence-living farms" as family farms. Both subsistence-production farms and subsistence-living farms tend to fall in the category of family farms. Furthermore, it is a well-known fact that the great majority of farms in the world are family farms, regardless of their degree of commercialization and of their level of income.

Schultz [1964, Ch. 3] strongly insisted that the economic behavior of farmers, even in underdeveloped societies, is quite "rational" in that the actual states of most of these farms are in the neighbourhood of a subjective equilibrium point. I agree with him in principle. However, he did not give a clear explanation of what the rationality in family farms is or what the subjective equilibrium of family farms is.

We may regard family farms as "firm-household complexes," using Tang's terminology [1959]. Our next question, then, is whether firm-household complexes are more alike to firms or to laborers' households in their nature. Of course, the similarity between

firm-household complexes and laborers' households is much greater than that between the former and firms. There are two major reasons. Firstly, both firm-household complexes and laborers' households get incomes by utilizing their own family labor. Secondly, both seem to have essentially the same objectives: they seem to aim at the maximization of their utilities which are the functions of income and of the quantity of family labor used or, instead of the latter, leisure. By "income" here I mean the sum of income in money and that in kind. The essential difference between firm-household complexes and laborers' households would consist in their way of getting incomes or, mathematically, in their income equations; while the income equation of the former contains the production function, that of the latter does not.

Each firm-household complex or family farm has its own particular utility function as well as its own particular production function. We can say that the economic behavior of a family farm is "rational" when the family farm has achieved subjective equilibrium, i.e. when it has realized the maximization of its utility, subject to its income equation. We economists cannot say anything about the "rationality" itself of the utility function or of the production function of a family farm, say, in an underdeveloped society, even if they appear to be somewhat queer from the point of view of people in an advanced society.[3] In this paper we shall assume that a family farm always strives to achieve utility maximization.

THE PURE COMMERCIAL FAMILY FARM WITHOUT A LABOR MARKET (MODEL 1)

ASSUMPTIONS AND THE SUBJECTIVE EQUILIBRIUM CONDITION

Let us begin with the analysis of the simplest model of a family farm (Model 1), i.e. a

2. A better continuum for classifying farms would involve three dimensions, taking in the third dimension either the proportion of total family labor utilized which is sold for use off the family farm or the proportion of nonfarm income in the total income of the farm family, as an index of the degree of being a "part-time farmer." Without the third dimension, we cannot distinguish, for instance, a "subsistence-production part-time family farm," which might be rather rich, from a "subsistence-production full-time family farm," whose income is likely to be low. In Japan there are about six million farms, and almost all of them fall into the following three categories—namely, "commercial full-time family farm," "commercial part-time family farm," and "subsistence-production part-time family farm." Roughly speaking, these three categories correspond, respectively, to "full-time farm household," "part-time farm household mainly engaging in farming," and "part-time farm household engaging in other jobs than its own farming," so termed in the Statistical Yearbook of the Ministry of Agriculture and Forestry, Japan. The proportion of these three categories in total farm households were 21 per cent, 37 per cent, and 42 per cent respectively in 1965. The proportion of the first category has been decreasing, and that of the last increasing rapidly in recent years.

3. In making such an assertion I feel some hesitation inwardly. Mathur and Ezekiel [1961] pointed out that most farmers in India have a tendency to hold their "savings in kind," even though they would have obtained considerable advantages by holding their savings in money. Such a tendency means a peculiar type of utility function (as a function of cash income and income in kind) that is expressed by Figure 17a. Is there no economically significant difference between such a tendency and a tendency, say, to like or dislike an automobile or a TV extraordinarily?

"pure-commercial family farm" in a society which has a perfectly competitive market for farm products but no labor market. The farm sells all its production, but it neither sells a part of its family labor for use outside the farm nor purchases labor from outside the farm.

Assumptions regarding the utility function of the farm family are as follows.

$$(1.1) \qquad U = U(A, M)$$

where A stands for the labor hours which the whole family members (including the operator) utilize in a year, and M for the amount of the farm family's income for the same period.[4]

$$(1.2) \qquad \bar{A} \geqq A \geqq 0, \quad M \geqq M_0 > 0.$$

$\bar{A}$ means "the physiologically possible maximum of labor hours for the whole family" and M_0 "the minimum subsistence standard of income for the whole family" at a particular level of consumer's price.[5]

4. As the utility function of a farm family, the following expression will be better than (1.1).

$$U = U\left(A, \frac{M}{P}\right)$$

where P stands for consumer's price level. However, for the simplicity of operation, I adopt (1.1), assuming P as fixed in this paper. One of my impressions from Rogers' paper in the present volume (Chapter 5) is that several of his ten propositions regarding characteristics of peasant farmers' behavior could be translated into economic language. My present paper seems to be closely related to two propositions, i.e. "familism" and "limited aspiration level." U in (1.1) in my present paper means, not the utility of a head of a family alone, but that of whole members of the family. That is to say, (1.1) involves the assumptions of "one pocket" and "one pain." By "one pain" I mean that the head will feel disutility of labor of, say, his wife as much as that of his own labor. Rogers' "aspiration level" may be regarded as equivalent in amount to my "achievement standard of income," as will be stated later.

5. "The minimum subsistence standard of income for the whole family" is equal in amount to Wharton's "minimum subsistence standard of living per family." [1963, pp. 52–54] Wharton presented the expression

$$S_{ms} = f(P, E. C) \qquad (1)$$

where S_{ms} represents the "minimum subsistence standard of living per person; P, physiologic requirements; E, economic well-being variable; and C, cultural variable." I prefer a modified formulation

$$S_{ms} = Pm + g(E, C), \qquad g \geqq 0$$

where P_m stands for the minimum physiologic requirements (below which, death). The minimum subsistence standard of income for the whole family is equal to the number of family members times the minimum subsistence standard, where a standardized adult unit is taken into account.

$$(1.3) \qquad U_A < 0, \quad U_M > 0$$

where U_A and U_M are written for $\partial U/\partial A$ and $\partial U/\partial M$ respectively.[6]

Measuring the amounts of family labor utilized, A, along the horizontal axis and the amounts of family income along the vertical axis, we have an indifference map (Figure 6.2) in which indifference curves should slope

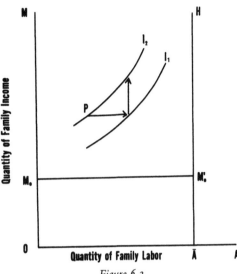

Figure 6.2.

upwards and to the right, due to assumption (1.3). Starting from any point P in the figure, an increase in A will decrease total utility, and so, in order to recover the initial level of utility U, M must also increase. In other words, it is possible to remain on the same indifference curve only if a rise in A is compensated by the corresponding rise in M. Therefore, indifference curves cannot but slope upwards and to the right.

The slope of indifference curve, being expressed by $-U_A/U_{M(>0)}$, measures that amount of M which is needed just to compensate the family for a small increase in the family labor utilized. The slope represents the valuation of a marginal unit of family labor utilized by the family itself. Therefore, we shall hereafter refer to $-U_A/U_M$ as "marginal valuation of family labor."[7] It

6. $U_A < 0$ means, of course, "disutility of labor," by which I imply both direct pain of labor and loss of leisure.

7. According to Hicks' terminology [1939, Ch. 1] $-U_A/U_M$ should be called "marginal rate of substitution of family labor for money."

follows directly from the assumption (1.3) that one reaches a higher level of utility as one moves from curve I_1 to I_2 (Figure 6.2).

As for the nature of utility function (1.1), we shall add the following assumptions:

$(1.4.1) \quad \dfrac{\partial}{\partial A}\left(\dfrac{U_A}{U_M}\right) > 0$

$(1.4.2) \quad \dfrac{-U_A}{U_M} = +\infty \qquad$ when $A = \bar{A}$

$(1.4.3) \quad \dfrac{\partial}{\partial M}\left(\dfrac{-U_A}{U_M}\right) > 0$

$(1.4.4) \quad \dfrac{-U_A}{U_M} = +0 \qquad$ when $M = M_0$ [8]

Assumptions $(1.4.1)$ and $(1.4.2)$ mean that a horizontal movement from any point to the right in the area $MM_0M_0'H$, for instance from P to Q (Figure 6.3), will increase the slope of

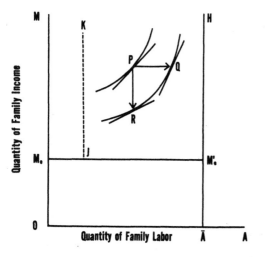

Figure 6.3.

indifference curves, and that, when one reaches the "maximum labor line" HM_0', the indifference curve will almost coincide with HM_0'. Similarly $(1.4.3)$ and $(1.4.4)$ imply that a vertical movement from P to R will reduce the slope of indifference curves and that, once one gets to the "subsistence line" M_0M_0', the indifference curve will be assimilated to

8. Assumptions $(1.4.1)$ and $(1.4.3)$ imply that both leisure (i.e., $\bar{A} - A$) and money M are superior goods for the farm family. These assumptions correspond to the assumption that both commodities x and y are superior goods for a consumer who is spending all of his income upon them. I owe the assumptions $(1.4.2)$ and $(1.4.4)$ to Tang [1959].

M_0M_0'.[9] It is obvious that assumptions (1.3), $(1.4.1)$, and $(1.4.3)$ result in indifference curves in the area $MM_0M_0'H$, being convex to the point M_0'.[10] Below M_0M_0', we shall assume, there are also indifference curves which are horizontal.[11]

So much for the utility function. Regarding the production and income of the farm family, or the family farm, let us make the following assumptions: (a) the farm produces a single product whose price, P_x, is given to the farm as determined on the market; (b) factors of production used are only land and labor; (c) land cannot be leased; (d) the acreage of farm land, B, owned and operated by the farm family under consideration is fixed; and (e) the technology of the farm is expressed by a production function, $F(A, B)$. From the above assumptions, it follows that gross farm income must be always equal to net farm income.

We shall assume, in addition, that the farm family is getting not only farm income, but also nonfarm income from nonfarm assets, E, whose amount is determined exogenously. We introduce such a variable because it enables us to analyze the effects of changes in prices (and other parameters) by dividing them into the effects of changes in E and other effects, a point to be developed later.

9. Taking into account the relationship between nutrition intake and the exertion of an individual or a family, the subsistence line M_0M_0' is likely to slope slightly upwards to the right, and at the same time the maximum labor line $\bar{A}M_0'H$ is probably just a little inclined upwards to the right until income reaches a certain amount.

10. Tang, in his discussion paper below, insists that we should take an assumption of "convexity of indifference curves" instead of my assumptions $(1.4.1)$ and $(1.4.3)$. He seems to think that (a) the fewer and simpler assumptions are the better; (b) assumptions $(1.4.1)$ and $(1.4.3)$ contain something more than the assumption of convexity; and (c) the latter is necessary and sufficient to my theory. Regarding (a) and (b), I agree with him, but not regarding (c): Because in my theory the sign of $\delta A/\delta E$ (2.2) can be determined only by having $(1.4.1)$ and $(1.4.3)$, as will be stated later, and $\delta A/\delta E < 0$ is one of my hypotheses.

The following type of expression

$$U = (\bar{A} - A)^\alpha (M - M_0)^\beta,$$

where $\bar{A} \geqq A \geqq 0$, $M \geqq M_0 > 0$, $\alpha > 0$, $\beta > 0$, $\bar{A}$, M_0, α and β are constant, will be suitable for the utility function of a farm family as well as a laborer's household, because it satisfies the assumptions (1.3) through $(1.4.4)$ to a great extent. I owe the expression to the suggestion of Takashi Takayama of Hokkaido University.

11. Reflecting upon human nature regarding work, it might be better to assume that in the area MM_0JK in Figure 6.3 (i.e. in the neighborhood of the vertical axis) indifference curves are horizontal [Jevons, 1879, Ch. 5].

Therefore, there is no restriction on E from having zero or any negative value.

We now have the following equation for the farm family's income:

$$(1.5) \quad M = P_x F(A, B) + E.$$

For the production function, let us assume the marginal productivity of labor is nonnegative and decreasing, i.e.

$$(1.6) \quad F_A \geqq 0, \; F_{AA} < 0.$$

Then, maximizing U of utility function (1.1) subject to income equation (1.5), we have

$$(1.7) \quad P_x F_A = - U_A / U_M.$$

This implies that for the family farm in equilibrium the "marginal productivity of labor" equals the "marginal valuation of family labor." The equilibrium values of A and M are determined by the simulataneous equations (1.5) and (1.7). Then the amount of output, F, is determined by the production function.

The equilibrium above stated is expressed by Figures 6.4a and 6.4b.[12] In both figures, the horizontal axes measure the amounts of labor input, A. Let us mark off a length OE along the M axis (Figure 4a) representing a given amount of E, nonfarm income from assets which we shall hereafter call "asset income," and let the production possibility curve, L_1, start from point E, then it is clear that any point on curve L_1 represents a set of A and M, which the farm family could choose. Hence, we shall call L_1, "family income curve."

Through any point on curve L_1 there will pass an indifference curve. Usually the indifference curve intersects curve L_1. It is only when an indifference curve touches L_1 that the family farm reaches a subjective equilibrium, in a sense that utility is maximized or that condition (1.7) is satisfied.

In Figure 4b, curve L_3 is the "marginal-productivity-of-labor curve" and L_2 (i.e. curve $O'DSQ'$) the "marginal-valuation-of-family-labor curve." Until A exceeds $A^\star$, the marginal valuation of family labor (i.e slope of indifference curves at any point on

the curve L_1 below $M_0 M_0'$) will remain zero. When $A = A_1$, the marginal productivity of labor is expressed by the slope of curve L_1 at point G (Figure 4a) or by the length KT (Figure 4b), and the marginal valuation of labor is represented by the slope of an indifference curve at G (Figure 4a) or by the length ST (Figure 4b). The point of equilibrium in Figure 4b is obviously at Q' where

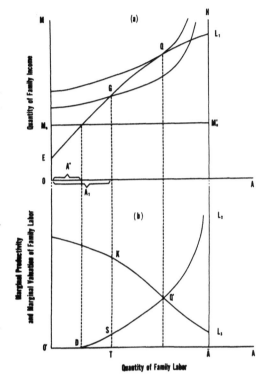

Figure 6.4.

the falling marginal productivity curve, L_3, intersects the rising marginal valuation curve, L_2.

Without a labor market, as is assumed here, the marginal productivity of labor in subjective equilibrium tends to vary from family farm to family farm. In most, the main causes will be the differences in (a) quantities of nonlabor resources farms have; (b) numbers of workers in farms; and (c) numbers of dependents in farms.[13]

12. Tanaka [1951] drew a figure which is essentially the same as Figure 6.4(a), though without the subsistence line $M_0 M_0'$ and the maximum labor line HM_0'. Insofar as I know, he is the first economist who applied the method of J. R. Hicks [1939, Ch. 1] to the family farm. Figure 6.4(b) was first presented in my paper [1957].

13. Mellor in the present volume says "Institutional rigidities stand in the way of the free transfer of resources which could prevent inequality among farms in marginal productivity of labor."

THE STABILITY CONDITION AND THE WORKING OF SUBJECTIVE EQUILIBRIUM

Let us now proceed to consider the stability condition and the working of the subjective equilibrium of the family farm above stated.

In order that U should be a maximum, it is necessary to have not only $dU = 0$, but also $d^2U < 0$. As the condition for $d^2U < 0$ for all values of dA and dM, such that $dU = 0$ (i.e. the stability condition of the family farm), we obtain

$$(2.1) \qquad V - U_M{}^3 P_x F_{AA} > 0,$$

where
$$V = \begin{vmatrix} 0 & U_A & U_M \\ U_A & U_{AA} & U_{AM} \\ U_M & U_{AM} & U_{MM} \end{vmatrix}$$

This stability condition is invariably satisfied by the foregoing assumptions (1.3), $(1.4.1)$, $(1.4.3)$, and (1.6).[14]

The graphic implication of the stability condition, (2.1), is that in the neighborhood of the equilibrium point "family income curve" L_1 (Figure 4a) should be below the indifference curve which touches the former.[15]

Effect of Changes in Asset Income

Let us now turn to consider the effects of changes in asset income, E. We shall consider the effects of price changes later, since price changes will be easier to deal with if we examine the effects of changes in E first. Let us continue to suppose, as before, that the price of the farm product, P_x, and the size of farm land, B, are given, but now suppose E to vary. Then the simultaneous equations (1.5) and (1.7) come to imply that each

14. Assumptions $(1.4.1)$ and $(1.4.3)$ result in

$$\begin{aligned} U_A U_{AA} &> 0, & U_A U_{AM} &> 0 \\ U_M U_{AM} &> 0, & U_M U_{MM} &> 0 \end{aligned}$$

respectively: by these, together with (1.3), the determinant V must be positive. On the other hand, from (1.6),

$$U_M{}^3 P_x F_{AA} < 0.$$

Hence (1.3), $(1.4.1)$, $(1.4.3)$, and (1.6) assure (2.1) to hold.

15. It is obvious that concavity of production possibility curve L_1 downwards to the right, i.e. $F_{AA} < 0$, is the stability condition of a "firm." On the other hand, convexity of indifference curves downwards to the right in the area $MM_0M_0'H$ (Figure 6.4a), i.e. $V > 0$, is the stability condition of a "laborer's household" earning wage income in proportion to the amount of its family labor supplied. We see that when both the stability condition of a firm and that of a laborer's household are satisfied, then the stability condition of a farm family must hold; but not conversely.

equilibrium value of A and M is a function of parameter E.

Differentiating (1.5) and (1.7) partially with respect to E and solving the resulting simultaneous equations, we obtain

$$(2.2) \qquad \frac{\partial A}{\partial E} = \frac{1}{\Delta} \frac{1}{U_M} \begin{vmatrix} U_A & U_{AM} \\ U_M & U_{MM} \end{vmatrix} \qquad (<0)$$

$$(2.3) \qquad \frac{\partial M}{\partial E} = \frac{1}{\Delta} \frac{1}{U_M} \begin{vmatrix} U_A & U_{AA} \\ U_M & U_{AM} \end{vmatrix} - U_M{}^2 P_x F_{AA} \qquad (>0)$$

where

$$(2.4) \qquad \Delta = \frac{1}{U_M{}^2} \{V - U_M{}^3 P_x F_{AA}\} \qquad (>0 .$$

Since
$$\begin{vmatrix} U_A & U_{AM} \\ U_M & U_{MM} \end{vmatrix} > 0, \qquad \begin{vmatrix} U_A & U_{AA} \\ U_M & U_{AM} \end{vmatrix} > 0$$

from the assumptions $(1.4.3)$ and $(1.4.1)$ respectively, A/E should be negative and M/E positive. This tells us that a rise in asset income E will make the farm family better off and thereby increase both leisure (i.e. $\bar{A} - A$) and total income M.

Figure 6.5 expresses these effects. When the asset income amounts to E_1 (Figure 5a), the point of equilibrium will be at R where the family income curve, L_1, touches an indifference curve. If now the asset income rises from E_1 to E_2, it will simply shift the family income curve upwards from L_1 to L_1', its shape remaining unchanged. The new equilibrium point will be at S. As the asset income continues to increase, the family income curve will continue to move upwards, and the point of equilibrium traces out a locus $M_0' RS$ which shows the way in which the quantities of both A and M vary when E increases. It is evident that if E is reduced so that the family income curve may just pass through point M_0', M_0' must be the point of equilibrium. Therefore, the locus must start from M_0'. Owing to the assumptions $(1.4.1)$ and $(1.4.3)$, the locus must always slope upwards and to the left, as shown by (2.2) and (2.3). With the shift upwards of family income curve in Figure 5a, the marginal valuation curve of family labor will shift upwards too from L_2 to L_2' in Figure 5b, owing to the assumption $(1.4.3)$, while the marginal productivity curve of labor, L_3, will

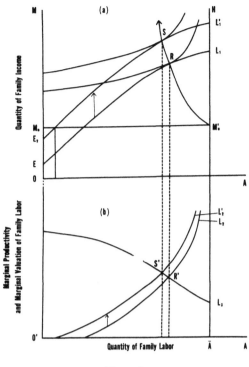

Figure 6.5.

not be affected at all. In consequence the equilibrium point will move from R' to S' along L_3.

It appears that the effects of change in asset income in the theory of the family farm have some similarity to what are called "income effects" in the theory of the consumer choice (household), and consequently curve $M_0'RS$ in Figure 5a is similar to the "income-consumption curve." Later, we shall again refer to the parallelism that appears to exist between the theory of the family farm and that of the consumer choice.

It is clear that $\partial A/\partial E < 0$ results in

$$\frac{\partial F}{\partial E} < 0 \quad \text{and} \quad \frac{\partial FA}{\partial E} \equiv \frac{\partial}{\partial E}\left(\frac{-U_A}{U_M}\right) > 0.$$

Effect of Changes in Price of Farm Product

Let us proceed to examine the effects of changes in the price of the farm product, P_x, supposing P_x to vary and E and B to be fixed. As before, differentiating equations (1.5) and (1.7) partially, but now with respect to P_x, solving the resulting simultaneous equations and applying (2.2) and (2.3), we obtain

$$(3.1) \quad \frac{\partial A}{\partial P_x} = F \cdot \left(\frac{\partial A}{\partial E}\right) + \frac{1}{\Delta} U_M F_A \ (\gtrless 0)$$

$$(3.2) \quad \frac{\partial M}{\partial P_x} = F \cdot \left(\frac{\partial M}{\partial E}\right) + \frac{1}{\Delta} U_M P_x F_A^2 \ (>0)$$

where Δ is the same as (2.4).

Since $F = -\partial E/\partial P_x$ from (1.5), when E is not taken as given but F and M are taken as given, it follows from (3.1) and (3.2) that the second terms of the right-hand sides of these equations represent respectively the effects on A and M of a change in P_x combined with such a change in E as would enable the farm family, if it chose, to have the same amounts of A and M as before, in spite of the change in P_x. For convenience, let us call the first terms of the right-hand sides of (3.1) and (3.2) "income-effect" terms and the second terms "substitution-effect" terms, though they are not so felicitous here. In (3.1) the income-effect term should be negative and the substitution-effect term positive, and hence the total effect is indefinite. On the other hand, in (3.2) both terms are positive, and consequently the total effect must be positive too.

These effects are expressed by Figure 6.6. Given a rise in the price of the farm product (from P_x to P_x') the family income curve will shift upwards from L_1 to L_1' in Figure 6a, and thereby in Figure 6b both the marginal (value) productivity curve and the marginal valuation curve will shift upwards respectively from L_3 to L_3' and from L_2 to L_2'. Consequently the equilibrium points will move from Q to S in Figure 6a and from Q' to S' in Figure 6b. In Figure 6a curve $L_1^\star$ passing through Q is drawn so that the vertical distances between curves L_1' and $L_1^\star$ at every value of A may be the same. $L_1^\star$ touches an indifference curve at point R. Thus R is the point of equilibrium if the asset income is reduced by the length $EE^\star$ and P_x remains unchanged.

We now see that a movement of the equilibrium point from Q to S is equivalent to a roundabout movement from Q to R and then from R to S. In Figure 6a it follows from the convexity of indifference curves and the concavity of curve $L_1^\star$ downwards to the right that point R must lie to the right of point Q. Point S in turn must be to the left of R, as shown before. Then a rise in the

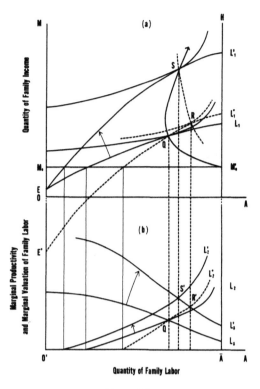

Figure 6.6.

price of the farm product affects the amount of family labor utilized in two ways. On the one hand, it raises the marginal value productivity of labor, and there will be an increase in family labor utilized (from Q to R), which we have called "substitution effect." On the other hand, a rise in the price makes the farm family better off by the length $EE^\star$, and thereby it will reduce the family labor input (from R to S); its effect along this channel is what we have designated as the "income effect." The total price effect on the amount of family labor utilized is the sum of these two opposite effects, and so its sign will be indefinite. The effect on the family income, however, will be definite. R invariably lies above Q and S above R, and hence S must be above Q. Consequently curve QS, i.e. the locus of points of equilibrium in response to the changes in the price of the farm product, P_x, may slope upwards either to the left or to the right. However, if P_x is reduced so that the family income curve may just pass through point M'_0 (such a price may be called "subsistence price" for the

farm family), the equilibrium point must be exactly at M'_0. Consequently curve QS, the locus of the equilibrium points, must start from point M'_0. Thus, curve QS is likely to be inclined upwards to the left, at least where P_x is not much above the "subsistence price."

It appears that there is some similarity between curve QS in Figure 6a and the "price-consumption curve" like the one between curve RS in Figure 6a (or curve RS in Figure 5a) and the "income-consumption curve." Here again we find a parallelism between the theory of the family farm and that of the consumer choice.[16]

The marginal productivity curves, L_3 and L'_3 (Figure 6b), correspond to L_1 and L'_1 (or $L^\star_1$) (Figure 6a) respectively. Similarly the marginal valuation curves, L_2, L'_2 and $L^\star_2$ (Figure 6b) correspond to L_1, L'_1 and $L^\star_1$ (Figure 6a) respectively. Thus, in Figure 6b, the substitution effect on family labor utilized owing to a change in P_x is represented by the shift of the equilibrium point from Q' to R', and the income effect by that from R' to S'.

The effects of changes in P_x on the equilibrium values of the output, F, and of the marginal value productivity of labor, $P_x F_A$, respectively are:

$$(3.3) \qquad \frac{\partial F}{\partial P_x} = F_A \cdot \left(\frac{\partial A}{\partial P_x} \right) \gtreqless 0$$

$$(3.4) \qquad \frac{\partial}{\partial P_x} (P_x F_A) = P_x F_{AA} F \cdot \left(\frac{\partial A}{\partial E} \right) + \frac{V}{\varDelta} \frac{F_A}{U^2_M} > 0.$$

The second term of the right-hand side in (3.4) means "substitution effect" and the first term "income effect." They are represented by the movement from Q' to R' and that from R' to S' respectively.

Since we are assuming output F as equivalent to the supply of the product of the family farm in this model, $\partial F/\partial P_x$ happens to

16. Compare Figure 6.5a and Figure 6.6a in this paper with Figure 5 and Figure 8 in Hicks [1939]. However, Figure 8 does not exactly coincide with the explanation in the mathematical appendix in his book. My Figure 6a corresponds to Hicks' Figure 8 so modified as to coincide with his explanation in the mathematical appendix. It is interesting that both the locus of the equilibrium points responding to changes in E (curve RS in Figure 6.5a) and the locus responding to changes in P_x (curve QS in Figure 6.6a) start from a single point E'_0 in the case of the family farm, whereas the "income-consumption curve" and the "price-consumption curve" start from different points in the case of the consumer choice.

represent the slope of the "individual supply curve" of the product. The implication of (3.3) is that it depends upon the relative weights of the income effect and the substitution effect whether the supply curve will slope upwards to the right or to the left. In the case of a firm, its supply curve usually slopes upwards to the right owing to the lack of income effects.

Tanaka [1962] advanced a theorem regarding the slope of curve QS in Figure 6a, as well as that of the supply curve of the single product in a purely commercial family farm, for the case where the farm's income is in proportion to the output. If the "income elasticity of the marginal valuation of family labor" is less (larger) than unity at any point, say Q, in the area $MM_0M_0'H$ in Figure 6a, then the slope of curve QS at Q must be positive (negative). It is obvious that in the range in which the slope of QS in Figure 6a is positive (negative), the slope of the individual supply curve of the product must be positive (negative). Tanaka's theorem [1962] will be expressed as follows:

(3.5) if $M = P_x \cdot F(A; B)$,

$$\frac{\partial Z}{\partial M} \bigg/ \frac{Z}{M} \lesseqgtr 1 \text{ results in } \frac{\partial A}{\partial P_x} \gtreqless 0 \text{ and } \frac{\partial F}{\partial P_x} \gtreqless 0,$$

where Z stands for $-U_A/U_M$ (the marginal valuation of labor).

Here we must recall that we are assuming in this model a single product and no home consumption of farm product. If a family farm is producing a number of products, a rise in the price of an individual product will induce not only the substitution of the product (or income) for leisure to which we have already referred, but also the substitution of the product in question for a wide range of other products. On the other hand, the income effect, owing to a change in the price of an individual product in the farm producing many kinds of products, is likely to be smaller than in the case of a farm practicing monoculture. Therefore, so far as the effects of a change in the price of a single product are concerned, the possibility that the substitution effect overwhelms the income effect will be larger in the case of a family farm producing a number of products than in the case of a farm family of monoculture [Krishna, 1963]. The problem of the relation-

ship between home consumption and the supply of the farm product will be considered later.

Effects of Changes in Farm Size

Our model will now be examined when there are changes in B, the size of farm land possessed and operated by the farm family, taking P_x and E as given. Following similar procedures with respect to equations (1.5) and (1.7) as before, we have

$$(3.6) \quad \frac{\partial A}{\partial B} = P_x F_B \left(\frac{\partial A}{\partial E}\right) + \frac{1}{\Delta} P_x F_{AB} \gtreqless 0$$

$$(3.7) \quad \frac{\partial M}{\partial B} = P_x F_B \left(\frac{\partial M}{\partial E}\right) + \frac{1}{\Delta} U_M P_x^2 F_{AB} F_A > 0$$

where Δ is the same as in (2.4). Let us assume

$$(3.8) \quad F_B > 0, \quad F_{AB} > 0.$$

The latter means that labor and land are cooperative with each other in production. Under these assumptions, the income term in (3.6) should be negative and the substitution term positive. Hence the total effect will be indefinite. On the other hand, in (3.7) both terms should be positive, making the total effect invariably positive.

Repeating the same procedure as before, we also have

$$(3.9) \quad \frac{\partial F}{\partial B} = F_A \left(\frac{\partial A}{\partial B}\right) + F_B \gtreqless 0$$

$$(3.10)$$
$$\frac{\partial}{\partial B}(P_x F_A) = P_x^2 F_B F_{AA} \left(\frac{\partial A}{\partial E}\right) + \frac{V}{\Delta} \frac{P_x F_{AB}}{U_M^2} > 0$$

Effects of Changes in Family Size

Now we shall turn to consider the effects of the changes in family size or in the number of family members. Let us divide family members into "dependents" and "workers" and begin with the effects of changes in the number of dependents. An increase in the dependent number will move the "minimum-subsistence-standard-of-income" line upwards from M_0M_0' to M_1M_1', but the "maximum labor line," $H\bar{A}$, will not be affected at all, as shown in Figure 6.7. Such an upward shift of the subsistence line is likely to reduce the slope of indifference curves (i.e. the marginal valuation of family labor) at every point in the area $MM_0M_0'H$. This is a near corollary of our assumptions (1.4.3) and (1.4.4). In consequence, the equilibrium point will move from point Q to R along the same family income curve (Figure 7a). At the same time, such a change in the slope of indifference curves will move the "marginal-valuation-of-family-labor curve" downwards to the right, and thereby the equilibrium point will shift from Q' to R' along the unchanged "marginal-productivity-of-labor curve" (Figure 7b). Thus, an increase in the number of the dependent members of a farm family will increase the family labor utilized, A; output, F; and income, M; but reduce the marginal productivity of labor (which in equilibrium always equals the marginal valuation of labor). Here we must not overlook that such a change is likely, not only to lower the income per family member, but also to increase the labor hours per worker.[17]

Let us turn to the effects of the changes in the number of workers in a farm family. The addition of a worker will not only raise the subsistence income line (usually more than that of one dependent will do) from M_0M_0' to M_2M_2', but also move the maximum labor line to the right from $H\bar{A}_0$ to $H_2\bar{A}_2$ (Figure 6.8a). Thereby it is likely to reduce the slope of indifference curves at every point in the area $MM_0M_0'H$ (usually more than an addition of one dependent will do). In consequence, the equilibrium point will shift from Q to S along the same family income curve, EQS. In Figure 8b, the marginal valuation curve will be moved downwards to the right (usually more than in the case of an addition of one dependent), and thereby the equilibrium point will shift downwards to the right from Q' to S' along the unchanged marginal productivity curve. Thus, an increase in the number of workers in a farm family is likely to increase the amount of family labor utilized, A; output, F; and income, M; but reduce the marginal productivity of labor. It is indefinite whether the amount of labor per

17. Although the addition of a child in a farm family is likely, not only to lower the income per family member, but also to increase the labor hours per workers, we economists can say nothing about whether the family would have become worse off or not; such addition of a child must have changed the family's utility function, and an inter-utility-function comparison (or an inter-indifference-map comparison) from outside will be impossible. It is a matter only the family itself can judge.

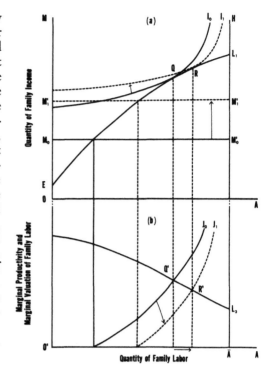

Figure 6.7.

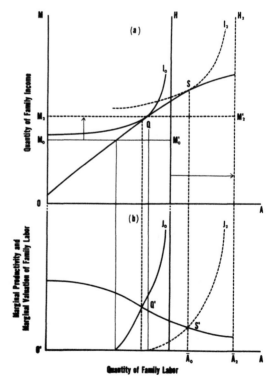

Figure 6.8.

worker will increase or decrease. However, the income per worker is likely to decrease, since the acreage of the farm land is fixed and the marginal productivity of labor is decreasing.

In Figures 6.9a and 6.9b, points Q and Q' are the initial equilibrium points. Suppose

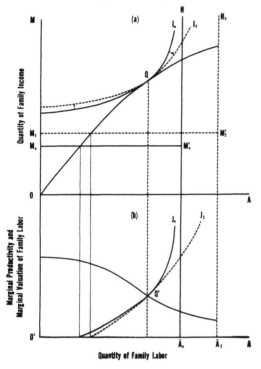

Figure 6.9.

that the addition of a worker has increased both the subsistence income standard and the maximum amount of available family labor and thereby changed the slope of indifference curves; but also suppose that the slope of the indifference curve at point Q has been almost unchanged—hence points Q and Q' continue to be the equilibrium points. Such a case will be very rare in reality, but its possibility cannot completely be denied. Then the marginal productivity (flow) of labor definitely remains to be a positive, while that of the labor force (i.e. stock of labor) happen to be zero.[18]

18. There have been disputes over the existence of the labor of zero marginal productivity. See Schultz [1964, Ch. 4] and Kao et al. [1964]. One point of importance will be distinguishing the marginal productivity of flow from that of stock, since they do not always go hand in hand.

Effect of Technological Innovations

Let us proceed to consider the relationship between technological innovations and the subject equilibrium of the family farm. We may distinguish "labor-saving innovation" from "production-increasing innovation."[19] In Figure 6.10, the horizontal axis measures

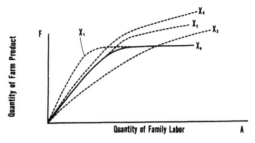

Figure 6.10.

labor input, A, and the vertical axis output, F, in a farm whose acreage of land is fixed. Curve X_0 is the initial production possibility curve. Curve X_1 stands for a labor-saving new technology; X_2 and X_3 for production-increasing new technologies; and X_4 for a new technology of a mixed type.

What will happen when we introduce these new production possibility curves into the indifference map of the family farm? In many (though not all) cases new technologies are accompanied by the introduction of capital goods which incur additional costs (e.g. depreciation, power, interest, and so forth). Suppose that the initial production possibility curve (i.e. the initial family income curve), X_0, starts from the origin in Figure 6.11, and that a labor-saving new technology is accompanied by additional costs, whose amount is represented by the length OD. Then the new production possibility curve (i.e. the new family income curve), X_1, must start from point D in the figure, and the new equilibrium point must be at R, at which the

19. Mellor [1963] insisted that it is a fallacy to distinguish labor-saving innovation from production-increasing innovation. I cannot agree with him completely. Under the circumstances where enlargement of farm size (i.e. increases in the acreage of farm land, the number of livestocks and that of fruit trees, and the like) is accessible to farmers, such a distinction actually may not be significant. But in many countries, especially densely populated underdeveloped countries, there are a number of obstacles to the enlargement of farm size; under such a circumstance, labor-saving innovations cannot be equated with production-increasing innovations.

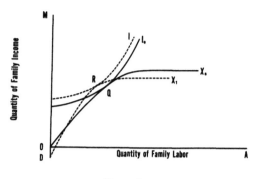

Figure 6.11.

whether or not the new family-income curve cuts the indifference curve, which touches the old family-income curve.[21]

Effect of Seasonality

It will be helpful to mention the relationship between the subjective equilibrium of the family farm and the seasonality which is one of the characteristic features of agricultural production. In Figure 6.13 the horizontal axis

new curve X_1 touches an indifference curve. The new equilibrium point, R, may be either above or below the old equilibrium point Q. But as long as the new family income curve intersects the indifference curve I_0, which touches the old family income curve X_0, there must exist a new equilibrium point that represents a higher level of utility than the old equilibrium point.[20] The new equilibrium point may be left-downwards or left-upwards or right-upwards from the old equilibrium point, as shown in Figure 6.12; it depends

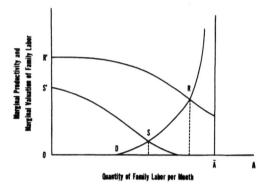

Figure 6.13.

measures the amount of family input for a month. Curve $R'R$ delineates the marginal productivity of labor for a month in the busy season, and curve $S'S$ that in the dull season. Curve $ODSR$ represents the marginal-valuation-of-family-labor curve, which may or may not shift from month to month.[22] The amount of family labor utilized and the marginal productivity of labor in the busy month in equilibrium is represented by point R, and those in the dull month by S. There is a likelihood of nearly zero marginal productivity of labor in a dull season, provided that the farm family are poor and there is no job opportunity anywhere else.

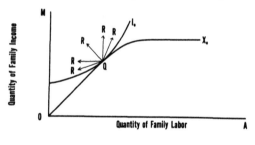

Figure 6.12.

upon what type of new technologies is adopted. The criterion for introducing a new technology for a family farm must be

20. In Japan we used to talk about "poverty by mechanization." In 1966 we have nearly three million small-type power cultivators for six million farms, whose average land size is just one hectare. The optimum acreage for such a type of cultivator is said to be about five hectares. Therefore, we have many cases in which introduction of the cultivator reduced farm income. Nevertheless, such mechanization may be regarded as "rational" so long as it raises the family's well-being. When the introduction of the cultivator lowers the farm income but raises the family's utility, such a machine appears to be similar to a labor-saving consumer's durable, like a washing machine, besides its nature as a producer's durable. Keep in mind the fact that four-fifths of total farms in Japan are part-time farms.

21. (This criterion was presented first in my paper [Nakajima, 1961].) Mellor [1963] took up the problem concerning technological innovation in a family farm using an indifference map. However, he did not take into consideration (at least explicitly) the additional costs which are likely to be accompanied by the introduction of new technology; in other words, he did not distinguish the "farm family's income curve" from the "production possibility curve."

22. In the month when labor is accompanied by more than usual disutility (whatever may the nature of the disutility be), the marginal valuation curve may lie above that in the normal month.

THE CAUSES OF POVERTY AND THE STAGES OF GROWTH

Now we shall consider the causes for the poverty in family farms in connection with their subjective equilibrium set forth above. Let us define the "farm in poverty" or the "subsistence living farm" as that farm whose equilibrium point comes very close to (or upon) the subsistence line $M_0 M_0'$ in Figure 6.4a. The causes for the poverty thus defined may be either or a combination of (a) scarcity of nonlabor resources (especially of land), (b) a low level of technology, (c) a low level of the price of the farm product, (d) a high level of the prices of goods and services purchased by the farm family, (e) zero or negative value of asset income, (f) high land rent and/or heavy taxation, (g) "surplus" family members (regardless of whether that of dependents or workers), (h) the relatively higher level of living in cities, (i) extreme shortage of farm workers, and (j) a too low "achievement standard of income." (We should keep in mind that we are now treating commercial full-time family farms only.) Conditions (a) through (f) are related to the shape and the position or the elevation of the family income curve, L_1, in Figure 6.4a. For instance, high fixed land rent in money terms will force the family income curve to start from a lower point than otherwise. Or a high rate of crop-sharing with a landowner or a high rate of tithe will affect the shape and the position of the family income curve almost in the same way as a low price of the farm product does.[23] Conditions (g) and (h) will push up the subsistence line, $M_0 M_0'$, the latter through the "demonstration effect." Condition (i), an extreme shortage of workers within the farm, will shift the maximum labor line to the left and thereby will curtail the effective length of the family income curve, i.e. production possibility curve. An extreme example of condition (i) is a farm operated by a widow. However, note that (i) does not always induce farms to be in poverty, since (i) will lower the subsistence income line at the same time.

By the "achievement standard of income" of (j) we shall mean that standard of income

at and above which the slope of indifference curves becomes nearly vertical (or the marginal valuation of family labor becomes nearly positive-infinite), regardless of distance from the vertical axis. The achievement standard of income thus defined is depicted by lines MM' in Figures 6.14a and 6.14b.[24] (Hereafter we shall call that the "achievement-income standard.") In Figure 6.14b it is obvious that the equilibrium point

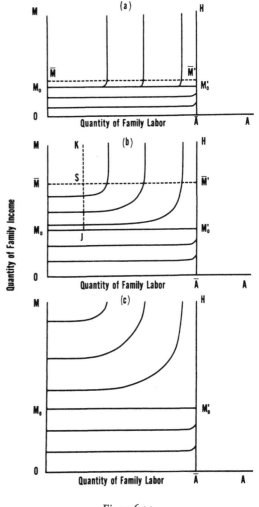

Figure 6.14.

must be below the achievement standard line MM' and above or at the subsistence line $M_0 M_0'$. If we denote the achievement income

23. Georgescu-Roegen [1960] presented an excellent analysis of tithe (or crop-sharing), combining its micro and macro aspects.

24. It may be well to regard our "achievement standard of income" as equivalent in amount to Wharton's [1963] "achievement standard of living."

standard by $\overline{M}$ and the actual income (in the sense of the income in equilibrium) by M, then it will be quite plausible to assume

$$(4.1) \qquad \overline{M} > M \geqq M_0$$

where M_0 stands for the subsistence income, as mentioned before.

Now, as is shown in Figure 6.14a, if the achievement standard line $\overline{MM'}$ is very close to the subsistence line $M_0M'_0$, the equilibrium point must be also very close to $M_0M'_0$, regardless of the shape and the position of the family income curve; i.e. the farm family is forced to be in a condition of poverty, as defined before. Thus, a too low achievement-income standard, i.e. (j), will be one of the causes which induce the farm family to be in poverty.

We may define "economic development" in many ways and in many aspects, and one of the definitions may be given in connection with the pattern of indifference maps. Figure 6.14a delineates the indifference map of the farm family (and, for that matter, of the laborer's household) in the first stage of economic development; here, the achievement-income standard is very close to subsistence-income standard.[25] Figure 6.14b stands for the second stage of economic development; the subsistence income standard has been raised, but the achievement income standard has been raised still more, and in consequence the difference between them has been widened. In the third stage, as is depicted by Figure 6.14c, the subsistence-income standard has been pushed up further, while we do not have the achievement-income standard any more! "The more, the better."[26]

Wharton [1963] insists that the "achievement standard of living" is always above the "actual level of living" and never reached, and also that successive improvements in the actual level of living induce an even higher achievement standard. On the other hand,

25. Georgescu-Roegen [1960] and Tanaka [1962] independently presented figures which are essentially the same as Figure 6.14a in this paper.
26. Line KSJ in Figure 6.14b is the same as line KJ in Figure 6.3. Taking into account what is stated in footnote 11, it is interesting that in the area $\overline{MM}SK$ in Figure 6.14b, there cannot be any indifference curve, because in this area any two points are indifferent for the family. This area means Paradise, or the goal of achievement, in the sense that the combination of labor and income designated by any point in this area represents the most desirable state for the family.

Mellor [1963] assumes that farmers in underdeveloped societies have "limited aspirations" because the marginal utility of added goods-and-services income drops substantially once his subsistence is met. Fisk's [1962] isolate group model also has a ceiling on the demand for food. The key to resolve these apparently divergent views will be found when we take into account the difference of "stages" as shown by Figures 6.14a and 6.14b. Mellor and Fisk seem to be bearing in mind implicitly the static societies in the first stage, while Wharton seems to be concerned with the dynamic societies in the second stage.

There is room to doubt whether or not there would be any society in the real world in which all families would have the indifference maps of such a pattern as shown by Figure 6.14c. It may be more realistic to assume that in advanced societies there are some families with the indifference maps like Figure 6.14c, while the rest have those like Figure 6.14b.

Mellor [1963] recommended the introduction of new forms of consumer goods into underdeveloped societies as a measure for increasing production as well as income in farms. Krishna [1963] gave the same recommendation for stabilizing the price fluctuation of foodgrains. Such a measure will be probably effective for those objectives. However, we must not overlook the secondary reaction which is likely to result from such a measure. If we define "felt poverty" as the ratio of the achievement income standard to the actual income (i.e. $\overline{M}/M$), the passing from the first stage to the second—assuming that such passing is induced by the introduction of new consumer goods—is likely to increase the "felt poverty" in the majority of farm families in the society, in spite of the probable rise in their actual income. Therefore it will be necessary to see to it that $\overline{M}$ does not increase too fast, while it is always important to try to raise M as rapidly as possible. It is interesting that Wharton seems to regard the gap between $\overline{M}$ and M as something good because the gap is presumed to stimulate economic activity. He stresses the bright side of the gap. Such a gap within a certain limit may be a necessary evil for economic development.

If we call $\overline{M}/M$ "felt poverty," what should we call M/M_0, the ratio of the actual income to the subsistence income standard? And what implications does the ratio have for the farm family in question? We may conceive three categories of poverty as follows. (a) A family whose income per capita does not reach some particular level may be regarded as a family in poverty, regardless of its subsistence income standard as well as its achievement-income standard. We shall call such a case *"temporary objective poverty."* (b) We may consider a family to be in poverty whose income is much below its achievement-income standard. Let us designate such poverty as *"upwards felt poverty."* (c) When a family's income is equal to or above but very close to its subsistence income standard, the family may be reckoned as in poverty. We may call such a case *"downwards felt poverty."* How do these three relate to each other actually? Which category of poverty is most significant in the real world will depend upon what type of society and which stage we are concerned with.

We must devise policy measures to alleviate "objective poverty" without aggravating both "upwards felt poverty" and "downwards felt poverty." In order to avoid increasing both kinds of felt poverty, heavy taxation on advertisements and no sanction of commercial broadcasting may be effective to some extent.

Another, presumably a more realistic, definition of achievement-income standard would be: Achievement-income standard is the income standard at which slopes of indifference curves just reach a certain large definite value.[27] However, insofar as we hold assumptions (1.4.1) and (1.4.3), the locus of the points at which indifference curves have slopes of a definite value must slope downwards to the right, as is shown by the curve $S\bar{M}'$ in Figure 6.14.2. But, if the locus can be regarded as being nearly horizontal in a good range, it may be well to call $\bar{M}$ (or the length of $\bar{M}O$) the "achievement income standard."

Not only Model 1, but also any other models, will be applicable to farm families even in feudal system. Insofar as Figure 6.14 is concerned, institutional factors will be reflected on the positions of subsistence-income-standard line, achievement-income-

27. This alternative definition is the result of a discussion with Tang during the conference.

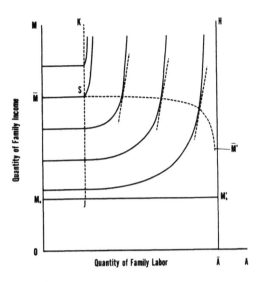

Figure 6.14.2.

standard line, and maximum-labor line, as well as on both the position and shapes of family-income curve and indifference curves.

THE PURE COMMERCIAL FAMILY FARM WITH COMPETITIVE LABOR MARKET (MODEL 2)

Hitherto we have assumed that a labor market for farm family labor did not exist. Let us proceed to Model 2 and suppose that there exists a perfectly competitive labor market around the farm family. The family, if it wants, may sell a part of the family labor for use outside the farm or may purchase some quantity of labor from outside the farm at a given wage rate determined in the market. For simplicity's sake we shall remove from our model the asset income, E; otherwise we shall continue with the same assumptions as before.

The equation for the farm family's income will be

$$(5.1) \qquad M = P_x F(A'; B) + W(A - A')$$

where A' represents labor input on the farm, whether it comes from the family itself or from off the farm, and A the amount of family labor utilized, whether it is used on the farm or elsewhere; and W stands for a given wage rate. Of course, $A \gtrless A'$. When $A > A'$ $(A - A')$ represents the amount of family labor supplied to outside; and when $A' > A$

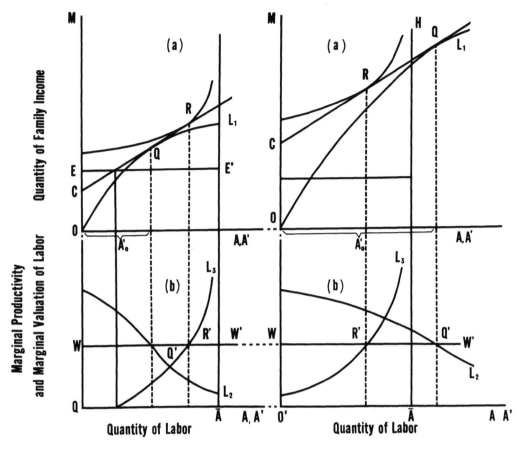

Figure 6.15.

Figure 6.16.

$(A' - A)$ stands for the labor hired from outside. Whichever of A and A' is larger will be determined internally in the model.

Maximizing U of utility function (1.1) subject to (5.1), we have

(5.2) $$P_x F_{A'} = W$$
(5.3) $$- U_A / U_M = W.$$

We see that (5.1), (5.2), and (5.3) are not simultaneous equations. At first, A' is determined by (5.2) alone; then by the simultaneous equations (5.1) and (5.3) both A and M are determined. It is clear that (5.2) is an equilibrium condition of a "firm" maximizing profit. On the other hand, (5.3) is the equilibrium condition of a "laborer's household," maximizing $U = U(A, M)$ subject to its income equation $M = WA$. Therefore the farm family may be regarded as an economic unit which behaves, in the first phase, as a "firm" maximizing profit (expressed by $P_x F - WA'$) and, in the second

phase, as a laborer's household with nonlabor income (in the amount of $P_x F - WA'$) maximizing utility.[28]

The equilibrium above stated is expressed by Figures 6.15a through 6.16b.[29] In Figure 6.15a, the curve L_1 delineates the production possibility curve. (It cannot be called family income curve in this model, as will be explained later.) The slope of line CQR represents W, the wage rate. (We may call it "wage line.") Condition (5.2) is satisfied at point Q at which the production possibility curve touches the wage line. Hence, Q must be the point of equilibrium with respect to labor input, A'.

Let the value of A' in equilibrium be denoted by A_0'. Then it follows that:

28. Thus, for the farm family under consideration "profit maximization" is a prerequisite to "utility maximization."
29. Tanaka [1951] presented figures which are essentially the same as Figures 6.15a and 6.16a.

a. When $A' = A'_0 = A$, we have

$$M = P_x F(A'_0; B),$$

and the values of A and M will be expressed by point Q in Figure 6.15a.

b. When $A' = A'_0$ and $A = 0$, M will be $M = P_x F(A'_0; B) - WA'_0$, and the combination of A and M will be expressed by point C.

c. Generally, when $A' = A'_0 \gtreqless A \geq 0$, we have

$$(5.4) \quad M = P_x F(A'_0; B) + W(A - A'_0),$$

and the values of A and M are represented by some point upon the wage line CQR in Figure 6.15a.

Equation (5.4) is the same as (5.1), provided $A' = A'_0$. The farm family can choose any point on the wage line, or below that, if it wants. But not any point above that. It is clear that a point of the most desirable combination of A and M will be on the line CQR. Therefore, the "family income curve" corresponding to the change in the amount of family labor utilized in this model must not be the production possibility curve, L_1, but the wage line CQR in Figure 6.15a. The point representing the most desirable combination of A and M above mentioned, i.e. the point of equilibrium with respect to the amount of family labor utilized, A, must be at point R in Figure 6.15a, at which the "family income curve," CQR, touches an indifference curve. In other words, at R condition (5.3) is satisfied.

The difference between Figure 6.15a and Figure 6.16a is whether point Q lies to the left or to the right of point R; or, expressed in another way, whether A'_0 is larger or smaller than the equilibrium value of A. In both Figure 6.15b and Figure 6.16b, the points of equilibrium with respect to A' are at Q', where the falling marginal-productivity-of-labor curves, L_2, intersect wage line WW'. (The lengths WO' measure the wage rate, W.) The equilibrium points concerning A are at R', at which the rising marginal-valuation-of-family-labor curves, L_3, cut the wage line.[30]

While the marginal productivity curves, L_2, correspond to the production possibility curves, L_1, the marginal valuation curves, L_3, correspond not to the production possibility curves, but to the family income curves, CQR and CRQ, whose expression is (5.4).[31]

It is obvious that the length $Q'R'$ in Figure 6.15b represents the amount of the family labor supplied to outside, and $R'Q'$ in Figure 6.16b stands for the amount of hired labor on the farm. Roughly speaking, Figures 6.15a and 6.15b depict the case of the farm whose ratio of the size of the family to that of the farm land is comparatively high, while Figures 6.16a and 6.16b depict the opposite case, where the ratio is comparatively low. In addition we may infer that, if labor is supplied and/or demanded only by family farms, the wage rate will be so determined that the aggregate demand for hired labor from family farms may be just met by the aggregate supply of labor from the rest of family farms.

Now let us introduce in our Model 2 another factor of production, say fertilizer, whose price is given as determined by its market. Then the equation for the farm family's income will take the form of

$$(5.5) \quad M = P_x F(A', C; B) + W(A - A') - P_C C$$

where C stands for the amount of fertilizer used and P_C its given price. As the equilibrium conditions we obtain

$$(5.6) \quad P_x F_{A'} = W = - U_A / U_M$$
$$(5.7) \quad P_x F_C = P_C.$$

Thus, with respect to the equilibrium condition for the factor of production to be purchased from outside, there is no difference between family farms and ordinary farms.

The Case of More Than One Product

Thus far we have assumed a commercial family farm producing a single product. If we introduce another product into the Model 2 and assume that both factors of production, labor and land, are divided into the two uses, then what will happen to the equilibrium?

30. We have been using the terms the "marginal-productivity-of-*labor*" curve and the "marginal-valuation-of-*family-labor*" curve because curves L_2 are the marginal productivity curves of A', labor input on the farm, regardless of whether it is the family labor or not; on the other hand, curves L_3 are the marginal valuation curves of A, family labor utilized, regardless of whether it is used on the farm or elsewhere.

31. The "marginal valuation curve" should never be called the "labor supply curve" in any sense. For one marginal valuation curve does correspond to one wage rate, and, when the wage rate changes, the whole curve is bound to shift.

The equation for the family's income will take the form of

$$(5.8) \quad M = P_1 F(A_1', B_1) + P_2 G(A_2', B_2) + W(A - A_1' - A_2')$$

where P_1 and P_2 represent the prices of the products, F and G the production functions for them A_1' and A_2' the amounts of labor inputs, and B_1 and B_2 those of farm land utilized in the two uses, respectively. Of course

$$(5.9) \quad B_1 + B_2 = B \text{ (where } B \text{ is constant)}$$

must hold. Maximizing U of utility function (1.1), $U = U(A, M)$, subject to (5.8) and (5.9), we have

$$(5.10) \quad P_1 \cdot \partial F / \partial A_1' = P_2 \cdot \partial G / \partial A_2' = W$$
$$(5.11) \quad P_1 \cdot \partial F / \partial B_1 = P_2 \cdot \partial G / \partial B_2$$
$$(5.12) \quad -U_A / U_M = W$$

The simultaneous equations (5.10), (5.11), and (5.9) determine A_1', A_2', B_1 and B_2. Then the equations (5.12) and (5.8) determine A and M.

The Semisubsistence or Semicommercial Family Farm (Model 3) (with Family Labor and a Single Product)

Hitherto we have assumed a purely commercial family farm, in a sense that the farm sells the whole amount of its product off the farm. Now we shall proceed to the next model and consider a family farm under conditions of semisubsistence production (or semicommercial production). Since the portion of the product consumed (whose amount we denote by X) means "income in kind," the farm family's income consists of two components, i.e. money income (denoted by M) and income in kind, X. Correspondingly, the utility function of the farm family may be assumed as

$$(6.1) \quad U = U(A, X, M)$$

where A stands for the family labor utilized, as before. Regarding this utility function we shall assume only

$$(6.2) \quad U_A < 0, \ U_x > 0, \ U_M > 0.$$

Here we will ignore asset income.

Except for the points above stated, we shall continue to employ the assumptions of Model

1, including the assumption of the nonexistence of the labor market. Then the equation for the farm family's income will be

$$(6.3.1) \quad M = P_x [F(A; B) - X] \quad \text{or}$$
$$(6.3.2) \quad M + P_x X = P_x F(A; B).$$

Obviously $(F - X)$ represents the quantity of the product to be sold, and $(M + P_x X)$ the family's total income in terms of money.

Maximizing U of utility function (6.1) subject to $(6.3.1)$ or $(6.3.2)$, we obtain

$$(6.4) \quad P_x F_A = -U_A / U_M$$
$$(6.5) \quad P_x = U_x / U_M.^{32}$$

The equation (6.4) is the equilibrium condition with respect to A, and (6.5) that with respect to X, the reservation demand for the product. It is clear that (6.5) is an equilibrium condition of a consumer's household. The above two equations, together with $(6.3.1)$ or $(6.3.2)$, will determine the values of A, X, and M in equilibrium. Then, total income, $(M + P_x X)$; output, F; and the quantity of the product to be sold, $(F - X)$, will be determined.

The Semisubsistence or Semicommercial Family Farm (Model 4) (with Family Labor and Two Products)

Next, let us introduce another farm product into the preceding model. Then the utility function and the income equation will respectively have the following forms:

$$(6.6) \quad U = U(A, X_1, X_2, M)$$
$$(6.7) \quad M + P_1 X_1 + P_2 X_2 = P_1 F(A_1, B_1) + P_2 G(A_2, B_2)$$

where suffixes 1 and 2 stand for the two products. Of course

$$(6.8) \quad A = A_1 + A_2$$
$$(6.9) \quad B = B_1 + B_2$$
[where B is taken as constant].

As the equilibrium conditions we have

$$(6.10) \quad P_1 F_{A1} = P_2 G_{A2} = -U_A / U_M$$
$$(6.11) \quad P_1 F_{B1} = P_2 G_{B2}$$
$$(6.12) \quad U_1 / U_M = P_1$$
$$(6.13) \quad U_2 / U_M = P_2$$

32. We may call U_x / U_M the "marginal valuation of X," instead of the lengthy Hicksian [1939] term, the "marginal rate of substitution of X for money."

where U_1 and U_2 stand for $\partial U/\partial X_1$ and $\partial U/\partial X_2$, respectively. Now, simultaneous equations (6.7) through (6.13) will determine the values of A, A_1, A_2, B_1, B_2, X_1, X_2, and M in equilibrium. Then, the equilibrium values of the outputs, F and G, the quantities to be sold, $(F - X_1)$ and $(G - X_2)$, and the total income $(M + P_1 X_1 + P_2 X_2)$, will be determined. It follows that the equilibrium values of $(F - X_1)$ and $(G - X_2)$ are functions of the parameters, P_1, P_2, and B.

Then it is clear that

$$(6.14) \quad \frac{\partial F}{\partial P_1}\bigg/\frac{F_1}{P_1}, \frac{\partial X}{\partial P_1}\bigg/\frac{X}{P_1} \text{ and } \frac{\partial}{\partial P_1}(F-X)\bigg/\frac{F-X}{P_1}$$

for instance, represent the direct price elasticities of output F, reservation demand X, and supply $(F - X)$, respectively. Krishna's econometric model for the price elasticity of the marketed supply of a subsistence crop appears to correspond, in principle, to our Model 4.[33]

In our Model 1 we have examined the signs of the effects of price changes by dividing them into "income effects" and "substitution effects." We could do it because we had sufficient—presumably plausible—assumptions, (1.2) through (1.4.4), concerning the utility function, (1.1) $U = U(A, M)$. Now, in order to make a similar examination as to the signs of the effects of price changes in Model 4, we must have sufficient—and even plausible—assumptions concerning (6.6) $U = U(A, X_1, X_2, M)$. What are the sufficient and plausible assumptions for such a utility function? The sufficient and plausible assumptions for (6.6) will certainly be more complicated than those for (1.1); moreover, the number of the former will be more than that of the latter. Thus, it appears exceedingly difficult to theorize on the working of subjective equilibrium in Model 4.

SOME FINAL REMARKS ON
EQUILIBRIUM VALUES IN THE
REAL WORLD

As stated above, the value of each variable is determined in equilibrium, mathematically.

33. See Krishna [1962]. He also estimated the elasticities which seem to correspond to

$$\frac{\partial B_i}{\partial P_i} \div \frac{B_i}{P_i}$$

(where $i = 1$ and 2) in this Model 4 [Krishna, 1963].

Here we should pause to consider the meaning such equilibrium values have in reality. They are ex ante values in that they are the values which the farm family is expected to determine—assuming that it behaves rationally—under a particular circumstance at some time before it starts the production. The weather conditions and other exogenous factors (pests, blights, and the like) during the production period are likely to affect the output, so that ex post output may differ from ex ante output. Besides, changes in prices and in other factors during the production period may induce the farm family to amend the production plan within possible limits. In consequence, it is highly likely for the ex post output of each product to be different from the ex ante output. If we denote the ex post output of each product by $\bar{F}$ and $\bar{G}$ respectively, in contrast to the ex ante outputs, F and G, it is obvious that

$$(6.15) \qquad \bar{F} \gtreqless F, \quad \bar{G} \gtreqless G.$$

Immediately just after the end of the production period, the farm family may well be regarded as a "consumers' household" having an income in kind of $\bar{F}$ and $\bar{G}$ and facing the markets for the two products as well as of other consumer goods. Let us assume the utility function of such a consumer's household as

$$(6.16) \qquad U^\star = U^\star(X_1^\star, X_2^\star, M^\star)$$

where $X_1^\star$ and $X_2^\star$ represent the amount of home consumption of (or the reservation demand for) each product, and $M^\star$ stands for the amount of money which will be received by the family by selling $(\bar{F} - X_1^\star)$ and/or $(\bar{G} - X_2^\star)$. The budget equation for the family in this phase will be

$$(6.17.1) \quad M^\star = P_1^\star(\bar{F} - X_1^\star) + P_2^\star(\bar{G} - X_2^\star) \quad \text{or}$$
$$(6.17.2) \quad P_1^\star\bar{F} + P_2^\star\bar{G} = P_1^\star X_1^\star + P_2^\star X_2^\star + M^\star$$

where $P_1^\star$ and $P_2^\star$ stand for the prices at that time. For simplicity of exposition, we shall substitute for (6.16) and (6.17.1), respectively,

$$(6.18) \quad U = U(X_1, X_2, M)$$
$$(6.19) \quad M = P_1(\bar{F} - X_1) + P_2(\bar{G} - X_2).$$

Maximizing U of (6.18) subject to (6.19) we have

$$(6.20) \qquad U_{x1}/U_M = P_1$$
$$(6.21) \qquad U_{x2}/U_M = P_2.$$

Simultaneous equations (6.19), (6.20), and (6.21) will determine the equilibrium values of X_1, X_2, and M. The supply of each product, $(\bar{F} - X_1)$ and $(\bar{G} - X_2)$, will be determined at the same time.

Thus, it will be reasonable to divide the decision-making of the farm family into two phases. The decision-making in the first phase will be made at some time *before* the start of production, from the standpoint of our original farm family or of a "firm-household complex," where the decisions concern both expected production and disposal (namely consumption and/or sales). Decision-making in the second phase occurs *after* production is completed, from the standpoint of a consumer's household having a given amount of income in kind, where the decisions do not have anything to do with production. Each decision may be called simply the "decision-making of production and disposal" and the "decision-making of disposal" respectively. It may be noted that in either case utility maximization is the objective.

We may also analyze decision-making

using Model 3, where we assumed a single product. In the second phase of decision-making the utility function of the farm family may be assumed to be of the following form

$$(6.22) \qquad U = U(X, M)$$

which is represented by Figures 6.17a and 6.17b. Figure 6.17a corresponds to Figure 6.14a, or to the first stage of economic development described previously, and Figure 6.17b to Figure 6.14b or to the second stage. In both Figures 6.17a and 6.17b, lines $X_0 X_0'$ represent the minimum requirement of variable X, which we may call "food." Lines $M_0 M_0'$ stand for the "subsistence-money-income standard," at and below which the slope of indifference curves become nearly horizontal. Lines $\overline{MM}'$ represent the "achievement-money-income standard," at and above which the slope of indifference curves become nearly vertical. If a farm family has a utility function as represented by Figure 6.17a, a rise in the price of the product will induce the family to sell less, and money income will increase little. This seems to be the case which Mathur and Ezekiel [1961] had implicitly in mind.

References

FISK, 1962. E. K. Fisk, "Planning in a Primitive Economy: Special Problems of Papua New Guinea," *Economic Record* (Melbourne, Australia), Vol. 38, No. 84 (December 1962), 462–78.

GEORGESCU-ROEGEN, 1960. Nicholas Georgescu-Roegen, "Economic Theory and Agrarian Economics," *Oxford Economic Papers*, Vol. 12, No. 1 (February 1960), 1–40.

HICKS, 1939. J. R. Hicks, *Value and Capital* (Oxford: Clarendon Press, 1939).

JEVONS, 1879. W. S. Jevons, *Theory of Political Economy* (2nd ed., London: Macmillan, 1879; 4th ed., London: Macmillan, 1911).

KAO, ANSCHEL and EICHER, 1964. C. H. C. Kao, K. R. Anschel and C. K. Eicher, "Disguised Unemployment in Agriculture: A Survey," in C. K. Eicher and L. W. Witt, eds., *Agriculture in Economic Development* (New York: McGraw-Hill, 1964), 129–44.

KRISHNA, 1962. Raj Krishna, "A Note on the Elasticity of the Marketable Surplus of a Subsistence Crop," *Indian Journal of Agricultural Economics*, Vol. XVIII, No. 3 (July–September 1962), 79–84.

KRISHNA, 1963. Raj Krishna, "Farm Supply Response in India-Pakistan: A Case Study of the

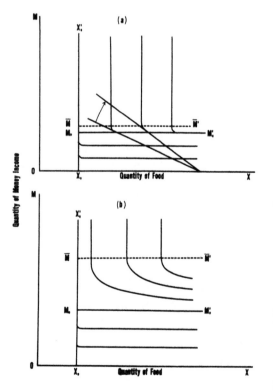

Figure 6.17.

Punjab Region," *Economic Journal*, Vol. LXXIII, No. 291 (September 1963), 477–87.

MATHUR and EZEKIEL, 1961. P. N. Mathur and Hannan Ezekiel, "Marketable Surplus of Food and Price Fluctuations in a Developing Economy," *Kyklos*, Vol. XIV, Fasc. 3 (1961), 396–408.

MELLOR, 1963. John W. Mellor, "The Use and Productivity of Farm Family Labor in Early Stages of Agricultural Development," *Journal of Farm Economics*, Vol. 45, No. 3 (August 1963), 517–34.

NAKAJIMA, 1957. Chihiro Nakajima, "Over-Occupied and the Theory of Family Farm," *Osaka Daigaku Keizaigaku* (in Japanese), Vol. 6, No. 2 & 3 (March 1957).

NAKAJIMA, 1961. Chihiro Nakajima, "Technological Innovation and the Subjective Equilibrium of Family Farm" (in Japanese), *Osaka Daigaku-Keizaigaku*, Vol. 11, Nos. 1 and 2 (October 1961).

OTSUKI, 1941. Masao Otsuki, *Farm Labor* (in Japanese), (Tokyo: Nishigahara-Kankōkai Press, 1941).

SCHULTZ, 1964. Theodore W. Schultz, *Transforming Traditional Agriculture* (New Haven, Conn.: Yale University Press, 1964).

TANAKA, 1951. Osamu Tanaka, "An Equilibrium Analysis of Peasant Economy," *Nogyo Keizai Kenkyu* (*Journal of Rural Economics*), Vol. 22, No. 4 (May 1951).

TANAKA, 1962. Osamu Tanaka, "Labor Supply and Farm Output," *Kobe University Economic Review* (Kobe, Japan) No. 8 (1962), 63–85.

TANG, 1959. A. M. Tang, "Economic Development and Changing Consequences of Race Discrimination in Southern Agriculture," *The Journal of Farm Economics*, Vol. XLI, No. 5 (December 1959), 1113–1126.

TSCHAJANOW (CHAYANOV), 1923. Alexander Tschajanow, *Die Lehre von der bauerlichen Wirtschaft, Versuch einer Theorie der Familienwirtschaft im Landbau* (Berlin: P. Parey, 1923).

WHARTON, 1963. Clifton R. Wharton, Jr., "The Economic Meaning of 'Subsistence'," *Malayan Economic Review*, Vol. 8, No. 2 (October 1963), 46–58.

COMMENT

Models of the Family Farm

RAJ KRISHNA

PROFESSOR C. NAKAJIMA has provided an interesting repertory of the basic theoretic models of the family farm. Before I offer a few comments on his models, I should like to digress for a while and try to define the nature of our field of discourse and the aims of our intellectual effort in this field.

THE NATURE AND PURPOSE OF THE THEORY OF THE FAMILY FARM

The theory of the family farm is essentially the theory of what may be called the "household firm" [Krishna, 1964a]. There are two characteristics of this conceptual creature which are crucial for economic theorizing: first, that a part of the output goes to the household; and second, that a part of the input comes from the household. The "pure" firm "purchases" almost all its inputs and "sells" almost all its outputs in the market at market prices against money payments. But the household firm simply *transfers in kind* a part of the household input potential to the firm and a part of its output to the household. The consequence of this institutional hybridization is that the models of the household firm have also to be hybrids of the theory of the productive firm and the theory of the consumer household. If the household firm is a farm, there are further theoretic complications, owing to the peculiar technical characteristics of agriculture, the institutional milieus governing the use of inputs and disposal of outputs, and the fact that the farm is usually a multiproduct firm. Therefore, theorizing about the family farm has to be more complex than theorizing about the pure consumer or the pure firm. This challenge we are now beginning to accept.

Recognizing the two theoretically crucial characteristics of the family farm, the ideal measure of the "degree of subsistence" must be the proportion of the output going to the household or the proportion of the input coming from the household or some weighted sum of the two. The sociological milieu of the family farm which inspires so much literature should reflect itself in these two critical ratios and need not enter the definition of a family farm in all its rich empirical detail. For the test of a theoretically useful definition is that, while catching the essentials of a phenomenon, it should allow the processes of deduction and prediction to move instead of cluttering them up. Therefore, Professor Nakajima starts with a two-coordinate definition of the family farm, the coordinates being the two ratios. He restricts the home-input ratio to the labor-input ratio only. But, in principle, the proportion of the *total* input coming from the household is the proportion required in the definition. When the purpose is merely to *measure* the degree of subsistence the proportion of output going to the household—*the home consumption ratio*—alone should suffice, for all inputs are rewarded by output. In terms of this measure, the pure subsistence farms (with a 100 per cent home-consumption ratio) must be a small and diminishing proportion of the farms of the farm world (the world, that is, where farms can be defined.) At the other end of the scale, the pure commercial farms (with a zero home-consumption ratio) are simply *firms*. The major part of the farm world seems to lie in the intermediate zone. (In the intermediate zone we can distinguish between *dominantly commercial* farms, with a less than 50 per cent home-consumption ratio, and *dominantly subsistence farms*, with a more than 50 per cent home-consumption ratio.) Hence our interest in what must be called "dual agriculture," the agriculture whose output partly goes home and partly goes out.

Almost everywhere "dual agriculture" is transitional agriculture, and it cannot be overemphasized that the transition is usually a one-way affair: the home-consumption ratio keeps falling (and the sale ratio rising) —not necessarily to zero, but to some critical limit. This unidirectional movement is forced fundamentally by three forces: the development of transport and communications, the monetization of economic relations, and technological change. There is stagnation mainly in areas which still remain unaffected by any of these forces. In all other areas, while "dual agriculture" may persist for a long time, the subsistence element of the duality (and with it the good old Peasant, with a capital P, and the anthropologico-sociological

picture of which he has been the centerpiece) is a slowly dying entity; and the market element is the growing part. The slow death of the reality corresponding to a conceptual category always disturbs the disciplines which have invested so much in the category. But our categories must die and develop with the realities which they are intended to comprehend.

Without being a crude Marxist, one can acknowledge the cold fact that techno-economic forces are storming or eroding the fortresses of the social-institutional deposits of history in large areas of the peasant world. The conservative, homosociologicus peasant, the market-insensitive, immutable, unpersuadable peasant, the kin-bound, caste-bound, contented peasant seems to be disappearing— slowly but unmistakably. Hence the need for dominantly economic models to predict the behavior of the "dual peasant" gradually shedding his old subsistence soul and strengthening his partly commercial soul.

In building and choosing our models, however, we have to bear some methodological norms in mind. First, as Marshall emphasized and recent econometrics has confirmed, relations can be found to be theoretically "normal" only for aggregates of a reasonable size. The single individual's supply-and-demand curves may be abnormal and yet the market supply-and-demand curves may be normal. Second, no matter how abstract our primary concepts (such as a utility function) are, the fruits of theorizing must, in the decades of econometrics, be predicted relations which are empirically testable. They must have variables whose empirical correlates exist in the available data or can be computed without prohibitive cost. Otherwise we remain stuck with verbal controversies about unverifiable *directional* statements. Third, we should give priority in theoretical and estimation work to relations whose implications aid the formulation of better growth policies (or the avoidance of bad policies).

MODEL I

The results of Professor Nakajima's basic model I are summarized in Table 6.1. The model is essentially the income-leisure model of the traditional texts, with the crucial

Table 6.1. Summary of Results of Model 1

RELATION NO.	GIVEN	AUTONOMOUS VARIATION	A	F	M	VMP_A	M/N	A/N	A/N_W	M/N_W
					CONSEQUENTIAL VARIATIONS IN					
I (a)	B, N, P	E increases	−	−	+	+				
I (b)	B, E, N	P increases	?	?	+	+				
I (c)	E, N, P	B increases	?	?	+	+				
I (d)	B, E, P	Nd increases	+	+	+	−		+		
I (e)	B, E, P	Nw increases	+	+	+	−			?	−
I (f)	B, E, P	Technological change	+	+	+					
I (g)	B, E, P	–do–	−	−	−					
I (h)	B, E, P	–do–	K	+	+					
I (i)	B, E, P	–do–	−	K	K					

Symbols

A	Family labor input		Nw	Number of workers in the family
B	Land input		P	Price
E	Asset income		VMP_A	Value of the marginal product of labor
F	Output		K	Constant
M	Money income		+	Increases
N	Number of family members		−	Decreases
Nd	Number of dependents		?	Uncertain

difference that while in the text models the equilibrium labor input is given by the tangency of the income-leisure indifference curve and the income line, representing a fixed wage, here the income line gives place to the family-income *curve* which, at a constant price of output, has the shape of the familiar product of labor curve. The (b) figures show the intersection of the "marginal valuation of income curve," depicting the increments of income required to induce additional work, and the marginal-product-of-labor curve depicting the increments of labor *needed* to earn additional income in the given technoinstitutional situation.

Table 6.1 shows that, ceteris paribus, the effects of an increase in asset income and of an increase in family size on labor input, total output, and income are what we would intuitively expect. An increase in asset income increases income and decreases output and labor input. An increase in family size increases the total labor input, income, and total output. But in the two important cases where intuition leaves us uncertain, calculus happens to do no better because the uncertainty is inherent in the cases. We cannot say for sure whether an increase in price increases or decreases the labor input and the total output (Case I (b) in Table 6.1). The signs of the slopes of the labor-supply curve and the output-supply curve, in which we are most interested as economists, remain

dubious. And when the land input is allowed to increase, we are again unable to say whether the labor input or the total output will increase or not (Case I (c)). Of course, it is nevertheless advantageous to know what we can and what we cannot infer rigorously from our assumptions. But it remains true that in the cases in which we are intensely interested, we cannot even make directional statements. It seems to me that we can go further if we write relations which have numerical counterparts, so that, from the known ranges of magnitude of the parameters which determine the labor-supply curve and the output-supply curve, we can predict the signs of the slopes of these curves under various constellations of those magnitudes. Thus by sacrificing some theoretical rigor, we can get a little more empirical predictive power.[1]

In the technological change cases, Professor Nakajima shows that, depending on the nature of the change, output will increase or remain the same, while the peasants may increase, decrease, or maintain their labor input. Figure 6.12 also indicates a possibility which seems highly improbable, viz. that following technological change, peasants *reduce* their labor input so much that output

1. It is this consideration which led me some time ago to write a set of relations determining the elasticity of the market supply of a subsistence crop in such a way that, from some known parameter ranges, I could compute the magnitude and sign of the elasticity [Krishna, 1962].

falls. But Professor Nakajima explains in a footnote that where, as in Japan, a majority of farms are part-time farms, peasants may use labor-saving mechanization to increase their leisure even to the point of reducing farm income (presumably because non-farm income can be increased, with a part of the labor saved by more than the decrease in farm income). The only possibility Professor Nakajima rules out is the one that involves peasants working more and earning less after technological change.

The analysis of the labor input in busy-season months and dull-season months is, I am afraid, very mechanical. We do not get anywhere by just drawing a higher marginal-product curve for a busy-season month and thus showing that more labor will be put in such a month than in a dull month (Figure 6.13), for there is surely some complementarity between the labor input of successive months over a crop season. This becomes clear if we consider what the "product" of labor in a dull month means, or whether all or most of the product is the product of the harvest labor month. Perhaps on technological grounds we should not disaggregate the labor input of a crop season. I wonder whether, given their technology and the crop complex, peasants have much choice in respect of the time distribution of the labor input over a crop season. And if they have, the explanation of this distribution will have to be very complicated. Indeed, one might go further and say that it might be a useful exercise to construct alternative models of the family farm in which the actual labor input (out of the total potential labor input of a farm family) is not a decision variable. Instead, we might postulate that what the farmer decides directly is an *output mix* achievable with the technology familiar to him and the resources available to him. He chooses this mix so as to maximize his income subject to certain limit constraints on input availabilities. Given the technology, the actual input levels are then determined implicitly.

Professor Nakajima's listing of the causes of poverty reflecting themselves in the family income curve or in the subsistence line or in the maximum-labor line is interesting (though it is inaccurate to mention the high prices of goods purchased by farmers and high rent and high taxation as causes of poverty within

the framework of the model under discussion, because one of the assumptions of the model is that all prices remain constant and gross farm income equals net farm income).

The introduction of an "achievement-income line" above the subsistence income line in Figure 6.14 enables Professor Nakajima to make the equilibrium income lie between the two and to philosophize about the effort-stimulating effect of "felt poverty" (defined as $\overline{M}/M$) and about "felt riches" (a phrase we might coin in answer to Professor Nakajima's query on page 178) measured by M/M_0. He also relates a low achievement-income line, a higher achievement line, and what I may call "the topless income-labor indifference map" (Figure 6.14c) to three successive stages of economic development. The oriental in Professor Nakajima insists that $\overline{M}$ should not "increase too fast" or disappear. Since this is subjective metaphysics, rather than economics, I may also enter my own subjective view that the aspiration maps of peasants go topless very soon after the growth of transport and communications, and what keeps the peasants where they are is not so much limited aspiration but limited resource availability. I may add, as another oriental being, that "felt riches" have little correlation with material income except a negative one at extremely low levels of the latter.

OTHER MODELS AND A FIFTH

In view of the two essential characteristics of the family farm (a part of the input comes from, and a part of the output goes to, the household), Models 2 and 3 are more important than Model 1. For while in Model 1 only output is marketable, in Model 2 labor is also *marketable*: a part of the farm labor can be hired in, and a part of the family labor can be hired out. And while in Model 1 all output is converted into money, in Model 3 only a part is sold, so that the utility function has three arguments: the labor input, the retained output, and the output sold.

Although Professor Nakajima makes labor marketable and output retainable separately in Models 2 and 3, I suggest that it is very useful to combine these two features in a single model. The synthetic model (let us call it Model 5) will then be the basic model of the family farm with one variable input (labor, partly family and partly hired) and one output (partly sold, partly retained). In Professor Nakajima's notation, in this new Model 5 we maximize

$$(5.1) \qquad U = U(A, X, M)$$

subject to

$$(5.2) \quad M = P[F(A'; B) - X] + W(A - A').$$

The first order equilibrium conditions of Models 2 and 3 will then hold together.

$$(5.3) \qquad PF_{A'} = W$$

$$(5.4) \qquad \frac{-U_A}{U_N} = W$$

$$(5.5) \qquad \frac{U_x}{U_M} = P$$

The labor input on the farm (A') is determined by the equality of its VMP (value of the marginal product) with the wage rate. The labor input of the family (A) is determined by the equality of the marginal valuation of family labor with the wage rate. And the retained output (X) is determined by the equality of the marginal (subjective) valuation of retained output with the price. The amounts of hired labor, the total output, the amount sold, and money income are then determined by $A - A'$, $F(A'; B)$, $F - X$, and 5.2, respectively.[2]

If we reflect on the results of the synthetic model, we find that as soon as any part of labor is marketable at all, the actual labor input on the farm must satisfy the marginality condition: $W = VMP_A$. And as soon as any part of output is marketable at all, the amount marketed or retained must satisfy the marginality condition that price equals the rate of substitution between money and consumption in kind. The first implication is testable with empirical cross-section production functions. And we find that in a number of recent production function studies in poor countries, the divergence between the VMP_L (of *actual* labour inputs on family farms) and the ruling wage has been found to be no greater than in richer countries [Heady and Dillon, 1961; Krishna, 1964b]. The second

implication is not testable because it is extremely difficult to estimate the empirical preference surface. And I have to repeat my plea that in order to increase testability, we should try to write models which have computable relations—between price and sales, for example.

When Professor Nakajima introduces an additional variable input (fertilizer) and an additional product in variants of Model 2, we only get the expected results: that the price of fertilizer has also to equal the value of its marginal product; and the value of the marginal product of each input has to be equal in producing every output. These are of course testable results, because empirical production functions (or their cross-sections) for farms with many inputs and outputs can be estimated.

In Model 4, with two variable inputs and two marketable outputs, again we find that the conditions involving utility terms are untestable, and Professor Nakajima candidly says that it is difficult to specify "plausible assumptions for a utility function" with four heterogeneous arguments; and "it appears exceedingly difficult to theorize on the working of the subjective equilibrium of Model 4."

The distinction between peasant decisions regarding ex ante output plans over several crop seasons and ex post disposal decisions within a season brought out in his conclusion is necessary. But I would avoid the highly restrictive Mathur–Ezekiel assumption that peasants sell mainly to meet more or less fixed money obligations [Mathur and Ezekiel, 1961]. It can be shown even without this assumption that within a season (with a fixed supply) the price elasticity of the marketable surplus of a subsistence crop can be negative. But over a number of seasons, when the output of a crop has some positive price elasticity, the elasticity of the marketable surplus of a crop is negative only under very special conditions.

CONCLUDING REMARKS

I would conclude by saying that, concerning the economic behavior of the "dualist" peasantry as a class, the following questions of a positive-quantitative nature need to be answered as early as possible:

___

2. There is another interesting result implicit in the first order conditions, viz. $\dfrac{-UA}{UX} = \dfrac{W}{P}$. The marginal subjective valuation of family labor in terms of output must equal the real wage.

1. Does the total agricultural output have some marginal, positive price sensitivity?
2. Does the acreage (output) of individual crops have it?
3. Does the marketable surplus (a) of a crop and (b) of all crops have it?
4. Is the allocation of land between crops technoeconomically rational in some measurable sense?
5. Is it true that the *VMP*'s of major inputs do not deviate from the ruling costs of their services in dual agriculture by more than they do in commercial agriculture?
6. Is the pick-up of government-supplied modern inputs positively related to the marginal return-cost ratios of these inputs?
7. Is the output elasticity of the marketable surplus greater than unity?

With some theoretically derived but empirically computable relations and a lot of rigorous empirical work to compute them, we can answer these questions. On the basis of some recent empirical work with Indian data, the answer to many of these questions seems to be positive.

Economists fully acknowledge the fact that the task of accelerating agricultural growth is primarily technoorganizational. But with the

knowledge of these relations, they can help the policy-makers to use prices to do their *little bit*, or, more important, avoid price policies which retard or frustrate the main technoorganizational effort.

References

HEADY and DILLON, 1961. E. O. Heady and John Dillon, *Agricultural Production Functions* (Ames, Iowa: Iowa State University Press, 1961).

KRISHNA, 1962. Raj Krishna, "A Note on the Elasticity of the Marketable Surplus of a Subsistence Crop," *Indian Journal of Agricultural Economics*, Vol. 17, No. 3 (July–September, 1962), 79–84.

KRISHNA, 1964a. Raj Krishna, "Theory of the Firm: Rapporteur's Report," *Indian Economic Journal*, Vol. XI, No. 4 (April–June 1964), 514–25.

KRISHNA, 1964b. Raj Krishna, "Production Functions for the Punjab," *Indian Journal of Agricultural Economics*, Vol. XIX, Nos. 3 & 4 (July–December 1964), 87–97.

MATHUR and EZEKIEL, 1961. P. N. Mathur and Hannan Ezekiel, "Marketable Surplus of Food and Price Fluctuations in a Developing Economy," *Kyklos*, Vol. XIV, Fasc. 3 (1961), 396–408.

COMMENT

On Subjective Equilibrium of the Subsistence Farmer

ANTHONY M. TANG

PROFESSOR NAKAJIMA's excellent paper deals with the equilibrium of the firm-household complex. In agriculture such a complex is found in the family farm. As a firm, the family farm makes production decisions. Under given resources of the farm, the relevant decision variable is the input of available family labor. As a household, the farm family must determine the amount of labor to be supplied. These decisions are inseparable within a firm-household complex. Although the family farm need not be a subsistence farm, the subsistence farm may be conveniently regarded as being always a

family farm; hence the relevance of Professor Nakajima's model to subsistence farms. This conclusion stands however one may wish to define "subsistence"—in terms of income level or the degree of home consumption of the output of the farm or both.

Professor Nakajima examines the behavior of the family farm under the following conditions: (1) rising nonfarm asset income, (2) increasing farm prices, (3) increasing nonlabor farm resources, (4) growing number of dependent nonworking family members, (5) expanding family labor force, (6) advancing technology, (7) seasonal fluctuations in farm activities, (8) limited "achievement standard" of the farm people as a constraint, (9) the presence of a labor market, (10) the use of purchased inputs, say, fertilizer, (11) multi-product enterprises, (12) "semicommercial" production (as opposed to the earlier assumption of complete disposal of the output in the market), and finally (13) disparity in anticipated and realized output.

This is a very tall order indeed. The present paper summarizes the fruits of several years of work by Professor Nakajima. We are fortunate to have his paper included in the program, and I consider it a privilege to be its discussant. After all, Professor Nakajima's work embodies the cumulative wisdom acquired over several years of intensive research, while my own interest in the "subjective equilibrium" of the family farm has been peripheral.

Despite the obvious fact that the interesting questions in this area of inquiry are largely empirical, theoretical frameworks of the sort Professor Nakajima is trying to build may provide bases for tentative explanations of certain phenomena observed in subsistence agriculture, as well as point up the meaningful questions to ask when one appeals to empiricism. Much more work can be done on the model-building level. Two aspects readily come to one's mind. First, it would be useful to try to reach the conclusions of this paper by means of fewer assumptions and/or less restrictive assumptions. Second, the present work deals with a subsistence farm's response (in terms of variable labor input) to a variety of disturbances, all of which are being taken as exogenously given or autonomously changing. Clearly several of these as listed above are subject to control by the farm operator and his family. Thus, embodied technology is an example in that the acquisition of the new inputs is a farm decision. The related but broader savings-investment decision is similarly subject to choice by a firm-household complex. So is perhaps reproduction of family members. It is hoped that Professor Nakajima, given his unusual comparative advantage in the field, will continue to exploit it and extend it to new areas of inquiry.

The specifics of my assigned task are: to summarize the major points of the paper and to spell out the implications as I see them; to suggest areas where empirical research is needed; and to check the validity of the model against what I know about the subsistence farmers in the southern region of the United States—an area on which I once made a study concerning the decision-making aspects of the family farm [Tang, 1958].

To those versed in Hicks' [1939] unrevised demand theory, Professor Nakajima's model no doubt strikes a familiar ring. Of the Law of Demand, Hicks says we can be pretty sure of its validity. A fall in the price of a commodity, other things remaining equal, leads to an increase in the quantity demanded. The substitution effect encourages us to consume more of this commodity at the expense of other commodities, taken collectively. The income effect also causes the consumption of the commodity to rise so long as the good in question is normal. Even if it were an inferior good, the negative income effect is likely to be small and consequently swamped by the positive substitution effect, since a single good usually occupies an insignificant position in the consumer's total budget. Of the Law of Supply, we are much less sure how it operates. For one thing, the income effect works in the same direction as the substitution effect only if the good is inferior. And if it is a normal good, one can no longer count on the opposing income effect's being insignificant, since the good or service one sells is likely to be his sole or major source of income. The supply of an individual's labor service is a case in point. Thus, an increase in the price of labor may cause the person to offer more, less, or the same amount of labor, so long as leisure is a normal good. The theory is consistent with an individual labor-supply curve of any inclination, including those with one or more backward bends. In terms of Hicks' "unreconstructed" terminology, the fundamental assumption for his theory is that the indifference curves are subject to decreasing marginal rates of substitution, i.e. they are convex to the origin.

The distinctive feature about a subjective equilibrium model for the family or subsistence farm is that—instead of an individual or a household trading leisure for income at some given wage rate—the farm family acquires income by varying labor input along a given production function. In other words, the income-leisure transformation is linear in the case of a household offering labor for sale; it becomes nonlinear and, under Professor Nakajima's assumption, concave in the case of a family farm. This difference, as Professor Nakajima's work shows, need not require any fundamental revisions of Hicks' theory for application to family farms.

Professor Nakajima, however, states the convexity condition for the indifference curves via a set of three assumptions: both leisure and income have positive marginal utility; leisure is a normal good anywhere on the indifference map (within the relevant plane as marked off by the income and leisure minima); and income is a normal good in the same sense. These three assumptions do indeed imply convexity. But convexity need not imply them. It seems to me, therefore, that Professor Nakajima's formulation may be in violation of the principle of Occam's Razor. To be sure, for peasants to show perverse output response under rising food prices, leisure must be a normal good. But there is no reason why it might not be an inferior good within certain ranges on the indifference map. The fundamental conclusion would remain unchanged. That is, the manner in which a family farm adjusts its labor input (hence, output) to a price change is purely an empirical question; in theory anything can happen.

Turning to the equilibrium income solution, Professor Nakajima shows that an increase in farm prices must lead to some increase in the income of the family regardless of the direction of labor adjustment. This follows directly from his assumption of incomes being a normal good. Here again, the question might best be left open.

The effects of a change in the family farm's nonlabor resources upon labor input and family income are similar to those obtained under a price change. Expansion in the number of nonworking dependents, by depressing the slope of the indifference curves, is likely to increase both family income and labor input. Similar results are expected if expansion in family size takes place among working members.

On the effects of a technological innovation, Professor Nakajima rightly concludes that the necessary and sufficient condition for its adoption is the attainment of a higher level of family satisfaction. As such the income and labor input under the new equilibrium relative to those under the old are indeterminate, depending upon the manner in which the new technology affects the slope and elevation of the family-income curve. Had he not been distracted by the dispute with John Mellor over the distinguishability between labor-saving and output-raising innovations, he might have stressed more a meaningful distinction based upon their effects on the slope of the production function. A labor-saving innovation raises average labor productivity but lowers marginal productivity for the most part. While an output-increasing innovation—say, an improved seed variety that raises yield by x per cent—improves both the marginal and average productivities. (The latter's effect is identical with that of a product price increase.) The implication of this distinction with respect to labor adjustment on family farms is clear. *Even more so* than an exogenous rise in nonfarm asset income, labor-saving innovations tend to (by Nakajima's assumptions, must) lower family labor input; whereas output-raising innovations may increase it. This is to be contrasted against Mellor's conclusion that "labor-saving tools *may* increase the marginal productivity of labor and thereby induce operation at a higher level of output" [Mellor, 1963]. Under the assumed shape for the production function, the statement is formally correct. But for densely populated agricultures, the relevant range of the function is almost certain to be the portion in which the marginal productivity of labor is lowered.[1] The orthodox policy prescription would seem to remain intact: stress output-increasing innovations in countries to which the theory of underemployment is addressed. To this an amendment may be added: begin to incorporate labor-saving innovations as the Fei–Ranis [1961] turning point is approached in order to smooth out the discreteness implicit in such a threshold theory and thus to prevent the economy from being subjected to possibly damaging jolts.[2]

1. The statement follows from the plausible notion of hardworking but poor peasants in overpopulated settings, where resource stringency forces the peasant family to apply labor to a point of near-zero marginal productivity in order to eke out a subsistence living. In such cases subjective equilibrium is obtained in a range of the total product curve in which marginal labor productivity is lowered by labor-saving innovations.

2. This point is developed at some length in my paper [Tang, 1965].

Professor Nakajima is next concerned with the equilibrium of subsistence farms under the constraint of a low "achievement income standard." This work parallels that of John Mellor [1963], whose concern was to explain a "puzzling" phenomenon in the under-developed countries: namely, a number of studies suggest rather high marginal labor productivity when the input is measured in flow terms, yet there was considerable idleness among the peasants, reckoned in stocks, even while the income level is depressingly low. The low achievement (or aspiration) standard is offered as a hypothesis. This is one of those really contentious aspects of economic development. For other writers have argued for the urgency of the development task on grounds that the gap between aspirations and performance is ever increasing, with the former, thanks to the "demonstration effect," rising much more rapidly. My view is that the seeming paradox is perhaps attributable to the problem of seasonality and to a failure to distinguish between idleness in peak labor input seasons and that in off seasons. I doubt that there is much idleness during the peak seasons when labor productivity is high. I also doubt that even in a poor isolated village there is not enough internal income variation and contact with the outside to keep income aspirations of the typical villager a safe distance ahead of his realized earnings, so that the constraint or discontinuity, even if present on the indifference map, does not serve as an effective constraint.

Professor Nakajima's next major pre-occupation has to do with the introduction of a labor market in which a farm family can either sell or buy labor at some given wage rate. Such an opportunity gives rise to part-time farming on farms too small to yield an equilibrium solution consistent with the market wage. The analytical framework is essentially that borrowed from trade theory. Again, the new equilibrium labor offer (input on family farm plus the amount sold) can be either greater or less than the initial input on farms. Professor Nakajima does not consider an alternative method of farm organization. Instead of selling part of the family labor to achieve equality between the wage rate, marginal valuation of labor, and labor's marginal productivity, the farm could accomplish the same end through enlargement and

operating it on a full-time basis. In reality one would expect both processes to proceed concurrently [Tang, 1958, Ch. 7].

In this section I shall attempt to place Professor Nakajima's work in a broader context. The low-level equilibrium trap theory, as expounded by R. R. Nelson, Harvey Leibenstein, E. E. Hagen, Stephen Enke, and others, has been given a fair amount of attention in growth literature. The trap takes on substance if at low income levels the rate of growth of endogenously generated income falls short of the induced population growth rate. In these circumstances, development efforts cannot lead to lasting income improvement unless they are massive enough to clear the trap in one jump.[3] This exception is conceded to be an academic proposition. One of the elements of the theory is the assumption of interchangeability between population and labor force or, more strictly, labor input. Now if agricultural development (Professor Nakajima's third case) leads to negative labor adjustment on family farms, the trap is thereby tightened. This was noted in one of my earlier writings [Tang, 1959]. Professor Nakajima's present paper adds additional dimensions to the trap theory. Concurrent population growth means at the farm level increases in the number of dependents and the size of family labor force. The resulting depression in the slope of the indifference curves may well give rise to an offsetting (positive) labor adjustment. So that as a crude statement one might regard these considerations as a vindication of the assumption employed by the trap theorists (as well as the two-sector model builders).

All this, however, is not very satisfying. One would like to be able to say something more than "anything can happen when it comes to labor adjustment on family farms." If I may say so, this is where one finds Professor Nakajima's paper unbalanced. For the purposes of our immediate interests in subsistence and peasant economics, one would like to know in particular whether at incomes near or at the subsistence level we can say something more definitive in this connection.

3. Hagen's model—which recognizes diminishing returns as population growth (and capital formation) pushes against a more or less fixed supply of land—precludes even this possibility. Formally, this can be represented as downward shifts in the population function, hence also in the income growth income [Hagen, 1959].

My own feeling is that in overpopulated subsistence agriculture labor adjustment in response to product-price increase or other more substantive development efforts is almost certain to be negative. Let me elaborate. Upon the opening of a new country, land would be a free commodity. Cultivation would be extensive and farm size optimum (probably small under primitive techniques). Population growth eventually exhausts free land. Further growth leads to subdivision of farms, reducing their size to less than optimum. The process continues until the farm is only big enough to yield a maximum output that just meets the minimum subsistence requirements of the family. So long as cultivation remains extensive, zero labor marginal productivity may be reached at a labor input level that leaves substantial leisure. Further population pressure brings into being intensive cultivation. The introduction of labor-intensive subsidiary enterprises—such as the virtually self-contained mulberry-silk-worm-fish sequence in China[4]—is a case in point. Its effect (and purpose) is to extend the range within which marginal labor productivity is positive. This permits further population growth and subdivision of farm land. Sooner or later a stage exists where the output needed to meet bare subsistence requires a labor input that leaves no leisure at all (other than the biological minimum for rest).[5] Such a situation is probably a reasonable approximation in the severely overpopulated farm area where the peasant works hard but remains poor. It existed in English cities among workers during the Industrial Revolution when men, women, and children had to work exceedingly long hours to keep the family's collective body and soul together. Under such circumstances any economic improvement must lead to negative labor response.

Stated within the context of a labor supply, it is plausible to postulate a function such that, as we move up along the wage axis, the quantity supplied would first decline, then increase, and finally decline again. Although the statistical findings from my study on the agriculture of southern United States are at best only suggestive, they are nonetheless consistent with the implications of such a labor supply [Tang, 1958]. It may be noted once again that the derivation of such a supply requires only that the indifference curves be convex.

Fei and Ranis in their excellent article, "A Theory of Economic Development" [1961], argued that the magnitude of development (industrialization) efforts needed to complete the take-off varies directly with the coefficient of labor redundancy in subsistence agriculture.[6] If our reading of the history of overpopulated agricultures as shown above is in general correct, then the redundancy (or the complement nonredundancy coefficient, as Fei and Ranis preferred it) coefficient would not be a good basis to use in gauging the size of the development task. In fact, it can be wholly misleading. An agriculture populated by exceedingly hard-working but poor peasants (hence, an agriculture with little or no redundant labor) offers far worse prospects for development than one which yields subsistence income under conditions of substantial labor redundancy. The former may also require a larger proportion of its labor force to be transferred to industry before completing the "take-off." This also means a relatively greater industrialization effort, the Fei-Ranis argument to the contrary notwithstanding.

As Professor Schultz [1964] cogently argued in writing on the transformation of traditional agriculture, the important thing is that farm people do adjust and optimize. Whether they reduce or increase labor input and production in response to, say, a price increase is of no particular significance. For even if they choose to respond in a perverse manner, one can always lower the price if greater output is deemed a paramount consideration in a development plan. This is all very well. But a planner would like to know which way he should go in using price incentive to get the desired result. And a prudent planner may not want to take our

4. Fish are raised in ponds that dot the countryside. The waste is used to fertilize mulberry trees, whose leaves feed the silkworms, whose waste in turn is fed to the fish.

5. This, of course, is a statement of a long-run tendency—a tendency that is no more inevitable than the Malthusian trap. Its validity is limited to those settings, for which the model is intended, where population growth is a historical fact and the state of the art has remained stationary or changed too slowly to overcome the above tendency.

6. The nonredundancy coefficient, preferred by Ranis and Fei, refers to the fraction of total available labor that has positive marginal productivity.

historical speculations and limited empirical evidence as sufficient bases for action. Must he, therefore, await new evidence before taking action?

Happily the answer is no. Given the convexity of the indifference curves and the concavity of the family income curve, the planner can, by means of a lump-sum tax together with a compensatory price increase, bring about some increase in family labor input and, hence, in output. This is without exceptions. By compensatory price increase we mean one such that the new family income curve, starting now from a lower intercept (by virtue of the tax) will pass through the initial equilibrium point. With reference to Figure 6.6a in Professor Nakajima's paper, if we use $E^\star$ as the new intercept for the income curve and S as the initial equilibrium point, then the new income curve intersects the indifference curve at S from a southwesterly direction. Hence, the new equilibrium point must be to the right of S. This means a greater labor input under the new equilibrium. Under such a compensatory scheme, the farm family's welfare is also always raised.

More important from the standpoint of growth and ease of application are the proposal's dynamic implications. It has been widely observed that in the underdeveloped countries the prices of the new inputs (which embody new technology) tend to be high in relation to the price of the output, as compared with similar ratios in the developed countries. This, of course, tends to discourage the much needed innovations on subsistence farms—the essence of Schultz's transformation. The situation can be corrected by precisely such a tax-plus-offsetting-price-adjustment procedure. However, in a dynamic context, the compensatory principle to be applied ideally to each individual farm family need no longer be given strict adherence. Instead, the focus is now on the play of incentive as a policy leverage to secure more rapid adoption of new inputs. The tax might be tied to an existing land tax or to the normal output of the farm as observed from the recent past. The lump-sum character of the tax can and should be maintained in either case. This tax is then coupled with either a general product price increase or, preferably, a subsidy on new inputs. The

play of incentive arises in that producers who respond vigorously to the lowered new input prices realize a cost saving in excess of their incremental tax burden. While those who do not, suffer a net penalty. Planners can lower or raise the play of incentive as they like. The exercise of this policy instrument is not subject to budgetary constraints. Cast in these terms, the question of labor adjustment, while still relevant, becomes a strictly secondary consideration.

This is not to say that further research on subjective equilibrium would not be worthwhile. The needed research, largely empirical, entails difficulties of a very high order, as labor economists who have done work on labor can readily testify. However, from the standpoint of separating out movement along a utility function from that between utility functions and from the standpoint of abstracting from such extraneous dimensions as wage legislation, overtime pay, moonlighting, nonhomogeneity of labor, fringe benefits, and the like, the subsistence agriculture has much to offer as an empirical setting.

As for the specifics of a workable empirical design, we shall leave them to Dr. Raj Krishna, in deference to his infinitely richer experience in this area of inquiry and to the content of his discussion paper on the subject. A general observation in this connection is in order, however. In appealing to the data, it would be necessary to distinguish between transitory and permanent shifts in the family income curve. Transitory shifts may be expected to lead to a positively inclined labor supply. Two plausible ways of looking at this are possible. First, a transitory change gives rise to little, if any, revision in one's sense of affluence. Hence the income effect may be largely inoperative. Second, when confronted with recurrent changes in yields and prices (and these changes need not be regular or periodical) from year to year, the farmer's problem becomes one of varying his labor input accordingly. An efficient intertemporal allocation of labor would seem to require larger input in years of high yields or prices and smaller input in years of low yields or prices. It may be worthwhile to suggest that Dr. Krishna's finding of a positive net relationship between output change and price change—to which he alludes in his paper—could be explained in these terms, since the disturbance (price change or shift in the family income curve) is clearly transitory. To shed light on Professor Nakajima's model, variations in permanent income functions are required. In this connection, an index of nonlabor resources per farm would be a more usable independent variable. A final observation is that, in line with our crude view of the historical process of agricultural reorganization under Malthusian population growth, it would be useful to try to identify subsistence farm areas under severe population pressure and those which allow substantial involuntary leisure, both in the sense explained earlier. The insight that such a classification may generate, with respect to both labor response and appropriate development effort, could be highly useful.

References

FEI and RANIS, 1961. J. C. H. Fei and G. Ranis, "A Theory of Economic Development,"

American Economic Review, Vol. 51, No. 4 (September 1961), 533–65.

HAGEN, 1959. E. E. Hagen, "Population and Economic Growth," *American Economic Review*, Vol. XLIX, No. 3 (June 1959), 310–27.

MELLOR, 1963. John W. Mellor, "The Use and Productivity of Farm Family Labor in Early Stages of Agricultural Development," *Journal of Farm Economics*, Vol. 45, No. 3 (August 1963), 517–34.

SCHULTZ, 1964. Theodore W. Schultz, *Transforming Traditional Agriculture* (New Haven, Conn.: Yale University Press, 1964).

TANG, 1958. Anthony M. Tang, *Economic Development in the Southern Piedmont, 1860–1950* (Chapel Hill, N.C.: University of North Carolina Press, 1958).

TANG, 1959. Anthony M. Tang, "Economic Development and Changing Consequences of Race Discrimination in Southern Agriculture," *The Journal of Farm Economics*, Vol. XLI, No. 5 (December 1959), 1113–1126.

TANG, 1965. Anthony M. Tang, "External Forces in Agricultural Development," in *Economic Development of Agriculture* (Center for Economic and Agricultural Development, Iowa State University, Ames, Iowa: Iowa State University Press, 1965).

CASE STUDY

Effects of Increasing Commercialization On Resource Use in Semisubsistence Farms in South Korea

JIN H. PARK

THIS PAPER HAS two main objectives. One is to observe the degree of commercialization of the general crop farms in Korean agriculture and to present empirical data on the effect of commercialization on farm resources. The second is to express my views on the applicability of the contemporary theories of economic analysis for the Korean agricultural setting.

The agricultural resources in Korea are mostly employed for food-grain production. Rice and barley are the most important crops. About 85 per cent of the total domestic consumption of food grains is supplied domestically. The nonfarm population in Korea is about 40 per cent of the total popula-

tion. Therefore, we would expect that around 30 to 40 per cent of the total crop production on farms would be marketed.

PROPORTION OF TOTAL KOREAN CROP PRODUCTION THAT IS MARKETED

Farm record data provide an estimate of the degree of commercialization for individual crop farms. Data are available for selected crop farms which kept records from 1955 to 1963.[1]

1. The number of farms in the annual sample averaged about 600, but the range was from 300 to 1,200.

Table 6.2. Proportion of Gross Earnings Received in Cash.
An Average for Crop Farms Keeping Records, 1955–1963

Year	Gross Earnings per farm 1,000 won	Cash Receipts per farm[a] 1,000 won	Cash Receipts per farm[b] As per cent of gross	Number of farm records[c] farms	Index of wholesale prices %
1955	35.0	12.0	34.2	392	100.0
1956	54.4	16.5	30.3	558	131.6
1957	59.9	18.2	30.4	571	152.9
1958	56.1	21.4	37.4	563	143.3
1959	57.3	21.8	38.0	630	146.7
1960	67.2	23.7	35.3	590	162.5
1961	64.2	26.0	40.4	620	192.3
1962	80.4	32.0	39.9	300	218.0
1963	111.7	38.1	34.1	1,200	NA

[a] The parts of farm products which were exchanged for goods and services were excluded.
[b] The cash receipts per farm were divided by the gross earnings per farm.
[c] The farm records-keeping project for 1955–1957 was conducted by the Bank of Korea, 1958–1961 by the Agricultural Cooperative Federation, and after 1961 by the Ministry of Forestry.
SOURCE: Agricultural Cooperatives Federation, *Agricultural Yearbook*, 1963.

Table 6.3. Components of Cash Receipts for Crop Farms Keeping Records, 1955–1963

Year	Crops sold %	Livestock products sold %	Nonfarm business %	Salaries, wages, rental revenues %	Total cash receipts %
1955	68.1	6.5	3.8	21.6	100.0
1956	67.9	5.9	3.3	22.9	100.0
1957	62.9	5.0	4.4	27.7	100.0
1958	54.2	5.6	10.7	29.5	100.0
1959	54.2	4.5	6.1	35.2	100.0
1960	50.6	4.7	7.4	37.3	100.0
1961	54.9	3.3	7.1	34.7	100.0
1962	55.2	6.6	6.4	31.8	100.0
1963	53.0	5.9	16.7	24.4	100.0

SOURCE: Agricultural Cooperatives Federation, *Agricultural Yearbook*, 1963.

Cash Receipts

The proportion of cash receipts to the value of total production among the selected record keeping crop farms is shown in Table 6.2. On the average, about 35 per cent of the gross value produced by the crop farms was exchanged for cash.[2] In the table, however, the value of farm products which were

2. If we define "commercialization" on the basis of cash sales, then Korean farms would fall into Wharton's "semi-subsistence" and "semi-commercial" portion of the spectrum [Wharton, 1963].

exchanged directly for goods and services was excluded. Considerable proportion of farm products are exchanged directly in kind for factors of production and for consumption goods and services. For example, the wages for hired labor are often paid in kind, part of the fertilizers needed by crop farms is exchanged for rice, part of the tax bill is paid in kind, rural boys and girls studying in city schools pay for room and board with rice. Therefore, the proportion of cash receipts to the value of total production on a farm will be significantly smaller than the proportion of value of "exchanged production."[3]

The most important part of the cash received by the crop farms comes from the crops sold (See Table 6.3). In 1955 the cash earned from crops sold was 68 per cent of the total cash receipts; it was 53 per cent in 1963. The relative importance of crops sold to total cash receipts has been decreasing during the period. On the other hand, the relative importance of the cash earned from nonfarm activities has increased. The cash earned from nonfarm business, salaries, wages, rental earnings, and the like was about 25 per cent in 1963. The cash earned from livestock was usually less than 6 per cent of the total cash receipts per farm.

As the Korean economy develops, the needs of farmers for cash to purchase goods and services for household consumption and for farm production tend to increase. In order to earn more cash income the crop farms have to sell more crops on the market. Given a desired level of farm prerequisites (farm-produced food consumed in the home), the cash income for crop farms can be increased by increasing farm production and/or by increasing cash income from nonfarm activities. For the record-keeping crop farms the cash earned from nonfarm activities was an important factor in increasing their cash receipts in recent years.

Cash Expenditures

The cash earned by the crop farms were spent both for consumption and production. On the average, about 55 per cent of the total cash receipts per farm was spent for farm household expenditures and 45 per cent for production requisites (See Table 6.4).

The consumer goods and services purchased by farmers from the industrial sector are naturally increasing as the economy develops and as farmer incomes rise. Clothing,

3. "Exchanged production" will be used to define that fraction of total production sold for cash plus that fraction of total production used to make payments in kind either for factor inputs or consumption goods. Thus "total value product" = "value of production sold" + "value product exchanged in kind for consumption goods" + "value of product exchanged in kind for production factors" + "value of product retained for farm family consumption" (farm privileges). "Exchanged production" is made up of the first three terms to the right of the equal sign.

Table 6.4. Use of Cash Receipts for Consumption and Production Requisites for Crop Farms Keeping Records, 1955–1963

	CASH EXPENDITURES FOR		
YEAR	Household consumption	Production requisites	Total cash expend.
	%	%	%
1955	59.5	40.5	100.0
1956	60.2	39.8	100.0
1957	64.1	35.9	100.0
1958	53.0	47.0	100.0
1959	57.2	42.8	100.0
1960	55.9	44.1	100.0
1961	55.9	44.1	100.0
1962	53.0	47.0	100.0

SOURCE: Ministry of Agriculture and Forestry, *Annual Report of Farm Record Keeping*, 1964.

housing materials, utensils, and often other foods such as fish, meats, fruits, are purchased. Moreover, the farmer who does not produce enough food grains for his farm family also needs to purchase part of the required food grains, in addition to the other foods. Above all, expenditures for education, health, transportation, and other services are increasing annually.

For the crop farms keeping records, 24 per cent of the total cash expenditures by farm households was spent for foods in 1962, about 20 per cent was spent for clothes, and 5 per cent was spent for other items (See Table 6.5). In recent years, the relative

Table 6.5. Cash Expenditures for Household Consumption for Crop Farms Keeping Records in 1955–1962

	CASH EXPENDITURES FOR				
YEAR	Farm food	Clothes	Lighting and Fuel	Other[a]	Total cash expend.
	%	%	%	%	%
1955	29.8	22.2	7.7	40.3	100.0
1956	32.9	22.4	7.1	37.6	100.0
1957	38.0	19.4	5.9	36.7	100.0
1958	32.3	16.0	7.6	44.1	100.0
1959	27.2	18.4	9.0	45.4	100.0
1960	28.9	19.2	8.9	43.0	100.0
1961	26.1	19.9	8.9	45.1	100.0
1962	24.1	19.5	11.4	45.0	100.0

[a] Include expenditures for education, health, transportation, housing materials, and so on.

SOURCE: Agricultural Cooperatives Federation, *Annual Report on Farm Record Keeping*, 1963.

Table 6.6. Cash Expenditures for Farm Operation and Nonfarm Business for Crop Farms
Keeping Records in 1955–1962[a]

CASH EXPENDITURES FOR

YEAR	Fertilizers	Hired labor	Feeds	Other inputs[b]	Nonfarm business	Tax charge	Interest payment
	%	%	%	%	%	%	%
1955	16.1	27.9	2.5	14.8	5.8	28.0	4.9
1956	24.0	28.7	2.3	11.7	6.1	22.2	5.0
1957	25.1	26.1	2.2	19.7	5.5	17.0	4.4
1958	35.0	18.3	5.1	18.2	8.1	11.4	3.9
1959	29.3	23.0	4.4	20.4	6.2	9.7	7.0
1960	28.9	21.9	6.1	23.1	7.7	7.5	4.8
1961	27.2	23.0	4.8	24.5	6.6	8.6	5.3
1962	34.3	15.5	5.2	23.8	11.0	7.5	2.7

[a] The money invested for purchase of farm properties was excluded.
[b] Include expense for seeds, insecticides, farm machinery, depreciation charges, etc.
SOURCE: Agricultural Cooperatives Federation, *Annual Report on Farm Record Keeping*, 1963.

proportion of cash expenditures for education, health, transportation, wedding and funeral ceremonies has been increasing.

The needs for cash in farm operation also increases as the farmer makes efforts to produce more. New seeds, new breeds of animals, fertilizers, insecticides, feeds, improved machinery and farming utensils, irrigation facilities, and so on are supplied mostly from outside the farm and are essential input factors to produce more on a given land.

The relative importance of cash expenses for the purchase of input factors is shown in Table 6.6. Chemical fertilizer is the most important item, and expenditure for it has been increasing significantly. In 1955 the cash expense for fertilizer was 16 per cent of the total cash expense for farm operation, and, in 1962 it was 34 per cent.

Also, the importance of cash expenses for seeds, insecticides, farm machinery, and feed has been increasing annually. On the other hand, the cash expenses for hired labor shows a declining trend.

These facts tell us that: the farmers in Korea are not cut off from the exchange economy, but are closely associated with it in production as well as in consumption; and the degree of association with the exchange economy increases as the agricultural economy develops.

As part of a developing economy, the farmer has to purchase increasing amounts of consumer goods and services and farm factor inputs. In order to purchase them, cash

income must increase. Basically he should produce more to increase his income from "exchanged production." To produce more from a given land area, the farmer has to use better or more input factors, which are mainly supplied from the outside of the farm [Hill and Mosher, 1963]. To purchase them, the farmer must sell more products. Consequently, increased farm production has a positive relation to increased commercialization.

Relationship between Marketed Production and Total Value of Product

The value of total production on crop farms consists of two components: the value of farm privileges, primarily the food consumed by the families, and receipts from exchanges. Since the income elasticity of demand for food grains for a crop farm household is positive, we would expect that, as total production on a crop farm increases, the value of farm privileges would increase along with increases in production exchanged; but exchanged production should increase more rapidly than the increases in farm privileges.

The author and Mr. S. Ban conducted a farm management study for four selected villages in 1963 to test this hypothesis.[4] Three of the four villages were typical Korean farm

4. The purpose of this study was to collect teaching materials for the National Training Center on Farm Management Analysis held at the College of Agriculture, Seoul National University, from July 13 to August 14, 1964. The villages are located near the college.

villages. Rice was the most important crop for the farmers in three villages, constituting about 60 to 70 per cent of the total value product.[5] The other village was made up of livestock and vegetable farms.

The Rice Farm Villages. Figure 6.18 shows the relationship in one of the three rice-

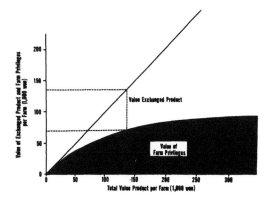

Figure 6.18. Relationship Between Total Value of Product and Exchanged Product per Farm for 84 Crop Farms in the Village of Chung Ja Ri, 1963.

producing villages between total value of product and exchanged production per farm. There were 84 farms in the village. The shaded area shows the value of farm privileges. The 45-degree line is the sum of the value of farm privileges and exchanged production, which is equal to total value.

On the average, the value of farm privileges and of exchanged production increase as total production on the farms increases, but the value of exchange production increases more rapidly than the value of farm privileges. The additional increment to value of exchanged production because of additional production on the farms becomes larger than the additional increment to farm privileges.

For the village as a whole, the total value of product per farm was 134,000 won, consisting of 66,000 won for farm privileges and 68,000 won for exchanged production.[6] The average index of commercialization

for the crop farms in the village was 51 per cent.

On the average, when total production increased from 134,000 won to 200,000 won, or an increase of 50 per cent, the value of exchanged production increased by about 70 per cent, while the value of farm privileges increased by about 30 per cent. This illustrates that, as the semisubsistence crop farms produce more, the importance of exchanged production increases more rapidly than that of farm privileges.

Although not reported on here, the same general relationship was observed for the crop farms in the other two villages.

The Livestock and Vegetable Farm Village. Among the four villages surveyed, an unusual one was made up of farms whose total value product came primarily from hogs, poultry, and vegetables.[7] There were 74 farms in the village, and they produced livestock and vegetables mainly for market. About half of the 74 farms sold more than 80 per cent of their total production.

The relationship between the value of total production and the value of exchanged production for the livestock and vegetable farms in the village is shown in Figure 6.19.

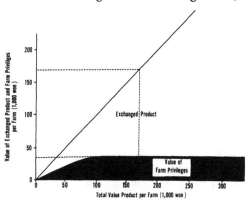

Figure 6.19. Relationship Between Total Value of Product and Exchanged Product per Farm for 74 Livestock and Vegetable Farms in the Village of Sinchun Ri, 1963.

A significant difference between Figure 6.19 and Figure 6.18 is that in the former, after

5. The three villages are Chung Ja Ri, Pajang Ri, and Homesil Ri. Chung Ja Ri was taken as the sample village for the Figure 6.18.
6. At the official rate of exchange, 250 won was equivalent to $1 in 1963.

7. The name of this village is Sinchun Ri. It is a newly settled village, and the average size of crop land for the farms in the village was about one-third of the average size in the other villages.

100,000 won, any increments in total production were exchanged at the market.

For the village as a whole, the total value product per farm was 169,000 won, of which the value of farm privileges was 32,000 won and the exchanged value was 137,000 won. Hence the average index of commercialization for the farms in the village was 81 per cent.

We can make the following statements:

1. For the general crop farms: The value of exchanged production increases more rapidly than for the farm privileges as total production increases. Hence the importance of the allocative functions of relative prices at the market on resource use will increase as total production increases.[8]

2. For the livestock and vegetable farms: Most of the additional production is sold at the market. The relative prices at the market will perform the major allocative functions of resource use on the farms which produce the products demanded mainly by the city consumers or by the industrial sectors.

3. Figure 6.18 represents the general picture in the Korean agricultural economy and Figure 6.19 the exceptional.

As urban population increases more rapidly than farm or rural population, and as the consumer income increases, the number of farmers who produce primarily for the market will (or should) be increasing. Particularly in rural areas near cities or where the transportation facilities are well developed, the number of farmers who allocate most of their farm resources to market production is increasing; and in such areas the index of commercialization of crop farms is significantly higher than that for crop farms in more distant local villages.

COMMERCIALIZATION AND LAND PRODUCTIVITY

The average index of commercialization for the general crop farms in Korea is estimated as somewhere around 40 to 50 per cent. The goal of production of the crop farms will be neither for farm food nor market alone. The

8. This statement may not be acceptable for the very small crop farms for which the increment to the farm privileges, due to an additional production of food grains, could be larger than the increment for exchanged production. Around 30 to 40 per cent of the total farms in Korea may belong to this category.

general farmers seek more cash income as well as more farm foods.

In order to sell more products at the market, the farmer must produce more by using new or more input factors. Therefore, we expect that the increasing commercialization of semisubsistence farms will raise the productivities of farm resources. For example, as commercialization increases, a unit of land or labor will produce larger output. As a consequence, the net family farm income will be increased by increasing commercialization.

Commercialization and the Yields of Rice and Upland Crops

In Korea, crop lands are classified into two kinds: paddy land and nonirrigated crop land. Rice is the chief crop produced from the paddies, and various other crops are produced from the nonirrigated crop land, which in Korea is called "upland." The effects of increasing commercialization on crop yields were observed for the two kinds of land separately.

On rice paddies. Out of 322 farms surveyed in the four villages, 277 farms produced rice in 1963. The 277 sample farms were sorted by two factors: per cent of rice sold and the size of rice paddies.

The distribution of 277 farms was as follows:

PER CENT OF RICE SOLD	SIZE OF RICE PADDIES (TANBO)			
	Less than 5	5 to 9	9 and over	All
	(Number of farms)			
Less than 20	60	27	10	97
20–50	34	28	45	107
50 and over	14	29	30	73
All	108	84	85	277

On the average, the farmers who sold larger percentage of rice secured higher yields per unit of land (Table 6.7). For example, the farmers who planted rice in less than 5 tanbo of paddies and sold less than 20 per cent of rice got a yield of 8 bushels of polished rice from a tanbo of land. (One tanbo is about one-tenth hectare.) On the other hand, the farmers who planted rice in the same amount of land but sold more than 50 per cent of the output got a yield of almost

Table 6.7. Relationship between Per Cent of Rice Sold, Size of Land, and Yield of Rice per Unit of Land for 277 Farms, 1963

PER CENT OF RICE SOLD	SIZE OF PADDIES (TANBO)			
	Less than 5	5 to 9	9 and over	All
	(Yield of polished rice per tanbo in bushels)			
Less than 20	8.0	5.8	7.4	7.8
20–50	8.2	8.1	7.8	8.0
50 and over	10.9	8.0	8.9	8.7
All	8.4	8.1	8.2	8.2

11 bushels from a tanbo of land. Namely, the yield of rice increased by about 30 per cent as the commercial index increased from less than 20 to more than 50.

For the other size groups the yields tend to increase as the per cent of rice sold increases. Increasing commercialization produced larger output per unit of land in rice production.

There seems to be no significant relation between the size of farm and the yield of rice, although it shows that the small producing units might have produced a higher yield per unit of land. The causal factors for these increases are difficult to measure satisfactorily. However, we would expect that, when the land area is given, the farmer who produced a larger output per unit of land would have used better or purchased more input factors on a unit of land than the farmer who produced less. In order to test this hypothesis, the relationship between the per cent of rice sold and the expense for fertilizers, manures, and insecticides per unit of land were observed. The results are shown in Tables 6.8 to 6.10.

On the average, the expense for the three

Table 6.8. Relationship between Per Cent of Rice Sold, Size of Land, and Expense for Fertilizers per Unit of Land for 277 Farms, 1963

PER CENT OF RICE SOLD	SIZE OF PADDIES (TANBO)			
	Less than 5	5 to 9	9 and over	All
	Expense for fertilizers per tanbo (won)			
Less than 20	372	358	283	343
20–50	418	298	343	333
50 and over	481	369	367	375
All	402	331	346	350

input factors increased as the per cent of rice sold increased. For example, the farmers who planted rice in less than 5 tanbo, and sold less than 20 per cent of the output, spent 372 won for fertilizers per tanbo of land. On the other hand, the farmers who had the same size of land, but sold more than 50 per cent of rice, spent 481 won for fertilizers per tanbo of land (Table 6.8).

Table 6.9. Relationship between Per Cent of Rice Sold, Size of Land, and Expense for Manures per Unit of Land for 277 Farms, 1963

PER CENT OF RICE SOLD	SIZE OF PADDIES (TANBO)			
	Less than 5	5 to 9	9 and over	All
	Expense for manure inputs per tanbo (won)			
Less than 20	400	476	426	435
20–50	650	372	453	444
50 and over	616	458	486	486
All	317	419	444	456

Table 6.10. Relationship between Per Cent of Rice Sold, Size of Land, and Expense for Insecticides per Unit of Land for 277 Farms, 1963

PER CENT OF RICE SOLD	SIZE OF PADDIES (TANBO)			
	Less than 5	5 to 9	9 and over	All
	Expense for insecticides per tanbo (won)			
Less than 20	52	28	9	32
20–50	46	34	37	37
50 and over	96	17	36	33
All	55	28	32	35

When the per cent of rice sold is given, the small-size farms spent a larger expense for fertilizers per unit of land. This implies that the small-size farmer might have used the rice paddies more intensively than the larger size farmers.

As for the manure inputs (Table 6.9), and for insecticides (Table 6.10), about the same relationships as for fertilizers are found—namely, the farmer who sold a larger per cent of his total output incurred a larger expense for manures and insecticides per unit of land than the farmer who sold less.

From such evidence we can say that the increasing commercialization in rice production is reflected in a larger output from a given land area by using better or more input factors on the land.

On Uplands. The upland farmer has a number of alternatives in choosing crops: barley, wheat, soybeans, potatoes, various kinds of vegetables and fruits, and industrial crops. Therefore the increasing commercialization on the upland crop production should affect the best choice of crops among the alternatives and the combination of crops grown.

In general, the index of commercialization is relatively low for upland crops which are demanded by *both* farm family and city consumers and is relatively high for upland crops which are demanded only by city consumers, who have higher incomes as well as different tastes compared to farm people.

The effects of increasing commercialization of the upland crops on the land productivity were observed for 313 farms. The hypothesis to be tested was: as the per cent of crops sold increases, a unit of upland will produce larger money value.

The relationship between the per cent of upland crops sold and the gross value produced per unit of land is shown in Table 6.11.

Table 6.11. *Relationship between Per Cent of Crops Sold, Size of Land, and Gross Value Produced per Unit of Land for 313 Farms, 1963.*

PER CENT OF CROPS SOLD	SIZE OF UPLAND (TANBO)			
	Less than 2	2 to 5	5 and over	All
	Gross value production per tanbo (won)			
Less than 10	11,241	7,920	5,497	7,588
10–20	14,413	7,877	6,632	7,961
20–50	15,815	9,513	7,086	8,486
50 and over	18,555	17,650	13,265	15,259
All	13,501	9,630	7,828	9,178

A tanbo of upland produced significantly larger money value as the per cent of crops sold increased. For example, among the farmers who had less than 2 tanbo of upland, the one who sold less than 10 per cent of the total crop produced 11,241 won from a tanbo of land, but the farmer who sold more than 50 per cent produced 18,555 won from the same amount of land. For the farmers

who had 2 to 5 tanbo of upland, the most commercialized farmer produced more than twice the money value from a tanbo than the least commercialized farmer. From this we can say that increasing commercialization in upland crop production causes farmers to produce more from a given area of upland.

Alternatively, small size-farms produced a larger money value from a unit of land than the large-size farms. Among the farmers who sold 20 to 50 per cent of the total output, the one who had less than two tanbo of upland produced 15,815 won from a tanbo of land, but the farmer who had more than 5 tanbo of land produced only 7,086 won from a tanbo of land. Hence, the small-size farms produced

Table 6.12. *Relationship between Per Cent of Crops Sold, Size of Upland, and Expenses for Fertilizers per Unit of Land for 313 Farms, 1963*

PER CENT OF CROPS SOLD	SIZE OF UPLANDS (TANBO)			
	Less than 2	2 to 5	5 and over	All
	Expenses for fertilizers per tanbo (won)			
Less than 10	590	481	398	469
10–20	951	371	343	409
20–50	785	556	344	444
50 and over	1,076	1,118	862	973
All	739	562	459	532

about twice what the large-size farms produced from a tanbo of land. This implies that the small-size farms used the land more intensively than the large-size farms.

We would expect that the farmer who produced more from a given land would have used better or more purchased input factors; and the farmer who produced more would have incurred a larger expense per unit of land than the farmer who produced less.

The relationship between the per cent of crops sold and expenses for fertilizers, manures, and insecticides per unit of upland are shown in Tables 6.12 to 6.14.

On the average, the expenses for fertilizers per tanbo of upland increased significantly as the per cent of crops sold increases. However, the small-sized farms had a larger expense for fertilizers per unit of land than the large-size farms. For example, among those who sold 20 to 50 per cent of the total

Table 6.13. *Relationship between Per Cent of Crops Sold, Size of Upland, and Expense for Manure Inputs per Unit of Land for 313 Farms, 1963*

PER CENT OF CROPS SOLD	SIZE OF UPLANDS (TANBO)			
	Less than 2	2 to 5	5 and over	All
	Expenses for manures per tanbo (won)			
Less than 10	1,513	889	578	875
10–20	1,570	936	555	849
20–50	1,482	1,088	574	802
50 and over	1,555	1,334	918	1,116
All	1,518	1,006	640	887

Table 6.14. *Relationship between Per Cent of Crops Sold, Size of Land, and Expense for Insecticides per Unit of Land for 313 Farms, 1963*

PER CENT OF CROPS SOLD	SIZE OF UPLANDS (TANBO)			
	Less than 2	2 to 5	5 and over	All
	Expense for insecticides per tanbo (won)			
Less than 10	20	6	8	9
10–20	13	5	12	8
20–50	33	14	7	14
50 and over	46	71	69	68
All	34	17	20	20

outputs, the farmer who had less than 2 tanbo of land spent 785 won for fertilizers per tanbo of land, but the farmer who had more than 5 tanbo of land spent 344 won on the same amount of land. The small-size farm produced larger output from a unit of upland by more intensive use of the land.

From the empirical evidence of our analysis, we can say that, as commercialization increases for the semisubsistence crop farms, the farmer produces a larger output from a given area of land by applying more or better purchased input factors.

Commercialization and Land Productivity in Different Enterprise Combinations. We have seen the effects of commercialization on the yields of individual crops. In this section the effects will be observed for the farms that have different enterprise combinations.

I have taken the village of Chung Ja Ri (Figure 6.18) as a typical village in Korea. Here rice production is the most important part of the total production, and the degree

of commercialization for rice farms is relatively low.

The village of Sinchun Ri (Figure 6.19) is an unusual village. Production from hogs, poultry, and vegetables is the major part of the total production, and the commercialization of the livestock and vegetable farms was relatively high.

The effects of commercialization on the land productivity of the two villages are shown in Table 6.15. (In the table the off-farm income was excluded.)

Table 6.15. *Relationship between Commercialization and Productivity of Land for Different Types of Farming in the Villages of Chung Ja Ri and Sinchun Ri, 1963*

INDEX OF COMMERCIALIZA- TION[c]	CHUNG JA RI[a] (rice farms)		SINCHUN RI[b] (livestock and vegetable farms)	
	Gross value product per tanbo	Farm expense per tanbo	Gross value product per tanbo	Farm expense per tanbo
Per Cent of Crops Sold	Won	Won	Won	Won
Less than 30	9,556	2,145	14,879	6,275
30–50	10,046	2,894	17,158	6,325
50–70	16,778	3,876	17,509	4,673
70 and over	18,261	5,325	65,753	36,593
All	12,541	3,180	31,517	14,741

[a] About 70 per cent of the total production was from rice.
[b] About 50 per cent of the total production was from hogs and poultry and about 35 per cent from vegetables.
[c] The value of marketed crops and livestock divided by the total value product.

The number of farms for Table 6.15 is as follows:

INDEX OF COMMERCIALIZATION (Per Cent of Crops Sold)	NUMBER OF FARMS	
	Chung Ja Ri Farms	Sinchun Ri Farms
Less than 30	23	15
30–50	35	18
50–70	22	16
70 and over	4	24
Total	84	73

On the average, the livestock and vegetable farms in the village of Sinchun Ri produced a significantly larger output from a unit of land than the rice farms in the village of Chung Ja Ri. The gross value per tanbo of land for the livestock and vegetable farms was 31,517 won; it was 12,541 won for the rice farms. The average size of crop land for the livestock and vegetable farms was 3.6 tanbo (about 0.36 hectare); and it was 11.2 tanbo (about 1.12 hectare) for the rice farms. Hence, the livestock and vegetable farms had about one-third of the size of crop land for the rice farms, but they produced about 2.5 times the money value from a unit of land that the rice farms did.

In order to produce larger income from a unit of land, the livestock and vegetable farms spent more per unit of land than the rice farms: 14,741 won per tanbo compared to 3,180 won, on the average.

The net family farm income per unit of land can be obtained by subtracting the expense per unit of land from the gross value production per unit of land. On the average, the livestock and vegetable farms produced 16,800 won of net family farm income from a tanbo of land, and the rice farms produced 9,400 won. Therefore, we can say that the livestock and vegetable farms earned significantly higher net income from a unit of land by using larger capital and labor on a unit of land compared to the rice farms.

The farmer who sold a larger percentage of crop and livestock production produced a significantly larger money value from a unit of land than the farmer who sold less. In the Chung Ja Ri village, for example, the farmers who sold less than 30 per cent of their total production produced 9,600 won from a tanbo of land, but the farmers who sold 50 to 70 per cent of the total production produced 16,800 won from a tanbo of land.

In the Sinchun Ri village, the most commercialized farm group produced a very large money value from a tanbo of land compared to other farmers. This was mainly due to the fact that specialized poultry and vegetable farms were included.

The farmer who sold a larger percentage of the total product incurred a higher expense per unit of land. In Chung Ja Ri, the farmers who sold less than 30 per cent of their total production spent 2,100 won per tanbo of land, while the farmers who sold 50 to 70 per cent of their total output spent 3,900

won. Subtracting the farm expense per unit of land from the total value product per unit of land, the farmer who sold a larger percentage of the total output earned a higher net family farm income per unit of land. In the village of Chung Ja Ri, for example, the farmer who sold less than 30 per cent of the total output earned 7,500 won of net family farm income from a tanbo of land, while the farmer who sold 50 to 70 per cent of the total output earned 12,900 won.

The case studies for the two villages provide us further evidence that increasing commercialization of the semisubsistence farms results in larger output from a given land area by using better or more purchased input factors.

COMMERCIALIZATION AND LABOR PRODUCTIVITY

What will be the effects of increasing commercialization of labor productivity?

The relationship between commercialization and labor productivity was observed for the 322 farms from the four villages. Labor productivity was measured by dividing the total value product on individual farms by the man-equivalent units which include the available family labor and the hired labor. The man-equivalent was calculated by weighing the differences in ages and sex of individual family labor and hired labor.

Table 6.16. Relationship between Commercial Index, Size of Land, and Production per Man-Equivalent for 322 Farms, 1963

INDEX OF COMMERCIALIZATION	SIZE OF CROP LAND (TANBO)			
	Less than 5	5 to 12	12 and over	All
(Per Cent of Crops Sold)	(Gross value production per man-equivalent in won)			
Less than 40	21,849	39,825	70,018	44,853
40–60	38,664	54,999	66,213	58,507
60 and over	60,918	91,197	86,754	78,000
All	48,716	59,301	72,314	61,379

All farms were sorted by two factors: the index of commercialization and the size of crop land. The distribution of the 322 farms for Table 6.16 is as follows:

INDEX OF COMMERCIALIZATION	SIZE OF CROP LAND (TANBO)			
(Per Cent of Crops Sold)	Less than 5	5 to 12	12 and over	All
	(Number of Farms)			
Less than 40	18	58	24	100
40–60	23	41	46	110
60 and over	52	37	23	112
All	93	136	93	322

As commercialization increases, the total value product per man-equivalent increases significantly. For example, taking the farm group which had less than 5 tanbo of crop land, the farmer who sold less than 40 per cent of his total production produced 21,800 won per man-equivalent, but the farmer who sold more than 60 per cent of the total production produced 60,900 won per man-equivalent. Namely, the production per man-equivalent for the most commercialized farm group was about three times that for the least commercialized farm group.

Alternatively, when the per cent of value of exchanged production to total production is given, the value production per man-equivalent increased significantly as the size of crop land per farm increased. For example, also among farmers who sold less than 40 per cent of their total output, those who had less than 5 tanbo of land produced 21,800 won per man-equivalent. Thus labor productivity increased by about 3.5 times, owing to the increase in the size of crop land.

From these facts we can say that the increasing commercialization of the semi-subsistence farms results in increasing labor productivity on a given land area.

IMPLICATIONS FOR ECONOMIC DEVELOPMENT

Increasing production from the agricultural sector is regarded as the key factor for the growth of the Korean economy. The domestic demand for foods is increasing more rapidly than the domestic supply, and the general price level in the economy is closely associated with the prices of food grains. The economy urgently needs enlarged foreign exchange earnings from exports of agricultural products. Cash income of farm

people needs to be increased to stimulate industrialization. Production per unit of farm labor should be increased to transfer the manpower from agricultural sector to non-agricultural sectors [Johnston and Mellor, 1961].

The above evidence indicates that the increasing commercialization of the semi-subsistence farms is an important factor in increasing production with a limited land area. With a given amount of land, the farmer who sold a larger proportion of his total product produced a larger output per unit of land and labor than the farmer who sold less. Hence we can say that the increasing commercialization is positively associated with the growth of the agricultural economy.

Any attempt to increase further the commercialization of semisubsistence farmers will encounter limitations or restrictional factors. To the individual farmer some of the restrictional factors will be external and others will be internal ones.

The market for the farmer must be enlarged, and at the same time, the efficiency in the marketing organization needs to be improved.

Since a large proportion of the consumers of agricultural products are within the agricultural sector, it will be difficult to enlarge the domestic market rapidly. Thus increasing the export of agricultural products will be an important strategy in enlarging the market for the semisubsistence farmer.

We have seen that the increasing commercialization requires increased expenditures per unit of land. Hence the need of credit by the semisubsistence farmer will be increased as commercialization increases.

The managerial ability of semisubsistence farmers must also be increased to cope with the uncertainties and risks that come with increasing commercialization. As commercialization increases, the uncertainties in technologies and the markets will be different from those with which the subsistence farmers are familiar. New products and new inputs will be continuously introduced on the farm; competition in the market will also increase. To bear the new kinds of uncertainties, technological and market information will need to be increased; and the dissemination of new knowledge will have to be speeded up.

THE TOOLS OF ECONOMIC ANALYSIS
FOR SEMISUBSISTENCE FARM
ORGANIZATION

So far we have investigated the nature of semisubsistence farm organization with particular reference to the commercialization of crop farms in Korea. We have seen that the increasing commercialization has an important impact on productivity of farm resources. This leads us to an important question: what will be the underlying principles of resource allocation on semisubsistence farms?

The number and kinds of variables which need to be taken into account for an economic study of a subsistence village will be different from those for the modern business sector. However, the underlying principles of economics are the same in both sectors; namely, the individual resource holders in both sectors are trying to utilize their limited resources among the best alternatives [Schultz, 1964].

In a significant degree the resource holders in the modern business sector may appear as more aggressive maximizers of economic returns from their resource use than the resource holders in the subsistence farm economy, mainly due to the various restrictional factors such as environmental, institutional, or structural factors in the latter sector. In such cases the restrictional factors ought to be freed and not the economic principles condemned.

The arguments for the applicability of contemporary economic theories to the subsistence nature of economic organization can be subdivided as follows: (1) the economics of resource use at firm and at aggregate level; (2) the institutional or structural variables of economic organization; and (3) economic development in general.

The economics of resource use at firm level have been developed based upon a profit maximizing representative firm. The arguments for the applicability of such theories to a subsistence farm in the traditional farm economic organization seem to concern the following points.

(a) The underlying assumptions, upon which the theory of firm was established, are criticized because the assumptions are often far from the realities facing the subsistence farmer. Rigid structural or institutional factors hindering resource mobility, high degree of imperfect knowledge by resource holders, narrow economic horizons in the subsistence economy, and the like are regarded as the characteristics of subsistence farm organization, which differ from the hypothetical representative firm of microresource economics.

I would agree that, if we could have analytical tools built under assumptions to fit into the reality of subsistence farms, there would be no reason why we should use tools built under unrealistic assumptions. But so far no replaceable tools have been built, and it seems to me that no realistically perfect tools which conform with the behavior of subsistence farmers will be made.

A possible solution for the problem might be to alter the unrealistic part of the assumptions so that the tools will be more useful for particular local conditions. The major tasks of economists in subsistence economies seem to be, not to invent new tools, but to become better users of the tools already invented.

(b) The choice criteria for the representative firm in microeconomic theory are criticized as unrealistic for a subsistence farm in a traditional economy. Relative prices at the market are the choice criteria for resource allocation of the representative firm, and this may not be the choice criteria for a subsistence farm.

This problem can be solved if we could have alternative choice criteria which fit into the reality of a subsistence farm. The subjective utility ratio could be an alternative choice criteria if the subsistence farm is entirely cut off from the market economy. My understanding, however, is that very few subsistence farms are entirely cut off from the market economy. Hence the criterion of subjective utility would be an equally, if not more, unrealistic choice for many areas in the world. For most cases of subsistence economy, a mixture of market-price ratios and subjective-utility ratios ought to be considered as the proper choice criteria.

The key for the issue of choice criteria seems to refer to the concept of price. If we define the concept of price in a broad sense, namely if we define the price as an opportunity cost, we would agree that the relative price is the choice criteria of resource allocation of subsistence farms.

(c) We may say that resource holders in a

subsistence economy have a limited amount of knowledge on the technical production function of his resources and on the choice criteria. Compared with the representative firm, the technological and market information available to a subsistence farm is limited, and because of this limitation, the subsistence farm may be using resources far from the optimum criteria of the representative firm. In this situation the answer would seem to be providing the needed information instead of condemning the optimum criteria of resource use.

(d) Some economists in a subsistence economy may hate to accept micro-resource economics, not because the subsistence farmers behave differently from economic theory, but because the terminologies appearing in economics differ from his vocabulary and from the language spoken by the subsistence farmers. In this situation the problem is a matter of techniques of communication. Because of poor communication, we should not condemn the principles of economics itself. Perhaps the real problem is the lack of economists who can communicate economic principles to subsistence farmers and understand farmers when they in turn seek to communicate back. Although the students of subsistence economies might fail to accept the concept of marginal analysis, opportunity cost principles, and so forth, the subsistence farmers are usually masters of these concepts in their daily behavior. Based on my observation, the farmers in the Korean agricultural economy are behaving in accord with the principles of economics; namely, the individual resource holders in the Korean agriculture are trying to utilize the limited resources for the best alternatives [Park, 1964].

The agricultural organization in Korea belongs to a semisubsistence category. About half of the value of total production on farms is sold. As the economy develops, the farmer's needs for cash income are increasing in order to purchase more consumer goods and services. To earn a larger cash income, the farmer has to sell more products by producing more on the farm. To produce more on a given area of land, the farmer uses better or more purchased input factors which are supplied from outside.

On the average, the additional increment to the income due to additional production on the farm was larger than the additional increment to the farm privileges. Thus, increasing production on the semisubsistence farm is closely associated with increasing commercialization.

As the level of commercialization increases, the farmers produced larger output from a unit of land and labor by using better and more input factors. The farmers who sold more of their total production earned higher net family farm income than the farmers who sold less.

Increasing agricultural production is a key growth factor for the Korean economy. Increasing commercialization in the semisubsistence farm sector is a strategic factor. To increase commercialization further, the market must be enlarged, efficiencies in the market organization improved, the supply of farm credit increased, and the managerial abilities of farmers increased.

The tools of economic analysis developed by economists in the last two centuries can be suitably used as tools of economic analysis for semisubsistence farms if the users of the tools know the assumptions upon which the tools were invented and make appropriate adjustments.

References

HILL and MOSHER, 1963. F. F. Hill and A. T. Mosher, "Organizing for Agricultural Development," Paper prepared for U.N. Conference on the Application of Science and Technology for the Benefit of the Less Developed Areas, Geneva, February 1963.

JOHNSTON and MELLOR, 1961. B. F. Johnston and J. W. Mellor, "The Role of Agriculture in Economic Development," *The American Economic Review*, Vol. 51, No. 4 (September 1961), 566–93.

PARK, 1964. Jin H. Park, "Behavior of Farm Resources in Livestock Production on Semi-Subsistence Crop Farms in Korea," A Case Study in the Village of Pajang Ri, Kyung Ki Do Province in Korea, 1964, Unpublished, Department of Agricultural Economics, College of Agriculture, Suwon, Korea.

SCHULTZ, 1964. T. W. Schultz, *Transforming Traditional Agriculture* (New Haven, Conn.: Yale University Press, 1964).

Wharton, 1963. Clifton R. Wharton, Jr., "The Economic Meaning of 'Subsistence'," *Malayan Economic Review*, Vol. VIII, No. 2 (October 1963), 46–58.

7

The Subsistence Farmer in Traditional Economies

JOHN W. MELLOR

FARMING IN THE TRADITIONAL agricultural economies dominant in much of Asia, Africa, and Latin America occurs largely on small farms with one- or two-man equivalent labor forces and on which the operational decisions and much of the labor come from the same household. Such farms are in that respect typical family or peasant farms. In addition, in the low-income traditional agricultures of the world the level of total output per farm is low, providing only modestly more than basic subsistence requirements to the family labor force. In part for this reason, a relatively high proportion of agricultural production from such farms is retained in the producing household for home consumption and a relatively small proportion is sold.

Typically, in low-income countries, some two-thirds of production is retained for home use and one-third is sold. On such farms the subsistence aspect of production is important and strongly influences the overall pattern of behavior. It is this type of subsistence farm to which this paper is addressed. The paper is not concerned, on the one hand, with large-scale operations, such as plantations, which are typical of certain regions of low-income tropical countries; nor, on the other hand, is this paper concerned with extremely low-income pure subsistence models. Although the dominant type of farm considered in this paper has an important subsistence element, it also is a type of farm which produces a significant marketable surplus and enters into the market economy, at least marginally.

This paper is concerned with the micro-economics of subsistence farms, with special reference to those aspects which are important to agricultural development policy. The discussion in this paper deals first with aspects of the values and objectives of farmers which are of particular significance in influencing their economizing decisions. Then, with the background of values and objectives given, the second section deals with four specific decision-making areas, allocation of resources initially controlled by the farmer, command of additional resources, response to prices and price relationships, and acceptance or rejection of technological change. The two major sections will be preceded by a brief introductory statement of the production process in a traditional agriculture. The emphasis of the paper is on traditional agriculture, which is the antecedent of a modern agriculture. It is necessary to understand this base, from which modernization departs, in order to understand the facilitators and inhibitors of modernization and to diagnose appropriate policy for agricultural modernization.

The Production Process in a Traditional Agriculture

The basic inputs of a traditional agriculture are land and labor. They are both considerably more important than the capital input. In any case, the capital input is primarily a relatively direct embodiment of labor in the form of land improvements, water systems, and very simple tools. To only a small extent is production a function of the extent to which the farmer is willing to save from present consumption for investment in forms of capital which are not created directly by farm family labor. The modernization of traditional agriculture is closely associated with increase in its use of forms of capital which are produced off the farm in complex production processes. Several of the problems associated with the transition to such agriculture will be discussed later in this paper.

The level of production and output on a farm in traditional agriculture is a function first of the size of the land base which an individual farmer commands. Secondly, and to a much lesser extent, it is a function of the input of labor provided by the farmer either directly or indirectly through the formation of capital through the use of labor. Labor plays a relatively more important role in determining increments to the aggregate level of production. Labor deserves special attention in economic analysis related to development because of the flexibility in its use, its relation to direct capital formation, and its implications for increases in the aggregate level of production.

In addition to measures for increasing production through increased input, production may be increased through greater skill in the use of inputs. Skill in husbandry is an important factor in traditional agricultures as well as in modern agriculture, although we do not know clearly how it compares in relative importance in these two types of agriculture. It is, however, particularly likely in traditional agriculture that the factors related to increased skill in husbandry of farming are closely related to increased labor input.

It is noteworthy that of the factors related to increased input the one most significant from the point of view of aggregate increase in production is that of labor. In general an increase in land quantity on an individual farm either does not increase the aggregate of production in an economy, because it represents a transfer from one farmer to another, or it is an indirect form of increase in labor input, reflecting the use of labor to bring more land into production. Particularly insofar as increased land input is the product of individual action by individual farmers, it tends, in a traditional agriculture, to involve expenditure of labor, with relatively little complementary input, in bringing new land to production through such labor-using devices as desalinization, clearing, leveling, and bunding land and so on. Thus we find that within the context of a traditional agriculture allocations regarding labor are of particular importance, and they remain important even after a large increase in use of the purchased inputs which accompany technological change and modernization.

Because technology is relatively static in a traditional agriculture, farmers' decisions are conditioned largely by gradual changes in factor proportions, caused by slow changes in population and land productivity, and derived changes in income and by weather and fluctuations in weather. Under such conditions the development of standard rules of thumb, which themselves become traditional, is a feasible and useful means of handling decisions and practice in farm management. Under such circumstances decision-making for a dynamic environment, in which the farmer has substantial control over a wide range of forces, may not be a highly developed skill, and thus emphasis on improved decision-making may be a necessary concomitant of modernization.

Farmers' Values and Objectives

Most governments of low-income countries formulate explicit development plans which include goals and objectives for agriculture in the aggregate and at least implicitly for individual farmers as well. Divergence between society's objectives, as expressed in economic plans, and farmers' practice and achievement is frequent. Such divergence may trace from inefficiency of farmers in meeting objectives they hold in common with government plans or from a divergence between the objectives of farmers and the objectives which society sets for farmers or of course, a combination of the two. It is important in forming sound public policy to diagnose what combination of the two factors explains observed divergence between behavior and objectives.

A divergence between farmers' objectives and those implicit in society's plans may arise because planners in essence set objectives which are sufficient oversimplifications of the collective values of society as to lose much validity. In particular, plans for agriculture often implicitly assume that farmers will maximize gross output or, slightly more complex, that farmers maximize gross output net of inputs purchased from other sectors. This in turn implicitly assumes that farmers attach very high utility to material goods available to them and the forms of output which can be sold to allow purchase of those material goods and attach very low value to idleness of labor and other resources which they control. In such cases farmers' objectives and society's objectives coincide. Divergence in achievement would then be due to inefficiency by farmers in meeting objectives rather than to a divergence in objectives. In fact, farmers' values and objectives generally do not conform with this presumption, and hence divergence in objectives does occur.

Although divergence in objectives may be substantial, it generally derives more from oversimplification of objectives by planners rather than a real divergence in underlying values. However, more basic divergence between farmers' and society's objectives may also occur. For example, society's objectives may imply a positive value to change and a low value to security in the status quo, but farmers may weigh these values differently. Likewise, society's objectives may implicitly place a high value on future income relative to present incomes as compared to the relative values ascribed to present and future income by farmers.

Clearly, judging performance by society's objectives for farmers may reflect divergence in achievement owing to the combined effect of inefficiency and differences in objectives. If the cause of failure to realize objectives set by society is inefficiency on the part of farmers in meeting commonly held objectives, then the solution lies with educational programs designed to achieve an increase in efficiency through farm-management analysis and teaching. The solution to a divergence of values and objectives requires much more complex efforts and adjustments.

The potential for divergence in objectives will be discussed under the three headings of material goods versus leisure, security versus change, and present income versus future income.

MATERIAL GOODS VERSUS LEISURE

Within the context of a traditional agriculture, farmer management decisions are importantly influenced by the relative weight farmers attach to the direct use of their labor in non-earning capacities (leisure in its broad sense)[1] and to material goods which may be produced or earned through transformation of labor in production processes. The special importance of these values in traditional agriculture derives from the importance of labor input in determining the production level. In a traditional agriculture, relatively few purchased inputs are used, so that little effect can be had on production by varying their quantity of input. In contrast, the level of production in a more developed agriculture may be importantly influenced by changing the level of input of fertilizer and other purchased inputs.

Within a traditional agriculture the farmer varies the level of production largely through the use of the resources which he supplies and controls himself—namely the land, capital, and family labor resources. There tends to be a very low and perhaps even a negative reservation price or value for idle land and capital resources, except as they may represent a direct embodiment of labor. Hence we find that in a subsistence agriculture the critical determinant of changes in the level of output is the input of family labor. This is in turn determined on the one hand by the relative values attached to leisure and material goods and on the other hand by the efficiency of the transformation of labor into material goods. This process may conveniently be seen in the form of a transformation of labor into material goods through five intermediate steps in the overall transformation. (For a fuller discussion see Mellor [1963].)

The intermediate transformations are as

1. See also the discussion by Jones below.

follows:[2] (1) the transformation of utility from leisure into labor; (2) the transformation of labor time into agricultural output; (3) the transformation of agricultural output into money; (4) the transformation of money into goods and services; and (5) the transformation of goods and services into utility. Of these transformations, (1) and (5) are the determinants of isoutility curves depicting lines of equal utility in the substitution of utility in the form of leisure for utility from material goods and services. The other three transformations represent, in essence, the production opportunities for converting man time, in the form of leisure, into goods and services as measured by market value. Transformation (2) is represented by the physical production function and (3) and (4) by the level of agricultural and consumer-goods prices.

Observed behavior of farmers regarding allocation of labor between leisure and production is thus a function of his values, his production possibilities, and the price relationships he faces. Since they are all interrelated, we cannot presume anything about the nature and effect of one of these without the knowledge of the nature and effect of the others.

The basis for farmers' decision regarding the allocation of labor between leisure and work can be depicted through the traditional representation of an indifference surface, as in Figure 7.1. On the horizontal axis, Oc demarcates the total man time available to be divided between labor and leisure. Increased labor is represented by a shift to the left. The vertical axis measures quantity of goods and services. In the particular representation in Figure 7.1, additional lines are drawn to demarcate the quantity of goods, Ox, required to provide minimal biological subsistence and the quantity of goods, Oy, to provide what is termed a culturally determined subsistence level.

The isoutility curves depicted $(T-Z)$ are drawn on the assumption that the utility from material goods is extremely high up to provision of biological subsistence, then drops significantly until the culturally determined subsistence is achieved, and then drops further. In actuality the transitions between these sectors would probably be gradual and hence

2. For alternative and related formulations, see Nakajima above and Fisk-Shand below.

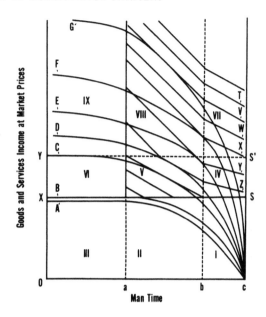

Figure 7.1. Hypothetical utility surface indicating the effect on labor input of various production possibilities.

the lines would curve gradually rather than experiencing the abrupt changes of the simplified presentation in Figure 7.1.

The slopes of the isoutility curves depicted also reflect a loss of utility as leisure is converted into work. The representation in Figure 7.1 depicts a relatively low utility to leisure in segments bc when little work is being done and a very high utility to leisure in segment ab. Line a represents a position of extreme utility to leisure set by the biological requirement of rest.

The transformation curves A–G convex to the origin reflecting declining marginal productivity of the labor resources as it is applied against fixed land and capital resources. The different transformation curves may reflect either different resource availabilities or different technologies. The curves reaching higher levels represent the presence of either more nonlabour resources or more labor-productive technology.

Given such an indifference surface, we can readily see the effect on allocation of labor, and hence on production, of various changes in the decision-making environment. It will be noted, however, that the effect of any one change in that environment will be influenced by the state of the other factors. For example, the effect of a technological change which increases the productivity of labor, represented by a shift from one production possibility curve to another, will depend on the nature of the isoutility curves as well as on the precise nature of the technological change. Thus, a technological change may result in a net withdrawal of labor, thereby in part counterbalancing the production-increasing effect of the change, or a net increase in labor input, thereby reinforcing the production-increasing effect of the technological change. Technological change tends to increase incomes which tends to cause operation at positions of lower utility to material goods and services and hence a decrease in labor input. But technological change also increases the marginal productivity of labor which encourages increased labor input. The resolution of these opposing forces depends on the specific environment in which they operate.

It is commonly argued that subsistence farmers in traditional economies in fact attach substantial value to leisure and relatively low value to additions of material goods and service beyond the requirements of subsistence. If we were to depict the extreme of such a situation on an indifference surface, the lines would be vertical lines terminating at the horizontal line of minimum subsistence. Operation would occur at the point at which the production possibility curve intersected the subsistence line. Availability of improved technology or more non-labor assets would provide an increase in utility by allowing a reduction in the labor input and no increase in production would occur.

It is of course unlikely that such an extreme form of limited aspirations exists. It is, however likely that in many low-income subsistence economies income pressures are suficiently severe to have, in fact, pushed the marginal utility of the last increments of material-goods income to unusually high levels. This causes at least those on small farms, and hence those under the severest income pressure, to introduce additional family labor into production even when the marginal returns are extremely low. In such a case there may be a reluctance to continue further input of labor at extremely low marginal returns if the resource position or the state of technology improves. This is not a condition of tightly limited aspirations so much as an unwillingness to work for extremely low marginal returns except when under the pressures of extreme poverty. The type of reactions which derive from this situation do, however, largely explain what may appear on the surface to be anomalous behavior—e.g. on very small farms substantial idle labor and great poverty (the marginal product of labor having been driven to zero); somewhat larger farms but still quite poor, all the labor force working hard (subsistence having been achieved by exactly using all the labor); and still larger farms with idle labor and relative prosperity (subsistence and somewhat more having been achieved, some of the added prosperity then being taken in greater leisure) [Mellor, 1963].

The preceding discussion of factors affecting allocations of family labor between leisure and productive work has a broad application. The following points have particular relevance to the subsistence farmer in a traditional economy.

This class of farmer is essentially by definition likely to include many poor farmers operating at points of unusually high but also rapidly declining utility to added material goods income, and hence they are particularly likely to respond to modest improvement in asset position or productivity by withdrawing labor from the production process. This tendency is certainly not universal, and certainly major increases in productivity or improvements in asset position may provide a shift to substantially different positions on the utility surface which will provide an increase in allocation of labor from leisure toward work.

Other factors within a subsistence farming system in a traditional economy which are likely to favor allocations of family labor toward leisure rather than work are: relatively narrow range and scant availability of attractive consumer goods, which lowers the utility of money earned from increased production; traditional attitudes concerning consumption which further lowers the utility of new forms of material goods and services; backward technology which lowers the productivity of labor and hence lowers the quantity of material goods and services which may be had for giving up a given quantity of leisure.

All these same factors, of course, also tend to encourage the use of hired labor to replace family labor. Such substitution of hired labor will occur whenever the marginal cost of the hired labor is less than the marginal value (based on utility and reservation price) of family labor. Problems of supervision and lower productivity of hired labor tend to provide some price and productivity discontinuity between family labor and hired labor, so that the analysis of the pure family labor case in fact has considerable relevance even when hired labor is available. In any case these phenomena explain why low-income subsistence agricultures typically include substantial use of hired labor even when family labor seems quite underemployed and consumption levels low. It is simply again a case of the marginal cost of hired labor's being extremely low and hence lower than the marginal utility of the family labor in leisure. This situation does not necessarily show an unusually high utility to leisure, since it occurs in a situation of very low cost of labor.

SECURITY VERSUS CHANGE

Society's values and objectives, as reflected in economic plans of developing nations, emphasize change, with particular emphasis on technological change in the rural sector. Such plans tend implicitly to place low weight on the risks involved in change or the converse value and objective of security. The subsistence farmers who must execute plans for technological change must weigh the risks and potential probabilities of gains and losses in any change. In addition, farmers' decisions, given certain probabilities, may vary when differing weights are attached to values concerning security and change. On the one hand, farmers may obtain special gratification from change itself and, given an even chance of gain, may choose change for the ancillary benefits of change and variety. On the other hand, farmers may attach special value to maintaining the status quo, and this may in part overbalance the other values and gains that change may offer. Thus, in deciding upon change, we have considerations not only of the economics of the probabilities of gains and losses, but also of the values of farmers regarding risks and risk-taking.

Subsistence farming in a traditional agriculture tends to be strongly influenced by features which encourage conservatism and thereby retard innovation and change. Special value tends to be attached to survival and maintenance of position as opposed to change and the improvement of position. Although such attitudes may be rooted in historic economic influences and relationships, the likelihood that they may have become institutionalized as a value and objective in themselves must not be ignored.

The economic basis for an attitude which is conservative and not oriented toward change lies with the high risks associated with change in a traditional agriculture and the potentially high penalty for failures in change. Firstly there is a high risk associated with innovation because of the lack of systematic research and testing. Presumably in any society a high proportion of initial ideas for change would not, in fact, provide improvement. Where institutionalized research and testing are carried on as in high-income commercial agricultures, the potentially successful innovations are systematically selected from a mass of possible changes, and hence those which are finally recommended have a high probability of success. In addition, innovation derived from institutionalized development of innovation may be derived from a systematic framework of past work and theory, which increase the likelihood of success for a given innovation. In contrast, innovation in a traditional agriculture will tend to have a high proportion of failures and is likely on the average not to pay. Development of societal values and institutions which protect individuals and the society itself from losses from innovation becomes strengthened in such cases.

In addition, the low-income characteristics of subsistence agriculture tend to place a heavy penalty for failure if an attempted innovation does not succeed. A failure which drives a farmer under the margin of subsistence or into debt in a system of high interest rates may be disastrous and thus eliminate the possibility of playing probabilities which would pay well over the long term.

Further, in a commercial economy some forms of change may be so institutionalized that the leads to inactivity by the farmer as a deliberate agent of change; for example, this happens with new seed varieties which become the principal ones available through normal commercial channels, and likewise for new forms of fertilizer, insecticides, and so on.

Having pointed out the factors which may drive farmers economic advantage and cultural values toward inertia, it is important not to overstate the inhibitions which this provides. Indeed, in most countries in the world farmers are already in transition from traditional to dynamic agricultures.

We find substantial evidence that in the modern world attitudes toward innovation in subsistence agricultures do change. For example, conditions can and do arise in which the innovator obtains greater prestige with the popularization of concern for development.

There is inequality of income distribution in most subsistence agricultures. Hence each community includes persons for whom the penalty of introducing an uneconomic innovation is not great. These persons may innovate and serve as the testers for others, thereby providing a sequence for innovation. With change in values and the availability of a class which can afford experimentation, a groundwork is laid for innovation and change at such time as profitable innovation is made available.

Finally some innovations may obviously represent a low-risk opportunity for large gain. Such innovations at least face little economic bar to acceptance.

PRESENT INCOME VERSUS FUTURE INCOME

An important ingredient of economic development is an increased stock of capital. Since agriculture is initially the dominant sector in most low-income traditional socieities, the agricultural sector is likely to have to provide much of the capital used in its own development [Mellor, 1966]. The extent to which subsistence farmers choose to save and invest depends on an economic factor—the rate of return which they can receive from saving and investing—and upon a value or objective factor—the relative weight which they attach to present and future income. There are likely to be a number of conflicting currents in regard to these factors.

As will be discussed later in the paper, the returns to investment by subsistence farmers tend to be relatively low, so that a high rate of investment would tend to require a relatively heavy weighing of future income as compared to present income.

Basic attitudes toward consumption, security, and fatalism, all have an important influence on farmers' values and objectives regarding saving and investment, and they are all inextricably interwoven with the economics of the rate of return on investment. Each of these attitudes is complex.

A strong drive toward improved material well-being might in itself discourage saving and investment as the farmer makes an effort to maximize his current level of consumption. On the other hand, more attractive consumer goods may encourage the farmer to reduce consumption now, so that a greater increase can occur later. With more attractive consumer goods he may aspire to reach a higher income level and be willing to wait to achieve it through investment. Particularly in this regard the effect of values and objectives may be so interwoven with the economics of the rate of return of investment that they cannot be separated empirically. Given two farmers with the same values and introducing more attractive consumption goods to them, one might increase consumption and decrease saving while the other acts conversely, with the only difference being different rates of return available in investment.

Conversely, a weak drive toward improved economic position may reflect itself in low rates of saving because the incentive to increase future incomes does not exist. But concurrently the low drive toward increasing consumption may place only a light burden on the current income and provide ease and scope for saving. If concurrently there is strong desire to maintain consumption levels, there may be an ancillary drive to save in order to assure maintenance of future consumption in the face of fluctuating income. However, such a situation may also result in decisions which withhold resources from production and provide low levels of income—levels which might be raised if increased incentives were provided. In this case the interaction with the rate of return will be less than in the case cited previously.

We can say further that if the rate of return

to investment is raised substantially, it may have a very favorable effect on saving and investment, provided there is a strong drive for increased material welfare, but very little effect if the values attached to material improvement are slight. Likewise, if material incentives are increased, subsistence farmers may channel savings more toward productive forms of investment and less toward hoarding. They may also put more inputs into the production process providing more income and then carry on more saving from that increased income.

Clearly another factor pushing toward emphasis on present consumption is the existing low level of incomes in a subsistence agriculture. However, income variability may provide substantial scope for some individuals to save, thereby reducing the risk for future investors and innovators by demonstrating the workability of innovation and investment.

Fatalism—the assumption that man has little opportunity for control of his own destiny—is, of course, not conducive to high rates of saving and investment. Such attitudes are likely to be reflected in input of resources sufficient to provide the culturally determined level of subsistence with no substantial margin beyond that.

In a subsistence agriculture we find the rate of saving and investment and the size of the capital stock to be small. This derives in significant part from the low rates of return to incremental investment typical of traditional economies. This tendency is probably reinforced by a greater tendency toward a fatalistic view of life, by relatively greater concern with maintaining income in contrast to desire to increase income, by a relatively greater weight to present income compared to future income, and by a relatively low level of income.

VARIABILITY AMONG SUBSISTENCE FARMERS

In regard to all the influences discussed above, there is likely to be considerable variability among farmers in observed differences in actions and in the underlying values and objectives. Substantial variability among farmers suggest that development programs will vary in success among groups of farmers.

An important research need is to study variability within communities in order to provide guidelines for action programs. Variables of particular importance are those associated with the economic factors of farm size and asset position and the related factors of income and educational level. A number of social factors are also of great importance in influencing farmers' values and objectives and in setting the environment in which values and objectives display themselves.

In addition, important changes in objectives and values occur over time. It is important that policy recognize and adjust to such changes.

FARMERS' DECISIONS

It has been clear from the preceding discussion that farmers' values and objectives are inextricably intertwined with the decision-making possibilities open to them. This section considers three important decision areas and examines the rationality of farmers' decisions in these areas. These decision-making areas are those of the allocation of existing resources, the command of additional resources, response to price, and response to technological change.

THE ALLOCATION OF EXISTING RESOURCES

Subsistence farmers normally have substantial allocative control over the land, labor, and capital resources they use. Controversy exists as to the extent to which subsistence farmers efficiently allocate these resources, given the existing environment in regard to values and objectives, resource productivity, and resource prices. Question is raised concerning farmers' efficiency regarding both the intensity of use of resources and the combination of enterprises and outputs. The controversy is important because it indicates the scope for development purely through educating farmers to make better decisions which increase production without further input as contrasted with the necessity to facilitate development by providing a basic and important set of changes in the environment within which farmers make decisions. Given a current high state of efficiency, requisite changes in the environment might range from providing new production possibilities through research, to providing new forms of inputs such as fertilizer, to new consumption possibilities, to education, and so on. Changing the decision-making environment normally requires a substantial planning and resource input by society.

Empirical studies testing farmers' decision for efficiency give conflicting impressions [Tax, 1953; Desai, 1963; Schultz, 1964; Heady and Randhawa, 1964]. This is true in both high- and low-income countries. Unfortunately, empirical studies of efficiency are subject to considerable hidden error. Any error in assumption concerning objectives, factor productivity, and factor costs on the part of the analyst is reflected in the finding of inefficiency on the part of the farmer (e.g. assuming an objective of money-income maximization, too high labor productivity, or too low labor costs will all result in showing optional cropping patterns more weighted to intensive crops than is found in practice). On one hand, incorrect criteria and assumptions will tend to show farmers acting inefficiently if they are in effect acting efficiently. But likewise, such incorrect criteria may also show farmers as acting efficiently when in fact they are not.

In this same vein it is also important to recognize that even to demonstrate that on the average within an area farmers allocate resources efficiently is not to argue against substantial opportunity for increased efficiency. Normally a sample will include substantial variability around that average. Thus, farmers may be efficient on the average *while all are individually inefficient*; this is analogous to the rabbit which was, on the average, shot by the two bullets which passed, respectively, one foot in front and one foot behind it. The question which must be answered is that of the extent to which variability in decisions and allocations by farmers arises from inefficient allocation on the part of many farmers and to what extent it reflects efficient allocation by individuals within a context of different conditions. It is indeed particularly likely, within a traditional agriculture, that the decision-making environment, and hence the nature of optimal decisions, will vary considerably from farm to farm. The emphasis in traditional subsistence agriculture on self-supplied inputs,

and the resultant scope for sharply different valuations of family labor with differences in values and incomes, is an important source of interfarm variation in environment and hence in the allocation of resources. These special factors are in addition to the usual ones of varying soils and other physical resources.

Thus, when we observe variability in allocations among farmers, we must be cautious in assuming that the variability in itself provides scope for increasing overall efficiency and production.

Except for a few unusually carefully performed and documented studies, we are forced to build our case regarding the efficiency of subsistence farmers in allocating their resources largely on a careful chain of logic. The primary argument for expecting high efficiency within the environment of subsistence agriculture is that the physical, economic, and cultural environment is relatively static over time, in contrast to its great geographic variability. Under such conditions we expect farmers, even through a process of trial and error and natural selection, to gravitate toward an optimal solution to resource allocation. Thus we should expect to find highly efficient allocation of resources in a subsistence agriculture in a traditional economy, as compared with commercial agriculture in a developed economy, not because subsistence farmers are better allocators, but because they have had considerable time to gravitate toward an optimal solution with a fairly constant technology.

Farmers in a dynamic agriculture are very likely to be out of adjustment even if they are efficient managers just because the environment is changing rapidly. Such farmers have to run quickly indeed just to hold a given degree of efficiency. This suggests an important caveat. Just because we often find farmers in traditional agricultures in good adjustment with their stable environment, we should not assume that they are quick and able decision-makers when their environment begins to change dramatically. And it follows that as economic development provides a dynamic environment, we may find a particular need for programs for helping farmers develop into better decision-makers.

Given the above argument, there seems little sense in teaching better decision-making to subsistence farmers as a first step in development and prior to changing the technological environment within which decisions are made. But as soon as the environment is changed, it may be important to help farmers improve their decision-making abilities. This will be less true with very simple or high rate-of-return innovations and more true for complex or lower rate-of-return innovations.

The preceding discussion is relevant to the role of farm management studies within the context of traditional subsistence agriculture. In such an economy the first role of farm-management studies is to study farmer decision-making within the context of the given decision-making environment, in order to discover what elements of that environment must be changed if farmers' decisions to increase production and income are to be made profitable and successful—this is, of course, policy-oriented farm-management research. Following such research and implementation of the prescribed policy, then, farm management research must follow quickly with programs for aiding farmers in adjusting their decisions to the new environment which has made production and income increasing innovation possible and profitable [Schickele, 1966].

THE COMMAND OF ADDITIONAL RESOURCES

The level of agricultural production is determined not only by the efficiency with which farmers use the resources which they command, but also by the willingness and ability of farmers to command additional resources. A principal possibility for command of additional resources to combine with labor lies with purchased forms of capital. Although initially of minor importance, such capital input grows in importance with development. Farmers may command more capital by increased saving, by borrowing, and by renting.

In the discussion of objectives and values, some of the complex considerations involved in saving and investment were reviewed. The main point which needs added emphasis in this context is the importance of the rate of return on capital in determining farmers' willingness to save and to invest. If, as appears likely from available empirical evidence, the returns to incremental investment are low, then there is little incentive to save for further investment [Stevens, 1959].

If the returns to capital are too low to be attractive for saving, it is unlikely that they will be attractive for borrowing, particularly since in most traditional agricultures the interest rates are high by the standards of high-income commercial agricultures. Of course it might be superficially argued that the high interest rates indicate high rates of return. However, it is likely that interest rates in traditional agricultures are made by the very high utility arising from consumption purposes on the part of the lower-income segments of the rural population and by the high risks and administrative costs of such lending. Thus, high interest rates do not necessarily reflect high rates of return to productive investment.

Many of the same problems arise in estimating the returns to any given resource which arise in making overall estimates of efficiency. An error in any number of respects is likely to cumulate upon the particular resource under examination. Again there is a tendency for the more carefully drawn studies to show surprisingly low returns to investment by individual farmers within the context of susbistence farms in a traditional economy [Schultz, 1964]. And here again a reasonable base of logical support may be provided. Firstly a high proportion of capital in a traditional agriculture represents a relatively direct embodiment of family labor —e.g. wells for irrigation, land leveling, and bunding. Such forms of capital are likely to have their returns driven to the low level normal for labor within a traditional subsistence agriculture. In these cases even the disutility of waiting for income is likely to be low, given the alternatives. Further, even those forms of capital which require investment of more than family labor in their creation usually have labor-input substitutes which will tend to hold down their returns, although the level may not be as low as in the case of capital directly formed by family labor.

Compounding the problem is the conservatism of peasant farmers, which makes them reluctant to add to their debt. This conservatism is based in part on economic factors, which require mitigation if the conservatism is to be released. The economic factors relate to the high risk of farming in most traditional agricultures. Farmers in traditional economies face much higher risk in regard to new technology than is true of farmers in commercial agricultures which have institutionalized the development and the testing of innovation so that the likelihood of recommendations actually being profitable is high.

Farmers also tend to face higher risk from natural hazards in traditional agricultures because investment has not been as heavily made in means of controlling the environment. Devices ranging from fully engineered irrigation works to broad programs of pest control all reduce the risk from natural hazards and are more widespread and effective in commercial agricultures. Subsistence agriculture in a traditional economy is likely to be caught in a vicious circle of low levels of technology, causing low returns to devices for reducing risk, and likewise low returns accrue to new technology due to the high risk—then all this is compounded by the scarcity of capital, technology, and administration for effecting devices for reducing risk.

Price risk may also be particularly high in traditional agricultures—and even "subsistence" farmers are subject to the market, since they normally have some marketed surplus and some requirements for cash purchases. Short-term volatility of agricultural prices arises from lack of knowledge of production prospects and storage stocks, the high risks from natural hazards and the relatively small proportion of production actually entering the market. The resultant volatility of market prices discourages farmers from further enlarging risks through borrowing.

PRICE RESPONSE

Change in the relative price of agricultural commodities may offer opportunity for farmers to increase incomes or prevent a decline in incomes through changing farm enterprise combinations. There is ample evidence that farmers in low-income countries observe such opportunities and act in an economically rational manner. Indeed, the greater flexibility of capital and management know-how in a traditional economy provides a basis for a more substantial response to price

is substitution of commodities, under given physical conditions, than is likely with the specialized highly crop-specific machinery and technical know-how of the modern, technologically advanced commercial agriculture. Thus, insofar as we deal with substitutions of commercial crops for which the production ratios are similar to the price ratios, we can expect subsistence farmers to exhibit high-price elasticities of supply [Bauer and Yamey, 1959; Krishna, 1963; Falcon, 1964]. The major complexities arise in regard to the case of aggregate response in production by farmers to an overall shift in the level of agriculture to nonagricultural prices and the case of subsistence crops. The aggregate case will be taken first.

The extent of response of the aggregate of agricultural production is, of course, the prime consideration if one is concerned with increasing the aggregate level of agricultural production or aggregate contribution to national income through price policy. The question of aggregate production response to price is best analyzed through analysis of the effect of price changes on the input of resources.

In a traditional agriculture there is by definition little scope for changes in production in response to change in the aggregate of agricultural prices through increased use of purchased fertilizer and similar inputs. As development occurs, such inputs increase in importance and aggregate price response should increase for this reason. There is scope in a traditional agriculture for price response through greater use of organic manures, increased weeding, and many similar practices. These, however, largely represent a direct embodiment of agricultural labor. Likewise the scope for greater use of land through bringing more land into cultivation and use of more capital in the form of land improvement largely involve relatively direct inputs of labor. Hence in a traditional agriculture the question of aggregate response to price resolves itself in large part to a question of labor response.

In an industrialized, commercialized economy some scope exists for changing the pace of labor shifts out of agriculture in response to changes in the relative level of agricultural prices. That this is a limited scope even in high-income countries is evidenced by the continuing resource maladjustments in the high-income economies of the United States and many European countries. The scope for such intersectoral shifts is, however, much more limited in low-income countries with chronic shortages of capital, rapid population growth, and substantial unemployment. In a low-income largely agricultural economy, the aggregate response of the agricultural labor force to price must be largely through a reallocation between agricultural labor and leisure or unemployment.

The extent to which farmers reallocate their family labor in response to changes in the marginal value productivity of their labor is a subject of complex counterforces. As indicated earlier in the case of technology, the effect of price changes can be broken into an income effect and a substitution effect. A price increase tends to have an income effect which is production-decreasing and a substitution effect which is production-increasing. The less the income effect and the greater the substitution effect, the greater will be the positive effect of price on production. If, for example, the marginal utility of added consumer goods and the marginal physical productivity of labor is relatively constant, then it is presumed that a rise in agricultural prices will raise the marginal value product of labor to the point at which the utility from the added income will be greater than the utility lost from the marginal labor. In that case there will be a positive response in production to a price increase. Since labor is an important input, and a substantial stock of relatively unutilized labor tends to exist in traditional agriculture, the potential for increased production through this means might be large. Clearly the response to price may be held down by two factors.

Firstly, it is possible that the marginal utility of added material goods may be declining significantly. This is particularly likely, as indicated previously, if the consumption patterns are relatively tradition-bound and if new, suitable forms of consumer goods are not made available. At the extreme a sharp drop in the marginal utility of added material goods and services may present the standard backward-bending supply curve as farmers' high-utility needs are met with higher prices and lower output.

A higher utility position is achieved by withdrawing labor from production to the point at which the marginal utility of the last increment of material goods derived through the production process is matched by the marginal utility of the last increment of leisure. This tendency may be counteracted on the price-utility side by making attractive consumer goods available or on the production side by increasing the marginal productivity of labor. The more sharply the marginal utility of material goods declines, the sharper the shift in prices must be to induce an aggregate increase in production. Large shifts in labor productivity, induced by technological change, are probably more economically and politically feasible than large shifts in relative prices.

Secondly, the effect of a price increase may be small on the aggregate of production if the marginal physical productivity of added labor is low or sharply declining. At the extreme, if labor has a zero marginal productivity, then price cannot cause an increase in production by attracting more labor into the production process. The effect will similarly be small if the marginal physical product is low and declining. Although it is unlikely that the marginal physical product of labor is zero, it is generally quite low in most agricultures and, in fact, sufficiently low so that labor is used in production only when the utility of consumer-material-goods income is very high or the disutility of sacrificing labor is unusually low. Thus an upward shifting of labor productivity functions may be necessary for major aggregate-production response from price increases. This analysis, of course, suggests that price policy will be more effective in effecting changes in aggregate production in agricultures with higher marginal products of labor—in parts of West Africa, for example, as compared to parts of South Asia.

In the aggregate there is, of course, little evidence of backward-bending supply curves. However, it is likely that there is considerable variability among farmers regarding supply response. The sum of some farmers responding positively to price but others in fact responding negatively probably results in a normal situation of very modest positive aggregate response of agricultural production to price. The aggregate response will probably increase as more purchased inputs are used in production and as the utility of material goods beyond those required for subsistence is raised through greater availability of a greater variety of attractive consumer goods. Raising labor productivity may also have this effect by shifting marginal decisions into areas of less sharply dropping utility schedules.

One of the arguments for assuming low responsiveness to price by subsistence farmers in traditional economies is that such farmers are concerned largely with production for their own use and hence attach special value to crops and livestock produced for home use relative to production for sale—what might be termed subsistence-mindedness (see Penny, above). In general however, subsistence farmers are not completely rigid in their production patterns for subsistence commodities. The apparent inflexibility arises from two sources, the first a matter of price relationships and the second a matter of forms of risk and uncertainty related to price.

In deciding upon relative emphasis on subsistence crops, it is economic for farmers to compare the farm price of crops they will sell and the retail price for crops they are to buy. Since there may be a significant difference between these prices because of marketing costs, there may well be a range of prices within these bounds within which individual farmers will not respond to price. The aggregate effect of this will be to reduce the average extent of response of supply to changes in price relationships at retail.

This tendency will be increased by farmers' reaction to risk and uncertainty. It is of great importance to peasant farmers that they be able to meet their subsistence needs. It happens that in most low-income countries there are great seasonal and year-to-year fluctuations in market availability of food crops and in market prices. As a result, farmers fear that if they produce certain crops for sale and then buy subsistence crops on the market, they will be caught purchasing at a time of seasonally or cyclically high prices or low supply. This simply means that farmers might restructure production with given price relationships if these prices were certain. But in the face of price uncertainty they will tend to favor the production of subsistence needs.

Finally, since subsistence crops normally dominate the total acreage, there is limited potential to shift production of these so that the crop-supply elasticity will respond more like the aggregate.

RESPONSE TO TECHNOLOGICAL CHANGE

The record in regard to acceptance of technological change by subsistence farmers in traditional economies is mixed. On the one hand we have the generally poor record in this regard of major programs of community development and extension. Such programs have normally included an effort to gain farmer acceptance of a wide range of innovations said to increase production and incomes, and yet the acceptance of change—and particularly the impact on production—has generally been rather small. On the other hand we have numbers of examples of individual innovations, including a number of mechanical innovations, improved seed varieties, inorganic fertilizers, and so on, which have in certain specific situations spread very rapidly even without formal programs of farmer education and exhortation.

In regard to the failures of community development and extension, it is easy to demonstrate that a high proportion of what has been recommended has not been economically or even technically suitable, and hence failure of farmer to accept such innovation appears more as a recommendation of their economic acumen than of their noneconomic drives. But on the other hand, a high proportion of the success stories tend to involve innovations which were very similar to practices already followed, which were simple and easy to apply, and which provided unusually high returns. The record for complex innovations providing more modest returns is not so clear. The record in regard to acceptance of innovation is further clouded by the wide range of factors which may inhibit acceptance of innovation.

Innovation may be accepted by farmers, not because of the direct economic benefits from the innovation itself, but because a acceptance of innovation brings ancillary benefits of favor from personnel and agencies fostering the innovation. The tying of extension programs with programs of government subsidized inputs, including credit, is an important case in point. Innovation may also be accepted or rejected on basically noneconomic grounds of traditionalism on the one hand or prestige of being an innovator on the other. (See the case studies, below, on Vicos, ACAR, and Comilla.)

Insofar as acceptance of innovation by subsistence farmers in traditional agricultures is based on the individual direct economic gains from the innovation, then three conditions must be met if innovation is to be accepted. There must be a desire for increased material welfare, there must be expectation that specific innovation will increase wealth, and there must be expectation that the farmer as innovator will participate in an increase in wealth from innovation.

The desire for increased material welfare may be weak in a traditional agriculture. An apparent attitude of uninterest in improved material welfare may grow in a situation in which there has been a history of no possibility of improved welfare through increased production—a condition common in traditional agriculture. Under such circumstances improvement in the position of one individual must come largely from taking income away from others—that is, by redistribution of wealth (see Rogers, above). The alternative of increasing individual wealth through expanding production is not thought to exist. In such circumstances a stable society requires conventions which inhibit desire for increased material welfare. Lacking such restraints, society will be constantly torn by strife as each attempts to benefit himself by taking advantage of others. Thus it is likely that, the longer the stable cultural history of an economically traditional society, the more inhibitions to incentives for change will have become institutionalized. In such societies the first requisite to increasing incentives is development of an awareness of the possibility of change and an awareness that this possibility can be positively rewarding both to the individual and to society as a whole and not just at the expense of the welfare of others. In most parts of the world enough has already been done in effectuating political and social change, and to a certain extent in introducing economic change, to achieve the requisite awareness.

A problem which was probably critical a few decades ago is probably now restricted in importance to scattered pockets of traditionalism.

Judging from past history, it is likely that political ferment plays an important role in developing a favorable personal and institutional attitude toward change. The very act of change in political leadership, the emphasis upon man's control of his own destiny which accompanies political ferment, and the rapid development and dissemination of ideas, must all play a role in the process of loosening men's minds and encouraging an attitude favoring change and improvement. In most parts of the world recent decades have seen substantial political ferment and it is likely that this has broad impact upon the motivation of men and their attitude toward change.

Given a general environment of ferment and change, the formal educational system may play an additional important role in shaping the development of broadened horizons. Education introduces a logic and rationale to many aspects of life, it opens up knowledge of different things, it demonstrates change, and, equally important, education itself provides one of the most important means of change by increasing mobility to other jobs and by providing a basis for understanding changes within agriculture which may improve welfare.

In addition to the political framework and education, physical health may play an important part in the development of positive motivation toward change. Where a population is heavily ridden with parasitic infections and debilitative disease, its physical energy is certainly sapped and its seems likely that an attitude of lethargy and inertia is created. It is difficult for persons ill and weak from such health conditions to develop an interest and enthusiasm for change. Indeed, in nations with substantial stock of unutilized manpower the favorable effect of control of disease on mental attitude may be much more important to the progress of development than its purely physical effect. Unfortunately little empirical study of this aspect of public health has been made, so we can do little more than speculate upon its significance.

It is also likely that the variety and quantity of consumer goods available has an important influence on the extent of desire for improved material welfare. Even where the possibility of change is accepted and education and health have broadened horizons and ambitions, the desire for increased material welfare may be small because of the lack of availability of consumer items of the type and units which are suitable to existing incomes. It is probably correct that the longer the history of cultural development of a society, the more standardized and traditional will be consumption patterns and the greater the inhibitions to the introduction of new consumption patterns. Again, however, most societies have now had sufficient history of new forms of consumption patterns to have at least seriously weakened the hold of traditionalism on consumption patterns. The problem nowadays in most areas is more likely one of providing the consumer-goods incentives in the appropriate price, quality, and quantity ranges rather than in breaking the hold of traditionalism on consumption patterns.

Thus, it is likely that subsistence farmers in a traditional economy are slow to innovate, even if innovation is highly profitable, because of various inhibitions to material improvement. Contemporary political ferment, expansion of education, widespread marketing of consumer goods, improved health and other factors, have all contributed to a much more encouraging current attitude toward innovation in most of the world's peasant economies.

Currently it is likely that a greater barrier to acceptance of technological change is that of the farmers' low expectations that specific technological changes will, in fact, increase wealth. Again there is a tendency in traditional agricultures with a long history of cultural development to have institutionalized resistance to innovation.

In a traditional agriculture the past evidence concerning innovation and change has generally been that it does not provide improvement. Until development of innovations (research) is institutionalized and based on a solid body of theory and tested thoroughly, it involves high risk. Under such circumstances, the group which is most likely to survive is the one which puts decision-making power into the hands of senior persons who have had ample opportunity to see innovation fail and who will

profit from that experience by extreme conservatism. Even initial efforts to institutionalize research are likely to include a relatively high proportion of failures. Hence, even as conscious development commences, the premium may still lie with the conservative rather than the innovative. It thus is important to the development of a desire for change, and motivation to change, that successful innovation be produced and demonstrated. And then a slow process of change in leadership patterns may be required.

Further inhibition to acceptance of innovation by subsistence farmers in traditional economies arises from the factors discussed in previous sectors dealing with labor allocation, borrowing of resources, and response to price.

Particularly in early stages of agricultural development, innovation may require additional labor input if it is to be profitable [Mellor, 1962]. In such a case innovation may not be accepted for the simple reason that it requires a substantial labor input and yet does not generate sufficient income to return the labor enough to attract it into production. In such a case farmers' actions seem uneconomic only if it is assumed that the labor has no opportunity cost or reservation price— a not uncommon error on the part of economists.

On the other hand, technological advance may provide the basis for shifting the labor-input, crop-output schedule up to the right sufficiently to raise the level of returns to the requisite additional labor input enough to attract it into use [Mellor, 1963]. Indeed, the expectation of very high returns to technological advance in low-income countries is based in part on the premise that such an effect will be had.

These points are illustrated in Figure 7.2. Function A represents the relationship between family labor input and output under conditions of traditional technology. Function B represents the situation with a new technology. If the configuration of the utility surfaces causes the level of labor input chosen for function A to be ox, then the new technology does not provide increased production unless labor input is increased as well. If the slope of the utility curves do not change over the relevant range, then introduction of the new technology will encourage input of

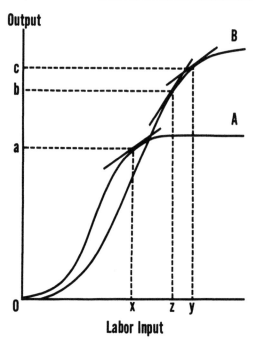

Figure 7.2. Hypothetical production functions indicating a possible effect of technological change on labor input and output.

additional labor xy. At labor input oy, the slope of *B* is the same as the slope of *A* at input ox. If, however, the slope of the utility curves drop sharply for output (income) higher than a, then the new technology may not elicit additional labor input and may therefore represent an inferior system.

If in reference to Figure 7.1 the utility curves are not vertical above the subsistence level and the change in the shape of the production function is as radical as depicted in the case of Function *A* and *B* in Figure 7.2, then an alternative position may be chosen. The sharp rise in marginal values on the new function may provide a new equilibrium point at which labor input is increased to a point such as ox and production to point ob. This represents a point of higher labor input, higher output, and higher marginal productivity of labor than the position previously occupied on Function *A*.

This discussion should clarify the potentially important, but often neglected, role of labor-saving tools. If farmers are operating at the top of the total product curve, labor-saving tools simply represent substitution of capital for labor with no effect on output. However,

if operation occurs below the top of the function, then labor-saving tools may increase the marginal productivity of labor and thereby induce operation at a higher level of output. Thus, if labor-saving tools account for the difference between production possibility *D* and *E*, Figure 7.1, they would not be yield-increasing. If they accounted for the difference between *E* and *G*, the effect would be yield-increasing and would also cause increased labor input. The role of labor-saving tools becomes particularly important when technical innovation of a yield-increasing type is highly labor-using, as in case *B*, Figure 7.2.

Farmers may, of course, also be inhibited from accepting innovation because of their reluctance to increase debt. In a subsistence economy special problems arise if innovation requires added cash expenditure and cash indebtedness and yet generates more output which is likely to be consumed in the farm household. The tendency for technological innovation to require increased monetary input also increases the problem of risk associated with price instability.

Finally, the profitability of innovation is affected by the skill and knowledge with which it is executed. In traditional subsistence agriculture the background of education or experience with change is such that innovation is often poorly executed and hence provides poor returns. In the case of very simple innovation, involving simple substitution of one seed for another, this may prove of small restrictive importance. However, with complex innovation, such as the complex package including hybrid maize, a major problem may exist which the standard institutions of a subsistence agriculture are not well adapted to meet.

Even if farmers are motivated to change and innovation is profitable, there remains a requirement for expectation on the part of the innovator that he will himself participate in the net increase in wealth which accompanies successful innovation. The innovator may fail to participate in the benefits of innovation for three sets of reasons: he may not have sufficient control of the factors of production to channel benefits to himself; he may not have sufficient control of the marketing process to channel benefits to himself; and he may not have sufficient control of his own consumption patterns to allow increased income to be used to his own benefit. All three of these influences are likely to be closely related to the system of land tenure, and all three are likely to represent a special problem in subsistence agriculture in traditional economies.

Land represents the key case of a factor of production which may be controlled by someone other than the innovator in such a way as to draw a disproportionate portion of benefits away from the farmer-innovator. Where population pressure is heavy, the bargaining power of the landowner may be such that he can control the division of benefits from innovation. Of course it appears to be against the landlord's own economic interest to take so much of the benefit of innovations as to remove all incentive from the farmer to innovate. Such practice may arise, however, because in fact the landlord is, on the one hand, not himself strongly motivated to increase his income from agriculture and, on the other hand, more concerned with maintaining subjugation of the tenant class. Such subjugation is likely to be reduced by improved economic position of the tenant class, and hence the landlord class may even have a positive incentive to prevent such improvement. Such restrictive practice may also arise simply from the institutionalization of the landlord-tenant relationship so as to load the costs of innovation on the tenant and the benefits on the landlord. In a traditional agriculture landlord-tenant relations may develop in a manner which is optimal for the given production conditions. Where purchased inputs are not important, there is unlikely to be an institutionalized means of dividing the cost of such inputs. With the introduction of change which requires substantial quantities of purchased inputs, the landlord may not understand the potential for return and may refuse to participate, even though he may still demand a full share of the total output, including that due to the purchased inputs.

In commercial agricultures technological innovation has been accepted for so long that land tenure institutions, including landlord-tenant relationships, have generally adjusted in a manner to encourage innovation to the benefit of both landlord and tenant.

Capital is another input over which the farmer may have little control but which is crucial to production. If capital is scarce and highly complementary with other inputs, the farmer may have to relinquish much of the benefit of innovation to the provider of capital. This problem is often tied to the problem of land tenure, since the capital input may be provided by the landowner. Where it is not tied in with land tenure, it is likely to be a limiting factor to incentives for only those farmers with relatively small holdings and lower-than-average incomes. These farmers are important from a welfare point of view but control too little land in the aggregate production.

A problem very similar to the credit problem is that of marketing. If the marketing channels are limited and entry is difficult or impossible, then the marketing agencies may draw off most of the benefit from innovation and thereby discourage application of innovation. Again, of course, it is never to the advantage of the monopolist to squeeze so tight that he prevents income-increasing innovation, but institutionalization of pressures, ignorance, and even a desire to maintain control through restriction of incomes and maintenance of dependency may all work to provide pressure restrictive of innovation. However, entry into agricultural marketing in low-income countries is generally relatively easy; and therefore it is unlikely that monopoly power will be wielded for any considerable period of time. Again, the hold of credit and marketing agencies on the very small, very low-income farmer may be strong and exploitative. It is important here, however, to distinguish between the welfare problem and the production problem. Such restrictions are not restrictive of the total volume of production even though they may inhibit improvement of conditions for a substantial number of people. Again it is likely that the worst abuses of market power occur in cases in which credit and marketing are tied to control of the land resource.

Restriction of consumption patterns is a less obvious but nevertheless potentially important factor which may remove expectation on the part of the innovator that he will benefit from increased wealth. Again, important restriction in this regard is likely to be tied in with control by the landlord or other power agents may restrict consumption from important outlets. A key example is schooling. In most low-income countries the drive to provide schooling is very high in rural areas. This continues from and grows out of the drive for providing alternative employment opportunities. If the political power structure, particularly including the landlord class, is opposed to the provision of rural schooling for fear that it will eventually upset the political power structure, then an important reason for generating additional income is lost. In a more general way, tight control of the availability of consumption goods and the general control of their own lives and destiny may lead to a sense of resignation which is discouraging to innovation even when a significant portion of the monetary benefits of innovation may come to the farmer decision-maker.

The preceding discussion indicates that subsistence farmers in traditional economies may appear to farm inefficiently because they are judged by criteria different from the ones they use in making their decisions; that farmers in fact are operating quite efficiently given their environmental conditions and objectives; that variability in decisions indicates more variability in environment and objectives than variability in efficiency; that economic efficiency in such traditional agricultures is the result more of the static nature of the environment than of excellence in decision-making, and hence a shift to a dynamic environment may require improved decision-making ability; that in a traditional agriculture farmers may be reluctant to borrow capital owing to a combination of low returns, high risks, and high penalties for failure; that farmers tend to respond significantly to relative changes in agricultural prices, but not to aggregate change in all agricultural prices relative to nonagricultural prices and that farmers face many inhibitory factors in regard to acceptance of single-factor high-return innovations but do inhibit acceptance of more complex, more modest-return innovation. In addition, the discussion shows close interaction of many economic and social influences, such as resource productivity and utility from leisure and material goods, so that judgment cannot normally be made about the influence of one of these factors without giving consideration to the others.

The discussion has emphasized traditional agriculture, although making it clear that in most low-income countries many of the features of traditional agriculture have been significantly modified. Nevertheless, the features of traditional agriculture continue with sufficient influence to suggest somewhat different policy recommendations for achieving particular goals in the transitional agricultures of today's low-income countries than in the fully commercialized agricultures of the world's high-income nations.

References

BAUER and YAMEY, 1959. P. T. Bauer and B. S. Yamey, "A Case Study of Response to Price in an Underdeveloped Country," *Economic Journal*, Vol. LXIX, No. 276 (December 1959), 300–305.

DESAI, 1963. D. K. Desai, *Increasing Income and Production in Indian Farming* (Bombay: Indian Society of Agricultural Economics, 1963).

FALCON, 1964. Walter P. Falcon, "Farmers Response to Price in Subsistence Economy: The Case of West Pakistan," *American Economic Review*, Vol. LIV, No. 3 (May 1964), 580–91.

HEADY and RANDHAWA, 1964. E. O. Heady and Narindar S. Randhawa, "Inter-regional Programming Model for Agricultural Planning in India," *Journal of Farm Economics*, Vol. 46, No. 1 (February 1964), 137–49.

KRISHNA, 1963. Raj Krishna, "Farm Supply Response in India-Pakistan: A Case Study of the Punjab Region," *Economic Journal*, Vol. LXXIII, No. 291 (September 1963), 477–87.

MELLOR, 1962. John W. Mellor, "Increasing Agricultural Production in Early Stages of Economic Development, Relations, Problems and Prospects," *Indian Journal of Agricultural Economics*, Vol. 27, No. 2 (April/June 1962), 29–46.

MELLOR, 1963. John W. Mellor, "The Use and Productivity of Farm Family Labor in Early Stages of Agricultural Development," *Journal of Farm Economics*, Vol. XLV, No. 3 (August 1963), 517–34.

MELLOR, 1966. John W. Mellor, *The Economics of Agricultural Development*, (Ithaca, N.Y.: Cornell University Press, 1966).

SCHICKELE, 1966. Rainer Schickele, "Farm Management Research for Planning Agricultural Development," ADC Reprint, (New York: Agricultural Development Council, December 1966).

SCHULTZ, 1964. Theodore W. Schultz, *Transforming Traditional Agriculture* (New Haven, Conn.: Yale University Press, 1964).

STEVENS, 1959. Robert D. Stevens, "Capital Formation and Agriculture in Some Lebanese Villages," Unpublished Ph.D. dissertation, Cornell University, Ithaca, New York, 1959.

TAX, 1953. Sol Tax, *Penny Capitalism: A Guate-* *malan Indian Economy*, Smithsonian Institution, Institute of Social Anthropology, Pub. No. 16 (Washington, D.C.: U.S. Government Printing Office, 1953), Republished, University of Chicago Press, 1963.

COMMENT

The Subsistence Farmer in Traditional Economies

CARL K. EICHER

PROFESSOR MELLOR'S paper is concerned with the microeconomics of subsistence farms and the implications for agricultural development policy. Since the implications for agricultural policy are underplayed, this paper should be viewed as a valuable survey paper which states a number of propositions to be tested in less developed countries.

I have four points to raise. The first point relates to the exclusion of shifting cultivators from the paper. Since Mellor informs us in his introduction that he is discussing subsistence farmers in Africa, Asia, and Latin America, I think that it is important to recognize that a substantial share of African subsistence farmers—especially in West Africa—have for many years produced export crops such as cocoa, oil palm, and rubber, on a small permanent land base while practicing shifting cultivation for the production of their staple foods, such as rice, yam, cassava, maize, and guinea corn.

My second point concerns the exclusive preoccupation with how subsistence farmers behave in ovepopulated countries. For example, the author states that, in general, an increase in land quantity on an individual farm "does not increase the aggregate of production in an economy because it simply represents a transfer from one farmer to another." Also he notes, "we find it likely that subsistence farmers are sharply limited in their freedom of action in regard to the use of land." There is, however, a large potential of expanding agricultural output in Latin America and Africa by bringing more land into production. The Congo has 16 million people and one-third the land area that India's 500 million people have at their disposal. Also, in the Sudan only about 10 per cent of the arable land is under cultivation. Mellor's paper would be more balanced if he extended his discussion to how subsistence farmers operate in land-surplus but still poor nations. Myint's vent-for-surplus labor leisure model of development is useful in analyzing how subsistence farmers bring new land into cultivation by adding export crops to their staple food crop production at very little risk [Myint 1964].

My third point concerns the framework of analysis and the logical development of the points which are supposed to lead us to "implications for agricultural development policy." Essentially, Mellor presents a string of propositions about subsistence economic behaviour which are almost always "counterbalanced," to use the author's words. The section on the "Production Process in Traditional Agriculture" does not seem to have any logical connection with "Farmers Values and Objectives" in Section III. In Section III, Mellor spends considerable time discussing the limited aspirations of subsistence farmers. Although this may be valid in many situations, there is ample evidence that subsistence farmers in West Africa, Burma, and other nations have not withdrawn labor from the production process following a modest improvement in their asset position. One cannot help but be struck in Africa by the intense drive to replace straw roofs with tin, and to purchase plastic sandals, and to finance the education of children. A few examples of the small holder "export explosion" in West Africa should be included in any discussion of limited aspirations. Next, Mellor states that the allocation of family labor between productive work and leisure has a broad application. This broad application, however, is not spelled out.

Mellor next turns to "security and change," with special reference to what he calls the institutionalization of research and testing. Since the research process has not been institutionalized in a traditional economy, he suggests that innovation will tend to result in a high number of failures. Therefore he notes that the process of introducing innovations in traditional agriculture is more difficult than in high-income agricultural countries. What does this tell us? In my judgment, the significant point is how do we explain the variance in the introduction of innovation within and between low income countries such as India, Pakistan, Nigeria, Ghana, and Brazil?

In Section IV Mellor discusses the rationality of farmers' decisions with respect to (a) allocation of existing resources, (b) acquisition of new resources, (c) price response, and (d) response to technical change. The author advances numerous sociological propositions to show that subsistence farmers have *mixed* rationality with respect to each of these four decision areas. Mellor states that empirical studies reveal conflicting impressions about the allocative efficiency of subsistence farmers in various countries. Since three of the four references refer to India, the reader could be helped if examples from countries in Latin America and Africa were included in this section.

My fourth and final comment on Mellor's paper concerns policy implications. The author states that one of his objectives is to discuss the implications of the microeconomics of such farms for agricultural development policy. The paper, however, presents a list of various characteristics of subsistence farmers rather than generalizations for agricultural policy.

In summary, Mellor has "counterbalanced" almost all of his propositions and has implied that we cannot make any definite generalizations about the microeconomics of subsistence farmers in traditional economies at this time. However, the propositions advanced are a valuable source of ideas for empirical testing in land and labor surplus economies.

Reference

MYINT, 1964. Hla Myint, *The Economics of the Developing Countries* (London: Hutchinson, 1964).

8

Supply Relationships in Peasant Agriculture

EDITOR'S INTRODUCTION

THE FUNDAMENTAL ISSUE of whether the peasant or subsistence farmer is an "economic man" has continued to be a major stimulus to empirical research. The measures chosen and approaches employed have varied considerably. Until recently research tended to concentrate upon empirical measures to assess efficiency in the allocation of resources within a sample of farms, either as a measure of the farmer's rationality or skill or both. (A good recent example is the article by Welsch [1965].) Estimated production functions and the derived marginal value productivities were the most common measures used. With a given level of technology and with market prices for products and inputs also given, the peasant farmer's performance was judged by the significance of his deviations from optimal allocations. One could assemble a respectable list of such studies conducted in the developing areas, and references will be found in several of the papers in this volume. As might be expected, the evidence cited is rather mixed, with cases of both malallocation and near-perfect allocation. Where the results revealed malallocations, they were usually attributed either to deficiencies in peasant managerial skill or to the influence of noneconomic factors impinging on economic decisions and behavior, such as irrationality, cultural barriers, illiteracy, institutional obstacles, and social disincentives. Alternatively,

those studies which revealed no significant malallocations in resource utilization were seen by partisans of peasants as "economic men" as proof that on net balance economic factors outweighed the noneconomic.

More recently the validity of the influence of economic incentives upon the behavior of peasant and subsistence farmers has been assessed by a growing number of studies dealing with the supply response of subsistence agriculture. (For a good summary see Krishna [1967], FAO [1967], and PSAC [1967].) The most influential early articles were by Bauer and Yamey [1959], dealing with cocoa and oil palm in Nigeria, and by Mathur and Ezekiel [1961] and Krishna [1962], dealing with the issue of "marketable surplus." Most of the early work, though highly imaginative and useful, did not seek exact measures of the elasticity of price response. However, following the pioneering work of Nerlove [1958], economists began to construct a number of more sophisticated empirical supply-response models of agriculture in developing areas.[1] From this burgeoning literature a number of conceptual issues have emerged to help refine the estimational approaches and to improve an

1. Venkataramanan, 1958; Stern, 1959, 1962, 1965; Chan, 1962; Krishna, 1963; Wharton, 1963; Falcon, 1964; Dean, 1965, 1966; Bateman, 1965; Behrman, 1966; Mangahas et al., 1966; Mubyarto and Fletcher, 1966.

understanding of the economic behavior of peasant farmers in response to economic incentives. Current research reveals that any proper assessment of the influence of economic incentives upon subsistence farmer supply behavior must make four critical distinctions.

1. *Acreage* response must be distinguished from *yield* response to economic incentives. Since most studies have tended to use land as the dependent variable, an important distinction must be made between the farmer's allocation of land and nonland resources in response to prices. An increase in the acreage devoted to a crop or the addition of new lands must be separated from an increase in output from an existing or unchanged acreage.

2. The elasticity of response by agriculture *as a whole* must be separated from that of a *single* crop. Most studies have involved a single commodity or a limited number of commodities in reaction to changing relative economic incentives, which is not the same as the response of all agricultural commodities.

3. Distinctions must be made as to the varying *lengths of time* involved in the estimated elasticity. Lengths of run and the time periods involved in adjustment to an economic stimulus are critical.

4. The elasticity of farm *production* as a whole must be distinguished from the elasticity of a *marketed surplus*. This distinction applies with acute force in conditions of subsistence and semisubsistence production. An alternative formulation of this distinction is between *food staples*, which are consumed by the family, and *commercial crops*, which are sold. Where the food staple is both consumed and sold commercially, the marketable surplus issues come into play, regardless of the fraction of total production sold (Krishna [1962]).

Many of these distinctions are handled by the proper specification of the variables and by the use of appropriate estimational techniques. Failure to make these distinctions has frequently led to differences in findings and consequently to disagreements as to the degree of price influence observed. Many disputes as to the significance of price response by peasant farmers are due to the inadequacies of the data employed and the statistical problems of estimation, but many

more disagreements are rooted in the improper handling of these four basic distinctions.

The two case studies presented here reflect a conceptual dichotomy of annuals vs. perennials, i.e. based upon the economic lifespan of the crop. This split also tends to cover the "food staples" vs. "commercial" distinction, since few perennials (or crops grown as perennials) constitute food staples.

Professor Behrman's study analyzes the supply response of four annual crops in Central and Northeastern Thailand—rice, cassava (manioc), corn, and kenaf. Rice, a traditional crop in Thailand and a major source of export revenue, showed a significant response to price; and the patterns of supply elasticities were highly correlated with the existence of profitable alternatives for the farmers. The rationality which these subsistence farmers revealed was particularly notable in the supply elasticities reflecting risk aversion. The median elasticity with respect to price was found to be 0.20, which is comparable to those estimated from grain crops in other lesser developed countries [Krishna, 1967, p. 504-07; PSAC, 1967, p. 527].

The phenomenal growth of the three Thai upland crops in response to a growing export demand is well known. For the 1956–1958 through 1961–1963 period, Behrman found that the production of cassava, corn and kenaf increased at average annual exponential rates, respectively, of 30, 32, and 46 per cent. Again, the estimated elasticities support the view of Thai farmers who are responsive to market incentives.

Professor Bateman undertakes a review of the empirical work which has been done on the supply functions of four tree crops—cocoa, rubber, lemons, and coffee. Although he finds a variety of estimational models and definitions of the relevant variables among the different studies, the picture which emerges from the review is again one of an economically rational and responsive farmer. This is true despite the time horizons involved, which tend to be longer than for annuals.

Despite the increased recent work on perennials, Bateman's review shows how little has been done, even though such crops as bananas, oil palm, tea, and coconuts are of considerable economic importance in tropical and subtropical areas. Based upon the work which has been done to date and in an effort to facilitate future empirical work in this area, Bateman puts forward four models for estimating planting decisions along with the planting-output relationship.

References

BATEMAN, 1965. Merrill J. Bateman, "Aggregate and Regional Supply Functions for Ghanaian Cocoa," *Journal of Farm Economics*, Vol. 47, No. 2 (May 1965), 384–401.

BAUER and YAMEY, 1959. P. T. Bauer and B. S. Yamey, "A Case Study of Response to Price in an Underdeveloped Country," *Economic Journal*, Vol. LXIX, No. 276 (December 1959), 300–305.

BEHRMAN, 1966. Jere R. Behrman, "The Price Elasticity of the Market Surplus of a Subsistence Crop," *Journal of Farm Economics*, Vol. 48, No. 4 (November 1966), 875–93.

CHAN, 1962. Francis K. W. Chan, "A Preliminary Study of the Supply Response of Malayan Rubber Estates between 1948 and 1959," *Malayan Economic Review*, Vol. 7, No. 2 (October 1962), 77–94.

DEAN, 1965. Edwin R. Dean, "Economic Analysis and African Response to Price," *Journal of Farm Economics*, Vol. 47, No. 2 (May 1965), 402–409.

DEAN, 1966. Edwin Dean, *The Supply Responses of African Farmers: Theory and Measurement in Malawi* (Amsterdam: North Holland Publishing Company, 1966).

FALCON, 1964. W. P. Falcon, "Farmer Response to Price in a Subsistence Economy: The Case of West Pakistan," *American Economic Review*, Vol. LIV, No. 3 (May 1964), 580–91.

FAO, 1967. Food and Agriculture Organization, *The State of Agriculture 1967* (Rome: Food and Agriculture Organization, 1967).

KRISHNA, 1962. Raj Krishna, "A Note on the Elasticity of the Marketable Surplus of a Subsistence Crop," *Indian Journal of Agricultural Economics*, Vol. XVII, No. 3 (July–September 1962), 79–84.

KRISHNA, 1963. Raj Krishna, "Farm Supply Response in India-Pakistan: A Case Study of the Punjab Region," *Economic Journal*, Vol. LXXIII, No. 291 (September 1963), 477–87.

KRISHNA, 1967. Raj Krishna, "Agricultural Price Policy and Economic Development," in Herman M. Southworth and Bruce F. Johnston, eds.,

Agricultural Development and Economic Growth, (Ithaca, N.Y.: Cornell University Press, 1967).

MANGAHAS, et al., 1966. Mahar Mangahas, Aida E. Recto, and V. W. Ruttan, "Price and Market Relationships for Rice and Corn in the Philippines," *Journal of Farm Economics*, Vol. 48, No. 3, Part I (August 1966), 685–703.

MATHUR and EZEKIEL, 1961. P. N. Mathur and Hannan Ezekiel, "Marketable Surplus of Food and Price Fluctuations in a Developing Economy," *Kyklos*, Vol. XIV, Fasc. 3 (1961), 396–408.

MUBYARTO and FLETCHER, 1966. Mubyarto and Lehman B. Fletcher, "The Marketable Surplus of Rice in Indonesia: A Study in Java-Madura," International Studies in Economics, Monograph No. 4 (Ames, Iowa: Department of Economics, Iowa State University, October 1966).

NERLOVE, 1958. Marc Nerlove, *The Dynamics of Supply: Estimation of Farmer's Response to Price* (Baltimore: Johns Hopkins University Press, 1958).

PSAC, 1967. Panel on the World Food Supply, "Production Incentives for Farmers," Chapter 9 in Report of the President's Science Advisory Committee, *The World Food Problem*, Vol. II (Washington, D.C.: The White House, May 1967).

STERN, 1959. R. M. Stern, "The Price Responsiveness of Egyptian Cotton Producers," *Kyklos*, Vol. XII, Fasc. 3 (1959), 375–84.

STERN, 1962. R. M. Stern, "The Price Responsiveness of Primary Producers," *Review of Economics and Statistics*, Vol. 44, No. 2 (May 1962), 202–207.

STERN, 1965. R. M. Stern, "The Determinants of Cocoa Supply in West Africa," in I. G. Stewart and H. W. Ord, eds., *African Primary Products and International Trade* (Edinburgh: Edinburgh University Press, 1965).

VENKATARAMANAN, 1958. L. S. Venkataramanan, "A Statistical Study of Indian Jute Production and Marketing with Special Reference to Foreign Demand," Unpublished Ph.D. dissertation, Department of Economics, University of Chicago, 1958.

WELSCH, 1965. Delane E. Welsch, "Response to Economic Incentive by Abakaliki Rice Farmers in Eastern Nigeria," *Journal of Farm Economics*, Vol. 47, No. 4 (November 1965), 900–14.

WHARTON, 1963. Clifton R. Wharton, Jr. "Malayan Rubber Supply Conditions," in T. H. Silcock and E. K. Fisk, eds., *The Political Economy of Independent Malaya* (Canberra: Australian National University Press, 1963).

CASE STUDY

Supply Response and the Modernization of Peasant Agriculture: A Study of Four Major Annual Crops in Thailand[1]

JERE R. BEHRMAN

THE ROLE OF EXPANDED agricultural production in economic development may be multifaceted. Expanded agricultural production may provide raw materials, unskilled labor, investment, foreign exchange, food and other consumption goods, and product markets for the nonagricultural sectors. Expanded agricultural production also may lead to increased welfare for the majority of the population of the lesser-developed world which now resides in rural areas [Mellor, 1966, pp. 1–132]. Although the role of agriculture in economic development was neglected somewhat in the immediate postwar period, in recent years this multifaceted role increasingly has been emphasized.

The increasing emphasis on the important contributions which agriculture may make to economic development has led to increasing efforts to understand the nature of agriculture in the lesser-developed world and to determine what government policies efficiently would be conducive to the expansions of agricultural production. Theodore W. Schultz and John W. Mellor, among others, repeatedly have emphasized the following general hypothesis about the nature of the large portion of the agricultural sector in the lesser-developed world which Schultz calls traditional agriculture: "*There are comparatively few significant inefficiencies in the allocation of the factors of production in traditional agriculture* [Schultz, 1964, p. 37 (italics in original)]." An

important implication of this hypothesis is that traditional agricultural production generally cannot be expanded so as to contribute significantly to economic development by the reallocation of traditional factors in the production of traditional products. Instead, relevant nontraditional factors for the production, in part, of nontraditional products must be introduced. These nontraditional factors have new technology embodied in them and frequently require the adoption of new cultivation practices in order to obtain sufficiently high returns to warrant their use. Given the Schultz-Mellor hypothesis and this implication, the modernization of traditional agriculture may be characterized as the introduction of such factors and such products.[2]

The modernization of traditional agriculture so defined has many aspects. Research must be undertaken in order to determine what nontraditional factors and products might be profitable under local conditions and to attempt to adapt the results of research in other localities to local conditions. The results of this research must be disseminated through markets and possibly through other institutions. Investment may be warranted in social overhead capital such as transportation, communication, education, and the provision of other factors for which externalities or decreasing marginal costs might be significant.

One very important aspect of such modern

1. This paper was originally given at the International Congress of Orientalists, Ann Arbor, Michigan, August 17, 1967 and presents in a very condensed form some of the results in Behrman [1966a; 1968b]. The author acknowledges the help of Prajiad Buasri, Prakorb Buasri, F. M. Fisher, M. Nerlove, C. R. Wharton, Jr., and the Computer Centers at the Massachusetts Institute of Technology and the University of Pennsylvania at various stages of this study.

2. Traditional agriculture may contribute substantially to economic development without such modernization if what Mellor [1966, p. 218] calls "an exploitive approach" of heavy taxation is adopted. One might argue, however, that even for an exploitive approach new factors in respect to organization may be necessary in order to increase the "surplus" which is squeezed out of the traditional sector (perhaps the Soviet reorganization under the First Plan is a relevant example).

ization is the question of whether or not peasants in traditional or near-traditional agriculture significantly respond to opportunities which are made available by changes in market conditions. The degree of supply response in such peasant agriculture has been a point of major controversy. Near one end of the spectrum of viewpoints are J. H. Boeke, L. Dabasi-Schweng, G. Dalton, J. P. Lewis, K. Nair, W. C. Neale, R. O. Olson, and others who suggest that cultural and institutional restraints limit° to insignificance any price response.[3] If the adherents of viewpoints near this end of the spectrum are correct, the Schultz-Mellor hypothesis about the efficiency of traditional agriculture is brought into question, and the transformation of traditional agriculture through the introduction of nontraditional factors and products is a very formidable task, because market incentives will not induce significant adoptions of innovations.[4] Near the other end of this spectrum of viewpoints (in addition to Schultz and Mellor) are P. T. Bauer, M. L. Dantwala, W. P. Falcon, B. S. Yamey and others who maintain that peasants in traditional and near-traditional agriculture respond quickly, normally, and efficiently to market incentives.[5] If the proponents of viewpoints near this end of the spectrum are correct, the Schultz-Mellor hypothesis is supported, and market incentives may play an important role in the transformation of traditional agriculture.

The present study is concerned with this supply-response aspect of the modernization of traditional and near-traditional peasant agriculture in central and northeastern Thailand. The supply response of the traditionally dominant crop, rice, is discussed in the first section. The supply responses of the three

major upland crops, the production of each of which has expanded tremendously in recent years, is examined in the following section. Conclusions and policy implications are presented in the third section. The major conclusion is that the traditional and near-traditional Thai peasants under study are quite rational in their response to market incentives, which supports the Schultz-Mellor hypothesis and its implications.

RICE SUPPLY RESPONSE IN CENTRAL AND NORTHEASTERN THAILAND, 1940–1963

Rice has long been the mainstay of the Thai economy. In the postwar period over two-thirds of the population lived in agricultural households which produced rice, and a significant per cent of the remainder was involved in rice trading, transportation, and milling. In the 1951–1963 period rice production occupied 82 per cent of the cultivated land and accounted for 54 per cent of the value of total agriculture production and 17 per cent of the national income. In the same 13 years rice processing accounted for 23 per cent of the value added in manufacturing, and rice exports represented 43 per cent of the total value of Thai exports. In the 1954–1963 decade export taxes on rice alone accounted for an annual average of over 15 per cent of total government revenue. In 1956 through 1960 rice accounted for over 50 per cent of the total food consumption by weight and over 60 per cent of the total food consumption by calories.[6]

In the period under study aggregate Thai rice production has been expanding regularly. As is indicated in the first row of Table 8.1, for example, in the 1951–1953 through 1961–1963 period rice production increased at an average annual exponential rate of over 2 per cent, and in the 1956–1958 through 1961–1963 period rice production increased at an average annual exponential rate of over 5 per cent. Despite this growth, however, the dominance of rice in Thai agriculture has decreased in the postwar decades. In Table 8.2 are presented some indices of the

3. Boeke [1953, pp. 3–5], Dabasi-Schweng [1965], Dalton [1962], Lewis [1964, p. 157], Nair [1965, n. 1, 44; n. 2, 139; 192] Neale [1959], Olson [1960]. For specific reference to Thailand, see Insor [1963, p. 149], Kingshill [1960, p. 46], Long et al. [1963, p. 107], and Somsakdi [1963].

4. Note also, however, that if adherents of viewpoints near this end of the spectrum are correct, substantial opportunities for increased traditional agricultural production may exist through the reallocation of traditional factors.

5. Bauer and Yamey [1959], Dantwala [1963], Falcon [1962, p. 324], Mellor [1966], and Schultz [1964; 1965, pp. 29, 49], for specific reference to Thailand, see Brown [1963, p. 18], Platenius [1963, p. 17], and Schultz [1965, p. 32]. For further discussion of hypotheses along this spectrum, see Behrman [1966a, pp. 4–10; 1968b, pp. 3–8].

6. Ayal [1965, Table 4], Chaiyong and Sopin [1965, p. 4, 10], Smith [1963, p. 67], and Thailand [1953, pp. 166, 232; 1962, p. 1; 1964]. For further details, see Behrman [1966a, pp. 111–140; 1968b, pp. 92–116].

Table 8.1. *Average Annual Exponential Growth Rates for the Four Major Thai Annual Crops:*
Quantity Produced, Area Planted, Yield, and Quantity Exported 1951–1953
through 1961–1963 and 1956–1958 through 1961–1963[a]

	Average Annual Exponential Growth Rate in Per Cent							
	1951–1953 THROUGH 1961–1963				1956–1958 THROUGH 1961–1963			
CROPS	Quantity Produced	Area Planted	Yield Per Unit Planted Area	Quantity Exported	Quantity Produced	Area Planted	Yield Per Unit Planted Area	Quantity Exported
	(1)	(2)	(3)	(4)	(5)	(6)	(7)	(8)
Rice	2.2	1.0	1.2	−0.3	5.6	2.8	2.8	1.4
Cassava	n.a.[b]	n.a.[b]	n.a.[b]	25.0	30.2	21.8	8.4	22.4
Corn	27.3	20.6	6.7	35.8	31.5	24.7	6.8	43.0
Kenaf	26.7	27.6	−0.9	43.8	46.2	47.6	−1.4	47.1

[a] Calculated from data in *Agricultural Statistics of Thailand 1963* (Bangkok: Division of Agricultural Economics, Ministry of Agriculture, 1963), Tables 11, 16, 20, 42, 81, 82, 83, and 86.
[b] Not available.

decline in relative importance of rice in Thai agriculture. On a more disaggregate level, moreover, the rates of growth and of change in the relative importance of rice have varied considerably. In the first two rows of Table 8.3 are presented statistics which relate to the distributions of growth rates in rice production and in rice production per agricultural resident across the 50 provinces (changwads) in central and northeastern Thailand for the 1940–1963 period. The exponential provincial growth rates in rice production over these 24 years ranged from −3.2 to 8.4 per cent, with the median and mean growth rates both equal to 2.8 per cent. The exponential provincial growth rates in rice production per agricultural resident

over the same years ranged from −7.4 to 4.6 per cent, with the median and mean growth rates both between −0.1 and 0.0 per cent.

In parts II and III of Table 3 the results of nonlinear maximum likelihood estimates of a Nerlovian dynamic supply response model for rice production in each of the 50 provinces in central and northeastern Thailand are summarized [Behrman, 1966a, pp. 182–220, 240–370; 1967a; 1968b, pp. 151–184, 200–315]. In part II the distribution of the coefficients of multiple correlation which were obtained from the estimates is summarized. The median and mean of this distribution reflect the fact that, for most of the provinces, the model which was used

Table 8.2. *The Relative Importance of the Four Major Thai Annual Crops:*
Total Value, Area Planted, and Exports 1951–1953 and 1961–1963

CROP	Per Cent of Total Value of Crop Production[a]		Per Cent of Total Area in Crops[a]		Per Cent of Total Value of Crop Exports[b]	
	1951–1953	1961–1963	1951–1953	1961–1963	1951–1953	1961–1963
	(1)	(2)	(3)	(4)	(5)	(6)
Rice	59.7	51.3	87.7	75.7	69.5	44.3
Cassava	0.1[c]	3.1	0.2[c]	1.4	0.8	5.6
Corn	0.7	4.2	0.7	4.1	0.8	8.3
Kenaf	0.4	4.0	0.1	2.1	0.2	6.7

SOURCE: Calculated from data in *Agricultural Statistics of Thailand 1961, 1963* (Bangkok: Division of Agricultural Economics, Ministry of Agriculture) as below:
[a] *Agricultural Statistics 1963*, Tables 4, 16, 20, 25.
[b] *Agricultural Statistics 1963*, Tables 81–89.
[c] Cassava production and area is that in Cholburi only, as reported in *Agricultural Statistics 1961*, Table 19.

*Table 8.3. Summary Statistics Relating to the Distributions of Estimated Mean Annual
Exponential Growth Rates in Rice Production and in Rice Production Per Agricultural
Resident, and of the Estimated Rice Supply Response Elasticities across the 50 Provinces in
Central and Northeastern Thailand for the 1940–1963 Period.*

Distribution	Range	Median	Mean[c]
I. Estimated mean annual exponential growth rate for 1940–1963 period (in per cent):[a]			
1. In rice production.	– 3.2 to 8.4	2.8	2.8
2. In rice production per agricultural resident.	– 7.4 to 4.6	– 0.1	– 0.0
II. Coefficient of multiple correlation for supply response model.[b]	0.03 to 0.96	0.73	0.70
III. Estimated short-run elasticity of area planted in rice (at point of means for 1940–1963 period) with respect to:[b]			
1. Deflated price of rice.	0.00 to 1.81	0.20	0.25
2. Expected yields per unit planted area.	0.00 to 1.94	0.00	0.21
3. Standard deviation in price over three preceding years.	0.00 to – 1.68	0.00	– 0.10
4. Standard deviation in yields over three preceding years.	0.00 to – 0.31	0.00	– 0.03
5. Population residing in agricultural households	0.00 to 8.31	0.59	0.76

[a] Estimated by ordinary least squares regressions. The data and the estimates are presented in Behrman [1966a, pp. 118–120, 402–428].

[b] Based on nonlinear maximum likelihood estimates of a Nerlovian supply response model. Short-run is defined to be one crop year. For details and the underlying estimates see Behrman [1966a, pp. 182–220, 240–370].

[c] Each province was weighted equally in the construction of the means.

explains a considerable portion of the variance in the rice supply. The proportion of the variance in rice supply across provinces which is explained by the model, moreover, is correlated positively at the 5 per cent level, with the per cent of the total land in field crops which is planted in rice ($\rho = 0.29$), with the mean rice production per provincial resident ($\rho = 0.30$), and with the exponential growth rates of rice production ($\rho = 0.41$) and of rice production per provincial resident ($\rho = 0.32$). The model thus tends to explain better the variations in rice supply in those provinces in which rice production was either relatively important throughout the period under study or increasing in importance at relatively high rates. No significant correlation at the 5 per cent level is present, however, between the coefficients of multiple correlation and other quantifiable provincial characteristics.[7]

In part III of Table 8.3 the distributions across provinces of the rice supply elasticities, which are implied by the nonlinear maximum likelihood estimates, are summarized. Primary interest in regard to the question of the response to market incentives is the response to price. For 96 per cent of the provinces an asymptotically significant response to

price was obtained.[8] Price thus seems to be a widespread determinant in Thai rice planting decisions. The elasticities with respect to price range from 0.0 to 1.81, but the median of 0.20 and the mean of 0.25 reflect a downward skewness in the distribution of these elasticities within this range. These elasticities are comparable in magnitude to those which have been estimated for grain crops in other lesser-developed countries.[9] The most interesting aspect of these price elasticities is the degree to which the distribution across provinces reflects the availability of alternative economic opportunities. The price elasticities tend to be high for those provinces in which the proximity of markets and the physiography make alternative crops economically attractive. The price elasticities tend to be relatively low, on the other hand, for those provinces which are relatively isolated from national and international markets and for those provinces in which large areas are inundated and urban pop-

7. The other possibly relevant quantifiable provincial characteristics are summarized in Behrman [1967a, Table 1; 1966a, Tables II–5, II–10, III–2, III–4, IV–2, and IV–3].

8. The exceptions are two fairly isolated, contiguous provinces (Phetchbun and Loei)—the only two provinces, incidentally for which the rice yield per unit planted area response to price is asymptotically significantly nonzero, (the implied elasticities of yield per unit planted area, with respect to price, are 0.20 and 0.12) [Behrman, 1966a, pp. 353, 459–462].

9. Falcon [1962, pp. 67, 130, 144; 1964], Fletcher and Mubyarto [1966], Hussain [1964, pp. 98, 101], Krishna [1961, pp. 482–485; 1963], and Mangahas, et al. [1966, pp. 694–695, 698]. These studies are summarized in Behrman [1966a, pp. 18–23; 1968b, pp. 14–19].

ulations are not sufficiently close to make truck farming profitable [Behrman, 1966a, pp. 353–370]. The distribution of rice-supply elasticities with respect to price across provinces thus suggests that Thai peasants react quite rationally to market conditions.

The second distribution of supply elasticities is with respect to expected yields per unit planted area. In the supply-response model that was estimated the dependent variable that was used is the area planted in rice because yields per unit area planted (and thus production) are subject to large variations, owing to environmental factors that are beyond the peasants control [Behrman, 1966a, pp. 182–187; 1968b, pp. 151–155]. If the area planted depends upon the expected revenue per unit area planted, then the expected yields per unit area planted and the expected price per unit of output both may be important determinants of the desired area planted.[10] The distribution of rice-supply elasticities with respect to expected yields per unit area planted in row 2 of part III in Table 8.3 indicates that the supply model estimates provide some support for the inclusion of the expected yields per unit area planted in the desired-rice-area-planted relationship. Although the coefficient of this variable is asymptotically significantly non-zero for only slightly less than half of the provinces (thus, the median of the distribution is zero), the magnitudes of the supply elasticities with respect to expected yields per unit area planted for such provinces tend to be larger than the magnitudes of the supply elasticities with respect to prices for the same provinces.

The distributions of elasticities in rows 3, 4, and 5 in part III of Table 8.3 all refer to risk aversion. For near-subsistence peasants risk aversion may be quite strong because the rewards for returns above the expected value may not offset the severe penalties for returns below the expected values.[11]

If harvest prices or yields per unit planted area are below their expected values, for example, the resulting inadequate income may force a near-subsistence peasant into burdensome debt, cause him to lose his land, or even result in his family's starvation. For such peasants characteristics of the probability distributions other than the expected values might be very important. The actual standard deviations of the price and of the yields per unit area planted in the last three crop years, therefore, were included in the supply model as proxies for the variances of the subjective probability distributions. This choice of proxies has some justification in that the variances of the subjective probability distributions probably are based largely on previous experience (although the choice of a three-year period is arbitrary). The distributions of rice-supply elasticities with respect to these standard deviations, however, provide but limited support for the hypothesis that higher moments of the subjective probability distributions of returns from crops are important in the decision to allocate area among crops. For both distributions an asymptotically significant response was obtained in less than half of the provinces (as indicated, once again, by medians of zero value). For both distributions the mean value of the implied elasticities with respect to the standard deviation is substantially smaller than the mean value of the implied elasticities with respect to the expected value of the same subjective probability distribution.

In addition to responding to the higher moments of the subjective probability distributions of expected returns, peasants also may attempt to lessen risks due to market fluctuations by first planting enough area in rice to assure sufficient food for the agricultural household residents, and only thereafter allocating the remainder of their land on the basis of expected returns.[12] To test this hypothesis, the population which resides in rural households was included in the supply model. The distribution of the implied elasticities of supply with respect to the population which resides in agricultural households is summarized in row 5, part III,

10. The expected price and expected yields per unit area planted refer to gross revenue. The available data do not permit the consideration of net revenue, which would be preferable. For a description of the construction of the expected yields series, see Behrman [1966a, pp. 243–254, 1968b, pp. 218–237].

11. Cochrane [1955, p. 1171], Dabasi-Schweng [1965, pp. 510, 515], Falcon [1962, pp. 18–21], Hansen [1960, pp. 157–158], Mellor [1966, p. 29], and Schultz [1964, pp. 31, 167–168]. In reference specifically to Thailand, see Breitenbach [1964, p. 76], Chaiyong et al. [1962 p. 10], Coleman [1963, p. 4], and Long et al. [1963, p. 20.

12. Chaiyong et al. [1962, p. 10], Coleman [1963, p. 4], Long et al. [1963, pp. 20, 37], and Pantum et al. [1963, Ch. 2].

of Table 8.3. For approximately 70 per cent of the provinces the estimated response to this variable was asymptotically significant. For most of these provinces, moreover, the response to this variable was substantially larger than the response to any other variable in the model. The magnitude of the population which resides in agricultural households thus seems to be an important determinant of planted rice area. The question arises, however, to what extent the population variable really represented population in the multivariate regression analysis. Because this variable is an exponential time trend, it may have served as a partial proxy for other determinants which are highly correlated with time. The geographical distribution of the estimates of the rice-supply elasticities with respect to the population which resides in agricultural households and the magnitudes of these estimates, however, both provide some support for the assumption that the population variable in fact generally did represent population changes. The distribution of these elasticities across provinces suggests that either no significant response or a very limited response is prevalent for those provinces in which rice production is largely for on-farm consumption. For every additional member of agricultural households in those provinces in which agriculture is relatively noncommercialized, moreover, the estimates imply that additional land has been planted in rice to provide an additional paddy supply of from 34 to 379 kilograms per year. In light of annual per capita paddy absorption estimates which range from 178 to 378 kilograms per year [Behrman, 1966a, pp. 112–115; 1968b, pp. 93–97], the order of magnitude of the above increases seem reasonable. The magnitude of these estimates, as well as the cross-section distribution, thus seems to support the hypothesis that near-subsistence Thai peasants do attempt to lessen risk by always planting enough area in rice to provide sufficient grain for on-farm consumption.

In respect to the supply of the traditionally dominant crop, thus, the traditional and near-traditional Thai peasants seem to respond quite rationally to market conditions. The Nerlovian dynamic supply-response model is consistent with a considerable portion of the variance in the rice supply for most of the provinces in central and northeastern Thailand. A significant response to price is almost universal. The pattern of rice-supply elasticities with respect to price, moreover, apparently is highly correlated with the existence of profitable alternatives. The results of this section, therefore, provide strong support for the Schultz-Mellor hypothesis and for its implications.

UPLAND CROPS SUPPLY RESPONSE IN CENTRAL AND NORTHEASTERN THAILAND, 1950–1963

The declining dominance of rice in Thai agriculture is emphasized in the previous section in reference to Table 8.2. Examination of the same table indicates that a major reason for the declining relative importance of rice has been the rapidly increasing importance of three upland crops—cassava, corn, and kenaf. The phenomenal growth of these three upland crops is made more explicit in Table 8.1. For the 1951–1953 through 1961–1963 period corn and kenaf production increased at average *annual* exponential rates of 27 per cent. For the 1956–1958 through 1961–1963 period cassava, corn, and kenaf production increased at average annual exponential rates, respectively, of 30, 32, and 46 per cent.

Prior to this expansion in the 1950's and early 1960's, each of these three upland crops had been grown in very limited quantities. The expansion of production represented such changes in scale and in the number of peasants who cultivated these crops, however, that the phenomena rightly can be considered to have been the widespread adoption of new crops. In the case of corn, moreover, the expansion of production coincided with the rapid acceptance of a new factor of production in the form of the relatively high-yielding Guatemalan flint seeds.[13] The adoption of kenaf and, to a lesser extent, of corn, furthermore, was predominantly by peasants in relatively remote areas, who previously had not been especially well integrated into the

13. The United States Operations Mission and the Ministry of Agriculture began experiments on various corn varieties in 1950. Guatemalan (Tequisate Golden Flint) seeds were multiplied by experimental stations and by selected farmers in 1952 and 1953 and sold on the market thereafter. By the early 1960's from 60 to 85 per cent of the rapidly growing corn production was Guatemalen flint [Behrman 1966a, pp. 53–59; 1968b, pp. 43–47].

national and international market. The rapid expansion of these three upland crops thus has several striking aspects. New products, which involved a new factor of production in one case, were adopted extraordinarily quickly and sold into market channels largely for export predominantly by peasants who previously had not been very active participants in commercialized agriculture.

The supply responses of each of these three crops in the relevant provinces in central and northeastern Thailand were examined by using procedures almost identical to those that were used for the rice-supply response. Two specific changes, however, should be noted. First, because none of the three upland crops is considered a basic staple in Thailand, the population residing in agricultural households was excluded from the model. Second,

because malaria control is hypothesized to have made possible expanded cultivation of upland areas [Breitenbach, 1964, p. 24], the annual provincial malaria death rates were included in the model. The nonlinear maximum likelihood estimates of the resulting Nerlovian dynamic supply-response model for the three major upland crops are summarized in Table 8.4.

In part I of Table 8.4 the distributions of the coefficients of multiple correlation for the three upland crops are summarized. The Nerlovian dynamic supply model that was used is consistent with a considerable proportion of the variance in the dependent variable. In fact, with the single exception of one data cell for cassava, in every cell for the upland crops a multiple correlation coefficient at least as high as the median (and

Table 8.4. Summary Statistics Relating to the Distributions of Estimated Supply Response Elasticities for the Leading Cassava, Corn, and Kenaf Producing Provinces in Postwar Thailand[a]

Distribution	Range	Median	Mean[b]
I. Coefficient of multiple correlation for supply response model			
Cassava	0.23 to 0.90	0.57	0.57
Corn	0.73 to 0.96	0.84	0.84
Kenaf	0.73 to 0.99	0.86	0.85
II. Estimated short-run elasticity of area planted (at point of means) with respect to:			
1. Relative product price			
Cassava	0.00 to 1.09	0.55	0.55
Corn	0.00 to 4.47	0.14	1.03
Kenaf	0.88 to 5.50	2.51	2.70
2. Expected Yields per unit planted area			
Cassava	0.00 to 0.60	0.30	0.30
Corn	1.36 to 7.73	3.06	3.56
Kenaf	0.00 to 3.71	0.00	1.05
3. Standard deviation in price over three preceding years			
Cassava	−0.46 to −0.50	−0.48	−0.48
Corn	0.00 to −1.69	−0.26	−0.44
Kenaf	0.00 to −3.63	−0.19	−0.70
4. Standard deviation in yields over three preceding years			
Cassava	0.00 to −0.09	−0.05	−0.05
Corn	0.00 to −0.35	0.00	−0.07
Kenaf	0.00 to −1.28	−0.33	−0.46
5. Annual malaria death rate per 100,000 inhabitants			
Cassava	0.00 to 0.00	0.00	0.00
Corn	0.00 to −12.27	0.00	−1.67
Kenaf	0.00 to − 1.39	−0.28	−0.46

[a] The underlying Nerlovian dynamic supply-response model and the nonlinear maximum likelihood estimating technique which was used are basically the same as was the case for rice. Short run is defined to be one crop year. For cassava the distributions are based on two provinces: Cholburi (1950–1963) and Rayong (1955–1963). For corn the distributions are based on seven provinces in the northeastern part of the Central Region plus Nakhornratsima in the southeastern part of the Northeast, all for 1950–1963. For kenaf the distributions are based on eight provinces in the southeastern half of the Northeast, all for 1954–1963. For all three crops the choice of provinces reflects the concentration of production of the crops. For further details concerning the underlying model, the estimation technique, the data, and the estimates, see Behrman [1966a, pp. 182–220, 240–334, 374–396; 1968b, pp. 151–184, 200–279, 316–333].

[b] Each province was weighted equally in the construction of the means.

higher than the mean) for the rice supply was obtained.[14]

In part II of Table 8.4 the distributions across the relevant provinces of the upland crop-supply elasticities that are implied by the nonlinear maximum likelihood estimates are summarized. Of great interest, once again, are the supply elasticities with respect to price. For one of the two leading cassava-producing provinces and for four of the eight leading corn-producing provinces no significant response to price levels is indicated by the econometric results. For the remaining leading cassava- and corn-producing provinces and for all eight leading kenaf-producing provinces, however, significant and substantial responses to price are implied. The implied short-run supply elasticities for the most part are greater than unity and are greater than similar estimates for advanced agriculture in highly developed nations [Nerlove, 1958, pp. 66–86]. Especially noteworthy in this respect are the kenaf supply elasticities with respect to price.

In addition to expected prices, the other determinant of expected gross returns per unit area planted is expected yields per unit area planted. For cassava and kenaf the estimates suggest that a significant response to this variable occurred in about half of the data cells. For corn, however, the estimates imply an elastic response to expected yields per unit area planted in each of the eight leading producing provinces. Because of the introduction of the Guatemalan flint seeds, expected aggregate corn yields presumably increased at annual rates of from 3 to 12 per cent.[15] The estimated corn-supply elasticities with respect to expected yields per unit area planted imply that in response to the growth in expected yields, area planted in corn increased at annual rates that were from four-thirds to eight times as high. The response to the profitable new opportunity which was present because of the availability of a

new factor of production in the form of new seeds thus apparently accounted for a large share of the phenomenal Thai corn expansion.

For the upland crops, as for rice, the response to the standard deviations in relative prices and in yields per unit planted area over the preceding three crop years is of interest because of hypothesized risk aversion. The responses to the proxy for the standard deviation in the subjective probability distribution of yields per unit planted area are very limited for cassava and corn but somewhat larger for kenaf. Of more interest, however, are the generally larger and more prevalent responses in the supply of the upland crops to the proxy for the standard deviation in the subjective probability distributions of relative prices. The estimated elasticities for these responses support the hypothesis of risk aversion in respect to market fluctuations. Note that such responses are more substantial and more common for the upland crops than for rice, as one might expect because almost the total upland crop production enters into market channels and is subjected to market-price fluctuations, while a substantial portion of the rice crop is consumed on the farm without passing through market channels.

The response to the last variable, the malaria death rate, is not significant for most of the leading upland crop-producing provinces. For several of the leading corn- and kenaf-producing provinces in which either land was relatively scarce or the malaria death rate declined substantially, a significant response was obtained. The results provide some support, therefore, for the hypothesis that malaria control contributed to the expansion of the three major Thai upland crops. To fully explore the effects of the malaria control program on Thai agriculture, however, one would need a more general model, which included other effects on the population.[16]

In respect to the supply of the new upland crops, thus, the traditional and near-traditional Thai peasants seem to be quite responsive to market incentives. The Nerlovian dynamic supply response model is consistent with a large proportion of the variance in the supply of the three major upland crops. The

14. Because more degrees of freedom were available for the rice estimates than for the upland crop estimates, however, on the basis of the comparison in the text one should not conclude too readily that the underlying supply model is more suited for upland crops than for rice.

15. Actual corn yields per unit area planted increased at average annual rates of from 3.3 to 11.9 per cent. Expected corn yields per unit area planted presumably increased at rates of the same order of magnitude [Behrman, 1966a, Table IV–8].

16. For an excellent study of the effects of malaria control in Ceylon, see Barlow [1967].

response to price, especially in the case of kenaf supply, has been very substantial. The response to the profitable opportunities presented by the availability of a new (and easily adopted) factor in the case of Guatemalan flint corn seeds also has been quite impressive. The results of this section, therefore, provide further support for the Mellor-Schultz hypothesis and its implications. New products and (at least easily adopted) new factors have been adopted readily by Thai peasants if market conditions have made such adoptions sufficiently profitable.

CONCLUSIONS

This study has concentrated on one aspect of the process of the modernization of traditional agriculture in one Asian country: the responsiveness of Thai peasants to market conditions. Even in respect to Thai agricultural supply response, the study has been far from exhaustive. Two important topics which have not been examined in the present study, for example, are the response of the marketed supply to market conditions [Behrman, 1966b] and the response of total agricultural production to changes in the terms of trade between agriculture and the rest of the economy.

Despite the limited scope of the study, however, the results have at least five important implications for those who are concerned with the modernization of Oriental peasant agriculture. First, the pervasiveness of the rice-supply response to prices and the apparent correlation of this response with the existence of profitable alternatives provide strong support for the Schultz-Mellor hypothesis that in traditional and near-traditional agriculture resources are allocated efficiently. Second, the three major upland crop-supply responses to market price—especially in the case of kenaf—suggest that traditional and near-traditional peasants will produce non-traditional products if market conditions suggest that sufficiently profitable returns may be expected. Third, the rapid adoption of the Guatemalan flint corn seeds because of the higher expected yields suggests that traditional and near-traditional peasants readily will adopt new factor inputs that are relatively simple to use and that promise

sufficiently high returns.[17] Fourth, the results of this study suggest that the government should avoid introducing distortions into the relative prices of products and factors because peasants do respond significantly to the existing price structure.[18] In the unlikely event that the government has sufficient information to stabilize market prices without incurring great costs in storage or in other activities, however, the strong responses of the supply of rice to the residents in agricultural households and of the supply of upland crops to the proxy for the variances in the subjective probability distributions of harvest prices suggest that medium-term stabilization may be desirable. Fifth, the results of the study suggest that the government need not utilize great quantities of resources in forcing peasants to adopt profitable innovations or in squeezing resources out of peasant agriculture so that agriculture will contribute to overall economic development. Government resources probably can be utilized much more efficiently (in a social sense) in agricultural research, in disseminating the results of such research if they are too complex to be disseminated sufficiently quickly through factor markets [Ruttan, 1967, pp. 10–31] and in investment in social overhead capital.

References

AYAL, 1965. Eliezer B. Ayal, "Economic Nationalism in Thailand," Cambridge: Harvard University, Center for International Studies, 1965. (Mimeographed.)

BARLOW, 1967. Robin Barlow, "The Economic Effects of Malaria Eradication," *The American Economic Review, Papers and Proceedings*, Vol. XLVII, No. 2 (May, 1967), 130–48.

BAUER and YAMEY, 1959. P. T. Bauer and B. S. Yamey, "A Case Study of Response to Price in an Underdeveloped Country," *The Economic Journal*, Vol. LXIX, No. 276 (December 1959), 800–805.

17. The results of this study may not be easily generalized to the perhaps more frequent case in which a whole complex of new factors and new skills must be introduced almost simultaneously in order for the venture to be profitable [Ruttan et al., 1966].

18. Two relevant examples of such distortions introduced by the Thai government are the suppression of the price that rice farmers receive through a large export tax on rice and the provision of irrigation benefits at no cost to the user [Behrman, 1966a, pp. 14–18, 59–64; 1968a; 1968b, pp. 11–13, 47–51].

BEHRMAN, 1966a. Jere R. Behrman, "Supply Response in Underdeveloped Agriculture: A Case Study of Four Major Annual Crops in Thailand, 1937–1963," Ph.D. dissertation (Cambridge, Mass.: Department of Economics, Massachusetts Institute of Technology, 1966).

BEHRMAN, 1966b. Jere R. Behrman, "The Price Elasticity of the Marketed Surplus of a Subsistence Crop," *Journal of Farm Economics*, Vol. 48, No. 4 (November 1966) 875–93.

BEHRMAN, 1967a. Jere R. Behrman, "The Relevance of Traditional Economic Theory for Understanding Peasant Behavior: A Case Study of Rice Supply Response in Thailand, 1940–1963," Philadelphia: Department of Economics, University of Pennsylvania, Discussion Paper No. 37; revised, January 1967. (Mimeographed.)

BEHRMAN, 1967b. Jere R. Behrman, "The Adoption of New Products and of New Factors in Response to Market Incentives in Peasant Agriculture: An Econometric Investigation of Thai Corn and Kenaf Responses in the Postwar Period," Philadelphia: Department of Economics, University of Pennsylvania, Discussion Paper No. 45, February 1967. (Mimeographed.)

BEHRMAN, 1968a. Jere R. Behrman, "Significance of Intracountry Variations for Asian Agricultural Prospects: Central and Northeastern Thailand," *Asian Survey*, Vol. VIII, No. 3 (March 1968), 157–73.

BEHRMAN, 1968b. Jere R. Behrman, "Supply Response in Underdeveloped Agriculture: A Case Study of Four Major Annual Crops in Thailand, 1937–1963" (Amsterdam: North-Holland Publishers, 1968).

BOEKE, 1953. J. H. Boeke, *Economics and Economic Policy of Dual Societies* (Haarlem: H. D. Tjeenk Willink, 1953).

BREITENBACH, 1964. Charles A. Breitenbach, *Crop Development in Thailand: A Report Written on Completion of Assignment* (Bangkok: U.S. Operation Mission, Agency for International Development, 1964).

BROWN, 1963. Lester R. Brown, "Agricultural Diversification and Economic Development in Thailand: A Case Study," Department of Agriculture, Foreign Agricultural Economic Report No. 8, Regional Analysis Division (Washington, D. C.: U.S. Government Printing Office, 1963).

CHAIYONG, et al., 1962. Chuchart Chaiyong, et al., "Production and Marketing Problems Affecting the Expansion of Kenaf and Jute in Thailand: A Report of the Preliminary Survey," Translated by Miss Bimpandha Sirivongse and Mrs. Gordon Sitton (Bangkok: Kasetsart University, Economics Report No. 7, 1962).

CHAIYONG and SOPIN, 1965. Chuchart Chaiyong and Tongkan Sopin, "Rice Premium: Policy to Support and Stabilize Prices and Incomes of

Thai Farmers" (Bangkok: Kasetsart University, 1965). (Mimeographed.)

COCHRANE, 1955. Willard W. Cochrane, "Conceptualizing the Supply Relation in Agriculture," *The Journal of Farm Economics*, Vol. XXVII, No. 5 (December 1955), 1161–76.

COLEMAN, 1963. P. G. Coleman, *A Report on Agriculture in Ubol Province*, Prepared for the Thai-SEATO Regional Community Technical Assistance Centre (Bangkok: 1963).

DABASI-SCHWENG, 1965. Lorand Dabasi-Schweng, "The Problem of Transforming Traditional Agriculture," *World Politics: A Quarterly Journal of International Relations*, Vol. XVII, No. 3 (April 1965), 503–21.

DALTON, 1962. George Dalton, "Traditional Production in Primitive African Economies," *The Quarterly Journal of Economics*, Vol. LXXVI, No. 3 (August 1962), 360–78.

DANTWALA, 1963. M. L. Dantwala, "International Planning to Combat the Scourge of Hunger Throughout the World," *Annals of Collective Economy*, Vol. XXXIV, No. 1 (January–March 1963), 71–96.

FALCON, 1962. Walter P. Falcon, "Farmer Response to Price in an Underdeveloped Area— A Case Study of West Pakistan," Unpublished Ph.D. dissertation, Department of Economics, Harvard University, 1962.

FALCON, 1964. Walter P. Falcon, "Farmer Response to Price in a Subsistence Economy: The Case of West Pakistan," *American Economic Review, Papers and Proceedings*, Vol. LIV, No. 2 (May 1964), 580–91.

FLETCHER and MUBYARTO, 1966. Lee Fletcher and Mubyarto, "The Marketable Surplus of Rice in Indonesia: A Study in Java-Madura," International Studies in Economics No. 4 (Ames: Department of Economics, Iowa State University, October 1966).

HANSEN, 1960. Alvin Hansen, *Economic Issues of the 1960's* (New York: McGraw-Hill, 1960).

HUSSAIN, 1964. S. M. Hussain, "A Note on Farmer Response to Price in East Pakistan," *The Pakistan Development Review*, Vol. IV, No. 1 (Spring, 1964), 93–106.

INSOR, 1963. D. Insor, *Thailand: A Political, Social, and Economic Analysis* (London: Allen and Unwin 1963).

KINGSHILL, 1960. Konrad Kingshill, *Ku Daeng— The Red Tomb: A Village in Northern Thailand* (Chiangmai, Thailand: The Prince Royal's College, 1960).

KRISHNA, 1961. Raj Krishna, "Farm Supply Response in the Punjab (India-Pakistan): A Case Study of Cotton," Unpublished Ph.D. dissertation, Department of Economics, University of Chicago, 1961.

KRISHNA, 1963. Raj Krishna, "Farm Supply Response In India-Pakistan: A Case Study of

The Punjab Region," *Economic Journal*, Vol. LXXIII, No. 291 (September 1963), 477–87.

LEWIS, 1964.   John P. Lewis, *Quiet Crises in India: Economic Development and American Policy* (Garden City, N.Y.: Anchor Books, Doubleday, 1964).

LONG, et al., 1963.   J. F. Long et al., *Economic and Social Conditions Among Farmers in Changwad Khonkaen*, Kasetsart University Economics Report No. 22 (Bangkok: Kasetsart University, 1963).

MANGAHAS, et al., 1966.   Mahar Mangahas, et al., "Price and Market Relationships for Rice and Corn in the Philippines," *The Journal of Farm Economics*, Vol. XLVIII, No. 3 (August 1966), 685–703.

MELLOR, 1966.   John W. Mellor, *The Economics of Agricultural Development*, (Ithaca, N.Y.: Cornell University Press, 1966).

NAIR, 1965.   Kussum Nair, *Blossoms in the Dust: The Human Factor in Indian Development* (New York: Praeger, 1965).

NEALE, 1959.   Walter C. Neale, "Economic Accounting and Family Farming in India," *Economic Development and Cultural Change*, Vol. VII, No. 2 (April 1959), 286–301.

NERLOVE, 1958.   Marc Nerlove, *The Dynamics of Supply: Estimation of Farmers' Response to Price* (Baltimore: The Johns Hopkins University Press, 1958).

OLSON, 1960.   R. O. Olson, "The Impact and Implications of Foreign Surplus Disposal on Underdeveloped Economics," *The Journal of Farm Economics*, Vol. XLII, No. 5 (December 1960), 1042–45.

PANTUM, et al., 1963.   Thisyanomdol Pantum, et al., "Agricultural Credit in Thailand: Theory, Data, Policy" (Bangkok: Kasetsart University, 1963). (Mimeographed.)

PLATENIUS, 1963.   Hans Platenius, "The Northeast of Thailand: Its Problems and Potentialities" (Bangkok: National Economic Development Board, 1963). (Mimeographed.)

RUTTAN, et al., 1966.   Vernon W. Ruttan, A. Soothipan, and E. C. Venegas, "Changes in Rice Growing in the Philippines and Thailand," *World Crops* Vol. XVIII (March 1966), 18–33.

RUTTAN, 1967.   Vernon W. Ruttan, "Notes on Agricultural Product and Factor Markets in Southeast Asia," Paper presented at Agricultural Development Council—University of Kentucky Seminar on "Adapting Agricultural Cooperatives and Quasi-Cooperatives to the Market Structures and Conditions of Underdeveloped Areas," Lexington, Kentucky, April 26–30, 1967. (Mimeographed.)

SCHULTZ, 1964.   T. W. Schultz, *Transforming Traditional Agriculture* (London and New Haven, Conn.: Yale University Press, 1964).

SCHULTZ, 1965.   T. W. Schultz, *Economic Crises in World Agriculture* (Ann Arbor, Michigan: The University of Michigan Press, 1965).

SMITH, 1963.   Harold D. Smith, *Agricultural Production and Consumption Patterns and Market Potential in Thailand* (College Park, Maryland: Department of Agricultural Economics, University of Maryland, Miscellaneous Publication No. 490, 1963).

SOMSAKDI, 1963.   Charvenvithya Somsakdi, "The Problem of Poverty in the Thai Rural Economy," *The Bangkok Bank Monthly Review* (September 1963), 78–88.

THAILAND, 1953.   *Thailand Economic Farm Survey, 1953* (Bangkok: Division of Agricultural Economics, Ministry of Agriculture, December 1953).

THAILAND, 1962.   *Thailand Population Census 1960: Whole Kingdom* (Bangkok: National Economic Development Board, Central Statistical Office, 1962).

THAILAND, 1964.   *National Income 1964* (Bangkok: National Economic Development Board, National Income Office, National Income Division, 1964).

CASE STUDY

Supply Relations for Perennial Crops
in the Less-Developed Areas[1]

MERRILL J. BATEMAN

THE RESPONSE OF FARMERS in underdeveloped countries to changes in economic variables has been a topic for discussion and study for years. The extent of the response in various countries and for different crops has not only analytical significance, but also bears on issues of political importance. In countries that are predominantly agricultural, problems of public finance and price and income stabilization relate directly to the supply elasticities of the relevant products.

Given the importance of supply information, the surprising element in any survey of the literature on perennials or tree crops is that so little is known about the elasticities involved, particularly those that apply to the long run. A number of factors have contributed to this void with respect to perennials, as Bauer and Yamey [1959, p. 800] note in the following:

There are . . . serious difficulties in measuring the degree of responsiveness of producers to price changes. There are the familiar problems arising from the usual absence in the real world of anything resembling closely the *ceteris paribus* of the theoretical formulations of functional relationships in economics. There are further difficulties created by the time lags between changes in agricultural capacity and changes in output; and also by the effects of uncertainty about the permanence of absolute and relative price changes. The problems of testing a hypothesis or of measuring the strength of a functional relationship make it difficult to reach objective assessments, and rival hypotheses are likely to flourish side by side, often deriving from opposing policy preconceptions and sometimes giving rise to opposing policy prescriptions.

In addition to the problems of measurement outlined, the lack of data, particularly

annual plantings, has hampered the quest for quantitative estimates of the parameters involved. The importance of the information, however, in the economic development of many low-income countries requires that more attention and effort be given to these problems.

The purpose of this paper is threefold. The first objective is to review some of the empirical work related to supply functions for tree crops. The second section outlines a few general models which can be applied to perennials, and the third section briefly reviews applications of some of those models to cocoa and coffee.

PAST STUDIES OF SUPPLY RELATIONS
FOR TREE CROPS

The supply functions for cocoa, rubber, and lemons have received more attention during the last two decades than have other tree crops. Recent efforts have also been made to examine the supply relations for coffee. Citrus fruits (other than lemons), bananas, palm oil, copra, tea, dates, and olive oil are other tree crops, important in many underdeveloped areas, that have received little, if any, study from a quantitative point of view.

This section of the paper is concerned with the models developed for cocoa, rubber, lemons, and coffee. The works of Ady, Bauer, Stern, Wharton and Chan, Arak, and French and Bressler are reviewed.

Cocoa

Numerous references have been made to the relative elasticity or inelasticity of cocoa producer response to changes in economic variables. One of the first serious attempts, however, to estimate the parameters of a supply function for a perennial was made by

1. An earlier version of this paper was given at the seminar sponsored by the Agricultural Development Council on Supply and Market Surplus Relationships in Peasant Agriculture, held at the University of Minnesota, February 19–20, 1966.

Miss Peter Ady of Oxford [1949]. The cocoa-supply model developed by Ady attempted to measure both the long- and short-run responses of farmers to changes in cocoa prices. As stated elsewhere [Bateman, 1965a], the Ady model is characterized by at least three different errors. Ady postulates that planting in a particular year is influenced by the prices that prevail in that year and that it takes nine years for cocoa to attain full bearing. Her model then relates total cocoa production in year *t* as a function of prices lagged nine years. If both initial assumptions were correct, the change in output rather than total output should be a function of lagged prices. The second error is one of misspecification. During the period of time under study by Ady, cocoa trees did reach maturity around the ninth or tenth year after planting; however, the trees had been producing some cocoa for at least four years prior to the tenth. In short, she failed to completely specify the output-planting relationship. A third error in the study involved the estimation techniques employed. After regressing output on prices lagged nine years, the residuals were regressed on current prices in an attempt to estimate the short-run response of the producer at harvesting time. Serious difficulties arise in using this methodology unless it can be shown that current and past prices are unrelated.

In spite of the criticisms outlined, Ady's work still stands as one of the few attempts to estimate the long-run supply elasticity of a tree crop.

Professor P. T. Bauer's writings [1954, Appendix 3] relative to the degree of responsiveness of producers provided the basis for studies that followed. Bauer argues persuasively that producer prices influence incentive and thus the level of production. Higher prices not only stimulate producers already engaged in production, but induce prospective producers who previously had not cultivated the crop to enter the market.

Although Bauer has never attempted to measure elasticities, he and Yamey did present statistical information in their 1959 article which leaves little doubt as to the responsiveness of Nigerian cocoa and palm-oil producers in the short run. During the 1950's the Nigerian produce-marketing boards widened the price differentials between various grades of the two products. The response by the farmer resulted in a significant increase in the proportion of top-grade produce submitted for purchase and the virtual elimination of the inferior grades. The response was short-run in the sense that output was responding to current price changes. The improvement in quality resulted from the employment of better harvesting and fermentation techniques.

Professor Stern's recent effort [1965a] to estimate the determinants of cocoa supply in West Africa did correct Miss Ady's first error by relating the change in output to past prices; he also failed to correctly identify the planting-output relationship. The only statistically significant results obtained by him for the post-1946 period involved the influence of time on output. Even the relationship between the trend variable and output is questionable, particularly in terms of usefulness. If the coefficient for the trend variable is the only significant parameter in a supply function, it would appear that little if any worthwhile information has been obtained.

The most recent efforts [Bateman, 1965b; Behrman, 1966] to estimate the supply parameters for cocoa will be presented below.

Rubber

Dr. Wharton [1963a], Mr. Francis Chan [1962], Professor Bauer [1948], and Professor Stern [1965b], all contributed to the development of supply functions for rubber. Chan was among the first to estimate the elasticities of supply. He tried both monthly and annual data, and his models were generally aimed at obtaining parameters which apply to the harvest or tapping response to price changes. The basic model employed related output in period *t* to the producer price of rubber in that period, the composition of the tree stand, mature acreage, and a trend variable. Separate regressions were run for estates and smallholders.

The use of annual data provided an imperfect estimate of the short-run (tapping) period, and the coefficients derived from this data were statistically insignificant for estates The price coefficient in the smallholder equation suggested an elasticity of 0.12, with a significance level of 10 per cent.

The regressions employing monthly data for the estates again failed to suggest significant response to current price changes. On the other hand, when monthly data were inserted into the smallholder model, statistically significant short-run price elasticities were obtained. The years 1949–1960 were subdivided into six different periods. Periods of rising prices were separated from periods of falling prices. The short-run price elasticities varied between 0.20 and 0.37 when the Korean War emergency was excluded.[2]

One important difference between rubber and many other tree crops is the flexibility the farmer has in controlling the flow of rubber output in the short run. The possibility of an almost immediate response of the rubber farmer to a price change contrasts with the lack of short-run flexibility (particularly with reference to price increases) inherent in the cultivation of a number of other perennials. Fertilizers and other soil additives can be used to stimulate output, but these efforts usually require from one to three years to be effective. The potential of the rubber farmer to respond almost immediately to price changes highlights the importance of examining short-run price elasticities for this product.

Stern has also attempted recently to estimate the short-run price elasticity of Malayan rubber. Using quarterly data for the period 1953–1960, he tests separate models for estate and smallholder production of rubber. The explanatory variables in the estate equation include current price deflated by estate wages for tappers and field workers, a ratio of beginning-of-quarter estate inventories to estate sales in the preceding quarter, and a time trend. The smallholder equation related output to deflated current price, the deflated current price of rice, and a trend variable.

In both Stern equations the trend coefficient was highly significant. The current price variable was not significant in the estate equation but was significant at the 1 per cent level in the smallholder equation and suggested a short-run price elasticity of approximately 0.20.

2. Wharton [1963b, p. 7] also reports similar short-run estimates for rubber supply in other Southeast Asian countries, using the same techniques, and found that none of the estimated price elasticities exceeded +0.21. (The reader should remember that, in the case of rubber, short-run estimates refer to the tapping or harvesting response.)

Lemons

An article by French and Bressler [1962] outlines a supply model for the lemon industry. Acreage data and age composition of lemon trees in California were available, allowing them to examine the relationship between the rate of planting and the farmer's long-run profit expectations. They assume that the rate of planting is a linear function of long-run profit expectations (a five-year average of past net returns per acre was selected after various tests) and the age composition of the tree stock. The latter variable was represented by the percentage of trees over 25 years of age, since the average life of a lemon tree is approximately 30 years.

Data covering the 1947–1960 period were analyzed using least squares. The age variable turned out to be nonsignificant; however, the profit variable was highly correlated with the rate of new plantings, as it explained about 86 per cent of the variance of the latter. No information was given regarding the elasticity that was generated by the model.

In addition to the planting model, French and Bressler also attempted to estimate the parameters of a removal equation. The removal function was similar to the planting one in that the rate of removal was assumed to be linearly related to profits and age. The attempt was unsuccessful in that none of the variables had significant coefficients.

Although the French-Bressler study did not involve an underdeveloped country, it did break new ground in formulating a model to measure long-run responses. Further, the study also highlights the types of data that are needed but not usually available in the developing countries.

Coffee

The first person to formulate an econometric model for the supply of coffee was Miss Marcelle Arak [1967]. In her dissertation she developed a number of different models to examine the planting, removal, and abandonment responses of coffee farmers in Brazil. The availability of planting data and the age composition of trees for the Sao Paulo region provided a basis for estimating the parameters of a number of different models. The period examined was 1930–1955. One Arak model assumed that planting in year t was a function of the farmer's price expectations in that year, the availability of suitable coffee land, and the age composition of the tree stock. A similar model assumed that the rate of planting, as opposed to the level of planting, was a function of the same set of variables. The short-run responsiveness of farmers to a change in expected coffee prices, as measured by the models, was relatively high. The elasticity of annual plantings with respect to coffee prices was 2.0 in one model and 2.3 in the other. The long-run price elasticities were not identifiable.

For the states of Minas Gerais and Espirito Santo, Arak utilized a different function. The change in the adult stock of coffee trees was assumed to be a function of expected prices for coffee and other agricultural products lagged four years, a similar vector of prices in the current year, and the acreage of adult trees in the previous year. The model attempted to separate the effects of plantings and the effects of eradication and abandonment on the changes in the adult stock of trees. Arak utilized a maximum likelihood procedure to estimate the parameters. The estimates generated by the model suggested long-run elasticities of 0.54 and 0.28 for Minas Gerais and Espirito Santo, respectively. The period of analysis was 1927-1959 for both states.

For the state of Parana, Arak specified a function different from those outlined above. For this region, the allocation ratio, $\Delta A_t/\Delta C_t$, was assumed to be a linear function of relative prices. The numerator, ΔA_t, was the change in the area of adult coffee trees, and the denominator was the change in the total agricultural area of the state. The results suggested a long-run elasticity equal to 0.955.

Mr. Edmar Bacha, a graduate student at Yale University, is currently completing a doctoral thesis that includes a demand-and-supply model for world coffee. As yet the results of his work are not available.

The author of this paper is currently engaged in estimating a supply function for Colombian coffee. The model employed is the third one outlined in this paper. Although the results are preliminary at this stage, early findings suggest elasticities in the neighborhood of 0.5 to 0.8

The reason for reviewing the above studies in detail has been to point out the few attempts made to estimate long-run elasticities, particularly during the period before 1965. When planting data have not existed, the models developed have taken one of two approaches. One approach involves the use of current price to explain the short-run response of output, plus a time variable to pick up the long-run movement. The latter variable worked reasonably well during the late 1940's and throughout the 1950's because prices lagged to ten years moved generally upwards. It should be noted at this point that Chan's work included composition and mature acreage variables. Both variables reflect long-run influences and improved the overall level of significance. The change in stock and its composition is the result of the farmer's response to price changes in an earlier period.

The second approach introduced lagged prices in an attempt to estimate the long-run response in addition to the short-run elasticities. In most cases, however, the author looked at the lag between planting and mature bearing and then introduced one price variable that was lagged the same number of years. Thus the second set of models hypothesized that the determinents of output were the current price and one lagged price. Ady and Stern in cocoa and Chan in rubber have all employed this technique.[3]

The objection to the first approach (i.e. the use of a time trend only to capture long-run movements) is that no information of a long-run nature is obtained. The outcome of the first type of model is that short-run elasticities are highly inelastic, and most of the explanatory power of the equation is the trend term.

The objection to the second model is the failure to identify the output-planting relationship. The assumption employed is that no output is obtained from the tree until it reaches a stage of mature bearing. If the tree crop in question has a very short lag between initial and mature output, the assumption is appropriate. For example, the length of time required for a rubber tree to achieve full flow once it has been tapped is very short. On the

3. Wharton mentions in a footnote [1963a, p. 144 that Chan has attempted to estimate the long-run elasticity, of rubber by introducing a price variable lagged seven years. The lag was based on the time it takes a rubber tree to reach mature bearing. The coefficient for the lagged price was not significant.

other hand, many tree crops require as long as four or five years to move from initial bearing to maximum yields. This is true for cocoa. For tree crops with long maturation periods, the assumption of no output until maturity is unrealistic. The problems encountered and the effort involved in identifying the output-planting relationship may also explain why some have used a trend variable to represent long-run influences.

The next section of the paper outlines four different supply models that may be used to estimate elasticities when planting and age data are not available. The relevance of a particular model depends on the tree crop in question and the socio-economic environment in which the response occurs.

GENERAL SUPPLY MODELS FOR TREE CROPS

There are two main points of interest in the development of a supply model for tree crops. First, one is concerned with the forces that motivate the farmer to plant; and the second area of interest is the relationship between acres planted and output harvested. The latter is particularly crucial when acreage data are not available.

Planting-Decision Models

The four supply models that follow relate to the first point. The models represent four different ways in which the farmer can react to economic variables during the planting decision. After the four supply models are developed, the relationship between acres planted and output harvested is examined.

Model No. 1—Gross Investment as a Function of Prices. The first model presented was first developed to explain the supply of cocoa [Bateman, 1965b]. The model is as follows:

$$(1) \qquad X_t = a_0 + a_1 \tilde{P}_t + a_2 \tilde{S}_t + u_t$$

where

$$\tilde{P}_t = \sum_{i=0}^{n} (P^{\star}_{t+i}) \Big/ n+1$$

$$\tilde{S}_t = \sum_{i=0}^{n} (S^{\star}_{t+i}) \Big/ n+1$$

$X_t =$ the number of acres planted in year t.

$P^{\star}_{t+i} =$ the expected real producer price in year $t+i$ of the product being planted.

$S^{\star}_{t+i} =$ the expected real producer price in year $t+i$ of an alternative crop.

$n =$ the expected age after which the trees planted in year t cease to bear.

The first equation states that the number of acres planted in any one year is a function of the mean value of future prices of the tree crop in question and of one or more alternative crops.

It is assumed that movements in actual producer prices shape the farmer's expectations concerning the future and that expectations are formed as follows:

$$(2a) \qquad \tilde{P}_t - \tilde{P}_{t-1} = \beta(P_t - \tilde{P}_{t-1})$$
$$(2b) \qquad \tilde{S}_t - \tilde{S}_{t-1} = \beta(S_t - \tilde{S}_{t-1})$$

The price-expectation models employ a distributed lag form common in the literature.[4]

The models suggest that the primary factor which causes a change in the farmer's price expectations from one year to the next is the movement in real producer prices.

Equations (1) and (2) can be combined to eliminate the price expectation variables. The final solution is:

$$(3) \quad X_t = a_0\beta + a_1\beta P_t + a_2\beta S_t + (1-\beta)X_{t-1} + v_t$$

where

$$v_t = u_t - (1-\beta)u_{t-1}.$$

It is assumed that the farmer desires to maximize the present discounted value of the returns from his investment. The model implicitly suggests that yields per acre and costs associated with planting and harvesting are not expected to change significantly during the relevant time period. The expected yield pattern of most tree crops is relatively stable, and changes in potential yield occur slowly. On the other hand, the cost stream associated with a particular

4. One could assume that the adjustment coefficient (β) in 2b is different from the coefficient in 2a and estimate them separately, using a long series of prices. On the other hand, the degrees of freedom are usually limited in any empirical analysis and the assumption that they are the same is convenient and, at the same time, may not distort reality severely.

investment in a tree crop will experience some fluctuations; however, the changes in costs may be a function of the changes in the price of the product. This is true particularly in underdeveloped countries where tree crops constitute an important segment of the economy. In summary, it is assumed that actual producer prices fluctuate more than do costs or yields.

Thus the major determinant of expected profits is the expected price stream. If the farmer expects future prices to be higher than past prices, expected profits will increase and the incentive to invest will induce more planting. On the other hand, if the farmer expects a downward trend in future prices and that the average price level will be low relative to past prices, gross investment in this product will fall and may even be zero or negative. Disinvestment occurs when the influence of S_t outweighs the impact of P_t and X_{t-1}.

On the other hand, one would expect some irreversibilities to exist between output and prices. One would not expect a small decrease in price in price to lead to a future decrease in output. This would imply that the farmer cuts down trees any time the crop price falls (the mortality factor is assumed to be zero for the present). The capital losses incurred in such a practice suggest the irrationality involved unless the fall in price is substantial. Still, if all variables are held constant except P_t and it is allowed to fall, the model indicates that the number of new acres planted this year will be less than last year—but could be positive. Thus a decrease in price may result in an increase in output. There may be objections to a supply model which is not more responsive to price decreases.

A supply model in which the stock of trees is a function of prices would eliminate this problem. The two models which follow employ this relationship.

Model No. 2—Stock of Trees as a Function of Expected Prices. The second model suggests that the farmer adjusts his stock of trees to movements in prices. Thus:

(4) $T_t = b_0 + b_1 \tilde{P}_t + b_2 \tilde{S}_t + w_t$

where

T_t = the total stock of trees in year t.

When the price-expectation models of (2a) and (2b) are added, then substituted and combined with equation (4), the expected price terms can be eliminated to give:

(5) $X_t = b_0\beta + b_1\beta P_t + b_2\beta S_t - \beta T_{t-1} + \tilde{w}_t$

where the error term

$\tilde{w}_t = w_t - (1 - \beta)w_{t-1}.$

Equation (5) indicates that new planting in period t is a function of the same variables that appeared in the first model with the exception of the lagged dependent variable. The lagged planting variable has been replaced by the stock of trees lagged one period and the parameter of the latter is a negative beta, the coefficient of adjustment in the price-expectation models.

The stock formulation does eliminate the problem which occurred in the planting model. A decrease in price, other variables remaining constant, may lead to a decrease in output. In fact, an objection to the stock model is that the output-price relationship may be too responsive to price changes—particularly on the downward side. A decrease in price may result in an immediate decrease in the stock of trees; hence future output will be negatively affected.

A more suitable stock model, which would allow more flexibility in the adjustment of stocks to changes in expected prices, is developed in the third model.

Model No. 3—Desired Stock of Trees as a Function of Prices. The desired stock model recognizes that certain constraints exist which keep the farmer from adjusting the actual stock of trees to the desired level given a change in price. The model is:

(6) $T_t^\star = c_0 + c_1 \tilde{P}_t + c_2 \tilde{S}_t + e_t$

where

$T_t^\star$ = the desired stock of trees in year t. This is the long-run equilibrium stock of trees, given the expected level of future prices.

It is further assumed that the actual stock of trees is adjusted in proportion to the difference between the stock desired in long-run equilibrium and the actual stock. The relation is:

(7) $T_t - T_{t-1} = \gamma(T_t^\star - T_{t-1})$

The constant γ is the acreage-adjustment coefficient and depends on the nature and type of constraints facing the farmer.

When the price expectation models of (2a) and (2b) are combined with equation (6) and (7), substitutions can be made to eliminate the desired stock and expected price variables. The result is:

$$(8) \quad X_t = c_0\beta\gamma + c_1\beta\gamma P_t + c_2\beta\gamma S_t \\ + (1-\beta-\gamma)X_{t-1} - \beta\gamma T_{t-2} + \tilde{e}_t$$

where the error term

$$\tilde{e}_t = \gamma[e_t - (1-\beta)e_{t-1}].$$

The desired stock model has been reduced so that new planting is once again the dependent variable. One of the interesting features of the desired stock model is that it contains the same variables as the planting equation, with one addition—the stock of trees lagged two periods. Although the coefficients appear complex, it is possible to solve for $\beta\gamma$ and then obtain the initial parameters of equation (6). On the other hand, it is not possible to separate the difference between the long-run and short-run elasticities of supply (γ) from the difference between the actual price and the expected level of future prices (β).[5]

The desired stock model is preferable to the other models developed in that it recognizes the constraints imposed on the farmer in adjusting his stock of trees and also provides for reversibility in the price-output relationship. If there is a strong presumption that the farmer reacts differently to increases in $\tilde{P}_t$ and decreases in $\tilde{S}_t$ than he does to opposite movements in these variables, the data could be separated into different time periods based on price trends. The degrees of freedom available in any long-run model, however, usually prevent such experimentation.

The final model suggests the importance of liquidity as a variable.

Model No. 4—The Liquidity Model. Given imperfect capital markets and limited funds, there is reason to assume that farmer income may be an important determinant of planting. Even though the farmer expects relatively

high prices to prevail in the future, he may lack the funds necessary to invest.

The planting model, previously developed, has been chosen to illustrate this effect; however, the income variable could be adapted to either of the other stock models. The planting model with the income variable added is:

$$(9) \quad X_t = a_0 + a_1\tilde{P}_t + a_2\tilde{S}_t + a_3Y_{t-1} + u_t$$

where

$Y_{t-1} =$ the income received by the farmer in year $t-1$. (This variable may be Y_t. The choice depends on the time relationship between harvesting and planting.)

Equation (9) relates planting to expected future prices and last period's income. Thus the model allows for the situation where Y_{t-1} is relatively large but price expectations are such that the farmer would not want to invest. In this case the influence of prices would outweigh the effect of income.

An additive formulation has been used in the presentation for reasons of convenience. In reality the functional form will vary from one environment and crop to another. Moreover, the applicability of the various models will depend on the tree crop, the particular time period, the income segment of the population devoted to farming, the stage of social and economic development of the society, plus many other factors. Yet the models are general enough in scope that sufficient effort should enable one to estimate the relevant parameters.

Before leaving this section, one final point should be noted. In the absence of data on the age composition of the tree stock, the stock-adjustment models implicitly assume that the trees have an infinite life. The mortality rate of trees because of old age, disease, and other factors has been omitted. Although this variable is difficult to quantify, a depreciation variable might be important for some crops, particularly when marginal lands are involved. On the other hand, some trees have an extremely long life span, and the mortality rate may be insignificant. The particular tree crop and its environment will determine the relevance of this variable.

If planting data were available, it would be

---

5. For a complete discussion of the impasse suggested above and some possible exceptions to it, one should consult Nerlove [1958, p. 64-5].

possible to obtain the long-run elasticities from the appropriate model above. In many areas, though, records have not been kept. In contrast, records of the annual quantity of the crop harvested are usually available; and by correctly specifying the output-planting relationship, the long-run supply elasticities may be estimated.

THE PLANTING-OUTPUT
RELATIONSHIP

Output in any one year is related to the sum of past plantings in a number of preceding years. This relationship may be expressed in the following way:

$$(10) \quad Q_t^{\star} = \sum_{i=k}^{\infty} (\gamma_i X_{t-i})$$

where

$Q_t^{\star}$ = the potential yield of the crop in year t.

γ_i = the potential yield per acre in year t of the acres planted in year $t-i$.

k = the age at which trees first begin to bear or produce.

The relation in equation (10) refers to potential output in the year of harvest. Actual output can be approximated by introducing the effects of climatic factors on yield and the impact of current economic factors on harvesting.

Once the relation between actual output and past plantings is correctly specified, it is possible to connect output and past prices in one of two ways. Since the sum of past plantings is the stock of trees, one alternative would be to rearrange the current and lagged dependent variables in the stock models to obtain the total stock of trees as the dependent variable. This relation could then be substituted for the stock of trees variable in the output-planting equation. One advantage gained from this approach is the degrees of freedom saved. The cost involves the submersion of the dynamic properties of the system. Moreover, you can not tell which prices are relevant, since there are other intermediate prices. A version of this approach, in fact, was adopted by Ady and Chan. The consequences suggest that the costs outweigh the gains.

The second approach requires that equation (10) be transformed into a first-order difference equation. This results in the elimination of almost all past plantings. The only planting variables that remain are those that belong to the tree's period of growth and decline. If the effects of the latter can be eliminated or estimated by a proxy variable, the four- or five-year period in which the tree's yield increases from zero to a maximum remains. And if the increases in yield are not smoothly distributed over the maturation period, additional variables may be eliminated.

All of the supply models presented previously have been derived in such a way that planting is the dependent variable. If information were available on new plantings, the age composition of trees, and other relevant data concerning the stock of trees, one could directly estimate the coefficients in the above models. In the absence of such information, it is necessary to combine the planting-decision models with the output-planting relation in order to estimate the price responsiveness of the producers.

The next section presents some results obtained from two of the models.

APPLICATIONS OF THE SUPPLY
MODELS

Four different attempts have been made to utilize the models outlined above. Table 8.5 summarizes results of the studies outlined earlier in this paper in addition to the efforts which will be described in this section. The reader can compare the elasticities generated by various models for three different tree crops: cocoa, coffee, and rubber.

As mentioned earlier in this paper, the author adapted the first planting model to Ghanaian cocoa. The results appear in Table 8.5 under the heading "Ghana (Model No. 1)." Since the coefficient for the lagged dependent variable was not statistically significant when this model was used, the elasticities for the various cocoa regions of Ghana are reported in the short-run column.[6]

6. Given a nonsignificant coefficient for the lagged dependent variable, one might assume that the coefficient of expectations is 1. This implies that the farmer's expected mean price in the future always equals the current price. Given the fluctuation in cocoa prices during the 1940's and 1950's, this conclusion does not appear tenable. For this reason the elasticities generated by the first model have been listed in the short-run column.

Table 8.5. Price Elasticity Estimates for Perennial Crops

CROP AND COUNTRY OR REGION	Period	ELASTICITY[a] Harvest and husbandry	Short-run	Long-run	Source
Cocoa					
Ghana	1930–40		0.43		Ady, 1949
Ghana	1920–39	0.17			Stern, 1965a
Ghana	1920–46	0.15			Stern, 1965a
Nigeria	1920–45		1.29		Stern, 1965a
Ghana (Model No. 1)					
Ashanti	1949–62		0.42		Bateman, 1965a
Brong-Ahafo	1949–62		0.87		Bateman, 1965a
Central	1946–62		0.44		Bateman, 1965a
Eastern	1946–62		0.32		Bateman, 1965a
Volta	1946–62		0.61		Bateman, 1965a
Western	1946–62		0.71		Bateman, 1965a
Ghana (Model No. 3)					
Central	1946–62		0.51	1.28	Bateman, 1968b
Eastern	1946–62		0.39	0.77	Bateman, 1968b
Volta	1946–62		0.53	1.06	Bateman, 1968b
Western	1946–62		0.31[e]	0.68[e]	Bateman, 1968b
Ghana (Model No. 3)	1947–64			0.71	Behrman, 1966
Nigeria (Model No. 3)	1947–64			0.45	Behrman, 1966
Ivory Coast (Model No. 3)	1947–64			0.80	Behrman, 1966
Cameroun Republic (Model 3)	1947–64	0.68		1.81	Behrman, 1966
Brazil (Model No. 3)	1947–64	0.53		0.95	Behrman, 1966
Ecuador (Model No. 3)	1947–64			0.28	Behrman, 1966
Dominican Republic (Model 3)	1947–64	0.03		0.15	Behrman, 1966
Venezuela (Model No. 3)	1947–64	0.12		0.38	Behrman, 1966
Coffee					
Brazil					
São Paulo[b]	1930–55		2.02		Arak, 1967
São Paulo[b]	1930–55		2.28		Arak, 1967
Espirito Santo	1927–55		0.08	0.54	Arak, 1967
Minas Gerais	1927–55		0.20	0.28	Arak, 1967
Parana	1945–62			0.96	
Colombia[c]	1947–65		0.47		Bateman, 1968a
Colombia[d]	1952–65		0.84		Bateman, 1968a
Lemons					
California	1947–60		No Estimates		French and Bressler, 1962
Rubber					
Malaysia					
Estates	1953–60	0.0			Stern, 1965
Smallholders	1953–60	0.02			Stern, 1965
Estates	1951–61	−.02[e,f]			Chan[h]
Smallholders	1948–61	0.12[f]			Chan[h]
Estates	1954–61	0.03[e,g]			Chan[h]
Smallholders	1953–60	0.34[g]			Chan[h]

[a] Three different price elasticities are distinguished for perennials. The first is the farmer response at harvest time to the current price. This response occurs over a time period too short for new plantings to come into bearing. The second is the response of planting or output to lagged prices without taking into account a Nerlovian adjustment mechanism. The long-run estimate allows for adjustment lags, provided they are real.

[b] Different models were used by Arak for São Paulo. The first utilized new acres planted as the dependent variable, while the second utilized new acres as a proportion of the total stock of trees.

[c] Output data are from the Colombian National Accounts and the price series is the producer price, deflated by a cost-of-living index for Manizales.

[d] The output data are from FAO publications, and the price series is the minimum producer price guaranteed by the government, which is deflated by a cost-of-living index for Colombia.

[e] Not significant at 10 per cent level.

[f] Based on annual data.

[g] Based on monthly data.

[h] Reported in Wharton [1963a, Tables 6–2, 6–3, 6–4]. Wharton also reports [1963b, 7] estimates of less than 0.21 for some other countries of Southeast Asia.

The elasticities range from 0.32 to 0.87, with the size of the elasticities varying inversely with the "cocoa age" of the region. The area where cocoa was first planted (eastern region) has the lowest response, with the newest region (Brong-Ahafo) exhibiting the largest.

The third model is currently being applied to the same Ghanaian cocoa areas. Preliminary results have been obtained, and the elasticities generated are listed in Table 8.5 under Ghana (Model No. 3). It is interesting to note that the short-run elasticities generated by the third model are very similar to the short-run elasticities of the first. In addition, the coefficients for the lagged dependent variable in the third model are statistically significant. When the adjustment lags are taken into account, long-run elasticities can be obtained, and these have been listed in the long-run column. Generally the long-run elasticities are approximately twice the short-run estimates.

Behrman [1966] has also utilized the third model to estimate cocoa-producer responses in a number of countries. In each country an aggregate supply function was estimated. When one compares his long-run estimate of 0.71 for Ghana with the long-run estimates the author obtained for various regions in Ghana, one notices that the regional estimates are somewhat higher. Two or three factors may explain the differences. Behrman's aggregate supply function does not allow for differences in soil and age of trees. In addition, he was not able to include the influences of weather on output. The regional data used by the author do allow for age and soil differences, and weather variables were included in each of the regional functions.

One interesting conclusion obtained by Behrman concerns the relative low elasticities for Ecuador, the Dominican Republic, and Venezuela. These are the oldest producing areas in the world. On the other hand, the cocoa producers in the other countries (Brazil and West Africa) are relatively responsive to prices in the long-run. This intercountry result agrees with the author's interregional findings for Ghana.

The third model has also been applied to Colombian coffee. The short-run elasticities are generally consistent with those obtained for cocoa. The coefficients for the lagged dependent variables are statistically significant; however, at this stage it is not possible to report the long-run elasticities because the effect of coffee's biennial yield cycle is combined with the coefficients of adjustment and expectation. This means that the coefficient for the lagged dependent variable includes all three factors. Additional information is needed before the effects of the biennial yield cycle can be separated from the other two coefficients ($\beta\gamma$). Thus estimates of the long-run elasticities are not available.

The attempts to use the models outlined in this paper by the author and Professor Behrman have proved rewarding. Reasonable estimates for the short-run and long-run producer responses in cocoa and coffee have been obtained, even though planting data and information regarding tree stocks have not been available. The possibility of determining such elasticities appears promising even in the absence of important information.

A major conclusion one arrives at when examining Table 8.5 is the lack of information for perennial crops that existed prior to 1965 and the significant amount of research since that time. Secondly, with the exception of the Arak models for Brazilian coffee and the Stern cocoa model for Nigeria, the short-run elasticities fall between 0.3 and 0.9. The long-run elasticities, on the other hand, vary between 0.15 for cocoa in the Dominican Republic to 1.8 for cocoa in the Cameroun Republic. In most of the cocoa- and coffee-producing countries producers are relatively responsive to prices in the long run. This suggests that government marketing boards have had considerable impact on the world production of coffee and cocoa, given their role in separating producer prices from world prices. By isolating producers from the world market, government agencies have had the power to control new plantings and supply of these products.

The final conclusion concerns the vast amount of work still to be done and the importance of additional information on tree crops. The responsiveness of producers in various countries still remains unexamined. The importance of future research regarding perennial crops is highlighted when one realizes that the pace of development in these countries is partially determined by the volume of foreign exchange the countries will earn from their perennial crops; secondly, their foreign exchange earnings are dependent on the price they receive for their products; the price the country receives is a function of world supply and demand conditions; and finally, these countries have the power to control their respective supplies.

References

ADY, 1949. Peter Ady, "Trends in Cocoa Production," *Oxford University Institute of Statistics Bulletin*, Vol. 2 (1949), 389–404.

ARAK, 1967. Marcelle Arak, "The Supply of Brazilian Coffee," Unpublished Ph.D. dissertation, Department of Economics, Massachusetts Institute of Technology, 1967.

BATEMAN, 1965a. Merrill J. Bateman, "Cocoa in the Ghanaian Economy," Unpublished Ph.D. dissertation, Department of Economics, Massachusetts Institute of Technology, 1965.

BATEMAN, 1965b. Merrill J. Bateman, "Aggregate and Regional Supply Functions for Ghanaian Cocoa," *Journal of Farm Economics*, Vol. 47, No. 2 (May 1965), 384–401.

BATEMAN, 1968a. Merrill J. Bateman, "A Supply Function for Colombian Coffee, 1947–65," a RAND Memorandum (Summer, 1968).

BATEMAN, 1968b. Merrill J. Bateman, *Cocoa in the Ghanaian Economy: An Econometric Model* (Amsterdam: North-Holland Publishing Company, 1968).

BAUER, 1948. Peter T. Bauer, *The Rubber Industry: A Study in Competition and Monopoly* (Cambridge: Cambridge University Press, 1948).

BAUER, 1954. Peter T. Bauer, *West African Trade* (Cambridge: Cambridge University Press, 1954).

BAUER and YAMEY, 1959. Peter T. Bauer and Basil S. Yamey, "A Case Study of Response to Price in an Under-Developed Country," *The Economic Journal*, Vol. LXIX, No. 276 (December 1959), 800–805.

BEHRMAN, 1966. Jere R. Behrman, "Monopolistic Pricing in International Commodity Agreements: A Case Study of Cocoa," Paper presented at the Ninth Annual Meeting of the African Studies Association, Indiana University, Bloomington, Indiana, October 29, 1966.

CHAN, 1962. Francis Chan, "A Preliminary Study of the Supply Response of Malayan Rubber Estates Between 1948 and 1959," *Malayan Economic Review*, Vol. 7, No. 2 (October 1962), 77–94.

FRENCH and BRESSLER, 1962. Ben C. French and Raymond G. Bressler, "The Lemon Cycle," *Journal of Farm Economics*, Vol. XLIV, No. 4 (November 1962), 1021–1036.

NERLOVE, 1958. Marc Nerlove, *The Dynamics of Supply: Estimation of Farmers' Response to Price* (Baltimore, Md.: Johns Hopkins University Press, 1958).

STERN, 1965a. Robert M. Stern, "The Determinants of Cocoa Supply in West Africa," in I. G. Stewart and H. W. Ord, eds., *African Primary Products and International Trade* (Edinburgh: Edinburgh University Press, 1965).

STERN, 1965b. Robert M. Stern, "Malayan Rubber Production, Inventory Holdings, and the Elasticity of Export Supply," *The Southern Economic Journal*, Vol. 31, No. 4 (April 1965), 314–323.

WHARTON, 1963a. Clifton R. Wharton, Jr., "Rubber Supply Conditions: Some Policy Implications," in T. H. Silcock, ed., *Studies in the Malayan Economy* (Canberra: Australian National University Press, 1963).

WHARTON, 1963b. Clifton R. Wharton, Jr., "Monocultural Perennial Export Dominance: The Inelasticity of Southeast Asian Agricultural Trade" (October, 1963). (Mimeographed.)

III

Theories of Change and Growth

9

The Early Stages of Development in a Primitive Economy: The Evolution from Subsistence to Trade and Specialization

E. K. FISK and R. T. SHAND

THIS CONTRIBUTION is a summary of three published papers dealing with problems in the development of a primitive economy, with special reference to the Territory of Papua-New Guinea [Fisk, 1962; 1964; Shand, 1965].

The first of the papers is concerned with an analysis of factors that determine the economic activity of a unit in a subsistence economy in isolation from modernizing forces. The resources available to a subsistence unit are considered, and by analyzing the factors that determine the unit's customary level of production, an indication is given of the type of resources liable to be available within such a unit for raising the level of production. The type and magnitude of external influences required to produce such an increase in production are also examined.

In the second paper, the subsistence group is in contact with the advanced sector. Conditions are analyzed under which units with "spare" resources—i.e. those not required for subsistence production—will be willing to utilize these in cash production as a supple-mentary activity to subsistence production.

The third paper takes the analysis a further step forward. The starting point is a stage where one or more of the resources initially available to a unit becomes fully employed. Three ways are examined in which further increases in production and income can be achieved—through technological change, through resource specialization and trade within the subsistence sector, and through additions to the resources available to a unit.

THE PRIMITIVE ECONOMY IN ISOLATION

In the first paper [Fisk, 1962] a simplified model of a pure subsistence unit is constructed entirely isolated in the first instance from the outside world, producing one product—food. Land available for cultivation by the subsistence unit is fixed, but it varies in quality, so that even when all the available land is not in cultivation, increments of labour will produce diminishing returns in

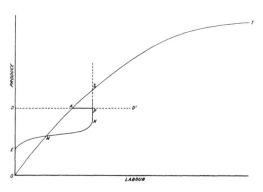

Figure 9.1.

terms of food output. In the initial stage of the analysis the level of technology is taken as given and unchanging, so that the physical relationship between the various levels of labor input and food output for the land available is given by the curve *O–T* in Figure 9.1.

There is assumed to be a certain quantity of labor potentially available. This is defined as the quantity of labor input that could be sustained by the subsistence unit if the incentive to work full time were present.

One factor limiting the potential supply of labor in a human society is the level of nutrition, which in a subsistence society can be roughly equated to the output of food. Below a certain level, work will be impossible, and the potential supply of labor will be nil. This is indicated in Figure 9.1 as point *E*. Above that level the potential supply of labor will increase as the supply of food increases, until a point *N* is reached at which the food supply, and the consequent level of nutrition, is adequate to maintain full physical activity for the length of the working period that is socially or otherwise acceptable. Once point *N* has been reached, further increments in the supply of food will not produce an increase in the potential supply of labor available, which will thereafter be limited by social and customary factors, such as the amount of leisure regarded as desirable for ceremonial and recreational activities, and not by the level of nutrition. This is represented graphically in Figure 9.1 by the composite curve *E–N–P–S*, on which *E* is the starvation point, *N* is the point at which nutrition is adequate for full activity, and *N–P–S* and onward represents the maximum potential supply of

labor available under the social and demographic conditions prevailing.

In our model demand is limited to the demand for food that, apart from the fixed level of clothing and shelter already provided for, is the only product the farmers know how to produce. Except for the minor short-term saving activities already mentioned, the food is for immediate consumption. In any society there is a definite limit to the amount of food that can be consumed with satisfaction, and if the diet contains as little variety as that of the average Highland subsistence unit in New Guinea, where sweet potatoes provide up to 90 per cent of the calorific intake, that limit should be reasonably well defined.

We may therefore expect a very distinct ceiling to the demand for food in a pure subsistence unit with adequate land. The level of this ceiling will be a function of population, physical activity, and a number of social and customary factors (including the pig cycle) and could be empirically established in any specific community. For the purpose of our model we shall assume that this ceiling is reached at a level of food consumption 25 per cent above that necessary to maintain the population in physical condition to provide their full potential supply of labor; viz. we shall assume that the demand ceiling is represented on Figure 9.1 by the horizontal line *D–D'*, which cuts the potential supply-of-labor curve at the point *P*, 25 per cent above *N*.

We now have sufficient data to determine both the maximum sustained level of production of which our model unit is capable and the actual level of production that will be reached. For brevity, let us refer to these two levels as "capacity production" and "actual production," respectively.

"Capacity production" is at S, where the potential supply of labor is fully employed. "Actual production" will only coincide with S when S occurs at a level of food production at or below the demand ceiling D–D'. This is not the case in our model as represented in Figure 9.1, nor, on the basis of the empirical studies available, is it the case in the major portion of the subsistence sector in the Territory. In Figure 9.1, as in the greater part of the New Guinea subsistence economy, the actual level of production will be limited by the demand ceiling rather than the potential supply of labor or labor ceiling. The actual level of production will therefore be at A, the intersection of the production curve and the demand-ceiling curve.

This means that there is a potential surplus concealed within the subsistence economy, comprising that portion of the potential supply of labor not required for production of food to the level of the demand ceiling. In Figure 9.1 this is represented by the horizontal line P–A, while the vertical line P–S represents the additional agricultural surplus that could be produced by that surplus labor, were there any incentive to produce it.

This is of special importance for development planning, particularly in the early stages, for this surplus labor is virtually the only substantial resource available for investment from within the subsistence sector itself. Therefore, where the advanced sector of the economy is small and external resources are limited, the rate of development of the subsistence sector, and thus of the major part of the economy, will depend largely on the effective exploitation of this resource.

A further fact of importance is that, given the necessary inducements and incentives, this resource can be made available without any reduction in the existing level of production or consumption, and without involving any serious hardship in the sacrifice of leisure, for the normal and essential requirements for social activities and recreation have already been taken into account in our concept of the potential supply of labor. This surplus of labor is therefore available at a very low opportunity cost.

Finally, with the simple form of the model in Figure 9.1 and given the incentive and opportunity, this resource of surplus labor can be converted into increased production and an increased level of income. In Figure 9.1 the potential increase in production is equivalent to the amount P–S, or an increase of about 28 per cent.

The development potential within the subsistence unit therefore takes the form initially of a pool of surplus labor available at low opportunity cost. This labor surplus will be converted into surplus agricultural production only when effective linkage for marketing the surplus has been established. Until that is done, the surplus is available in the form of unskilled labor to contribute to the investment required for the establishment of that linkage, through the construction of roads and tracks and the like.

This basic model may be employed to consider how variations in two factors—population and technology—would affect the availability of surplus labor and the quantity of surplus agricultural product that this labor could produce, and also what kinds of external assistance would have the greatest effects on total production under the various situations considered.

A change in population alters the position of the curve E–N–P–A, while the T–P curve remains undisturbed. Beyond a certain particularly favorable population-land ratio, a marginal increase in population would: reduce the surplus labor available; reduce the surplus of agricultural output that this labor could produce; and reduce the return per unit of labor so used.

A change in applied technology, on the other hand, alters the position of the T–P curve. Some innovations, such as the introduction of steel ax heads in place of stone, will operate primarily as a labor-saving device and will have little effect on the level of output at which the marginal productivity of labor approaches zero. Other innovations —such as the introduction of fertilizer, irrigation schemes, land improvement, and conservation schemes—have the effect of raising the overall productivity of land, so that the marginal productivity of land approaches zero at a higher level of total production. Under this head could also be included schemes for settlement of surplus

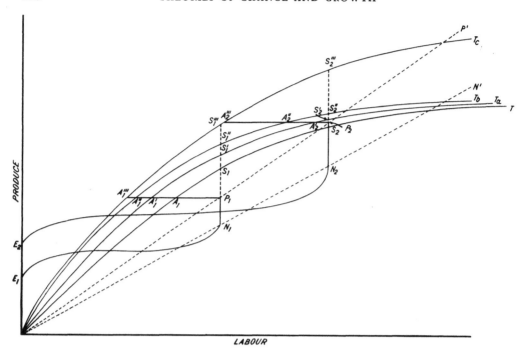

Figure 9.2.

population and for the opening up of new land, which have a somewhat similar effect. Referring back to Figure 9.1, innovations of the first type tend to change the *T–P* curve in such a way as to increase the length of *AP* without greatly increasing *PS*. Innovations of the second type tend to have the reverse effect.

The principles developed in the consideration of variations in these two factors may be combined and applied to the problems presented by two different types of subsistence units encountered in Papua-New Guinea. The first type is exemplified by the Siane, as described by Salisbury in *From Stone to Steel* [1962]. The second type we shall take as the Chimbus, as described by Brookfield and Brown in *The Struggle for Land* [1963]. The situations are shown in Figure 9.2, in somewhat exaggerated form, in order to emphasize the distinctions that affect the planning situation.

The Siane situation is shown by the curve E_1–N_1–P_1–A_1–A'_1 and so on. The production curve *O–T* represents the original precontact technological situation, before the introduction of steel ax heads, and the curve O–T_a that after steel axes were in full use but

before steel-bladed spades had replaced the digging stick as the woman's agricultural implement. The situation at the time of Salisbury's field work is therefore described by P_1–A'_1 and S'_1. The production curve T_b represents a further technological advance of a mainly labor-saving nature, such as the introduction of metal-bladed spades or other improved implements, while the curve T_c represents a technological advance of the more expensive and capital-consuming nature, such as irrigation, use of fertilizer, land development, and the like.

The model shows that the Siane situation at the time of Salisbury's field work contained a considerable internal-development potential. Given the establishment of effective linkage by the extension of the government road system from Goroka, and the normal extension services provided by the Department of Agriculture and Fisheries, production should rise approximately to the level of S''_1, involving an increase of approximately 35 per cent, without requiring any of the more expensive forms of external assistance. Moreover, in the initial stages, before effective linkage has been established, the labor surplus available for the formation of social capital and to help in the completion of the linkage would be very considerable, rising to as much as $A''_1 - P_1$ at technological level t_b.

However, if the more expensive external capital assistance is applied to the Siane at this stage, the additional advantage will be relatively very much smaller. The initial labor surplus would be increased only by the very small increment $A''\,'_1 - A''_1$, and the potential production surplus by $S'\,''_1 - S''_1$. If external resources for this type of technological improvement are scarce in the economy as a whole, it is clearly unwarranted to apply them to the Siane, at least until their production has been stabilized at the higher level S''_1.

The Chimbus situation, shown by the curve $E_2 - N_2 - P_2 - A'_2$, and so on, is very different. At the time of Brookfield and Brown's field work, steel ax heads and metal-bladed spades were in wide use, and there was a fairly substantial potential of surplus labor that was then being diverted to cash cropping. The position at that time was therefore the situation $P_2 - A''_2 - S''_2$ in Figure 9.2. The situation at the time of Brown's further visit in 1962 is therefore not surprising, for the increase in production potentially available from the investment and application of this labor surplus at technological level T_b would be only the very small amount $S_2 - S''_2$, which on the position depicted in the diagram would be about 6 per cent, and the return per unit of additional labor so employed would be less than one-third of that in the case of the Siane.

On the other hand, if external capital assistance were made available to enable the change to technological level T_c, the situation of the Chimbus would be transformed. The potential labor surplus would increase very substantially to A''_2, and the potential production surplus would rise by at least 20 per cent, making real progress possible for the first time. The return per unit of additional labor employed would also improve dramatically, rising to a level not very far short of that in the Siane situation. It is clear, therefore, that if the scarce resources available from the advanced sector have to be allocated on a highly selective basis, they will have a much greater effect on total production and progress if applied to the Chimbu-type situation than to that of the Siane.

The first problem in raising the production of the subsistence sector is to establish an effective and economic linkage with the exchange economy of the advanced sector. This mainly requires the provision of necessary communications, marketing, and distribution facilities. The magnitude of the problem is in the main a function of the degree of physical isolation of the subsistence units concerned. In Papua-New Guinea isolation varies greatly from an extreme in the Southern Highlands, where there has been no effective penetration of the advanced sector, to the Goroka Valley, where penetration in the form of commercial agricultural estates and the provision of airfields and roads has been substantial.

Once linkage is established, the second planning problem is to insure that the development potential available within the subsistence sector is maximized. The model may be used to provide guidance to policy formation in this respect. In particular it shows that where population pressure on the land has not yet developed, as with the Siane, a great deal can be achieved by the introduction of simple technological improvements of the labor-saving variety, which can be effected with little drain on the scarce capital resources of the advanced sector. However, it shows that where population pressure on the land is considerable, as with the Chimbus, technological change of this type has little effect on productive capacity; in such cases considerable additional assistance from the advanced sector is essential, for the required increase in production can only be achieved by increasing the effective quality of the land available. This means either investment in land improvement (such as irrigation, fertilizer, drainage) or in settlement of part of the population on new land—all of which are liable to be expensive.

THE PRIMITIVE ECONOMY IN CONTACT WITH ADVANCED SECTOR

Given that there is a development potential concealed within the subsistence sector, in the form of a surplus of available labor and unused productive capacity of tribal lands, the next question is how these resources can be utilized for additional agricultural or other production.

Total production in the second article [Fisk, 1964] is made up of two components: subsistence production and supplementary cash production. The former will be determined by the level of internal demand for subsistence products. The latter will be determined by a number of factors affecting either the size of the surplus productive capacity available or the ability and willingness of the members of the subsistence group to put that surplus to productive use.

When the isolation of the pure subsistence group is invaded by contact with the advanced sector, the group becomes subject to a number of external influences, and supplementary cash production, if it develops, is a response of the subsistence group to these influences. These are of two types: there are the market forces that reach the subsistence group from the exchange economy of the advanced sector and provide an incentive for supplementary cash production; there are also the external nonmarket forces that modify the ability and willingness of the members of the subsistence group to respond to that incentive. As the market forces are also subject to modification by external nonmarket forces, there is in fact quite a complex interplay of forces and influences involved in the growth of supplementary cash production.

In its simplest form, the basic proposition is that supplementary cash production is the response of the subsistence group to the force of incentive. The growth of cash production is therefore dependent on the relative strength of two factors. On the one hand, there is the strength of the incentive transmitted to the subsistence group by the market forces, which may be termed the *incentive factor*. On the other, there is the strength of the resistance or inertia of the subsistence group to changes of the types required for supplementary cash production, which may be termed the *response factor*.

However, both these factors are resultants of a complex manifold of components, which may broadly be classified as internal and external. They are illustrated diagramatically in Figure 9.3. In the case of the incentive factor, the internal components are the market forces that operate in a deterministic

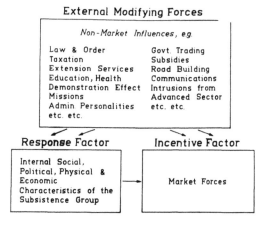

Figure 9.3.

fashion in accordance with known laws. The external components are the nonmarket forces through which the effect of the market forces can be modified and by which intervention is possible. In the case of the response factor, the internal components are the cultural, political, physical, and economic characteristics of the subsistence group itself, and in the absence of external influences, these also can be taken as largely deterministic and given. The external components are the nonmarket forces that influence and modify the internal characteristics of the group and through which intervention in the response factor is possible.

Attention will be concentrated in the main on the incentive factor, not because the response factor is less important, but rather because the incentive factor is less understood and because it is in that field that a new economic analysis is most needed.

The strength of the incentive factor depends ultimately on a comparison by the subsistence producer of the disutility of additional labor (or negative leisure) necessary to earn money, with the utility of the goods and services that money will enable him to buy. Although the rationale of such a decision is, in fact, a single comparison of the disutility of labor with the utility of its return, it is convenient to consider it in two steps, with money in the middle. One is to consider the disutility of money in terms of the cost in additional labor input necessary to earn it. The other is to consider the utility of money in terms of the additional satisfactions it makes available.

In the initial stages of linkage with the advanced sector, the cost of earning money within the subsistence unit may be particularly high. In other words, the cash return per unit of labor expended in supplementary cash production may be particularly low. Some of the causes of this phenomenon belong to the response factor and can be tackled through education, agricultural extension services, and the like, as already discussed. There are, however, other major causes that belong properly to the market sector in a free-enterprise society, and it is with these that the present discussion is concerned. The range, accessibility, cost, and efficiency of processing, marketing, transport, and distribution services are the main factors under this head and, for a given level of technology and a given population-resources ratio, will largely determine the net price in money that the producer in the subsistence unit will obtain for the labor he devotes to supplementary cash production. In the analysis that follows, this net price will be taken to refer to the price received by the subsistence producer himself, and will be termed the "cash return per unit of labor."

Similarly, in the initial stages of linkage the return in terms of satisfaction per unit of money within the subsistence group may be expected to fall off sharply at quite a low level of income. Here, again, some of the causes belong to the response factor. However, the market factors—such as the range and appropriateness of the goods and services offered for money, their availability at the time and place they are required and the cost of retailing—are the major economic factors that give money its utility for the producer in the subsistence unit. In what follows, the net effect of these factors will be referred to as the "utility of money" to the subsistence producer.

The operation and interaction of these two major components of the incentive factor will now be examined in the form of a simple model in order to see how effective incentive is produced and how planned intervention can make it more effective.

In the model for this paper the main assumptions are that the economy comprises an advanced and a subsistence sector. The advanced sector is thoroughly monetized, trades internationally, and there is a scarcity in capital and entrepreneurship within it. The subsistence sector comprises numerous self-sufficient subsistence production units, with initially no economically significant trade between themselves or with the advanced sector. Surplus capacity, after subsistence needs have been met, is assumed. Physical isolation from the advanced sector is a characteristic of the typical subsistence group.

Supplementary cash production is assumed to take the form of a cash crop produced primarily for export, for which prices are fixed by world conditions. Money capital is not a limiting factor in cash cropping. This applies only to the preparation and planting of the land and to the husbandry and gathering of the crop. In a nonmonetized subsistence group this is quite realistic. The only factors for which money payment is necessary—such as planting materials, technical advice, and perhaps some improved tools—will normally be available free or on credit, as for example from the agricultural extension service and associated institutions. Processing, marketing, transport, and distribution, for which money capital is often a limiting factor, are here treated as ancillary services and not as part of cash cropping. Finally, constant returns to scale in terms of physical output of cash crop per unit of labor input (but excluding processing, transport, marketing, and so on) are assumed throughout the limited range of production possible with the surplus labor available.

Having assumed constant returns to scale in the physical production of the raw crop, the cash return per unit of labor within the subsistence group will vary with the net price per unit of production received by the subsistence producer and with the amount of additional labor necessary to market it at that price. The price at the port of export is taken as fixed, and the cost in terms of labor per unit of the raw product at the farm gate is also taken as fixed. The variable factors are therefore the costs, in terms of money (a reduction in the net price) or labor (an increase in the total labor input), of the market factors linking the producer with his export market. These factors, such as processing, grading, storage, transport, packaging, and marketing, are poorly developed in the initial stages of linkage; their cost, in terms of money or labor, is high, and the net return per unit of labor is correspondingly low.

When linkage with the advanced sector is at an early stage, the returns per unit of labor in the subsistence unit are likely to be low, owing to high costs of transport and marketing. As output in the sector expands, there are likely to be considerable external economies of scale. These will eventually lead to increases in the cash return per unit of labor in the subsistence unit. Under practical circumstances, these increases are likely to occur as a series of more or less discontinuous jumps.

The first part of the model is illustrated diagramatically in Figure 9.4. The total labor input for supplementary cash production by the whole subsistence group is shown as L on the horizontal axis. The total expendable cash income of the group is shown as Y on the vertical axis. The radials OC_1, OC_2, OC_3, OC_4, and OC_n represent five different rates of cash return per unit of labor. L_1 is the labor input necessary to produce the level of output at which an entrepreneur will introduce a scale-economizing service sufficient to raise the cash return per unit from OC_1 to OC_2. L_2, L_3, and L_n indicates the labor inputs necessary to reach the level of output at which the next jumps in return will take place. The point L_p is the maximum input of labor available for supplementary cash production within the group without encroaching on subsistence production. It will be noted that L_p is shown as substantially below L_n, which should be taken as implying that a subsistence group, utilizing only surplus resources available after meeting its subsistence needs, is unlikely on its own to reach a level and concentration of cash production at which the major economies of scale can be fully exploited. In the diagram the total cash income that can be earned by the group at different levels of labor input in the available range $O–L_p$ is shown by the zig-zag line in heavy dashes, $O–P$ (hereafter referred to as the C path).

The second part of the model considers the market forces that give money its utility for members of the subsistence group. The amount of money the members of a subsistence units will want to earn will depend to a very large extent on the range of goods and services they can buy with it, on the price, and on the facility with which they can be obtained when and where they are wanted. Subsistence producers will be resident in the subsistence-producing area, and what will matter to them most are the goods and services available where they live. The availability of a cinema show, kerosene fuel, cigarettes, and soap within a few minutes' walk of their home will make money very much more useful to them than the availability of the same range of goods and services several days' march away. The greater the range of goods and services available and the more readily they are available, the greater the utility of money to them and the more they will wish to earn.

On the other hand, the supply of such

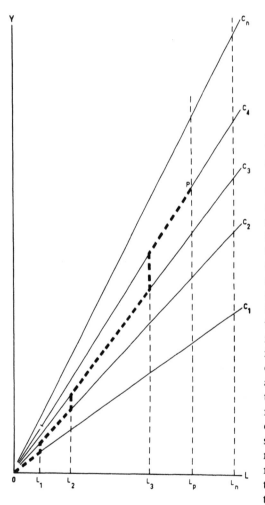

Figure 9.4.

goods and services will normally depend on entrepreneurship and capital. In the very early stages of economic development, entrepreneurship and capital are usually very scarce factors and command a high price. A certain minimum turnover will be necessary to attract them, the minimum varying for different classes and grades of goods and services. As the potential turnover in any given area depends upon the amount of spending money available in the area, which in turn is related directly to income, then the utility of money will be a function of the total spendable income in the area. This is a chicken-and-egg type of problem, and the answer to it is that once some effective contact or linkage is established between the subsistence unit and the advanced sector, money acquires some value and a utility egg is introduced into the subsistence unit as part of the process. It may, and probably will, be a very small and insignificant egg, but it will be there and, eventually with luck, a small and insignificant chicken will hatch out of it. The question is how the opportunity to buy an occasional odd stick of tobacco, and the desire to earn the odd shilling to do this, can develop into substantial participation in the monetized economy of the advanced sector.

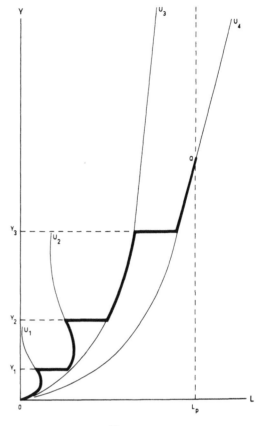

Figure 9.5.

The utility of money in the group can be expressed in terms of indifference curves plotting income against leisure, and a large number of curves could be plotted for any given unit, showing the effect of increases in the utility of money as the range, accessibility, and price of the goods and services available for money improve. Alternatively, and this will suit the model better, utility can be expressed in terms of the amount of labor that the people of the group would consider it just worthwhile to devote to earning any specific income. In this case also there could be a large number of curves indicating the different level of utility as the goods and services available for money improve. These would be total supply curves of labor at different levels of utility of money. Four such curves are shown in Figure 9.5 as $O-U_1$, $O-U_2$, $O-U_3$, and $O-U_4$.

The curve $O-U_1$ represents the situation when the utility of money in the subsistence group is very low. The group will find it worthwhile to devote a certain amount of labor to earning the price of the odd stick of tobacco, but will rapidly reach the point where the utility of an additional unit of income will fall off rapidly. In fact, so long as the range and quantity of goods and services available in exchange for money remain restricted to the very low level, it is probable that beyond a certain quite low total income the utility of incremental units of money will fall below the utility of incremental units of leisure (or negative labor). When this happens, the U curve will turn backward, and the effect of an increase in the return per unit of labor, that lifts total income above this turning point, will be to reduce rather than increase the total labor input. Under these circumstances the phenomenon of the backward-sloping curve is a perfectly rational response to market conditions, at least in the short run.

The curves $O-U_2$, $O-U_3$, and $O-U_4$ represent the supply of labor at successively higher levels of utility of money. When and if the total income in the area reaches Y_1, it may just become worthwhile for an itinerant trader to call once a month or so, offering a modest range of simple consumer goods for sale. This will rapidly raise the utility of money in the area, and the utility curve for the subsistence unit will move from $O-U_1$ to $O-U_2$ in a nearly horizontal jump, starting at income level Y_1. Subsequently when total income reaches Y_2 it may pay an entrepreneur to establish a full-time trade store in the area, with a wider range of goods available at all times. At this point the utility curve will move almost horizontally from $O-U_2$ to $O-U_3$. When total income reaches Y_3, there will perhaps be several better-class stores in the area, together with certain services such as a weekly cinema show, a coffee shop, or a hairdresser, which will further raise the utility of money in the subsistence unit from curve $O-U_3$ to $O-U_4$. Accordingly, the total labor input that the subsistence group will find just worthwhile at varying levels of total income is indicated in Figure 9.5 by the heavy zigzag curve $O-Q$ (hereafter termed the U path).

In this part of the model also the real situation has been simplified by eliminating some of the steps. There would clearly be some intermediate utility curves, particularly between $O-U_3$ and $O-U_4$. This simplification enables the principal characteristics of the situation to be brought out more clearly. The points for emphasis are the following:

1. In the initial stages of linkage with the advanced sector the utility of money in the subsistence unit is liable to be very low and the supply curve of labor may slope backward sharply after reaching a quite small value of total income.

2. The utility of money within the subsistence unit will depend very largely on the range, quality, and accessibility of goods and services available for purchase in the area, which in turn will depend on the total money income available for expenditure on such goods and services in the area. The utility of money will therefore be some function of total income in the area.

3. The change from one level of utility of money to the next higher level will tend to take place suddenly, in the form of a discontinuous horizontal jump from one utility curve to the next, at specific levels of total income. Here again external economies are responsible.

The two halves of the model from Figures 9.4 and 9.5 have combined in Figure 9.6.

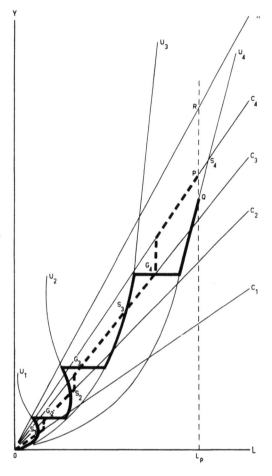

Figure 9.6.

The horizontal axis measures the total labor input into supplementary cash production by the subsistence group, while the vertical axis measures the total expendable cash income for the area. The zigzag curve $O-Q$ (in heavy continuous line) traces the U path and indicates the supply of labor that the group will find just worthwhile for the purpose of earning various levels of total cash income, while the zigzag line $O-P$ (in heavy dashes) traces the C path and indicates the total cash income that can be earned by the subsistence producers for varying levels of labor input. Where the C path lies to the right of the U path, this means that the amount of labor input necessary to earn that amount of income is greater than the amount such an income would make worthwhile, and therefore the market forces would provide no incentive for that level of labor input. Conversely, where the C path lies to the left of the U path, the amount of income earned by such a labor input would be greater than the minimum necessary to make it worthwhile, and the market forces would provide an effective incentive to increase the labor input up to the point where the C path and the U path coincide. Moreover, the strength of that incentive will in general be proportional to the amount by which the actual income return exceeds the minimum income necessary to make that level of labor input worthwhile (i.e. proportional to the horizontal distance between the C and U paths).

In Figure 9.6, therefore, there are four growth points, the origin O and points G_2, G_3, and G_4. These are points of instability, above which the market factor will provide incentive for labor input, and hence output of cash production, to increase up to the next point of stagnation—S_1, S_2, S_3, or S_4, as the case may be. These points of stagnation are positions of stable equilibrium, beyond which the market factor provides no incentive for growth.

These points of growth and stagnation are of considerable interest. Most people who have been directly concerned with the encouragement of cash production amongst subsistence producers have encountered the exasperating "stop-go" type of response to their efforts. For example, the agricultural officer of one district of New Guinea complained to the writer that after years of intense and patient effort by his department a number of tribes had been enabled to plant groundnuts as a commercial cash crop. The crop was successful, and output grew until one year quite a respectable sum was realized, and it looked as though further progress was assured. Considerable trouble was taken to obtain orders to provide an assured market for an even greater output in the next year. However, planting for the next season was actually reduced. In another instance a medium-scale planter in the

Markham valley, who took considerable trouble to provide good conditions for his labor, complained of the difficulty of operating with directly recruited labor because the laborers would come to work only until they had earned a specific and quite small sum, say five pounds, when they would return to their home village, irrespective of the inducements and opportunities for greater earnings. Another commonly heard complaint is that tree crops planted at considerable cost in labor, whether under compulsion or persuasion, are neglected and only partially harvested, with the result that the money income of the subsistence units is far below the potential of their standing trees.

Figure 9.6 shows not only how such phenomena arise, but that they are to be expected. In the case of the highland groundnuts, the agricultural officer had been operating with considerable effect on the response factor, and through his persuasion and enthusiasm had temporarily succeeded in raising groundnut production to a point to the right of the U path but not quite sufficiently to reach a higher growth point. Consequently the market forces provided no incentive to maintain production at this level and drew it back to the next point of stable equilibrium below.

The model also shows what is necessary to overcome stagnation at these points and gives a clear pointer to the formation of policy for stimulating a higher level of participation in the exchange economy. The problem is either to lift the subsistence group over the humps where the incentive factor is inadequate or to remove the humps. External nonmarket influences must be applied to produce one or more effects:

1. An artificial increase in the level of cash production to lift it sufficiently above each stagnation point to reach another growth point (e.g. by persuasion or compulsion).

2. An artificial increase in the cash return per unit of labor, thus effecting the jump from one C curve to the next at a lower labor input (and hence crop output) than would happen in response to market forces alone. This may be effected by temporarily subsidizing the development of marketing, transport and processing facilities, and the like,

or by providing government-operated services for these purposes prepared to operate at a loss for some years.

3. An artificial increase in the utility of money, thus effecting the jump from one U curve to the next at an earlier point (lower total income) than would have happened in response to market forces alone. This may be effected by subsidizing temporarily the provision of goods and services for money in the area or by setting up government retail stores prepared to operate at a loss for some years.

All three methods have been attempted in various places and at various times, though seldom in concert to obtain the greatest effect, and often on an inadequate scale. The model makes it clear that, unless intervention is on a scale sufficient to force the subsistence unit right over the hump to the next growth point, natural growth cannot be resumed. It also shows clearly the advantages and economies to be gained from concerted three-point intervention rather than a piecemeal approach.

In the foregoing, the subsistence unit has been considered in isolation, and the development of the market forces in the area has depended on the development of cash production by the subsistence producers themselves and on the level of income earned by that production. In such cases the subsistence producers have to be coaxed and assisted up the stairs. However, in some cases an elevator can be installed.

In most primitive economies there are areas where the development of cash cropping as a supplement to subsistence production has been very much more rapid than in others. For example, in some parts of the Goroka subdistrict of the Eastern Highlands of New Guinea supplementary cash cropping has developed to a relatively high level in the short period of about 15 years, despite the remoteness and inaccessibility that kept the region from effective contact with the advanced sector for many decades. This rapid development was made possible largely by an intrusion from the advanced sector, in the form of substantial European investment in small and medium coffee estates in the area.

The effect of this investment was twofold.

First, the investment brought relatively highly paid managers and technicians into the area, and created a demand for local labor for construction, planting, and maintenance work on the estates. This produced a very substantial inflow of income into the area that was not dependent on cash crop production by the subsistence units themselves, which induced the provision of goods and services for sale in the area on a scale that rapidly raised the utility of money to the potential cash cropper from the subsistence units, even before he had commenced production for the market. Second, it rapidly raised production of the cash crop in the area to a high level quite independently of cash cropping by the subsistence units, thus inducing the provision of processing, transport, and marketing facilities, with the economies of scale developed to a higher point than mere supplementary cash cropping by the subsistence producer could have reached alone. Returning to our model in Figure 9.6, this means that, during the time the subsistence producers were beginning to develop supplementary cash cropping, the operative curves for the subsistence groups most directly affected were not the zigzag C path and U path, with all their stagnation points and humps to be overcome, but the labor-supply curve U_4 and the cash return curve C_n. Under these circumstances the humps and stagnation points are eliminated, and the incentive factor is strongly operative without impediment straight from O to R.

Therefore, where availability of land, capital, and enterprise makes possible an intrusion from the advanced sector in this way, encouragement of such an intrusion is in many respects an effective answer to the chicken-and-egg problem. Even where political and economic conditions are unfavorable to a large-scale intrusion from the private or foreign sectors (as is at present the case in Papua-New Guinea), a similar effect can be obtained by large-scale intrusion from the public sector, in the form of assisted land development and settlement schemes established under government control and with government finance, or even in the form of large state-owned and operated farms.

The report [International Bank, 1964] of the recent World Bank Mission to Papua-New Guinea contains two major types of recommendations that could assist in stimulating a higher level of participation of subsistence producers in the exchange economy. First, the Mission favors a greater intrusion of the advanced sector, not in the form of assisted land settlement schemes, which it regards as being too expensive, but through the encouragement of the private sector, in the form of more numerous and expanded estates. Second, the Mission advocates increased expenditure on roads, coastal shipping and port facilities, airfields, and so on. Both of these factors will tend to strengthen the incentive for participation.

The Primitive Economy with Advanced Sector Contact and with Full Employment

In the third article [Shand, 1965] the factors are examined whereby production and income can be further increased in the primitive unit. In particular the question is analyzed of how further increases can be achieved once the "spare" labor resources within the unit have become fully employed. The factors examined include the development of specialization and trade within the subsistence sector, the application of improved technology, and the augmentation of available resources. Examples are again drawn from the rural sector of the economy of Papua-New Guinea. Use is made of concepts drawn from economic theory, especially from international trade theory, and these are applied with the aid of a simple model.

Many assumptions in the third model are of course the same as those employed in the second. Additional assumptions are as follows:

1. The *economic unit* in the subsistence sector is the single household.
2. *Total supplies of land and labor for the rural sector* as a whole are fixed, though their allocation between units within the sector may change.
3. There are two commodities which can be produced by household units in the subsistence sector: one is a single composite of all subsistence products denoted by S, the other is an export product which can only be marketed in the advanced sector, denoted by X, and that prices for X are determined internationally.

4. The terms of trade between the two sectors are sufficiently unfavorable to make the purchase of substitutes for S from the advanced sector unprofitable. Favorable terms would allow units to reduce the production of S to some extent below needs, to transfer the resources to the production of X, and thereby to earn more than enough additional income to replace the deficit of S with purchases from the advanced sector. This situation, however, is not commonly encountered in the early stages of development. The high cost of transporting goods in and out of the subsistence sector both reduces prices received by producers of the commodity in trade and substantially raises the cost of goods from the advanced sector, especially bulky perishables.[1]

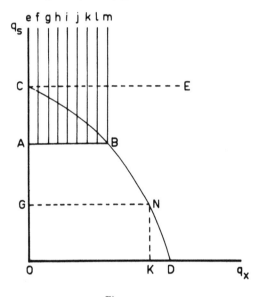

Figure 9.7.

In Figure 9.7, for any unit let $O\text{--}q_s$ represent production of subsistence products, and $O\text{--}q_x$ represent production of export products. Then the situation of a particular unit (household) is represented as follows:

OC is the maximum quantity of subsistence

1. This is not, of course, to argue that foodstuffs are rarely bought from the advanced sector, but only that it is relatively uncommon for consumption to occur in this "replacement" sense. Most of the purchases that do occur are in a luxury or prestige class and are supplementary to the customary levels of consumption.

products that the unit could produce at the existing level of technology with the resources initially available to the unit employed solely for subsistence production. OD is the maximum quantity of export products that the unit could produce at the existing level of technology, with its resources exclusively employed in export production.

The curve C–B–N–D therefore represents the maximum range of production of S and X open to the unit with the resources available to it. At point N, for example, the available resources are so distributed that the unit produces OG of S and OK of X, and production of neither S nor X can be further increased, under the limitations assumed, without a reduction in production of the other.

The model will now be applied to the situation where subsistence production does not exhaust the unit's resources. This is illustrated in Figure 9.7. The internal demand for subsistence products, assumed constant in the model, requires OA of S. The unit could produce OC of S if it devoted all its resources to this end; however, since the consumption of more than OA of S adds nothing to the satisfaction of the unit and since there is at this juncture no trade in S with other units, the unit will not gain by producing more than OA of S. It can only improve its economic welfare by producing X for sales to the advanced sector.

This rather restricted choice system is indicated in Figure 9.7 by the range of indifference curves e to m. Emerging from the pure subsistence stage at point A, the unit would be on an indifference curve e. Production of X, supplementary to OA of S, takes the unit to higher indifference curves (i.e. through income earnings which are spent on goods from the advanced sector). Since there is no satisfaction in consuming more than OA of S, the indifference curves rise vertically from OA. The lack of trade in S and the unwillingness to reduce consumption of S below OA mean that these indifference curves terminate at the level A. Expansion of the production of X finally becomes limited by the scarcity of resources, e.g. limited to AB in Figure 9.7. This would place the unit on an indifference curve m.

The starting point for the analysis in this paper is a point on the production-possibility curve (such as B) where a surplus of resources over and above those required for subsistence was available and has been diverted to production for export, but where one or more of the inputs initially available to the unit is already fully employed. A further increase in total production is barred by the scarcity of that factor.

Other less favorable situations can be envisaged where there are few resources remaining after subsistence needs are satisfied. At the extreme there may be none at all, owing perhaps to land shortage, possibly coupled with low resources productivity. This is illustrated in Figure 9.7 where OC of S is required by the unit and there is no possibility of producing for the market from the initial resource supply.

In Papua-New Guinea[2] it is exceptional to encounter units which have no residual resources after meeting their subsistence production requirements. There are, however, wide differences between units in their capacities to produce a market surplus. Some are particularly favored by a high land-population ratio and a high productivity of physical resources. Some are limited by land scarcity because of population pressure or inequalities in the distribution of land ownership, in some cases exacerbated by low yields from poor soil fertility and the like. Significant for this analysis is the growing number of farmers who are faced with the question of how to expand income once they have reached the limits of their initial resources and who need to find ways to do this, such as through technological change, resource or product specialization, and additions to resources.

TECHNOLOGICAL CHANGE

Technical innovations may be applied either to subsistence production or to export production.

The application of an innovation to subsistence production can be of particular value. For units with all, or practically all, of

2. These and later observations in this section of the paper are based to a large extent on field work carried out as part of an investigation of indigenous cash cropping in Papua-New Guinea by R. T. Shand and W. Straatmans on a grant from the Reserve Bank of Australia.

their resources tied up in subsistence production, such innovations may provide the first opportunity for export production. In less extreme cases technological innovation may add substantially to their capacity to produce a surplus. Thus in Figure 9.8 a unit

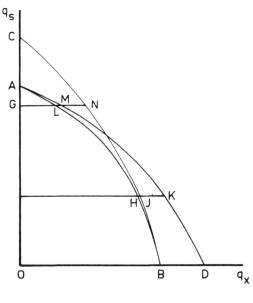

Figure 9.8.

which initially has production possibilities denoted by the curve *AB* may be able to move to a new set of production possibilities shown by *CB*. Where a high proportion of resources are engaged in subsistence production, e.g. at *G*, the unit is initially confined to the production of *GL* of *X*, but with the adoption of the innovation and with the release of resources, considerably more (*LN*) of *X* can be produced.

The importance of this type of innovation is often not fully appreciated, probably because the assistance it offers to a developing unit is indirect. In the early stages of development in Papua-New Guinea this type of innovation has been of great importance. An outstanding example has been the labor-releasing effect that followed the substitution of steel for stone axes in the Highlands. The introduction of hoes and spades has also had an appreciable labor-saving effect.

The adoption of a technological change for export production offers a direct opportunity to expand production and income. In Papua-New Guinea there is great scope for raising yields on small-holdings of cocoa, coffee, and other cash crops. Yields are generally very low, owing to lack of experience with new crops and to the fact that agricultural extension staff and facilities are scarce.

The impact of an innovation on export production also depends on the proportion of resources required for subsistence. Referring again to Figure 9.8, let the innovation change the production possibility curve from *AB* to *AD*. Clearly the effect of such an innovation will not be great where there are few resources initially available for export production, e.g. a unit at point *L* would produce only *LM* more of *X*. Conversely, the innovation will most benefit those who are fortunate enough to have a low proportion of resources tied up in subsistence production, e.g. a unit at a point *H* would benefit to the extent of *HK* more of *X*.

RESOURCE AND PRODUCT SPECIALIZATION

Under certain circumstances greater commodity specialization by individual units within the subsistence sector can lead to an expansion of income, especially where self-sufficiency for each household unit, with the production of X as a mere supplement to subsistence production, constitutes an inefficient allocation of resources. When such specialization does take place, the subsistence commodity will become a cash crop for some producers, a local market will be established for the first time, and some producers will then become dependent upon the local market for a proportion of their supplies of this commodity.

The rural sector of Papua-New Guinea has as yet shown practically no tendency toward specialization and trade between units in the subsistence sector. An attempt should be made to explain the underlying reasons for this. In the following analysis the simplest case will be taken where there are only two units in the subsistence sector.

Specialization is profitable where there are *increasing returns* to factor inputs. Increasing returns could make specialization profitable, for example, between units within the same village. Unfortunately there is not enough evidence available at present to show under what circumstances a range of increasing returns would exist for smallholders at an early state of development.

Specialization can also be profitable in the familiar case where differences in physical conditions of production bestow a *comparative advantage* on one unit in the production of a particular commodity. Comparative advantage could also make specialization worthwhile within the village, for example where one unit has good coffee land and another has land better suited to subsistence production. In some areas of Papua-New Guinea there are social institutions that tend to eliminate comparative advantage at the village level. It has been recorded in at least two areas that the various land types tend to be shared by the groups in the localities, so that no one group owns a particular land type [Brookfield and Brown, 1963, 102–104; Howlett, 1962, 136].

Commonly comparative advantage will be the result of a combination of ecological factors—e.g. soil, climate, and altitude—and specialization will tend to develop on a broader geographical basis.

The effect of this type of comparative advantage is illustrated in Figure 9.9, where

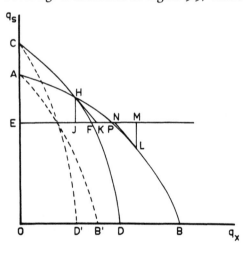

Figure 9.9.

one unit, U_s, has a comparative advantage in the production of S with a production possibility curve CD, and the other unit, U_x, has a comparative advantage in X and a production possibility curve AB. Both units

are assumed to have the same internal demand of OE for S.

U_s could reach a point F on CD, and U_x a point P on AB without trade within the subsistence sector. With specialization, however, there could be trade to the extent of $JH\,(=ML)$ of S and a greater total production of X. As a result, U_s would be better off at K and U_x at N. All the production effects of greater specialization would go to expand the output of X, total production and consumption of S would remain unchanged, though there would be a partial inclusion of output in the exchange economy $(HJ$ in Figure 9.9).

It has been shown above how, without trade between units in the subsistence sector, the proportion of available resources required to meet subsistence needs plays a crucial role in determining the extent to which a unit can expand production and income. The same factor affects the extent to which specialization and trade within the subsistence sector can profitably take place.

If all the resources of U_s are required to meet its own subsistence needs, there is no opportunity for trade, and the development of both units is thereby obstructed. For example, in Figure 9.9 production unit U_x can only increase its production of X from EP to EM if it can purchase subsistence commodities from U_s to the extent of ML. In other words, it is dependent for its expansion of production on the ability of U_s to produce a surplus of S.

On the other hand, the reverse does not hold. If, before trade takes place, U_s has the capacity to produce a surplus of S but the resources of U_x are fully employed in producing its subsistence needs, trade and specialization can take place with profit to both. This again emphasizes the vital role played by the ability to produce a surplus of subsistence commodities as an enabling factor for development under the conditions being examined.

The influence of this factor was fully examined in this third paper. It is summarily presented here so that a greater emphasis can be given to the major factors that affect the course of economic development in Papua-New Guinea.

The absence of specialization in Papua-New Guinea is not due to difficulty in the production of a food surplus. Most farmers are well enough supplied with resources to be able to produce a surplus if this is in their interest. Three factors appear to explain the lack of specialization: low resource productivity in cash cropping, uncertainties in market dependence for foodstuffs, and the high cost of transporting commodities within the subsistence sector.

The comparative advantage of a unit in a particular commodity depends both on the physical environment of production and on the *technology* employed in the production process. An area might be highly favoured ecologically for the production of a cash crop, but the use of low-yielding plant material and poor cultural methods can seriously reduce or even eliminate the advantage which the physical conditions may offer. This is illustrated in Figure 9.9. If two producers were to use approved planting material and to follow rigorously recommended cultivation procedures, they might have production possibilities denoted by the curves *AB* and *CD*. By the use of inferior plant material and unsatisfactory cultivation procedures, production possibilities are much reduced and might appear as the curves *AB'* and *CD'*. Potentialities for specialization between the two units are reduced as a result.

This situation appears to be common in Papua-New Guinea. There are large areas physically suited to the production of cash crops such as coffee, cocoa, and rubber, but despite the efforts of the administration, smallholder production is often characterized by low yields, arising sometimes from low inherent yielding capacity of plant material and sometimes from suboptimum techniques used in establishment, maintenance, and harvesting operations. Consequently the incentive for specialization between producers is greatly reduced.

Since there is no regular trade in foodstuffs between units in Papua-New Guinea, producers are likely to regard dependence upon others for subsistence needs as a somewhat risky venture and tend to discount heavily possible profits from specialization due to the *uncertainty factor*.

The third important factor in Papua-New Guinea is *the high cost of transportation*. Communication between groups in the subsistence sector is made difficult by a particularly mountainous terrain. The transport system has not as yet overcome this problem. There are few links between regions and in any one region, and the links between the subsistence and the advanced sectors are also poorly developed.

ADDITIONS TO RESOURCES

The third way of increasing production and income is the expansion of a unit's resource base. Additions to resources can be made in the traditional forms of land and labor or in the form of investment of capital.

In Papua-New Guinea it is not typically land shortage that first impedes the economic expansion of the household unit, but rather the limitations of the household labor supply. A relatively small number of more enterprising units have overcome this problem by hiring extra labor. Howlett [1962, 198–200] has reported units near Goroka in the Eastern Highlands employing labor for coffee production both on a casual and regular basis. The largest units "regularly employ labor lines of twenty or more men." This labor comes from nearby areas where opportunities for earning money are absent. Hogbin[3] encountered examples in the same area where units added land as well as labor.[4] Further examples were found by Shand and Straatmans in other areas, e.g. in the Gazelle Peninsula of New Britain and on Karkar Island. One large landholder on Karkar Island left a legacy of about 100 acres of coconut and cocoa trees, established by the use of hired labor from the island and from the mainland.

There has been little investment as yet in durable or nondurable inputs among units within the rural sector of Papua-New Guinea. The investment that has taken place has been almost exclusively in simple tools, such as the steel ax, hoes, and spades, which have had an important effect on productivity in the sector but have necessitated only small outlays. One notable exception is a large-scale mechanized farm in the Markham Valley, New Guinea (see Crocombe and Hogbin [1963a]).

Resource expansion among units in Papua-

3. G. R. Hogbin, verbal communication, 1964.
4. It was clear in these cases that managerial inputs were also an important factor in the utilization of the increased resource supply.

New Guinea has not yet led to substantial investment of money. As noted above, expenditures on durable and nondurable inputs have been small, and in areas where land is plentiful, units can often still obtain extra land by agreement with other members of the social group to which they belong without money payment [Howlett, 1962, 198–200]. There are signs, however, that this situation is changing. Money payments are becoming a more common element in land transfers, particularly between units belonging to different clans or tribes [Crocombe and Hogbin, 1963b]. Money payments are also becoming customary for labor services. It is clear that with an increasing number of units endeavoring to expand their resource base, there will be a growth of markets for labor and land that will lead to a greater degree of commercialization of units on the factor side of production.

This third paper examines the problem of how to expand production and income of economic units in the subsistence sector once one or more of the factors of production initially available have become fully employed. Three ways of obtaining further growth are considered: the adoption of new techniques, greater specialization in resource use among units, and additions to the resources of units.

The analysis shows that where, as is usual, a large proportion of the resources initially available to a unit are absorbed in subsistence production, the application of technical innovations to such production are of particular importance for the development of cash cropping. This means that subsistence production should receive at least as much attention in programs of research and extension as is given to other (e.g. export) crops.

The importance of the proportion of initially available resources used in subsistence production is again evident in the analysis of resource specialization between units in the subsistence sector. The opportunity for the overall development of the sector by this means depends, in the first instance, upon the capacity of units to produce a surplus of subsistence products. It is only when the production of such a surplus is possible that other factors, such as the levels of technology in export production and of transport costs, will commence to influence the degree to which specialization and trade will develop. Intervention is thus not only needed to increase resource productivity in export production and to reduce prohibitive transport costs, but also to increase resource productivity in subsistence production. In many cases the latter type of intervention may be an essential prerequisite to the development of internal trade and specialization.

References

BROOKFIELD and BROWN, 1963. H. C. Brookfield and Paula Brown, *The Struggle for Land* (London: Oxford University Press, 1963).

CROCOMBE and HOGBIN, 1963a. R. G. Crocombe and G. R. Hogbin, "The Erap Mechanical Farming Project," *New Guinea Research Unit Bulletin* No. 1, Australian National University, Canberra, Australia (April 1963).

CROCOMBE and HOGBIN, 1963b. R. G. Crocombe and G. R. Hogbin, "Land, Work and Productivity at Inonda," *New Guinea Research Unit Bulletin* No. 2, Australian National University, Canberra, Australia (August 1963).

FISK, 1962. E. K. Fisk, "Planning in a Primitive Economy: Special Problems of Papua New Guinea," *Economic Record* (Melbourne, Australia), Vol. 38, No. 84 (December 1962), 462–78.

FISK, 1964. E. K. Fisk, "Planning in a Primitive Economy: From Pure Subsistence to the Production of a Market Surplus," *Economic Record*, Vol. 40, No. 90 (June 1964), 156–74.

HOWLETT, 1962. D. R. Howlett, "A Decade of Change in the Goroka Valley, New Guinea," Unpublished Ph.D. dissertation, Australian National University, Canberra, Australia, 1962.

INTERNATIONAL BANK, 1964. International Bank for Reconstruction and Development, *The Economic Development of the Territory of Papua and New Guinea* (Baltimore, Md.: Johns Hopkins University Press, 1965).

SALISBURY, 1962. R. F. Salisbury, *From Stone to Steel: Economic Consequences of a Technological Change in New Guinea* (Melbourne: Melbourne University Press, 1962).

SHAND, 1965. R. T. Shand, "The Development of Trade and Specialization in a Primitive Economy," *Economic Record*, Vol. 41, No. 94 (June 1965), 193–206.

COMMENT

The Demand for Food,
Leisure, and Economic Surpluses

WILLIAM O. JONES

STUDENTS OF THAT PART of the less developed world which is located in subsaharan Africa have long been dissatisfied with development models deriving from a situation in which increased output with existing techniques is thwarted by lack of uncultivated land. This undoubtedly is the situation in much of southern and eastern Asia, and experience there has inspired models of the Fei and Ranis type [1964], in which the marginal productivity of labor in agriculture is forced to zero by population pressure on the land. But in most of tropical Africa, in parts of Latin America and Southeast Asia, and in other scattered parts of the world uncultivated land is still plentiful enough that increased populations could be fed by the simple expedient of bringing more land under cultivation. It is with such a situation that Fisk and Shand are concerned; in parts of the New Guinea Highlands development can proceed for a time at least with only moderate decline in the marginal productivity of land.

W. H. Nicholls [1963 and Chapter 10 below] discusses a similar situation in an article on the agricultural surplus as a factor in economic development, published at about the same time as Fisk's first article, but dismisses it with the assertion that under such circumstances in an isolated population "there would be a maximum incentive for population growth" [1963]. The rest of Nicholls' discussion of "underpopulated" countries is concerned with open economies that can sell their food surpluses in a world market. Nicholls assumes "that any given agricultural population maximizes its food output"; if a surplus of foodstuffs results, it is either absorbed by rapid population growth or moves into international trade. Fisk and Shand, however, are faced with a situation where surplus food could be produced but is not, and they undertake to determine why.

They find the answer in "the narrow capacity of the human stomach." They make this error by confusing quantity with value;[1] and by assuming that the demand for nonfood products is fixed. As a result, they conclude that man's desire for economic products is satiated before labor is fully employed. As in development with unlimited supplies of labor, a labor surplus exists that "is of particular importance for development planning" [Fisk, 1962].[2] The greater part of the three articles, like that of the chapter presented here, is devoted to discussions of ways to direct this surplus labor to production for market. Correct understanding of why labor is in surplus, if in fact it is, therefore becomes critical.

THE DEMAND FOR FOOD

Fisk and Shand make a significant contribution by introducing a function, EMN, which relates the level of nutrition to the potential supply of labor that is available—or better, perhaps, to the potential effectiveness of a total supply of labor (Figure 9.1). They explain that "the shape of the curve . . . is purely formal," but it is probably not unrealistic.[3] It can be expected that for a population at the "starvation level"[4] a rather

1. Adam Smith did not make this mistake. What he said was: "The rich man consumes no more food than his poor neighbour. In quality it may be very different, and to select and prepare it may require more labour and art; but in quantity it is very nearly the same" [Smith, 1937, 164]. For quality read value, for quantity read calories.
2. Quotations in text are from the original Fisk [1962; 1964] and Shand [1965] articles published in the *Economic Record*. Although the main argument of these three papers is presented verbatim in the chapter in this volume, some pertinent details, particularly about the pig cycle, are not. Chart references are to those published in this volume.
3. The middle portion of EMN should probably have a steeper slope.
4. As described in A. B. Keys et al. [1950].

large increase in the amount of food ingested will be required to realize any labor output at all; further increments in calorie consumption are unlikely to contribute as much to labor output, and if too great, may actually reduce it. Improvement in the quality of the diet, however, may bring substantial benefits once the basic calorie supply is assured, but at a decreasing rate. If the vertical axis against which EMN is drawn is thought of as primarily measuring total calories of the minimum quality required up to the point above M where EMN turns sharply upward, and thereafter mainly improved quality of the calories (better balanced protein, vitamins, and minerals), it is a useful concept and certainly a closer approximation to reality than the dichotomy between "minimum subsistence" and "fully fed" in calorie terms that is invoked by Nicholls. In particular it directs attention to the fact that large labor inputs are possible even though food intake is considerably less than the standards for adequate diets (presumably N) that may be set by nutritionists. It also suggests that at points between M and N the consumer could, if he wanted, substitute consumption of other goods for that of food without disastrous—perhaps without serious—consequences. But this anticipates the discussion of the next section.

Up to this point Fisk and Shand are talking about consumption of food in terms of adequacy for physical activity, and they are measuring it somehow in physical units. It is at the next step that Adam Smith is called in, and we are told that "In any society there is a definite limit to the amount of food that can be consumed with satisfaction, and if the diet contains as little variety as that of the average Highland subsistence unit in New Guinea, where sweet-potatoes provide up to 90 per cent of the calorific intake, that limit should be reasonably well defined." They therefore define a maximum demand for food that is a function of "population, physical activity and a number of social and customary factors (including the pig cycle)," all of which are taken to be exogenously determined. The demand for food is completely inelastic, and it is in fact so represented in Figure 9.1; N is required for full activity; P, a constant multiple of N (1.25), is the most that can be consumed. Surprising as this assumption is to

students of the economics of food consumption, it could conceivably be true some place of some people at some time; not, it seems almost certain, of the inhabitants of the Highlands of New Guinea, who have a "pig cycle."

In setting up this basic model, Fisk assumes that:

1. The requirements of clothing and shelter are met "to the customary standards of the tribe," by a fixed expenditure of labor.
2. The only other economic activity is the provision of food.
3. Ceremonial activity and the preparations therefore can be treated as leisure "and affecting economic activity only to the extent that certain amounts of leisure activity are socially regarded as necessary, and that the amounts of labour available for economic activities are socially limited thereby."

They find that the third assumption presents little difficulty, except for the pig.[5] Pigs are consumed during certain "ceremonial" activities, and their production requires inputs of land and of labor. They provide periodic feasts, when members of the community prodigally glut themselves on pork. Fisk and Shand are uneasy because the consumption of pigs is cyclical; they fail to recognize the clear evidence of a usually unsatisfied demand for at least one kind of food—for pig meat is food—and in a diet with a starchy-staple ratio of 90 (unbelievably high if the starchy staple is a root) they must be strange human beings indeed who would not like to see the pig cycle shortened.

The demand for food is *not* limited by the capacity of the human stomach [Davis, 1954]. In value terms—and these are economic terms—it may not be limited at all.[6] As incomes rise, or prices fall, consumers are quite willing to consume ever more costly delicacies, be they pig meat or caviar. Except at the very lowest incomes, the value of food consumed tends to rise less rapidly than

5. In all fairness it must be pointed out that Fisk and Shand ask no more of their model than that it be "a caricature, rather than a picture, of the real life situation" and that it not omit details affecting the principles governing the main interactions of the model. My argument here is that certain omissions do in fact critically affect inferences drawn from the model.

6. These issues are discussed further by Nakajima in the present volume and Wharton [1963].

the total value of all consumption, it is true, but it rises nevertheless, as thousands of household expenditure studies have shown. D–D' therefore is not completely determined by physiology or custom, but is functionally related to income, which in this model is approximated by OT. If we are to explain why actual production of food is less than it could be, why P lies below S, we must look elsewhere.[7]

CLOTHING AND SHELTER

The only activity other than farming that Fisk and Shand specifically regard as economic is the provision of food and shelter. This, they assume, will require a fixed amount of labor for a given population to meet "the customary standards of the tribe." As with foods, it is assumed that once these socially dete mined requirements have been satisfied, no addition to them or improvement in them is wanted or would be accepted. In a tropical climate, with modest development of the building arts, this assumption may not be too unrealistic. Once it is recognized, however, that clothing may serve other ends than utilitarian protection against heat, cold, and thorns or the demands of modesty, the assumed limitation on demand for it becomes less convincing. Perhaps New Guinea Highlanders are different, but the almost universal experience has been that items for personal adornment are among the first objects of trade and frequently serve as a store of wealth as well. Ornamentation, which is a principal component of clothing in Western and non-Western societies alike, is certainly income-elastic.

It is a serious mistake, however, to assume that food, clothing, and shelter exhaust the range of material goods desired by men, even men in the most "primitive" economies. Material provisions of nomadic and hunting people may be kept to the barest minimum by the exigencies of constant movement, but even such people need weapons for defense and hunting and utensils for transporting, preparing, and serving food and drink; they may also have minimum furniture—such as stools and beds, curtains, floor coverings—

and at least a few objects prized for their artistic merit. Sedentary people, like the sweet-potato farmers of interior New Guinea, can permit themselves a greater number of such articles, if they can obtain them, and they must of necessity have tools for farming. Unlike the normal pastoralist, who stores his food supply on the hoof, they must also provide for the storage of their harvests from one year to the next. Variation in the number of these items that may be owned by one household is large [Jones, 1960]. They include such commonplace things as pots, baskets, spoons, plates, porridge stirrers, sifters, cups, knives, stools, beds, and skins. They may also vary in quality of workmanship, as judged either by their effectiveness for the task they are designed to perform or by their esthetic appeal. A member of a "primitive" economy is not supplied with a uniform kit of necessaries, like that of an army private, and then required to be content with that and no more. It is primitive economics to think so.

All of these material possessions—houses and storehouses, clothing and ornamentation, and a variety of implements, weapons, and utensils—have a cost. As incomes rise, the consumer will acquire more in terms of numbers or in terms of quality; i.e. the demand for material possessions, like the demand for food, is income- and price-elastic. Engel's law asserts that as income rises, the share that is spent on food declines; this can only mean that the share spent in some other way rises, and this other way can only be expenditure on nonfood goods and on services. That some of these other goods may represent investment—and many of them do—is irrelevant here, except that Fisk and Shand abstract from all saving, except storage of food for a rainy day or in preparation for a feast.

If we recognize that the demand for food is income-elastic both above and below N, and that food is competing with a fairly wide range of other consumer goods, it is easy to understand why food consumption may not be maximized. If a handsome nose plug can only be got by stalking a wild animal for days, killing and butchering him, and then polishing and shaping one of his canines, and if the nose plug is valued more than the additional amount of pig meat that the same amount of labor might produce, where is the

---

7. If the supply function (OT?) and the demand function ($EMNPS$?) were drawn in value terms, would the gap PS appear?

wonder that our New Guinea Highlander produces less food than he could if he would?

Fisk and Shand dispose of the demand for other goods than food by the device of lumping them together in a customary bundle of fixed cost that is determined outside their system. But they do recognize some of this production as economic, how much is not clear. With another group of activities, normally considered to be economic in Western economies, they are less tolerant. This is a group called "ceremonial activities" (unspecified except for feasting), which are thrown into a larger and even less clearly defined category called leisure activity.

The physiocratic willingness of many two-sector modelers to divide all human behavior into farming and everything else—usually designated as leisure—and to regard only the first as economic, suggests a picture of preindustrial man as existing in only two states—either vigorously engaged in unspecified activities having to do with growing food crops or supine beneath a tree in a state of suspended animation.[8] This casts out of the economic calculus a wide range of activities, including not only socially important ones, but economically important ones as well. Perhaps this categorization results from a form of cultural blindness that prevents the observer from seeing old men who sit by the campfire telling stories and posing riddles as being both the transmitters of history and the instructors of the young. It is reflected in the young teachers' college graduate who cannot see the educational process going on about him as fathers and mothers, uncles and aunts, grandfathers and grandmothers, through demonstration, remonstrance, and precept, acquaint the boys and girls of the village with knowledge of farming, hunting, building, carving, housekeeping, and all the complex skills of their society, in addition to manners, morals, governance, and religion. Discussion and palaver may be dismissed as time wasted

8. Fisk and Shand present the "Song of the Tribal Economist" (Fisk? or Shand?) to introduce their discussion of the utility of money; it incidentally illuminates their picture of what the New Guinea Highlander does when not working in his fields [Fisk, 1964].

> If I act in a rational way
> I'll just sit on my backside today,
>   When I want a good feed
>   I've got all I need
> Piping hot, and there's nothing to pay.

without being recognized as the way in which a community arrives at consensus, or peace-disturbing arguments before the whole village as a way of settling legal disputes before one's peers. So-called leisure-time activities include as well the settlement of disputes before more formal courts; the transmission and creation of oral literature through storytelling and song; entertainment and recreation through music and dance and relaxation through drink; healing of the sick by treatments both medical and psychological and the propitiation of the supernatural either directly or by proxy.

It is our custom, when computing the economic product of Western societies, to take into account the services provided by teachers, writers, composers, musicians, actors, artists, congressmen, doctors (including psychiatrists), priests and ministers, lawyers, and judges; why should they be excluded when considering the economic activities of other societies? Most of these services compete for labor time with the production of food, with the construction of dwellings, and with the manufacture of pots and baskets, spears and arrow points, shell necklaces and body paints. And the demand for most, if not all, of these services increases with income—increases more rapidly than income, in fact, if Engel's law is to hold.

For the modeler who is aware of them, this welter of other activities is a nuisance at best, and the temptation to assume them away may be strong. Economic models are by their nature simplified versions of reality (but good ones are not caricatures), abstracting from a complex of interactions in order to identify the principal determinants of economic change. Fisk and Shand have set aside all activities other than food farming as not pertinent to the problem in hand; the difficulty is that such activities *are* pertinent and will *not* be set aside. "Social and customary factors (including the pig cycle)" require that D–D' be set, not at the level dictated by physiological considerations, but 25 per cent above it. This, of course, is no solution at all, for the labor required to provide these other goods and services reduces that employed in farm production, rather than increasing it. And if, as has been argued here, the demand for these goods and services is income-elastic, the labor required to produce them is not 25 per cent or 50 per cent or any other constant fraction of labor employed in agriculture or of total employment.

ON SURPLUSES

The interpretation of economic behavior presented here is of an economy in which limited labor resources must be allocated among a number of productive economic activities, only one of which is farming, and it implies that a large part of the labor resources not devoted to producing food are in other productive employment. If more labor is to be found for farming, it is to be won by offering higher economic incentives than it earns in its present employment. The "incentive factor" and the "response factor" [Fisk, 1964] both lie in the economic sector, and the balance between employment in agriculture and other employment is *determined by marginal principles*.[9] If surplus is "that which remains when use or need is satisfied," there is no surplus. The means to be used in increasing agricultural output, and the economic costs of doing so, are considerably different from what they would be if there were in fact a considerable reservoir of labor, eager to work but nevertheless idle because no remunerative opportunities for employment exist.

Examination of the kinds of goods that are purchased when a community is first opened to trade bears out the notion that imported goods are essentially substituted for goods previously produced because they are better in quality or cheaper or both. Lists of goods considered to be most suitable for trading along the West African coast in the seventeenth century, for example, include many kinds of cloth for clothing and for bedding; metal and crockery, cauldrons, buckets, vats, bowls and dishes; knives, axes, cutlasses, and sabers; fishing lines; iron and lead for working; sheepskins; and a few objects for ornamentation. They include a very few items that probably did not have their counterpart in traditional manufacture, such as looking glasses and perhaps trumpets [Jones

and Meret, 1962]. This being true, the gains from trade should take into account any reduction in supply of home-produced goods and services, as well as increases in the supply of imported ones. They should also, no doubt, make allowances for the redistributive effects of trade, for those who produce the additional export commodities are not necessarily those who formerly produced the domestic goods for which they are substituted.

The dichotomy between agricultural work and leisure that characterizes the model developed by Fisk and Shand to explain the workings of an economy with idle land is also found in models, such as that of Fei and Ranis, that are primarily directed at economies where uncultivated land is scarce, economies with "unlimited supplies of labor." Fei and Ranis use diagrams much like those of Fisk and Shand, but they spend more time in discussion of the situation when the marginal physical productivity of labor in agriculture is zero and the average physcial product of agriculture just equals (or determines) "an institutionally determined real wage" or a "constant institutional wage" similar in concept to Fisk and Shand's D–D'. That part of the population which grows no food or less food than it consumes is "redundant" and "parasitic"; where Fisk and Shand find idle hours, Fei and Ranis find idle men. But just as "idle" hours may be devoted to other economically productive and socially essential activities, so may the hours of "idle" men. In both models a part of the population produces enough food for all the population. The difference is that in Fisk and Shand's case, agricultural output could be raised by transferring labor from "ceremonial" activities to the cultivation of idle land, whereas in the Fei and Ranis model, like Fisk and Shand's Chimbu case, technical change is necessary if more labor is to be productively employed in farming.

Farm laborers in the Fei and Ranis model do, in fact, produce a food surplus which is consumed by their followers who grow less food than they consume.[10] It is the existence of this food surplus that permits "parasitic"

9. There should be no reason for surprise, therefore, when an increase in productivity of labor in agriculture leads to a transfer of labor from farming to other productive activities, as is said to have occurred among the Siane.

10. Fei and Ranis designate as agricultural surplus (*TAS*) only that part of this food surplus which accompanies redundant laborers who move from the agricultural to the industrial sector, i.e. that part which is surplus to the agricultural or traditional sector [Fei and Ranis, 1964, 24–27, 205–208].

labor to survive, and it is in this traditional sense that the concept of economic surplus has perhaps most often been used. Nicholls [1963, 1], for example, defines agricultural surplus as "the physical amount by which, in any given country, total food production exceeds the total food consumption of the agricultural population" and argues that "until underdeveloped countries succeed in achieving and sustaining . . . a reliable food surplus, thay have not fulfilled the fundamental pre-condition for economic development." Presumably Nicholls intends only that farmers should produce more food than they consume, not that the entire country should produce more food than it consumes, but his diagrammatic model seems to make no allowance for producers of nonagricultural products. In fact, this diagram resembles closely Figure 9.2 of Fisk and Shand, with P' defined as food consumption per capita when the population is "fully fed," and N' defined as the biological minimum food consumption per capita. Nevertheless, the balance of his text is devoted to discussion of situations in which farmers are productive enough to provide their own food requirements and those of persons working in other sectors as well.

This biological-evolutionary concept—that a society must first satisfy its food requirements before it can provide itself with other human requirements, classed by Fisk and Shand as clothing and shelter on the one hand and ceremonial activities (including the pig cycle) on the other—certainly seems reasonable at first glance; if men cannot produce enough food to maintain themselves, they will surely perish, and certainly they will have no time to devote to furniture, ornaments, utensils, and tools. Tools? How can man secure food without tools or weapons? How can he keep it without pots or baskets? Perhaps he can, if he lives like the beasts; but where can we find men without tools? And if we could, would they then still be men?

The Robinson Crusoe model has been a favorite device for introducing novices to notions of economics and economizing. It is interesting to read again Defoe's account of how the original Robinson Crusoe went about providing for his wants. His concern for tools and materials is simultaneous with

his concern for food, and the manufacture of implements, utensils, storage pots and sheds goes on, along with hunting and planting. It is true that later, when his efforts at crop-farming had succeeded, Crusoe says:

Upon the whole, I found that the forty bushels of barley and rice was much more than I could consume in a year; so I resolved to sow just the same quantity every year that I sowed the last, in hopes that such a quantity would fully provide me with bread, etc. [Defoe, 1895, 155]

Robinson Crusoe had no need to produce a surplus until he met Friday.

This fictional account is less inconsistent with reality than theories assuming all energy to be devoted to food until some undetermined minimum is reached. In every society of which we have knowledge, food production and other economic production go hand in hand. H. W. Pearson [1957, 339], in a chapter which he has entitled "The Economy Has No Surplus," asserts flatly, "There are always and everywhere potential surpluses available," and although he is concerned primarily with a somewhat broader problem than ours—the conditions that permit the development of trade and markets, money, cities, differentiation into social classes, and civilization itself—his basic argument is germane. He first examines the usefulness of the concept of subsistence requirements and concludes that it is so elusive as not to permit any direct determination of whether a society is producing more of this minimum requirement or not, citing as an example in support of this argument J. S. Davis's [1954] comments on food supply and population growth in India. On the other hand, "If it is held that subsistence needs are not biologically but socially defined, there is no room for the concept of absolute surplus, for then the distribution of economic resources between subsistence and other requirements is determined only within the *total* context of needs thus defined" [Pearson, 1957, 323]. If this is true, "Man, living in society, does not produce a surplus unless he names it such, and then its effect is given by the manner in which it is institutionalized" [p. 326].

Pearson's chapter has been severely criticized by Marvin Harris, primarily because it subordinates the role of "techno-environmental adaptations" in the evolution of human societies and because it "leads to the conclusion that cultural phenomena are essentially the result of whimsical and capricious processes" [Harris, 1959]. This is a debate with which we need not concern ourselves here,[11] but it is of some significance, given Harris's general reaction to Pearson's chapter, that he finds in it "one grain of irrefutable truth."

The members of simple societies do not merely stay alive; they carry on numerous activities requiring the expenditure of energy which from a strictly biophysical point of view are irrelevant to the business of food production. Yet from psychological, social, and cultural points of view, these additional activities ... may be of decisive importance for determining the ability of even the simplest society to use its technological equipment effectively in relation to the natural and cultural environment.

Harris's grain of irrefutable truth and Pearson's surplus that exists only when man says it does are something quite different from the labor surplus of Fisk and Shand that results from underproduction of food or the agricultural surplus of Nicholls that results from man's determination to maximize food production at all times. But the views of Harris and Pearson are not inconsistent with the maximizing behavior of man as traditional economic theory conceives it and as empirical investigation finds it.

John Stuart Mill would have been as disturbed as Harris and Pearson undoubtedly would be by Nicholl's absolute maximization assumption. Mill also points out clearly that imported goods compete with home-produced goods and that the alternative to purchasing for export is not idleness but the production of domestic substitutes for the unavailable imports. His comments on "Adam Smith's theory of the benefit of foreign trade ..., that it afforded an outlet for the surplus produce of a country," are so appropriate that they are quoted at length:

The expression, surplus produce, seems to imply that a country is under some kind of necessity of producing the corn or cloth which it exports; so that the portion which it does not itself consume, if not wanted and consumed elsewhere, would either be produced in sheer waste, or, if it were not

produced, the corresponding portion of capital would remain idle, and the mass of productions in the country would be diminished by so much. Either of these suppositions would be entirely erroneous. The country produces an exportable article in excess of its own wants from no inherent necessity, but as the cheapest mode of supplying itself with other things. If prevented from exporting this surplus, it would cease to produce it, and would no longer import anything, being unable to give an equivalent; but the labor and capital which had been employed in producing with a view to exportation would find employment in producing those desirable objects which were previously brought from abroad or if some of them could not be produced, in producing substitutes for them. [Mill, 1902, 387]

The labor surplus found by Fisk and Shand, and perhaps that found by Fei and Ranis, may be an illusion resulting from their refusal to take seriously, when performed by non-Europeans, a group of productive activities that account for the largest part of the national income of developed countries. When isolated communities are brought into trading contact with the world economy, they may increase their economic product rapidly, not by substituting productive labor for idleness, but by turning from activities that are less highly valued in the world market to those that are more highly valued. Trade is not a substitution of new goods and services for the joys of leisure, but of preferred or cheaper new goods and services for old ones. A great deal may be gained, but much may be lost too. Those who are convinced of the economic advantages of specialization and exchange are convinced that, when trade is engaged in freely, the gains will more than offset the losses, but they may not when trade is imposed from outside or economic transformation is attempted by technocratic decree and associated penalties for nonconformance.

Fisk and Shand seem at times to recognize that customary activities must be suspended or curtailed if more labor is to be employed in agricultural production. When discussing the "response factor" in the second article in this series, they point out that the change to active participation in the monetized economy "will, in many cases, do violence to the very culture of the society concerned, as well as to its economic organization" [Fisk, 1964]. In the third article comparative

11. A reply to Harris, by Abraham Rotstein, and a rejoinder by Harris appeared in the *American Anthropologist*, June 1961.

advantage is evoked to determine the benefits that are to be found in specialization and trade, and they devote their attention to clearly recognizable market incentives throughout most of the excellent discussion of increasing engagement in the market economy. Here the labor-leisure assumption is little used and therefore causes them little trouble, except in understanding the pig cycle and the reaction of the aberrant Siane to the introduction of steel ax heads. Nevertheless they find the strength of the "incentive factor" to depend on comparison of the disutility of labor (or negative leisure) with the utility of its return, rather than on comparison of the utilities to be obtained from time spent in alternative employment. The frequent failures of plans for the betterment of colonial peoples have many causes, but surely one of them has been this arbitrary classification of activities as nonproductive, with the corollary that time devoted to them is free time, to be brought into "productive" employment at no cost. The assumption that most nonagricultural activities of subject populations are also noneconomic and that the allocation of time among various activities is uninfluenced by economic considerations provides a convenient rationalization for compulsory labor and imposed cultivation, even for hut or poll taxes and exploitative wages.

So-called primitive economies can alter their production patterns, even without external trade, to the extent that they direct resources now used in one kind of economic activities—Pearson's surplus—to new activities. If it is the wish of the society, however determined, that this is desirable, then total product will have increased.[12]

There is, then, in most societies the capability of increasing the labor resources that are brought into a desired employment. Does it matter whether these resources are drawn from a surplus of idle labor, as Fisk and Shand believe, or are drawn from other productive activities? If policy conclusions would be unaffected, it does not matter,

and the simple assumption may be preferred. But it is suggested here that policy recommendations will be different depending upon the resources of the increased labor input, if only in the relative emphasis given to market forces and to direct intervention. If members of a "subsistence economy," like members of a market economy, are driven by the desire to improve their material well-being by fashioning new ways of combining the resources available to them, they must not be regarded as passive recipients of change, but active initiators of it.

Contrary to current doctrine, and contrary to Fisk and Shand, "effective linkage with the external exchange economy" and increased consumption of commodities moving in international trade are not the only means by which a society can be induced to increase its production of material goods. A new style in pottery or carving, the discovery or invention of new gods and of new ways to worship them (witness the medieval cathedrals), a charismatic leader with enthusiasm for war, or a new obsession with competitive feasts can provide the opportunity and incentive to direct labor in new directions, and so, in the view of the populations engaged, to enhance the national product. A new technique, whether for making fetishes or growing sweet potatoes, can do the same; and a new way of combining the factors of production can be equally effective.

Economies are poor to the extent that their members find themselves unable to make reasonable progress toward satisfying their wants. If the world were made up of thousands of isolated communities, relative wealth or poverty would not depend upon levels of living measured absolutely, but upon the degree to which each community approximated its standard of living. Rapid change could come when new elements appeared in the standard, if there was knowledge of how to achieve them or if new means for achieving the old standard were discovered. Under these circumstances the surplus, in Pearson's sense, would be redefined or redirected, and the economy would advance. This can be said differently and more prosaically: when relative costs and prices change, resources will be reallocated to achieve a new equilibrium.

12. It is assumed throughout this paper that a society's economic requirements are determined somehow by the free exercise of consumers' choice; but only the exposition, not the argument, is affected by this. The argument would be the same if the economic ends of the society were determined by a dictator, a gerontocracy, a communist party, or a democratically elected government.

In the world of today when there are few isolated communities, most standards of living have incorporated new and similar elements. If this were not so, would we be so concerned about economic growth? But although knowledge of ends becomes increasingly universal, knowledge of means lags far behind. It is not the responsibility of the development economist to teach people to want more, but to assist them in making some heartening progress toward achieving what they want now. He cannot do so if he misunderstands the essential problem that a society faces when it redeploys its productive resources—to gain as much as possible of the new satisfactions without sacrificing more than is necessary, or desired, of those it now has.

The paternalism that is so characteristic of recent colonial policy and that colors many contemporary development policies, both national and international, grows in part at least from the belief that backward societies are static and that their members must be exhorted and coerced to better themselves. Some of the devices to be used are mentioned by Fisk and Shand in their discussion of the response factor: "tact and understanding . . . the demonstrative effect of a higher standard of living . . . the work and influence of missions . . . the imposition of a poll tax" are suggested as ways of altering the "passive or inert factor" [Fisk, 1964]. Noneconomic and nonmarket forces, of course, influence response to economic stimuli in market as well as in nonmarket economies and must be taken into account in any development program. The danger is that they may be emphasized at the expense of market forces and that planners and government may unnecessarily make economic decisions that could be better made by the people who are affected.

References

DAVIS, 1954. J. S. Davis, "Adam Smith and the Human Stomach," *Quarterly Journal of Economics*, Vol. 68, No. 2 (May 1954), 275–86.

DEFOE, 1895. Daniel Defoe, *The Life and Strange Adventures of Robinson Crusoe of York, Mariner* (Boston: Houghton, Mifflin, 1895).

FEI and RANIS, 1964. J. C. H. Fei and Gustav Ranis, *Development of the Labor Surplus Economy: Theory and Policy* (New Haven, Conn.: Yale University Press, 1964).

FISK, 1962. E. K. Fisk, "Planning in a Primitive Economy: Special Problems of Papua New Guinea," *Economic Record* (Melbourne, Australia), Vol. 38, No. 84 (December 1962), 462–78.

FISK, 1964. E. K. Fisk, "Planning in a Primitive Economy: From Pure Subsistence to the Production of a Market Surplus," *Economic Record* (Melbourne, Australia), Vol. 40, No. 90 (June 1964), 156–74.

HARRIS, 1959. Marvin Harris, "The Economy Has No Surplus?" *American Anthropologist*, Vol. 61, No. 2 (April 1959), 185–98.

JONES, 1960. W. O. Jones, "Economic Man in Africa," *Food Research Institute Studies*, Vol. I, No. 2 (May 1960), 107–34.

JONES and MERAT, 1962. W. O. Jones and Christian Merat, "Consumption of Exotic Goods as an Indicator of Economic Achievement in Ten Countries of Tropical Africa," *Food Research Institute Studies*, Vol. III, No. 1 (February 1962), 35–60.

KEYS, et al., 1950. A. B. Keys, et al., *The Biology of Human Starvation*, Vol. I (Minneapolis, Minn.: University of Minnesota, Laboratory of Physiological Hygiene, 1950).

MILL, 1902. J. S. Mill, *Principles of Political Economy*, Abridged . . . by J. L. Laughlin (New York: Appleton, 1902).

NICHOLLS, 1963. William H. Nicholls, "An Agricultural Surplus as a Factor in Economic Development," *Journal of Political Economy*, Vol. 71, No. 1 (February 1963), 1–29.

PEARSON, 1957. H. W. Pearson, "The Economy Has No Surplus: Critique of a Theory of Development," in Karl Polanyi, C. M. Arensberg, and H. W. Pearson, eds., *Trade and Market in the Early Empires: Economies in History and Theory* (Glencoe, Ill.: Free Press, 1957).

ROTSTEIN, 1961. Abraham Rotstein, "A Note on the Surplus Discussion," *American Anthropologist*, Vol. 63, No. 3 (June 1961), 561–63.

SHAND, 1965. R. T. Shand, "The Development of Trade and Specialization in a Primitive Economy," *The Economic Record*, Vol. 41, No. 94 (June 1965), 193–206.

SMITH, 1937. Adam Smith, *An Inquiry into the Nature and Causes of the Wealth of Nations*, Edwin Cannan, ed. (New York: The Modern Library, 1937).

WHARTON, 1963. Clifton R. Wharton, Jr., "The Economic Meaning of 'Subsistence'," *Malayan Economic Review*, Vol. 8, No. 2 (October 1963), 46–58.

CASE STUDY

Subsistence and Transition in Agricultural Development among the Ibaloi in the Philippines

MILTON L. BARNETT[1]

THIS ESSAY IS concerned with selected aspects of agricultural development among the Ibaloi, one of the several ethnic groups known collectively as "Igorot," or "mountain people," in northern Luzon, the Philippines. While most of their more than 200 communities are still engaged in subsistence agriculture, an increasing number are rapidly being drawn into a network of commercial farming as new experiences, newly available knowledge and ideas, and new needs have repercussions on traditional Ibaloi behavior.

The materials used here are drawn from a current study of three communities, each manifesting a different level of economic activity—subsistence farming, "mixed" subsistence and cash crop, and solely commercial farming. The first community is called Kadasan; the second, Balbalikong; and the third, Atok.

A pattern of culturally homogeneous communities, sharing the same social structure but evidencing differing degrees of integration and linkage with the modern sector despite a common heritage and even a similar resource base, is a frequent developmental phenomenon. Such divergencies in rapidity of integration occur even where there has been no planned change or external growth catalyst deliberately introduced. The three Ibaloi communities have all experienced growth, but their degree of commercialization and economic integration with the outside world differs considerably. A relatively homogeneous culture and generally similar land resource base is possessed by the Ibaloi of the first two communities, Kadasan and Balbalikong. They are linked by kinship and frequent ritual and social contacts. Personnel in Atok, the commercial farming

community, are extremely mobile, coming from different parts of the highland area. The wage laborers periodically return to their home villages, especially at the time of planting and harvesting, or that of life crises. Our study of the third community emphasizes the economic activities of those Ibaloi farm workers and operators who come from Kadasan and Balbalikong. The present paper will only report on our interim research findings in Kadasan, the subsistence village.

THE IBALOI

The Ibaloi live in the southernmost heights of the Cordillera Central of northern Luzon. Most of the 55,000 Ibaloi inhabit Benguet subprovince. They are also to be found in the foothills of the mountain range that begins to rise in Pangasinan to the south, in the adjacent slopes of the range in La Union to the west and Nueva Vizcaya to the east. To the north of Benguet is Bontoc subprovince, with its Northern Kankanai and Bontok villages, and in the northeast lies Ifugao.

Benguet has a rough topography. The extremely mountainous terrain is marked by rugged, sharply sloped ridges and deep valleys. The sole exception is La Trinidad Valley, which is the only plateau of any size in Benguet. Here is the center of intensive commercial vegetable production, stimulated primarily by Chinese entrepreneurs and truckers, who employ local labor in their rented fields and who purchase produce for shipment and subsequent sale in Manila and elsewhere in the lowlands. Just south is Baguio, summer capital of the country and gateway to Mountain Province. The city is the major center for marketing, secondary education, and nonagricultural employment

1. Acknowledgment is gratefully made to Patricia Afable and Dora Smith, both of whom know Kadasan well.

and for obtaining a glimpse of the world beyond the Cordillera.

The commercial mining of gold in the vicinity of Baguio produces more than 75 per cent of the gold output of the Philippines and provides one employment outlet for Ibaloi men, but lowlanders by far preponderate in the local mining work force. Lumber camps cutting shaft timber for the mines and finished wood for regional consumption offer some employment. Two dams in eastern Benguet—Ambuklao and Binga—permit the generation of electric power, shipped largely to Manila. Some employment is to be found here as well as in the reforestation projects maintained in the watershed. The dams' concomitant function of water control little affects agriculture in the region, except along the Agno River, where population can scarcely be described as dense.

Injudicious timber operations, *kaiñgin* (slash-and-burn) agriculture, and the ever present use of pine for fuel and illumination have had deleterious effects on the forests. Where they still exist, they have been decimated; where they no longer exist, they have been replaced by grasslands used by some for limited grazing of livestock and for farming of taro, sweet potatoes, and other root crops.

Benguet is a region of distinct seasonal differences in rainfall and flow of streams. About 35 per cent of the typhoons visiting the Philippines cross over Mountain Province. Strong winds and the excessive precipitation carried by them wreak havoc on fields, crops, and irrigation systems. The annual threat posed by typhoons, it will be seen, has considerable influence on decision-making with respect to farm enterprises. The skillful utilization of water resources, dramatically exemplified by the irrigated rice terraces of the Ifugao, is nevertheless limited by a dry season, which in western Benguet enables the use of only 10 per cent of the area employed for rice cultivation during the rains. Apart from those fortunate few whose paddies are close to those streams still flowing in the dry season, thereby permitting irrigation, most Mountain Province farmers must depend upon a single rice crop.

Kadasan, one of the villages under study in western Benguet and the focus of our attention here, is located about 30 kilometers by road and trail from Baguio. Like most Ibaloi settlements, it is rather small, with 19 households nestled in a narrow valley about 3,800 feet above sea level. Most of the houses are clustered together above a stream running 50 feet below them. Terraced rice fields, some with stone walls 10 feet in height, extend up the slopes on both sides of the stream, terminating on the farther side at the edge of a wood lot and ridge top and on the closer side reaching to the houses and gardens of the 99 people who live in the hamlet. (The average size of the Kadasan household, 5.2 persons, is lower than that of our second village under study, where an average of 6.3 persons per household prevails.)

The Ibaloi household generally comprises parents and their unmarried offspring. Occasionally a widowed parent of one of the spouses will also reside there. The marriage of a daughter often results in her husband's coming to live in her home, but matrilocal residence seldom lasts beyond a year or two, with the couple then moving to their own place of residence. Shift in residence usually occurs when the newly married pair are given their inheritances in land.

The typical Ibaloi home has two buildings, one used for sleeping and the other for cooking and eating. The buildings are rectangular in shape, averaging about 9 to 12 square feet in size. The range of house sizes in Kadasan extends from 8 by 10 feet to 17 by 26 feet. The floor is of wood, built on posts, and elevated from the ground a meter or more. Roofs are gabled, with most constructed of thatched *cogon* grass (Imperata cylindrica). (The ubiquitous metal sheets used for building construction have begun to find their way into villages of the interior but more frequently are to be seen near or along the road.) The frame of the house is wooden, with panels of woven split bamboo or *cogon* grass serving as walls. Older houses tend to be more substantially built, with plank walls. The interiors of both houses are scantily furnished, with a few short stools, chests, and kerosene cans used for storage of those items not easily hung on walls or strung from a line.

In most houses rice is stored in the *sapatan*, the space between the horizontal rafters connecting the upright walls and the gabled roof. Those who have larger quantities to store will construct granaries of wood. Rice is stored in bundles, or *tan-ay*, and not threshed until needed for actual consumption. In this fashion during the rainy season rice is kept dry above the earthen hearth in the cookhouse, blackened by soot, to be removed *tan-ay* by *tan-ay* as required. From this usage one Ibaloi criterion in the evaluation of desirable rice varieties emerges: rice grains should not easily shatter. (In contrast, rice in the Luzon lowlands is more often threshed after harvest, either in the fields or at home, to be stored in baskets or other containers.)

In the vicinity of the household will grow some taro, as well as papaya, jackfruit, or bananas. A few homes have coffee shrubs growing nearby. Most food for family consumption, however, is cultivated away from the house. In the *uma*, or hillside clearing, are raised the *camotes* or tropical sweet potato, cassava, taro, and other root crops. The cultivation of the *uma* is the responsibility of women. These crops and the irrigated rice grown in the terraced fields provide the basic subsistence of the Ibaloi. Some beans, pepper, and sometimes field corn supplement the diet. Chickens, dogs, pigs, and water buffalo are raised, primarily for ritual consumption, but also for sale to those celebrating a rite requiring animal sacrifice. The buffalo, of course, are also used for labor. Cattle and a few goats are reared, largely for sale, again for religious use. Only recently have beans and green peppers been raised by a few households with possible sale in mind.

Kadasan diet is a restricted one, based chiefly on the crops grown locally, with meat consumed only when an animal is slaughtered on the occasion of a sacrifice. Wildlife is scarce, but field snails are collected, and bats and rice birds provide some added protein to meals. The streams are nearly depleted of fish; only fingerlings, tadpoles, crawfish, and small eels are caught, though in small quantities. When some cash is available in the household, dried fish will be purchased and consumed sparingly.

THE ROLE OF RICE IN IBALOI AGRICULTURE

Prior to the turn of the nineteenth century wet rice cultivation had diffused throughout most Ibaloi communities, probably coming from their neighbors in the north of the mountain range [Scott, 1958]. Villagers in Kadasan maintain that the construction of their terrace walls began in 1913, when a small group moved from Balbalikong to settle down in the small valley. *Camote* (sweet potato) had earlier replaced taro as the major root crop (although the latter retains its ritual importance) and still occupies this position, but rice, above all, has become the cultural focus of Ibaloi society. While tubers are used in daily fare, the ability to serve rice obtains prestige. More time is spent on rice cultivation than on other enterprises; an activity concerned with rice production takes precedence over any other crop. Planting and harvesting, cultivation and distribution, are central to the maintenance and reinforcement of the Ibaloi bilateral kinship system. Rice and rice products are the most significant gifts sent to those who have left the area for urban centers; seasonal farming requirements are the most compelling force, apart from occasions like the death of a family member, bringing urban sojourners and others back to Kadasan. Despite the intrusion of the cash crop and its attendant values, rice remains the center of Ibaloi interests and beliefs.

As one might expect, rice plays a significant role in Ibaloi folktales, but the current importance of rice is seen in the detailed phraseology and lexicon employed to describe rice and the work required to secure it. There are the more obvious terms for the work cycle and terms for the general type of crop—*talon* for the rainy season and *kintoman* for the dry winter season—or names of specific varieties, many of which merely describe their source, like *bontok*. There are also words describing the condition of the panicles, ease of shattering of grains, shape of the grain, health of the plants, and the like.

Shortly after the study had begun in 1963, specimens of 20 varieties of rice, glutinous and nonglutinous, were gathered from Kadasan fields and *sapatan*, storage places. Three early-maturing varieties, three medium varieties, and fourteen late varieties were being grown in the terraces whose total area falls short of 10 hectares. (Other varieties have been tried in the past but were found unsuitable to local conditions and withdrawn from cultivation.)

Opinions on the characteristics of each variety used in Kadasan are generally shared, not only on objectively measurable traits such as average number of grains per panicle or length of time for maturation or productivity per given unit of land area for a particular variety, but also on matters of taste and consistency, persistence of flavor after extended periods of storage, or ease in pounding rice in the stone or wooden mortars possessed by every household.

Evaluations of rice varieties employ numerous criteria. *Bago-an*, for example, is a nonglutinous variety that produces more grains in a panicle than any other local variety. One *tan-ay*, bundle of harvested rice, will provide its owner with a greater volume of cleaned rice than a sheaf of some other variety. It is easier to pound and thus possesses an additional asset for the user. Moreover, *bago-an* is *ma-shek*, "not easily consumed," which makes it clear to the Ibaloi that when prepared for eating, it will produce a greater volume of cooked rice. It remains one of the oldest and most popular varieties in the locality. To cite another set of judgments, *bayabas* is an early-maturing variety, so it is especially useful for planting in a period of anticipated water shortage. It is hard to pound and its flavor is not highly regarded. On the other hand, it is a variety preferred by some because it is *enkanalkal*, hard and dry when cooked. *Bayabas*, people say, is not easily digested and therefore hunger will be delayed. It is considered particularly desirable for feeding young men, whose appetites are more voracious and lasting. It tends to be rather low-yielding, but it goes a long way at a meal. Older persons consistently praise glutinous *betalka* and *balatinaw* because of the softness of the grains. These are more easily consumed by those with poor teeth and will be planted with this end in mind. The softer-grained rice may also be mixed with tougher ones to make a more edible meal. Glutinous rice has its limitations. These varieties attract rice birds and rats more than do the nonglutinous varieties, making for serious depletion of the amount of harvested grain from these lower-yielding plants.

Decisions on which varieties to plant are not capricious nor are they wholly reliant on factors such as taste or softness of grain. One main consideration is the suitability of the variety to the season. Although no local Ibaloi can expound on varietal differences in sensitivity to sunlight, most are aware of the fact that, given adequate water, some varieties perform better in the dry season, when solar energy is plentiful, than during the rainy period, when sunlight is diminished. Similarly, it is well known that some varieties lodge more easily than others in heavy rainfall or wind, making for difficulty in harvesting or for loss of crop.

Ease in harvesting is a major consideration, not only from the viewpoint of one's own labor, but especially when there is a need for assistance from others. The position of the flagleaf in relation to the panicle must be taken into account if one wishes to bind sheafs of equally long stalks. In addition, those varieties having short distances between panicle and flagleaf cause blistering and soreness of the fingers, especially the thumb. Harvesting is quicker and easier when this problem does not exist.

Varietal variations in toughness and smoothness of the stalk pose two other problems. A fine and smooth stalk creates difficulty in binding the *tan-ay* and retards the tempo of the harvest. A different type of problem arises from the unwillingness of livestock to eat the tough stalks. When farmers are forced to rely upon the harvested fields as a source of fodder, especially during the dry season following harvest when hillsides are burned in preparation for tuber cultivation, this characteristic assumes considerable importance in the selection of a variety. The use of harvested fields for foraging, incidentally, creates another problem for the farmer, namely that of selecting varieties whose maturation rates will be similar to those of his neighbors'. The fields of a man who has planted late-maturing rice can be overrun by water buffalo released to forage on a nearby harvested paddy. Either coordination of planting or fence building is required, and generally the latter step will be avoided if possible.

As farmers begin to venture into a second crop on their harvested paddy, such as planting beans or peppers, a new aspect of farm management emerges—the need to consider the maturation period of the rice in order to accommodate the second crop. Conscious decisions to utilize early-maturing varieties, even though they tend to be less productive than later ones, have been made by those planning the raising of vegetables. In all cases, however, final selection of the appropriate variety is determined by the availability of the desired seeds, either in one's own granary or by borrowing from neighbors.

What is appropriate from the viewpoint of biological growth has no necessary relationship to social requirements. Ibaloi religious life requires the availability of *tapuy*, rice wine, made best from glutinous and semiglutinous varieties. Virtually no ritual would be proper without it. Propitiation of the ancestral spirits, so important to the well-being of the community and the individuals who compose it, would be seriously incomplete without the offering of *tapuy* to the dead.

Fully one-fourth of the total land area devoted to rice is given over to the production of glutinous varieties, even though they are low-yielding.[2] The factor of softness satisfying the dentally inadequate can be regarded as inconsequential in accounting for their persistently growing of quantities of glutinous rice. Similarly, such reasons as the making of rice cakes, alleviating the monotony of everyday fare by eating a rice with a different consistency and flavor, and even the making from the glutinous varieties of rice yeast, sometimes to be sold in the Baguio market, also appear to be secondary explanations for growing glutinous rice. It is the religious purpose that is the paramount motivation for the cultivation of glutinous rice. A farmer who anticipates the offering of a memorial ceremony for a deceased parent will, accordingly, plant more glutinous rice. The intense respect for ancestors and the lively role the ancestral spirits play in influencing daily behavior and thought of their descendants is a major theme continually evidenced in Ibaloi life.

During the course of the study, questions were asked of the researchers about rice varieties in the lowlands and particularly those being grown in Los Banos, at both the College of Agriculture and the International Rice Research Institute (IRRI). At the latter, efforts are being made to develop varieties which will be early-maturing, high-yielding, disease-resistant and insensitive to length of day, in addition to having stalks which will not lodge easily in heavy rainfall and strong wind [IRRI, 1962, pp. 13–14]. This program was related to residents of both Kadasan and Balbalikong, the "mixed economy" community. Casual mention was made that of the thousands of varietal tests, a number seemed to combine several of the desired characteristics and showed promise of high yields. Inevitably requests for some of the seeds were forthcoming, and no great effort was made to forestall these. An experiment initiated by the writer with the assistance of IRRI staff members in the area was already in progress on a different problem, which involved the use of trial plots made available by interested Ibaloi farmers. Local testing would not only be of value for the intrinsic merit of determining the suitability of some of the more promising varieties tested at the Institute, but at the same time it would provide an opportunity to study Ibaloi reactions to innovation in rice production. Known Ibaloi experiences with both success and failure of different varieties minimized the danger of repercussions in the event of negative results. Essentially the variety testing was perceived as experimentation by the farmers themselves. A sufficient number elected to attempt the trials, thus spreading the risk of possible crop loss.

Five varieties considered suitable for testing were chosen by the author at the suggestion of members of the IRRI staff. These included one semiglutinous variety that might lend itself to making *tapuy*, rice wine. The varieties initially were planted during the dry season with two applications of ammonium sulphate. Seed and fertilizer were provided without cost to the farmers. With the exception of one variety, results were at least moderately successful, sufficient to warrant retrial in the following planting season.

The results of these trials, which continue at time of writing, will be reported elsewhere, but a number of relevant observations may be made here:

1. Despite early enthusiasm, which seemed to indicate a lack of concern for the risks

---

2. An 800-square-meter paddy produced 30 *tan-ay* of nonglutinous rice, but only 18 of glutinous. It is interesting to note that while the former sells at ₱2.50 a *tan-ay*, glutinous varieties obtain ₱3.50. But this is token; the supply of the latter is limited and not often made available for sale.

involved, there indeed was anxiety. This was explicitly demonstrated by several farmers who chose to plant locally used varieties with known potentialities rather than chance uncertainty.

2. Several of those who chose to try the new varieties selected paddies in which soil was less fertile or where water was available in lesser amounts.

3. For those who participated in the trials, the risk was less than if they had planted the new varieties during the wet season when the major crop is planted. Winter cultivation is at best a gamble: the water supply is limited and unreliable, yields are generally poor, and the worst is expected.

4. Where the new varieties were tried, there were uneven responses in following the recommended practices. Periodic weeding was neglected by some farmers, and the recommended spacing of shoots at the time of transplanting was ignored in favor of the traditional pattern.

5. Unique results were carefully considered by the farmers and not dismissed. For example, the variety Chianung 242 had full but short panicles. The farmers counted samples of these, grain by grain, and compared them with local high-yielding varieties.

6. Single favorable qualities were weighed against other traits by the cooperating farmers. Although Chianung 242 had an extremely high yield and a large number of tillers, farmers pointed out that:

   a. The short-stalked plant compelled harvesters to stoop or bend over when cutting. The new posture was considered more tiring and annoying.

   b. The smooth, hard stalk made binding of sheaves difficult.

   c. Livestock refused to forage on Chianung 242 stalks in the harvested paddy.

   d. The tendency for grain to shatter easily was considered a liability by most harvesters.

The newly introduced varieties illustrate a conflict between differing sets of criteria employed for selecting ideal rice types: the goals of the plant breeder who is production oriented and those of the Ibaloi whose traditional criteria favor a tall, easily bound stalk, which is usable as fodder, a long, awned panicle with nonshattering grains. Length and type of panicle should offer no serious problem; the Ibaloi are sufficiently pragmatic to recognize and utilize a high-yielding variety. Shattering of the grain, while irritating to some, will be overlooked by others as they begin to adopt field threshing as a new technique. Three farmers have already begun field threshing, and the practice will probably spread. Conflict with the present storage system is not anticipated; the *sapatan* is still useful during the rains, for drying and storing those varieties which retain their grains after having been harvested. The acquisition of containers for the clean grain presents no problem.

Two major problem areas remain to be solved: those presented by the short, hard stalk and the required use of fertilizer to maintain the high-yielding character of the varieties. As for the first, development of alternative pasture on the barely utilized grass-covered hills might solve the cattle-grazing problem and could have far-reaching consequences in raising the economic level of the Ibaloi. The presence of livestock and the desire to have greater numbers offers a motivational set that may be used to advantage by extension workers. The sickle could conceivably be introduced to help solve the stooping problem of the harvesters, the sickle is not unknown in the region, though not employed in the harvest.

The purchase of commercial fertilizer appears doubtful, given the present economic level of most Kadasan farmers. Moreover, while nitrogen-producing fertilizer is used in vegetable production, strong resistance to its use in the cultivation of rice prevails. Although wet-rice cultivation partially diffused to the Ibaloi from the Bontok, the composting practices of the latter have never been adopted. Fertilizer, it is claimed, encourages excessive foliation at the expense of grain yield. For this and other reasons the Ibaloi forbear using it. In any case, the major problem of the locality is water, and the shortage of this vital input precludes the extensive use of fertilizer-requiring varieties of rice. Water management could be improved in Kadasan, but it is doubtful that this alone would suffice to increase significantly rice-producing acreage during the dry period. Only when the key problem of water supply is solved will innovations such as multiple cropping be effectively introduced.

In the traditional Ibaloi system of values at Kadasan, quantity in rice production is not more important than quality. Larger stores of rice are wanted, but variety is not chosen merely on the basis of higher yields. Productivity, limited by a not too beneficent environment, is only one of the several factors to be considered in the Ibaloi rice-growing complex.

WORK AND INCOME IN RICE CULTIVATION

Tiglaw, a woman in Kadasan, seldom commits herself to others about plans for working her rice fields. Direct questions are answered with vagueness or evasion. Her reluctance is understandable. If she were more specific, she and her husband would obtain assistance from her neighbors. What is involved here is not labor exchange, like *revuelta mano* in the Andes or as in the case of the two *compadres* in a lowland Luzon community who feel free to call upon one another when help is needed. Assistance in Kadasan involves payment in kind or in cash, and Tiglaw knows this. She also realizes that if she appears to invite help, she will very likely get more than she and her husband require. Refusal is impossible; the arrival of volunteer labor must be accepted as politely as possible. It would seem that no matter how numerous the supply of workers from one's own household or how small one's landholdings in rice paddy, the probability is great that one will also have volunteer labor to feed and pay. Tiglaw may discourage a few by her reticence, but never entirely. At least her close kin will appear, and they are to be welcomed—as well as fed and paid.

Actually a distinction may be drawn between two types of work. With the exception of planting of the seedlings and harvesting of the crop, when labor is needed, it is arranged through direct contact with the desired workers. Some preference is given to kinsmen, but wherever possible this decision is tempered by knowledge of the work ability of the individual. Cleaning fields prior to breaking the soil, plowing and harrowing,

preparation of the seedbed, cleaning of terrace walls and construction or repair of paddy dikes, and weeding of the fields when the plants are two months old fall into this category of planned labor. While the general work cycle of land and seed preparation are determined by anticipation or presence of the rains, no one step is demanded on a particular day.

Transplantation of the seedlings cannot be delayed for long without risk, nor can the harvest wait many days after the plants have matured and are ready for cutting. Vicissitudes of weather, the larger numbers of people needed to perform these tasks, and the uncertainty of their availability, are all conducive to the more general invitation to help. A man lets it be known he will be harvesting on a particular day, and people arrive to assist him.

Weeding is the only activity paid for in cash, one peso for a day's work. All other labor, including that of borrowed water buffalo, is reimbursed with rice. Work in the seedbeds, terrace walls, and paddy embankments gain one bundle of rice daily. The rental of a water buffalo earns its owner two *tan-ay* for each day of labor. The person who helps in a day's harrowing or plowing will be paid two rice bundles at harvest time, provided that he helps harvest for one day; if he should not, he is paid one bundle for that day's work.

Payment for work in planting and harvesting is somewhat more complicated. An individual providing one day's labor in planting is expected to work one day at the harvest. One bundle of rice is forthcoming for the two days of work, with the planter expected to return for the harvest. At this time payment is made, and if he or she should not return, no payment is given for the work of planting. Occasionally one may be ill at the time of harvest or otherwise unable to attend. In such cases an effort is made by the person to find a substitute. The landowner seldom gains the free labor of one day by failure to appear at the harvest. On the contrary, the whims of harvesters are such that they may not appear on a day when a field with a less popular variety is being harvested but descend *en masse* on the day when a favored rice is desired as payment. Payment is equal irrespective of age, sex, or speed and ability of the harvester. Although the average rate of harvesting is three bundles a day per worker, children and laggards may produce considerably less.

There is some tendency in the rice fields toward division of labor by sex, but this is by no means consistent. In general, women weed, transplant, and harvest the paddy. It is believed that women are better at cleaning terrace walls. On the other hand, men plow, harrow, loosen the earth in those corners of the field where the soil cannot be turned by the plow. They build the embankments and tie the sheafs of rice—that is, make the *tan-ay*. But the work is interchangeable. Men work at harvesting and women bind bundles of rice and, if a man is not available, plow or harrow. Equal pay for equal work is the general rule.

In the light of the foregoing, what happens at the extremes of size of landholdings at the time of harvest? Daksit, a young man of about 26 years of age, is married and has three children living with him. The youngest of five children, he and a sister dispute the ownership of an 800-square-meter parcel of rice land. He and his wife use it intermittently, but primarily for vegetables after the sister has harvested a rice crop. To supplement his income, he works a field in Balbalikong for the elderly widowed sister of his father. It is understood that they will share the proceeds of the harvest. Instead of working the field alone with his wife, Daksit, who is rather shy and retiring, found himself assisted by seven planter-harvesters. The parcel yielded a return of 20 bundles of rice, seven of which were given to the *mengetang*, helpers. One bundle went to the woman who had provided him with rice seed. The remainder was shared evenly between him and his aunt, so he received a total of six *tan-ay* for the work which he and his wife had put into the field. Daksit is land-poor and needs to spend little time on his own field. Uusally he is off working for others, to obtain the rice he needs for his household.

Pangulo, one of the largest landholders in Kadasan, has a total rice-paddy area of about 1.2 hectares. In 1964 *talon* production (rainy season), he began his seedbed on June 6, using 12 bundles of rice. Plowing his fields began two weeks later, with the assistance of three men, and after this was completed, four days were spent at harrowing. Planting of the rice

shoots lasted two days. In terms of man days of work, the necessary tasks were handled thus:

Activity	No. of Man Days
Seed Preparation	18
Plowing	7
First Harrowing	9
Second Harrowing	8
Cleaning of Walls	19
Planting-Harvesting	105

Of the 61 persons participating in the planting and harvesting, 32 came from communities other than Kadasan. The large response had not been expected by Pangulo, who was obliged to accept all despite the fact that 24 of the group were 15 years of age and younger (a child of ten years of age is considered ready to harvest); 11 people came from a community nearly an hour's walk from Kadasan. How did this happen? Pangulo had met two of the residents of that place on the trail one day and asked them to inform their neighbors that he would be harvesting. In the previous year (1963) only 41 persons appeared in order to help with the planting; in 1962, there were only 33 helpers.

A total of 388 *tan-ay* of rice were harvested, and Pangulo, after discharging his obligations including those for the renting of three water buffalo, distributed 144 bundles to his *mengetang* and retained 244 for himself.

The uncertainty of the situation for the cultivator can be seen in the output differences between 1964 and other earlier years. For example in 1955–1956 Pangulo's total harvest was 423 bundles, with 100 of these going to helpers. The following year he harvested 383 *tan-ay*, with 101 of these distributed to harvesters.

Pangulo is a methodical man, deliberate in his ways and, although highly respected for his knowledge of custom law and cultural lore, iconoclastic. No Ibaloi in Western Benguet is more ready for rational farm management than he. But the rational man in an Ibaloi setting must cope with social reality. If he is chagrined at the unexpected numbers of helpers who will unnecessarily cut into his net gains from the harvest, he stifles his disappointment, although he may mention it to those close to him, and looks for other ways of supplementing his income. Pangulo, better than most, can closely estimate how many persons are needed to harvest a given area of paddy. He also knows that if the number who arrive far exceed his calculations, he has no choice but to accept them.

RITUAL DETERRENTS TO THE ACCUMULATION OF SAVINGS

Older Ibaloi speak of the *peshit*, a series of rituals designed to enhance a man's prestige in the community. The first occurs some time after marriage, when relatives from outisde the community are invited to the home of the couple. Three pigs are butchered, along with any other animals that might be available. The occasion is festive, with traditional dancing taking place for the first time in the home of the celebrant. The next *peshit*, with an offering of five pigs, comes within the next three years—earlier if the means to offer the celebration are possible. The cycle continues with six, eight, and then ten pigs being slaughtered at similar intervals of time. Once terminated, a man might begin the series once more, entrenching his sound and prestigeful status in the community.

Peshit are no longer held in this part of Benguet, the last elaborate one having been given shortly after the end of World War II. An older person recently remarked to some students, "You practice the *peshit* by going to school, having learned to read and write." The implication was that a formal education provided the prestige of today. This may very well be the case; but advanced schooling offers more tangible rewards than prestige. Those few who manage to be sent by their parents move into the civil service or obtain teaching posts in schools. *Peshit* no longer exists except in the rare reminiscences of the past, when questions may stimulate discussion. The function of the *peshit* cycle, however, has been absorbed by the *kapi*, a memorial service for a deceased spouse or parent.

But rituals still persist, with a majority manifesting concern for the well-being of the dead. To cite one example, the *kemstad*, or ritual to cure illness, is held after a local diagnostician determines which of the deceased relatives is causing difficulty by not having his or her wants satisfied. The *kemtad*

is not excessively demanding. The offering of a clean, if not new, dress, a pair of chickens, a blanket, rice wine, some money, and the sacrifice of a small female pig will suffice. Having performed the *kemtad*, a mother may take her ailing child to the hospital several kilometers away, but the formal propitiation of the deceased relative is still deemed necessary for the good health of the child. Such minor ceremonials, when they occur not too frequently in one household, cause no serious drain on the economic means of the family.

The funerary service, which is unanticipated except in the case of the aged or infirm, does create hardship in subsistence level families. The ceremonial lasts for days, depending upon the desire and means of the bereaved. Expenses are high; the costs involved in feeding guests, who may number 100 and more, frequently require the mortgaging of rice lands or the renting of them to others. The latter recourse further weakens the ability to recoup the funds expended on the funeral. A funeral for an aged parent not long ago cost ₱520.00, not including the individual contribution of the children in the form of livestock, stores of rice, and other foods. Neighbors and kin will ceremonially offer gifts to the deceased and this collective contribution helps defray expenses, but it seldom is adequate. For example, the expenses of another funeral in the barrio reached ₱615.30 (apart from offerings of individual children), but the *upu*, contribution of mourners and nonkin guests, only reached ₱148.90. On the occasion of a death, close kin may not permit the incurrence of any new debts "by the deceased" to help defray the costs of the funeral. Money must somehow be raised to satisfy creditors—meager savings are tapped, an animal or valued possession may be sold, or land mortgaged— one way or another, the death ceremonial is termined with no outstanding debt.

The funeral of one man lasted 12 days. During this period three pigs, two cows, three horses, three dogs, a female water buffalo, and a rooster and hen were slaughtered as ritual offerings to the deceased man. Livestock is expensive, and to this must be added the cost of *camote*, rice and taro, along with the alcoholic beverages served to guests.

Much has been written about the excessive expenditures and debts incurred by grieving families among the Chinese and lowland Filipinos. The same problem exists among the Ibaloi and requires no further elaboration here.

For a *kapi*, or memorial service, held for a woman who had died three years earlier, all the men of Kadasan, with the exception of those away at work in the sawmills and mines, gathered and chopped firewood at the home of the celebrant, made seats and tables of bamboo poles for the invited guests. Forty bundles of rice had already been pounded the week before the *kapi*, and a sack of milled rice was purchased. For three days and two nights, the celebration went on.

The only discordant note came from the grandson of the dead woman, a young man who observed that if his parents had not planned the *kapi*, he might be attending school in Baguio. Other strictures usually come from those young adults who have embraced Christianity. They attend the rituals but protest their pagan nature or their unnecessary high cost. On the whole, conversion does not greatly deter most people from either attending or even participating in the several rituals mentioned here.

It is striking to note that in the vicinity of Atok, where men go to obtain employment in commercial farming operations and thus would appear to be in closer contact with modernizing influences, rituals seem to have increased in number and frequency, rather than to have declined. With the availability of cash, more rituals have been undertaken. But seldom does anyone undertake the sponsorship of a ceremonial with all expenses at hand. One consequence of this reported increase has been an even greater incurrence of debt by agricultural workers.

Traditional religious beliefs among subsistence agriculturists often provide dramatic examples of conservatism and the retarding of agricultural development. The widespread refusal of the Ibaloi to use poisons in combating rat infestations so destructive to crops and stored cereals has its roots in religious convictions. For example, one suicide after a crop failure owing to the imposition of a taboo occurred not long ago. Although numerous instances could be found to support the notion that Ibaloi religion is antipathetic to change, our own position disagrees. Ibaloi values and behavior are remarkably resilient. The fact that one's ancestors did something one way does not restrict an individual from trying alternative ways of doing things.

NONAGRICULTURAL SOURCES OF INCOME

Those who leave Kadasan to find permanent employment in activities other than agriculture in effect are lost to the community, returning home only on the occasion of an important ritual and making the contribution that situation may demand, but seldom remitting much of their wages. The man who is employed in a gold mine earns at least ₱80 each month but contributes to his wife and children only when she visits him in quest of funds. She will return with ₱10 or 15, but seldom more. On his infrequent trips to his own household he is berated by his family and neighbors for his drinking, his gambling, his indifference about the welfare of his children. Alienation is only intensified.

Many young men and women who find work in Baguio also lose their ties with the village and their families. Their new places of residence at best become a center for the occasional Kadasan visitor who has come to the Baguio market on some quest. Personal ties are maintained through gossip and the recounting of events of interest, but really little happens in Kadasan other than birth and death and occasional tragedy. They may return home for a *kapi* or other ritual, but interest in local affairs lags after a day or so, and they go back to Baguio, divorced from the agricultural life that they chose to leave. The sole college student, who has been an undergraduate for more than seven years, comes home on occasion to stay indoors, play his guitar, and perhaps visit with friends. He seldom helps around the house and certainly not in the fields of his father. If he should return to reside in Kadasan, it will be only because he has found no adequate alternatives in Manila, where his social life appears to consist of going to the movies and visiting with other Mountain Province friends. It is implausible to expect him to farm; he has lost many of the skills and has no desire to reside in the village.

Only those who leave temporarily in search of cash, while still carrying on the planting and harvesting activities on their fields, contribute to the cash income of the community and their families through their earnings. The periods between the termination of harvesting and the beginning of a new planting season leave Kadasan a community of old people, women, and children. The interim and dry season are the periods of outmigration for jobs. As the latter go to school and develop new interests and perspectives, it is likely that the hamlet will retain only a skeletal working force, sufficient to keep the fields at a minimum productive level. But perhaps this is as it should be, since the land base is much too small to maintain more than a small population.

SOME PERSPECTIVES

Of the 19 households, only four seem to be in a position to maintain a viable economic position. This is done by hard work, ingenuity in developing sources of income, or to some extent having reasonable landholdings, favorable in size and proximity to water.

Pangulo, whose lands yield about 400 *tan-ay* of rice, lives alone most of the time and has no additional mouths to feed. Moreover, he is enterprising. He constructs a bed frame when other activities are not pressing and sells it for 30 pesos. He moves out of the village in search of cows or water buffalo, buys them for fattening, and gains about 50 or 75 pesos on each head. Although these activities are limited, the difference in additional income that they provide is critical. He gathers the manure of his livestock, works it into the earth of a paddy, and discovers that the increase in yield is about 50 per cent. He reads avidly whenever he can, visits in Balbalikong and talks farming, then decides to raise some pigs in an enclosure, providing them with feed instead of allowing them to the fields and be destructive. He tries a variety of chicken that is new to the area, uses the rice bran that normally may be tossed away. He is able to sell his chickens more readily and at better prices than his neighbors.

Bakbak is an assiduous worker. His holdings are small, but he and his children eke out every possible bundle from the paddy. They all appear at planting time in the fields of others and thus contribute to the family larder. He earns money by cutting lumber or in any way that he can. Frugality and hard work seem to be the mainstays of this family. The house is orderly, not reflecting the confusion that one finds in the homes of those who are less organized and successful.

On the other end of the scale is Daksit, whom we discussed earlier. He, too, works hard whenever he can but somehow does not manage to find the same opportunities discovered by Bakbak. The *uma* (garden) is the major source of diet for him and his children. He is back, as it were, in the period before the Ibaloi embraced rice cultivation. But the *camotes* are not sufficient in quantity to keep the family together. One child was given away for adoption. Daksit and his wife frequently quarrel. She goes off to pick coffee beans at her father's place to sell them. Daksit obtains some help from his widowed aunt and, less frequently, his sister. Efforts to grow beans for sale resulted in the young plants being washed away in a storm, making for a total loss of labor and zeal. The family barely manages to maintain itself at the subsistence level. But it is not only Daksit who lives this way of life. It is shared by other Kadasan households. This economic level is found in other Ibaloi communities throughout Benguet.

The condition of subsistence in Kadasan appears at first glance to offer little possibility of development. The soil which is not overly fertile in the first place continually suffers depletion of its nutrients, with only insignificant effort made to restore them. The pattern of inheritance extends the problem of land fragmentation. The water supply is limited, permitting only one rice crop. Growing vegetables is often in vain because of the danger of destruction by wind and rain. This threat inhibits attempts to grow cash crops in lieu of rice; you can always store and eat rice, but this cannot be done with green peppers or beans; moreover, the prices of these in the local market are unstable, while rice rarely shifts in price. Rice remains the crop most suitable for the wet season.

More careful evaluation of the situation suggests that a planned program of extension education and activity could provide the stimulus for realistic change and, more important, the possibilities for that change. The present water supply is not hopeless but requires assistance from a hydraulic-engineering standpoint. Cisterns and a wooden dam could make a significant difference in water supply. Education in better water management would then have some realistic basis for taking root.

Given these prerequisites for agricultural development, the question of enterprise alternatives become more meaningful. It is very likely not a matter of rice *or* cash crops but both, in a planned cycle of activities taking into account varietal differences that would best lend themselves to an optimal agricultural timetable.

Conversion of underutilized rough grasslands to pasture appears to be feasible. Indeed, interest in livestock, now so closely related to ritual ends, can readily be reoriented into a profitable money enterprise. Obviously such a program requires work, time, the investment of personnel, and probably some grants-in-aid for waterworks. The final question arising, then, is, "Is it worth it?" At the risk of sounding cavalier, would it not be easier and cheaper to relocate Kadasan Ibaloi elsewhere? If the people had wanted to leave their homes, they would have already migrated to the Cagayan Valley or north to Apayao in search of new lands. But they have chosen to stay, and this, in its own right, becomes a social asset well worth utilizing.

References

IRRI, 1962. International Rice Research Institute, Annual Report 1961–62 (Los Banos, Philippines: IRRI, 1962).

SCOTT, 1958. W. H. Scott, "A Preliminary Report on Upland Rice in Northern Luzon," *Southwest Journal of Anthropology*, Vol. 14, No. 1 (1958), 87–105.

IO

Development in Agrarian Economies:
The Role of Agricultural Surplus,
Population Pressures, and
Systems of Land Tenure[1]

WILLIAM H. NICHOLLS

IN THE PRESENT ARTICLE I shall define (with occasional modifications) an "agricultural surplus" as the physical amount by which, in any given country, total food production exceeds the total food consumption of the agricultural population. "When by the improvement and cultivation of land . . . the labour of half the society becomes sufficient to provide food for the whole, the other half . . . can be employed . . . in satisfying the other wants and fancies of mankind" [Adam Smith]. This concept might appear to be too simple and obvious to warrant serious consideration. Unfortunately what was obvious to Adam Smith in 1776 is easily overlooked amid the agricultural affluence of today's advanced countries. As a consequence Western economists have tended to ignore or seriously underestimate the importance of an agricultural surplus both in the earlier economic history of today's developed countries and in those countries that still remain at or

near the bare subsistence level of food consumption.

My own reading of economic history, developed at length elsewhere [Nicholls, 1964], has led me to the conclusion that "until underdeveloped countries succeed in achieving and sustaining (either through domestic production or imports) a reliable food surplus, they have not fulfilled the fundamental pre-condition for economic development." Kuznets reached a similar conclusion on the basis of his comparative studies of economic development: "an agricultural revolution—a marked rise in productivity per worker in agriculture—is a pre-condition of the industrial revolution in any part of the world" [Kuznets, 1959, 59–60]. If Kuznets and I are correct, much mischief has resulted from the fact that most Western policy-planners and theorists have misread the Law of the Declining Relative Importance of Agriculture, tending to emphasize the existence of a *labor* surplus in agriculture, while taking a surplus of *food*

1. Reprinted from *The Journal of Political Economy*, LXXI, 1 (February 1963), 1–29.

output (except in a very long-run context) for granted. They have thereby reinforced the predilections of economic planners in the underdeveloped countries for all-out emphasis on industrial development.

Few theorists have incorporated the production side of agriculture into their models. Insofar as policy-planners have done so, they have largely proposed means of raising

agricultural productivity, notably mechanization and land consolidation, which require drastic structural changes in agriculture and presuppose the massive absorption of surplus agricultural labor by prior industrialization. Thus, in theory and policy, economists have largely neglected the *initial* importance of the production side of agriculture, which they try to make the cart behind an industrial

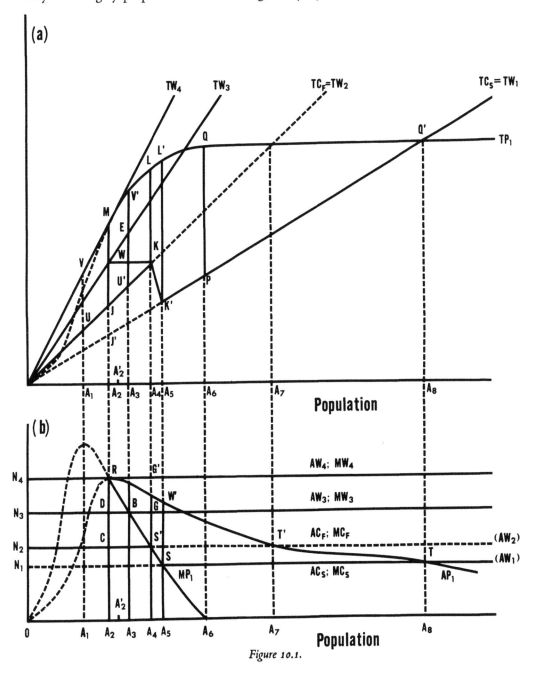

Figure 10.1.

horse. Fortunately those so oriented are now finding that history is catching up with them. The current news from Communist China, India and Pakistan, Turkey, Russia, and even Argentina and Brazil offers mounting evidence that agriculture cannot be so easily dismissed as they had once supposed.

With this jeremiad off my chest, let me turn to my principal objective—the development of some partial analytical models that give greater precision to the concept of an "agricultural surplus." I shall give special attention to determinants of the size, and potential contributions to economic growth, of the agricultural surplus under various conditions of population pressure and under different systems of land tenure. I shall particularly emphasize the opportunities for, and limitations of, making agriculture a positive generating force instead of a needless drag on general economic development.

THE BASIC TOOLS

For present purposes my graphic techniques may easily be confined to those familiar from elementary production theory. However, it is well to make explicit at the outset my basic assumptions and the special definitions of particular curves that will hold throughout the entire analysis which follows.

Let us assume that (1) all agricultural land is of homogeneous quality; (2) agricultural techniques are given; (3) only food crops are grown, industrial crops (if any) being treated as a separate part of the agricultural sector; (4) food output is produced by a large number of identical production units, each of whose acreage of land is the optimum amount (small) for the given level of techniques (primitive); (5) a constant proportion of the agricultural population participates in the farm-labor force; (6) per capita food consumption is given and identical for all individuals in any given agricultural population; and (7) labor and land are so combined that any given agricultural population maximizes its food output. If assumptions (5) and (7) are inconsistent with each other, as they may be under special circumstances, we shall abandon (5) in favor of (7).

Under these assumptions, the product curves would take the following form. The annual total product curve (TP_1 in Figure 10.1a) will follow the path $OMQQ'$, the linear portions OM and QQ' following from our maximizing assumption (7). This means that all agricultural land will be in actual use only for populations of OA_2 or greater. As population increases from nil to OA_2, land is brought under cultivation (and the number of identical farms increased) in the same proportion as population is increasing, so that total food output increases along OM proportionately with population. For a population of OA_6, total product will be at its maximum A_6Q, which level will presumably be maintained for still larger populations by avoiding further increases in the amounts of labor actually used in production. With TP_1 so defined, the average product curve (AP_1 in Figure 10.1b) will be $N_4RT'T$ and the marginal product curve (MP_1 in Figure 10.1b) will be $N_4RS'SA_6A_8$.

On the consumption side, the annual total consumption curves (TC_s and TC_f in Figure 10.1a) depend upon the levels of food consumption that prevail. Let us suppose that per capita food consumption may vary from a minimum biological subsistence level (say 2,000 calories per day) to a maximum, "fully fed" level (say, 3,000 calories per day). In Figure 10.1b let ON_2 measure (on an annual basis) these two extremes of per capita food consumption, as represented by the average consumption curves AC_s and AC_f, respectively. The vertical level of these AC curves then determines the slopes of the corresponding linear total consumption curves of Figure 10.1a.

The slope of each of the several annual total wage curves (TW_1 to TW_4) in Figure 10.1a is similarly dependent upon the relevant annual wage rate (ON_1 to ON_4) as determined by the intersection of the supply-and-demand curves for labor in Figure 10.1b.[2] In the latter figure, the various vertical lines beginning at A_1, A_2, and so on, may be considered the shifting short-run supply curves of labor. For populations up to OA_5 the demand curve for labor will correspond to the marginal product curve $N_4RS'S$. Thus the real annual wage rate will be ON_4 for all populations up to

2. As we shall see later, wages need not be separately considered under a system of owner-operated farms but become highly relevant where the agricultural land is owned by rent-maximizing landlords who hire their farm workers.

OA_2 and ON_3 for a population of OA_3. When population reaches OA_4, the annual wage (ON_2) will be just sufficient to provide a "fully fed" diet. Hence any further increase in population A_4A_5 must mean not only a fall in the wage rate to ON_1, but a deterioration in the diet itself to the subsistence level.[3] Thus AC_s represents the minimum (subsistence) annual wage. For any population in excess of OA_5 (for which $MP_1 = MC_s$) some farm workers must receive more than their specific contributions to food output ($MC_s > MP_1$) in order to survive. Agriculture having thus become "overpopulated," the phase of the MP_1 curve SA_6A_8 loses all relevance as a factor in wage determination, social necessity forcing the abandonment of all efforts to maximize anything but total food output.[4] We shall therefore assume that, for the entire range of possible populations, the average consumption curve is $N_2S'ST$ (Figure 10.1b) and the total consumption curve $OKK'Q'$ (Figure 10.1a).

We now have all the tools necessary to determine the *agricultural surplus*. The annual (total) agricultural surplus is the vertical difference between the total product curve (TP_1) and the relevant total consumption curve (TC_f or TC_s)—VU for a population of OA_1, KL for a population of OA_4, $K'L'$ for a population of OA_5, and PQ for a population of OA_6. The agricultural surplus will entirely disappear only when population reaches its maximum level—OA_7 for a "fully fed" population ($TP_1 = TC_f$), OA_8 when the diet is at the subsistence level ($TP_1 = TC_s$). Thus there will normally be some range of population (such as OA_8) within which there are annual agricultural surpluses of varying but positive magnitude.[5] Each surplus will also be subject to various alternative uses, some of which will promote economic

3. We ignore the possibility that, for any given level of population, food output would fall because workers will have lower energy levels as they become less adequately fed. Otherwise, for populations in excess of OA_4, the total product curve would be lower than that indicated by TP_1.

4. Nicholas Georgescu-Roegen demonstrates convincingly on both empirical and theoretical grounds why this is normally so. Here, our initial assumptions being in conflict, we retain assumption (7) while dropping assumption (5).

5. We shall, however, have occasion later to recognize the possibility that some or all of a particular country's agricultural land might be so infertile that TP would coincide with, or lie entirely below, the TC_s curve (cf. footnote 23).

development more than others. To this problem we now turn, first considering conditions of *under*population, then conditions of *over*population.

In the section that immediately follows, we shall limit ourselves to that range of agricultural populations (OA_5) for which the marginal product of farm labor equals or exceeds the subsistence wage rate. Countries whose agricultural population is so large (greater than OA_5) that the marginal product of farm labor falls below the subsistence wage will be considered "overpopulated" and analyzed in a later section.

"AGRICULTURAL SURPLUS" IN AN UNDERPOPULATED COUNTRY

Let us first consider the case of an "underpopulated" country—that is, one in which land is initially so relatively abundant that it is a "free good." We shall analyze the economic development of such a country and the role an agricultural surplus can play in that development. We will consider two types of agriculture—that consisting of one sector (food production only) and that having two sectors (food and industrial crops).

A ONE-SECTOR AGRICULTURAL ECONOMY

Let us assume a newly settled country whose entire population is engaged in food production. Suppose further that there is an agricultural surplus—that is, more food production than the existing population needs for its own subsistence—but no opportunities for international trade. Since the food surplus would then have no alternative value in the form of imported consumer or producer goods, it would be extremely difficult, if not impossible, to develop a domestic nonfood sector beyond the handicraft stage. Under these circumstances any population of less than OA_7 would be surfeited with food, and there would be a maximum incentive for population growth. Thus, starting with a relatively small population of (say) OA_2, one might expect population to follow an equilibrium adjustment path (Figure 10.1a) along TP_1 from M to the intersection with the TC_f curve.[6] Up to this point $(TP_1 = TC_f)$ at which population was OA_7, there would also be no incentive to improve farming techniques. If the population grew beyond OA_7, the path would (unless techniques were now improved) move horizontally along TP_1 to Q' as the TC curve gradually swung down to its minimum level, TC_s. With $TP_1 = TC_s$, an absolute maximum population of OA_8 would have been reached.

Fortunately such "new" countries as those of the Americas and Australia were born after channels of international trade had been well developed. Let us therefore assume instead that any food surpluses produced in our newly settled country may be freely and profitably exchanged for foreign-produced goods under constant terms of trade. The relatively high levels of living which such exchangeable food surpluses (over and above complete satisfaction of food needs) make possible would then probably become habitual, thereby favoring voluntary restraints on population growth in order to enjoy further material progress. By what process might such material progress take place? Since our analysis depends in part on the land-tenure system assumed, we shall consider separately the situation in which all farms are owner-operated and that in which farm workers do not own the land they cultivate.

A System of Agricultural Freeholders

Let us assume in this section that the "new" nation has a liberal and equalitarian land-settlement policy, distributing all available "free land" in units of family size, so that the prevailing system of land tenure is one of owner-operated farms. Each farmer, being at once landlord and laborer, will then seek to maximize his total returns from land and labor combined. This means that he will maximize his *average* (not total) agricultural surplus. For any population up to OA_2, farming techniques remaining constant, the average agricultural surplus $(AP_1 - AC_f)$ will

be at a maximum RC (Figure 10.1b). Per capita real income (which may be measured by the height of AP_1, since the economy is entirely agricultural) will also be at its maximum level, RA_2. Hence, OA_2 may be considered the optimum population, for the given technology, in a nation of agricultural freeholders.[7]

There is no reason to assume, however, that population growth will cease when it has reached OA_2. To be sure, agricultural freeholders—having become habituated to a high real level of living and mindful of the dangers of their landholdings becoming fragmented through inheritance—might be expected to impose considerable voluntary restraints upon further population growth. However, even a moderate increase in population from OA_2 to OA_4 would significantly reduce the per capita agricultural surplus if nothing is done to raise agricultural productivity or to create nonagricultural employment. For, while the *total* agricultural surplus would continue to increase from MJ to LK, the *average* surplus would fall from RC to GS'. Thus, if the entire current agricultural surplus is consumed (presumably in the form of imported consumer goods), it must be at the expense of lower per capita real income as population grows beyond OA_2.

This need not happen, however, if part of the agricultural surplus is accumulated and directly or indirectly invested in essential

---

6. This particular adjustment path follows from our initial assumptions (5) and (7). The assumption that labor is a constant fraction of population is somewhat awkward, however, given the significant time lag before newly born children can become part of the labor force. If we recognize such discontinuities in the adjustment of the size of the labor force by dropping assumption (5), the adjustment path might alternatively run horizontally from M to the TC_f curve, vertically to the TP_1 curve, horizontally to the TC_f curve, and so on, until $TP_1 = TC_f$.

7. Any population smaller than OA_2 will surely grow to that level, since (given constant international terms of trade) population increase costs nothing in per capita real terms. Strictly speaking, there will be certain necessary social overhead costs associated with population growth. An important example is investments in transportation, since the available land is "free" only after it and its product have been made accessible. Similarly, the population will probably not reach OA_8 (at which all "free" land has been taken up) before agricultural techniques are improved. Indeed, each farmer—having all the land he needs but being unable to hire farm workers at a wage below their maximum average product (RA_2)—can increase his real income *only* by improving his techniques. In both instances, however, accumulation and direct or indirect investment out of agricultural surplus will probably pay off handsomely by way of the growth in the size of that agricultural surplus. In addition, with the concomitant growth in the size of the domestic market, increasing opportunities for development of an industrial sector (again financed initially out of agricultural surplus) will probably already have been seized before the population reaches OA_2. For reasons of convenience, however, let us assume that, at a population of OA_2, TP_1 reflects the effects of any prior investment in social overhead and in agricultural techniques and that the nonagricultural sector employs a negligible part of the total population.

types of social overhead, in a domestic nonagricultural sector, and in improved agricultural techniques. More specifically, farm owner-operators need not become progressively worse off as population grows from OA_2 to OA_4: (1) if A_2A_4 jobs can be created in the nonagricultural sector, the *agricultural* population remaining constant at OA_2; (2) if, through investment in better agricultural techniques, farmers can raise the total product curve (TP_1) sufficiently to permit an agricultural population of OA_4 to enjoy an average product of at least A_4G' ($=A_2R$); or (3) by some combination of the two. Given an initial agricultural surplus of MJ, the initial financing for one or both of these alternatives (and associated social overhead investments) can be found.

Let us look first at social overhead investment, since, if wisely made, it may contribute significantly to both industrial development and agricultural improvements. A nation of agricultural freeholders, producing a substantial agricultural surplus, is in an unusually favorable position to minimize the role of government. To a very large extent the achievement of an optimum allocation of the agricultural surplus among nonfood consumption, nonagricultural investment, and agricultural investment can be left to the voluntary decisions of private enterprise. Nonetheless, an agriculture of equalitarian structure is likely to be particularly aware of the need for certain public services that individual farm families cannot provide for themselves satisfactorily, if at all. At the same time an equalitarian agriculture will probably be associated with a democratic sociopolitical environment, in which government is responsive to demands for the public services that a majority of small landowners want and are willing (through taxes) to pay for.

Hence, at a minimum, government will probably be called upon to assume the role of assuring an optimum rate of direct or indirect public investment in transportation, education, agricultural research and extension services, banking and credit institutions, and other types of social overhead. To provide such social services for any given population, government will presumably tax away some part of the agricultural surplus. To that extent the funds immediately available for imported consumer goods and private domestic invest-

ment will be reduced. However, subsequent returns on private investment in either agriculture (whose TP_1 curve will rise, increasing the agricultural surplus for the given population) or the nonagricultural sector will presumably be higher.

Let us now consider more generally the contributions that an initial agricultural surplus can make to both nonagricultural development and to agricultural improvements. For analytical purposes, let us incorporate social overhead and government into our model by the following assumption. Any given investment is allocated between tangibles (plant and equipment) and intangibles (social overhead) in such a way as to maximize the response in terms of productivity, the sources of that investment —whether private (voluntary savings) or public (taxes)—being in the proportions consistent with its optimum allocation.

It seems reasonable to suppose that as population grows to OA_2 and beyond, there will be an increasing number of opportunities for profitable investments in a nonagricultural sector. This is particularly likely under our assumption of an equalitarian land ownership pattern, the equitable distribution of incomes favoring the development of a demand for a broad range of goods and services. While initial opportunities will lie primarily in the residentiary industries (retail and wholesale trade and other services, and in the manufacture of bulky goods too costly if imported from afar), the growing size of the domestic market will increasingly permit import-substituting manufacturing enterprises to achieve an efficient scale of operations.

Suppose then that, with an entirely agricultural population of OA_2, enough of the initial agricultural surplus MJ is shifted from consumption to nonagricultural investment to provide nonfarm employment for a small increment of population A_2A_2' at a real wage of A_2R. Insofar as this initial investment goes into industrial *fixed* capital, an equivalent part of the food surplus will now have to be exchanged for imported industrial producer goods instead of imported consumer goods. In addition, part of the initial investment will take the form of advances of a major component of industrial *working* capital—the food needed to feed the nonfarm population. As the consequence of such investment, exports

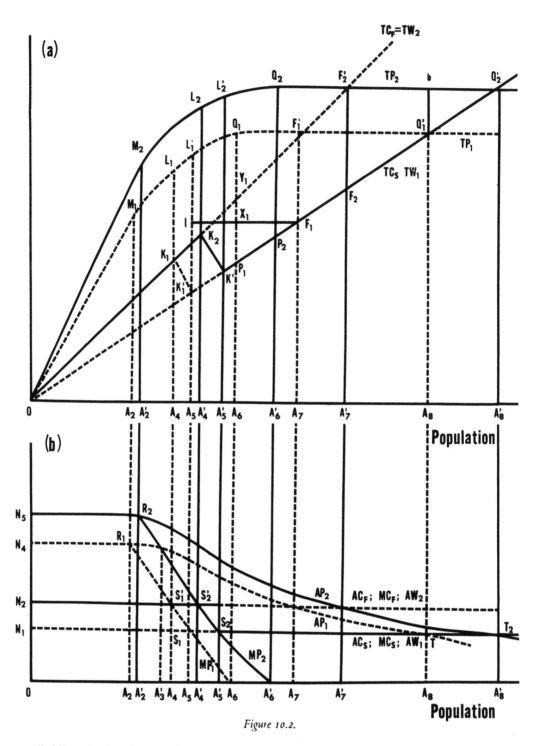

Figure 10.2.

will fall as food is diverted from the export market to domestic consumption. While initially small, this loss of export revenue will become increasingly significant as the non-agricultural population grows toward A_2A_4, at which level WJ of the constant agricultural surplus MJ will be consumed as food by the nonagricultural sector.

Declining food exports need cause no problem, however, if farmers shift their expenditures for industrial consumer goods from foreign to domestic sources in step with the shifts in the market for food from foreign to domestic outlets. Thus, by the time total population reaches OA_4, OA_2 farmers may meet the nonagricultural sector's needs for WJ food by purchasing an equivalent amount of domestic industrial goods, the exchange having to that extent become internal rather than international.[8] By such import replacement the agricultural population can also provide the nonagricultural sector with a major part of the market needed for its growing output of industrial goods. In addition, the investment in the nonagricultural sector will have generated income that —whether accruing to manufacturers and industrial workers or (as nonfarm investment income) to farmers—will presumably not only maintain but increase the effective demand for industrial goods, domestic or foreign.

Unless the "new" nation's natural endowment for agricultural production is exceptionally poor, however, it is unlikely that a population increase from OA_2 to OA_4 would be entirely absorbed in the nonagricultural sector. More likely, at some intermediate point, if not at the outset, the relative returns on capital investment in agricultural improvements would exceed those on nonagricultural investment. This being so, suppose that part of the export revenue derived from the agricultural sector, raising the total product curve of agriculture from TP_1 to TP_2 (Figure 10.2a). The optimum agricultural population would then increase from OA_2 to OA_2',[9] its per capita farm income at the same time increasing from $R_1 R_2$ to $R_2 A_2'$ (Figure 10.2b). In this case, of the assumed increment of total population $A_2 A_4$, $A_2 A_2'$ would find profitable employment in agriculture, reducing to $A_2' A_4$ the number of farm people who would have to find nonfarm employment in order to prevent per capita income in agriculture from declining along AP_2.

Whether any given agricultural surplus would be sufficient to provide the nonagricultural investment needed to employ a given number of people (such as $A_2' A_4$) at a *given* wage ($R_2 A_2'$) cannot be determined a priori. However, the chances of doing so would have been considerably improved as the result of the agricultural improvements assumed, since the size of the agricultural surplus (and food supply) would have substantially increased. Hence, greater resources than before would be available for nonfarm investment and further agricultural investment. In any case, a population of OA_4 (even if entirely in agriculture) would be better off than was the smaller farm population OA_2 before the agricultural improvements were made.

However, achievement of an optimum allocation of the agricultural surplus might be prevented by certain institutional factors. Thus, the equalitarian structure of agricultural surplus might tend to favor excessive investment in agricultural improvements, since farmers would have a particularly strong interest in improving their own land, while perhaps lacking full knowledge of alternative investment opportunities in the nonagricultural sector. On the other hand, if a political majority can be won for public policies that use taxes, import duties, direct public subsidies, or inflation to provide funds for nonagricultural investment, there may well be excessive investment in the industrial sector. An agrarian democracy would presumably be in the best political position to prevent unduly heavy taxation of agriculture to promote industry. However, commercial-industrial minorities have historically shown surprising success in winning sufficient political support from agriculture—through appeals to national pride, considerations of national security, and persuasion of farmers to ignore their own immediate economic self-interest[10]—to establish such public policies at an early stage.

8. Farmers will have no reason voluntarily to avoid such import replacement if the prices and qualities of domestic industrial goods are the same as those of foreign origin and if the domestic product mix corresponds to farmers' preference patterns. However, if domestic manufacturers can produce profitably only with tariff protection, internal terms of trade will turn against agriculture and encourage its premature contraction at the expense of the agricultural surplus and food exports. While there will be a considerable incentive on the demand side for the industrial sector to produce the product mix desired by farmers, comparative advantages within the industrial sector may favor a somewhat different product mix. In this case, however, parts of the nonagricultural sector will have to find sufficient export markets to earn the additional exchange which that sector needs for purchasing its residual food needs from the domestic agricultural sector.

9. This would correspond with the empirical fact that, in the earlier stages of economic development, the agricultural population continues to grow absolutely but not relatively.

10. The willingness of the corn and wheat farmers of the United States Midwest to adhere for over a century to high-tariff policies, despite their heavy dependence on export markets, is a classic example. Regional differences in comparative advantage and consequent economic interests; the greater political and cultural leadership of coastal regions and capital cities, which earliest experience commercial, industrial, and urban development; and disenfranchisement of illiterates and slaves (which works to the political disadvantage of rural areas) have also been historically important factors favoring industrial interests in largely agricultural countries.

By such means "infant" industries may be created before they are yet profitable enough to attract adequate private funds in the absence of public protection and subsidies. If so, the short-run effect will be a shift in the terms of trade against agriculture, a decline in the level of voluntary savings by farmers out of a given agricultural surplus, discouragement of investments in agricultural improvements, and a slower rate of expansion (perhaps even a reduction) in food output and the size of the agricultural surplus. Hence, unless the "infant" industries are capable of rather quickly becoming self-sustaining, the potential contributions of the agricultural surplus to general economic development may not be fully realized, food exports falling more rapidly than their equivalent in terms of import replacement.

Despite this danger, a system of agricultural freeholders would appear to be most favorable to the establishment of a process of "balanced" growth, during which excesses of investment in either agriculture or industry are largely avoided. In such a favorable politicoeconomic environment an initially large and growing agricultural surplus can serve as the principal means of getting industrial (and general) development under way.

International terms of trade remaining constant, the extent to which it will continue to pay to allocate investment to agriculture will, of course, depend in considerable part on the richness of the nation's natural endowment. If this endowment is sufficiently rich (as in the United States or New Zealand), agriculture's TP curve will continue to respond satisfactorily to further investment in improved techniques until very late in the development process. In nations with a less rich endowment (England or Japan) agriculture's initial role may be no less important. However, relatively larger allocations of investment to the industrial sector will be warranted at an earlier stage of development, such nations perhaps ultimately even becoming net importers of food. If the international terms of trade shift in favor of food products, any given TP curve for agriculture, while constant in physical terms, will be shifting upward in value terms, encouraging greater relative emphasis on agriculture. The opposite will be true if the terms of trade

move against food products, particularly if the given country becomes a sufficiently large food exporter that, by its own increased exports, it lowers the world price.

While agriculture's physical productivity (TP) can be progressively raised only by capital investment, the form that such investment should take will vary with the changing relative scarcities of the several productive factors. Once all available land has come under cultivation, investments in land-saving improvements will immediately become appropriate. Whether early capital investments in agriculture should also be labor-saving will depend upon whether agriculture's capital stock or its population is growing more rapidly. At the outset population may be outpacing capital, in which case capital investments that are labor-saving should be avoided, since the result would be the creation of a redundant labor force and enforced (unwanted) leisure in the absence of sufficient alternative nonfarm job opportunities. As economic progress brings a faster rate of capital accumulation than of population growth in agriculture, however, investment in that sector can take on a progressively more labor-saving character, this tendency being greatly accelerated once the nonagricultural sector has developed so far that the *absolute* agricultural population begins to fall. Only at that stage will the size of the farm (in terms of land) begin to increase, opening the way for full-scale mechanization of farming operations. Similar principles hold for the nonagricultural sector.[11]

A System of Landlords and Tenants

How will our previous analysis be affected if we assume that individual farms are operated by renters or hired workers rather than by

11. As Fellner [1956, Ch. viii] has shown, under conditions in which capital has begun to grow more rapidly than labor as well as land, uninterrupted growth requires that cost-saving innovations in both agriculture and industry be sufficiently plentiful to absorb all new savings without permitting the yield on the growing stock of capital in the two sectors to fall below some necessary minimum level of return. The form that such improvements take must also change in order to be compatible with changing relative scarcities. In the absence of government interference, which prematurely promotes the adoption of labor-saving types of improvements, however, forms of improvements are likely to be *induced* that are compatible with a fairly constant rate of return on investment and continuing full employment at *rising* real wages.

their owners? Given a landlord-tenant system, landlords would seek to maximize the returns (rent) on their land (the vertical difference between TP_1 and the relevant TW curve in Figure 10.1a) for any given agricultural population by equating MP_1 and the going wage rate.

Let us first note, however, that, given a society of free men and an equalitarian land-settlement policy, a landlord-tenant system could be established in an "underpopulated" country only under special circumstances. Given constant agricultural technology, an agricultural population of OA_2 or less would result in a real wage so high (AW_4) that the corresponding TW_4 curve would coincide with the TP_1 curve along OM and landlords would receive *no* rent. Land would be too plentiful to have any scarcity value, so that the entire agricultural surplus would accrue to farmers as workers $(AP_1 = AW_4)$ even if they did not own the land. Not only would there be no economic incentive for the creation of a separate landlord class but, at the same time, agricultural workers would certainly not be available for hire, since they could freely acquire land of their own.

Once a system of freeholders had thus been established, it could be *generally* displaced by a new landlord class only if some special group (domestic or foreign) had superior access to the knowledge, capital, and markets needed to raise agricultural productivity substantially, particularly by achieving certain potential economies of scale. Presumably owner-operators would be willing to sell their land only if they were offered a price that would give them a stream of discounted future annual incomes greater than that based on their current return (the vertical difference between AP_1 and the appropriate AW) on the land by a premium sufficient to compensate them for their loss of satisfaction when they give up their status as landowners. Thus, for any given agricultural population, would-be landlords would have to anticipate having TP and AP curves that were higher than TP_1 and AP_1 by at least the amount of this premium if they were to be able to offer a price sufficient to persuade owner-operators to give up their land. This premium would presumably be greater the greater the agricultural population, for population growth would bring increasing rewards for

land ownership and declining labor income, with a consequent enhancement of the social status associated with working one's own land.

Let us pursue this matter further by supposing that a landlord class could achieve a total product curve of TP_2, while owner-operators (lacking equal access to the means of achieving such agricultural improvements) continued to produce according to TP_1 (Figure 10.2a). For populations of less than OA_2', there would be no incentive (apart from possible speculative motives) for a landlord class to establish itself in the absence of a bonded labor force (indentured workers, peons, or slaves). In a free labor market wages would rise from R_1A_2 to R_2A_2' (Figure 10.2b), absorbing all the gains in productivity that the landlord-tenant system was capable of achieving.[12] If the population increased beyond OA_2', however, wages under the new system would fall below R_2A_2' and landlords could anticipate some rent insofar as former owner-operators had not captured part of this rent as a premium for selling their land.

For purposes of further analysis, let us assume that AP_1 includes this necessary premium for each agricultural population. Then OA_3' becomes the critical level of

12. For agricultural populations of less than OA_2 the major problem facing would-be landlords would be a scarcity of wage labor, not land. Land would be no less "free" to them than to the original owner-operator class unless application of their superior techniques required landholdings larger than some prevailing legal ceiling on the size of settlement unit specified in the nation's public land policy. In the latter case, they might have to resort to land purchase from earlier settlers (cf. footnote 14 below), even though unsettled land was still available to others and was not of a quality less than that of settled land. In any case, if those having access to superior techniques could also meet their labor requirements from their own families, two separate classes of owner-operators (operating at sharply different levels of technique and productivity) might emerge. However, if the class with superior techniques had the desire or necessity of hiring much or all of its farm labor force, the profitability of its doing so in a free labor market would depend upon the level to which it bid up wage rates. At best, would-be landlords could hire former owner-operators at slightly above their opportunity cost of R_1A_2; at worst, they would force the wage rate up to its maximum level of R_2A_2'. Initially, the number of hired workers demanded might be so small a proportion of the agricultural population that the wage rate would be only slightly above R_1A_2, permitting partial replacement of the owner-operator system on a profitable basis. However, in the text we suppose that the would-be landlords' demand curve for labor would be shifting to the right sufficiently more rapidly than the supply curve of labor (population) so that the wage rate would quickly rise to and remain at its maximum level of R_2A_2', thereby bringing such displacement to a halt long before it had become general.

population at which the wages (MP_2) that can be earned by working the landlords' land are just sufficient to compensate for the loss of wages, rent, and status (AP_1) that could be earned under the less productive owner-operator system. For populations between OA'_2 and OA'_3, workers would be better off under a landlord-tenant system than if they operated their own farms. Therefore, within this range of populations the purchase of land by would-be landlords would be facilitated by the fact that sellers would enjoy a wage premium, as a result of which the extent of their encroachment (via the selling price of land) on the landlords' rental income would probably be reduced. If the owner-operator system remained intact until the agricultural population had grown beyond OA'_3, however, the increasing gap between AP_1 and MP_2 would have to be compensated for by increasing land prices. Thus, for populations in excess of OA'_3, the landlords' rent would be restricted to the vertical distance between TP_2 and TP_1, lessening the opportunities for the more productive landlord class to establish itself.

We may conclude that, for any given difference in productivity (level of TP) assumed for the two systems, the opportunities for a change to a landlord-tenant system would be best when the agricultural population had grown slightly beyond OA'_2, particularly if the owner-operators showed less foresight than the would-be landlords about the consequences of further population growth. A change to landlordism would also be more likely, the greater its superiority in terms of productivity, since the more TP_2 exceeded TP_1, the greater the initial wage premium and the greater the range of populations (the farther right A'_3) within which it would pay owner-operators to sell their land.

Finally, it is worth noting that, under certain special circumstances, a landlord-tenant system might replace an owner-operator system even for populations of less than OA'_2. If one allows for some differences in the quality (including locational advantages) of the land, it might be easier for landlords to persuade certain freeholders to sell their land while they still have the opportunity of moving with an advancing "frontier," where they can again set themselves up as owner-operators on still available "free

land."[13] However, the landlord class would still have to solve the problem of labor scarcity, since the free agricultural work force on the older lands would decline as former freeholders (except for the impecunious) either reestablished themselves elsewhere in agriculture or used their newly won capital to establish nonagricultural enterprises. Thus, even if the opportunities for agricultural reorganization were very large, the partial displacement of a system of owner-operators for populations of less than OA'_2 would probably be possible only if accompanied by the introduction of a system of indenture, peonage, or slavery.

Insofar as the initial freeholders succeeded at an early date in winning public investments in social overhead (which would help to equalize differences in knowledge, foresight, site value, and the like), the original freeholding system would probably be preserved unless potential economies of scale in agriculture were considerable. There are few types of food production for which economies of scale are so great as to require such an outcome. If an increasingly unequal distribution of land ownership ultimately grew out of initial equality in the food-producing sector, it would therefore be largely the cumulative result of actual differences in the quality of land, social-overhead investment, and the like, which we have assumed to be absent. On the other hand, certain industrial crops may be of such a nature that large-scale production on a landlord-tenant basis may produce substantial economies. In an "under-populated" country well suited for such industrial crops, therefore, agriculture might ultimately take on a dual character, with one sector producing food on family-sized farms under a freeholding system and another sector producing industrial crops on large-scale plantations, whose workers did not own their own land. We shall return briefly to this case of a two-sector agricultural economy in a later section.

But what if the original land-settlement policy was oligarchic rather than equali-

13. This actually happened in the Southern Piedmont during 1830–1850. Tidewater cotton planters bought and consolidated the land of small, largely subsistence freeholders (who had settled the Piedmont in the latter part of the previous century), the latter moving west, where they could take up "free" land once more. This process might not have been possible, in spite of the high profitability of cotton at that time, if the planters had not been able to bring their labor supply (slaves) in with them

tarian? For example, assume that, as in much of Latin America, most of the initially unsettled land was granted by the Crown to a few favored individuals. Such a situation would probably tend to lead to an agricultural structure characterized by a very few landlords, renting many operating units to an equal number of worker families, who supply all of the farm labor. Before analyzing this important special case, we must make certain special assumptions if the curves of Figure 10.1 are to be as valid for a landed oligarchy as for a system of agricultural freeholders. First, if we define the agricultural population as the total of the landlord and tenant populations, the landlord population must constitute a negligible proportion of the whole.[14] Second, there must be no difference in the productivity of renters (workers) and owner-operators, so that TP_1 is equally valid for either. Finally, let us assume that the landlords either hire their workers for the lowest possible wage in kind or achieve the same effect by rent charges (whether in cash or crop shares) for use of the land that net the tenant an equivalent to the going wage.[15]

14. A more general solution would require drawing a negative coordinate to the left of o in Figure 10.1a measuring the landlord population to the left and only the worker population to the right of the origin. Then, the subsistence of the landlord population being a fixed charge on the economy, the TC_f (or TC_s) curve would begin at the (negative) point representing the landlord population, with the same slope ($=MC_f$ or MC_s) as before.

15. This assumption means that, even if land is rented on the basis of crop shares (that is, a fixed proportion of the total output for any given population), the landlords can exact an increasing share as population increases—at least so long as the residual left to the tenant is above the subsistence level ON_1. Such an assumption appears to be eminently reasonable, particularly in a new country in which noneconomic factors would be least likely to have caused the establishment of "traditional" shares unrelated to market conditions. Even so, however, suppose that for some reason a customary landlord's share of $1/k$ was established that was constant regardless of population. Whatever the value of k, tenants would (like owner-operators) prefer an agricultural population of OA_2 or less, since they would then be best off per capita; but the landlord class would prefer that tenant population (OA_6 in Figure 10.1a) that would maximize $1/k$ of TP ($=1/k$ of A_6Q), hence TP. However, k remaining constant, population cannot exceed that level at which $(1-1/k)TP$ falls below TC_s. If this critical level of population is less than OA_6, the landlords would have to settle for a total income less than the maximum. The smaller the value of k (the larger the landlord's share), the more likely this outcome would be. Alternatively, if the tenant population grows beyond the critical level, the threat of starvation might generate social pressures or force that would reduce the landlord's share, thereby permitting the larger population to persist at the expense of the landlord's income.

Given oligarchic control of all land from the outset of settlement, the few landlords might be able to extract considerable rent for populations well below OA_2. Thus they might exploit their monopoly of land by releasing it for use by would-be settlers in only that quantity that would maximize their rent, using private armies or other devices to protect unused land against squatters and interlopers. Given the settlers' derived demand curve for land, suppose that a settler population of OA_1 would maximize total rents at VU (Figure 10.1a). That low level of population would then net as wages only ON_2 instead of ON_4, the difference accruing to the oligarchy as rent.[16] The total agricultural surplus available for purchase of foreign industrial goods would initially be considerably smaller (VU instead of, say, MJ) than under a "free"-land policy. However, because of the highly unequal distribution of income, the landlord class could already live in comparative luxury if it chose to do so.

Nonetheless, insofar as population grew beyond OA_1 without the necessity of increasing the wage above ON_2, the landlords' total rents would (up to a population of OA_4) be increasing. Hence, the oligarchy might find it profitable to introduce a positive

16. For purposes of this analysis, we assume that the supply curve of land coincides with the horizontal axis up to the point at which all land is in use, where the supply curve becomes vertical. Assuming, as before, that there is a constant ratio of labor to land for populations less than OA_2, we can measure settler population as well as quantity of land horizontally, so long as all land is not in use. Furthermore, the marginal product of land will be constant over the same range. The settlers' demand curve for land can be derived from this constant gross product by subtracting from it vertically the supply curve of settlers, which presumably must cut the vertical axis at a wage equal to at least the subsistence wage ON_1. (The example in the text implies that a higher wage ON_2 is required to attract OA_1 settlers.) Unless this supply curve of settlers is completely elastic, the demand curve for land will be falling. If this demand curve cuts the horizontal axis at or to the left of the point at which all land is in use, it will determine the number of settlers who will be attracted by a "free"-land (no-rent) policy. Given oligarchic land ownership, however, the amount of land (hence number of settlers) would be sharply restricted to the point at which *marginal* (not average) revenue equals zero. Only if the supply curve of settlers were very elastic, so that marginal revenue equaled zero to the right of the point at which all land had been released for use, would it pay landlords to cease their restrictive practices. If the population grew sufficiently beyond OA_1, whether because of the increasing ease of attracting immigrants or natural increase, this would in any case be the ultimate outcome as the demand curve for land shifted to the right.

recruitment program to shift the supply curve of settlers (hence the demand curve for land) to the right. Given more time, the same result might be achieved through natural increase, either that of the original settlers or that of more heavily populated countries, increasing the numbers who would be willing to migrate to the new country at the given wage rate.

But suppose the landed oligarchy were unable to attract the desired number of free immigrant workers (perhaps in part because its efforts to bar squatters were not wholly successful) and were too impatient to depend upon the natural increase of the initial settlers? Alternatively, it might find it possible to reduce any indigenous labor to peonage or might import slaves, turning such artificially cheap sources of labor (at the minimum possible wage AC_s) to the production of a larger agricultural surplus. For example, for a peon or slave population of OA_2, they might win for themselves MJ', even larger than the agricultural surplus MJ that the same number of owner-operators (preferring a more generous diet) would choose to produce. Even if the peons or slaves were less productive than free men, so that TP_1 were lower, the landlords would probably retain a considerable part of the lower agricultural surplus, none of which they could capture if they had to hire an equivalent number of unbonded settlers at the necessary market wage A_2R. Insofar as the indigenous population proved to be a passable labor force, as in Mexico or Peru, such a latifundium system might well be ended only by revolutionary methods. However, insofar as slavery was the preferred source of agricultural labor, the system might gradually die out, through a tendency for the cost of slave labor to rise toward the alternative of hiring free men; in the United States and Brazil the historical trend well before abolition was toward rising import prices of slaves (as an increasing demand faced an increasingly restricted supply).

In any case, let us now assume that, by the time the agricultural population actually reaches OA_2, the landlord class must (for whatever reason) man its agricultural operations with completely free labor hired at the going market rate A_2R. Whatever their previous success in exacting income by means

that made land artificially scarce and labor artificially cheap, the landlords can now regain their advantage only if the agricultural population grows further. Should the population grow to OA_3, the real wage will fall from AW_4 to AW_3, and the rent will rise from nil to $V'F$. For a still larger population, the real wage will decline to $AC_f(=AW_2)$ and the rent will increase to KL. The size of the agricultural surplus for any given population will be the same (assuming TP_1 constant) as under an owner-operator system, the only difference being in how the surplus is distributed. For a population of OA_2, the workers will capture the entire surplus MJ. For an intermediate population of OA_3, the surplus will be $V'U'$, of which the landlords will receive $V'E$ as rent and the workers EU'. For a population of OA_4, the entire surplus KL will accrue to the landlords.

Thus, unlike either owner-operators or agricultural workers, the landlord class will benefit from an increase in the agricultural population beyond OA_2 because it has a strong interest in cheap labor and dear land. Such an increase in the worker population, unless accompanied by the creation of an equivalent number of nonfarm jobs, must mean a rapidly increasing concentration of agricultural income in the hands of the few landlords. Under these circumstances is an agricultural surplus of equal magnitude likely to serve with the same effectiveness in contributing to nonagricultural and agricultural improvements, hence to general economic growth?

Let us begin with social overhead investment. At a population of OA_2, since the agricultural workers command the entire agricultural surplus, they are as able as the same number of owner-operators to finance such investment. Hence, if the worker class is equally cognizant of the advantages to itself of public outlays for the general welfare, it may be quite willing to pay the necessary taxes if government is responsive to its wishes. It is possible, however, that the landed oligarchy (while currently deriving no *economic* advantages from land ownership) will dominate the political process. If so, the landlords as politicians will be happy to tax away part of the initial agricultural surplus enjoyed by the worker class. But they will probably direct the resulting public revenues largely toward those types of social overhead which primarily benefit the landowner and toward subsidies for the establishment of importing firms, agricultural trading and processing enterprises, and banks, which they themselves dominate. They will probably see little advantage to themselves in public investments in the education of the masses or workers. Insofar as they are able to gain control of the marketing and banking process, they may even be able to squeeze out part of the (real) agricultural surplus for themselves by paying abnormally low prices for the workers' products and charging the workers abnormally high prices for imported merchandise and for credit.

If the worker population of OA_2 is unable to overthrow such "taxation without representation" when its economic power is greatest, its chances of breaking out decline rapidly as its numbers grow beyond OA_2. As this happens, the economic power of the landlord class quickly increases at the expense of the workers. Increasingly the principal source for financing social overhead, the sociopolitically dominant landlord class will rarely be willing to tax itself in order to support such public services as education and agricultural extension. Hence social overhead investments are likely to lag far behind the levels that a democratic society dominated by agricultural freeholders would be able to achieve.[17]

To what extent might the workers be able to avoid such an outcome by financing investment in nonagricultural enterprise out of the agricultural surplus? At a population of OA_2, the worker class would capture the entire surplus. If the landed oligarchy were willing to sell its land,[18] the workers might give first priority to using the surplus to enable them to become owner-operators, in which case the analysis of the previous section

would become appropriate. However, if we assume that land purchase is not possible, one might expect the workers to be particularly interested in nonagricultural investment, since they have no incentive to invest in permanent improvements in land that they do not themselves own. Such investment would give them protection against exploitation by any trading monopolies controlled by the landlord class, and initially at least, there would be the same effective demand for a broad range of goods and services as under an owner-operator system.

The barriers to such investment by agricultural workers would be considerably greater, however. First, the landlord class might use its political power to bar their direct entry into nonagricultural enterprise and its economic power (through control of the banking system), to frustrate their choice of the nonagricultural investments best serving their own needs and interests. Second, the workers' initially favorable economic condition would be more likely to encourage a higher rate of natural increase (at the expense of accumulation) than if they owned the land they cultivated. Third, given their lower social status and lesser educational advantages, they might be less aware of nonagricultural investment opportunities and less self-reliant, venturesome, and foresighted.

Given such barriers, they would probably be less successful than owner-operators in preventing the agricultural population from increasing beyond OA_2. If their numbers did increase, they would have much less financial staying power for creating enough nonfarm employment to keep their real wage from falling, since their share of the agricultural surplus would decline rapidly. Any nonagricultural investment they might have made at the outset would have to have been sufficiently profitable to become almost immediately self-sustaining. For they probably could not long maintain at initial levels the investments out of their rapidly falling annual farm income, even if this income were supplemented by some nonfarm investment income. Furthermore, their original nonagricultural investments could easily prove to have been misdirected in view of the rapidly growing concentration of income in the

---

17. I have argued elsewhere that this actually happened in the United States South [Nicholls, 1960, 106–113].

18. At a population of OA_2, the landlords might be expected to be most willing to sell their land, since it produced no rent. If they had accumulated sufficient wealth from the past, however, they might choose to hold on to their land in anticipation of a rapid rise in land values as population increased beyond OA_2, or if significant population growth was not expected, they might see opportunities for investing in agricultural improvements that would produce rents at a population of OA_2 or slightly more.

hands of a few rich landlords, who would presumably want a very different product mix than the masses of workers. For such reasons, nonagricultural enterprises based on investment and consumption by agricultural workers might easily die aborning.

If, then, the agricultural population grows well beyond OA_2, the key factors determining whether or not the given country enjoys economic growth or stagnation are the attitudes and motivations of the very small but rich landlord class. If the landlords choose to invest their increasingly great wealth in industrial development and/or agricultural improvements, a process of economic growth may get under way. Where this has happened historically, it has usually been because the landlord class abandoned long-held agrarian (and often hedonistic) values in response to some competing value system whose growing acceptance threatened the landowners' traditional dominance. In both eighteenth-century England and nineteenth-century Japan a new value system—oriented toward concepts of thrift, efficiency, and profit and largely industrial-urban in both origins and objectives—broadly affected the aspirations of the landed oligarchy and enlisted its powerful backing for both agricultural improvement and industrial development.

Here, however, we are primarily concerned with the more typical case, in which landed oligarchies are a strong restraining force on economic development. At a population of OA_2, they would have the greatest incentive to invest in agricultural improvements but, because they receive no rent, lack the resources to do so unless they have previously accumulated wealth. If agricultural population grows from OA_2 to OA_4, their incentive to invest in agricultural improvements will probably decline because, without any effort or sacrifice on their part, their rental incomes will be burgeoning. Furthermore, even if investments in agricultural improvements would increase their incomes (as well as those of their workers) further, they may already be so rich that they are insensitive to such opportunities. The same may be true for investments in the nonagricultural sector, particularly since the landlords may view industrial development as a threat to their socioeconomic power and (because it would raise the cost of agricultural labor) to their

economic well-being as well. In addition, the opportunities for developing domestic industrial enterprises will be greatly limited by the fact that the worker class has few if any resources with which to purchase off-farm goods and services.

Under such circumstances the landlord class will have little incentive to invest in domestic enterprises other than plantation-based agricultural processing or export-import agencies that facilitate the exchange of their large food surplus for foreign industrial goods, mainly luxuries for their own consumption. Otherwise they may invest largely in "safe" bonds and shares in more developed countries, exporting most of the benefits of the increasing income from food exports to other countries. There will be little or no internal multiplier effect by which the export base might be broadened, the size of the domestic market expanded, and the growth of complementary and subsidiary industries encouraged. The neglect of investment in social overhead (especially education) will impose another important barrier to economic growth [North, 1961, Ch. 1].

In such a static situation it is quite conceivable that an originally "underpopulated" country can slip over into a condition of "overpopulation." The crucial question here is what happens during the phase of population growth A_4A_5. The landlord class may even view favorably the further growth of agricultural population from OA_4 to OA_5 since total land rents will become even larger (growing from LK to $L'K'$) as the workers' diet is squeezed down to the bare subsistence level AC_8. Even so, such a view will prove to be shortsighted from the standpoint of the landlords' own self-interest. First, the deterioration of the workers' food intake may affect worker energy and productivity, lowering the TP curve. Second, once the agricultural population has reached OA_5, any further increase will mean that the marginal productivity of labor (MP_1) falls below the subsistence wage AC_8. At this point, social pressures for "make work" and dangers of worker revolt will probably cause nonmarket forces to take over, reducing the landlords' agricultural surplus in proportion as population grows.

Hence, as agricultural population grows

beyond OA_4, a prudent landlord class would be moved to bestir itself at last to seek ways of developing nonagricultural employment for an otherwise redundant labor force and of improving agricultural techniques. While it will now have maximum resources for investing in both domestic industry and its own agriculture, it may well have delayed too long. Given past neglect of opportunities for investing in human capital, for developing necessary economic, social, and political institutions; and for preventing increasing inequalities of income distribution that narrow the domestic market, the pattern of demographic behavior and the whole sociocultural framework may make a transition to a condition of "overpopulation" more probable than achievement of a successful turnabout at this late date.

We must therefore conclude that, with rare exceptions, a landed oligarchy will not be conducive to turning an initially large agricultural surplus into a primary generating force in getting a process of self-sustaining economic growth under way.

A TWO-SECTOR AGRICULTURAL
ECONOMY

Thus far we have assumed that the agriculture of the given country is entirely engaged in food production, any agricultural surplus consisting only of food. Let us consider briefly an alternative situation, in which the agriculture has two sectors—one engaged in food production (largely for domestic consumption) on small owner-operated farms, the other producing industrial crops (largely for export) on large-scale, highly capitalized, well-managed, and highly productive plantations.[19]

In countries in which a sector of the latter type has become important, it has typically been based on foreign capital and management, freeing its initial development from dependence upon domestic financing out of an agricultural surplus in the food-producing sector. However, we need not preclude the possibility that the large-scale sector was developed by a domestic landed oligarchy

that was initially able, on the basis of peon or slave labor, to squeeze out a considerable agricultural surplus in the form of industrial crops (sugar, cotton, tobacco, or coffee) that were readily and profitably exchangeable for any necessary food imports. We might further suppose that the oligarchs lacked sufficient control (or the will to enforce it) over the entire land supply to prevent settlement by owner-operators on the residual unutilized lands. We shall here treat industrial-crop production as if it were part of the nonagricultural sector, centering our attention once more on the food-producing sector. To simplify our analysis, let us assume that the large-scale sector of agriculture produces no food of its own.[20]

In this situation, we may take the curves of Figure 10.1 as representing only that part of agriculture that is engaged in food production on owner-operated farms. Since the large-scale sector has ample resources for meeting its food needs by imports, the food-producing sector need not be more than self-sufficient. For example, suppose that the subsistence wage were ON_4 instead of ON_2 in Figure 10.1a, so that TC_s (now TW_4) coincided with TP_1 over the phase OM. Then, any food-producing population up to OA_2 could produce enough barely to subsist. Suppose instead that ON_3 represented the subsistence diet and ON_4 the "fully fed" diet, so that TW_3 became TC_s and TW_4 became TC_F. Then, a food-producing population of OA_2 or less could enjoy an optimum diet unless it chose to squeeze that diet in order to acquire a minimum amount of nonfood goods by exchange. Any population growth beyond OA_2, however, would have to be at the expense of a poorer diet.

Even if such low productivity in the food-producing sector is due to primitive techniques

19. The analysis that follows would be equally applicable if the large-scale sector produced primary products of nonagricultural origin, such as petroleum or minerals.

20. In large-scale agriculture, this assumption is often approximated in fact because the use of land for industrial-crop production is usually much more profitable; unskilled gang labor of the type used in producing most industrial crops is usually unsuitable for efficient cereal and livestock production; and subsistence food production by workers on plots assigned them by the landlord may, in the latter's view, unduly divert them from their obligations to work at producing the major cash crop. Where the use of such plots is a major part of the total compensation to workers, however, it may be viewed as essentially the equivalent of a subsistence wage, although the quality of the workers' diet would probably be higher than if all food needs had to be met by off-farm purchase.

rather than to an inherently poor natural endowment, the large-scale sector might not be inclined to use any of its resources to improve the situation. To be sure, if TP_1 were raised sufficiently, the large-scale sector would be able to meet its food needs more cheaply through domestic exchange than through imports. Then, by three-way trade, it would (wages remaining constant) command more foreign industrial goods than before, while the food-producing sector could now also import some industrial goods for its own consumption. However, the small-scale structure of the latter sector would in any case discourage direct private investment by the large-scale sector. Furthermore, since wages in the large-scale sector would depend upon the alternative returns that its workers could earn by cultivating their own land, it might consider agricultural improvements in food production unfavorably because they would raise the labor costs. For this reason, it might be reluctant to support (through taxes) *public* investment in the food-producing sector.

The possibility that part of the surplus of the large-scale sector of agriculture will be voluntarily directed into domestic industrial development may also be rather remote. If the large-scale sector is foreign-based, it may be an important adjunct of the colonial policy of the mother country, which may explicitly discourage industrial development of its colony. Even if the large-scale sector is dominated by *indigenous* capital and management, however, the difficulties of mobilizing its surplus for industrial development may be equally great, for the same reasons as those already discussed in the previous section on oligarchic food production. In either case, this sector may make certain important capital investments in irrigation works, railroads, warehousing, docks, and other valuable assets that directly facilitate its operations. But such investments may be too specialized to provide broader benefits to the economy at large. Indeed, such a large-scale sector of agriculture is usually so little integrated with the domestic economy that is only nominally indigenous rather than foreign.

However, one important exception might be noted. If the particular industrial crop becomes less profitable—because of soil exhaustion, plant disease, falling export prices, or otherwise—indigenous capital and management in the large-scale sector will probably seek better alternative domestic investment opportunities elsewhere. This possibility is especially likely if the country produces so large a part of the world supply of the given crop that, by its own expansion, it causes the world price to fall. Such a turn of events may (perhaps in combination with production controls) encourage the strongly profit-motivated entrepreneurs of the large-scale sector to shift resources either into food production or into nonagricultural enterprises.

With this possible exception, effective mobilization of the surplus of large-scale agriculture for general economic development must usually await such political reforms as the winning of national independence or the broadening of the electorate. Only then is it possible to capture through taxation, tariffs, exchange controls, and other political devices this surplus for purposes of general economic development. When this happens, however, there is a strong danger that the effectiveness of the highly productive large-scale sector in earning foreign exchange will be seriously impaired by nationalization (accompanied by inefficient indigenous management), by enforced division into small properties, or by political harassment of foreign capital and management. Even if such a dissipation of the large-scale sector's surplus is avoided, there is a further danger that it will be too largely allocated to industrial development, cutting food imports sharply without sufficient offsetting investment in the domestic food-producing sector. There are probably few countries in which, taking international comparative advantage and alternative domestic investment opportunities fully into account, it will not pay to invest part of the surplus produced by the large-scale agricultural sector in means of raising the food-producing sector's TP curve. In the absence of such investment, the food-producing sector can easily become a serious bottleneck, interrupting a smooth process of industrial-urban development.

Given these problems of mobilizing the surplus of a highly productive large-scale agricultural sector for general economic development, a country that also has from the outset a relatively productive and equalitarian food-producing sector is indeed fortunate. For then the agricultural surplus of the food-producing sector can play the same active role as that already discussed in an earlier section, serving as the principal source for financing both agricultural and nonagricultural investments and providing a broad market for domestic manufactures. Initially the large-scale sector of agriculture would itself play a passive role in getting economic development under way, little if any of its own large surplus being directed voluntarily into agricultural improvements in food production or into the establishment of domestic manufactures. Politically its influence would probably be negative as it actively opposed public policies which would provide social overhead for the benefit of the food-producing sector and promote industrial development.

However, the coexistence of an equalitarian sector of agriculture would provide an important political offset to such oligarchic tendencies. As a consequence, it might prove possible politically to establish public policies by which the large-scale sector's surplus would be partially mobilized (albeit involuntarily) for general development purposes. As the food-producing sector and domestic manufactures developed, the large-scale sector might gradually become integrated into the national economy, increasingly meeting its need for both food and manufactures from domestic rather than foreign sources.

We may conclude that even a substantial exportable surplus of industrial crops, produced by the large-scale sector of agriculture, can usually be effectively mobilized for general economic development only by political means. Hence the political environment must be such as to permit the capture of part of that surplus for developmental purposes, while avoiding its dissipation, misallocation, or destruction. Perhaps most favorable to such an outcome is the coexistence of a productive and equalitarian food-producing sector, whose agricultural surplus can be the prime generating force for developing and integrating the national economy, and through whose moderating democratic political influence, contructive

rather than disruptive public development policies can evolve.[21]

"AGRICULTURAL SURPLUS" IN AN OVERPOPULATED COUNTRY

Let us now consider the situation of a country which suffers serious overpopulation. For

21. In his analysis of the early economic development of the United States, North [1961] concludes that the oligarchic South's highly profitable export trade in cotton was the prime generating force, but only because of the spread of the internal market economy by interregional trade among the plantation South, the equalitarian Midwest food sector, and the industrial Northeast. Application of my own analysis to the same case would require giving greater credit to the Midwest food sector as an initiating economic and political force. As the Midwest's rich natural endowment came under exploitation, its increasing agricultural surplus quickly condemned to near extinction the agriculture of New England. The latter region was thereby forced to concentrate even more on trade and manufacturing, in which its comparative advantage was strong, in the process creating an important political bloc favorable to industrialization. Thus the Midwest and Northeast complemented each other in ways favorable to balanced economic growth of "the North." While interregional trade undoubtedly had an accelerating effect on all three regions, the South from an early date was inclined toward economic, political, and cultural separatism. While resisting politically many public policies favoring the development of other regions, it bought New England (rather than English) manufactures, largely because the hated tariffs forced it to, and bought Midwestern foods because they were then the world's cheapest. The Civil War offers the ultimate proof that interregional trade had not sufficed to mobilize adequately the South's agricultural surplus for national economic development or to integrate it fully into the national economy [Nicholls, 1960, Ch. 2]. Brazil's economic development offers an interesting comparison. Historically, the Brazilian economy was largely dependent on the production for export of sugar, coffee, and other industrial crops on a large-scale basis. Until recent decades, probably little of this large agricultural surplus found its way into the development of either sufficient food production or manufacturing. After 1929, with public policies directed toward maintaining the incomes of coffee planters in the face of heavy overproduction, the latter's interests first began to turn toward direct investments in urban real estate and industrial enterprise. Only after 1947, however, did the national government—through large-scale deficit financing, high tariffs, and a system of multiple exchange rates that discriminated against domestic coffee planters—begin to capture much of the coffee sector's surplus for use in promoting industrial development. Under such stimuli, southern Brazil has recently enjoyed considerable industrial (and general) development. Meanwhile, however, its older sugar- and cotton-exporting northeastern region has remained feudal and backward, in part because it has never been adequately integrated with the food-producing and industrializing south, and in part because the latter proved to be more efficient even in those major industrial crops produced in the northeast. Even in the south, the historical lack of an equalitarian food-producing sector is only very gradually being overcome through public investments in social overhead and the use of taxation to discourage large landholdings. Despite these recent advances, investment in Brazil's food-producing sector clearly appears to be lagging behind the optimum level needed for achieving a maximum rate of economic growth.

this purpose, let us return to Figure 10.2, once more assuming in turn an agricultural structure of owner-operator farms and one of landlords and tenants. We need not this time distinguish between one-sector and two-sector agriculture, since we shall analyze food production under a landlord-tenant system in a way that is equally applicable to food production under a two-sector situation.

We have already defined "overpopulation" for the level of agricultural technique represented by TP_1 as any population greater than OA_5, at which MP_1 equals the subsistence wage AC_s. Let us suppose that out particular country is initially suffering from maximum possible overpopulation, with OA_8 people in the food-producing sector. At this level, the entire food output $(A_6Q_1 = A_8Q_1')$ is required to feed the people at a bare subsistence level $(AP_1 = AC_s$ at T_1 and $TP_1 = TC_s$ at $Q_1')$. Under these circumstances A_6A_8 of the agricultural population would be redundant in the sense that it could be removed from agriculture without lowering total output, TP_1 being constant and MP_1 zero.[22]

Would there, then, be any agricultural surplus out of which to finance economic development? If we continue to define (1) the agricultural surplus as the excess of food output over the food needs of the agricultural population, *including those who are redundant*; and (2) the TP_1 curve as including the share paid to landlords (if any), the answer is no. We shall, however, have occasion to modify these definitions.

THE CASE OF A PEASANT AGRICULTURE

Suppose first that there are no landlords, all farms being owned and operated by peasant families. Then, by the time the agricultural population reaches OA_8, the entire agricultural surplus will have been exhausted by the peasants' own food needs. However, if we

classify the population from the point of view of productive activity as distinct from place of residence, we might as accurately consider the redundant portion A_6A_8 to be *nonagricultural* population. So viewed, the agricultural population having been redefined as OA_6, an agricultural surplus of P_1Q_1 might be said to exist. Certainly the existence of a food surplus which will at least feed the redundant population—should ways be found to use it in initiating agricultural improvements or the production of nonagricultural goods—has considerable potential value. However, this surplus will be insufficient to provide any investment funds for importing (or otherwise obtaining) industrial production goods. Hence nonagricultural and industrial-crop sectors being here assumed absent, the given country has (apart from birth control) few routes for escaping stagnation: depopulation resulting from disaster, the mobilization of redundant labor for direct capital formation through sheer muscle power, and the receipt of private philanthropy or public grants-in-aid from abroad. Let us consider these several alternatives briefly.

Suppose that a sudden disaster reduces the population from OA_8 to OA_7. The redundant population would then become smaller (A_6A_7), requiring only P_1X_1 of the agricultural surplus for its food needs and freeing as much as Q_1X_1 for investment in production goods. However, this potential gain could easily be wiped out entirely if the smaller population increased its food consumption to the maximum $(F_1F_1' = Q_1X_1)$ or to a lesser level, spending the difference on nonfood consumption; or if natural increase restored its numbers to their former level OA_8. In the event of such a disaster, therefore, the government would be fully warranted in trying to prevent either eventuality by taxing away the full agricultural surplus P_1Q_1 and devoting it to the reemployment (in industry or agriculture) of the redundant population A_6A_7. However, in today's world, where famine relief and public health services can be so quickly mobilized internationally, unplanned disasters are much less likely to occur than formerly. Furthermore, few countries (Stalinist Russia and Communist China may represent partial exceptions) would willingly engage in *planned* disaster as a solution to overpopulation.

22. This principle of maximizing total output under conditions of overpopulation might, under the assumed circumstances, also warrant the cultivation of a second class of land so much less fertile than that (homogeneous) land assumed in Figures 10.1 and 10.2 that its TP curve lay below its TC_s curve for all possible populations. Rather than keep the entire redundant population A_6A_8 on the better land and [leave] the poorer land to idle, it would pay to divert redundant workers to the poorer land so long as their marginal productivity was greater than zero, even though none of the diverted workers produced enough for his own subsistence.

On the other hand, the potential of "bootstrap" operations as a means of creating fixed capital is far greater than commonly believed. Unused or underutilized labor represents a stupendous waste. If properly organized and motivated, such labor can be turned to direct capital formation. Communist China appears to have recognized this opportunity by making extensive use, especially in construction, of a considerable volume of unpaid or underpaid labor on a largely involuntary basis; by its emphasis on labor-intensive methods of expanding production; and by the development of small-scale rural industries [Malenbaum, 1959]. However, China's recent difficulties in maintaining agricultural output suggest that its coercive methods of labor recruitment and its excessive zeal in diverting labor from agriculture have done much to undermine the motivations of its once energetic, resourceful, and individualistic peasantry.

The Chinese experience offers both a challenge and a lesson to other overpopulated countries that seek to develop within a democratic rather than totalitarian framework. The challenge lies in finding democratic organizational techniques for recruiting redundant rural labor effectively on a voluntary basis. One can find in most overpopulated countries isolated situations in which, usually owing to the accidental emergence of outstanding local leadership, such techniques have been found and effectively applied. But few, if any, overpopulated countries have found democratic means of generalizing such favorable local experiences, in large part because of the inadequacies of public investments in education, agricultural research and extension services, and the like.

The lesson of the Chinese experience is that, for good or ill, the motivations of the peasantry are important. Hence, given appropriate organization and leadership, the problem is how to enlist these motivations as a positive factor in expanding productive activity. From this standpoint, despite all the disadvantages of small-scale farming units, a system of peasant owner-operators has, under conditions of severe overpopulation, much to recommend it. Having accepted the principle that *all* family members will share and share alike in the distribution of the total output, the family will have the maximum incentive

both to save, instead of consuming any fortuitous surplus which it may produce, and to forego leisure in favor of investing otherwise redundant labor in private and community capital projects that add (however little) to productivity.[23] By just such a slow accretionary process of investing small annual increments of savings and larger amounts of underutilized labor, peasant families can gradually raise the stock of agricultural capital substantially, to the lasting benefit of agricultural productivity.

If full advantage is to be realized from such favorable private motivations, however, social overhead investment becomes essential, both to speed the process of making agricultural improvements and to prevent population growth from dissipating any initial gains. Hence, insofar as a poor and overpopulated country is able to attract foreign aid, it will usually be wise to direct a major part into such public services as agricultural research and extension, farm credit, and marketing improvements. Suppose now that through some combination of "bootstrap" operations and foreign-financed social overhead investment, the total product curve in Figure 10.2 is raised from TP_1 to TP_2. The given agricultural population OA_8 will now produce A_8b instead of A_8Q_1'. While still formidable, the redundant population at least will have been reduced from A_6A_8 to $A_6'A_8$.

Population remaining constant at OA_8, $Q_1'b$ of agricultural surplus will now be available as a potential source of investment funds for either creating nonfarm jobs or achieving further gains in agricultural productivity. Unfortunately, this entire surplus could quickly disappear as a result of diet improvement or the growth of the agricultural population to OA_8', at which no one would be better off than before. Hence, insofar as possible the government must tax away the entire gain $Q_1'b$. Since such a tax policy would seriously weaken peasant incentives to make further agricultural

23. Even in the poorest countries of the world there is probably a small, largely invisible agricultural surplus that is too widely dispersed among cultivating families to be captured through normal taxation procedures [Panikar, 1961]. If such funds are to find their way into capital formation at all, therefore, they will probably do so in the form of minor improvements in the peasants' own land or (given effective local leadership) in community projects that require cooperative effort but convey considerable private benefit [Raup, 1960].

improvements, however, certain offsetting tax credits should be offered to farmers who adopt approved farming practices, accept effective methods of birth control, and the like, so that what they retain from the agricultural surplus (including more food) will be used to maximum advantage.

THE CASE OF A LANDLORD-TENANT SYSTEM

But what if the structure of the food-producing sector is such that the cultivators do not own their own land, instead renting the land from a relatively few landlords? In previous analysis, we assumed that TP_1 *includes* the landlords' share and that, once the agricultural-worker population exceeds the level OA_5 at which the agricultural surplus is maximized, the landlords will have to give ground to noneconomic considerations by abandoning the marginal principles of distribution followed in a market economy. Then further population growth beyond OA_5 will have to come out of the landlords' share (the entire agricultural surplus), since workers receive *only* a subsistence wage.

If we continue to make these assumptions, the landlord (like the owner-operator) will now take as his objective *maximum total output*, not maximum agricultural surplus. He will therefore also choose, for populations of OA_6 or greater, to use labor until its marginal product is zero.[24] For example, if the total worker population that landlords must feed is OA_7, they will prefer to use OA_6 rather than OA_5 workers, since the increment of labor input A_5A_6 (Figure 10.2) will, while producing less than the subsistence wage, *add something* to total food output ($AC_8 > MP_1$ but $MP_1 > 0$). Therefore, the residual (IL_1') accruing to landlords from the maximum agricultural surplus $L_1'K_1'$ produced by OA_5 labor will be less than the residual (X_1Q_1) which they can capture from the smaller agricultural surplus P_1Q_1 produced by OA_6 labor.

Carried to their logical conclusion, however, these assumptions would mean that when the worker population reached OA_8, the landlords' share would be completely exhausted. That this should happen in spite of the ever increasing scarcity of land relative to population hardly seems credible. Let us therefore assume instead that, for populations of OA_5 or greater, the landlords receive as rent a crop share that is a certain percentage of any given total output. At a population of OA_5, the landlords could exact a crop share of $L_1'K_1'/L_1'A_5$ (slightly over half as the curves of Figure 10.2 are drawn). If the landlords were willing and able absolutely to enforce this share, it would be impossible for the worker population to grow beyond OA_5. This barrier to further population growth would not be fully effective, however, if the landlord class (as is not improbable) gave ground (motivated by paternalism or fear) as an alternative to permitting some of their workers to starve as their numbers increased. Insofar as they did, the landlords' percentage share would have to be reduced. Let us assume that this happens as the population grows to OA_8 but—redefining the TP_1 curve to represent only the sharecroppers' *net* product —suppose that even at OA_8 the landlords' share is significantly positive.[25]

If the landlord population is relatively small, virtually all of its total share rents representing agricultural surplus, a source of investment funds for economic development will exist in spite of the subsistence level of the great masses of the agricultural population.[26] Suppose first that the landlord class decides voluntarily to invest a major part of its surplus in nonagricultural development (which would reduce the redundant agricultural population for a given level of techniques) and/or in improvements in food-

---

24. Georgescu-Roegen [1960], insists that, even under a system of landlords, overpopulation requires capitalistic principles to give way to "the feudal system of distribution," in which some workers are paid more than their specific contribution to output. According to him, "Striking historical evidence of this aspect of feudalism is provided by the gleaners, who received a share greater than the quantity of corn gleaned. In contrast with this, capitalism has no place for gleaners."

25. As we saw earlier (footnote 16), this maximum population will be larger the smaller the landlords' percentage share, while whatever the latter share, landlords will also maximize their rents by maximizing total output. It is also worth noting that if we took the subsistence requirements of landlord families into account, the greater their numbers relative to sharecropper families, the greater the landlords' percentage would have to be.

26. In the remainder of this section the analysis will in general be equally applicable if one substitutes "the management class of the large-scale industrial-crop sector" for "the landlord class'—assuming once more that the food-producing sector consists of owner-operated farms—considers that the TP curves represent *gross* output and that all redundant population is in the latter sector.

producing techniques. Suppose it does the latter, so that gross productivity increases, raising the sharecroppers' net-product curve from TP_1 to TP_2 in Figure 10.2. For a population of OA_8, the agricultural surplus (entirely at the disposal of the landlords) would then be further increased by Q'_1b. With so large a redundant population, the landlord class would not have to share any of this gain with its farm workers. However, it might find that it paid to divert this increment of surplus (or even more) to workers in the form of incentive payments by which they would be encouraged (through an improved diet or the adoption of better practices) to produce more food and fewer children, raising the total product curves further. By such a process they might overcome some of the motivational disadvantages normally associated with cultivators who did not own their own land. By becoming willing to devote its accumulation to domestic investment rather than to lavish living, a landed oligarchy *could* provide out of its agricultural surplus the stimulus for helping an overpopulated country to move from a state of initial stagnation into one of ultimately self-sustaining economic growth.[27]

However, for the various economic and political reasons already considered, the landlord class is not often likely to play this important role voluntarily. This is unfortunate, since where it does not, an overpopulated country can usually escape from stagnation only by the more difficult and initially disruptive route of sociopolitical revolution. Given such a revolution, the landed oligarchy's surplus can at last be taxed away; or (by agrarian reform) its land can be expropriated and operated collectively by the state or redistributed to small owner-operators.

Where private landholdings have been very large and inefficiently managed, as here assumed, a good case can be made that collective farming (as in Mexico) is a more efficient method of providing agricultural workers with social overhead investment and of capturing the agricultural surplus than land redistribution on a private basis. On the other hand, particularly given the temptation to mechanize agriculture prematurely on state collective farms, the problem of redundant population is likely to plague even the collectives, while the superior motivations of small owner-operators (especially in livestock production) are largely absent.[28] If large landholdings are broken up in favor of small owner-operated units, however, the latter motivations can be effectively mobilized only if the government supplies the small holders (through public research, extension, credit, and marketing facilities) with the managerial and financial assistance that the private landlord class had formerly failed to provide.[29]

CONCLUSION

In view of the diversity of population and land-tenure situations with which I have dealt in this paper, I will not attempt to

27. According to Ranis [1959] the Japanese landlord, far from being "Ricardo's wastrel type," from 1868 on devoted himself to agricultural improvements and (shunning the diversion of his respectable surplus to high living or speculation) invested a large part of his surplus in non-agricultural industries as well. Beginning its modern period in "a classic Malthusian situation," Japan quickly found ways of tapping previously underutilized reserves of productivity with a minimum need for additional investment. It centered its initial efforts on agriculture, raising yields per acre as well as per man remarkably without disturbing the very small size of cultivating unit. Having raised agricultural productivity substantially, however, Japan effectively channeled most of the gains into nonagricultural development. Ranis further says of the Japanese agricultural worker: "Before 1868 he supported the feudal ruling classes in the cities; after the Restoration he became the prime source of developmental capital. Good returns to be obtained from the soil—through his labor—were gathered up by means of high rents and the tax on the land." (Cf. the similar findings of Johnston [1951]).

28. Much the same arguments apply to large-scale mechanized state farms built up (as in Russia) by collectivizing small owner-operated units. This latter procedure is almost certain to meet greater political resistance (and have a more deleterious effect on worker incentives) than one by which government simply displaces the private large landlord in an otherwise unchanged large-scale agricultural structure. The Soviet Union's current agricultural difficulties—with 45 per cent of its labor force still in agriculture and its farm-labor productivity scarcely 10 per cent that of the United States—hardly recommend collectivization of small holdings. The striking agricultural progress of Japan and, more recently, of Poland suggest that the alleged advantages of collectivization of small-scale private operating units are easily exaggerated.

29. Nationalization or division of large-scale agricultural organization engaged in industrial-crop production is, however, likely to have serious effects on the size of the agricultural surplus. Since such commercial enterprises are often well financed and efficiently managed while serving as a major source of foreign exchange, their potential contribution to economic development can easily be destroyed before equally satisfactory finance and management can be provided from alternative public or private sources; an example is Cuba's sugar industry at the present time.

summarize my findings. Let me only express the hope that by its very diversity this analysis has demonstrated the almost universal importance of having a substantial and reliable agricultural surplus as the basis for launching and sustaining economic growth. Admittedly I have passed over lightly or taken for granted the several important allocative criteria that would have to be applied in assessing properly the relative merit of agricultural and industrial development in any particular instance. Among these criteria I would particularly specify the relative dynamic (accelerating) character, relative marginal productivities of capital, and relative international comparative advantages of the two sectors. I would insist as much as the next economist that, insofar as information permits, such criteria should be applied faithfully in policy formulation for underdeveloped countries. However, in actual practice, judgments and guesses must often be substituted for nonexistent facts and empirical knowledge. Where this is done, I believe that usually agriculture is unduly undervalued.

The undervaluation of agriculture is particularly likely to occur within the *short-run* context of the next several five-year plans of most of today's overpopulated countries. This outcome would be unfortunate for three reasons. First, even if agriculture is in fact more traditional and static than industry, plans that fail to do anything about it can quickly bring any initial growth of the industrial sector to a halt as further natural increase, compounded by a high income-elasticity of demand, turns a modest food surplus into a food deficit, with concomitant inflation and diversion of scarce foreign exchange. Second, because their agricultural techniques are typically still so primitive and productivity so low, the overpopulated countries still have tremendous opportunities to increase food output by relatively moderate injections of capital into small-scale operating units, taking supplies of agricultural land and labor as given. Finally, for such countries international comparative advantage is far more likely to rest initially in agriculture (especially in industrial crops) than in manufactures.

Within a sufficiently long-run context, of course, the policy objectives of today's underdeveloped countries *must be* substantial industrial-urban development, a smaller agricultural force, and larger-scale mechanized farms. In the process, these countries may ultimately become major customers, on a strictly commercial basis, for food produced by nations now plagued with large agricultural surpluses. In the interim, however, they cannot hope to offset their entire food deficit by imports, whether purchases or gifts, even if they are willing and able to do so. First, the food deficits they face in the near term are of a magnitude far beyond the physical (if not fiscal) capacity of the advanced countries to cover out of either present huge stocks or annual surpluses. Second, until they have taken up the great slack in their own under-utilized national endowment, the overpopulated countries have a substantial potential for increasing their food supply on an economic basis. Under these circumstances, the most that the current food surpluses of the United States and other advanced countries can do is to tide the overpopulated countries over until they can put their own agricultural houses in order. Beyond this immediate necessity, the advanced countries primarily need to supply such countries with the resources (other than land and labor) for producing food, rather than the food itself. The sooner this is done, the sooner will public foreign-aid programs make their optimum contribution to the achievement of sustained economic development in the world's overpopulated countries [Heady, 1962].

References

FELLNER, 1956. William Fellner, *Trends and Cycles in Economic Activity* (New York: Henry Holt, 1956).

GEORGESCU-ROEGEN, 1960. Nicholas Georgescu-Roegen, "Economic Theory and Agrarian Economics," *Oxford Economic Papers*, Vol. 12, No. 1 (February 1960), 1–40.

HEADY, 1962. Earl O. Heady, "Food for Peace—Boon or Bane to the Economy of the United States," Paper presented at a symposium of the Ohio State University Land-Grant Centennial, 1962.

JOHNSTON, 1951. Bruce F. Johnston, "Agricultural Productivity and Economic Development of Japan," *Journal of Political Economy*, Vol. LIX, No. 6 (December 1951), 498–513.

KUZNETS, 1959. Simon Kuznets, *Six Lectures on Economic Growth* (Glencoe, Ill.: Free Press, 1959).

MALENBAUM, 1959. Wilfred Malenbaum, "India and China: Contrast in Development Performance," *American Economic Review*, Vol. XLIX, No. 3 (June 1959), 284–309.

NICHOLLS, 1960. William H. Nicholls, *Southern Tradition and Regional Progress* (Chapel Hill: University of North Carolina Press, 1960).

NICHOLLS, 1964. William H. Nicholls, "The Place of Agriculture in Economic Development," in Kenneth Berrill, ed., *Economic Development with Special Reference to East Asia* (New York: St. Martin's, 1964).

NORTH, 1961. Douglas C. North, *The Economic Growth of the United States, 1790–1860*

(Englewood Cliffs, N.J.: Prentice-Hall, 1961).

PANIKAR, 1961. P. G. K. Panikar, "Rural Savings in India," *Economic Development and Cultural Change*, Vol. X, No. 1 (October 1961), 64–85.

RANIS, 1959. Gustav Ranis, "The Financing of Japanese Economic Development," *Economic History Review*, Vol. II, No. 3 (April 1959), 440–54.

RAUP, 1960. Philip M. Raup, "The Contribution of Land Reforms to Agriculture: An Analytical Framework," Paper presented at conference of Social Science Research Council's Committee of Economic Growth at Stanford University, November, 1960.

CHAPTER

11

The Role of Agriculture in Economic Development:

Classical versus Neoclassical Models of Growth

DALE W. JORGENSON

As a branch of general economic theory, the theory of development of a dual economy is of very recent origin. As recently as five years ago the theory of economic growth consisted of two essentially unrelated parts—theories for an advanced economy and theories for a backward economy. It was widely recognized that under contemporary conditions most backward economic systems have important relations with advanced economies, either through international trade or through the establishment of a modern "enclave" in an otherwise backward social and economic setting.[1] Either relationship gives rise to economic and social "dualism," in which a given economic or social system consists of two component parts—an advanced or modern sector and a backward or traditional sector. Neither theories of economic growth for an advanced economy nor theories of development for a backward economy are directly applicable to the development of a dual economy.

Beginning in 1961 a series of papers on the

theory of development of a dual economy have appeared. These papers may be classified, perhaps somewhat arbitrarily, into two groups. The first begins with the framework of the theory of growth for an advanced economy and builds toward the theory of development for a backward economy [Jorgenson, 1961]. The second begins within the framework of the theory of development and builds toward the theory of growth [Fei and Ranis, 1964].[2] The principal difference between these two approaches to the theory of a dual economy is in conditions governing the supply of labor to the advanced sector. In the first approach labor may be removed from the backward sector only by reducing the output of that sector. In the second approach labor may be removed at no sacrifice in output; in this sense labor in the backward or agricultural sector is surplus.

In view of the substantial disparities between theories of development of a dual economy with and without surplus agricultural labor, the possibility of testing the two theories empirically suggests itself. However, before empirical tests can be carried out, the theories must be developed

1. This point of view is elaborated in my paper [Jorgenson, 1961]. The same point of view is expressed by Spaventa [1959, especially, pp. 386–390]. An excellent review of the literature on economic dualism through 1960 is given by Ellis, [1961, pp. 127–141].

2. See also Fei and Ranis [1961a; 1961b; 1963].

within a common theoretical framework. Within such a framework the empirical implications of the set of assumptions underlying each theory may be compared. Some implications of the two theories will be identical; other implications will contradict each other. Only after the implications of both theories are compared can empirical tests to discriminate between the theories be designed. The first objective of this paper is to present a new version of the theory of development of a dual economy with surplus agricultural labor. This theory is developed within a framework that also includes a theory of development of a dual economy without surplus labor. Within this framework the two alternative approaches to the development of a dual economy may be compared with each other. The two theories are intimately related, since development with surplus labor leads to the elimination of the surplus. Once the surplus is eliminated, the two alternative approaches lead to identical conclusions. It is only where agricultural labor is alleged to be in surplus that the implications of the two approaches are different. Empirical tests capable of discriminating between the two theories in these circumstances may be suggested. The second objective of this paper is to carry out these empirical tests and to assess the empirical validity of the two alternative approaches to the development of a dual economy.

ALTERNATIVE THEORIES OF A DUAL ECONOMY

As an introduction to the development of a dual economy, it is useful to review the theory of economic growth for both advanced and backward economic systems. The modern literature on theories of growth originates with essays by Harrod [1939] and Tinbergen [1942]. Both Harrod and Tinbergen assume that investment is a constant fraction of national output. The chief difference between the theories proposed by Harrod and by Tinbergen is in the description of technology. Harrod assumes that labor and capital are perfectly complementary; such a technology is characterized by "fixed factor proportions." Technological change is assumed to be equivalent to an increase in the labor force or "labor-augmenting." Tinbergen assumes that technology may be characterized by substitution between labor and capital or "variable factor proportions." Technological change is assumed to be equivalent to a proportional increase in output for any combination of labor force and capital stock.

For present purposes the similarities of theories of growth for an advanced economic system are more important than the differences. For future reference we may note that theories within Harrod's framework are usually labeled as "Keynesian," while theories within Tinbergen's framework are described as "neoclassical." A list of important contributions within the Keynesian framework would include those of Domar [1946], Duesenberry [1958], and Smithies [1957]. The most significant recent contributions within the neoclassical framework would include the work of Swan [1956], Tobin [1955], and Solow [1956]. The perils of this particular choice of language may be illustrated by attempting to classify the theory of growth of Kaldor [1957, 1961, 1962]. Kaldor combines a neoclassical description of technology with a theory of saving different from that considered by either Harrod or Tinbergen; he labels this theory of saving "Keynesian." We will use the terms "Keynesian" and "neoclassical" to distinguish alternative descriptions of technology. By this convention Kaldor's theory of growth is solidly neoclassical.

One branch of the modern literature on theories of development for a backward economic system originates with the articles on "Economic Development with Unlimited Supplies of Labour," by W. A. Lewis [1954, 1958]. Lewis postulates that the fundamental characteristic of a certain class of backward or traditional economies is the existence of disguised unemployment. Arguing that the resulting theory of economic growth is neither Keynesian nor neoclassical, Lewis states that "from the point of view of countries with surplus labour, Keynesianism is only a footnote to neo-classicism—albeit a long, important and fascinating footnote. The student of such economies has therefore to work right back to the classical economists before he finds an analytical framework into which he can relevantly fit his problems."

Lewis clearly intended to depart entirely

from the theory of economic growth for advanced economies as embodied, for example, in the work of Harrod. He describes his research program as follows: "Our present task is not to supersede neo-classical economics, but merely to elaborate a different framework for those countries which the neo-classical (and Keynesian) assumptions do not fit." In its original version Lewis' model of economic growth postulates the existence of an advanced or capitalistic sector and a backward or traditional sector. However, there is no relationship between activity in the backward part and that in the advanced part of the economic system. The population of the backward sector of the economy functions as the empirical counterpart of Marx's reserve army of the unemployed. Lewis' analysis of the role of the unemployed in the determination of wages during economic development is strictly analogous to that of Marx. The only purpose of introducing a backward sector of the economy as distinct from an advanced sector is to provide a physical location for the industrial reserve army. It may be noted that in Lewis' theory of development population growth is treated as exogenous or shunted aside as a qualification to the main argument.

A second branch of the theory of development originates with Leibenstein [1954, 1957]. In this branch of the theory the two most important relationships are between labor and output on the one hand and income per capita and the rate of population growth on the other. In Leibenstein's theory emphasis is laid on the balance between growth of income and the growth of population, each adjusting to the other. Disguised unemployment is an inessential feature of the model. The flavor of Leibenstein's theory of development of a backward economy, like that of Lewis, is distinctly "classical." The practical implications of Leibenstein's theory are not, however, the dismal implications of the classical economists. The central result of Leibenstein's theory is the existence of a low-income equilibrium of the model, called the "low-level equilibrium trap." The low-level equilibrium trap is a kind of Malthusian equilibrium of population and sustenance. This equilibrium is stable for initial levels of income, up to a second equilibrium that defines the critical minimum effort required

for sustained economic growth. The Malthusian equilibrium level of income is stable for small changes in income; to achieve sustained economic growth, something like a massive infusion of capital is required. Such a "big push" development strategy had been recommended earlier by Rosenstein-Rodan [1943] and by Nurkse [1953] on somewhat different grounds.

One may characterize theories of development for backward economies as classical and theories of growth for advanced economies as neoclassical without accepting Lewis' viewpoint on neoclassical theory, namely: "When the labour surplus disappears our model of the closed economy no longer holds. Wages are no longer tied to a subsistence level. The neo-classicists invented the doctrine of marginal productivity. The problem is not yet solved to anyone's satisfaction, except in static models which take no account of capital accumulation and of technical progress" [1954]. Lewis was writing 12 years after the appearance of Tinbergen's fundamental essay on the theory of economic growth; since Tinbergen's theory, which is definitely not static and which does take account of capital accumulation and technical progress, is not mentioned by Lewis, one may suggest that Tinbergen's model is an exception to Lewis viewpoint on neoclassical theory. The recent contributions of Swan, Tobin, and Solow could also serve as exceptions.

In Lewis' view a backward economy eventually develops into an advanced economy; the boundary between the two is marked by the disappearance of disguised unemployment. Similarly, in Leibenstein's theory the transition from a backward economy to an advanced one takes place at the level of income per head corresponding to the critical minimum effort. The theory of development of a dual economy is an important departure from either of these views of the relationship between a backward and an advanced economy. The starting point of the theory is the observation that the backward and advanced sectors of an economy exist side by side in most developing economies. Empirically the two most important characteristics of a backward or underdeveloped economic system are low income per head and a relatively large proportion of the total population engaged in agriculture. It is possible to conceive of an economic system with high income per head and a predominance of employment in the agricultural sector. However, the best-established empirical regularity in the study of economic growth is the close association between low income per head and a high proportion of employment in agriculture.[3] The process of economic development may be studied as an increase in income per head and a high proportion of employment in agriculture. Alternatively, the process may be studied as an increase in the role of industrial activity relative to that in agriculture. In the theory of development of a dual economy these two developments are intimately related. The development of a backward or traditional economic system consists of establishing modern modes of economic organization in a backward or traditional setting and of transforming the traditional or backward sector itself. These processes may proceed simultaneously or may occur in either order. In any event the phenomenon of economic dualism is an intrinsic characteristic of the developmental process.

The theory of development of a dual economy has been approached within both classical and neoclassical frameworks. Lewis' approach to the development of a backward economy was first applied to the development of a dual economy by Fei and Ranis in their essay, "A Theory of Economic Development" [1961b]. A complete presentation of the work of Fei and Ranis is contained in their monograph, *Development of the Labor Surplus Economy* [1964]. The work of Fei and Ranis is much more than a mere elaboration or refinement of Lewis' model of economic development. Fei and Ranis attempt to study the detailed interrelationships between the backward or traditional sector of a dual economy and the advanced or modern sector. The interrelationships include not only the sharing of a common supply of labor, as in the most rudimentary form of the Lewis model, but also consumption of the goods produced by one sector by workers in the other sector, investment by property owners in one sector in assets of the other sector, and

so on. However, Fei and Ranis retain the fundamental postulate of Lewis' theory of economic development; in their words: "With regard to real wages, to the extent that there exists a reserve army of the disguised unemployed in the agricultural sector, it is unlikely that significant upward pressures on the industrial real wages will persist. It is the recognition of this that led to the celebrated condition of an unlimited supply of labor (i.e., the constancy of the real wage level) by Professor Lewis. This assumption, truly essential for the analysis of the development process in a dualistic economy, will be accepted as the starting point [of our theory] [1963]."

The theory of development of a dual economy has been approached within the neoclassical framework by the present author in an essay, "The Development of a Dual Economy" [Jorgenson, 1961]. In this theory of development a neoclassical description of technology and the labor market is combined with a demographic theory in which population growth depends on the supply of agricultural output per head and the birth rate.[4] Disguised unemployment is assumed to be nonexistent. The real wage rate depends on the marginal productivity of labor in manufacturing, which bears a certain fixed relation to the average level of agricultural income. The birth rate is assumed to be given and may be changed only by an alteration in medical technique or in social institutions. The force of mortality depends on the supply of food per head; however, it may attain a minimum that depends on the state of medical knowledge, provided that the supply of food is sufficient. This demographic theory is similar to that employed by Leibenstein [1954] and suggested by Lewis [1954].

The chief difference between the classical and neoclassical approaches to the development of a dual economy is in conditions governing the supply of labor to the advanced sector. In the Fei and Ranis or classical approach to the theory, the real wage rate is assumed to be fixed. From the point of view of the industrial sector, labor is available in unlimited amounts at a fixed real wage. For

3. For empirical support of this association, the following may be consulted: Dovring [1959], Chenery [1960]; Kuznets[1957]; C. Clark [1957].

4. This demographic theory is formally identical but different in interpretation from the theory presented in my earlier paper. For the previous interpretation, see Jorgenson [1961].

the agricultural sector two phases of development may be distinguished. In the first phase the level of population exceeds that which can be employed in agriculture with positive marginal productivity. The excess labor may be removed from the agricultural sector with no loss in agricultural output and no additional nonlabor input into agriculture. In the second phase the marginal product of labor in agriculture is positive but below the fixed real wage rate. In the neoclassical approach labor always has positive marginal productivity in agriculture, so that labor is never available to the industrial sector without sacrificing agricultural output. From the point of view of the industrial sector the real wage rate rises steadily over time, depending on the rates of technological process in both sectors and the rate of capital accumulation.

In the following section a new version of the classical approach to the development of a dual economy will be presented. This version of the classical approach will preserve the most essential features of Lewis' theory of economic development—namely an unlimited supply of labor at a fixed real wage. Following the presentation of a classical theory of development of a dual economy, the neoclassical theory will be reviewed. Finally, these two approaches to the theory of development of a dual economy will be compared with each other and with the results of recent empirical research. To facilitate comparison between the two theories, the technology for the classical theory will be assumed to be similar to that for the neoclassical theory. In the writings of Lewis and of Fei and Ranis theories of development with and without technical change or with and without population growth are treated in detail. For present purposes only a single version of the classical theory, including each of these separate theories as a special case, will be presented.

DEVELOPMENT OF A DUAL ECONOMY

A CLASSICAL APPROACH

The purpose of presenting a new version of the classical approach to the theory of development of a dual economy is to provide a basis for comparison with the neo-classical approach and with empirical data. This purpose is not the same as to provide a theory that represents what Lewis or Fei and Ranis "really meant." In the present version of the classical approach the "essential" assumption proposed by Lewis and by Fei and Ranis, unlimited supplies of labor at a fixed real wage rate, will be retained. Some of the other elements of the Fei and Ranis theory of development of a dual economy will be retained, others will be replaced. It is obvious, but should perhaps be mentioned, that in interpreting the conclusions derived from the present version of the classical approach, it must be borne in mind that a different set of assumptions could lead to different conclusions.

In the theory of development of a dual economy, the economic system may be divided into two sectors—the advanced or modern sector, which we will call, somewhat inaccurately, the manufacturing sector, and the backward or traditional sector, which may be suggestively denoted agriculture. This terminology has been used by Lewis [1954] and by Fei and Ranis [1961, pp. 533–534] as well as by the present author [1961]. It is clear that manufacturing includes a good many traditional activities and that these activities have many of the characteristics of the backward sector; similarly, the agricultural sector may include a relatively advanced subsector. Examples of the former would include small-scale industry in Japan; examples of the latter would include plantation agriculture in Asia and agriculture in areas of European settlement in parts of Africa. Nevertheless, it is useful to regard the backward sector as mainly agricultural and the advanced sector as primarily industrial.

Productive activity in each sector may be characterized by a function relating output to each of the factors of production—land, labor, and capital. The special character of the theory of development of a dual economy is an asymmetry in the productive relations. The output of the traditional sector is a function of land and labor alone; there is no accumulation of capital except in the form of land reclamation. This assumption is made by the present author [Jorgenson, 1961] and also by Lewis [1954] and by Fei and Ranis [1964, p. 16]. Of course other assumptions are possible. Even in relatively primitive societies, there are important uses of capital in agricultural production [Firth and Yamey, 1964]. Capital is accumulated in the form of land reclamation and in the form of equipment for agriculture, fishing, and hunting. In the study of primitive societies, saving and investment, ownership of property, and even credit cannot be ignored. For present purposes, the assumption of no capital in agriculture is useful. The essential distinction is between agriculture that uses capital produced in the advanced or modern sector and agriculture that uses only traditional forms of capital. We will refer to an agricultural sector utilizing modern forms of capital as commercialized agriculture. For present purposes the special role of commercialized agriculture will be ignored. In principle this type of agriculture could be included in the modern or advanced sector of the economy.

It will be assumed that land is fixed in supply. Further, it is assumed that agricultural activity is characterized by diminishing returns to scale. The assumptions are made by the present author [1961] and by Fei and Ranis [1964, pp. 15–16]. Although there are many ways to account for diminishing returns—e.g. declining quality of land as more and more is put under cultivation as in Ricardo's extensive margin—the initial assumption that land is fixed in supply implies that the diminishing returns arise at the intensive margin of the Ricardian scheme. In the neoclassical theory of development of a dual economy it is assumed that the marginal productivity of labor in agriculture is always positive. In the classical theory it is assumed that there is some point at which the marginal productivity of labor becomes zero. If population exceeds the quantity at which the marginal productivity of labor becomes zero, labor is available to the manufacturing sector without loss of agricultural output. This assumption, made by Lewis [1954] and by Fei and Ranis [1961a] will be retained in the present version of the classical theory of development of a dual economy.

Land does not appear as a factor of production in the manufacturing sector; the level of manufacturing output is a function of capital and labor alone. In manufacturing, expansion of productive activity proceeds with constant returns to scale. This appears to be a reasonable assumption, at least on the basis of evidence from the manufacturing

industries of advanced economies.[5] A second feature of the production functions for agriculture and manufacturing is that each function will shift over time, so that a given bundle of factors will generate a higher level of output at one date than at an earlier date. In short, technological change will be assumed to take place in the manner indicated by Tinbergen and other contributors to the neoclassical theory of economic growth. A special problem arises in applying this assumption to the classical theory of development of a dual economy. For simplicity, it will be assumed that the point at which the marginal productivity of labor becomes zero remains the same for all technological changes. Of course the output of the agricultural sector at this point increases over time as the agricultural production function shifts upward.

In the classical approach to the theory of development of a dual economy, population growth is ignored or shunted aside as a qualification to the main argument. Lewis discusses a demographic theory quite similar to that of Leibenstein, as outlined above. However, this demographic theory is not integrated into the theory of economic development in a satisfactory way. For Lewis' main line of argument it suffices to assume that unlimited quantities of labor are available to the industrial sector at a fixed real wage; an unlimited supply of labor may have its origin in population growth, but population growth is not affected by activity in either the agricultural or industrial sectors until the phase of disguised unemployment is completed. A similar assumption is made by Fei and Ranis: "Population growth will be treated as a known phenomenon exogenous to our model" [1961b]. This assumption must be qualified in that so long as the real wage remains fixed, the consumption of workers consists entirely of products of the agricultural sector. In the words of Fei and Ranis: "as a consequence of the natural austerity condition arising from the same unlimited supply of labor situation, much industrial output must take the form of capital goods due to the absence of a domestic market for consumer goods" [1964, p. 118]. For simplicity it will be assumed that so long as there is disguised unemployment, population

5. See Jorgenson [1961], and the references given there.

expands at the same rate as the growth of agricultural output. This is the only assumption that is consistent with the view of Lewis and of Fei and Ranis that the real wage rate remains fixed and equal to the initial level of real income in the agricultural sector. At this level of income all of the income of workers in either sector is used for consumption of agricultural products.

The chief difference between the classical approach to the development of a dual economy and the neoclassical approach is in the conditions governing the supply of labor. In the classical theory labor is available to the industrial sector in unlimited quantities at a fixed real wage rate, measured in agricultural goods. Lewis suggests that it is immaterial to his argument whether the marginal productivity of labor in agriculture is zero or simply less than the real wage rate [1954]. Fei and Ranis distinguish between phases of development in which the marginal productivity of labor is zero and in which the marginal productivity of labor is positive but less than the real wage [1961b]. In the first of these phases labor may be supplied to the industrial sector at no loss in agricultural output; in the second of these phases labor may be supplied to the industrial sector only at some sacrifice in agricultural output. In both phases labor is available to the industrial sector at a fixed real wage rate only if the terms of trade between agriculture and industry remain fixed and if population growth is precisely equal to the growth of agricultural output. If the terms of trade should turn against industry, a constant real wage (measured in agricultural goods) will imply a rising price of labor relative to the price of industrial goods.

Finally, in the present version of the classical approach to the development of a dual economy it will be assumed that saving is equal to total profits in the industrial sector. This assumption is consistent with Lewis' observation that "We have seen that if unlimited labor is available at a constant real wage, the capitalist surplus will rise continuously, and annual investment will be a rising proportion of the national income" [1954]. As Lewis emphasizes, "Practically all saving is done by people who receive profits or rents. Workers' savings are very small" [1954]. The present assumption implies that agricultural rents, insofar as they exist at all, are exchanged for goods produced by the industrial sector. The agricultural products represented by these rents are then provided to the industrial workers. The institutional mechanism by which this transaction takes place may vary from one economy to another. For example, agricultural rents may be taxed away and the proceeds spent on governmentally financed investment; alternatively, landlords may themselves invest in the industrial sector, becoming industrial capitalists; finally, landlords may consume goods produced by the industrial sector, so that all investment is done by the owners of industrial capital. For present purposes it suffices to assume that saving is equal to total profits in the industrial sector without specifying whether the resulting accumulation of capital is owned by the government, the landlords, or the industrial capitalists.

We are now in a position to lay out a more concrete version of the classical approach to the development of a dual economy. To begin the analysis, we consider an economic system in which no development of manufacturing activity has taken place; all productive activity is concentrated in the traditional or backward sector. We will assume that there is some maximum quantity of labor that may be employed in the agricultural sector with positive marginal productivity; the agricultural labor force, say A, is always less than this maximum quantity of labor. If we let Y be the level of agricultural output and L the fixed quantity of land available to the economy, then a simple version of the production function for agriculture, characterized by constant returns to scale with all factors variable, is given by the Cobb-Douglas function:

$$Y = e^{\alpha t} L^{\beta} A^{1-\beta},$$

where $e^{\alpha t}$ represents the shift factor corresponding to technological progress. Changes in techniques are assumed to take place at a constant percentage rate, α. The constant β represents the elasticity of output with respect to an increase in the supply of land; if the supply of land is fixed, it is possible to choose the origin for measuring the passage of time so that the production function can be rewritten in the simpler form:

$$Y = e^{\alpha t} A^{1-\beta}.$$

For a total population in excess of the maximum quantity that may be employed at positive marginal productivity, we may distinguish between the labor force employed at positive marginal productivity—say A—the agricultural labor force, and the labor force that is redundant—say R. Then total population is the sum of the agricultural labor force and redundant labor:

$$P = A + R.$$

If we represent the maximum labor force that may be employed at positive marginal productivity by A^+, then the agricultural labor force is the minimum of total population and this maximum labor force:

$$A = min \begin{cases} P \\ A^+ \end{cases}.$$

Of course, if the agriculture labor force is equal to total population, disguised unemployment is zero; if the agricultural labor force is equal to the maximum level, A^+, redundant labor is equal to the difference between total population and this maximum level.

Under the assumptions that the rate of technological progress in agriculture is positive and that the maximum quantity of labor that may be employed with positive marginal productivity is fixed over time, the development of an economy in which all productive activity is concentrated in the traditional or backward sector is simple to describe. At a constant real wage rate, measured in agricultural goods, population increases at the same rate as agricultural output. In the presence of redundant labor, the rate of growth of agricultural output and population is constant and equal to the rate of technological progress in agriculture, α. In the absence of redundant labor, population growth can exceed the rate of technological progress, since the rate of growth is equal to the rate of technological progress, α, plus the elasticity of output with respect to labor, $1-\beta$, multiplied by the rate of growth of population. With a constant real wage rate, the rate of growth of pop-

ulation is simply $\alpha/1-\beta$, a positive quantity. Hence, in an economy in which there is no redundant labor initially, population will grow at a positive rate until the maximum quantity of labor that can be employed with positive marginal productivity is reached. After this point the rate of population growth will slow to the rate of technological progress, α, and all increments in population will become part of the redundant labor force.

We next consider an economic system in which development of manufacturing activity has taken place. Conditions of production in the manufacturing sector must be described. We have assumed that the production function in manufacturing exhibits constant returns to scale. We have also assumed that the output of manufactured goods for a given bundle of capital and labor increases over time. If we denote the quantity of manufacturing output by X, the manufacturing labor force by M, and the quantity of capital by K, then a simple version of the production function for manufacturing is given by the Cobb-Douglas function:

$$X = e^{lt} K^\sigma M^{1-\sigma},$$

where e^{lt} represents technological change, as before, and the constant σ represents the elasticity of manufacturing output with respect to an increase in the supply of land.

With respect to the supply of labor to the manufacturing sector, we have assumed that redundant labor is available to the industrial sector at a fixed real wage, measured in agricultural goods. We may also assume that the terms of trade between agriculture and manufacturing are fixed. If we assume further that competitive conditions prevail in manufacturing, the marginal product of labor is equal to the fixed real wage, measured in either agricultural or manufacturing goods. This assumption is made by Lewis [1954] and by Fei and Ranis [1964, pp. 16–19]. If we denote the fixed real wage measured in manufactured goods by w, the marginal product of labor in the manufacturing sector is then:

$$\frac{\partial X}{\partial M} = (1-\sigma)\frac{X}{M} = w.$$

If there is no redundant labor, the marginal productivity of labor in the agricultural sector may still be below the real wage rate, measured in agricultural goods. However, labor may be transferred from the agricultural sector to the industrial sector only by sacrificing agricultural output. Under these conditions it may still be assumed that the terms of trade between agriculture and manufacturing are fixed, this assumption is made by Lewis [1954]. Alternatively, it may be assumed that the terms of trade turn against manufacturing, so that the wage rate measured in manufactured goods increases, this assumption is made by Fei and Ranis [1964, p. 209]. In the present version of the classical approach to the theory of development of a dual economy, the terms of trade between agriculture and manufacturing cannot be determined endogenously. For simplicity we will begin with Lewis' assumption that the terms of trade are fixed; under this assumption the marginal product of labor in manufacturing is fixed. Using the marginal productivity relationship given above to eliminate the manufacturing labor force from the production function for manufacturing, we may write:

$$X = \left(\frac{1-\sigma}{w}\right)^{(1-\sigma)/\sigma} e^{(\lambda/\sigma)/t} K.$$

If we assume that saving is equal to the share of profits in the industrial sector, ignoring depreciation, we may set the rate of change of capital equal to the share of profits in manufacturing output:

$$\dot{K} = \sigma X,$$

so that the rate of growth of capital may be written:

$$\frac{\dot{K}}{K} = \sigma\left(\frac{1-\sigma}{w}\right)^{(1-\sigma)/\sigma} e^{(\lambda/\sigma)t}.$$

Using the production function and the fact that the output per man remains constant, the rate of growth of manufacturing output may be written:

$$\frac{\dot{X}}{X} = \frac{\lambda}{\sigma} + \sigma\left(\frac{1-\sigma}{w}\right)^{(1-\sigma)/\sigma} e^{(\lambda/\sigma)t}.$$

The rate of growth of manufacturing employment is, of course, equal to the rate of growth of manufacturing output.

For an economy with total population in excess of the maximum quantity that may be employed at a positive marginal productivity in agriculture plus the manufacturing labor force, there is redundant labor. Total population is the sum of the agricultural labor force, the industrial labor force, and redundant labor:

$$P = A + M + R.$$

The agricultural labor force is the minimum of total population less the manufacturing labor force and the maximum labor force that may be employed at positive marginal productivity:

$$A = min\begin{cases} P\text{-}M \\ A^+ \end{cases}$$

So long as there is redundant labor in the agricultural sector, manufacturing output and manufacturing employment grow at a rate that is positive and increasing. Capital in manufacturing also grows at a rate that is positive and increasing, but always less than the rate of growth of output. This implies that the capital-output ratio is always falling; a similar result is obtained by Fei and Ranis [1963]. Since agricultural output is increasing at a constant rate, equal to the rate of technological progress in agriculture, population is increasing at this same rate. Whatever the initial value of the rate of growth of manufacturing output, this rate of growth eventually exceeds any fixed rate of growth. The sum of redundant labor and manufacturing employment grows at a rate that exceeds the rate of growth of population; but this rate must fall to the rate of growth of population. Hence the rate of growth of manufacturing employment eventually becomes so large as to force the rate of growth of redundant labor to become negative and decreasing. Under these conditions redundant labor eventually disappears altogether. This concludes the description of the first phase of development with unlimited supplies of labor. The point at which redundant labor disappears is called the "Lewis turning point." by Fei and Ranis [1961b].

After the Lewis turning point is reached, the marginal productivity of labor in the agricultural sector is positive but less than the real wage rate, measured in agricultural goods. Under the assumption that the real wage rate remains fixed when measured in agricultural goods, the rate of growth of population is equal to the rate of technological change in the agricultural sector less the elasticity of agricultural output with respect to labor multiplied by the rate of decline of the agricultural labor force. Where w_A is the proportion of the agricultural labor force in total population and w_M the proportion of the manufacturing labor force, this condition on the rate of population growth implies:

$$\alpha + (1-\beta)\frac{\dot{A}}{A} = w_A\frac{\dot{A}}{A} + w_M\frac{\dot{M}}{M},$$

or, simply:

$$\alpha + (w_M - \beta)\frac{\dot{A}}{A} = w_M\frac{\dot{M}}{M}.$$

For this condition to be satisfied, the manufacturing proportion, w_M, must be such that the rate of growth of the agricultural labor force is negative at the Lewis turning point. Furthermore, the rate of growth of the agricultural labor force must remain negative until the labor force itself reaches the level at which the marginal product of labor in agriculture, measured in agricultural goods, is equal to the real wage. For this it suffices to assume that the share of manufacturing in the total labor force exceeds the elasticity of agricultural output with respect to land. Under this condition the agricultural labor force declines at an increasing rate until the marginal product of labor is equal to the real wage. At this point a third phase of the development of a dual economy is reached, in this phase the wage rate of labor is the same in agriculture and in manufacturing.

The third phase of development of a dual economy under the classical approach is described by Lewis [1954] as follows: "When capital catches up with labor supply, an economy enters upon the [third] phase of development. Classical economics ceases to apply; we are in the world of neo-classical economics, where all the factors of production are scarce, in the sense that their supply is inelastic. Wages are no longer constant as accumulation proceeds; the benefits of improved technology do not all accrue to profits; and the profit margin does not necessarily increase all the time." Fei and Ranis [1961b] describe the third phase as follows: "The transition into phase [three] constitutes a

major landmark in the development process. With the completion of the transfer of the disguisedly unemployed, there will occur a switch, forced by circumstances in employer behavior, i.e., the advent of a fully commercialized agricultural sector. This landmark may be defined as the end of the take-off process. We know of no other way to establish a nonarbitrary criterion for an economy reaching the threshold of so-called self-sustaining growth." The basic point made by Lewis and by Fei and Ranis is that a neoclassical theory of growth for an advanced economy applies after the third phase of development has been reached. Hence, further discussion of this phase will be postponed until the neoclassical theory of development for a dual economy has been discussed.

Parenthetically, it should be remarked that Fei and Ranis attempt to combine Lewis' notion of disguised unemployment with the critical minimum effort hypothesis of Leibenstein [Fei and Ranis, 1963]. Their criterion for a critical minimum effort is that the rate of growth of population must be less than the rate of growth of the industrial labor force. In the presence of disguised unemployment, this condition is always satisfied, provided only that the rate of technological change in the industrial sector is positive. With a positive rate of technological change, the rate of growth of the industrial labor force eventually exceeds any fixed rate of growth; with a fixed real wage, measured in agricultural goods, the growth of population is limited by the rate of technological change in the agricultural sector. In the absence of disguised unemployment, the critical minimum-effort criterion is satisfied only under a somewhat different set of conditions. We will return to the discussion of this problem after our review of the neoclassical theory is complete.

A NEOCLASSICAL APPROACH[6]

The distinguishing characteristics of the neoclassical theory of the development of a dual economy are the technology of the agricultural sector and the conditions governing the supply of labor. First, in the neoclassical approach it is assumed that the

6. This section is based on my paper "The Development of a Dual Economy" [Jorgenson, 1961].

productivity of labor in agriculture is always positive so that labor is never redundant. Secondly, it is assumed that the real wage rate is variable rather than fixed; wage rates in the backward sector are assumed to be proportional to those in the advanced sector. The interpretation of this relationship will be discussed below. Finally, at very low levels of income it is assumed that the rate of growth of population depends on the level of income. This feature of the theory is not a distinguishing characteristic of the neoclassical approach as such; however, none of the proponents of the classical approach has integrated a demographic theory of this type with a theory that embodied Lewis' assumption of an unlimited supply of labor at a fixed real wage. The reasons for this are obvious; according to the demographic theory utilized in the neoclassical approach, a fixed real wage implies a constant rate of population growth. So long as the wage remains unchanged, population growth may be treated as exogenous, as in the classical approach of Lewis and of Fei and Ranis. Significantly, it is only in discussing the neoclassical phase of economic growth that Lewis suggests an endogenous determination of the rate of growth of population [1954].

We will begin discussion of the neoclassical theory by considering an economic system in which no development of manufacturing activity has taken place. Except for the possibility that labor may be redundant, the description of technology for the agricultural sector is the same for both classical and neoclassical theories. In the neoclassical approach there is no level of the agricultural labor force at which the marginal productivity of labor is zero. It is assumed that the agricultural production function for any level of the agricultural labor force may be characterized by the Cobb-Douglas production function:

$$Y = e^{\alpha t} L^{\beta} A^{1-\beta},$$

where variables and parameters have the same interpretation as in the classical approach. Assuming that the supply of land is fixed, this production function may be rewritten in the form:

$$y = e^{\alpha t} A^{-\beta},$$

where $y = Y/A$ is agricultural output per head.

A second characteristic of a backward economic system is the relationship between the rate of growth of population and the level of agricultural output per head. The birth rate is assumed to be given and may be changed only by an alteration in medical technique or in social institutions. The force of mortality depends on the supply of food per head; however, mortality may attain a minimum, provided that the supply of food is sufficient. The minimum value of the force of mortality depends on the state of medical technique. If there is literally no agricultural production, the net reproduction rate falls to the level $-\delta$, where δ is the difference between the maximum possible force of mortality (mass starvation) and the fixed birth rate. As the supply of food per head increases, the force of mortality gradually declines; it will be assumed that mortality eventually attains a minimum determined by the state of medical technique. As the force of mortality declines, the net reproduction rate rises; it will be assumed that the minimum level of the force of mortality corresponds to a positive level of the net reproduction rate, say ϵ, where ϵ is the difference between the fixed birth rate and the minimum level of the force of mortality.[7] If the rate of increase in the net reproduction rate is constant as agricultural output per head increases, this demographic relationship may be written in the form:

$$\frac{\dot{P}}{P} = \min \begin{cases} \gamma y - \delta \\ \epsilon \end{cases}$$

where γ is the rate of increase in the net reproduction rate or the rate of decrease in the force of mortality with respect to an increase in the output of food per head. The net reproduction rate, $\dot{P}/P$, is equal to the fixed birth rate less the force of mortality.

For the first phase of development, in which the force of mortality is above its minimum, the production function for the agricultural sector and the demographic relationship may be combined to yield a differential equation in agricultural output per head:

$$\frac{\dot{y}}{y} = \alpha - \beta(\gamma y - \delta) = \alpha + \beta\delta - \beta\gamma y.$$

7. As noted above, the interpretation of this demographic theory is not the same as that presented in my paper "The Development of a Dual Economy" [Jorgenson, 1961]. However, the two theories are formally identical.

Multiplying by agricultural output per head, y, we obtain the fundamental differential equation for the development of a backward economy:

$$\dot{y} = (\alpha + \beta\delta)y - \beta\gamma y^2.$$

There are two stationary states for a backward economy—that is, there are two levels of agricultural output per head that, once established, will maintain themselves. All such stationary states may be obtained by setting the rate of change in agricultural output per head equal to zero:

$$(\alpha + \beta\delta)y - \beta\gamma y^2 = 0.$$

This equation has two roots, namely output per head equal to zero and output per head equal to $(\alpha + \beta\delta)/\beta\gamma$, which is necessarily positive. If agricultural output is zero, the rate of population decline is equal to a fixed constant, δ. This stationary state corresponds to mass starvation; the whole population dies off at a constant exponential rate, finally becoming extinct. For the second stationary state, agricultural output per head remains constant; however, the rate of population growth is positive. This may be seen by inserting the stationary value of agricultural output per head into the equation for determining the rate of growth of population:

$$\frac{\dot{P}}{P} = \gamma[(\alpha + \beta\delta)/\beta\gamma] - \delta = \frac{\alpha}{\beta} > 0,$$

so that population and sustenance grow at the same positive rate, with no increase in agricultural output per head. The situation in which output per head remains constant with a growing population is precisely that envisioned in Leibenstein's low-level equilibrium trap [1954, p. 15]. Although there are important differences between theory of development of a backward economy described here and that suggested by Leibenstein, the existence of a "trap" level of income under certain circumstances suggests the following problem: under what conditions is the low-level equilibrium trap stable? The answer is straightforward, if a low-level equilibrium trap exists, it is stable.[8] To complete the analysis of a purely traditional or completely agricultural economy, it is necessary to determine the conditions

8. A proof of this proposition is given in Jorgenson [1961].

under which a low-level equilibrium trap exists.

We will denote the minimum level of agricultural output per head at which the net reproduction rate achieves its maximum by y^+. Then, using the demographic relationship given above, we may determine the value of y^+ as follows:

$$\frac{\dot{P}}{P} = \gamma y^+ - \delta = \epsilon.$$

Hence

$$y^+ = (\epsilon + \delta)/\gamma$$

is the value of production of food per head at which the net reproduction rate attains its maximum. If the critical level of output, y^+, is below the positive stationary level of output per head corresponding to the low-level equilibrium trap, $(\alpha + \beta\delta)/\beta\gamma$, this stationary level will never be attained. To attain such an equilibrium, a rate of growth in population higher than the maximum possible rate, ϵ, would be required. If population growth attains its maximum, the production function for the agricultural sector and the demographic relationship may be combined to yield a differential equation in agricultural output per head:

$$\dot{y} = (\alpha - \beta\epsilon)y,$$

which has the general solution:

$$y(t) = e^{(\alpha - \beta\epsilon)t} y(0);$$

the rate of growth in agricultural output per head, $\alpha - \beta\epsilon > 0$, will be attained from any positive initial level of output per head. If this rate of growth is positive, no positive stationary equilibrium level of agricultural output per head exists; if this rate of growth is negative, a stationary state with positive agricultural output per head, corresponding to the low-level equilibrium trap, does exist.

If the low-level equilibrium trap exists, it is stable in the large, since the trap level of agricultural output per head will be approached from any initial level of output per head. If the initial level of output per head is higher than the critical level, y^+, output per head declines at the rate $\alpha - \beta\epsilon$ to the level at which population growth reaches its maximum. From this point the original fundamental differential equation for a backward economy describes the movement of agricultural output per head to the stationary level, $(\alpha + \beta\delta)/\beta\gamma$.[9] If the initial level of output per head is lower than the critical level, γ^+, the movement of agricultural output per head to the trap level of income is described by this same equation. Obversely, if the low-level equilibrium trap does not exist, then the rate of growth of output per head for initial levels of output greater than the critical level, γ^+, is positive and equal to $\alpha - \beta\epsilon$. For initial levels of agricultural output per head higher than γ^+, output per head grows at this rate. For initial levels of output per head lower than γ^+, the movement of output per head to the critical level γ^+ is described by the fundamental differential equation for a backward economy.

The interpretation of the low-level equilibrium trap in the neoclassical theory of the development of a dual economy is entirely different from that of the low-level equilibrium trap in Leibenstein's theory of economic development. For Leibenstein, the trap level of agricultural output per head is stable for any changes in output per head up to the level associated with the critical minimum effort. In the neoclassical theory a low-level equilibrium trap is stable in the large, provided that it exists. There is no level of output per head which corresponds to a critical minimum effort. To escape from the low-level equilibrium trap of the neoclassical theory, changes in the rate of introduction of new techniques of agricultural production or changes in medical knowledge are required. Unless changes in medical technique reducing the force of mortality are accompanied by changes that reduce the birth rate even more, such changes make the escape from a trap level of agricultural output per head more difficult. An alternative policy for escape from the low-level equilibrium trap of the neoclassical theory is to introduce capital as a factor in agricultural production. This policy is one form for the introduction of nontraditional factors into the agricultural sector. Such a policy has been suggested by T. W. Schultz in his book, *Transforming Traditional Agriculture* [1964].

9. Where $\gamma_2 = (\alpha + \beta\delta)/\beta\gamma$, the solution to this differential equation may be written:

$$\gamma(t) = \gamma_2 + \frac{1}{e^{(\alpha+\beta\delta)t}[(\beta\gamma/\alpha + \beta\delta) + (1/\gamma(0) - \gamma_2)] - (\beta\gamma/\alpha + \beta\delta)}$$

Up to this point we have considered an economic system in which no development of manufacturing activity has taken place. Next we consider an economic system consisting of two sectors—a backward agricultural sector and an advanced manufacturing sector. The technology of the agricultural sector has already been described. Conditions of production in the manufacturing sector are the same as those of the classical theory. We have assumed that the manufacturing production function may be characterized by constant returns to scale and that the output of manufactured goods for a given quantity of capital and labor increases over time; a simple version of the manufacturing production function is the Cobb-Douglas function:

$$X = e^{lt} K^\sigma M^{1-\sigma},$$

where variables and parameters have the same interpretation as in the classical theory. This production function may be rewritten in the form:

$$x = e^{lt} k^\sigma,$$

where $x = X/M$ is manufacturing output per head and $k = K/M$ is capital per head in the manufacturing sector. Secondly, we assume that saving is equal to the share of profits in the manufacturing sector; as before, we ignore depreciation, so that the rate of change of capital may be set equal to the share of profits in manufacturing output:

$$\dot{K} = \sigma X.$$

This assumption is identical to that made in the classical approach.

To close the model for the neoclassical theory of the development of a dual economy, it is necessary to describe the allocation of labor between the backward and advanced sectors of the economy. To simplify the discussion, we will assume that as agricultural output per head increases, all output is consumed, until the force of mortality reaches its minimum; this occurs at a level of agricultural output equal to the critical value, γ^+. We assume that once the critical value is attained, all further increases in consumption per head take the form of manufactured goods. Under these assumptions agricultural output per head in excess of the critical value, γ^+, constitutes a surplus; we may define the agricultural surplus per head, say s, as the difference between agricultural output per head and the critical value, γ^+:

$$s = \gamma - \gamma^+.$$

If agricultural output per head exceeds the critical level, part of the labor force may be released from the land to produce manufactured goods with no reduction in the rate of growth of total population.[10]

As before, we denote agricultural population by A and manufacturing population by M; total population, say P, is the sum of these two components:

$$P = A + M.$$

The demographic theory for the development of a dual economy is the same as that for a backward economic system: The net rate of reproduction is the minimum of the rate corresponding to the minimum force of mortality and the rate that corresponds to output of food per head, as indicated above; the basic demographic relationship may be written:

$$\frac{\dot{P}}{P} = \min\begin{cases} \gamma\gamma\dfrac{P}{A} - \delta \\ \epsilon \end{cases}$$

where $\gamma A/P$ is output of food per head for the whole economy. Where total population is equal to the agricultural population alone, this model of population growth reduces to that for the backward sector alone. For an economy with an agricultural surplus, total food consumption is the critical level, γ^+, multiplied by total population; the proportion of the total labor force employed in agriculture is the ratio of this critical level of agricultural production per head to the actual level of output per head:

$$\frac{\gamma^+}{\gamma} = \frac{A}{P}.$$

Of course this relationship holds only when an agricultural surplus exists—that is, if $\gamma > \gamma^+$. Under these assumptions the relationship governing the distribution of labor

between the backward sector and the advanced sector may be represented by:

$$\frac{A}{P} = \min\begin{cases} 1 \\ \gamma^+/\gamma \end{cases}.$$

To study the development of a dual economy for the case in which the advanced sector is economically viable, we must assume at the outset that an agricultural surplus eventually emerges—that is, that $\alpha - \beta\epsilon > 0$, which is both necessary and sufficient for the emergence of an agricultural surplus. The case in which the advanced sector is not economically viable will be treated subsequently. We assume first that the initial level of agricultural output per head is below the critical level, γ^+. Provided that $\alpha - \beta\epsilon > 0$, output per head increases along a path given by the fundamental differential equation for a backward economy.[11] An industrial labor force comes into being when agricultural output per head attains the critical value, γ^+—that is, when agricultural output attains the minimum level necessary for population to grow at its maximum rate. From this point forward, population grows at the maximum rate of net reproduction, ϵ, so that:

$$P(t) = e^{\epsilon t}P(0),$$

where the origin for measurement of time is taken to be that point at which agricultural output per head is equal to the critical value, γ^+.

From the fact that population is growing at a constant rate and the assumption that consumption of food per head is stationary it is clear that food output and population must grow at the same rate; hence,

$$Y = P\gamma^+ = P(0)e^{\epsilon t}\gamma^+.$$

Given the agricultural production function, we may calculate the rate of growth of the agricultural labor force required to maintain the growth of the agricultural surplus as follows:

$$Y = e^{\alpha t}A^{1-\beta} = P(0)e^{\epsilon t}\gamma^+,$$

so that:

$$A^{1-\beta} = P(0)\gamma^+ e^{[\epsilon - \alpha]t},$$

which may be simplified:

$$A = [P(0)\gamma^+]^{1(/1-\beta)}e^{[(\epsilon - \alpha)/(1-\beta)]t}.$$

10. The relationship between the existence of an agricultural surplus and development of the advanced sector has been discussed by Lewis and by Fei and Ranis. This relationship is also discussed by Nicholas Kaldor [1960]. The necessity of an agricultural surplus has been emphasized by William H. Nicholls [1963; 1964] (reproduced as Chapter 10 in this volume).

11. See footnote 9.

Using the fact that the origin of time is taken to be the point at which population growth first attains its maximum rate, we have the following:

$$\gamma^+ = P(0)^{-\beta} = A(0)^{-\beta};$$

substituting this expression for the critical value of agricultural output per head, γ^+, in the formulas given above, we obtain the following expression for the growth of the agricultural labor force:

$$A = P(0)e^{[(\epsilon-\alpha)/(1-\beta)]t} = A(0)e^{[(\epsilon-\alpha)/(1-\beta)]t}.$$

Agricultural population may grow, decline, or remain constant, depending on the magnitude of the parameters ϵ, the rate of growth of total population, and α, the rate of technological progress in agriculture.

The manufacturing population is equal to total population less agricultural population; hence the growth of the manufacturing labor force is governed by the following expression:

$$M = P(0)[e^{\epsilon t} - e^{[(\epsilon-\alpha)/(1-\beta)]t}],$$

which is zero at time $t = 0$ and grows at a rate which is always more rapid than the rate of growth of total population. To show this, we begin with the assumption that an agricultural surplus eventually emerges, namely:

$$\alpha - \beta\epsilon > 0,$$

which implies:

$$\epsilon - \alpha < \epsilon(1 - \beta),$$

so that:

$$\epsilon > \frac{\epsilon - \alpha}{1 - \beta}.$$

The rate of growth of population is greater than that of the agricultural population alone; hence the manufacturing labor force is growing at a rate which exceeds that of total population. The rate of growth of the manufacturing labor force is always declining and approaches, as a limit, the rate of growth of population, ϵ.

To study the growth of manufacturing output, it is necessary to characterize the process of capital accumulation in the advanced sector of the economy. The fundamental relationships include the expression given above for the growth of the manufacturing labor force, the production function

for the manufacturing sector, and the savings function. Combining these relationships, we may eliminate the output of the manufacturing sector and the manufacturing labor force to obtain a differential equation in capital alone:

$$\dot{K} = \sigma K^\sigma P(0)^{1-\sigma} e^{lt}[e^{\epsilon t} - e^{[(\epsilon-\alpha)/(1-\beta)]t}]^{1-\sigma},$$

which is the fundamental differential equation for the neoclassical theory of development of a dual economy. From this fundamental equation it may be deduced immediately that there is no stationary situation for any economy in which the advanced sector is economically viable; that is, provided that there is a positive and growing agricultural surplus, the advanced sector must continue to grow. The pattern of growth of the advanced sector is determined by two initial conditions, the size of total population at the time that the growth of the advanced sector begins and the size of the initial capital stock. Only the initial size of the population has any effect on the long-run pattern of growth of the economy; the influence of the initial size of capital stock eventually dies out.[12] Secondly, it may be shown that there is no critical minimum level of the initial capital stock required for sustained economic growth. Given any positive initial capital stock, no matter how small, the existence of a positive and growing agricultural surplus generates sustained economic growth.

For the neoclassical theory of the development of a dual economy, capital and output grow at the same rate in the long run, namely $l/(1 - \sigma) + \epsilon$, where l is the rate of technological progress in industry, $1 - \sigma$ is the share of labor in manufacturing output and ϵ is the rate of growth of population. Population grows at the rate ϵ; since the share of labor in manufacturing output is constant, the wage rate of the manufacturing labor force eventually grows at the rate $l/1 - \sigma$. In the short-run the beginning of the growth of the advanced sector is always characterized by a "big push"—that is, an extraordinarily high rate of growth of manufacturing output. From the viewpoint of the neoclassical theory of the development of a dual economy, such a high initial rate of growth may be interpreted as a statistical artifact. Using the production

12. A proof of this proposition is given in Jorgenson [1961].

function for the advanced sector, we may derive the relation:

$$\frac{\dot{X}}{X} = l + \sigma \frac{\dot{K}}{K} + (1-\sigma)\frac{\dot{M}}{M}$$

so that the rate of growth of manufacturing output is equal to the rate of technological progress plus a weighted average of the rates of growth of capital stock and of the manufacturing labor force. But the initial rate of growth of the manufacturing labor force is essentially unbounded; this rate of growth declines gradually, approaching a long-run equilibrium value equal to the rate of growth of total population. The existence of a statistically observable "big push" is no evidence for the necessity of a massive infusion of capital from outside the system for a "take-off" into sustained growth; sustained growth depends on the economic viability of the advanced sector and not on the initial level of capital stock. The advanced sector is economically viable if and only if there is a positive and growing agricultural surplus.

We have assumed that wage rates in the backward sector of a dual economy are proportional to those in the advanced sector. Using this relationship and the saving function, it is possible to determine the terms of trade between agriculture and industry. The balance of trade between agriculture and industry requires that the value of labor income in both sectors is equal to the value of manufacturing output not used for additions to capital together with the value of total agricultural output. This balance relation may be written:

$$wM + \mu wA = (1-\sigma)X + qY,$$

where q is the terms of trade between agriculture and industry and μ is the constant of proportionality between wage rates in the agricultural sector and wage rates in the industrial sector.

This constant of proportionality may be interpreted in a number of different ways. First, in a "strict" neoclassical theory, wage rates in the two sectors must be equal. In this case the constant of proportionality, μ, is unity. Alternatively, if the process of development of a dual economy is characterized by a steady flow of labor from agriculture to industry, a differential between agricultural and industrial wages may be required to

sustain this flow [Jorgenson, 1961]. As a third alternative, if land is owned by the cultivators but the full value of the land cannot be realized by outright sale, the industrial wage rate must be sufficiently high to cover both labor and property income for a member of the agricultural labor force [Lewis, 1954]. If nothing can be realized by the sale of land, the industrial wage rate would have to be equal to unity divided by the share of labor in total agricultural output. Other interpretations of the constant of proportionality could doubtless be given. Provided that μ is a fixed constant, the balance relation may be rewritten in the form:

$$\mu wA = qY,$$

so that:

$$\frac{\dot{w}}{w} + \frac{\dot{A}}{A} = \frac{\dot{q}}{q} + \frac{\dot{Y}}{Y}$$

and

$$\frac{\dot{q}}{q} = \left[\frac{\epsilon - \alpha}{1-\beta} - \epsilon\right] + \frac{\dot{w}}{w}.$$

In the long run the rate of growth of the wage rate in manufacturing is equal to $l/1-\sigma$, so that the rate of growth of the terms of trade is the sum of a negative and a positive quantity; hence the terms of trade may turn in favor of agriculture or industry, depending on the relative magnitude of the two quantities.

BEYOND DISGUISED UNEMPLOYMENT

Where the advanced sector is already in existence, wage rates in the advanced and backward sectors may be taken to be equal, as in the "strict" neoclassical approach. Then the neoclassical theory of the development of a dual economy may be reinterpreted as a theory of the neoclassical phase of Lewis' theory of economic development. Such a theory of the neoclassical phase would also be consistent with the first two phases of the Fei and Ranis version of the classical theory of development of a dual economy. Fei and Ranis associate equality between the marginal products of labor in the backward and in the advanced sectors with the commercialization of agriculture; hence they refer to the point at which equality between the marginal products is achieved as the "commercialization point" [1961b]. However, any association between equality of marginal products of labor in the two sectors and the beginning of the use of capital in the backward or traditional sector is purely fortuitous. Commercialization of agriculture can precede, coincide with, or lag behind the disappearance of disguised unemployment. A complete classical theory of the development of a dual economy should include a separate theory for each of these alternative possibilities. Here we will consider only the situation in which commercialization of agriculture lags behind the disappearance of disguised unemployment.

Interpreting the neoclassical theory of the development of a dual economy as the neoclassical phase of the classical theory, the growth of the manufacturing labor force and manufacturing output and the accumulation of capital are described by the relations given above for the neoclassical theory. However, the initial phases of the development of the advanced sector are not the same as in the neoclassical theory. In the classical theory the phase of redundant labor initiates the development of manufacturing. This sector develops further in the phase of disguised unemployment, where there is no redundant labor but the marginal product of labor in the agricultural sector is below the real wage rate, measured in agricultural goods. Finally, the marginal products of labor in both sectors are brought into equality with the fixed real wage rate. By this time a certain amount of capital has been accumulated in the manufacturing sector. Given the manufacturing labor force, the second initial condition for the fundamental relations of the neoclassical theory of development of a dual economy—namely, the size of total population when agricultural output per head reaches its critical value, y^+—can be computed by inserting the manufacturing labor force into the equation:

$$M(t) = P(0)[e^{\epsilon t} - e^{[(\epsilon-\alpha)/(1-\beta)]t}],$$

by inserting total population into the equation:

$$P(t) = P(0)e^{\epsilon t},$$

and by computing $P(0)$ and the origin for the measurement of time. These constants may then be used to determine the course of

economic growth in the neoclassical phase of the classical theory of the development of a dual economy. Of course the fundamental relations of the neoclassical theory are valid for the classical theory only *after* the beginning of the neoclassical phase.

Up to this point we have considered only the case in which the advanced sector is economically viable. A necessary and sufficient condition for the economic viability of the advanced sector is the eventual emergence of a positive and growing agricultural surplus. Provided that an agricultural surplus eventually emerges, the development of a dual economy may be characterized in two ways. If there is disguised unemployment, as in the classical approach, the manufacturing sector develops in three separate phases. First, manufacturing output and employment grow at a rate that is positive and increasing. Capital in manufacturing also grows at a rate which is positive and increasing, but always less than the rate of growth of manufacturing output. Redundant labor eventually disappears. Secondly, provided that the share of manufacturing in the total labor force exceeds the elasticity of agricultural output with respect to land, the agricultural labor force declines at an increasing rate, until the marginal product of labor is equal to the real wage in both sectors. The realization of this condition marks the end of disguised unemployment. Finally, the manufacturing sector enters into the neoclassical phase. This phase is the same as the phase of "dualistic" development in the neoclassical theory, provided that the initial conditions of the fundamental relations of the neoclassical theory are properly reinterpreted. If there is no disguised unemployment, as in the neoclassical approach, the backward sector develops according to the fundamental relations describing an increase in agricultural output per head until the critical level, y^+, is reached. At this level the force of mortality reaches its minimum, and the net reproduction rate for total population reaches its maximum. From this point forward the development of the manufacturing sector is described by the fundamental relations for capital accumulation and for the growth of manufacturing output and employment. These relations are the same as those describing the neoclassical phase of development of a dual economy in the classical approach.

We may now consider the case in which the advanced sector is not economically viable. First, we will describe the neoclassical theory of development for this case. If capital for the advanced sector is already in existence, the condition for economic viability of this sector, $\alpha - \beta\epsilon > 0$, is not satisfied. There are two possibilities. First, suppose that $\alpha = \beta\epsilon$; then the manufacturing labor force is equal to zero and there is no manufacturing production. Secondly, suppose that $\alpha < \beta\epsilon$ and the initial value of the manufacturing labor force is positive. Then this labor force declines to zero, after which there is no further manufacturing production. Total population becomes entirely concentrated in the agricultural sector and agricultural output per head eventually declines to that associated with the low-level equilibrium trap.

The classical theory of development where the advanced sector is not economically viable at the maximum net reproduction rate is somewhat more complex. We consider development only in the third, or neoclassical, phase. In this phase the development of a dual economy is characterized by the same fundamental relations as in the neoclassical approach. If the advanced sector is not economically viable, two possibilities exist. First, if $\alpha = \beta\epsilon$, the existence of a positive manufacturing labor force contradicts the fundamental differential equation for the neoclassical theory of development of a dual economy. Hence, for the classical approach this condition must be ruled out by assumption. Secondly, if $\alpha < \beta\epsilon$, the manufacturing labor force begins to decline as soon as disguised unemployment is eliminated. This decline continues until the agricultural labor force reaches its maximum level, so that further increases in the agricultural labor force are redundant. Throughout the decline of the manufacturing labor force the real wage in both sectors remains constant, with no disguised unemployment.

With a fixed real wage, measured in agricultural goods, the rate of population growth must decline to the rate of technological progress in agriculture when the agricultural labour force reaches its maximum, so that $\epsilon = \alpha$ from this point forward. At this lower rate of population growth the advanced

sector is always economically viable. The labor force in manufacturing begins to grow at a rate exceeding that of population growth but eventually declines to this rate of growth. The renewed growth of the manufacturing labor force is characterized by a "big push"— that is, an extraordinarily high rate of growth of the manufacturing labor force. As in the neoclassical theory of the development of a dual economy, this high initial rate of growth may be interpreted as a statistical artifact. The existence of such a statistically observable "big push" is no evidence for the necessity of a massive infusion of capital from outside the system for a "takeoff." Sustained growth depends on the economic viability of the advanced sector at the new rate of population growth and not on the initial level of capital stock.

In the second phase of growth in the manufacturing labor force the labor force in agriculture remains constant at its maximum level, while agricultural output grows at the same rate as population. Manufacturing output and capital stock eventually increase at the rate $l/(1 - \sigma) + \alpha$, and the real wage, measured in manufacturing goods, grows at the rate $l/1 - \sigma$. Throughout the second phase of growth in the manufacturing labor force, the real wage, measured in agricultural goods, is increasing at the rate of technological progress in agriculture, α. The terms of trade between agriculture and industry eventually grows at the rate $l/(1 - \sigma) - \alpha$. This rate may be positive or negative, depending on the relative rates of technological progress in the two sectors.

In the classical theory of the development of a dual economy, the phase of development beginning with no manufacturing production but with redundant agricultural labor or disguised unemployment is characterized by a rate of growth of the manufacturing labor force that exceeds the rate of growth of population. This characterization is a necessary consequence of the classical theory, whether or not the advanced sector is economically viable at the maximum rate of net reproduction. If the advanced sector is not economically viable at this rate of population growth, the initial phase of disguised unemployment is followed by a phase of absolute decline in the manufacturing labor force that terminates with the agricultural labor force at its maximum level and with a reduced rate of population growth. This phase is followed by a second phase of growth in the manufacturing labor force. Again, the rate of growth of the manufacturing labor force exceeds the rate of growth of population.

We conclude that the criterion for a critical minimum effort proposed by Fei and Ranis, that the rate of growth of population must be less than the rate of growth of the industrial labor force, provides no indication whatever concerning the economic viability of the advanced sector. The advanced sector is economically viable if and only if there is a positive and growing agricultural surplus— that is, $\alpha > \beta \epsilon$. During the phase of disguised unemployment, the critical minimum effort criterion of Fei and Ranis is satisfied whether or not the advanced sector is economically viable. Where their criterion is satisfied, the elimination of disguised unemployment may be followed by sustained economic growth or by a period of absolute decline in the manufacturing labor force. Only the existence of a positive and growing agricultural labor force assures that growth will be sustained.

SUMMARY

In the preceding sections we have described two alternative approaches to the theory of development of a dual economy. In order to facilitate comparison of the two approaches, we have attempted to develop both within the same framework. Within this framework the basic differences between the two approaches are in assumptions made about the technology of the agricultural sector and about conditions governing the supply of labor. In the classical approach it is assumed that there is some level of the agricultural labor force beyond which further increments in this labor force are redundant. In the neoclassical approach the marginal productivity of labor in agriculture is assumed to be always positive, so that labor is never redundant. In the classical approach the real wage rate, measured in agricultural goods, is assumed to be fixed "institutionally" so long as there is disguised unemployment in the agricultural sector. In the neoclassical approach the real wage rate is assumed to be variable rather than fixed; it is further assumed that at very low levels of income the rate of growth of

population depends on the level of income. These are the basic differences between the neoclassical and classical approaches to the theory of development of a dual economy.

The neoclassical and classical theories differ in the characterization of the backward or traditional sector of the economy. These differences have implications for the behavior of the backward sector. Among the implications we may note that according to the classical approach, the agricultural labor force must decline absolutely before the end of the phase of disguised unemployment; in the neoclassical approach the agricultural labor force may rise, fall, or remain constant. The differences between the two approaches also have implications for the behavior of the advanced sector; unfortunately these implications depend on the actual behavior of the terms of trade between the backward and advanced sectors. In the neoclassical approach the terms of trade may rise or fall. In the classical approach the terms of trade cannot be determined endogenously. Alternative assumptions about the course of the terms of trade may be made. Corresponding to each assumption about the terms of trade, there is an alternative theory for the behavior of the advanced sector. Since any assumption about the course of the terms of trade is consistent with the classical approach, the behavior of the terms of trade cannot provide a test of this approach. The classical approach may be tested only by deriving the implications of this approach for the advanced sector, given the observed behavior of the terms of trade, and confronting these implications with empirical evidence.

We have developed the classical theory in detail only on the assumption that the terms of trade between the backward and advanced sectors remain constant. Proceeding on this assumption, we have derived the following implications of the classical approach: (1) output and employment in the advanced sector grow at the same rate so long as there is disguised unemployment in the backward sector; that is, labor productivity in the advanced sector remains constant; (2) capital grows at a slower rate than output and labor, so that capital-output ratio falls; this result corresponds to that of Fei and Ranis [1961b]; (3) the rates of growth of manufacturing output, employment, and capital increase during the phase of disguised unemployment. For the neoclassical approach, the corresponding results are: (1) output and capital in the advanced sector grow at the same rate, asymptotically, so that the capital-output ratio remains constant; (2) manufacturing employment grows more slowly than either output or capital, so that labor productivity in the advanced sector rises; (3) the rates of growth of manufacturing output and employment decrease throughout the development process. Since the classical approach reduces to the neoclassical approach after the phase of disguised unemployment is completed, the two approaches have different implications only for situations where it is alleged that disguised unemployment exists.

In view of the similarities between classical and neoclassical approaches to the development of a dual economy, it is not surprising that many implications of one model are also implications of the other. For example, both models imply that if the proportion of manufacturing output to agricultural output increases, the share of saving in total income also increases. Thus, either model suffices to explain an increase in the fraction of income saved in the course of economic development. The fact that the implications of the two approaches for the share of saving are identical is of considerable significance. According to Lewis [1954]: "The central problem in the theory of economic development is to understand the process by which a community which was previously saving and investing [four or five percent] of its national income or less, converts itself into an economy where voluntary saving is running at about [twelve to fifteen percent] of national income or more. This is the central problem because the central fact of economic development is rapid capital accumulation (including knowledge and skills with capital)." Both classical and neoclassical theories of the development of a dual economy provide an explanation of an increase in the share of saving. In each case the explanation is based on the relationship between saving and industrial profits. Disguised unemployment is neither necessary nor sufficient to generate a sustained rise in the share of saving. Ultimately a sustained increase in the saving share depends on a positive and growing agricultural surplus, and not on the presence or absence of disguised unemployment.

EVIDENCE

We have concluded that tests of the classical versus the neoclassical approach to the development of a dual economy can be carried out only for situations in which it is alleged that disguised unemployment exists. For all other situations the implications of the two approaches are identical. Even where disguised unemployment is alleged to exist, some implications of the two approaches are identical. The implications that are different may be classified into two groups: direct implications of the basic assumptions about agricultural technology and the conditions governing the supply of labor; and indirect implications about the behavior of both backward and advanced sectors of the economy. In reviewing the evidence pertaining to the development of a dual economy, we will first discuss the evidence for and against the existence of disguised unemployment and historical evidence for and against the constancy of the real wage rate in certain historical circumstances where disguised unemployment allegedly exists. Secondly we will discuss the evidence for and against the indirect implications of the two alternative approaches. Since the indirect implications refer mainly to historical trends in economic development, we will concentrate on the historical development of the Japanese economy, which is cited in support of the classical approach by Fei and Ranis [1964, p. 134, 263–64] and by Johnston [1962].

In Lewis' [1954] original presentation of the classical approach the scope of validity of the assumption of disguised unemployment is delimited as follows: "It is obviously not true of the United Kingdom, or of North West Europe. It is not true either of some of the countries usually now lumped together as under-developed; for example, there is an acute shortage of male labour in some parts of Africa and of Latin America. On the other hand it is obviously the relevant assumption for the economies of Egypt, of India, or of Jamaica." In Lewis' treatise *The Theory of Economic Growth*, he characterizes the phenomenon of disguised unemployment as follows: "This phenomenon is rare in Africa and in Latin America, but it repeats itself in China, in Indonesia, in Egypt and in many countries of Eastern Europe" [1955, p. 327]. In a later presentation he states that "More than half of the world's population (mainly in Asia and in Eastern Europe) lives in conditions which correspond to the classical and not to the neoclassical assumptions [1958]. Fei and Ranis are not so specific in delimiting the scope of application of their version of the Lewis model. However, they state that "The empirical support of both our theory and policy conclusions draw heavily on the experience of nineteenth century Japan and contemporary India" [1964, p. 6].

Lewis' allegations that disguised unemployment exists in Asia and Eastern Europe are based on a substantial literature on the problem dating from the 1930's and early 1940's. This literature has been surveyed by Kao, Anschel, and Eicher [1964]. Estimates of disguised unemployment in the early literature are based on what Kao, Anschel, and Eicher call the indirect method of measurement. In this method labor requirements for production of the current level of agricultural output and labor available from the agrarian population are estimates; the difference between labor available and labor required is called "disguised unemployment." One fallacy underlying this method is that agricultural work in all countries is highly seasonal. Substantial parts of the agricultural labor force may be unemployed in agriculture during a part of the year without being redundant. The critical test is whether the agricultural labor force is fully employed during peak periods of demand for labor, such as planting and harvesting. Only if labor is redundant during periods of peak demand could the agricultural labor force be reduced without reducing agricultural output. A second fallacy underlying the indirect method is that all members of the agricultural population older than some minimum age, usually fifteen, are treated as members of the agricultural labor force and that younger members of the population are not treated as members of the agricultural labor force. All of the studies of the 1930's and early 1940's are based on the indirect method of measurement. Examples are provided by the

work of Buck [1930] on China and the work of Warriner [1939], Rosenstein-Rodan [1943], and Mandelbaum [1945] on southeastern Europe. More recent examples may be found in the work of Warriner [1948] on Egypt, Mellor and Stevens [1956] on Thailand, and Rosenstein-Rodan [1957] on southern Italy.

Warriner [1955] has subsequently withdrawn from her position on disguised unemployment in Egypt, noting that her earlier estimate was based on a fallacious set of assumptions. Kenadjian [1961] has corrected Rosenstein-Rodan's estimate of disguised unemployment for southern Italy to take seasonal demands for labor into account. By this single adjustment the estimate of disguised unemployment is reduced from 10 to 12 per cent of the agricultural labor force to less than 5 per cent. Pepelasis and Yotopoulos have attempted to measure disguised unemployment in Greece from 1953 to 1960, taking into account the seasonal pattern of demand for labor. Their conclusion is the following: "From the eight years of our series, [disguised unemployment] existed only in 1953 and 1954 to a degree of 3.4 and 2.3 [per cent] respectively. The other years of the period are marked by a seasonal shortage of labor" [Kao et al., 1964, p. 136]. A corrected version of Buck's estimate of disguised unemployment has been presented by Hsieh: "the conclusion that in the majority of the localities . . . there was at the seasonal peak a shortage of male labor, which had to be reinforced by a large number of female workers, probably applies not only to many other areas of China but also to other Asian countries. Field investigations of several other localities in China and the rural districts of Bengal in India reveal a similar situation. Considering the extremely intensive input of labour in their farm operations, this is not unexpected" [Hsieh, 1952]; [Oshima, 1958]. We conclude that estimates of disguised unemployment based on the so-called indirect method of measurement always overestimate the amount of disguised unemployment. When these estimates are corrected to take into account the seasonality of demands for agricultural labor, the situation in southeastern Europe, Egypt, China, and Southeast Asia appears to be one of labor shortage rather than labor surplus.

Almost all of the evidence for the existence of disguised unemployment is based on the indirect method of measurement. However, attempts have been made to test for the existence of disguised unemployment by examining historical instances in which substantial parts of the agricultural labor force have been withdrawn in a short period of time. This type of test is always subject to the criticism that one cannot generalize from isolated historical examples. Nonetheless, the evidence is worth reviewing. One class of examples consists of studies of agricultural production after labor is withdrawn for a public works project. Two such examples are summarized by Schultz, as follows: "In Peru a modest road was recently built down the east slopes of the Andes to Tingo Maria, using some labor from farms along the way mostly within walking distances; agricultural production in the area dropped promptly because of the withdrawal of this labor from agriculture. In Belo Horizonte, Brazil, an upsurge in construction in the city drew workers to it from the nearby countryside, and this curtailed agricultural production" [1956, p. 375; 1964, p. 62].

Another class of examples consists of studies of the effects of famines and epidemics. Schultz [1964, 66–67] has studied one such example in detail, the effects of the influenza epidemic of 1918–1919 in India on agricultural production. He summarizes the results as follows: "The agricultural labor force in India may have been reduced by about 8 per cent as a consequence of the 1918–19 epidemic. The area sown to crops was reduced sharply the year of the influenza, falling from 265 million in 1916–17 to 228 million in 1918–19. This drop, however, is confounded by some adverse weather and by the many millions of people who became ill and who were therefore incapacitated for a part of the crop year. For reasons already presented, 1919–20 is the appropriate year to use in this analysis. The area sown in 1919–20 was, however, 10 million acres below, or 3.8 per cent less than that of the base year 1916–7. In general, the provinces of India with the highest death rates attributed to the epidemic also had the largest percentage declines in acreage sown to crops. It would be hard to find any support in these data for the doctrine that a part of the labor force in agriculture in India at the time

of the epidemic has a marginal productivity of zero."[13]

A third type of evidence used to test for the existence of disguised unemployment consists of anthropological studies of peasant agriculture, 18 studies by anthropologists and economists are cited by Oshima [1958] in support of the following position: "Despite the limitations of the empirical material, there is no denying the general picture that emerges for Asia. The labor requirement during busy seasons exceeds the male, adult population so that female and juvenile labor must be recruited into the labor force. And, from the description found in the book, cited, no part of this larger labor requirement seems redundant, given the existing technology and organization. A withdrawal of portions of the labor force may be expected to reduce total output (in the sense that insufficient plowing, inadequate planting, and untimely harvesting will diminish the size of the final crop)." The studies reviewed by Oshima refer to India, China, and southeast Asia. Schultz gives a detailed summary of two exceptionally complete anthropological studies, that of Panajachel, Guatemala, by Sol Tax and that of Senapur, India by W. David Hopper. Schultz [1964, p. 52] concludes "that no part of the labor force working in agriculture in these communities has a marginal productivity of zero."

Evidence from anthropological studies is subject to the same criticism as the examination of historical instances of rapid withdrawal of agricultural labor—namely that one cannot generalize from particular examples. However, in view of the consistency of the evidence from indirect estimates of disguised unemployment for the entire agricultural labor force of countries such as Greece, southern Italy, Egypt, and China with

13. Amartya K. Sen has pointed out to me that the estimates of changes in working age population used by Schultz are too high, since only deaths between 1917–1918 and 1918–1919 are recorded as changes in the labor force. The natural increase of the population from 1916–1917 and 1919–1920, the base dates for the measurement of acreage sown, are ignored. Taking 8.35 per cent per decade as the rate of natural increase, Schultz's estimates of changes in the agriculture labor force should be reduced by 2.4 per cent. Making these changes, Sen obtains an estimate of the labor coefficient of .412±.252, Sen's estimate is closer to the a priori value of 0.4 given by Schultz than Schultz's own estimate of 0.349±0.152. Sen's results, like those given by Schultz, support the conclusion cited in the text.

the evidence from both historical and anthropological studies, it may be concluded that disguised unemployment simply does not exist for a wide range of historical and geographical situations where it has been alleged to exist. Lewis admits that disguised unemployment is not typical of Africa and Latin America. This is consistent with the historical and anthropological evidence for Brazil, Mexico, and Peru cited by Schultz. Lewis claims that disguised unemployment exists in southeastern Europe, Egypt, and Asia. But this is inconsistent with the evidence from indirect measurement in the case of southeastern Europe, Egypt, and China and both historical and anthropological evidence in the case of India, China, and Southeast Asia. We may conclude, with Kao, Anschel, and Eicher [1964, p. 141], that "it is an understatement to say that the development literature in [the early 1950's] was optimistic about development through the transfer of redundant agricultural labor to other occupations. We have shown that the empirical studies supporting this optimism were often poorly conceived. In addition, we have noted that by considering temporary rather than permanent labor transfers and by allowing some reorganization of production, various writers have arrived at a high percentage of disguised unemployment. To date, there is little reliable empirical evidence to support the existence of more than token—5 per cent—disguised unemployment in underdeveloped countries."

We have reviewed the evidence for and against the existence of disguised unemployment. The evidence suggests that the conditions governing the supply of labor in southeastern Europe and Asia are no different from those in Latin America and Africa to which Lewis refers. This evidence does not demonstrate that disguised unemployment never exists in any historical or geographical circumstances, but only that the scope of applicability of the classical approach to the development of a dual economy is severely limited. More specifically, the classical assumptions do not apply to Latin America, Africa, southeastern Europe, India, China or Southeast Asia. Thus far we have reviewed evidence for most of Asia except for Japan. For Japan it is possible to check out the indirect implications of the classical and neoclassical approaches for historical trends in economic development. Japan is the only Asian country for which long-term data exist for trends in agricultural and nonagricultural labor force, agricultural and nonagricultural output, and capital formation. Furthermore, Japanese historical development has been cited in support of the classical approach by Fei and Ranis [1964, pp. 134, 263–264] and by Johnston [1962]. Fei and Ranis state that "Continuous capital shallowing in Japanese industry between 1888 and the end of World War I is evidence that Japan made maximum use of her abundant factor, surplus agricultural labor" [1964, p. 132]. They go on to say that "The empirical evidence on Japan . . . indicates clearly that . . . a change of regime from capital shallowing to capital deepening occurred at about the end of World War I. Moreover, we have convincing evidence that Japan's unlimited supply of labor condition came to an end at just about that time. . . . The virtual constancy before and rapid rise of the real wage after approximately 1918 is rather startling. We thus have rather conclusive evidence in corroboration of our theoretical framework" [1964, pp. 263–264]. Since the Japanese data are the only empirical support offered by Fei and Ranis in support of their assumption of an unlimited supply of labor at a constant real wage, Japanese economic development up to 1918 provides an important test case for the classical approach to the theory of development of a dual economy.

We first consider the implications of the classical approach for the agricultural sector. For this sector Fei and Ranis [1964, p. 22] assume that there is an institutionally fixed real wage, equal to the initial average productivity of labor. Ohkawa and Rosovsky provide data from which real labor income per capita in agriculture for the period 1878–1917 may be estimated. The share of rents in agricultural income fluctuates during this period, beginning at an average level of 59 per cent in 1878–1887 and ending at an average level of 58 per cent in 1908–1917 [Ohkawa and Rosovsky, 1964, p. 54]. Labor income may be estimated by deducting the share of rents from real income per capita. This results in the series for labor income presented in Table 11.1. Total real income per capita is 100.0 in 1913–1917 [Ohkawa and

Table 11.1. Real Labor Income per Capita in Japanese Agriculture, Five-Year Averages 1878–1917.

1878–82	18.0
1883–87	18.1
1888–92	18.2
1893–97	21.1
1898–02	27.0
1903–07	31.3
1908–12	39.4
1913–17	42.0

SOURCE: Computed from K. Ohkawa and H. Rosovsky [1964, Table 6, p. 54; Table 10, p. 57].

Rosovsky, 1964, p. 55]. We conclude that for the period 1878–1917 the assumption of of a constant real wage rate in the agricultural sector is inconsistent with the evidence. The hypothesis of a constant real wage rate in the agricultural sector where disguised unemployment exists is the most important assumption underlying the classical approach to the theory of development of a dual economy. The classical approach stands or falls on this hypothesis.

A second implication of the classical approach for the behavior of the agricultural sector is that the agricultural labor force must decline absolutely as redundant labor leaves the land and, later, as disguised unemployment is eliminated. This decline must include all of the redundant labor force, together with that part of the labor force with marginal productivity less than the real wage rate. The typical pattern of economic development in Europe is a constant or moderately rising agricultural labor force until just before or just after the relative importance of nonagricultural population surpasses that of agricultural population. Subsequently, the agricultural labor force begins to fall [Dovring, 1959].[14] In short, absolute reductions in the size of the agricultural labor force occur after industrialization is well under way rather than during the early stages of industrialization. This pattern also characterizes Japan. The agricultural labor force is essentially constant from 1878–1882 to 1903–1907, falling slightly from an average level of 15,573 thousand to

15,184 thousand over this period of 25 years. From 1903–1907 to 1913–1917 the agricultural labor force falls from an average level of 15,184 thousand to an average of 14,613 thousand. The total decline over the 35-year period is 7 per cent [Ohkawa and Rosovsky, 1964, p. 46]. Since Fei and Ranis date the end of the surplus labor period at 1918, we may conclude that 7 per cent can serve as an upper bound for the percentage of the labor force that could be classified as redundant at any time during the period 1878–1917. A second useful comparison may be made between the number of farm households in 1884, a total of 5,437 thousand, and the number in 1920— 5,573 thousand, a slight increase [Ohkawa and Rosovsky, 1964, p. 49]. The movement of labor from the rural areas to the advanced sector did not involve the transfer of a reserve army of the disguised unemployed. The process is described by Ohkawa and Rosovsky as follows: "During the early period of industrialization necessary increases in the labor force did indeed come from the rural areas. But laborers were usually young and left single. There was only very little movement in terms of family units, and no formation of an agricultural proletariat. Thus, a fairly typical Asian type of agriculture remained in existence and was utilized to promote impressive increases in productivity, while Western technology was making rapid progress in manufacturing" [1964, p. 48]. The Japanese pattern may be regarded as similar to that of many European countries, including countries of northwestern Europe, where the period preceding the predominance of the nonagricultural labor force in the total labor force is characterized by a stable agricultural labor force, rising or declining at very moderate rates throughout the period of initial industrialization. This pattern is inconsistent with the hypothesis of redundant labor or of disguised unemployment. However, the pattern is entirely consistent with the neoclassical theory of the development of a dual economy. We may conclude with Ohkawa and Minami [1964] that "in the light of Japanese experience with the initial phase of economic development, traditional agriculture based on household production grew at a considerable rate in terms of both output and productivity; technological progress had taken place and the level of living

14. For a study of the development of agricultural population during the English industrial revolution revealing a similar pattern, see Chambers [1953]. I am indebted to Henry Rosovsky for this reference.

and wage rates increased to a certain extent. These responses occurred together with the increase in population. In view of this, it seems that the features of models of the Lewis type are too rigorous to be applied to such historical realities."

We have discussed the empirical validity of the implications of the classical approach to the theory of development of a dual economy for the agricultural sector. These implications the constancy of the real wage rate, measured in agricultural goods, and the absolute decline of the agricultural labor force during the phase of disguised unemployment—are directly contradicted by the evidence we have reviewed. In particular, the interpretation of Japanese economic development prior to 1917 by Fei and Ranis is inconsistent with the evidence on real labor income in agriculture. The pattern of development of the agricultural labor force up to 1917 is inconsistent with the existence of substantial surplus labor in the agricultural sector during the initial period of industrialization. The development of the agricultural labor force follows the pattern of most European countries. This pattern is fully consistent with the neoclassical approach to the development of a dual economy. At this point we turn to the development of the advanced or nonagricultural sector of the Japanese economy during the period preceding 1917. As we have already pointed out, the implications of the classical approach for the advanced sector depend on the historical development of the terms of trade between agriculture and industry. Data on the terms of trade are presented by Ohkawa and Rosovsky [1964, p. 48]. These data are consistent with the assumption that the terms of trade are essentially constant throughout the period before 1917. Accordingly, the implications of the classical approach on this assumption may be confronted with data on the development of the nonagricultural sector of the Japanese economy for this period.

The first implication of the classical approach for the advanced sector is that labor productivity remains constant during the phase of disguised unemployment. The corresponding implication of the neoclassical approach is that labor productivity is always rising. Real income per member of the labor force in secondary and tertiary industry for

the period 1878–1917 are given by Ohkawa [1957, p. 34]. These data are presented in Table 11.2. The data show an increase in

Table 11.2. Real Income per Capita in Japanese Industry Five Year Averages, 1878–1917.

	Secondary industry	Tertiary industry
1878–82	137	156
1883–87	173	199
1888–92	189	197
1893–97	217	227
1898–02	268	261
1903–07	237	261
1908–12	266	313
1913–17	327	333

SOURCE: Ohkawa [1957, p. 34].

labor productivity from 1878–1882 to 1913–1917 of 239 per cent in secondary industry and 213 per cent in tertiary industry. These increases in productivity are inconsistent with the implication of the classical theory that labor productivity remains constant throughout the phase of disguised unemployment. Increases in labor productivity are a direct implication of the neoclassical approach. We conclude that the data on labor productivity provide very powerful support for the neoclassical theory.

A second implication of the classical approach for the advanced sector is that the rates of growth of output and employment increase over time. The corresponding implication of the neoclassical approach is that rates of growth of both variables decline over time. Rates of growth of real income and occupied population in secondary and tertiary industry for the period 1878–1917 are presented in Table 11.3. The rate of growth of real income has a substantial downward trend for this period. This trend is inconsistent with the implications of the classical approach. The rate of growth of the nonagricultural labor force shows a high initial value but declines monotonically as development proceeds. This trend is also inconsistent with the implications of the classical approach. We conclude that data on the rates of growth of output and employment provide additional support for the neoclassical theory. It should be pointed out that for the period subsequent to 1918, the date at which disguised unemployment disappears according to Fei and

Table 11.3. Rates of Growth of Output, Employment, and Capital in Japanese Industry Five Year Averages, 1878–1917.

	Output	Employment	Capital
1878–82 to 1883–87	10.1	5.4	—
1883–87 to 1888–92	4.4	4.4	4.7
1888–92 to 1893–97	6.3	3.8	5.2
1893–97 to 1898–02	6.7	3.4	5.7
1898–02 to 1903–07	1.9	3.0	4.6
1903–07 to 1908–12	5.8	2.6	6.5
1908–12 to 1913–17	5.2	2.4	5.8

SOURCE: Rates of growth of output and employment computed from Ohkawa [1957, p. 20, p. 34]; rate of growth of capital computed from Ishiwata [n.d. p. 12].

Ranis, there is an increase in the rates of growth in the secondary and tertiary sectors. This is evidence neither for nor against the classical as opposed to the neoclassical approach, since the implications of these approaches are identical for periods in which there is no disguised unemployment.

A third implication of the classical approach for the advanced sector is that the capital-output ratio falls throughout the phase of disguised unemployment and that the rate of growth of capital increases over time. The corresponding implications of the neoclassical approach are based on asymptotic results; the capital-output ratio eventually becomes constant, since the rate of growth of output and the rate of growth of capital tend to the same limit. Data on net capital stock for the period 1883–1917 are given by Ishiwata [n.d., p. 12]. Rates of growth computed from these data are presented in Table 11.3. There is essentially no trend in the rate of growth of capital during this period. We conclude that data on the rate of growth of capital stock are inconsistent with the implications of the classical approach. The capital-output ratio for the advanced sector may be computed from the data on capital given by Ishiwata and the data on real income given by Ohkawa. The resulting capital-output ratios are presented in Table 11.4. The capital-output ratio for the advanced sector computed by

Ishiwata from an alternative set of data on real income are also presented in this table [n.d., p. 15]. For the period as a whole, both series of capital-output ratios show a substantial increasing trend. For Ishiwata's series of capital-output ratios the trend is especially strong. We conclude that the implication of the classical approach of "capital-shallowing" throughout the period prior to 1917 is inconsistent with the evidence. The data on capital-output ratios provide additional support for the neoclassical theory.

We have considered implications of the classical and neoclassical approaches to the development of a dual economy for both agricultural and nonagricultural sectors. The assumption of a constant real wage rate in the agricultural sector made in the classical approach is inconsistent with the evidence presented by Ohkawa and Rosovsky. Real labor income per capita in agriculture more than doubles during the period 1878–1917. The implication of the classical approach that the agricultural labor force must decline absolutely as redundant labor leaves the land is also inconsistent with the evidence. Data on the occupied population in agriculture shows a decline from 1878–1917 of only 7 per cent; data on the number of farm households shows a 2.5 per cent increase. The Japanese pattern is similar to that of many European countries where the agricultural labor force is essentially stable throughout the period of initial industrialization.

Implications of the classical approach for the nonagricultural sector are also inconsistent with the evidence. First, the implication that labor productivity remains constant is in-

Table 11.4. Capital-Output Ratio in Japanese Industry, Five Year Averages, 1883–1917.

	Ohkawa real income	Ishiwata real income
1883–87	1.96	1.56
1888–92	1.99	1.51
1893–97	1.88	1.53
1898–02	1.80	1.52
1903–07	2.03	1.72
1908–12	2.10	1.82
1913–17	2.24	1.79

SOURCE: Computed from Ohkawa [1957, p. 34] and Ishiwata [n.d., p. 15].

consistent with the data presented by Ohkawa; these data show an increase in labor productivity over the period 1878–1917 of 239 per cent in secondary industry and 213 per cent in tertiary industry. Secondly, the implication that rates of growth of output and employment increase over time is inconsistent with evidence on the growth of real income and employment in the non-agricultural sector presented by Ohkawa. Finally, the implications that the rate of growth of capital increases over time and that the capital-output ratio falls is inconsistent with the data of Ishiwata on capital stock for the period 1883–1917. The rate of growth of capital stock shows no trend over this period; the capital-output ratio actually rises substantially over the period 1883–1917.

The evidence on Japanese economic development from 1878–1917 supports the neoclassical rather than the classical approach to the theory of development of a dual economy. The basic assumptions of the classical approach are inconsistent with the evidence. The implications of the classical approach are also inconsistent with the evidence, while the implications of the neoclassical approach are strongly supported by the evidence. The evidence on Japanese economic development corroborates the evidence we have reviewed for and against the existence of disguised unemployment in Latin America, Africa, southeastern Europe, India, China, and Southeast Asia. We conclude that the neoclassical theory of the development of a dual economy is strongly supported by the empirical evidence and that the classical approach must be rejected.

References

BUCK, 1930. John Lossing Buck, *Chinese Farm Economy* (Chicago: University of Chicago Press, 1930).

CHAMBERS, 1953. J. D. Chambers, "Enclosure and Labour Supply in the Industrial Revolution," *Economic History Review*, Second Series, Vol. 5, No. 3 (1953), 319–43.

CHENERY, 1960. H. B. Chenery, "Patterns of Industrial Growth," *American Economic Review*, Vol. 50, No. 4 (September 1960), 624–54.

CLARK, 1957. C. Clark, *The Conditions of Economic Progress*, 3rd ed. (London: Macmillan, 1957).

DOMAR, 1946. E. D. Domar, "Capital Expansion, Rate of Growth, and Employment," *Econometrica*, Vol. 14, No. 2 (April 1946), 137–47.

DOVRING, 1959. F. Dovring, "The Share of Agriculture in a Growing Population," *Monthly Bulletin of Agricultural Economics and Statistics*, Vol. 8, No. 8/9 (August–September 1959), 1–11.

DUESENBERRY, 1958. J. S. Duesenberry, *Business Cycles and Economic Growth* (New York: McGraw-Hill, 1958).

ELLIS, 1961. Howard S. Ellis, "Las Economías Duales y El Progreso," *Revista de Economia Latinoamericana*, Año I, No. 3 (Julio–Septiembre 1961), 127–41.

FEI and RANIS, 1961a. J. C. H. Fei and G. Ranis, "Unlimited Supply of Labour and the Concept of Balanced Growth," *Pakistan Development Review*, Vol. 1, No. 3 (Winter 1961), 31–58.

FEI and RANIS, 1961b. J. C. H. Fei and G. Ranis, "A Theory of Economic Development," *American Economic Review*, Vol. 51, No. 4 (September 1961), 533–64.

FEI and RANIS, 1963. J. C. H. Fei and G. Ranis, "Capital Accumulation and Economic Development," *American Economic Review*, Vol. 53, No. 3 (June 1963), 283–313.

FEI and RANIS, 1964. J. C. H. Fei and G. Ranis, *Development of the Labor Surplus Economy* (Homewood, Ill.: Irwin, 1964).

FIRTH and YAMEY, 1964. Raymond W. Firth and B. S. Yamey, eds., *Capital, Saving and Credit in Peasant Societies* (Chicago: Aldine 1964).

HARROD, 1939. R. F. Harrod, "An Essay in Dynamic Theory," *Economic Journal*, Vol. 49, No. 193 (March 1939), 14–33.

HSIEH, 1952. C. Hsieh, "Underemployment in Asia: I. Nature and Extent," *International Labor Review*, Vol. 65, No. 6 (June 1952), 703–25.

ISHIWATA, n.d. S. Ishiwata, *Estimation of Capital Stocks in Prewar Japan (1868–1940)*, Unpublished Paper D 27 (Tokyo, Japan: Institute of Economic Research, Hitotsubashi University).

JOHNSTON, 1962. B. F. Johnston, "Agricultural Development and Economic Transformation: A Comparative Study of the Japanese Experience," *Food Research Institute Studies*, Vol. 3, No. 3 (November 1962), 223–75.

JORGENSON, 1961. Dale W. Jorgenson, "The Development of a Dual Economy," *Economic Journal*, Vol. 71, No. 282 (June 1961), 309–34.

KALDOR, 1957. Nicholas Kaldor, "A Model of Economic Growth," *Economic Journal*, Vol. 67, No. 268 (December 1957), 591–624. Reprinted in *Essays in Economic Stability and Growth* (Glencoe, Ill.: Free Press, 1960), 259–300.

KALDOR, 1960. Nicholas Kaldor, "Characteristics of Economic Development," *Essays on Economic*

Stability and Growth (Glencoe, Ill.: Free Press, 1960), 233–42.

KALDOR, 1961. Nicholas Kaldor, "Capital Accumulation and Economic Growth," in F. A. Lutz and D. C. Hague, eds., *The Theory of Capital* (London: Macmillan, 1961).

KALDOR and MIRRLEES, 1962. N. Kaldor and J. Mirrlees, "A New Model of Economic Growth," *Review of Economic Studies*, Vol. 29, No. 80 (June 1962), 174–92.

KAO, ANSCHEL and EICHER, 1964. C. H. C. Kao, K. R. Anschel and C. K. Eicher, "Disguised Unemployment in Agriculture: A Survey," in C. K. Eicher and L. W. Witt, eds., *Agriculture in Economic Development* (New York: McGraw-Hill, 1964).

KENADJIAN, 1961. B. Kenadjian, "Disguised Unemployment in Underdeveloped Countries," *Zeitschrift für Nationalökonomie*, Band 21, Heft 2 (September 1961), 216–23.

KUZNETS, 1957. S. Kuznets, "Quantitative Aspects of the Economic Growth of Nations, II. Industrial Distribution of National Product and Labor Force, *Economic Development and Cultural Change*, Vol. 5, No. 4 Supplement (July 1957).

LEIBENSTEIN, 1954. H. Leibenstein, *A Theory of Economic-Demographic Development* (Princeton, N.J.: Princeton University Press, 1954).

LEIBENSTEIN, 1957. H. Leibenstein, *Economic Backwardness and Economic Growth* (New York: John Wiley, 1957).

LEWIS, 1954. W. A. Lewis, "Economic Development with Unlimited Supplies of Labour," *Manchester School of Economics and Social Studies*, Vol. 22 (May 1954), 139–91.

LEWIS, 1955. W. A. Lewis, *The Theory of Economic Growth* (London: Allen and Unwin, 1955).

LEWIS, 1958. W. A. Lewis, "Unlimited Labour: Further Notes," *Manchester School of Economics and Social Studies*, Vol. 26 (January 1958), 1–32.

MANDELBAUM, 1945. K. Mandelbaum, *The Industrialization of Backward Areas* (Oxford: Blackwell and Mott, 1945).

MELLOR and STEVENS, 1956. J. W. Mellor and R. D. Stevens, "The Average and Marginal Product of Farm Labor in Underdeveloped Economies," *Journal of Farm Economics*, Vol. 38, No. 3 (August 1956), 780–91.

NICHOLLS, 1963. William H. Nicholls, "An Agricultural Surplus as a Factor in Economic Development," *Journal of Political Economy*, Vol. 71, No. 1 (February 1963), 1–29.

NICHOLLS, 1964. William H. Nicholls, "The Place of Agriculture in Economic Development," in C. K. Eicher and L. W. Witt, eds., *Agriculture in Economic Development* (New York: McGraw-Hill, 1964).

NURSKE, 1953. Ragnar Nurske, *Problems of Capital Formation in Underdeveloped Countries* (New York: Oxford University Press, 1953).

OHKAWA, 1957. K. Ohkawa, *The Growth Rate of the Japanese Economy since 1878* (Tokyo: Kinokuniya, 1957).

OHKAWA and MINAMI, 1964. K. Ohkawa and R. Minami, "The Phase of Unlimited Supplies of Labor," *Hitotsubashi Journal of Economics*, Vol. 5, No. 1 (June 1964), 1–15.

OHKAWA and ROSOVSKY, 1964. K. Ohkawa and H. Rosovsky, "The Role of Agriculture in Modern Japanese Economic Development," in C. K. Eicher and L. W. Witt, eds., *Agriculture in Economic Development* (New York: McGraw-Hill, 1964). First published in *Economic Development and Cultural Change*, Vol. 9, Part 2 (October 1960), 43–67.

OSHIMA, 1958. H. Oshima, "Underemployment in Backward Economies: An Empirical Comment," *Journal of Political Economy*, Vol. 66, No. 3 (June 1958), 259–63.

ROSENSTEIN-RODAN, 1943. P. N. Rosenstein-Rodan, "Problems of Industrialization of Eastern and South-Eastern Europe." *Economic Journal*, Vol. 53, Nos. 210–211 (June–September 1943), 202–211.

ROSENSTEIN-RODAN, 1957. P. N. Rosenstein-Rodan, "Disguised Unemployment and Underemployment in Agriculture," *Monthly Bulletin of Agricultural Economics and Statistics*, Vol. 6, Nos. 7/8 (July–August 1957), 1–7.

SCHULTZ, 1956. T. W. Schultz, "The Role of the Government in Promoting Economic Growth," in Leonard D. White, ed., *The State of the Social Sciences* (Chicago: University of Chicago Press, 1956).

SCHULTZ, 1964. Theodore W. Schultz, *Transforming Traditional Agriculture* (New Haven, Conn.: Yale University Press, 1964).

SMITHIES, 1957. A. Smithies, "Economic Fluctuations and Growth," *Econometrica*, Vol. 25, No. 1 (January 1957), 1–52.

SOLOW, 1956. R. M. Solow, "Contribution of the Theory of Economic Growth," *Quarterly Journal of Economics*, Vol. 70, No. 1 (February 1956), 65–94.

SPAVENTA, 1959. Luigi Spaventa, "Dualism in Economic Growth," *Banca Nazionale del Lavoro-Quarterly Review*, No. 51 (December 1959), 386–434.

SWAN, 1956. T. W. Swan, "Economic Growth and Capital Accumulation," *Economic Record*, Vol. 32 (November 1956), 334–61.

TINBERGEN, 1942. J. Tinbergen, "Zur Theorie der langfristigen Wirtschaftsentwicklung," *Weltwirtschaftliches Archiv.*, 55 Band (1942), 511–49. Translated and reprinted as "On the Theory of Trend Movements," in L. H. Klaasen, L. M. Koyck and H. J. Witteveen, eds., *Jan Tinbergen Selected Papers* (Amsterdam: North-Holland, 1959), 182–221.

TOBIN, 1955. J. Tobin, "A Dynamic Aggregative

Model," *Journal of Political Economy*, Vol. 63, No. 2 (April 1955), 103–15.

WARRINER, 1939. Doreen Warriner, *Economics of Peasant Farming*, (London: Oxford University Press, 1939).

WARRINER, 1948. Doreen Warriner, *Land and*

Poverty in the Middle East (London: Royal Institute of International Affairs, 1949).

WARRINER, 1955. Doreen Warriner, "Land Reform and Economic Development," Fiftieth Anniversary Commemoration Lectures (Cairo: National Bank of Egypt, 1955).

COMMENT

Sectoral Interdependence, Structural Transformation, and Agricultural Growth

BRUCE F. JOHNSTON

AT THE OUTSET of his paper Jorgenson explains that he is concerned with the role of subsistence agriculture in the *theory* of economic growth rather than its role in the process of economic growth. Perhaps this explains why this brilliant exercise in model-building seems to have only limited relevance to the important policy issues in the field of agricultural development.

My own interest in seeking to understand the changing nature of the interrelationships between agriculture and the rest of the economy in the course of development has been quite different. My preoccupation has been to derive insight with respect to the choice of measures for promoting agricultural development and with the issues involved in determining an appropriate balance between agriculture and nonagriculture in the allocation of resources and in the tax burden of the two sectors. That the issues of sectoral balance are exceedingly difficult is obvious; and for reasons that Tolley and I have recently tried to elaborate [Johnston and Tolley, 1965], it is also singularly difficult to establish suitable criteria for devising an efficient strategy for promoting agricultural development. Hence I am prone to take a very pragmatic view of theoretical models.

If a model seems to illuminate certain essential features of the growth process, I am not greatly disturbed if it is not a complete model or even if it fails to give a complete description of reality in all respects. Thus I continue to believe, in spite of Jorgenson's ingenious effort at refutation, that the Lewis two-sector model affords important insights, although it certainly needs to be refined and supplemented. Incidentally, I am intrigued by the fact that Jorgenson apparently does not even regard Lewis' formulation as a "dual-economy model," asserting that his only purpose for introducing a backward sector was "to provide a physical location for the industrial reserve army." (Presumably Jorgenson disregards Lewis' consideration of the role of the backward sector in providing the food supplies of the modern sector, because this is handled as a verbal supplement to the more formal part of the analysis.) I would have supposed, on the contrary, that the backward sector figures prominently in Lewis' model because he had observed that such a sector is a huge, palpable fact in most underdeveloped countries and that the overwhelming importance of the agricultural sector in the early stages of growth is a highly significant initial condition that has important implications for the process of development.

Let us now turn to what I regard as the central feature of Jorgenson's neoclassical model. In the present paper this is summed up with breathtaking brevity: "Given any positive initial capital stock, no matter how small, the existence of a positive and growing agricultural surplus generates sustained economic growth." Elsewhere he notes that the necessary and sufficient condition for the emergence of a positive and growing agricultural surplus, and therefore a necessary and sufficient condition for sustained economic growth, is that $\alpha - \beta\epsilon > 0$—that is, that the rate of technical progress in agriculture exceeds the exogenously determined rate of population growth multiplied by the elasticity of output with respect to land. (I will have a few words to say later about Jorgenson's handling of population growth, but I will note in passing that his population relation is not as important—nor to my way of thinking, troublesome—as appears to be the case on a first reading.)

This conclusion is, of course, diametrically opposed to Lewis' view. For both Jorgenson and Lewis, an essential feature of sustained economic growth is the structural transformation of an economy that takes place with the emergence of an expanding industrial sector. Lewis characterizes this as the "capitalist sector" to emphasize the difference in technology between the two sectors: the fact that this modern sector utilizes appreciable quantities of capital, whereas production in the traditional sector is based on land and labor, with scarcely any use of reproducible capital. Lewis also emphasizes a difference in employment arrangements between the two sectors, viz. the fact that the capitalist sector is based on wage labor hired only up to the point where its marginal productivity is equal to the wage rate, whereas his "subsistence sector" is, as Ohkawa [1964, pp. 201–212] expresses it, the "self-employment sector" in which the bulk of the population is able to eke out an existence, even though the marginal product of some of its members may be less than the average product that they consume. The fundamental contrast is that in Lewis' view the transfer of manpower to the capitalist sector is limited by the *demand* for labor, which in turn is limited by the rate of capital accumulation.

Now within the assumptions of the respective models, each of the two views is correct. And as a description of reality, both views are quite obviously wrong. Or to be a bit more precise, an accurate description of the real world has to take account of the element of truth contained in both views. The emergence of a growing nonagricultural sector necessarily depends upon the availability of food supplies for the increasingly large fraction of the population employed in that sector. But it is equally true that sustained economic growth and the process of structural transformation depends upon the

expansion of output and employment in the nonagricultural sector, i.e. the rate of increase in the *demand* for labor in the secondary and tertiary sectors. This aspect of the problem was, in fact, vividly expressed by Jorgenson in his first article on the dual economy [1961]: "Of course, if the growth of manufacturing is not sufficiently rapid some of the excess labor force will remain on the land and part or all of the surplus may be consumed in the form of increased leisure for agricultural workers." That is to say, a necessary, though obviously not sufficient, condition for the emergence of a positive and growing agricultural surplus is a growing nonagricultural sector dependent upon purchased food. The growth of demand must provide "scope" for an increase in agricultural productivity to occur.

In short, in a given time or place the limiting factor in the process of structural transformation and economic growth may be either an inadequate rate of increase in food supplies for a growing nonagricultural population *or* an inadequate rate of expansion of the capitalist sector. A one-sided view of causation, as with the concept of "agriculture's contributions" that a number of us have used, is inadequate for reasons that have been well expressed by Ohkawa [1964]. As is usual in economics, we need a concept that recognizes the reciprocal relationships involved. And in this instance we need to think in terms of the sectoral interdependence between agriculture and the rest of the economy—and of the implications of the changing nature of those interrelationships.

In my own thinking, influenced considerably by study of Japan's experience, I have tended to focus my attention in the direction emphasized by the Lewis model. But before I indicate why I attach particular importance to factors relevant to the growth of demand for labor outside of agriculture, let me take pains to disassociate myself from the naive view that a substantial fraction of the farm labor force can be removed, without appropriate measures to increase agricultural productivity, and expect to maintain the level of agricultural output unchanged. Even though Lewis started with the assumption of "unlimited supplies of labor," he qualified this by the proviso that the workers remaining in agriculture could sustain output because they would be able and willing to work harder [Lewis, 1954]. Mellor and I argued in our 1960 treatment of this issue that, although a more intensive rate of utilization of the existing stock of farm labor might be of appreciable importance in some situations, a much more significant consideration is the potential that exists for expanding farm output and productivity by methods that make only minimal demands on capital and other scarce resources [Johnston and Mellor, 1960].

Although it is difficult to specify formally, there is an important distinction to be made between the notion of disguised unemployment in the static sense and the proposition that, owing to the limited rate of growth of demand for food and the potential that exists for increasing output per unit of input, there is often a relative surplus of labor in agriculture. (The special significance of agricultural exports in most underdeveloped countries is, of course, related to the fact that expansion of production for export is not limited by the rate of increase in the size and per capita incomes of the domestic population dependent upon purchased food.) If the notion of "rural underemployment" or, in its extreme form, the idea of redundant rural labor of zero marginal productivity is taken to mean that the agricultural sector can be ignored, the idea is fundamentally and disastrously wrong. But on the other hand, there is likely to be a "surplus" of labor in traditional agriculture in a *relative* sense during the earlier stages of development; and this proposition has significant implications for many less-developed countries. I find the large body of literature discussing the existence or nonexistence of surplus labor in agriculture under static *ceteris paribus* assumptions largely irrelevant, although I must concede that there are undoubtedly "industrial fundamentalists" at large who need to be disabused of the notion that a sizable fraction of the rural population in underdeveloped countries is idle and can simply be transferred to industry with no adverse impact on agricultural output. No doubt there are many areas where there is significant underemployment except at the seasonal peaks in labor requirements. There are also, or have been, areas where most farming activities are "woman's work," so that there is, or was, a potential surplus of male labor. But to translate that potential into a participating role in the farm labor force requires a change in attitudes, most commonly sparked in tropical Africa by the introduction of high-value export crops and a sharpened interest in acquiring money incomes.

The principal implication of this concept of a relative surplus of labor in agriculture at the early stages of development concerns the choice of measures or the appropriate strategy to be pursued in fostering agricultural development. This is a subject on which I have written at length, and I only propose to mention briefly two aspects of the problem at this time.

As a result of the primacy of man's need for food and the limited extent to which secondary wants can be satisfied in a pre-industrial economy, countries at an early stage of economic development have some 70 to 80 per cent of their labor force in agriculture. (A number of Latin American countries are not, in this sense, underdeveloped—or certainly not an early stage of development.) The change in size of the agricultural labor force can be indicated very simply by a relation suggested by Dovring, viz: $P'_A \equiv (P'_T - P'_N)(P_T/P_A) + P'_N$, where P'_A, P'_T, and P'_N are the rates of change in the agricultural, total, and nonagricultural population respectively, and P_T/P_A is a weighting coefficient equal to the total population divided by the farm population [Dovring, 1959; Johnston and Nielsen, 1966]. This relationship is, of course, merely an identity; but I will argue that for countries at an early stage of development there are cogent reasons for assuming that the causal factors work in such a way that the rate of change in the agricultural population (or labor force) is the dependent variable. That is, owing to institutional arrangements such as the family farm or "communal" systems of land tenure, which give agriculture its special character as the "self-employment sector," the size of the agricultural labor force is determined essentially as a residual. Furthermore, where little structural transformation has taken place, the agricultural labor force will continue to increase in absolute size for many years, and there is real danger that it may not even decrease as a percentage of total population unless employment opportunities in the nonagricultural sectors increase at a fairly rapid rate.

Jorgenson asserts that the classical model implies an immediate *absolute* decline in the farm population; but given a high rate of population growth and a situation where agriculture weighs heavily in the total population, this seems highly unlikely. There are, in fact, three considerations (in addition to agriculture's special character as the self-employment sector), which suggests that the farm population will continue to increase in absolute size until considerable structural transformation has taken place.

First, extraordinarily high rates of population growth are to an increasing extent characteristic of the less-developed countries; and there are very strong indications that for the short and medium term the population growth in these countries must be regarded as an essentially exogenous variable, determined mainly by rapid and large reductions in mortality rates that are not dependent on any major change in economic and social structure. Although Jorgenson seems to attach a good deal of importance to a functional relationship between per capita food supplies and the death rate, the relationship appears to be relevant only to his "failure" cases. I will, therefore, not pause to take issue with this assumed relationship, although I will say in passing that it seems a little more defensible than the functional relationship between per capita food supplies and birth rates postulated in his 1961 article. The second reason is that the rate of absorption of labor by the nonagricultural sectors seems to be primarily a function of the rate of capital formation and the degree of capital intensity of investment in the nonagricultural sector; and this rate of absorption appears to be remarkably slow even in those underdeveloped countries that have witnessed fairly rapid rates of capital formation and output in their industrial sector. Owing to higher rates of natural increase and slower growth of employment in the nonagricultural sector, underdeveloped countries today do not seem to display the high coefficients of differential growth (i.e. the difference between the rate of growth of the total and the nonagricultural population) that were experienced in Meiji Japan. The third consideration is simply the fact that, for a given coefficient of differential growth, the change in P'_A is very sensitive to the weighting coefficient, P_T/P_A. For example, an extremely high coefficient of differential growth of 4 per cent associated with a P'_T of 2 per cent and P'_N of 6 per cent means that the absolute size of the farm population will *increase* at a rate of 1 per cent if agriculture still accounts for as much as 80 per cent of the population; but it will decrease at a 4 per cent rate if the farm population's share has fallen to 40 per cent of the total.

The second implication of the changing nature of the interrelationships between agriculture and nonagriculture that I want to mention concerns the increase in agricultural productivity that must occur in order to support a growing nonfarm population. Tolley has presented a two-sector model that shows how the percentage change in the proportion of the population in the agricultural and nonagricultural sectors will depend upon changes in productivity in the two sectors, the income elasticity of demand for food, and the proportion of the population in the agricultural sector in the year being considered [Johnston and Tolley, 1965]. If we make the rather unrealistic assumption—although it is in line with Jorgenson's "success" case and the Ranis-Fei model—that the income elasticity of demand for food is zero, Tolley's model gives the following simple relationship:

$$S_g = (f'/f)(N_f/N_g),$$

where S_g is the percentage rate of increase in the proportion of the population in the non-food sector, f'/f is the annual percentage increase in productivity in the agricultural sector (and thus equivalent to Jorgenson's α), and N_f and N_g are the proportion of the population in the agricultural and non-agricultural sectors respectively.

The first point that is relevant here is simple that at the early stages of development achievement of even a high rate of growth of the nonagricultural sector and in the population dependent upon purchased food requires only a fairly modest increase in agricultural productivity because the second term, N_f/N_g, is very large. But as structural transformation proceeds, the required increases in agricultural productivity increase at an accelerating rate. (More realistic assumptions concerning the change in the income elasticity of demand for food over time would, of course, make the changes in the required increase in agricultural productivity less spectacular.)

The other point to be emphasized is that the rate of change in agricultural productivity (Tolley's f'/f or Jorgenson's α) should be regarded as an important policy variable, not a constant. There is striking historical evidence, derived especially from the experience of Japan and the United States, that the potential for increasing output per unit of input is very substantial. It is because of this evidence, of course, that such importance attaches to what Schultz [1953] has described as the process of producing and distributing new production techniques. And another part of Tolley's model draws attention to the fact that when the agricultural sector bulks large in the total economy, it should receive priority in the allocation of resources directed at increasing output by shifting production functions.

In conclusion, I would like to make two brief observations with respect to Jorgenson's attempt to invoke certain aspects of Japan's experience to demonstrate that his neoclassical model gives a more faithful approximation of reality than the classical models of Lewis or Ranis and Fei. First, I would like to suggest that the notion of a constant real wage in agriculture and non-agriculture is a simplifying *assumption*, not an implication of these models. And I find it very easy to agree with the analysis by Ohkawa and Minami [1964] that suggests that it is a very difficult assumption to defend. I will therefore only mention in passing that, as Ohkawa would readily agree, the rate of increase in per capita food consumption in Japan, suggested by the figures that he published in 1957, exaggerate the rate of increase because of underestimation of agricultural output in the early years of Meiji.

Inasmuch as Jorgenson supports his argument by citing the statement in the Ohkawa and Minami article that "the features of models of the Lewis type are too rigorous to be applied to such historical realities," it seems appropriate to quote a more general conclusion by Ohkawa concerning the relevance of the Lewis model to Japan's experience. Speaking of the characteristics

of the Japanese labor force in terms very similar to my general discussion of the determinants of the agricultural labor force in an underdeveloped country, Ohkawa concludes:

In a broad sense, it was "a labour market with an unlimited supply of labour," in Arthur Lewis' terminology. The supply price of labor was basically determined by the level of subsistence of the people on the land. With real wage rates determined correspondingly by it, the enterprisers in the non-agricultural sector could employ their required labour force in an almost perfectly elastic manner.

Ohkawa goes on to note that, contrary to the Lewis assumption, real wages increased in Japan. He then concludes, with a somewhat cavalier attitude toward models that is much to my liking, "that the notion of an unlimited supply of labor can still be applied in this case on the assumption of a trend line of an increasing supply price of labor at a certain rate" [1964, 207].

Jorgenson's neoclassical model, on the other hand, assumes that agricultural wages are determined as a proportion of wages in the nonagricultural sector. The first comment here is that it is usually more meaningful to think in terms of per capita incomes of the farm population rather than a wage rate since wage employment is generally of minor importance in the agricultural sector of less developed countries, and the major component of income of farm families in such economies is their own consumption of their own subsistence production.

The basic point, however, is that it seems most unlikely that the level of agricultural incomes would adjust to industrial wage levels. At least to the extent that there is validity in the view that the transfer of population out of agriculture is limited by the rate of growth of demand for industrial labor, we have a disequilibrium situation in which such equilibrating adjustments in the allocation of labor to the two sectors are not to be expected. It thus seems much more plausible to argue, with Lewis and Ohkawa, that the supply price of labor is "basically determined by the level of subsistence of the people on the land." In fact, it would seem that at the present time the principal anomaly that calls for explanation is the extent of job rationing and the fact that industrial wages in industrial countries often seem to be two or three times as high as average farm incomes, instead of the 30 per cent differential suggested by Lewis in 1954.

References

DOVRING, 1959. F. Dovring, "The Share of Agriculture in a Growing Population," *FAO Monthly Bulletin Agricultural Economics and Statistics*, Vol. 8, No. 8/9 (August–September 1959), 1–11.

JOHNSTON and MELLOR, 1960. B. F. Johnston and J. W. Mellor, "The Nature of Agriculture's Contributions to Economic Development," *Food Research Institute Studies*, Vol. I, No. 3 (November 1960), 335–56.

JOHNSTON and NIELSEN, 1966. B. F. Johnston and S. T. Nielsen, "Agriculture and Structural Transformation in a Developing Economy," *Economic Development and Cultural Change*, Vol. 14, No. 3 (April 1966), 279–301.

JOHNSTON and TOLLEY, 1965. B. F. Johnston and G. S. Tolley, "Strategy for Agriculture in Development," *Journal of Farm Economics*, Vol. XLVII, No. 2 (May 1965), 365–79.

JORGENSON, 1961. Dale W. Jorgenson, "The Development of a Dual Economy," *Economic Journal*, Vol. LXXI, No. 282 (June 1961) 309–334.

LEWIS, 1954. W. A. Lewis, "Economic Development with Unlimited Supplies of Labour," *The Manchester School*, Vol. 22 (May 1954), 139–91.

OHKAWA, 1964. K. Ohkawa, "Concurrent Growth of Agriculture with Industry: A Study of the Japanese Case," in R. N. Dixey, ed., *International Explorations of Agricultural Economics* (Ames, Iowa: Iowa State University Press, 1964) 201–212.

OHKAWA and MINAMI, 1964. K. Ohkawa and R. Minami, "The Phase of Unlimited Supplies of Labor," *Hitotsubashi Journal of Economics*, Vol. 5, No. 1 (June 1964), 1–15.

SCHULTZ, 1953. T. W. Schultz, *The Economic Organization of Agriculture* (New York: McGraw-Hill, 1953).

COMMENT

Two Sector Models and Development Policy

VERNON W. RUTTAN[1]

THIS PAPER WILL EXAMINE the potential contribution of two sector models to the formulation of agricultural development policy. In evaluating the potential contribution of two sector models, or any other analytical scheme, to agricultural development policy, it is desirable to maintain a sharp distinction between economic analysis and economic policy or planning. Analysis implies the breaking down of a complex phenomenon, such as the process of agricultural or general economic development, into its components in order to achieve an understanding of fundamental elements, relationships, and processes. Economic policy or planning involves utilization of the growth components, relationships, and processes to design new patterns of organization leading to more rapid development.[2]

If this symbiotic relationship between economic analysis and economic planning is to persist, the analyst must identify those strategic variables that will have a relatively high pay-off when they are manipulated by those engaged in economic policy-making and planning. And the economic policy-maker and planner must develop sufficient sophistication to recognize and use the insights that the analyst can provide.

During the last three decades economics has been involved in a major revolution and, in the last decade, has resolved a major intellectual crisis.[3] After two decades of intensive testing and elaboration, a new integration of Keynesian and classical economics has been achieved. This integration has resulted in a new consensus regarding the broad monetary and fiscal policy measures appropriate to the achievement of relatively high rates of economic growth in modern

1. The author is grateful to Raj Krishna, A. Weisblat, and Jose Encarnacion, Jr., for helpful comments during the preparation of this paper.

2. This distinction is similar to that made in biology between genetics and plant breeding [Chang, 1964, 48–49; Jennings, 1964].

3. For a discussion of the concept and characteristics of scientific revolution," see Kuhn [1962].

capitalist economies [Johnson, 1961; 1962].[4]

As economists have been asked to extend their services to policy-makers and planners in countries that are just beginning to experience modern economic growth, a new crisis has developed. Something approaching a consensus has begun to emerge to the effect that economic analysis conducted within the framework of either the older developments associated with the "marginal revolution" or post-Keynesian income, employment, and growth theory has been less effective than anticipated in providing the knowledge needed by policy-makers and planners in solving the development problems of the emerging non-Western economies [Lewis, 1955, 140–141; Bauer, 1963; Robinson, 1962, 99–123; Seers, 1962].

No clear-cut system of "new development economics" has emerged to dominate the field as completely as the "new economics" based on Keynes' work dominated economic thought after 1936. Two approaches have established a substantial "claim," however, in the race to stake out the boundaries of a "new development economics."

One of these approaches is the "growth stage" or "leading sector" approach, which in recent literature, has been closely identified with Rostow [1956; 1960]. Agricultural development stages have been elaborated by Johnston and Mellor [1961], Mellor [1962a; 1962b] and by others [Perkins and Witt, 1961]. I recently examined the potential contribution of the growth stage approaches to agricultural development policy in another context [Ruttan, 1965]. Two major conclusions emerged from this examination: the growth-stage approaches have played a positive role in focusing attention on the critical importance of the agricultural sector in the development process; and the basic limitation of the growth-stage approach is that it substitutes a search for economic doctrine in the form of historical generalizations for the development of analytical power.

The two- (or multiple-) sector approach that Jorgenson employs in the paper being reviewed represents a second major approach to the formulation of a new development economics. As with the growth-stage approach, primary emphasis is placed on the

dynamics of the transition or "takeoff" into sustained growth. Whether the multiple-sector models will be more successful than the growth-stage scheme in establishing a valid claim as the foundation for a "new development economics" will depend on the ability of economic analysts, working within the context of two or multisector development models, to provide policy-makers and planners with effective guides to the policy decisions and program choices necessary to achieve more rapid growth in a specific economy at a particular time.

THE JORGENSON NEOCLASSICAL TWO-SECTOR MODEL

In his paper for this conference, and in his 1961 article in the *Economic Journal*, Jorgenson presented an excellent review of the evolution of the "Keynesian" and "neoclassical" growth models and of the dual economy development models. He has also made a major contribution to the theory of growth of the dual economy.

In Jorgenson's neoclassical model, the classical assumption of zero marginal productivity of labor and an "institutionally determined wage-rate" in the subsistence sector are dropped, and wage rates are determined in an intersector labor market. As a result, labor is never available to the industrial sector without sacrificing agricultural output, and the terms of trade move against the industrial sector continuously throughout the development process.

In Jorgenson's system an economy's ability to generate an agricultural surplus depends on only three parameters: the rate of technical progress in agriculture; the rate of population growth (when population growth is not limited by food shortages); and the elasticity of output in the agricultural sector with respect to changes in the agricultural labor force. For an economy caught in a low-level equilibrium trap, an escape is possible only through changes in the rate of introduction of new technology in agricultural production, and changes in medical knowledge and practices, which lowers the birth rate more rapidly than mortality.

If these two policies can be pursued with sufficient vigor, either singly or in combination, an agricultural surplus can be produced.

---

4. It is perhaps more correct to refer to a consensus with respect to the Keynesian "paradigm" rather than to Keynesian theory.

And production of an agricultural surplus is both a necessary and a sufficient condition for the generation of growth in the total economy. No initial minimum level of capital stock is required to induce a "takeoff" into sustained economic growth. The rate of growth of output in the nonagricultural sector, given the existence of an agricultural surplus depends on the rate of technological progress in the nonagricultural sector; the elasticity of output growth with respect to the growth of labor inputs; and the elasticity of output growth with respect to the growth of capital inputs.

The Jorgenson model has clearly moved at least two steps beyond the Ranis and Fei model toward the objectives of operational relevance.[5] The Fei-Ranis assumption of an "institutionally determined" wage rate and a horizontal labor supply curve to the industrial sector, which persists until agricultural employment begins to decline absolutely, is difficult to defend empirically.[6] And historical research, stimulated by Rostow's emphasis on the "takeoff," casts considerable doubt on the significance of models that depend primarily on dramatic shifts in saving and/or capital accumulation to escape from a low-level equilibrium trap [Rostow, 1963; Strassmann, 1964].

There are a number of aspects of the model, however, that imply that further elaboration is needed before the potential of the two-sector model can be fully realized. Let me enumerate:

1. *The model is for a closed economy.* Oshima's criticism [1963] of the Fei and Ranis "classical"

model in this respect would also seem to apply to the Jorgenson model. Trade may represent a substitute for either a domestic agricultural surplus or a domestic industrial sector.[7]

2. *The shift from a high- to a low-income elasticity of demand for agricultural products by the agricultural sector is discontinuous.* In both models all increases in per capita agricultural income are consumed by the agricultural sector until limitations on population growth imposed by food shortages are eliminated. Beyond this point the income elasticity of demand for agricultural output in the agricultural sector declines to zero, and all increases in per capita agricultural production beyond this point become available as a surplus to support the growth of the nonagricultural labor force. Historical experience is consistent with a more gradual shift from high- to low-income elasticities of demand for farm products [Goreux, 1960; FAO, 1957].

3. *Resource use in the intersector commodity market is ignored.* In most underdeveloped countries substantial labor and capital resources are absorbed in the storage transportation and trading activities involved in making the marketable surplus produced by the agricultural sector available to urban consumers. The shift of workers from a rural or village location to an urban location associated with growth in nonfarm employment typically requires an even more rapid rate of growth of resource use in the marketing sector than the rate of growth in marketable surplus from the agricultural sector [Stevens, 1963; USDA, ERS, 1965].

4. *The terms of trade move against the industrial sector continuously.* This appears inconsistent with the growth experience in the presently advanced countries. In the United States, for example, the terms of trade moved against the industrial sector from the closing of the land frontier (about 1890) until the beginning of rapid production advance in the 1920's. Since the mid-1920's the terms of trade have generally moved in favor of industry, except during World War II [Ruttan and Callahan, 1962; Potter and Christy, 1962].

5. Modifications in their more recent work have tended to reduce some of the differences between the Jorgenson "neoclassical" and Fei and Ranis "Keynesian" two sector models [Fei and Ranis, 1966; Jorgenson, 1966].

6. Jorgenson argues that even the Japanese data, on which Fei and Ranis depend for historical support, is inconsistent with the hypothesis of a fixed wage rate in the agricultural sector during the development process. Gaps in the historical record do leave some room for disagreement, however. Additional evidence against the institutionally determined wage rate is provided by two types of studies: Kao et al. [1964] argue that there is little reliable empirical evidence to support the existence of zero marginal productivity of labor in agriculture in underdeveloped countries and regions. Work on the impact of urban-industrial development on agricultural wage rates and incomes demonstrates a close association between the level of local urban-industrial development and farm wage rates in underdeveloped countries and regions. This is inconsistent with a perfectly classic supply curve of labor to the industrial sector [Ruttan, 1955; Nicholls, 1960; 1963; Fonollera and Ruttan, 1965].

7. Since this paper was written, several papers exploring the economics of the open dualistic economy have been prepared by D. S. Paauw and J. C. H. Fei [Paauw, 1966; Fei and Paauw, 1966].

5. The rate of growth of population and labor force are identical. I would anticipate that prior to maximum population growth, and for some period thereafter, the rate of growth of population, and hence demand for agricultural output, would be higher than the rate of growth of the labor force. A lagged relationship would represent at least a perfunctory recognition of population dynamics [Encarnacion, 1967].

Although it would be possible to elaborate on each of these points, I would like to focus the rest of my discussion on what Jorgenson has identified as "the fundamental characteristic of a dual economy"—asymmetry in the productive relations.

TWO-SECTOR MODELS AND
DEVELOPMENT POLICY

In the two-sector models reviewed here, the production relation for the agricultural sector is defined to include only land and labor. Land inputs in the aggregate are considered to be fixed—to have a zero supply elasticity. The production relation for the nonagricultural sector is defined to include only capital and labor. Land or, more broadly, resource inputs are not represented in the production function for the nonagricultural sector.

Land in the Nonfarm Sector

Unless we are prepared to ignore the nonsubsistence resource sectors such as mining, forestry, and plantation agriculture (activities that have been defined out of the agricultural sector in two-sector models in order to maintain the convention that the *subsistence sector* and the *agricultural sector* are identical), the production function for the nonagricultural sector should be expanded to include land and other natural resources.

This is particularly important during the early stages of development, when output of the nonsubsistence *resource* sectors may be large relative to the output of the manufacturing sector. At present, when some authors would argue that the Philippine economy has "taken off" into self-sustained growth [Itchon, 1962], the nonsubsistence agricultural and resource sectors (mining, forestry, fishing, and plantation agriculture) account for roughly

15 per cent of GNP as compared to approximately 18 per cent by manufacturing.[8]

Capital in Agriculture

Any model that is expected to have operational relevance must include, as elements in the agricultural production function, terms that permit an evaluation of the elasticity of output with respect to: capital investment in land; capital equipment purchased from the nonfarm sector; and inputs of operating expense items, such as fertilizer and insecticides, purchased from the nonfarm sector.

The classical distinction between land and capital—land being identified as the "original and indestructible powers of the soil"— represents an untenable analytical distinction. Knight insisted at least 30 years ago that the notion that land is not produced, in the same sense that other capital goods are produced, is false [Knight, 1956, 53-54]. The only distinction between land and other inputs that is significant for economic policy is their relative elasticity of supply and their relative output elasticity coefficients.

A review of recent Asian experience impresses one with the extent to which increases in output continue to be accounted for by increases in land inputs, even in the most densely populated countries of the region During the last decade increases in area planted accounted for roughly one-fourth of the growth of rice output in Japan, for one-third of the growth in India, and for the entire increase in rice output in the Philippines [Venegas, 1964].

Even in Taiwan, the only country of the region in which yield increases were sufficient to account for the entire increase in the growth of rice production, the increases were not achieved by a simple upward shift of the production function. The yield increases were achieved primarily by investment resulting in expansion of irrigation systems and more effective delivery of irrigation water to increase the land area double-cropped; increases in the use of fertilizer, an input purchased from the nonfarm sector; and introduction of new rice varieties characterized by a high-yield response to fertilizer [Hsieh and Lee, 1958].

8. Calculated from data presented in National Economic Council [1964].

It is possible, of course, to take the position that even if output can be increased by capital investment in the agricultural sector or in the agricultural supply sector, it is much more efficient to obtain the same output increases through pure shifts in the production function. The production of technological change in agriculture is itself, however, a relatively capital-intensive activity (particularly when one considers the human investment involved). Furthermore, it frequently requires a relatively long gestation period and has highly uncertain returns. The supply of new technical knowledge is relatively inelastic with respect to increases in expenditure on research over the short run because of the inelastic supply of competent research personnel in most less-developed countries. Technological change is, itself, one of the more difficult products for a country in the early stages of economic development to produce. In fact, it sometimes appears that an industrial economy is a prerequisite for technological change in the agricultural sector.[9]

A NEW DIMENSION IN THE GROWTH OF DEMAND FOR FARM OUTPUT

The importance of expanding the dual-economy model to include resource flows from the nonagricultural to the agricultural sector becomes particularly important for those countries in which the elasticity of supply of land is relatively low or where land development is shifting from a labor intensive to a capital intensive activity, and which are, at the same time, experiencing population growth rates approximating the biological maximum. (Philippine population is now growing at more than 3.2 per cent per year and is expected to approximate 4.0 per cent per year during 1975–1980. [Ramachandran, 1963].) In such economies even modest increases in per capita income imply annual rates of growth in the domestic demand for agricultural output of 4.0–6.0 per cent per year. Rates of growth of domestic demand in this range are completely outside the experience of most presently developed countries either during recent years or during the time they were making the transition from predominantly agricultural to industrial economies. Among non-Western economies, only those that have been able to achieve rapid increases in land in cultivation have experienced agricultural output growth rates in this range in recent years [USDA, ERS, 1965].

To achieve agricultural growth rates in this range, I would anticipate the necessity for two types of capital investment:

1. *Rapid increases in capital intensive land development.* In the past, land development has been relatively labor intensive in most Southeast Asian countries. In Japan and Taiwan, the climate and topography lent themselves to labor-intensive land development even during the later stages of agricultural development. Climatic and topographic considerations in the monsoon areas are such, however, that I would anticipate that the investment required to bring substantial new areas into production or to make water available during the dry season in areas presently cultivated would be much more capital-intensive in the future.

2. *Rapid increases in capital investment by the nonfarm sector to support technological change in agriculture.* Such investment must be directed into the support of agricultural research; into investment in industries that produce the equipment and materials (fertilizer, insecticides) in which the new technology is embodied; and into the development of the effective transport, market or credit, and tenure facilities and institutions.

The net effect of such capital flows into the agricultural sector could even reverse the investment flow from the farm to the nonfarm sector assumed in most two-sector models as well as in most growth-stage approaches.[10]

I urge Jorgenson to expand his two-sector model, in order to explore the effects of reducing the asymmetry in the production relations. He could then hope to deal operationally with situations where an industrial surplus represents a prerequisite for surplus production in the agricultural sector at certain stages in the development of low-income agricultural economies. Tolley and Smidt

9. Even in Japan the rate of growth of total productivity in agriculture remains low relative to the rate of growth of total productivity in the rest of the economy [Domar, 1964].

10. I understand from Raj Krishna that such a reverse flow may be under-way in India at the present time.

[1964] recently produced and implemented empirically a two-sector model for the United States economy that includes capital and other inputs purchased from the non-agricultural sector in the agricultural production function. The only alternative I see to this suggestion is to build a three-sector model in which the pure subsistence sector is separated from the rest of agriculture.

SUMMARY

It is now time to return to the issue posed in the introduction. What guidance can the dual-economy models provide the policy-maker or the planner in making the policy decisions and formulating the program designs necessary to achieve more rapid agricultural development? My answer can be summarized in three points.

1. Deductions from the dual-economy models can provide formal confirmation of the policy-makers' intuitive judgment that the rate of technological change and the rate of population growth represent important instrumental variables in any effort to achieve surplus production in the agricultural sector. This is a solid but hardly remarkable achievement.

2. The promise of the dual models to replace the historical generalizations of the growth-stage approaches with relevant empirically testable analytical relationships remains inadequately realized.

3. At least part of the failure of the dual-economy models has been due to the empirical techniques employed by their builders. Instead of the historical generalizations about growth-stage sequences, construction of dual-economy models tends to proceed on the basis of rather casual empirical generalizations about the variables to be included and the form of the relationships appropriate to the models.

There are also two additional points that have implications both for the general discussion of the last several days as well as for the paper being reviewed and the broader issues of transforming subsistence agriculture:

1. There are *no* theoretical propositions that can provide operational guides to economic policy in the absence of empirical knowledge regarding the magnitudes of variables and parameters in the *specific* economy for which the policy choices are relevant. Let me draw an analogy from biology. Knowledge of the principles of plant nutrition does not permit the extension worker or farmer to recommend accurately the appropriate application of nitrogen to rice on a *specific* field; it can only guide him in designing an efficient trial or test in the farmer's field to provide the relevant empirical information. Similarly, the role of growth models or theories is not to provide direct insight regarding policy choices; rather, it is to serve as a *guide* for the empirical research needed to project the quantitative effects of the manipulation of alternative instrumental variables.

2. I seriously object to the use of generalized historical tests as a device for selection among alternative models. The lack of conclusiveness of such tests is illustrated by the disagreement between Jorgenson and Fei and Ranis regarding the support they derive from their "classical" and "neo-classical" formulation from Japanese historical experience. Since it is usually possible to build several logically consistent models that are not contradicted by historical data, such tests are inherently weak. A stronger test must involve the response to deliberate changes in instrumental variables. The work at Vicos that Holmberg reports in his chapter illustrates the systematic testing of the consequences of the use of economic policy to modify the parameters of a microeconomic system. At the macroeconomic level, more attention needs to be given to the consequences of deliberate policy changes than to the imperatives of self-contained models.

References

BAUER, 1963. P. T. Bauer, "The Study of Underdeveloped Economies," *Economica*, Vol. 30, No. 120 (November 1963) 360–71.

CHANG, 1964. T. T. Chang, *Present Knowledge of Rice Genetics and Cytogenetics*, Technical Bulletin #1, International Rice Research Institute, College, Laguna, Philippines (August 1964).

DOMAR, et al., 1964. E. D. Domar, et al., "Economic Growth and Productivity in the United States, Canada, United Kingdom, Germany and Japan in the Post-War Period," *Review of Economics and Statistics*, Vol. 46, No. 1 (February 1964), 33–41.

ENCARNACION, 1964. José Encarnacion, Jr., "Two-Sector Models of Economic Growth and Development," *The Philippine Economic Journal*, Vol. IV, No. 1 (First Semester 1965), 1–13.

FEI and PAAUW, 1966. J. C. H. Fei and D. S. Paauw, "Analysis of the Open Dualistic Economy: An Application to the Philippines," Field Work Report No. 9, Center for Development Planning, National Planning Association, Washington, D.C., August 1966. (Mimeographed.)

FEI and RANIS, 1966. J. C. H. Fei and Gustav Ranis, "Agrarianism, Dualism and Economic Development," in Irma Adelman and Erik Thorbecke, eds., *The Theory and Design of Economic Development* (Baltimore: Johns Hopkins University Press, 1966), 3–41.

FAO, 1957. Food and Agriculture Organization, United Nations, "Factors Influencing the Trend of Food Consumption," *The State of Food and Agriculture* (Rome: Food and Agriculture Organization, 1957), 70–110.

FONOLLERA and RUTTAN, 1965. Raymundo Fonollera and Vernon W. Ruttan, "Agricultural Wage Rates and Non-Farm Development in the Philippines," International Rice Research Institute, Agricultural Economics Staff Memorandum (February 1965).

GOREUX, 1960. L. M. Goreux, "Income and Food Consumption," *FAO Monthly Bulletin of Agricultural Economics and Statistics*, Vol. 9, No. 10 (October 1960), 1–12.

HSIEH and LEE, 1958. S. C. Hsieh and T. H. Lee, *An Analytical Review of Agricultural Development in Taiwan—an Input-Output and Productivity Approach*, Economic Digest, Series #12 (Taipei, Taiwan, China: Chinese-American Joint Commission on Rural Reconstruction, July 1958). (A 1964 supplement to the above report was released in 1965).

ITCHON, 1962. G. Y. Itchon, "Philippines: Necessary Conditions for 'Take-Off'," *The Philippine Economic Journal*, Vol. 1 (First Semester, 1962), 28–37.

JENNINGS, 1964. P. R. Jennings, "Plant Type as a Rice Breeding Objective," *Crop Science*, Vol. 4, No. 1 (1964), 13–16.

JOHNSON, 1961. H. G. Johnson, "The General Theory After Twenty-Five Years," *American Economic Review*, Vol. 51, No. 2 (May 1961), 1–17.

JOHNSON, 1962. H. G. Johnson, "Monetary Theory and Policy," *American Economic Review*, Vol. 52, No. 3 (June 1962), 335–84.

JOHNSTON and MELLOR, 1961. B. F. Johnston and J. W. Mellor, "The Role of Agriculture in Economic Development," *The American Economic Review*, Vol. 51, No. 4 (September 1961), 566–93.

JORGENSON, 1961. Dale W. Jorgenson, "The Development of a Dual Economy," *Economic Journal*, Vol. 67, No. 268 (June 1961), 309–34.

JORGENSON, 1966. Dale W. Jorgenson, "Testing Alternative Theories of the Development of a Dual Economy," in Irma Adelman and Erik Thorbecke, eds., *The Theory and Design of Economic Development* (Baltimore, Md.: Johns Hopkins University Press, 1966), 45–66.

KAO, et al., 1964. C. H. C. Kao, K. R. Anschel and C. K. Eicher, "Disguised Unemployment in Agriculture: A Survey" in C. K. Eicher and L. W. Witt, eds., *Agriculture in Economic Development* (New York: McGraw-Hill, 1964), 129–41.

KNIGHT, 1956. F. H. Knight, "The Ricardian Theory of Production and Distribution," *On The History and Method of Economics*, University of Chicago Press (Phoenix Books, 1956), 37–88. First published in *Canadian Journal of Economics and Political Science* (February and May 1935).

KUHN, 1962. T. S. Kuhn, *The Structure of Scientific Revolutions* (Chicago: University of Chicago Press, 1962).

LEWIS, 1955. W. A. Lewis, *The Theory of Economic Growth* (London: Allen and Unwin, 1955).

MELLOR, 1962a. John W. Mellor, "Increasing Agricultural Production in Early Stages of Economic Development, Relations, Problems and Prospects," *Indian Journal of Agricultural Economics*, Vol. 27, No. 2 (April–June 1962), 29–46.

MELLOR, 1962b. John W. Mellor, "The Process of Agricultural Development in Low-Income Countries," *Journal of Farm Economics*, Vol. 44, No. 3 (August 1962) 700–16.

NATIONAL ECONOMIC COUNCIL, 1964. National Economic Council, Office of Statistical Coordination and Standards, "Analysis of National Income of the Philippines for 1961–63," *The Statistical Reporter* (Bangkok), Vol. 9 (April–June 1964), 1–26.

NICHOLLS, 1960. W. H. Nicholls, "Industrialization Factor Markets and Agricultural Development," *Journal of Political Economy*, Vol. 69, No. 4 (August 1960), 319–40.

NICHOLLS, 1963. W. H. Nicholls, "Industrial Urban Development and Agriculture in San Paulo, Brazil, 1940–50," (Department of Economics, Vanderbilt University, 1963). (Mimeographed.)

OSHIMA, 1963. H. T. Oshima, "The Ranis-Fei Model of Economic Development: Comment," *American Economic Review*, Vol. 53, No. 3 (June 1963), 448–52.

PAAUW, 1966. D. S. Paauw, "A National Income Accounting Framework for the Open Dualistic Economy," Field Work Report No. 1, Center for Development Planning, National Planning Association, Washington, D.C., June 1966, (Mimeographed.)

PERKINS and WITT, 1961. Maurice Perkins and Lawrence Witt, "Capital Formation: Past and Present," *Journal of Farm Economics*, Vol. 43, No. 2 (May 1961), 333–42.

POTTER and CHRISTY, 1962. Neal Potter and F. T. Christy, Jr., *Trends in National Resource Commodities* (Baltimore, Md.: Johns Hopkins University Press, 1962).

RAMACHANDRAN, 1963. K. V. Ramachandran, "Population Projections for the Philippines, 1960–1980," *The Philippine Statistician*, Vol. 12 (December 1963), 145–68.

ROBINSON, 1962. Joan Robinson, *Economic Philosophy* (Chicago: Aldine, 1962).

ROSTOW, 1956. W. W. Rostow, "The Take-off into Self-Sustained Growth," *The Economic Journal*, Vol. 56, No. 261 (March 1956), 25–48.

ROSTOW, 1960. W. W. Rostow, *The Stages of Economic Growth* (London: Cambridge University Press, 1960).

ROSTOW, 1963. W. W. Rostow, ed., *The Economics of Take-off into Sustained Growth* (London: Macmillan, 1963).

RUTTAN, 1955. Vernon W. Ruttan, "The Impact of Urban Industrial Development on Agriculture in the Tennessee Valley and the Southeast," *Journal of Farm Economics*, Vol. 37, No. 1 (February 1955), 38–56.

RUTTAN, 1965. Vernon W. Ruttan, "Growth Stage Theories and Agricultural Development Policy," *Australian Journal of Agricultural Economics*, Vol. 9, No. 1 (June 1965), 17–32.

RUTTAN and CALLAHAN, 1962. Vernon W. Ruttan and J. C. Callahan, "Resource Inputs and Output Growth: Comparisons Between Agriculture and Forestry," *Forest Science*, Vol. 8, No. 1 (March 1962), 68–82.

SEERS, 1962. Dudley Seers, "Why Visiting Economists Fail," *Journal of Political Economy*, Vol. 70, No. 4 (August 1962), 328–32.

STEVENS, 1963. R. D. Stevens, "The Influence of Industrialization on the Income Elasticity of Demand for Retail Food in Low Income Countries," *Journal of Farm Economics*, Vol. 45, No. 5 (December 1963), 1495–99.

STRASSMAN, 1964. W. P. Strassmann, Book Review of "The Economics of Take-off into Sustained Growth," Proceedings of a Conference Held by the International Economic Association, Edited by W. W. Rostow, *American Economic Review*, Vol. 54, No. 5 (September 1964), 785–90.

TOLLEY and SMIDT, 1964. G. S. Tolley and S. Smidt, "Agriculture and the Secular Position of the U.S. Economy," *Econometrica*, Vol. 32, No. 4 (October 1964), 554–75.

USDA, ERS, 1965. U.S. Department of Agriculture, Economic Research Service, "Factors Associated with Differences and Changes in Agricultural Production in Underdeveloped Countries," Third Progress Report on Participating Agency Agreement Between the Agency for International Development and the Economic Research Service, USDA (Washington, D.C.: January 1965).

VENEGAS, 1964. E. Venegas, "The Relative Influence on Acreage and Yield on World Production of Rice," International Rice Research Institute, Agricultural Economics Staff Memo (Manila: January 1964).

IV

Developing Subsistence Agriculture

12

Transforming Traditional Agriculture

EDITOR'S INTRODUCTION

THE IDEAS EXPRESSED by Professor T. W. Schultz in his recent book, *Transforming Traditional Agriculture* [1964], have been singularly influential in current programs and policies for developing subsistence agriculture. His provocative ideas have also been the cause of extended debates regarding a number of major issues.

Professor Schultz seeks to explain the economic behavior of farmers in poor, long-settled, agricultural communities and emphasizes a number of facts regarding traditional or subsistence agriculture that were previously ignored or not recognized. He defines "traditional agriculture" as that sector of a poor, underdeveloped country which has attained a particular long-run equilibrium with respect to the allocation of factors of production at the disposal of farmers and with respect to investment to increase the stocks of such factors.

Professor Schultz' analysis focuses on economic behavior as merely one of the subsets of human behavior, but he does not assume that this economic subset is independent of other noneconomic subsets. Whether the other subsets are to be put aside by abstracting from them or introduced explicitly depends upon the particular problem under analysis. Schultz thus recognizes that his definition of "traditional agriculture" has connotations which go far beyond economics, even though he delimits it as a purely economic concept that abstracts from particular cultural components.

Similarly, although the term "transforming" may connote a cultural or institutional or a purely technological transformation, Professor Schultz prefers to define a transformation as one that is in response to new economic opportunities. He maintains that although this type of a transformation may gradually alter particular noneconomic cultural components, it is not dependent upon changes in the underlying preferences of farm people. The sources of the new economic opportunities are predominantly improvements in the state of the productive arts.

As set forth by Schultz, the economic logic underlying the particular economic equilibrium of traditional agriculture is closely akin to that of the classical long-run stationary state. It is a type of equilibrium at which an economy, or a sector of an economy, arrives if it has exhausted all of the economic opportunities inherent in the state of the productive arts at its disposal. Thus, if farmers have been responding to the relevant economic incentives, enough time has elasped for them to have arrived at a relatively efficient allocation of the agricultural factors of production at their disposal, and to have equalized their marginal satisfactions from additional savings and the marginal value productivities of additional investment to increase the stocks of agricultural factors of production. Thus in traditional agriculture there are no unexploited opportunities that could be used by traditional farmers to promote increases in agricultural productivity and agricultural production.

From this chain of economic logic Schultz derives the following two critical hypotheses:

1. There are comparatively few significant inefficiencies in the allocation of the factors of production in traditional agriculture.
2. The price of the sources of income streams from agricultural production is relatively high in traditional agriculture.

To support the first hypothesis Schultz relies primarily upon two studies of peasant farming in India and Guatemala. These studies confirm the view that traditional farmers are using their present resources very efficiently and that better resource allocation under existing traditional technologies will provide very little growth. In addition, more savings and investment in the presently available factors of production offer little growth opportunities because they offer a low rate of return. Within the available state of the arts, the farmers have exhausted all the profitable production and investment opportunities. These facts account for Schultz' view that traditional or subsistence farmers are "efficient but poor."

Because the reshuffling of traditional agricultural techniques offers very few possibilities for significant growth, Schultz argues that greater growth prospects are to be found in new techniques, new inputs, and new market opportunities. The key to generating a dynamic process is an advance in knowledge that makes it possible to improve the productive arts.

From these basic hypotheses Schultz develops and espouses three critical policy prescriptions on the importance of prices, investment in research, and investment in human capital.

Given the already optimum allocation of productive resources, savings, and investment in agriculture, traditional farmers display the characteristics of "economic men" and therefore will be responsive to economic incentives. Although Schultz relied upon very few empirical studies, there has been considerable additional evidence generated since that time, much of it summarized in Chapter 8. These studies conclusively show that prices are just as important in traditional agriculture as in modern agriculture.

The search for new agricultural inputs is seen by Schultz as a necessary part of the process of modernizing traditional agriculture. To acquire these improvements in the productive arts, it is necessary to invest in new forms of material things and in new skills.

These improvements in technology—whether in farm practice or embedded in new farm inputs—are considered of major importance in providing the economic opportunities that will induce farmers to increase agricultural production. Thus investment in research is seen as a first step to raise the technological levels of poor communities now dependent upon traditional agriculture.

His advocacy of the importance of education or investment in human capital for the transformation of traditional agriculture is central, and his arguments both follow and build upon his previous work in this area [Schultz, 1963].

These three policy prescriptions reflect his ranking of the probable causes for the observable differences in the amount and growth rate of agricultural production between nations and regions. Based on his analysis, Schultz believes that "differences in land are the least important, differences in the quality of material capital are of substantial importance, and differences in the capabilities of farm people are the most important" [Schultz, 1964, p. 16].

As would be expected, Professor Schultz' iconoclastic views have been criticized on several scores. One major criticism concerns the absence of any allocative inefficiency in traditional agriculture, the limited empirical evidence cited (two village studies), and the extrapolation of the Guatemalan and Indian evidence to other regions, especially Africa [Eicher, 1965; Massell, 1964]. The Indian evidence has also been criticized as being non-representative of traditional agriculture [Mosher, 1967]. Another major criticism has concerned his relegation of land to a position of lesser importance [Plath, 1967] and the significance of his analysis for large landlords, especially for Latin American *latifundistas* [Beckford, 1966; Feder, 1967]. The two village studies upon which he relies have been criticized as well for masking what may be significant variations from the "average" within the sample, for ignoring the possibility of allocative inefficiencies within enterprises, and for not recognizing enterprise adoptions and responses which may have been culturally neutral [Mosher, 1964; 1967]. A final critique has concerned the need for greater attention to the allocative inefficiencies that may be due to a wider economic decision-making unit leading to allocative inefficiencies in resources at the sectoral level as opposed to the individual farm level [Adams, 1967].

Schultz' views continue to be provocative and stimulating. Since they are influencing much current policy on the transformation of subsistence agriculture in the developing world, a critical examination of these views in depth will serve as a useful backdrop for an understanding of the problems of developing subsistence agriculture. Two leading agricultural economists have undertaken this task.

Professor V. M. Dandekar takes issue with certain conceptual notions advanced by Schultz and makes a strong plea for the inclusion of population as a significant variable that affects the development pattern of subsistence agriculture. While he agrees that farmers in traditional agriculture are efficient though poor, Dandekar does not agree with Schultz that this efficiency necessarily results in the full employment of all factors of production (especially labor) or in levels of living that are at or above subsistence levels. Dandekar believes that the pressure of population upon traditional agriculture is of a special nature and, because it is mainly self-employed, permits the employment of residual labor on the basis of survival irrespective of its marginal productivity. He is particularly critical of *why* traditional agriculture should arrive at a long-term stationary equilibrium and why technological stagnation occurs. In analyzing the impact of population growth upon traditional agriculture, Dandekar distinguishes two sectors:

one where population pressure is not excessive and which produces a surplus; and the other where the population pressure is excessive, leaving no surplus and leading to dissaving and disinvestment.

Professor J. Leonard Joy also examines Schultz' analysis. He broadly agrees with Schultz' propositions regarding the efficiency of traditional farming systems. However, he doubts the extent to which "poor country farmers" are in long-run stable equilibrium. While scientific research may be essential to transformation, there may be circumstances where other programs would be productive without waiting for scientific breakthroughs. Also much scientific research in the past has failed to have an impact because it did not relax the constraints inhibiting farming development. Advice given has frequently been uneconomic, for a variety of reasons that Joy indicates. He notes, too, that there are social costs of development that Schultz neglected.

Perhaps the greatest difference between Joy and Schultz is on the question of the implications of Schultz' analysis for policy and economics research. While as a generalization it may be true that there should be heavy emphasis on agronomy research and a concern to avoid inhibiting development by unfavorable price and taxation policies, the policy decisions which need to be made cannot readily be resolved by such generalizations. While Schultz emphasizes the need for historical studies of farmer responsiveness, Joy advocates microeconomic studies exploring farmer behavior and identifying the constraints on farming systems, using this to identify priorities for agricultural research and to measure the significance of changes in resources, techniques and prices on the opportunities available to farmers. He stresses, too, the need for such studies to take account of the social implications of innovation, especially as they affect the material rights and obligations of the innovators.

India is one of the major nations of the world facing severe problems with subsistence agriculture. In a brief but thoughtful paper, Prof. M. L. Dantwala advances the basic thesis that the transformation of agriculture, at least in the Indian case, must be accompanied, if not preceded, by general economic development. He examines three of the commonly prescribed measures—reform of agrarian structure, provision of adequate credit, and guaranteed minimum support prices—and finds that none of them offers a solution to the problems of the Indian subsistence farm unless the general problems of underdevelopment are also attacked.

References

ADAMS, 1967. Dale W. Adams, "Resource Allocation in Traditional Agriculture," *Journal of Farm Economics*, Vol. 49, No. 4 (November 1967), 930–32.

BECKFORD, 1966. George L. Beckford, "Transforming Traditional Agriculture: Comment," *Journal of Farm Economics*, Vol. 48, No. 4, Part I (November 1966), 1013–15.

EICHER, 1965. Carl K. Eicher, Review of "Transforming Traditional Agriculture," *Nigerian Journal of Economic and Social Studies*, Vol. 7, No. 1 (March 1965), 81–3.

FEDER, 1967. Ernest Feder, "The Latifundia Puzzle of Professor Schultz: Comment," *Journal of Farm Economics*, Vol. 49, No. 2 (May 1967), 507–10.

MASSELL, 1964. B. F. Massell, Review of "Transforming Traditional Agriculture," *Journal of the American Statistical Association*, Vol. 59, No. 308 (December 1964), 1308–10.

MOSHER, 1964. Arthur T. Mosher, Review of "Transforming Traditional Agriculture," *Annals of the American Academy of Political and Social Science*, Vol. 356 (November 1964), 108.

MOSHER, 1967. Arthur T. Mosher, *Promoting Agricultural Growth, A Framework For Organization and Planning* (First Draft), (New York: Agricultural Development Council, Inc., August 1967). (Mimeographed.)

PLATH, 1967. C. V. Plath, "On the Economic Importance of Land: Comment," *Journal of Farm Economics*, Vol. 49, No. 3 (August 1967), 734–35.

SCHULTZ, 1963. Theodore W. Schultz, *The Economic Value of Education* (New York: Columbia University Press, 1963).

SCHULTZ, 1964. Theodore W. Schultz, *Transforming Traditional Agriculture* (New Haven, Conn.: Yale University Press, 1964).

COMMENT

Questions of Economic Analysis and the Consequences of Population Growth

V. M. DANDEKAR

THE PURPOSE OF THIS PAPER is to examine critically the thesis Professor Schultz has developed in his celebrated book, *Transforming Traditional Agriculture* [1964]. The discussion is divided into two parts. In the first I examine the economic logic underlying Schultz' thesis. My contention is that Schultz has neglected or missed the consequences of population growth and hence has arrived at an oversimplified understanding of the causes underlying traditional agriculture. In the second I indicate how, once we explicitly take into account the consequences of population growth, the complexity of the phenomenon becomes evident.

QUESTIONS OF ECONOMIC ANALYSIS

The economic-analytical apparatus set up by Schultz seeks to explain the production behavior of farmers who are bound by traditional agriculture. His point of departure from conventional explanations is to reject cultural and institutional differences as necessary explanations. He bases his economic concept of traditional agriculture on the fact that an economy characterized by traditional agriculture does not grow or is stagnant. This means that in such an economy the stock of reproducible means of production does not grow or remains unchanged. Because this is a condition at which traditional agriculture arrives gradually over a long period and presumably stays there indefinitely, Schultz refers to it as a condition of long-term equilibrium. Such a condition is reached and maintained, provided the conditions of supply of and the demand for reproducible means of production in an economy remain constant over a sufficiently long period. That the conditions of supply remain constant is expressed by means of Schultz' first "critical condition," namely that "the state of the arts remains constant." By the state of the arts is meant "the state of the arts underlying the supply of reproducible factors of production." The requirement that the conditions of demand remain constant is expressed by means of his second "critical condition," namely that "the state of preference and motives for holding and acquiring sources of income remains constant." His third condition expresses the requirement that the first two conditions prevail over a long enough period for the economy to arrive at an equilibrium [Schultz, 1964, p. 30]. The equilibrium, derived following Friedman [Friedman, 1962, Ch. 13], is stationary and is characterized by zero net savings and investment, and consequently by a stationary stock of reproducible means of production. Schultz emphasizes throughout that the reproducible means of production include not only the material factors but also the skills and capabilities of man which are augmented by investment in him and which are useful to him in his economic endeavor.

In an economy characterized for a long enough period by a stationary stock of the reproducible means of production it seems reasonable to assume that "a state of equilibrium exists in the sense that productive services are being combined in the right proportions to produce the right amount of goods" [Friedman, 1962, p. 246]. Schultz expresses this by means of the first of his two "critical hypotheses" derived from his concept of traditional agriculture, namely that there are comparatively few significant inefficiencies in the allocation of the factors of production in traditional agriculture. But Schultz recognizes that "Since the productive agents include the human agent, the knowledge (or know-how, or 'instruction') of how to employ each of the productive agents including himself is also an integral part of the factors of production" [Schultz, 1964, p. 134]. Hence this particular hypothesis cannot in fact mean very much, for it signifies no more than that the allocation of factors of production in traditional agriculture is as efficient as the managerial ability in it is capable of. It seems, however, that Schultz means a little more than that. One implication

of this hypothesis is that "an outside expert, however skilled he may be in farm management, will not discover major inefficiency in the allocation of factors" [Schultz, 1964, p. 39]. I completely agree with Schultz on this point, though I must make it clear that if managerial ability is itself regarded a part of the reproducible factors of production, this is not a necessary implication of the hypothesis derived from the initial concept of the stationary equilibrium. It means that, in the matter of farm management, the farmers in traditional agriculture, through a long process of trial and error, have learned all that can be learned and that therefore the new mathematical techniques of farm planning and farm budgeting have not much to offer to them. Personally, I believe this to be so, and I agree that it is worth stating, particularly in view of the rather wild promises that a school of agricultural economists appears to be holding for obtaining substantial and often surprisingly large increases in agricultural production through a mere reallocation of the existing factors of production.

Schultz spells out yet another implication of this hypothesis, namely that "no productive factor remains unemployed," and with particular reference to labor, he interprets this to mean that "each laborer who wishes and who is capable of doing some useful work is employed." He proceeds to observe as follows: "The efficient but poor hypothesis does not imply that the real earnings (production) of labor are not meager. Earnings less than subsistence are not inconsistent with this hypothesis provided there are other sources of income, whether from other factors belonging to workers or from transfers within the family or among families in the community" [Schultz, 1964, p. 40]. Does this last proviso mean that, in poor communities characterized by traditional agriculture, no one in fact lives below subsistence? How is it that living below subsistence is inconsistent with the "efficient but poor" hypothesis? Why is it inconceivable that in relation to the existing stock of reproducible means of production, which in terms of the equilibrium concept has long ceased to grow, the burden of population may be so large that even the most efficient allocation and use of these factors does not permit any useful employment of the whole labor force or at any rate does not produce enough for the subsistence of the whole population? Schultz does not ask himself these questions. Instead he proceeds to dispute and refute what he calls "The Doctrine of Agricultural Labor of Zero Value."

While disputing this "doctrine," Schultz opines that what is "typical of many poor agricultural communities because they are in a stable state of long-run equilibrium" is that "marginal product of labor in agriculture is very low" but that nevertheless "labor in agriculture produces as much as does comparable labor in other sectors" of the economy. He concedes a situation where "the marginal product of labor in agriculture is less than that of comparable labor in other sectors of the economy," [Schultz, 1964, p. 56] but he interprets it as follows: "The second is related predominantly to growth and to lags in adjustment, and it represents one of the disequilibria that is rooted in economic growth. It can persist for decades, and is presently most evident in some of the countries in which agriculture is technically in the vanguard" [Schultz, 1964, p. 57]. This may be so. However, it seems to me that the second situation is more general than the first, and that the underlying reason is that the conditions of employment and the pressure of population in agriculture and in other sectors of the economy in relation to their productive resources are very different. In traditional agriculture, along with traditional industry, employment is primarily self-employment, wherein no clear distinction between employment and unemployment is possible. In the other sector, namely of organized modern industry and trade, employment is for a regular wage, which in general cannot be less than subsistence. Moreover, this latter sector is so organized that it will not employ labor beyond the point where its marginal productivity equals the wage. In contrast, traditional agriculture must accept the entire residual labor force on the basis of self-employment and survival, quite irrespective of its marginal productivity. Here the marginal productivity is often below subsistence, and even if it were zero, there is no way by which this sector may throw off or disown any part of the labor force that seeks self-employment in it. Whether in fact the marginal productivity is close to zero will naturally depend upon the size of the labor force in relation to the stock of the reproducible capital in this sector. If, in a particular case, it is in fact zero, it is not inconsistent either with the long-term stationary equilibrium that traditional agriculture is postulated to be or with the derived hypothesis regarding the efficient allocation of the existing factors of production. In disputing at such length what he calls the "Doctrine of Agricultural Labor of Zero Value," Schultz seems to have been carried away by the energy of his own argument. He undertook this task because, as he states, "To build where there are obsolete structures one must first demolish and remove them, which can be costly" [Schultz, 1964, p. 8]. A little reflection on his part would have convinced him that this little structure was not, indeed, in his way. However, if he must demolish it anyhow in the belief that it was obsolete, I am afraid the cost might be very heavy.

So much for the first of the two "critical hypotheses" derived by Schultz from his economic concept of traditional agriculture. His second hypothesis is that the price of the sources of income streams from agricultural production is relatively high in traditional agriculture. Again, this hypothesis cannot mean much. The price is relatively high; relatively to what? In point of fact, the price is the stationary equilibrium price at which the existing stock of reproducible means of production remains constant with zero net savings and investment. Having postulated this, the hypothesis that the price is relatively high makes little sense. Nevertheless, Schultz puts forward this hypothesis because he thinks that still "The analytical task is to explain a low rate of net investment in traditional agriculture or even no net investment whatsoever." He believes that "a low rate of return would provide a logical basis for a low ratio of savings to income" and hence proceeds to "present a theoretical basis for a low rate of return to investment in factors of production in traditional agriculture" [Schultz, 1964, pp. 72–73]. A full theoretical basis for zero net savings and investment is provided as soon as the condition of long-term stationary equilibrium is postulated. Therefore, if there is any further analytical task left, it is to explain why traditional agriculture gradually arrives at a long-term stationary equilibrium, or if we know that this is because, in traditional agriculture, the conditions of supply of and demand for the reproducible means of production remain constant over a long period, to explain why these conditions of supply and demand remain constant for such a long period.

Schultz' formulation of the conditions of demand for the factors of production is that "the state of preference and motives for holding and acquiring sources of income remains constant" [Schultz, 1964, p. 30]. His explanation is: "That the basic preferences and motives under consideration may remain constant over long periods is highly plausible, if for no other reason than that it is difficult to conceive of developments that could change them" [Schultz, 1964, p. 31]. On the conditions of supply of the factors of production, Schultz' formulation is that "the state of arts remains constant" and he does not raise the question why. Does he imply that this is something which simply happens? If he does, then by including it as a critical condition underlying traditional agriculture or in other words as an explanation of what he calls the condition of long-term equilibrium, which is another name for stagnation, I am afraid Schultz is playing the same game, namely "The Game of Concealing Factors," that he accuses others of playing when they use the concept of technological change as an explanatory variable of economic growth. He warns: "The advance in knowledge and useful new factors based on such knowledge are all too frequently put aside as if they were not produced means of production but instead simply happened to occur over time. This view is as a rule implicit in the notion of technological change" [Schultz, 1964, p. 136]. For this reason he rejects the concept of technological change as an explanatory variable of economic growth. "To use it for this purpose is a confession of ignorance, because it is only a name for a set of unexplained residuals" [Schultz, 1964, p. 137] and hence: "Analytically it conceals most of the essence of economic growth" [Schultz, 1964, p. 138].

However, if technological change is not something that simply happens outside the production process, then its absence cannot merely be the negation of something which otherwise simply happens. It is something

more and worse than that. In order to emphasize this active aspect, we should refer to this condition as the condition of "Technological Stagnation" rather than referring to it by such neutral terms as "the constancy of the state of arts" or "the absence of technological change." If we do this, then a full economic explanation of the phenomenon of traditional agriculture will require us to raise the question as to why and how technological stagnation occurs and to try to answer it within the framework of economic analysis. If this does not seem possible, then we must agree that an appeal to certain cultural and institutional attributes of the communities concerned is necessary.

In the economic logic developed by Schultz, there is discernible apparently another variation of this "Game of Concealing Factors" and which, for want of a better name, we may call the "Game of Missing Factors." After outlining the critical conditions underlying the type of economic equilibrium which he postulates for traditional agriculture, Schultz points out that "In the process of reaching this type of equilibrium, the stock of material factors of production and the labor forces are the principal variables." [Schultz, 1964, p. 30]. His subsequent analysis is based on a concept of capital that is all-inclusive, "including human as well as non-human capital" [Schultz, 1964, p. 78], and closely following Friedman [1962, pp. 247-248], he derives a horizontal demand curve for permanent income streams. However, when he comes to the supply curve, he assumes it to be "slope positively" [Schultz, 1964, p. 77]. If he had been consistent with his concept of capital to be all-inclusive, and followed Friedman, he would have obtained an equally horizontal supply curve and would have found it hard to arrive at the long-term stationary equilibrium he postulates [Friedman, 1962, pp. 252, 257].

Thus it seems that Schultz did not mean to use the all-inclusive concept of capital "including human as well as non-human capital." He requires the concept of capital to include all reproducible means of production but, apparently, he has no intention of including in that concept those factors which cannot be augmented; for what is under consideration is a supply of these factors, and this is meaningful only in the context of reproducible factors. Schultz observes:

Nevertheless, there are particular qualities in the natural environment and in human beings which are not augmentable; they are therefore qualities that represent factors, the supply of which is essentially fixed. . . . In the case of man, the qualities that are not acquired but are inherited biologically are for all practical purposes "fixed" per man in any large population over any time span that matters in economic analysis. . . . Capital goods are always treated as produced means of production. But in general the concept of capital goods is restricted to material factors thus excluding the skills and other capabilities of man that are augmented by investment in human capital. The acquired abilities of a people that are useful in their economic endeavor are obviously produced means of production and in this respect forms of capital, the supply of which can be augmented. [Schultz, 1964, pp. 135-136]

If Schultz had firmly held to this concept of capital as comprising all reproducible factors of production, he would have found it necessary and useful to distinguish the following factors of production: (1) Land, i.e. the particular qualities in the natural environment that are not augmentable; (2) labor, i.e. the particular qualities in human beings that are not acquired but are inherited biologically and that for all practical purposes are fixed per man; and capital, i.e. all reproducible means of production, including: all improvements in land as a factor of production that can be augmented by investment; all improvements in man as a factor of production, i.e. his acquired skills and capabilities that can be augmented by investment; and finally all other reproducible material means of production. In this classification, labor is not nonreproducible. What is not reproducible in labor are the particular qualities per man. However, men can be reproduced and their number increased. Nevertheless, the reason to distinguish labor from other reproducible means of production is that, within the existing social and institutional framework in which human reproduction takes place, we do not expect it to respond to economic pressures and incentives in the same manner as the supply of other reproducible means of production does.

Let us therefore distinguish the factors of production into three broad categories—called land, labor, and capital—and follow Friedman in his treatment of the theory of capital. After a preliminary exercise in which an all-inclusive concept of capital including human as well as nonhuman capital leads to a horizontal demand curve, Friedman [1962, pp. 247-248] considers the slightly more real case wherein factors of production are distinguished into two categories, namely human and nonhuman wealth. Friedman then confines the term capital to nonhuman wealth and derives a zero-net-saving demand curve for the same. With a given income from human wealth, this demand curve is negatively sloping. He follows the same procedure with the supply curve; given a fixed income from human wealth he derives a positively sloping zero-net-investment supply curve. The intersection of the two curves gives the required long-run stationary equilibrium.

With the distinction between factors of production as suggested above, we could somewhat improve upon this but would obtain basically the same result. Capital would include all forms of reproducible means of production, embedded in land, man, and other materials, and we would get a negatively sloping zero-net-saving demand curve and a positively sloping zero-net-investment supply curve for capital with income from land and labor given and fixed, the intersection giving the required equilibrium. Although this is not much, this is as far as we could go following Friedman in clarifying an important issue.

The whole analysis—or the "Theoretical Scaffold," as Schultz calls it—is based on the condition that income from land and labor is given and fixed. I shall not raise here the question of how and in what sense one allocates incomes to different factors and I shall also not raise questions regarding the income from land. I shall, however, ask this question: whatever the meaning we may attach to the term "income from labor," in what sense do we expect it to remain fixed? In particular, under a growing labor force do we expect the per capita labor income to remain constant? In fact, once the stage is reached when the reproducible factors of production, called capital, cease to grow, do we expect even the per capita total income from all sources to remain fixed? If not, does agriculture, under these conditions, at all reach the long-term stationary equilibrium that Schultz postulates it to be?

Throughout this exercise in economic logic purported to clarify the economic character and nature of traditional agriculture, Schultz makes no reference to the consequences of population growth. He seems to have missed this crucial element in the situation, partly through an early and unnecessary decision that the problem of surplus labor is nothing but an obsolete doctrine that must be demolished and partly through total dependence on a classroom treatment of the subject of the theory of capital, which again Schultz apparently did not pursue beyond an elementary proposition. Having missed the consequences of population growth, Schultz has arrived at an oversimplified understanding of the causes underlying traditional agriculture and the measures necessary to transform it into a highly productive sector.

He derives a state of long-term equilibrium as arising out of constant conditions of demand for the supply of capital—that is, reproducible means of production. Consequently, the only way to break through this state of stagnation is to alter the conditions of demand for and supply of capital, as for instance by shifting the demand curve up and the supply curve down. Apparently Schultz does not think that much can be done to the demand curve. The only thing to do is therefore to shift the supply curve downward, which in other words means to reduce the supply price of reproducible means of production. This step requires development of new means of production with higher rates of return, which is another name for technological progress. Thus, having got into a situation of stagnation arising out of technological stagnation, the only way to break through it is to achieve technological progress. The only substantial point gained through this rather long-winded argument is that technological progress is not something that simply occurs over time but something that can be attempted and achieved by well-conceived investment. Further, this effort is not something that can be done only once, for then we reach another state of stagnation, though with a larger stock of capital than before. Continued progress along this direction requires sustained technological progress, which requires basic long-term investment to promote knowledge, science, and skills. Hence education, beginning with primary education, must receive a high priority.

This conclusion is well taken, though it seems one could reach the primary school more directly. As an analysis of the problems of traditional agriculture, it suffers from oversimplification and hence from incomplete understanding. The reason is the missing factor, population. As soon as population is introduced into the analysis, the complexity of the situation becomes evident.

CONSEQUENCES OF POPULATION GROWTH

Let us suppose, as Schultz postulates, that traditional agriculture is a stationary state of economic equilibrium characterized by zero net savings and investment and consequent stationary stock of capital. Let us further suppose that, under these conditions, the population does not itself reach a state of stationary equilibrium but continues to grow more or less independently of the stock of capital, as seems to be happening with a number of poor countries characterized by traditional agriculture. Because the stock of capital is supposed to have become stationary, the flow of income will in general not expand in proportion to population. Hence, with increase in population, per capita income will fall, and hence savings will fall. In other words, the equilibrium price of the stock of capital, at which the stock was maintained stationary with zero net savings and investment, will no longer be an equilibrium price, because at that price net dissavings will occur and the stock of capital will be reduced. The process will continue inexorably as the pressure of population grows further. There will thus be no state of stationary equilibrium, but a state of continuous deterioration with negative net savings and investment and a steady reduction in the stock of capital. Thus the characteristic condition of traditional agriculture turns out to be that it fails to produce a surplus over subsistence and hence soon begins to live on capital consumption.

The phenomenon might be explained more simply as follows. In the early stages of settlement of people on land, when the pressure of population is not great, even traditional agriculture produces a surplus over the subsistence of the population. As population increases, in response to growing demands of its subsistence, a part of the surplus is saved and invested mainly in the extension of cultivation, but also in the development of improved cultural practices enhancing the productivity of land. Through this process traditional agriculture has been able to provide subsistence to a growing population for a surprisingly long period of its history. At the beginning the growth of agriculture was probably more rapid than the growth of population, so that agriculture could provide either a higher standard of living or a larger surplus over subsistence for investment. But sooner or later a stage is reached when growth in population overtakes the growth in agriculture, and the surplus over subsistence is gradually reduced. There are two reasons. Firstly, because of settled conditions of life, improved standards of living, better health, and reduced mortality, population might grow faster than before. Secondly, extension of cultivation might reach its natural limits, and further improvement in cultural practices might become increasingly more difficult within traditional knowledge. Moreover, once the process is begun by which the surplus over subsistence is reduced, it becomes cumulative and itself causes a further reduction in the surplus. In due course the surplus over subsistence is reduced to zero, and we reach the stage of zero net savings and investment. My contention is that, having reached this stage, there is no reason to suppose that this would be a state of stationary equilibrium with constant stock of capital, unless at this stage the population ceases to grow as well. If population continues to grow, as in fact it would, a state of continuous deterioration sets in with negative net savings and investment and a steady reduction in the stock of capital. This seems to be the characteristic condition of traditional agriculture in most developing countries today.

That dissaving and disinvestment occur progressively is discernible to anyone who is familiar with the field conditions at first hand, and innumerable instances may be cited. One merely has to notice the state of repairs in which in a majority of cases land, equipment, living houses, livestock, and finally the health of men lies. Repairs are not attended to, not because investment in repairs does not pay nor because knowledge and skills are lacking, but because no surplus over subsistence is available for investment. So fences, bunds, and sources and channels of irrigation are not mended; implements, cattlesheds, and living houses are not repaired; animals are famished and are let into one another's fields for grazing; and men are undernourished to the point that often good seed is eaten. All this happens with full knowledge of what is happening.

We do not have to assume that in traditional agriculture every inch of soil is under pressure of excessive population, so that it does not produce any surplus over the subsistence of the population with which it is burdened. This is not true either. Thanks to the very unequal distribution of land among the people dependent upon it, the pressure of population in traditional agriculture is very unevenly distributed. At one extreme there are a few large farms owned by a few people and where therefore the pressure of population is very light. Naturally these farms produce a surplus over the subsistence of the population they support. At the other extreme there are numerous small farms owned by a large majority of the population. Here the pressure of population is excessive. The farms fail to produce enough for the subsistence of this population, and capital consumption becomes inevitable. In between there is a whole continuum of farms with the pressure of population on land increasing from one end to the other, and consequently the surplus over subsistence going down from a positive high to a negative low. Somewhere in the middle we have a point where the surplus over subsistence is zero.

This point provides a convenient division of traditional agriculture into two sectors: a sector that is not overburdened with population and that therefore produces a surplus of varying degree over subsistence of its population; and another sector where pressure of population is excessive, agriculture fails to produce a surplus over the subsistence of this population, and dissaving and disinvestment of varying degree prevail. Obviously the two sectors within themselves are not homogeneous but contain a wide range of variation in respect of the pressure of population on land. Indeed, the two sectors are two divisions of a continuum and merge into one another at the margin. Further, though the point of division between the two sectors is, at any given time, logically clear and operationally determinable, it is not fixed and static. With growing pressure of population, the margin between the two sectors recedes, and the surplus-producing sector continually shrinks. Finally we should note that both the sectors are sectors of traditional agriculture and that therefore agriculture in one sector is as traditional as in the other sector. The reason why one sector produces a surplus while the other does not is that one bears a small population in relation to its land resources, while the other is burdened with a large population, and not that agriculture is more productive in one than in the other. In fact, with regard to the character of their reproducible means of production, the nature of their agricultural inputs and returns to them, the two sectors are basically similar.

The two sectors are not physically segregated, and a great deal of traffic, both in land and labor, takes place between the two. The surplus-producing sector rents out part of its land resources to the other sector and hires labor from that sector. Undoubtedly, this helps equalize the pressure of population in the two sectors. However, for several reasons there are distinct limits to this process. Firstly, we should note that, barring conditions of feudalism and slavery, hired labor in general has to be paid at least a subsistence wage. Therefore, when the surplus-producing sector hires labor from the other sector, the quantum of hired labor is limited by the condition that its marginal productivity remains above subsistence. Thus, in spite of the surplus-producing sector's hiring labor from the other sector, the marginal productivity of labor in the surplus-producing sector necessarily remains above subsistence, while in the other sector it is below subsistence and often close to zero. In other words, the burden of population on the two sectors remains still quite unequal. The surplus-producing sector admits population only to the extent where it maximizes the surplus of that sector; the other sector must accommodate all the residual population, irrespective of its marginal productivity.

Secondly, even within the limits set by considerations of marginal productivity, the quantum of hired labor that is employed in the surplus-producing sector remains rather limited. The reason is the very low productive efficiency of the labor that is available on hire. The productive efficiency of this labor is often below its own subsistence, not because of any inherent inferiority of its natural endowment, but because of a long process of disinvestment to which it is subjected through malnutrition and hunger. Therefore, except for crucial operations such as harvesting, it is not generally profitable to employ this labor. If its productive efficiency were better, more of it could be hired and employed in the other sector.

Finally, there are other circumstances that inhibit the hiring and employment, on any scale, of unskilled labor that is very poor and that through chronic hunger has been reduced to very low productive efficiency. In the midst of poverty and hunger, it is always difficult to protect visible prosperity. A good standing crop is frequently in danger of being trespassed by hungry men and hungry cattle, and a good prosperous farmer often finds himself surrounded by latent hostility. Therefore, in his farm operations, even a farmer with means and ability is unwilling to enter into commitments that he with his own labor and the labor of the members of his family cannot meet.

Under the circumstances, for a farmer owning land beyond the physical capacity of the members of his family, the simplest method of managing his farm is to keep in self-cultivation what he can with the help of his family members and a certain amount of casual labor and rent out the rest to a sharecropper; and here I am referring to, not a landlord in the sense of an idle, nonworking landowner, but to a farmer proper, the tiller of the soil. The reasons are not far to seek. Renting out to a sharecropper is a method by which labor might be hired at below-subsistence wage and the surplus reaped more quietly and by less ostensible means. Therefore, when the surplus-producing sector rents out its surplus land to the other sector, superficially it makes available to that sector additional land resources and thus helps equalize the pressure of population in the two sectors. In fact, while renting out its surplus land, the surplus-producing sector keeps to itself the surplus and passes on less than bare subsistence to the other sector.

Thus the two sectors exist side by side, not in mutually complementary relationship, but a relationship based on exploitation, callous disregard, resentment, and latent hostility. Even the barest analysis of the nature of traditional agriculture in the modern world must take cognizance of these facts. Schultz has missed them either because of unfamiliarity with field conditions or through the analytical error of omitting population as a factor of any consequence.

Let us now examine the consequences of population growth in the two sectors and first consider the sector that produces surplus over subsistence. At any given time this sector does not suffer from an excessive pressure of population. As population grows, the farms at the margin of this sector are pushed below the subsistence level, and they join the other sector. Thus the margin between the two sectors recedes, and the surplus-producing sector shrinks. This is the consequence of growth of population on this sector. The sector shrinks in size but does not, at any given time, suffer from excessive pressure of population. Therefore, I think, the nature of traditional agriculture here comes close to Schultz' concept. For instance, in this sector, in spite of its savings potential, little net investment takes place, because any further additions to the stock of capital of the traditional kind are not worth making, and supplies of improved inputs are not readily available. Existing stock of capital is kept in repair and is maintained, and there is no net disinvestment as in the other sector, but there is no net investment either. Hence the sector may be supposed to be in a state of long-term equilibrium of the kind postulated by Schultz. Secondly, all available labor in this sector is fully utilized, and its marginal productivity is not zero and, in fact, can be well above subsistence. In short, there is no surplus labor. On the contrary, there is a shortage of labor, and the sector employs varying quantities of labor hired from the other sector, severely limited by the extremely low productive efficiency of the hired labor and several institutional factors inhibiting the employment of such labor. Finally, management is reasonably efficient in the sense that all available factors of production are properly allocated and utilized. Thus the sector clearly satisfies all the major requirements of traditional agriculture as postulated by Schultz.

Before considering measures necessary to transform this sector into a modern sector of agriculture, we should ascertain what happens to its savings potential. Of course, in the first instance, the full potential is not realized, and considerable part of it is frittered away in ostensible and wasteful consumption. A part of the savings also flows out of agriculture, as for instance in the training and education of sons for eventual moving out of agriculture. But there are three main channels of investment in which a large part of the savings flows: buying or acquiring of additional land for renting out; moneylending for consumption purposes at exorbitant rates; and trading and shopkeeping. Poverty and hunger existent in the other sector provide ideal conditions to pursue these activities, and for a competent operator, the returns to investment in these lines far exceed any conceivable returns to even improved inputs in agriculture. Therefore, as investment decisions they are completely justifiable. It is unfortunate that they add little to the total wealth of the community, for basically their function is exploitative, and they inevitably result in further deprivation of the poor and the hungry. In traditional societies this reality is well recognized and understood by both parties to the process, and they will be surprised if they are told that a school of modern economists does not believe it to be a fact.

The possibilities of earning such lucrative returns to investment in land acquisition for renting, moneylending, and trading is a principal reason why savings in this sector do not flow into more productive investment. One of the first measures to transform this sector into a sector of modern agriculture is, therefore, to regulate these activities to eliminate exploitation and to insure that the returns are in consonance with the economic service performed.

Ignoring for a moment the excessive burden of population thrown on the other sector, one can make a good case for keeping the agriculture in this sector in family farms. There are, then, two principal problems of transforming traditional agriculture in this sector into a more productive one. One is the providing of channels for productive investment. The other is the supply of enough labor. For reasons already explained, the sector will not be able to make much use of the surplus labor in the other sector. Therefore the solution to the twin problems lies in mechanizing the agriculture in this sector. Mechanization will provide, in the first instance, a channel for productive investment for the savings in this sector. Secondly, it will reduce the dependence of this sector on the poor and unskilled labor from the other sector. Mechanization in this sector will undoubtedly aggravate the pressure of population in the other sector, but it must be ignored if traditional agriculture in the surplus-producing sector has to be transformed within the framework of family farms.

Let us next examine the situation in the other sector—namely the one that, burdened with excessive population, does not produce any surplus over its subsistence. Here traditional agriculture is characterized, not by a state of equilibrium, but by a state of continuous deterioration, with negative net savings and investment. Because it does not produce enough for its subsistence, it lives and survives by capital consumption. Superficially there is a surplus of capital, in the limited sense of material equipment and implements. This condition arises mainly because of certain indivisibilities and because every farmer, however small his holding, strives to possess his own implements and cattle. Consequently, in relation to the size of land, the number of cattle is large, but it is famished; and so also the number of implements is large, but they are often not in good repair. In relation to its land resources, the sector also has a surplus of labor, but its productivity is very low, and under its own growing pressure the productivity declines progressively. Thus man lives and survives by cheating land, cheating cattle, and finally cheating himself. Here man works on land with a continually declining stock of reproducible means of production, including those qualities of land and man that can be maintained and augmented by investment; and in the absence of such investment, both land and man move inexorably toward the ultimate equilibrium, where both are reduced to their irreducible minima.

Of all the disinvestment that occurs, the most serious is that one that occurs in man himself. Schultz attaches great importance to the investment in man. Therefore he should have no difficulty in appreciating the danger

of disinvestment in man that goes on in this sector. Even a cursory glance at these men would show that not merely no net investment has been made in them since they were born, but further, through a process of disinvestment, even their natural endowment has been eroded. Hence, if one is talking of investment in man, the first priority must be given to assuring a minimum subsistence to these people and thus halting the process of erosion. This is the first step essential to transform traditional agriculture in this sector into a more productive one.

The second problem is how to make better use of the labor in this sector. Properly fed, this labor would soon turn itself into good productive labor. It must therefore be put to good use. The land resources in this sector are not adequate for this labor to be fully engaged in cultivation. Therefore a part of it will have to be withdrawn from current cultivation and employed on works that will directly create capital, mostly embedded in land. Depending upon the size of the labor force to be thus handled, this program will require an effort of organization in order to withdraw the surplus labor from current production, to hold it in appropriate organizations for employment on capital works and to train it for eventual withdrawal from agriculture for employment in the industrial sector as it grows. I am not sure that all this can be done without disturbing the family farm organization at least in this sector.

I have raised these issues only to indicate the complexity of the phenomenon called traditional agriculture and of the all-out effort that will be needed to transform it into a more productive agriculture. One may differ on the details of this description, or even more so on the remedial measures to be adopted. However, neglect of these complexities will result in a statement not adequate even for a classroom understanding of the subject, let alone for deliberating on questions of policy and program in this field.

References

FRIEDMAN, 1962. Milton Friedman, *Price Theory, A Provisional Text* (Chicago: Aldine, 1962).

SCHULTZ, 1964. T. W. Schultz, *Transforming Traditional Agriculture* (New Haven, Conn.: Yale University Press, 1964).

COMMENT

Diagnosis, Prediction, and Policy Formulation

J. LEONARD JOY

IN APPRAISING Professor Schultz' work [1964],[1] I have tried to ask how far his approach would get us in enlightening policy decisions.

THE ANALYTICAL FRAMEWORK

The analytical framework underlying Professor Schultz' argument is that elaborated in his work *Transforming Traditional Agriculture* [1964].

"TRADITIONAL" AGRICULTURE AS A DESCRIPTION OF "POOR COUNTRY" AGRICULTURE

It is important to recognize with Professor Schultz the degree to which subsistence farming systems are typically adapted to their natural environment. More than this, it is important to recognize in relation to some of the situations that concern us—especially in India—the degree to which opportunities to improve such farming systems have been exhausted.

However, his model of "traditional agriculture" does not by any means cover all "underdeveloped" farming situations, for there are examples of subsistence agricultures where opportunities are not fully exhausted and where farming has not reached a long-run equilibrium. Various parts of Africa, especially, have in the past century been offered opportunities for change, which have in part been accepted and which in some places have still to be fully exploited. The most important of these have almost certainly been market opportunities, and farmers have responded by investing spare capacity in labor and land in the production of new crops, as well as in the production of traditional crops for local markets. Although new techniques and new "material forms" have been introduced, it seems most unlikely that these account for anywhere near the enormous increases in output experienced in many parts of Africa in, say, the past 30 years.

Possibly Professor Schultz would consider that where farmers have responded, there is no problem, and that his model is intended to cover the problem situations where output is not increasing. Even so, Africa's experience suggests that farmers respond to new opportunities other than changes in the state of the arts. This observation carries policy implications that are to my mind understressed by Professor Schultz, who concludes: "*The* sources of the new economic opportunities are improvements in the state of the productive arts" [1964, p. 3]. This statement and the policy conclusions that this leads him to seem to me to show a misplaced emphasis: partly because it is allowed to overshadow other possible policy measures that may be more important, or perhaps complementary, and partly because it shows an unwarranted faith in the possibilities of improving the state of the productive arts.[2]

1. The original version of this paper (of which this is a much condensed version), was prepared as a commentary on a paper by Professor Schultz summarizing the arguments expressed in his *Transforming Traditional Agriculture* [1964] and considering explicitly the research and policy conclusions that they implied. Parts of this paper that related directly to that of Professor Schultz have been omitted from this presentation which discusses the views set out in *Transforming Traditional Agriculture*.

2. In retrospect, I am impressed by the extent to which my view has been colored by my East African experience of the 1950's. Plant breeding had scored some successes, but there were no breakthroughs. Attempts to encourage more intensive farming by Africans had more notable failures than successes, for in many areas poor rainfall regimes inhibit intensive cultivation. While one hoped for plant breeding successes, there seemed—wrongly?—little scope for breakthroughs where rainfall was not reliably sufficient. However, one could only see limited practical scope for irrigation in East Africa, and it seemed that even where it was feasible, the prospect of economic viability was often to be discovered, if at all, only after sustained and comprehensive research.

If I were writing this afresh today, my emphasis would be different, for I would give new weight to the possibilities of genetics research. Broadly speaking, however, my argument still seems relevant to areas where available moisture—or sunshine—are limiting.

It must not be forgotten that ideas of scientific husbandry are not new. There have been agronomists pursuing scientific investigation at research institutes and university colleges throughout Africa, Asia, and elsewhere for many decades, and their impact on traditional agricultures has generally been very disappointing. It is tempting to suggest that our scientific knowledge has improved and that we should expect greater success in future. It is no doubt true that even the last few years have seen considerable strides in the understanding of biological fundamentals, and our earlier knowledge now appears in some respects rather crude. But the failures of science have in the past been less attributable to scientific misinformation than to the fact that much of the information sought and found was largely irrelevant. One example, from Tanganyika, relates to the discovery, repeatedly confirmed, that groundnut yields were considerably increased by weeding within a few days of crop germination. Efforts to persuade farmers to undertake timely weeding were, however, largely unsuccessful, for it meant persuading them to switch their attention from urgent digging, that would extend the area planted before the rains petered out. Where labor is scarce and land plentiful, there is little thanks for advice that increases the productivity of land at the cost of reducing the productivity of labor. In this sense the subsistence farmer is efficient and the research scientist inefficient. The scientist needs not only to apply himself to those constraints that effectively limit farm production; he needs also to relate advice on crop husbandry to farming systems *as a whole*. Past failure to meet these two requirements—which reflects a failure to relate agronomy research to effective farm economics analysis—has rendered much agricultural research abortive. There is sadly little evidence that this deficiency is being made good.

But even where research is able to relieve existing constraints and push out the production possibility frontiers, there are other *economic* reasons why farmers might decline *objectively* to adopt innovations. We may distinguish three:

1. that they increase gross returns by less than the increase in costs;
2. that they increase long-run average net return but only at the risk of short-run calamity;
3. that the prospective increases yield an unattractively low present net worth in the light of the farmers' high rates of time preference.

COSTS AND RETURNS

There should be universal agreement about the need for new inputs to increase yield values by more than their costs. However, I think that Schultz generally overestimates the possibilities of finding innovations where this condition is satisfied. It should be noted that the *percentage* increases in yields necessary to cover the *absolute* costs of new inputs may be very high indeed. Compare the situation of a technically advanced farmer in the United States experiencing yields of, say, 2000 pounds of seed cotton per acre with that of an African farmer averaging 300 pounds seed cotton per acre. If the commercial farmer needs a 10 per cent yield increase to justify the use of fertilizers or insecticide, the same absolute increase (200 pounds) is to the subsistence farmer a forbidding requirement of 66 per cent yield increase. Sometimes such increases may be possible, but we have come to realize that the genetic capacities of crop and stock varieties to be found in subsistence farming are low because they are geared to low inputs. Their capacity to respond to higher inputs is limited. In recognizing this we have become increasingly aware of the need for "package deals"—e.g. irrigation plus improved seed plus fertilizers plus insecticide. None of this denies in the least the need for investment in research and in human skills that Professor Schultz so strongly advocates. It does, however, qualify our optimism in situations where *all* inputs have to be stepped up.

UNCERTAINTY

One issue that I consider to have been treated too lightly by Professor Schultz is that of uncertainty. We might postulate that farmers' willingness to innovate for an increase in the long-run average net return is subject to the condition that the risk of reducing the net return in any one year should not exceed some given value. Further we might postulate that the degree of risk that farmers are willing to incur is related to their nearness, in some sense, to "biological" subsistence. If we then recognize the possibility that proposed innovations might involve a risk of lowering net outputs, then we may conclude that where these assumptions are relevant, farmers will not adopt new techniques.

In a Ph.D. thesis Sipra Das Gupta [1964] has shown that farmers' refusal to innovate that appeared irrational was consistent with a desire to avoid increasing risk. Her thesis shows Punjab farmers' cropping patterns to be efficient, in the sense that no possibilities of raising farm incomes can be seen that do not also increase risk.[3] We thus have a hypothesis that subsistence farmers may resist innovation because it means departing from a system that is efficient in minimizing the risk of catastrophe for one that significantly increases this risk.

There are good grounds for supposing that many innovations that might be advocated would in many cases significantly increase risk. Improved seed, fertilizers, and insecticides might increase long-run returns by more than long-run costs but, in the year when costs are not covered, the loss and debt incurred may be very considerably greater than was conceivable under the traditional system. Subsistence systems are low-cost systems: commercial systems may be high-cost systems. For this reason alone the risks of commerce—especially on the threshold—

3. In one section of the thesis quadratic programming is used to generate farming patterns that give maximum long-run returns for any value of variance. Existing farming patterns were found to be very close to the calculated maximum efficiency patterns but showing a high aversion to variance. Diagrammatically: E = long-run average return; V = variance of returns. It is impossible

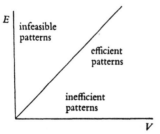

to find farming systems that will give higher average returns for any degree of variance than those plotted by the "efficient patterns" boundary. Any point on this line is uniquely associated with a farming system. Farmers were found to be following systems on the efficient-patterns boundary but low down to the left—thus demonstrating risk aversion.

may be forbiddingly high,[4] and farmers may well be willing to give up unproductive assets (cash, cattle, or gold ornaments) that yield an invaluable precautionary liquidity for productive assets that they may reasonably see as a potentially calamitous gamble. This gamble may well be aggravated if, because of their innovations, farmers are disowned by their community and lose their claim to social security.

TIME PREFERENCE

A third reason for thinking that it may not be as easy to offer innovations acceptable to the rational subsistence farmer, as Professor Schultz appears to suggest, is that the farmer might have a high rate of time preference. Not only may he be in equilibrium now with regard to his allocation of resources to future production, but innovations may well fail to disturb this equilibrium. The rate at which farmers replace low-yielding cocoa or coffee for high-yielding trees may be understandably slow or zero if for four or five years there are only extra costs and no extra returns. The future stream of net returns may need to be considerably raised if its present net worth is to exceed the small but immediate returns of existing assets. I suggest that it is typical of a near-subsistence economy that the demand for current consumption is so high that it pays to lend rather than to invest. Even where direct interest rates are not charged, lending may be an investment if it increases, by social convention, the obligations of the rest of the community to the leader.

CULTURAL AND SOCIAL FACTORS

A point that Professor Schultz seemingly fails to recognize is that the relinquishing of social institutions and cultural values may in itself be counted as a cost. Where this is so, it may

4. In the course of an evaluation of the economics of irrigation in a place where farm production was largely for subsistence, preliminary calculations suggested that, although the value of marketable surplus on a peasant smallholding might, with irrigation, be raised from Shs300 to Shs2400, the costs involved would absorb 85 per cent of the gross returns. In my view, it would require a high degree of confidence in the expected returns to induce these farmers to commit themselves to costs of this order. Shs = East African shillings. At that time Shs1 East African was worth £0.05 sterling or about $0.14.

be true that a cultural revolution would be necessary for there to be economic progress, but it would not follow that such a revolution would be desirable. Whether or not a cultural revolution is a precondition for economic progress, it is almost invariably a consequence. Subsistence farmers are often able to anticipate such consequences, and doing so, they may resist economic change and obstruct the innovator.

As an example of social resistance to private innovation, I would quote the Acholi of Northern Uganda, where resistance manifested itself in a number of ways. Here a man may claim the usufruct to land for as long as his hoe or axe marks are visible. In such a situation, and where wide areas of land are freely available, the introduction of tractor plowing by private individuals has obvious implications. Thus, although a pioneering individual received permission from his chief to open land by tractor, his neighbors attempted to forestall him by themselves hiring a tractor—not to plow the land, but to leave the marks of a plow on the land, so that the pioneer would be unable to claim it. In spite of this opposition, the man proceeded and met much resentment when he contracted out from his own customary obligation to join reciprocal work parties and, worse, enticed others to repudiate their customary obligations for paid labor on his land. Those who had accepted casual labor were warned by those who had not that by working for the innovator they were condemning their sons to work for his sons. The innovator saw himself as an example to his people. In this role he was prepared to face ridicule, ostracism, and even personal violence. But he was deeply concerned that there might be nobody attending his funeral.

The point that I am making here is that these subsistence farmers were correct in identifying the innovator as a menace to their society. However, their concern was not over the tractor per se, but over the emergence of a local capitalist. Economists would do well to study problems of innovation, not simply in relation to specific techniques and their material forms, but also in relation to their social and organizational forms. This, of course, can only be done with reference to specific cases, but it is clear that the evaluation of an irrigation or mechanization project should be related to alternative forms of social organization by which such enterprises could be developed.

Thus, although I agree with Professor Schultz in a predisposition to ascribe to subsistence producers the characteristics of rationality, efficiency, and responsiveness, there are important differences between us. Whereas he implies that all subsistence farmers are in efficient equilibrium, I believe that the efficiency of subsistence farming relates in a general sense to the systems followed, seen in the context of the environment in which they were developed; not only are individual farmers inefficient, but in many cases the environment has changed so that traditional systems are no longer efficient. Whereas we both see the subsistence farmer as responsive to opportunities, I believe that Professor Schultz and I might differ both as to what constitutes an opportunity and as to the ease with which new opportunities can be generated. Above all, we differ with regard to our assessment of the usefulness of this view of farmer rationality for illuminating the choices that policy decision-makers have to face and also with regard to the role of economic analysis in assisting with these decisions.

POLICY IMPLICATIONS

At first sight there seems everything to commend the policy conclusions that emerge from Professor Schultz' analysis. In general, there cannot be much wrong with the idea that one should:

1. identify agricultural inputs that are unmistakably rewarding;
2. insure a supply of these inputs to farmers;
3. teach farmers to use them efficiently;

especially if one proceeds with this as a continuous policy in the context of:

4. positive measures for population control;
5. policies to reduce price fluctuations; and
6. abstention from all measures that would depress farm prices or raise input prices.

By such policy measures agricultural development will become a dynamic and ongoing process.

The difficulty with this policy prescription is to know what it means in particular situations. Indeed, it works better as a troubleshooting chart than it does as a guide to positive policy recommendations. An agriculture that is not developing may not have available new and unmistakably rewarding techniques; or their material embodiment may not have been provided for; or farmers may not have the appropriate skills. But it could be that the new techniques are not rewarding because of tenure or social arrangements that reduce the reward to the entrepreneur; or that, although economic, their introduction is resisted by those who stand to lose (as the machine pressing of oil kernels was resisted by the women who formerly did the pressing and who stood to lose their pin money); or that farmers are indeed "irrational," as were those who were reluctant with the use of seed treatment to exorcise their grandfathers' ghosts that materialized as maize rust. In short, Schultz' policy advocacy begs the question of what is meant by "unmistakably rewarding" inputs and assumes that we have the techniques of analysis for identifying these. Insofar as we have such techniques, their application and articulation should be the central theme of economics research.

RESEARCH PRIORITIES

What we need to know is the relative significance of resources devoted to plant breeding or research on soil fertility; to credit policies or land registration; to land reforms or marketing reforms; to farm extension services or to primary schooling. How do we resolve the choice among guaranteeing minimum product prices, subsidizing inputs, and offering inputs on credit, when encouraging the adoption of new techniques? What we need to know is what is stopping farmers from producing more *now*, and what alternative ways there are of inducing them, or making it possible for them, to produce more. Having diagnosed current limitations, having identified alternative policies for relieving these, we need next to predict the consequences of alternative policy measures; and finally we need to evaluate them in the light of explicit objectives.

Thus, whereas Professor Schultz would wish to see economics research focus on the confirmation of his assumption of rationality,

I would wish to start by interpreting the nature of farmers' rationality in particular situations. I would not collect evidence of farmers who had behaved as "economic men." I would instead seek to understand how, in particular situations, farmers' behavior was related to their physical environment, resources, techniques, exchange opportunities, their objectives, and the way in which these are in turn related to custom, social values, and institutions. We need to identify the constraints on farmer behavior and the policies and research achievements that might most effectively relax these constraints. Were we to do so, we should, I am sure, discover situations where price and tax policies were critically inhibiting and situations where only a technological breakthrough would permit an agricultural transformation. But we might also discover situations where progress depended on other policies or where even a technological breakthrough *presupposed* investment in new resources. Broad generalizations deriving from a vaguely specified belief in farmer rationality are of limited value, even though they are acceptable.

I believe that we should aim to predict, for particular situations, farmers' responses to new resources, new techniques, new market opportunities, and new institutions (including land reform), and to introducing these in different ways. The analytical framework necessary for such predictions needs to be considerably more elaborate than that used by Professor Schultz, and it needs to contain, endogenously, values, customs, and institutions.

In order to make effective predictions about farmers' responses we need tools adequate for the analysis of farming systems of a high degree of complexity. Subsistence and semi-subsistence farming systems are, generally, highly complex—more so than commercial systems if only because their analysis can be more reasonably premised on the separation of commercial from non-commercial activities. Production function analysis cannot begin to cope with such complexity. Linear programming can in principle cope with a good deal of it, although its development for the study of peasant farming has not, so far, been very effectively explored. There have, indeed, been numerous programming studies of peasant farming but these applications have generally been unsatisfactory insofar as they have mis-specified the decision making environment in various ways. The major common defect has been gross oversimplification of both activity choices and constraint specification. Matrices of the order of 200 × 200 seem to be necessary for the effective description of a "peasant" farm situation and it is hardly surprising that studies based on matrices of the order of 20 × 20 produce little insight or conviction. The definition of the objective function presents particular problems also for near-subsistence farm analysis. Yet programming formulations have, so far, been used primarily to solve optimizing problems rather than to explore choice boundaries and farmers' behavior in relation to them.

As with any tool, programming is open to misuse but I believe that, by diligently attempting a full specification of the farm decision-making environment, programming can lead us to an improved understanding of the possibilities for raising farm outputs. One important point is that programming models can very readily take account of values, customs, and institutions within the analysis. Techniques, resources, and the natural environment impose the ultimate (short-run) bounds to production possibilities. Farmers may not reach these bounds because of constraints imposed by customs (e.g. which dictate that men or women should or should not undertake certain types of work) and social institutions (e.g. which impose constraints on land use or govern the share of the product received by the farmer). The extent to which these social considerations affect production possibilities both currently and potentially with net techniques, market prices, and the like, can be assessed [Joy, 1967].

Although programming—and the simulation models to be developed from it—will not provide all the answers, it is a most powerful technique for the analysis of farm situations, and the most promising in terms of the illumination that it could yield. But peasant farm situations are complex, and existing studies have hardly begun to reflect this complexity.

The development of programming is but one particular suggested approach by which the economist might contribute to the formulation of relevant strategies for agricultural development. In general, we need tools for diagnosis and prediction. We need procedures for listing and appraising alternative policies. I would commend policy formulation based on diagnosis and prediction, rather than on generalizations about the lessons of history. I would therefore commend research on diagnosis and prediction aiming at immediately useful results and the long-run improvement of the techniques.

References

DAS GUPTA, 1964. Sipra Das Gupta, "Producers' Rationality and Technical Innovation in Indian Agriculture," Unpublished Ph.D. dissertation, London School of Economics and Political Science, 1964.

JOY, 1967. J. Leonard Joy, "One Economist's View of the Relationship Between Economics and Anthropology," And "An Economic Homologue of Barth's Presentation of Economic Spheres in Darfur," in Raymond W. Firth (ed.), Themes in Economic Anthropology, ASA Monographs No. 6 (London: Tavistock, 1967).

SCHULTZ, 1964. T. W. Schultz, Transforming Traditional Agriculture (New Haven, Conn.: Yale University Press, 1964).

CASE STUDY

The Problems of a Subsistence Farm Economy: The Indian Case

M. L. DANTWALA

THE MAIN CONTENTION of this paper is that the problem of transformation of subsistence agriculture into viable commercial farming cannot be solved merely through measures like reform of the agrarian structure, provision of adequate credit and marketing facilities, extension of know-how for the use of nontraditional inputs, and the like, unless accompanied, if not preceded, by economic development in general, which would relieve the pressure of population from land.

AGRARIAN STRUCTURE: 1955 AND 1975

In discussing the subsistence nature of agriculture of many developing countries, it is necessary to make a distinction between the problem of small farms and that of small farmers. Table 12.1 [India, 1961, 18–19] gives the distribution of rural households in India according to the size of their ownership holding. As many as 23 per cent of rural households do not own any land. Further, it is interesting to note that, whereas 38 per cent of farms—farmer[1] households are below 2.5 acres and 52 per cent below 5 acres, as much as 65 per cent of the area is cultivated in holdings of 10 acres and more (see Table 12.1). A size of 10 acres may not appear impressive in the context of Western economies, but in India we consider a size of holding of 10 acres and more as a viable unit, whereas holdings below 5 acres, at the current intensity of cultivation, are by and large uneconomic, in the sense that they have hardly any surplus to effect transformation from subsistence to commercial farmers. In the above statements, the quality of land is ignored. If a holding has perennial irrigation

and grows high-yielding crops like sugarcane, a size of 5 acres would be viable.

In formulating a plan for agricultural development in India, it is necessary to take a view on the pattern of the size of holdings that is likely to materialize, say, during the next two decades. This will depend not so much on what the land reformer wishes, but on the objective conditions as determined by the growth of the labor force and its disposition between the agricultural and the nonagricultural sectors. According to the 1961 census, the number of agricultural workers in 1961 was 135.3 million (see Table 12.2). On the assumption that the population will increase at the compound rate of 2.35 per cent per annum and that the proportion of workers in the agricultural and the nonagricultural sectors would remain the same, the number of workers in 1970–1971 will be 170.7 million and in 1975–1976, 191.7 million—an increase of 56.4 million in 15 years. Correspondingly, the nonagricultural sector will have to employ as many as 22.1 million additional people. If the proportion of agricultural workers to the total declines from 71.8 to 66.6 in 1975, the additional employment in the agricultural and the nonagricultural sector would be 42.7 million and 35.8 million, respectively. Thus there seems to be no escape from having to accommodate millions of more people in the agricultural sector, which would inevitably lead to a further shrinkage in the unit of cultivation. Full cognizance will have to be taken of this fact in any scheme for the transformation of subsistence agriculture into modern commercial enterprise.

If past experience is any indication, it is likely that the pressure of agricultural population will fall mainly on small holdings below 5 acres and on large holdings of 50 acres and above. Both the number of house-

---

1. By definition, there are as many farmer households as there are farms.

Table 12.1. Estimated Number and Cumulative Percentage of Households and Area Owned by Size Limits of Household Ownership Holdings (1953-1954 Crop Season)

Holding size (acres)	No. of households (000)	Area owned (000 acres)	Cumulative households	Percentage area
			Percentages	
1. 0.001	14,669	—	23.09	—
2. 0.01–0.99	15,360	4,166	47.26	1.37
3. 1.00–2.49	8,879	14,839	61.24	6.23
4. 2.50–4.99	8,569	30,821	74.73	16.32
5. 5.00–7.49	4,966	30,411	82.55	26.28
6. 7.50–9.99	2,972	25,766	87.23	34.72
7. 10.00–14.99	3,207	39,053	92.28	47.50
8. 15.00–19.99	1,690	29,253	94.94	57.08
9. 20.00–24.99	929	20,623	96.40	63.83
10. 25.00–29.99	636	17,480	97.40	69.55
11. 30.00–49.99	1,051	39,439	99.06	82.46
12. 50.00 and above	604	53,580	100.00	100.00
13. Total	63,532	305,431	—	—

SOURCE: *National Sample Survey Report on Land Holdings* (3) Number 36. Cabinet Secretariat, Government of India, 1961.

holds and the area comprised by small holdings below 5 acres will increase, but the area under units between the size of 5 and 50 acres may not be adversely affected. Between 1953–1954 and 1959–1960—when more than a score of land reform laws were operating with full steam—the total number of operated holdings increased by 4.8 million; the percentage of holdings in the size group of 5 acres and below increased from 60 to 63, and the percentage of area operated therein from 15.4 to 18.9. At the other end the percentage of operated holdings in the size group of 50 acres and above came down from 1.53 to 1.07, and the area comprised by it from 17.1 to 12.2 per cent. The percentage of total area comprised by units of the size between 5 and 50 acres actually increased from 67.5 to 68.9 [India, 1960; 1967].

Now if we have to take the pattern of the size of cultivation units—a large number of very small farms and a large portion of cultivated area in the middle-sized group—as given, our developmental plans have to be such as would be appropriate and feasible for such an agrarian structure.

GROWTH VERSUS SOCIAL JUSTICE

Let us try to spell out with a little more precision what this means with reference to some specific policy issues. First and foremost, we have to make up our mind whether our policy should be to operate on the entire

agricultural base or concentrate on areas of the largest potential. The Intensive Agricultural District Programme derives its rationale from the choice of the latter alternative. There are distinct advantages in this line of action, but its implication should be clearly understood. There are well-recognized shortages in improved inputs and administrative skill. If

Table 12.2. Work Force Disposition (in Millions)

Year	Total work force	Workers in agriculture	Workers in nonagri. sector
1950–51	139.5	100.6	38.9
1960–61	188.4	135.3	53.1
1970–71	237.7	170.7	67.0
1975–76	266.9	191.7	75.2

Assumptions:
(1) Population increases at the compound rate of 2.35 per cent per year.
(2) Work force increases at the same rate as that of population.
(3) Proportions of workers in agricultural and nonagricultural sector remain the same as in 1961 (71.8 and 28.2).

Note: Increase between 1950–51 and 1960–61 is partly owing to change in definition. The participation rate is said to have increased from 39 in 1951 to 42.98 in 1961.

Increase in Number of Workers

	Agriculture	Nonagriculture
1951–61	34.7	14.2
1961–75	56.4	22.1

Assuming that the proportion of work force in agriculture is reduced to 66.6, increases would be as follows:

1961–75	42.7	35.8

this limited supply is to be made available in adequate doses to select areas, there is no escape from the relative neglect of the larger subsistence sector of agriculture. When this comes to be fully realized, the developing countries will be confronted with the issues of welfare and social justice. Given a democratic framework with adult franchise, this can be an explosive issue, and the government may be compelled to seek a compromise between a policy that stimulates growth and one that meets the immediate demand for social justice.

LAND REFORM

How far can the reform of the agrarian structure help to alleviate, if not solve, the problem of subsistence farming? The economists and other technical experts, given a free choice, would like to reorganize the agrarian structure in a manner that would provide a production base most suited for progressive and efficient agriculture. Even if they reconcile themselves to the inevitability of retaining a large number of relatively small farms in view of the population pressure, they will certainly not like the continuation of palpably uneconomic dwarf farms that would be incapable of absorbing the improvements in technique and production practices. They will perhaps take a view regarding the size range —the minimum and the maximum—of holdings that would be most appropriate from the economic and agronomic points of view. Even if their recommendation involves elimination or merger of farms of one acre and below, it will affect 24 per cent of the total (or about 15 million) cultivator households. These had between them only 4 million acres of land. If they opt for a minimum of 5 acres, the percentage would go up to 52 per cent and attach about 33 million farm households with an owned area of 50 million acres.[2] On the other hand, the politician and the policy-maker, confronted with the stupendous problem of rural poverty and unemployment, would be under tremendous pressure to equalize ownership of land and provide land to the landless. In view of the numbers involved and the total inadequacy of

surplus land that would be available through the imposition of ceilings on existing large holdings, this is an impossible task. In spite of this, he will be tempted to temporize on the question to assuage the pressure of public opinion and egalitarian urges—so powerful in poor countries—and seek to reconcile the requirement of efficiency with that of social justice *here and now*. In the process he will tend to favor an agrarian structure that will perhaps be neither efficient nor would satisfy the land hunger. There is, however, no point in putting the blame for such an equivocal policy on the political leadership. The technician and the land reformer have a solution for subsistence farmers. The search for a type of reform, say for Indian agriculture, that would give an efficient agrarian structure yet does not involve uprooting millions of people from their farms has so far not yielded any precise solution.

REFORM OF CREDIT INSTITUTIONS

The dilemma of other reform measures is equally frustrating. The cooperative credit institutions, whose avowed purpose is to help the weaker—and therefore the subsistence—section of the agriculturists, end up by discovering that because of the inherent uneconomic character of their enterprise, even its most liberal banking attitude does not make it possible to render any assistance to it. This is now recognized even by the most ardent supporters of the cooperative movement. It is contended that the problem of the subsistence farms is one of rehabilitation, and the credit institutions by themselves can do very little, even with the best of intentions. Professor D. R. Gadgil, one of the foremost innovators in the cooperative movement, states this problem with commendable frankness in his recent article [1964]. He admits that the Report of the Committee of Direction of the Rural Credit Survey of the Reserve Bank of India, on which present policies are largely based, "does not adequately deal with the problem of subsistence and uneconomic farms, the problem of consumption loans and the problem of cooperative backward states."

The smaller cultivator and the cultivators who grew the less costly crops, did not equally benefit from the crop-loan system. This was because

2. Both these calculations leave out another 14 to 15 million households of landless persons in the rural area (see Table 12.1).

production credit needs played a relatively small part in his total requirement of credit. If the cooperative structure makes credit available for all the production *and consumption* needs of the farm family, the security and repayment base of the crop-loan system becomes nonapplicable, inasmuch as it is highly unlikely that the proceeds of the sale of farm produce by the small farmer will cover his total requirement of credit. The financial problem of the weaker sections of the rural community thus becomes in a large part the problem of consumption finance to wage-earning classes. It is thus not only fraught with more risk, but requires for administration a much more detailed and individualistic approach. In a sense, therefore, developments required for this purpose are in the same direction of supervised individual credit. Ultimately the only development that can help substantially in this matter is a more close-knit organization of the weaker sections themselves, such as of the small farmers in types of cooperative farming or cooperative bullock or labor-sharing units and of wage-earners in labor contract societies.

In plain words, this amounts to shifting the responsibility to assist the subsistence sector to other institutions, most of which are not even in existence!

PRICE INCENTIVE

Lastly, let us see whether the oft-recommended policy of incentive prices can be of any avail to the subsistence farmer. Farm Management and Cost-Production Studies in India have revealed that the cost of production of the last decile of farmers ranked by efficiency is anywhere between five to seven times higher than that of the most efficient farmers—even in as small an area as a district. If the average cost of production is taken as the basis for fixing the support prices, according to the Farm Management Study in West Bengal, 50 per cent of the farmers will have a deficit economy in the cultivation of *aman* paddy. The same principle, applied to jute, would leave out nearly 58 per cent of the producers. If instead, what is known as the bulkline cost is made the basis—covering about 85 per cent of the most efficient production—about 26 per cent of the paddy growers and 32 per cent of the jute growers will not have their cost covered. Going to the extreme, if prices were to be fixed at levels that would cover the cost of production of the last 20 per cent of cultivators, Indian

prices will perhaps be twice, if not three times, the prices prevailing in international markets (see Table 12.3 [Agriculture, 1963, pp. 142, 257]).

Table 12.3. *Bulkline and Average Cost of* Aman *Paddy—Hoogly and 24-Parganas Districts—1955-56 and 1956-57 Average*

Bulkline Cost		Average Cost	
Rs. per maund	13.1	Rs. per maund	10.4
% of Production Covered	85.0	% of Production Covered	59.3
% Farms Covered	73.8	% Farms Covered	50.6
% Area Covered	80.2	% Area Covered	54.9

AMAN PADDY

COST OF PRODUCTION PER MAUND (Rs)	CUMULATIVE % OF AVERAGE OF TOTAL		
	Production	No. of Farms	Area
3.00–4.99	3.01	4.49	2.29
5.00–6.99	19.40	17.20	15.98
7.00–8.99	47.68	37.10	37.90
9.00–10.99	66.78	56.45	62.03
11.00–12.99	84.56	73.39	79.75
15.00–16.99	95.06	85.21	92.25
21.00–22.99	98.37	92.20	96.69
23.00 and up	100.00	100.00	100.00

SOURCE: *Studies in Economics of Farm Management in West Bengal, Years 1954-55 to 1956-57.* Directorate of Economics and Statistics, Ministry of Food and Agriculture, Government of India, 1958.

Thus, it would seem that none of the known devices—like reform of the agrarian structure, reorganization of credit and marketing system, guarantee of minimum support prices—offer any solution to the problem of the subsistence farm. But this should not be in any way surprising if we bear in mind the factors that were responsible for the emergence of subsistence sector in the agriculture of the underdeveloped economies. In fact, the main characteristic of underdeveloped economies is the pervasiveness of subsistence agriculture. It should, therefore, be obvious that the one cannot disappear without the other's disappearing. One finds very little of subsistence agriculture in a developed economy, or much of advanced agriculture in an underdeveloped economy. If so, it is futile to search for the solution of subsistence agriculture that is not also a solution of general underdevelopment. Correspondingly, that which is a solution for general economic underdevelopment will also be a solution for subsistence agriculture. The end of subsistence farming will be coterminous with the end of underdevelopment. This may appear tautological; but any dichotomy in the approach to the problem of subsistence agriculture and that of general economic underdevelopment would be sheer escapism.

References

AGRICULTURE, 1963. Ministry of Food and Agriculture, *Studies in Economics of Farm Management in West Bengal, Report for the Years 1954–55 to 1956–57* (New Delhi, India: Directorate of Economics and Statistics, Ministry of Food and Agriculture, 1963).

GADGIL, 1964. D. R. Gadgil, "Prospective Developments in Co-operative Finance," *The Maharashtra Co-operative Quarterly* (Bombay), Vol. XLVII, No. 3 (January 1964), 156–59.

INDIA, 1960. Government of India, Cabinet Secretariat, *The National Sample Survey: Eighth Round: July 1954–April 1955*, No. 30, "Report on Land Holdings (2) (Operational Holdings in Rural India)" (New Delhi, India: Government of India, 1960).

INDIA, 1961. Government of India, Cabinet Secretariat, *The National Sample Survey: Eighth Round: July 1954–April 1955*, No. 36, "Report on Land Holdings (3) (Some Aspects of Ownership Holdings)" (New Delhi, India: Government of India, 1961).

INDIA, 1967. Government of India, Cabinet Secretariat, *The National Sample Survey: Sixteenth Round: July 1960–June 1961*, No. 113 "Tables with Notes on Agricultural Holdings in Rural India" (New Delhi, India: Government of India, 1967).

13

The Execution of Agricultural Development: Case Studies of Planned Change

EDITOR'S INTRODUCTION

SUBSISTENCE AGRICULTURE has changed and developed in the past, even in situations where there was no deliberate or conscious effort to achieve development. But the rates of growth were in most cases almost imperceptible, leaving most areas still without adequate levels of living. The rates of growth desired by the peoples and nations where subsistence agriculture predominates today are considerably higher than the historical ones that they have experienced. To accomplish the demanded rates of growth will involve various approaches to planned change.

The deliberate or planned development of subsistence agriculture requires more than theories and empirical evidence supporting them. Even if there were complete agreement on both the facts and theories about subsistence agriculture (which as we have seen, there is not) the task would still remain to derive useful operational approaches to bring about the more rapid development desired. The changes must be planned and organized into policies, programs, and projects.

Intervention into the growth process in agriculture has taken a variety of forms and has operated at several levels. There have been governmental schemes and private activities by the agribusiness community.

There have been national schemes and regional or state schemes. There have been commodity approaches concentrating upon particular crops and factor-input approaches concentrating upon fertilizer or mechanization. There have been health programs and tube-well projects. There have been land-settlement schemes and marketing boards. There have been extension programs and cooperatives. Each of these efforts represents a program or activity for the purpose of stimulating more rapid rates of agricultural development. Each has also met with varying degrees of success or failure.

Attempts at planned change in agriculture face a number of problems.[1] Three explanations are currently being advanced to explain the difficulties faced in programming developmental assistance in this field.

One difficulty is what I call the "microheterogeneity" of agriculture. The physical inputs and climatic factors in agriculture are not homogeneous. The quality of labor and management ability varies considerably among farm people. Equally important, the microenvironment—soil, rainfall, humidity, hours of sunshine, and the like—also varies

1. For a useful review of the literature, see Gittinger [1966].

considerably from place to place, though it may seem uniform to the untrained eye. As a biologic process, agriculture is far more subject to environmental factors. Although improved technology has reduced somewhat the influence of climate and environment upon agricultural production, the peasant farmer is still very much controlled by the microenvironment where the biological process takes place. Such "microheterogeneity" restricts severely the effectiveness of many central plans that cannot take account of these factors.

Secondly, agriculture involves a large number of geographically scattered decision-makers and a large number of different kinds of productive decisions temporally dispersed. In a typical developing country, agricultural production is carried out by millions of farmers who are widely scattered. Planning or controlling the activities of such large numbers over such a wide area is extremely difficult. Further, the time span required in agricultural production involves numerous and varied decisions because most agricultural products have a crop cycle or a time lag between planting and harvest. The production decisions of the cultivator throughout the crop cycle are different and require different skills and knowledge: which crops to choose, which variety, when to plant, when to weed, when to fertilize, when to harvest. An exclusively "top-down" developmental planning effort that does not take account of microenvironmental differences and the important localized knowledge of the farmers themselves will only end in frustration.

Another recent explanation is an outgrowth of the 1964 MIT conference: namely that agricultural development is a "systems problem," involving the interaction of a large number of variables, both economic and noneconomic [Hapgood and Millikan, 1965]. Two complexities are involved: the very large number of interrelated factors and the unique importance of any one factor or series of factors in any given situation. An exhaustive and almost comprehensive list of the relevant factors and variables that affect agricultural development can be prepared and has been attempted (see Table 13.1). But the importance of any particular factor or of any set varies through time and from place to place. Solutions that concentrate

upon a single factor while excluding all others rarely are successful. Furthermore, the critical problem in any one country or region need not be the same as in another. Merely because a program attacks successfully a combination of critical factors in one place does not mean that it can be transferred to another problem situation. *Agricultural development programs must, therefore, be based upon an analysis of the developmental process in its complex totality, concentrating upon the key interacting factors, each of which must be studied in all the uniqueness of each particular situation.*

In his recent book, *Getting Agriculture Moving* [1966], Dr. A. T. Mosher has attempted to unravel these complexities and to reduce them to a basic, simplified level. He has identified five "essentials" and five "accelerators" that are universal for agricultural development. The five essentials are (1) markets for farm products; (2) constantly changing technology; (3) local availability for supplies and equipment; (4) production incentives for farmers; and (5) transportation. One or more may be crucial in any given situation, or at any given time, but all are equally important determinants in that they are interrelated with each other in making growth possible. The accelerators are those factors that, while not absolutely essential for agricultural growth, can make a contribution to speeding up the rate of growth once the essentials are met. The five accelerators are: (1) education for development; (2) production credit; (3) group action by farmers; (4) improving and expanding agricultural land; and (5) national planning. Note that traditional economic variables are involved in only two of the essentials—markets for products and incentives—and only two of the accelerators—production credit and planning.

The complexities and interrelatedness of developing subsistence agriculture help to explain the considerable variation in focus, emphasis, and approach that can be found among the programs of planned change around the world. They also help to explain why so many "pilot projects" or programs have concentrated upon smaller, more manageable, and homogeneous areas or upon particular facets of the problem that were considered to be "the" critical problem or "the" magic answer to development.

Table 13.1. Classification of Factors Affecting Agricultural Development

Physical Input Factors

1. Nonhuman physical inputs
   - a. Land
   - b. Climate
   - c. Seeds
   - d. Water
   - e. Fertilizer
   - f. Pesticides
   - g. Structures
   - h. Work animals
   - i. Other animals
   - j. Tools and machinery
   - k. Fuel and power other than animal power
2. Labor.

Economic Factors

1. Transport, storage, processing, and marketing facilities for products.
2. Facilities for the supply and distribution of inputs including credit.
3. Input prices, including interest rates.
4. Product prices, including prices of consumer goods.
5. Taxes, subsidies, quotas.

Organizational Factors

1. Tenure, land.
2. Farm size and legal form.
3. General government services and policies.
4. Voluntary and statutory farmers' organizations for:
   - a. Coordinating physical input use, e.g. irrigation associations, tractor stations.
   - b. Economic services, e.g. purchase, sale, credit associations and cooperatives.
   - c. Social services, e.g. health centers, schools, family planning centers.
   - d. Local government.
   - e. Diffusion of knowledge, e.g. adult-education classes, youth clubs.

Socio-Psycho-Cultural Factors

1. Integration of agricultural institution, practices, and values within the technosocial matrix of the nation.
2. Public administration factors, structure, values, mode of operation of the innovating bureaucracy.
3. Social structure, cultural values, and dynamics of peasant communities.
4. Process of sociocultural change, barriers, and motivations in the innovative sequence, functional harmony or disharmony in society as its constituent parts change.

Knowledge Factors

1. Organization of basic and applied research.
2. Diffusion of knowledge relating to:
   - a. Technical knowledge, e.g. agronomy, plant genetics, soil science, water management, agricultural engineering, pest control, home technology.
   - b. Economic knowledge, e.g. land economics, general economics, farm management.
   - c. Policy, e.g. politics, public administration, planning.
   - d. General education, e.g. literacy, adult education, mass communication.

SOURCE: Hapgood-Millikan [1965, 13]. Prepared by a Classification Committee at the MIT Conference composed of J. D. Montgomery, C. R. Wharton, L. R. Martin, Raj Krishna, and G. M. Foster.

Four case studies have been selected out of the many that could have been considered as being particularly relevant to the problems of developing subsistence agriculture.[2] The focus and emphasis of each differs from the others, as does the area covered and length of operation. They have been arranged in accordance with their size and scope. The Vicos project in Peru is concerned with a single small community of 1,800 people; the Comilla program in East Pakistan with an administrative unit of 107 square miles; the ACAR program in Brazil with a state larger than France; and the Rockefeller Foundation program with two major crops in Mexico as a whole.

VICOS IN PERU

The Cornell program in Vicos, Peru, which began in 1952, is an excellent case study of a program initiated primarily by anthropologists under the leadership of the late Prof. Allan R. Holmberg of Cornell University.[3] The twofold objectives of the program were, first, to convert the Andean Indians resident on a traditional manor under conditions to serfdom into commercial agricultural producers, and thereby improve their levels of living; and second, to study the independent

2. Over 50 case studies will be discussed at the International Seminar on Change in Agriculture at the University of Reading, England, September 3–14, 1968. Other interesting ones will be found in Borton [1967].

3. During his terminal illness, Prof. Holmberg was assisted in the preparation of the case study by Prof. Henry F. Dobyns.

variables involved in raising the levels of agricultural and human productivity.

When Cornell University first leased the manor, the manor Indians practiced primitive technology on their small subsistence plots and were effectively isolated from the wider regional and national community because of language, illiteracy, and social, ostracism imposed by serfdom. The conditions of tenure and traditional manorial controls reduced economic motivations, discouraged the introduction of new technology, and inhibited capital accumulation (except livestock). The condition was what the authors call "the vicious circle of serf servility."

The Cornell Peru Project leased the manor but did not force changes among the Indian serfs by the traditional power and sanctions of the manor "lord." The project sought to effectuate change in four ways. First, relying upon a participant-intervention approach, they used explanation and enlightenment to encourage the serfs to innovate and to change. Second, they made realistic provision of new technologies and factor inputs, such as improved seeds, fungicides, and fertilizers. Third, they changed certain "rules of the game" that had been previously followed in manorial relationships with the serfs and that obviously had operated as disincentives to changes. Fourth, they used their power as "manor lord" to exclude other external power foci that had previously merely exploited the serfs and fostered the latter's greater integration into the wider commercial world and their greater direct contact with the institutions of government.

Today the serfs own their own land, are self-sufficient in food, produce an agricultural surplus that is marketed regionally and nationally, and have acquired a greater sense of independence and control over their lives.

COMILLA IN PAKISTAN

The program of the Pakistan Academy for Rural Development began in 1960 as a pilot experiment for the development of subsistence agriculture in the county, or *thana*, of Comilla, East Pakistan. The Academy is basically a research and training institution with experimental project activities directed by a central cooperative association in which are federated a system of primary cooperatives. The Comilla *thana* was set aside by the government of Pakistan to serve as an experimental "laboratory" where the Academy could develop and test patterns and procedures that might be suitable for developing East Pakistan's agriculture. Under the leadership of social scientists, the 100-square-mile area became both a laboratory to experiment with new approaches to development as well as a training ground for the capacitation of the personnel engaged in rural development in East Pakistan.

Of the three activities described in some detail, perhaps the most interesting is the Comilla approach to extension education. The managers of the cooperative societies come to the office of the Central Association each week and receive special training in new farm practices, new farm inputs, and demonstrations at the Association's farm. This information is then spread by the manager after his return through the meetings of the cooperative society, and if there are problems, these are taken up by the manager on his next visit to the Central Association, where all the government technicians are located.

Although the Comilla experiment has been operating for a very few years, the project staff has already developed some interesting guidelines based upon their experience. The program has relied primarily upon group organization and action at the local level through the mechanism of cooperatives, which have been integrated into a central system, and the system has been structured so that the available technical talent and administration is centralized in one location plus coordinated in their overall efforts. The two-way flow within the system has facilitated the introduction of new technology and the training of farmers for more modern agriculture.

Another interesting aspect of the program has been its ever-broadening scope and activities as the program developed. Beginning with a cooperative pilot project, the "experiment" quickly added pilot projects in a wide range of problem areas—rural education, family planning, irrigation, women's education. This pattern of a widening scope as a program evolves is also demonstrated in the third case study.

ACAR IN BRAZIL

The ACAR program in Minas Gerais, Brazil, is an interesting example of a program that largely began with a major focus upon a single problem—credit—but then gradually broadened its scope to include a wide array of rural development services. The program began in 1948 under joint sponsorship of and financing by the American International Association for Economic and Social Development and the state government of Minas Gerais. The ACAR program gradually expanded its concept and approach in the fields of credit and technology over the years. From a modest beginning of three local offices in 1949, the program today has a staff of almost 600 persons operating through 14 regional offices and 120 local offices, reaching more than three million people a year in the state.

In its extension education work, the program has used youth clubs, men's and women's clubs, nutrition and health projects, community exhibits, demonstrations, technical bulletins, and radio programs. Special attention has been given to rural extension committees in each community and similar leadership groups.

In its credit work, the original supervised credit approach has been modified and three other forms of credit provided—"oriented," housing, and for youth. The repayment records of the borrowers has been outstanding. As of November 30, 1964, loan maturities totalled some Cr$563 million, with 99.95 per cent of this amount repaid. The cost of providing the supervision or educational component with the credit represented between 7 and 11 per cent of the cost of the loan but brought a return of 6.5 fold.

The history of the ACAR program is an interesting example of how a responsive and flexible institution that begins with a limited or single-focus approach to a problem necessarily finds itself forced into a wider network of service, owing to the complexities of the problem of developing traditional agriculture and its changing character through time.

THE ROCKEFELLER FOUNDATION IN MEXICO

Intensive agricultural research to develop dramatic improved agricultural technology is frequently advocated as indispensable for a breakthrough from subsistence to commercial agriculture. The prototype for most current approaches is the work of the Rockefeller Foundation in Mexico, which began in 1943 as the Office of Special Studies and is now being continued as the International Center for Maize and Wheat Improvement.

In his case study of the Mexican program, Dr. Delbert T. Myren examines the 20-year experience of the program in an attempt to unravel the puzzle of its greater success in the case with wheat than with corn, despite almost identical professional resources and research approaches which led to equally significant technological breakthroughs. Dr. Myren advances four main explanations:

1. Between the two crops there were important locational differences, with attendant differences in the quality of the land, especially irrigation. More wheat was irrigated than corn; and corn was predominantly dependent upon rainfall.

2. Corn producers are different from wheat producers because the former are heavily subsistence while the latter are commercial and have a higher level of literacy.

3. Probably the most important explanations for the differential success of wheat over corn lie in certain technical differences between the two crops: (a) In wheat the new varieties gave protection against heavy disease losses, whereas in corn there was no single serious disease problem. (b) The seeds for the new hybrid corns had to be purchased each new planting season, whereas the open pollinated wheat could, if necessary, be duplicated by the farmer or by his neighbors. (c) In the case of wheat, the genotype maintains itself for an indefinite period, whereas the hybrid corns require a highly competent and efficient seed-multiplication agency to maintain their hybrid vigor. (d) The new hybrid corn had inherently lesser ecologic adaptability than the improved wheat varieties, which meant that corn required greater local-specific research and development to accommodate for its greater temperature sensitivity.

4. Finally, there is eight times as much corn acreage as wheat, and there are forty times more corn farmers than wheat farmers. These important differences in numbers and size between the two crops seriously affect the

ease with which the new technology can be spread utilizing accepted methods of extension education.

Dr. Myren's case study offers an excellent analysis of the important considerations that must enter into the strategies involved in an intensive concentration of resources to achieve major technological breakthroughs.

References

BORTON, 1967. Raymond E. Borton, ed., *Case Studies to Accompany Getting Agriculture Moving* (New York: Agricultural Development Council, 1967).

GITTINGER, 1966. J. Price Gittinger, "The Literature of Agricultural Planning. Notes on Its Usefulness," Planning Method Series No. 4 (Washington, D.C.: Center for Development Planning, National Planning Association, September 1966).

HAPGOOD and MILLIKAN, 1965. David Hapgood and Max F. Millikan, *Policies for Promoting Agricultural Development*, Report of a Conference on Productivity and Innovation in the Underdeveloped Countries (Cambridge, Mass.: Center for International Studies, Massachusetts Institute of Technology, January 1965).

MOSHER, 1966. Arthur T. Mosher, *Getting Agriculture Moving: Essentials for Development and Modernization* (New York: Praeger, 1966).

CASE STUDY

The Cornell Program in Vicos, Peru[1]

ALLAN R. HOLMBERG and HENRY F. DOBYNS

THIS PAPER IS AN analysis of a case in transition by a population of Andean Indian farmers from less than subsistence production, incapable of even feeding themselves, to commercial agricultural producers on a modest scale. We need first to describe briefly the characteristics of agricultural production in the Andean area, by which we mean principally the mountain areas of Bolivia, Peru, and Ecuador, plus the fertile Pacific coastal plain west of the Andes.

CHARACTERISTICS OF ANDEAN AGRICULTURE

PRODUCTION UNITS

Several types of production units engage in agriculture in the Andean region, which has

1. We acknowledge our debt to Dr. Mario C. Vazquez for his advice in revising this analysis after its oral presentation as well as to his long-term substantive contributions to the Cornell Peru Project. We are indebted to the organizations whose financial support made this analysis possible: the Carnegie Corporation of New York, which supported the Cornell Peru Project for many years; an anonymous donor; and the Office of Technical Cooperation and Research of the Agency for International Development, whose contract AID/csd-296 permitted us to prepare this paper as one of the contributions of the Comparative Studies of Cultural Change of Cornell University's Department of Anthropology. We alone bear full responsibility for the conclusions presented.

been farmed for thousands of years [Bird, 1951], so that the present ecology is one that has been seriously affected by human exploitation. Many areas, e.g. the densely populated high-altitude plateau and principal agricultural valleys of Bolivia [Junta Interministerial Directiva, 1963, p. 38], have been virtually completely deforested.

Only a few of the various types of production units found in the Andes are truly subsistence farms. The types range along a continuum of productivity from those that cannot feed their resident farming population (so that members of farm families must resort to wage labor off the farm, so as to earn cash with which to purchase supplementary foodstuffs) to those which produce tremendous surpluses of agricultural commodities beyond local consumption that are sold externally, often outside the country on the world commodity market.

Beginning at the more productive end of the continuum, we may identify first of all the "factory in the field" [McWilliams, 1939], as a highly capitalized, technologically complex and relatively efficient agricultural enterprise operating on an extensive land base. There are at least two geographically specific forms of such enterprise in the Andean region: plantations and ranches.

Plantations

Plantations are characteristic of the Pacific coast littoral of tropical Ecuador and Peru and the relatively recently developed portions of the lowland jungles of eastern Peru and Bolivia. They typically cultivate row crops with high yields of products in demand on the world commodity market—sugar, cotton, rice, bananas, and coffee. These products bring in significant sums in foreign-exchange credits to both Ecuador and Peru.

Ranches

The ranch is another of these geographically specific forms. Much of the Andean mountain complex rises so high in altitude that cropping is not possible over broad expanses, but forage plants do grow there. Thus specialized stock-production enterprises have been developed in a number of high-altitude areas. They produce significant portions of the national commercial wool clip and mutton, llama meat, goat, and the like.

Both the plantation and ranch forms of field factory produce primarily to sell outside the production unit. Production for immediate consumption is secondary to the main business of growing plants or animals for external sale. Both forms are characteristically organized as corporations and obtain short-term operational capital from commercial banks. Both hire wage labor for relatively specialized tasks, aided by mechanization, and occupy a strongly paternalistic position in terms of supplying the labor force with housing, educational, and medical facilities. The labor force is typically unionized.

Medium Farms

A variety of "medium farmers" occupies the next-lower position of the continuum of production. These farm units typically exploit a smaller land base than the ranch or plantation. They are for the most part privately owned and owner-operated with the aid of farm laborers employed for cash wages, as on plantations and ranches. They are capitalized, but less heavily than plantations or ranches.

They also produce primarily for external sale but include agricultural activities carried on to sustain the farm population. The range of crops grown by medium farmers is, therefore, considerably greater than that grown on plantations. Medium farmers are more reliant than larger producers upon crop loans from government agricultural banks than upon commercial banks. They depend more on agricultural extension-service personnel for technical advice than upon the company agronomists hired by plantation managements, and their children attend public schools rather than company-financed schools.

Peasants

Less productive than the medium farmers are a vast multitude of several millions of peasant farmers. The peasantry is made up of independent small landowners, or farmers who hold lands within special legal entities called Indigenous Communities in Peru and Bolivia and Communes in Ecuador. The peasant farm is not, of course, capitalized in any conscious sense. It is characteristically small, often extremely tiny, as a result of fractionalization of titles [Junta, 1963, pp. 37–38]. The technology employed in its exploitation is traditional and typically brings little non-human energy into play in carrying out farm tasks, so that they are physically arduous and time-consuming.

Some Indigenous Communities retain communally owned lands, some of which are exploited by individuals under assignment or lease, others of which are exploited by community labor. Except for this last characteristic, these lands generally fall into the same category as peasant production units.

The Andean peasantry constitutes today, after the abolition of serfdom in Bolivia, the greatest single reservoir of unskilled or semi-skilled labor in the region. Quite typically, the peasant who cannot grow sufficient food to subsist his family must find alternative sources of income. He hires out by the day on nearby plantations or ranches, or in accessible towns, in order to earn cash with which to purchase additional food, clothing, and an occasional luxury [Faron, 1960; Patch, 1959b; Beals, 1952]. If industrial or mine employment is available, the peasant becomes a worker.[2] Alternatively, the less-than-subsistence farmer signs up as a sharecropper on a neighboring plantation, ranch, or manor, in order to gain additional cultivable land or pasturage rights,[3] or rents wood-cutting rights [Buitron, 1947], or specializes in some branch of cottage industry or traditional artisanry in order to capitalize on his surplus labor and bring in cash. This means making hats in Chinchera and Araque; baking bread in Chupaca; weaving cord sandals in Pomasqui, canvas and cotton goods in San Juan; blankets in Carmen Alto, Quinchuqui, and Punyaro; ponchos in La Bolsa, Iluman, Carabuela, and La Compania; shawls and yard goods in Agato and Peguche; mats in San Miguel, San Roque, and Maji-pampa; baskets in Santiaguillo; dressmaking in Sicaya; pottery making in Peguche and Cotocollao; pottery, brick, and tile in Tani-tan; stoneworking in Amantani.[4] It means carrying on petty trading expeditions, turning a profit buying and reselling manufactured goods and agricultural commodities,[5] or hiring out as a burden-bearer [Buitron, 1947] or migrating seasonally to plantation zones to work in harvests requiring numerous hands, such as cotton [Tschopik, 1947, p. 41], rice [Saunders, 1961], and coffee [Martínez, 1961, p. 160]. Sometimes it means settling permanently on a plantation as a hired hand[6] or moving into special occupational niches that happen to be open in towns, such as butchering [Preston, 1963]. The peasantry also provides the bulk of rural-urban migrants who have been gradually abandoning the farms of the Andes and bursting the cities in the area at their seams.[7]

Manors

Least productive of the Andean agricultural units are the traditional manors. This comment is generally true for both types of production unit found within the manor—the manor fields or flocks and the subsistence plots of the manor serfs. The manor field farmed with obligatory labor of the serfs (or the manor flocks pastured by the manor/serfs in the special case of high altitude estates) yield little. They are destined primarily for external sale after the owner's family is subsisted, if the estate is in private hands and the family resides in a provincial city near enough to it to make provisioning feasible. The pre-revolutionary latifundia[8] in Bolivia were, it is said [Heath, 1959], "invariably self-supporting," producing a small surplus to sell in the cities.

Manors are not, however, typified by the kind of capitalization that Simon Patiño poured into his Pairumani showplace. Unskilled hand labor constitutes an unproductive substitute for mechanization and technification of agricultural practices. If serf labor costs were charged against sales returns, many manors would operate at a loss [Vásquez, 1961]. Instead of employing rotation grazing on fenced, seeded pastures with professional shepherds, typical *páramo* or *puna* high-altitude range management consists of little or no attention to tufted grasses native to the areas overgrazed by too many serf-owned as well as manor livestock. Even on the Ecuadorian coast, where cattle graze cultivated but rarely fertilized pasture down to guinea grass and elephant grass, exploitation remains extensive [Miller, 1959].

The subsistence plots assigned to the manor serf population are farmed with the least capital, the most traditional simplest technology [Vasquez, 1952], for the most limited

2. Alencastre Montúfar [1960, p. 6]; Allred et al. [1959, p. 68]; Llosa Larrabure [1962]; Marus and Monje Rada [1962, p. 139]; Montalvo Vidal [1958, pp. 2–3, 9]; Tschopik [1947, pp. 24, 28]; Adams [1959, pp. 93–94].

3. Buitrón [1947]; Holmberg [1950]; Patch [1959b, p. 16]; Stein [1961, pp. 38–43].

4. The individual references for each example are: Buitron [1947]; Montalvo Vidal and Galdo Pagaza [1960, pp. 2–3, 6 ff]; Tschopik [1947, p. 41]; Hearn [1950]; Collier and Buitron [1949, p. 163]; Rubio Orbe [1956, p. 156]; Collier and Buitron [1949, pp. 163–164]; Dobyns [1965b, p. 4]; Tschopik [1947, p. 45]; Parsons [1945, pp. 24–25]; Cisneros Cisneros [1949]; Ortiz Vergara and Galdo Pagaza [1958a, p. 29].

5. Kuczynski-Godard [1944, p. 14; 1945, pp. 13–21]; Tschopik [1947, pp. 30–31]; Buitron [1947]; Beals [1952]; Preston [1963].

6. Cheng and Portugal [1963, p. 105]; Ghersi Barrera [1963, p. 131]; Ghersi Barrera and Dobyns, 1963, pp. 155–156]; Patch [1959a, pp. 3–14]; Soler Bustamente [1963, p. 83].

7. Adams [1959, p. 117]; Dobyns [1963, p. 20]; Doughty [1963b; 1963a, pp. 113–115]; Hickman [1963, pp. 123–124]; Stein [1961, pp. 20, 43]; Ghersi Barrera [1963, p. 131]; Preston [1963]; Heath [1959]; Espinosa Zevallos [1965, pp. 185–188].

8. The term "latifundia" is used in Latin America to describe the large manorial-type plantation, ranch, or estate, while the term "minifundia" embraces the small-scale peasant farmer.

objectives of any Andean farms. The productivity of the serfs' plots is so low that very frequently the manor serf population must go outside the manor to seek labor for wages with which to purchase foodstuffs to make up for the deficit in family production.

FARM PRODUCTIVITY

It must never be forgotten that the serf, unproductive though he may be, always reserves certain kinds of farm production for external sale, even under starvation conditions. Let us cite a simple example. When the Cornell Peru Project undertook to change the culture of one Andean manor population, that of Vicos, it was necessary to *teach* the Indian serfs to eat eggs and cheese. The serf population did not know what chicken eggs tasted like except as medicine for certain illnesses [Vazquez, 1952], even though 85 per cent of the households raised farmyard flocks. Eggs were always in demand and could be sold for cash or bartered almost like money. So eggs produced in Vicos were almost all sold outside the manor, and "constitute the principal article of commerce" [Vasquez, 1952]. Even though fresh cows were always milked and cheese made, these were also sold or traded during the Sunday market [Vasquez, 1952].

Vicos lies in a mixed farming area, with extensive high-altitude pastures where manor management and serfs alike grazed livestock. The serf diet was, however, a very nearly vegetarian one [Alers, 1965] save for the few families owning enough cattle to afford to eat beef regularly [Vasquez, 1952]. Animals comprised the principal form of investment and saving by the serfs, who preferred to invest in goods which could move off the manor should the serf flee intentionally or be evicted. Animals also comprised the principal source of ready cash for serfs, to finance emergency expenditures [Vasquez, 1965a], such as the purchase of grain to sustain themselves during the famine of the winter of 1949-1950 [Vasquez, 1952]. Thus livestock was raised for external sale rather than home consumption. Kitchen herds of guinea pigs provided the main source of animal protein in the serf diet, augmented from time to time when a large animal died and the meat was salvaged or one was slaughtered for

feasting during a religious festival. All other animals not held on pasture were sold outside the manor.

At the same time the Vicos serfs sold livestock to raise cash, they spent part of their money purchasing cereal grains for their own consumption. The manor was a grain-importing agricultural unit, not just under famine conditions but regularly. This paradox characterizes not only Vicos, but also the Andean region. Bolivia grew about 39 per cent of the wheat tonnage it consumed in 1949 (that which entered into commercial channels) and imported 61 per cent by weight [Keenleyside et al., 1951, p. 54]. Wheat imports into Peru regularly cost that country more foreign exchange than its imports of automobiles, trucks, buses, delivery vans, pickups, jeeps, ambulances, and fire engines [Garayar Pacheco, 1961, 550, 552, 615-617]. Peru grew not quite 30 per cent of its wheat consumption tonnage in 1961, importing just over 70 per cent. The value of domestic wheat was, moreover, even lower relative to imported wheat, at 25.6 per cent of the total value [Garayar Pacheco, 1962, pp. 409, 532]. Wheat production has hardly improved at all in Ecuador, even though the introduction of chemical fertilizers has greatly increased potato yields—from 85,000 to 208,000 metric tons between 1951 and 1954 [Miller, 1959].

If even the least productive of agricultural units in the Andes produces some things for external sale, then the key to agricultural development in the region is not the *kind* of agricultural enterprise per se, but the degree to which agricultural production units enter into the commercial exchange system.

One measure of this sort comes, again, from Vicos. In 1951, only 7.7 per cent of the serfs on that manor owned 11 head or more of livestock, counted in cow units [Vasquez, 1965a]. The fact that 328 families of 363 owned some cows [Alers, 1964, p. 33] did not mean that they owned enough cattle to sell a cow oftener than very rarely. The truly and regularly productive portion of the serf population was quite small.

PEASANT PRODUCTIVITY

Among the next group, the peasantry, the level of productivity appears to be only slightly higher than among manor serfs, as

Table 13.2. Peasant Agricultural Production Sold by 50 Mountain Communities in Peru, by Type of Commodity

Community	1	2	3	4	5	6	7	8	9	10	Total number products sold
1. Carcas	+	–	+	+	+	+	–	–	+	+	7
2. Mito	+	+	+	–	+	+	–	–	+	+	7
3. Accopata	+	+	+	–	+	–	–	–	+	+	6
4. Chupaca	+	+	–	–	+	+	–	–	+	–	5
5. Camicachi	+	–	+	–	+	+	–	–	+	–	5
6. Palca	+	–	–	+	+	+	–	+	–	–	5
7. Acobamba	+	–	–	+	+	+	–	–	–	–	4
8. Palcamayo	+	–	–	+	+	+	–	–	–	–	4
9. Llambilla	+	–	+	+	+	–	–	–	–	–	4
10. Tupe	+	+	–	–	–	–	–	–	+	+	4
11. Mayobamba	+	+	+	–	+	–	–	–	–	–	4
12. Huayre	+	+	–	–	+	–	–	–	–	–	4
13. Amantani	+	–	–	–	+	–	–	–	+	+	4
14. Allauca	–	+	–	–	+	+	–	–	–	–	3
15. San Pedro de Cajas	+	+	–	–	+	–	–	–	–	–	3
16. Castrovirreyna	+	+	–	–	+	–	–	–	–	–	3
17. Huancaire	–	–	+	–	+	–	+	–	–	–	3
18. Huanec	–	+	–	–	+	+	–	–	–	–	3
19. Huaychao	+	+	+	–	–	–	–	–	–	–	3
20. Muquiyauyo	–	–	+	–	–	–	–	–	+	+	3
21. Paucartambo	–	–	–	–	+	–	+	+	–	–	3
22. Pucara	–	–	–	+	+	+	–	–	–	–	3
23. Huaylas	?	+	–	–	–	+	–	–	–	–	3
24. Chaupi	?	?	–	–	–	?	–	–	–	–	3
25. Pichqachuri	?	?	–	–	–	?	–	–	–	–	3
26. Qayao	?	?	–	–	–	?	–	–	–	–	3
27. Qollana	?	?	–	–	–	?	–	–	–	–	3
28. Santa Barbara	+	+	–	–	+	–	–	–	–	–	3
29. Huayllay	+	+	+	–	–	–	–	–	–	–	3
30. Chinchera	+	+	+	–	–	–	–	–	–	–	3
31. Cuyo Chico	–	–	+	+	–	–	–	–	+	–	3
32. Huancaya	–	–	+	–	–	+	–	–	–	–	2
33. Rimac	+	–	+	–	–	–	–	–	–	–	2
34. Sicaya	–	–	–	–	+	+	–	–	–	–	2
35. Yungalla-Primo	+	–	+	–	–	–	–	–	–	–	2
36. Chaquicocha	–	–	–	–	+	+	–	–	–	–	2
37. Hualcan	+	–	–	–	–	–	–	–	+	–	2
38. Taquile	–	–	–	–	+	–	–	+	–	–	2
39. Huarochiri	+	–	+	–	–	–	–	–	–	–	2
40. Choclococha	+	+	–	–	–	–	–	–	–	–	2
41. Hualcaralla	–	–	+	–	–	–	–	–	–	–	1
42. Andarapa	–	–	–	–	–	+	–	–	–	–	1
43. Lupo	–	–	+	–	–	–	–	–	–	–	1
44. Lurinsayac-Anansayac	–	–	–	–	–	+	–	–	–	–	1
45. Suni	–	–	+	–	–	–	–	–	–	–	1
46. Pararin	+	–	–	–	–	–	–	–	–	–	1
47. Ayamarca	–	–	–	+	–	–	–	–	–	–	1
48. Ichupampa	+	–	–	–	–	–	–	–	–	–	1
49. Chinchero	–	–	–	–	+	–	–	–	–	–	1
50. Cajacay	–	–	–	–	–	–	–	future	–	1

TYPE OF COMMODITY[a]

a. Key for Products

1. slaughter animals and dried meat; 2. hides and wool; 3. cheese and milk; 4. fresh vegetables; 5. potatoes and other tubers, including oca and ollucu; 6. cereal grains; 7. peppers (aji, rocoto); 8. timber or firewood; 9. eggs; 10. chickens or other fowl, or guinea pigs.

SOURCE: (Numbers in parentheses refer to the community.)

(1) Castillo, Castillo, and Revilla [1964a, 22–23]. (2) Castillo et al. [1964a, 48–49]. (3) Castillo et al. [1964b, 15–16]. (4) Tschopik [1947, 40]. (5) Montalvo Vidal [1958, 5–11]. (6, 7, 8) General Engineering Laboratory [1962, 158, 3]. (9) Matos Mar [1953]. (10) Matos Mar [1951, 8–29]. (11) Morris [1964, 7ff]. (12) Alencastre Montúfar [1960, 11–12, 15, 22]. (13) Ortiz Vergara and Galdo Pagaza [1958a, 17, 19]. (14) Castro Pozo [1946]. (15) General Engineering Laboratory

[1962, 167]. (16) Tschopik [1947, 26]. (17) Soler Bustamente [1954]. (18) Castro Poze [1946]. (19) Tschopik [1947, 54]. (20) Pulgar Vidal [1945]. (21) Andrews [1963, 144]. (22) Alers Montalvo [1960], Sabogal [1962]. (23) Doughty [1963b, 186–192]. (24, 25, 26, 27) Arguedas [1956]. (28) Tschopik [1947, 22]. (29) Tschopik [1947, 52]. (30) Ortiz Vergara and Galdo Pagaza [1958b, 80]. (31) Oscar Nuñez del Prado [1960, 11]. (32) Cotler [1961, 140–142]. (33) Boluarte [1959, 287]. (34) Tschopik [1947, 44]. (35) Boluarte [1959, 287]. (36) Castillo et al. [1964b, 24]. (37) Stein [1961, 32]. (38) Matos Mar [1957]. (39) Guillén Araoz [1961]. (40) Tschopik [1947, 23]. (41) Cotler [1961, 143]. (42) Wilfredo Nunez del Prado [1959, 22–25]. (43) Guillén Araoz [1961]. (44) Tschopik [1947, 32–33]. (45) Guillen Araoz [1961]. (46) Doughty and Negrón [1964, 22]. (47) Allred et al. [1959, 60]. (48) Kuczynski-Godard [1945, 46]. (49) Oscar Nuñez del Prado [1949, 28, 35]. (50) Obando [1961].

far as available data indicate. Even in the lush eastern lowlands of Bolivia, cattle hides and alcohol constituted the primary exports until modern transportation became available in the mid-1940's, and farming was mainly a matter of subsistence diet [Weeks, 1946].

The independent Andean peasant farmer has been so little studied that our remarks on this type of farming will necessarily be based largely on studies of members of Indigenous Communities. Our characterization of the peasantry is based upon a 2.2 per cent sample (38) of the 1,662 Indigenous Communities officially registered by the government of Peru (see Table 13.2), supplemented by information from 12 other farming communities. Anthropological studies of these settlements, not specifically directed toward exploration of the question now under discussion, have recorded that all those in our sample sell or barter outside the community at least one type of food produced locally. Some stock-raising communities located at elevations above the limits of agriculture [Tschopik, 1947, p. 23] or above the limits for certain crops [Alencastre Montúfar, 1960, p. 12] trade animals and animal products for agricultural commodities in order to achieve a more varied diet, while some Indian farm populations caught in a particularly repressive network of social subordinance to mestizos have been forced to barter their products

Table 13.4. Peasant Farming Communities Exporting Products for External Sale in Peru (N=50)

A. Animal and Animal Products

Products sold by			Per cent of communities
Wool and Hides	Meat and Animals	Cheeses and Milk	14
Wool and Hides	Meat and Animals		22
	Meat and Animals	Cheeses and Milk	12
		Cheeses and Milk	14
	Meat and Animals		14
Wool and Hides			4
	None		20
			100

B. Staple Agricultural Commodities

Products sold by			Per cent of communities
Vegetables	Tubers	Cereals	10
	Tubers	Cereals	14
Vegetables	Tubers		2
		Cereals	16
	Tubers		22
Vegetables			4
	None		32
			100

instead of selling them for cash, receiving a third or less of the cash price [Oscar Nuñez del Prado, 1960, p. 11]; 36 per cent of the sample communities report selling three different types of agricultural commodities outside the community, while 38 per cent sell one or two commodities outside (see Table 13.3). As might be expected of a regional economy in which livestock constitutes the most easily marketable agricultural commodity, 80 per cent of the sample communities export animals or animal products (see Table 13.4), but one must keep in mind that highland livestock is "small in size and light in weight,

Table 13.3. Degree of Peasant Community Participation in the Commercial Market Economy in 50 Mountain Communities in Peru

Number of agricultural commodities sold	Number of communities	Per cent of communities
1	10	20
2	9	18
3	18	36
4	7	14
5 to 7	6	12

SOURCE: Table 13.2.

with very low yields of meat, milk, wool"
[Junta Interministerial Directiva, 1963, p. 39].
The number of communities exporting live
animals for slaughter, fresh and dried meat, is
greater than the number of exporters of any
other commodity, 62 per cent (see Table
13.5). Similar evidence on surplus sales can be

Table 13.5. *Proportion of 50 Peruvian Peasant
Communities Selling Agricultural Commodities
Outside, by Type of Commodity*

Agricultural Commodity	Per cent of communities
1. Slaughter animals and meat	62
2. Grains	40
3. Potatoes or other tubers	48
4. Cheeses and milk	40
5. Wool, hides, or leather	40
6. Fresh vegetables	16
7. Fowl or guinea pigs	12
8. Eggs	20
9. Timber or firewood	8
10. Peppers	4

SOURCE: Table 13.2.

assembled for other communities and countries (see Tables 13.6 and 13.7). Such figures
clearly support our assertion that no Andean
farming community lives in a purely subsistence economy.

More accurate as an index of development,

of course, is the proportion of the total farm
population in any given community that
produces for export. A milk-powdering
plant built near Cochabamba remained idle
for several years because the surrounding area
produced no surplus after the agrarian reform
[Heath, 1959]. Information on the proportion
of surplus producers is not available for
many communities. In a hat-making Indian
hamlet on the Peruvian shore of Lake
Titicaca, only 5 per cent of the families are
considered well-to-do because they produce
an agricultural surplus for sale from landholdings larger than usual in Chinchera
[Ortiz Vergara and Galdo Pagaza, 1958b,
pp. 64–65; Montalvo Vidal and Galdo
Pagaza, 1960, p. 2].

The prevailing view of the peasant farming
community is that of a settlement of agriculturalists, all of whom produce at least
some surplus over family subsistence needs
for sale. Indeed, in the Cuatro Ojitos colony
in eastern Bolivia, commercial sales are
reported to be from 60 per cent to 90 per cent
of family production; peasant consumption
ranging from 40 per cent down to 10 per cent
of the harvest is perhaps the nearest approach
of reality to theory [Marus and Monje Rada,
1962, p. 50].

The typical ethnography of an Andean
settlement reports the number of small

Table 13.6. *Jungle Settler Agricultural Production for Sale by Selected
Settlements in Peru, Bolivia, and Ecuador, By Type of Commodity*

Colony	TYPE OF COMMODITY										Total number products sold
	1	2	3	4	5	6	7	8	9	10[a]	
1. Tingo Maria, Peru	+	+	+	+	+	+	−	+	−	−	7
2. Tambopata Valley, P.	−	−	−	−	−	−	−	+	−	−	1
3. Cuatro Ojitos, Bolivia	+	+	+	−	+	+	+	−	+	+	8
4. Yapacani, Bolivia	−	−	−	−	+	+	−	−	−	−	2
5. Cotoca, Bolivia	−	−	−	−	+	+	+	−	−	−	3
6. San Luis (6 colonies)	−	−	−	−	+	−	−	−	−	−	1
7. Todos Santos (7 colonies)	−	+	+	+	+	+	−	+	−	−	6
8. Villa Tunari (6 colonies)	−	+	+	+	+	+	−	+	−	−	6
9. Chipiriri, Bolivia	−	+	−	+	−	+	−	−	−	−	3
10. Santa Fe sector	−	+	+	−	+	+	+	+	−	−	6
11. Carrasco sector	−	+	+	−	+	+	+	+	−	−	6
12. Caranavi sector	−	+	+	−	+	+	+	+	−	−	6
13. Santa Clara, Ecuador	−	+	+	−	+	−	+	−	−	−	4

[a] For Commodities: Column 1 = vegetables; 2 = fruits; 3 = yuca; 4 = coca; 5 = maize; 6 = rice; 7 = sugar cane; 8 =
coffee; 9 = eggs; 10 = fowl.
SOURCE (Numbers in parentheses refer to the community):
(1) Ministerio de Agricultura [1962, p. 17] (this area also exports cacao, rubber, tea, and livestock); (2) Martinez [1961,
p. 154]; (3 to 12) Marus and Monje Rada [1962, pp. 12, 50, 84–86, 111, 199, 225]; (13) Sherman [1963, p. 82].

Table 13.7. *Peasant Agricultural Production For Sale by Selected Mountain Communities in Ecuador and Bolivia, By Type of Commodity*[a]

	TYPE OF COMMODITY										
Community	1	2	3	4	5	6	7	8	9	10[b]	Total number products sold
1. Nayon, Ecuador	–	–	–	–	–	+	–	–	–	–	1
2. Punyaro, Ecuador	+	+	–	–	+	+	+	–	+	+	7
3. Cotocollao, Ecuador	–	–	–	+	+	+	–	–	–	–	3
4. Pilacumby, Ecuador	+	–	–	–	–	–	–	+	–	–	2
5. Chimbo Canton, Ecuador	+	–	–	+	–	+	–	–	+	+	5
6. Pillapi, Bolivia	+	–	+	–	–	–	–	–	+	–	3
7. Aiquile, Bolivia	+	+	–	–	+	+	–	–	–	–	4

[a] This sample is too small to permit significant comparison with the Peruvian pattern, other than in very general terms. The emphasis on sales of animals and animal products is similar, but agricultural commodities appear somewhat more important in this small sample.

[b] For commodities: Column 1 = slaughter animals, dried meat, or lard; 2 = hides and wool; 3 = cheese and milk; 4 = fresh vegetables or fruit; 5 = potatoes and other tubers; 6 = cereal grains, including green corn; 7 = peppers; 8 = timber or firewood; 9 = eggs; 10 = chickens, other fowl, guinea pigs.

SOURCE (Numbers in parentheses refer to the community):
(1) Beals [1952]; (2) Rubio Orbe [1956, p. 163]; (3) Hearn [1950]; (4) Cisneros [1949]; (5) Bazante [1963, 134]; (6) Martinez [1962, p. 5]; (7) Suarez Agnez [1958, p. 67].

general stores in the population studied and outlines production activities in general terms, without actually defining what proportion of the farm families in fact produces a surplus and sells it outside.

A monograph on a coastal farming community in Peru reports family production in generalized terms; each family is reckoned as possessing at least two fresh milch cows, the wife is considered to earn cash income half the days of the month vending maize beer or buying and reselling vegetables. Poultry is sold, as is garden truck [Gillin, 1947, pp. 78–79].

Where the proportion of farmers producing a surplus for sale in a given area has been reported, it turns out to be, on the other hand, much less than 100 per cent of the farm families in the Andean highlands, although seldom as low as in Chinchera.

In a farming community in central Peru studied by Cornell Peru Project anthropologists, Carcas, only 11 of 101 families, or 10.9 per cent regularly sell produce outside the community [Castillo, Castillo, and Revilla, 1964a, pp. 6, 22]. In a relatively developed peasant community on the Peruvian coast, studied 20 years ago, family productivity ranged widely, even though all families appear to have been already involved in commercial activity. In Moche, about 3.4 per cent of the families were estimated, however, to produce 32.5 times as much milk per day as the typical dairyman [Gillin, 1947, pp. 8, 24]. Their 10-milch-cow herds coincided

closely with the Vicos definition of wealth as 11-cow units. Thus the bulk of commercial production came from a few families. In the Andes themselves there are, on the other hand, farm communities where only a small proportion of the families even feed themselves from their fields, so members of most households must labor for wages with which to purchase food to make up the production deficit. In a Puno population, also studied 20 years ago, only 13.6 per cent of the families harvested enough to feed themselves or produced any surplus. All the rest produced less than their own subsistence needs [Kuczynski-Godard, 1945, p. 43].

Technological differences aside, Andean agricultural and livestock production suffers from time to time what are called "bad crop years." These are periods when natural phenomena affect agricultural production. Hail storms, droughts, excess rainfall causing landslides that destroy the crop at the same time that they give rise to serious erosion are recurrent problems. In this respect, one agronomist has written that "if there are abundant rains and warmth in the Andes, there is a good crop year on the Coast, as that of 1961–1962; but if there is drought and cold in the Andes, the crop year is bad on the Coast" in Peru [Aguilar Dávila, 1963, p. 32].

Economic development in the Andean region has not come and is not yet coming from or through the traditional highland peasantry. Agricultural development in this region has occurred and is occurring primarily through the medium farmer and the large plantation or ranch.

The distribution of land ownership is in general very unequal in Peru and Ecuador, varying from extreme latifundium to extreme minifundium. Great estates "dominate the landscape" in the Andean valleys, while tiny plots "crowd up the mountainsides" [Saunders, 1961].

In Peru 1.4 per cent of the farmers—large landlords and leasors—control 62.8 per cent of the cultivated area, while only 25.4 per cent of the cultivated area holds 94.5 per cent of the farmers who hold less than 25 hectares. Medium farmers (26 to 249 hectares) hold 11.8 per cent of the land [Seoane, 1963, 74–76]. Minifundium characterizes all three major geographic zones of Peru, according to the Agrarian and Housing Reform Commission [Comisión, 1961, p. 18]. The coast has 35,964 properties averaging 1.39 hectare each. The Andes have 16,436 properties averaging 2.10 hectares each, and 8,362 properties in the jungle average 4.96 hectares apiece. This phenomenon is most accentuated, however, in the central and southern Peruvian Andes, where 64.6 per cent of the properties have areas of less than 5 hectares, with an average of 1.62 hectares each [Seoane, 1963, p. 139].

In Ecuador, only 705 properties, a mere 0.17 per cent of the total in 1954, took up 37.4 per cent of the farm land holdings of 1,000 hectares and more which averaged 3,180.1 hectares in size. Holdings larger than 200 hectares comprised only 1.1 per cent of all those in Ecuador but covered 56.7 per cent of the country's farm land. At the opposite extreme, over a quarter of a million holdings, constituting 73.1 per cent of the total number, took up only 7.2 per cent of the farm land and averaged only 1.7 hectares each. Medium farmers (with holdings between 5 and 200 hectares) occupied 25.8 per cent of the farm units comprising 35.8 per cent of the total area. The inequality of land distribution is even greater in the Ecuadorian Andes than on the coast. In the highlands, 81.7 per cent of the holdings occupied less than 5 hectares, averaging only 1.6 hectares

each and covering 11.3 per cent of the farmland. On the other extreme, 0.7 per cent of the holdings occupied over 200 hectares, averaging 1,032 hectares each and covering 58.4 per cent of the farm land [Saunders, 1961, p. 59].

In Bolivia, the agrarian reform program has established legal maxima for various types of agricultural enterprises in various parts of the country, from 35 to 80 hectares for the small property from the altiplano to the subtropical zone, from 350 to 600 for the medium property, and 150 to 2,000 for modern enterprises [Heath, 1959]. Since peasants in some valleys seized properties as small as 3 or 4 hectares [Suarez Arnez, 1958, p. 140], it remains difficult to tell just how far the former latifundia of Bolivia have been reduced.

Peasantry

It has been asserted that any landholding smaller than 5 hectares cannot maintain a family at even a low level in Ecuador, especially in the Andean highlands, so that the owners of such farms are in fact laborers because they depend upon working for others to subsist [Saunders, 1961]. The density of rural population rises as the farm population increases, and cultivable land is lost by unchecked erosion. In one Ecuadorian Indian town members of the present generation can expect to inherit 0.1485 hectare, compared to their parents' 0.1757 hectare, their grandparents' 0.2681 hectare, and their greatgrandparents' 0.6401 hectare [Beals, 1952]. These generalizations may certainly be extended to Peru and, with modification, to Bolivia.

Yet the typical Andean peasant farms an area smaller than 5 hectares. Peasant farms in an Indian hamlet on the Peruvian side of Lake Titicaca range in size from 0.5 to 5 hectares [Montalvo Vidal, 1958, p. 6]. In one Peruvian coastal valley oasis, Viru, 20 years ago 80 per cent of the properties on the Irrigators' Register consisted of less than 5 hectares, descending in size to 0.20 hectare [Oscar Nuñez del Prado, 1951, p. 9]. This was still the situation in this valley in 1964 [Vasquez, 1965b, p. 139, Anexo I].

The peasant migrant into the Amazon basin appears to be in transition from the traditional production minifundia with a deficit of the highlands to a fuller life, if not yet to a very significant commercial production.

In the area of colonization of the Peruvian sector of the Amazon basin around Tingo Maria, simple subsistence farmers were estimated to constitute half the farm families in 1962 [Ministerio de Agricultura, 1962, p. 80]. Many of these jungle settlers came from Andean mountain areas, where Indian landholdings typically consist of four or five tiny plots, scattered at distances of three or four kilometers from one another, that total perhaps a single hectare all together. In the Tingo Maria area they enjoy a much richer subsistence economy, with a whole hectare planted to maize, another to yuca (a starchy tuber), with a few banana plants, orange trees, vegetable garden, and a farmyard flock of chickens and a pig or two [Ministerio de Agricultura, 1962, p. 81].

The typical pattern in other colonization areas is still one where farmers cultivate two to four hectares (see Table 13.8). In the eastern Bolivia area, where highland colonists reportedly sell 60 per cent to 90 per cent of their agricultural production, plots average slightly less than 4 hectares per family [Marus and Monje Rada, 1962, pp. 38, 50].

Settlers at Cuatro Ojitos and Yapacani appear to be increasing their planted area at the rate of one hectare per farmer per year, but those at Cotoca only half a hectare annually, having achieved a total cultivated area averaging only 2.1 hectare per family during the 1961–1962 season [Marus and

Monje Rada, 1962, pp. 38, 80, 110]. In the Todos Santos and Villa Tunari sectors of the Chapare colonization area, settler families cultivating an average of 3.54 hectares in 1962 were adding 0.7 hectare per year to their farms [Marus and Monje Rada, 1962, p. 190]. Farms in the San Luis colonization area average from 2 to 2½ hectares [Marus and Monje Rada, 1962, p. 139]. A sample of the settlers in 11 colonies in the Santa Fe, Caranavi, and Carrasco sectors of Bolivia cultivated an average of 2.8 hectares per family in 1962, while farmers in the Chipiriri sector averaged 4.8 hectares [Marus and Monje Rada, 1962, pp. 254, 226]. These figures suggest that in the course of a few years many highland colonists in these areas will subjugate more than five hectares and really pass out of a peasant style of farming into truly commercial medium farming.

Medium Farmers

Medium farmers may be reckoned as cultivating from 5 to 100 hectares, a unit frequently labeled a "fundo" in Peru [Oscar Nuñez del Prado, 1951, p. 10]. In the lower range of medium farmers, "family farms" of 5 to 10 hectares may be distinguished in coastal Peru, at least [Vasquez, 1965b, p. 132]. In eastern Bolivia, the *quinta* is usually 8 to 10 hectares, less than half cultivated, and never more than 20 hectares [Heath, 1960]. This distinction among farm units between 5 and 10 hectares in size is also useful in Ecuador

Table 13.8. Area Cultivated by Settlers in Selected Settlements in Eastern Bolivia[a]

Hectares	Cuatros Ojitos		Todos Santos		Villa Tunari		Chipiriri		Santa Fe[b]	
	No.	Ha.	No.	Ha.	No.	Ha.	No.	Ha.	No.	Ha.
0.5	1	0.5	2	1.0	8	4.0	6	3.0	17	8.5
1.0	4	4.0	4	4.0	19	19.0	14	14.0	70	70.0
2.0	16	32.0	11	22.0	51	102.0	39	78.0	87	174.0
3.0	12	36.0	14	42.0	36	108.0	49	147.0	63	189.0
4.0	16	64.0	2	8.0	29	116.0	18	72.0	29	116.0
6.0	14	84.0	9	54.0	41	246.0	51	306.0	42	252.0
9.0	8	72.0	1	9.0	7	63.0	16	144.0	7	63.0
13.0	1	13.0	—	—	3	39.0	12	156.0	—	—
18.0	—	—	—	—	—	—	3	54.0	1	18.0
Average		4.24		3.26		3.54		4.76		2.8

[a] Hectares cultivated by sample (72 of 675) in 1961–1962 season.
[b] Caranavi and Carrasco sectors.
SOURCE: Marus and Monje Rada [1962, pp. 37, 188–189, 226, 254].

[Saunders, 1961]. The medium farmers cultivate a sufficiently large land base to escape
the economic confines of minifundium, the
general characteristic and developmental
curse of the peasantry.

In a Peruvian coastal irrigation project
opened to settlement in 1929, the 404 lots
comprising the 3,679 hectare project are
now farmed by only 196 proprietors (average 18.7 hectares) despite a 15-hectare limitation imposed in 1935 [Revilla Corrales and
Ramón Cordova, 1964]. A parallel concentration of land ownership is already under way
in the Cuatro Ojitos colony in eastern
Bolivia, which started in 1957 with uniform
assignments of 20 hectares [Marus and
Monje Rada, 1962, pp. 3, 30]. Some colonists
have been selling their 20 hectares to others
when they give up the struggle, while others
have lowered their aspirations and sold half
their original areas to more ambitious and
successful colonists. The same process is
occurring in the Cotoca colony, where the
International Labour Organization Administration fixed 9 hectares as the original equal
plot area [Marus and Monje Rada, 1962,
p. 107].

The farm consolidators are members of
the rural middle class, standing socially
and economically between the peasants and
the proprietors of the great estates. They
invest in the education of their children in
accord with middle-class values. They exhibit
their solvency by driving pickup trucks. They
may, in areas where high-unit value cash
crops can be profitably grown, enjoy an
annual income up to nearly $5,600 (S/.150,000)
in Peru [Ministerio de Agricultura, 1962,
p. 82]. They may live in the capital city,
leaving their fields to be cultivated by permanently settled peons, both in the coastal
valleys and in the less densely settled mountain valleys [Revilla Corrales and Ramon
Cordova, 1964; Tschopik, 1947, p. 39]. In
Peru's Tingo Maria colonization area, medium
farmers constitute approximately 35 per cent
of the farm families [Ministerio de Agricultura, 1962, p. 81]. Although 9 per cent of
Ecuador's highland holdings are between
10 and 200 hectares in size (and 33.6 per cent
of those on the coast are), "there are very few
family-sized farms in Ecuador" because
owners of farms large enough to maintain a
family comfortably play the traditional

owner's role of supervising hired labor
[Saunders, 1961].

LATIFUNDIUM

According to the Peruvian Commission for
Agrarian and Housing Reform, the number
of properties classified as large and very
large, whose size varied from region to
region, was as follows [Comisión, 1961,
13–16] :

GEOGRAPHIC ZONE	LARGE PROPERTIES		VERY LARGE PROPERTIES[9]	
	No.	Hectare range	No.	Hectare range
Coast	692	(100–500)	181	(over 500)
Andes	258	(200–500)	99	(over 500)
Jungle	905	(100–1000)	300	(over 1000)
Totals	1855		580	

The largest fincas of the Camba area in
eastern Bolivia reach 50,000 hectares in
area [Heath, 1960].

The "factories in the field," large-scale
plantations and ranches, constitute only a
very small percentage of the farm families in
the Andean region, but they cultivate or
graze a significantly high proportion of the
total agriculturally exploited area. This concentration of ownership is, of course, now
more pronounced both in Peru and Ecuador
than in Bolivia. In Peru's Viru Valley, four
proprietors owned 75 per cent of the irrigated
area inscribed in the Irrigator's Register 20
years ago [Oscar Nuñez del Prado, 1951,
p. 9]. Their plantations constituted only
1.7 per cent of the number of irrigated properties on the register. Their reported areas
averaged 805 hectares per plantation, but
their actual areas were considerably greater.
In this same valley in 1964, properties of 100
hectares and over constituted 87.8 per cent
of the total area cultivated and belonged to
only 3.4 per cent of the proprietors even after
several estate divisions. On the other hand,
77.6 per cent of the proprietors owned barely
3.6 per cent of the cultivated area, an extreme
example of minifundium. Within this large
group of very small holders, 31.5 per cent
possess only 0.5 per cent of the cultivated

9. The inconsistent definition of size of large and very
large properties stems from environmental differences
that policy-makers perceive in the coastal littoral, the
Andean mountains, and the Amazon rain forest.

area, holding less than 1 hectare each. Between these extremes in size of landholdings, the family farms (5–10 hectares) and the medium holdings (10–100 hectares) constituting 19 per cent of the proprietors occupied 8.6 per cent of the cultivated area [Vazquez, 1965c].

In Peru's Ica Valley, 94 per cent of the landowners in 1940 had less than 6.88 hectares each and together held only 16 per cent of the cultivated area, while at the other extreme, 68 per cent of the area was held in estates of 111 hectares or larger size [Smith, 1960].

In Huamanga Province, Ayacucho Department, Peru, 28.3 per cent of agricultural land belongs to 1.3 per cent of the land-owning population (*hacendados*); 71.7 per cent of the land belongs to 81.9 per cent of the landowning population; 16.8 per cent of the total population is landless, living as peons on lands of the haciendas [Díaz Martínez, 1962]. In Huanta Province in the same department, 15.6 per cent of the agricultural lands are in the hands of 0.5 per cent of the landowning population; 84.4 per cent of cultivated lands are owned by 85 per cent of the landowning population; 13.8 per cent of the agricultural population is landless, living on hacienda lands. In La Mar Province of this department, 22.4 per cent of agricultural lands are owned by 0.2 per cent of the total landowning population; 77.6 per cent is in the hands of 86.4 per cent of the small- and medium-sized property owners; 13.4 per cent of the remaining population is composed of serfs living on haciendas [Díaz Martínez, 1962].

In Cotopaxi Province, Ecuador, 82.7 per cent of the farm units are reported to cover less than 5 hectares. Another 8.1 per cent fall into the "family farm" category of 5 to 10 hectares; and 8.2 per cent of these cultivation units are between 10 and 100 hectares in size. Only 0.96 per cent of the units are larger than 100 hectares, yet these 256 units cover 60 per cent of the area farmed, while all the units of less than 20 hectares (94.6 per cent of the farm units) cover only 10 per cent of the area cultivated [Díaz B. and Cordova, n.d., 47]. The total surface area of 70 manors in public ownership in this country averages 1,857 hectares each, but manors of 9,350 and 9,586 hectares are included in the range [Casals et al., 1964, pp. 48–50].

Near the bottom of the socioeconomic group of owners of plantations are many of those engaged in coffee and tea production on newly subjugated jungle lands in the Amazon basin. In the Tingo Maria area, about 10 per cent of the farm families operate true plantations, or large-sized holdings in the process of being converted into true plantations. These production units contain a minimum of 100 hectares, the minimum plantation size. They operate with credit from the national agricultural development bank. They hire numerous migratory laborers from the Andean highlands but sometimes lose half their coffee crop for lack of sufficient harvest hands [Ministerio de Agricultura, 1962, p. 83]. The process of consolidation has enabled some farmers to accumulate over 100 hectares of land in the La Esperanza irrigation project on the Peruvian coast, which started with colonists on 15 hectare plots [Revilla Corrales and Ramón Córdova, 1964].

At the more prosperous and spectacular extreme of plantation characteristics, the large, highly capitalized and industrialized plantations on Peru's west coast include one family agricultural complex that reportedly cultivates 32,213 hectares [Malpica, 1964, pp. 31–33]. There are at least four other enterprises cultivating more than 10,000 hectares each: 12,399; 11,163; 10,145; and 10,707, respectively [Malpica, 1964, pp. 26, 16, 42, 39].

A total of 200 coastal plantation owners cultivate a reported area of 338,266 hectares, an average of 1,691 hectares per plantation [Malpica, 1964, pp. 11–61]. The preponderant role these plantations play in Andean agriculture may be deduced from figures on their participation in the world commodity market. Sugar exports comprised 12.9 per cent of all Peruvian export value in 1961 [Garayar Pacheco, 1962, pp. 527, 608], compared to 30 per cent some 20 years ago, when half a dozen firms dominated production [Ford, 1955, pp. 57–58], and one boasted that it refined over one-third of all the sugar made in the country [Sainte Marie S., 1945, p. 121].

A review of key agricultural exports is revealing [Garayar Pacheco, 1962, pp. 575, 606–617]. Cotton exports brought 16.4 per cent of the value of all Peruvian exports in 1961. These proportions are lower than in earlier years because of a spectacular increase in offshore fishing, which has raised Peru to a foremost world fishing nation. Edible fish, fish oil, and fish meal exports comprised 14.4 per cent of all Peruvian exports in 1961. Another plantation and medium-farm crop, coffee, made up a significant 4.6 per cent of Peruvian export value in 1961. The major single Peruvian export is copper. Ore, concentrates, blisters, sheets, and the like, exported made up 21.9 per cent of the value of Peruvian exports in 1961. Thus one mineral, three fisheries products, and three agricultural commodities constituted 70.2 per cent of Peru's 1961 exports. Yet this agricultural production comes from the relatively small part of the nation's acreage under plantation management.

Peruvian agricultural production in 1960 followed this pattern [Seoane, 1963, p. 80]:

Commodity	Percentage of cultivated area
Food crops (potatoes, maize, barley, etc.)	73.8
Industrial food and fiber crops (cotton, coffee, sugar cane, grapes, etc.)	23.2
Industrial crops (sugar cane for alcohol, coca, jute, etc.)	2.7
Other	0.3

Food crops are grown mainly in the Andes and by the small farmers of all three zones. Livestock production for slaughter predominates in the Andes, and milk production predominates on the coast. Low yields per hectare are notorious, confirming the backwardness of cultivation techniques employed by the small farmers [Seoane, 1963, p. 78]. In Ecuador, on the other hand, dairying is important in the Andes near the major cities. There a man will consider himself well off if he has a dairy farm near Quito, Latacunga, Riobamba, Cuenca, Loja, Cayambe, or Tulcan [Miller, 1959]. The larger the landholding in Ecuador, the higher proportion of it is rangeland. In the highlands in 1964, farm units under 100 hectares cultivate more than half their area, but 65.9 per cent of holdings between 100 and 500 hectares are pasture, 80.8 per cent of those from 500 to 1,000 hectares, and 86.7 per cent of those from 1,000 to 2,500 hectares, and 93.8 per cent of the holdings over 2,500 hectares were grazed. The same breaking point was recorded on the coast, but pasture occupied 55.3 per cent of the 100–500 hectare units, 57.4 per cent of

those from 500 to 1,000 hectares, 52.9 per cent of 1,000 to 2,500 hectare units, and 60.2 per cent of those over 2,500 hectares [Saunders, 1961].

Ranch sizes are, of course, much larger than row-crop plantation sizes. A much smaller sample of the more or less modernized high-altitude ranch operations in Peru—24 cases for which approximate areas have been reported—utilizes a land base of 2,883,290 hectares, or an average of 120,137 hectares per ranch [Malpica, 1964, pp. 20–75; Patch, 1958, p. 8].

The concentration of land ownership in Peru is indicated by the fact that at least 8 of the 24 ranch owners are also among the 200 coastal large plantation owners.

Figures cannot be given for manor size. The number of manors in Peru and Ecuador is another figure that we would like to cite but cannot. Estimates for Peru have varied from 1,198 [Vazquez, 1961, p. 9] to 3,777 [Kantor, 1961].

This, then, is the national and regional context in which some 1,800 Indian serfs of the manor of Vicos, Peru, struggled for a livelihood in 1951. Their subsistence plots did not provide adequate food, and they barely survived by dint of hard work outside Vicos during the four days of the week they did not have to work for the manor.

THE CORNELL PROJECT IN VICOS, PERU

VICOS UNDER THE MANORIAL SYSTEM

Lest the thought that the Andean manor is a tremendous expanse of land occupied by few people confuse the reader, we wish to make it clear here that an outstanding characteristic of manors such as Vicos is overpopulation, in terms of agricultural carrying capacity permitted by the traditional farming technology. The principal value of the Vicos manor to its exploiters was its large serf labor force rather than the land itself [Vazquez, 1952].

The 1952 Vicos labor force of 363 men (or grown boys or adult female substitutes) was obligated to labor three days each week, or 156 days per year, for the manor management, in return for a token payment of 20 Peruvian centavos per day and the family house lot and farm plot or plots. This labor could be applied anywhere the manor management wished, within Vicos or outside, on fields or in factories. The manor management could and did rent out the serfs to labor on other manors, receiving payment in cash that was pocketed as pure profit or in kind convertible into such cash. None of this profit went to the serfs who performed the actual labor. They were hired out with approximately as much voice in the matter as oxen hired out to do a neighbor's plowing.

Given such circumstances of management interest in a large labor supply, it is not surprising that there were 363 families in Vicos at the beginning of 1952 when the Cornell Peru Project intervened there [Alers, 1964, p. 4]. These families occupied approximately 85 per cent of the area of cultivable land in the Vicos manor. Only some 15 per cent of the cultivable area was farmed for the profit of the manor management.

The plots of the serfs, which in theory should have provided their subsistence, in fact did not support them because of the failures in their technological control of the natural environment. Agricultural technology for their own subsistence was so inefficient that their potato crops were failing because unprotected plants succumbed to blight.

While the manor management in legal fact controlled all of the lands of the manor, and could eject a serf at any time or reassign serfs to different plots, in social fact this power had seldom been exercised. Most serf land tenure resulted from the operation of a traditional system of customary serf land-tenancy law.

Moreover, the plots were extremely fractionalized. No one has yet succeeded in counting all of the particular little plots into which the minifundium cultivated by the serfs of Vicos has been divided through the years. It has been estimated that there are upwards of 10,000 individual identifiable cultivated plots in Vicos today. The new peasants of Vicos cultivate a few square meters in four, five, or six areas, at distances of from a few yards to several kilometers from their farmsteads.

This miniscule agriculture—or gardening, to place a more accurate label upon it—is in fact the predominant form of agriculture in the Andean region, at least in number of farmers employed. It is the least productive form of agriculture but absorbs the energies of the great bulk of the farm population.

Manor serfs, judging from the Vicos example, farm with a traditional and simple technological kit that provides little control over the natural environment beyond that attained several thousands of years ago during the beginning stage of the Neolithic Age in the Old World. The serf farms in profound ignorance of most, if not quite all, of the advances in farm production technology that have occurred during the past century. He has been shut off from technological change by the cultural barriers of illiteracy and language, speaking only an Indian language, as well as by the social barriers of serfdom.

The serf lacks knowledge that selected seed should correct deficiencies of deteriorated local seed stocks, because he lacks scientific knowledge about the genetic inheritance of traits and even the Spanish to learn about genetic processes. The pressures of hunger drive him to dig potato tubers to eat long before they are mature, reducing his ultimate harvest and tending to bring about the saving of selectively smaller seed for the next season's planting.

The serf lacks knowledge that fungicides can protect seed potatoes in the furrow and that insecticides can halt potato plant diseases, being unfamiliar with the subvisible world of disease agents for lack of microscopes and even magnifying lenses.

The serf may not lack knowledge that fertilizers besides animal manure exist, but he does lack knowledge that he might be able to afford to purchase them and apply them to his own fields.

The serf lacks knowledge that slow irrigation with heavy field soaking can increase production, being accustomed merely to open the ditch at the top of the field and let the water rip. Erosion is a concept foreign to the serf's comprehension in terms of reduced soil fertility and crop yield, and he has no conception of how to prevent or control erosional processes.

The serf lacks knowledge that crop loans might be obtained to purchase such modern aids to agricultural productivity, and he certainly lacks the confidence that an Indian serf might qualify for a loan from a mestizo-operated bank. Even more seriously, the serf lacks knowledge of the market outside his immediate neighborhood, where the demand that would absorb commercial production must be found.

Quite aside from his sheer ignorance, the serf is an inefficient farmer because of lack of motivation. Virtually the only property of value that a manor serf can accumulate is livestock and a few changes of homespun clothing made in traditional local style. In legal theory, at any rate, all land within the manor belongs to the management, and a serf may be ejected therefrom at any time at the pleasure of the management. This is particularly true in the absence of any written contract governing management-serf relations. Yet the profit to be gained from serf labor leads manor managers to attempt to keep all serfs on their manors rather than to eject them, save on those high-altitude manors in the process of conversion into modern ranches. In the latter cases, the traditional serf shepherd population is being forced off the land in several instances and professional shepherds hired on salary to pasture much larger flocks than before. Pastures are being improved and fenced and grazed in rotation by manor animals, while serf livestock is done away with.

The serf builds his own house, but the lot it occupies is assigned to him by the manor management and remains its property. There is, therefore, little motivation for the serf to invest labor and money for materials in constructing a very good house.

On the other hand, animals may be owned by serfs and pastured on manor lands at most manors, although often only upon payment of a grazing fee in cash or labor. Animals bring social prestige to their owner, and economic power as well. For, being always in demand at the urban market, animals may be sold at virtually any moment for ready cash. The serf who has cash or can obtain it by selling livestock attains a significant amelioration of his condition within the manor socioeconomic system—as long as he escapes either the notice or the wrath of the management. With cash, the serf can dominate other serfs who lack livestock. He can lend them cash to meet emergencies such as curing fees, funeral expenses, marriage costs. Such a loan between serfs places the debtor in a position of socioeconomic subservience to the lendor. The debtor must respond to the lendor's calls for assistance in his agricultural tasks or risk being unable to obtain future loans. The livestock owner is also sought after by poor serfs without oxen, who seek to borrow such animals to plow their fields.

Finally, of course, cattle tend to reproduce and increase in numbers, which provides an analog to bank interest on savings, and cattle are self-transported commodities. If the serf should be thrown off a manor, he can hope to take his cattle with him, even though his house, his fields, his trees, and even his tools remain behind.

The manor system of agriculture seems to entail at least two other phenomena of importance in agricultural development— indeed, in the agricultural contribution to the national economy. Manors typically have a set of local serf authorities charged by priest and manor management with responsibility for everyday religious instruction of the serfs, and even with some rituals. These religious authorities are also typically held responsible for carrying out certain kinds of maintenance —repairing and decorating the manor chapel, bridges, even roads. Other repairs are carried out by the serfs during their days of obligatory work for the manor management. If neither the management nor the series of serf authorities takes a serious interest in the physical maintenance of the manor, it may fall into serious disrepair. Serfs who have little or no acquaintance with motor vehicles and seldom even ride in one tend to let farm-market access roads develop a fatal line of hard-ridged ruts. Terraces constructed in prehistoric times may fall from lack of simple annual maintenance.

In addition, the efficiency of the manor production unit is seriously impaired by the systematic and often even desperate theft by the serfs. If the manor grows an edible cash crop, particularly, its produce is subject to being halved before reaching the market by serf looting.

As long as serf women enjoy the right to glean the manor fields already harvested by the men paying their obligatory labor, it is little wonder that the men manage to rebury half the potatoes they dig up for their wives to uncover during the gleaning. The same process occurs at planting time, when the manor seed goes to sow serf fields when manor seedlings are transplanted.

While women are shelling maize for the manor management in its warehouses, it is not surprising that the folds and pockets of their voluminous woolen skirts become filled with corn kernels.

Such thievery by manor serfs is usually carried out in terms of a conception of the economic sphere of life as a relatively fixed quantity. This means that the serf regards himself as competing with the manor management for a nearly fixed amount of agricultural production harvested from the manor fields. The cultural focus of the small-scale subsociety is upon doing the other fellow out of part of his share for one's own benefit, rather than upon increasing the productivity in order to augment the share of each and all. The conception extends not only to the manor management, but also to other serfs. This theft from serfs by other serfs is quite common. Manor managers are constantly besieged by serfs seeking adjudication of disputes over ownership of animals thought to have been rustled or of damages to be assessed against the owner of animals that strayed into a field and damaged a standing crop. During the harvest season, serfs build small thatched huts in the fields to sleep there at night, so as to guard against loss of their ripening grain to man as well as birds. Within this stringent cultural context, the manor serf lives with certain minimal needs for purchased items not produced on the manor.

Chewing the leaves of the coca plant mixed with slaked lime is a typically Indian trait throughout the Andean highlands save Ecuador. Coca only grows in tropical or subtropical habitats, however, so that it is imported into the higher altitudes where it is consumed. Serfs who chew coca have to pay for it.

Salt is not readily obtainable in more than a few areas of the Andean region—a few rock-salt mines, Pacific coast salt-drying pans, and high-altitude salt lakes in Bolivia and Ecuador. Most manor serfs must purchase salt.

The ignorance of the manor serf is so profound that often he must purchase his clothing. The farm wives on such manors simply do not know how to sew on machines, nor can they afford to purchase sewing machines. They buy cloth and pay seamstresses in nearby towns to make their clothing, even though the design follows a traditional and distinctive local pattern.

Such necessities force the serf to produce at least a small amount for sale on the external market in order to obtain cash with which to purchase coca, pepper, salt, distilled liquor, cloth, festive bread, and services.

As already indicated, the most important single source of serf cash income is the sale of livestock. This includes the sale of chickens and other barnyard fowl where they are successfully raised by serf wives, and especially the sale of their eggs. It includes the sale of cheese.

Cash is also earned by serfs working outside the manor for daily wages, usually quite low because of labor surpluses and the traditional social dominance of those who hire labor in the mestizo trading towns where serfs seek unskilled jobs. Inevitably, the necessity for able-bodied serfs seeking wage labor outside the manor leads to neglect of the serf subsistence plots, to their being farmed by women and children at something less than maximum efficiency. So productivity remains low for another reason in the vicious circle of serf servility.

PARTICIPANT INTERVENTION

The Cornell Peru Project stepped into the kind of manor serf agricultural and social situation just outlined at Vicos in 1952 with a twofold objective. First, the project was a bilateral endeavor of Cornell University and the Peruvian government, initially through the Peruvian Indian Institute and later the National Plan for Integrating the Aboriginal Population, to improve the standard of living of the Vicos population. Second, the Project was a joint scientific endeavor designed to study the independent variables involved in increasing agricultural and human productivity starting from the base just outlined [Holmberg and Vazquez, 1951].

A bilateral organization was established known as the Cornell Peru Project, with scientific objectives as well as practical ones, with the participation of a prestigeful North American institution of higher learning and of officials of the national government of Peru [Holmberg and Monge, 1952]. This form of organization carried with it a fundamental importance, to which we shall allude later on.

Change was achieved in the situation of the Vicos serfs by leasing the manor itself for a five-year period. This placed the Cornell Peru Project in the position of manor manager for five years, so it was able to institute sweeping innovations from a status with powerful leverage. In fact, the reader may conclude that the Cornell Peru Project was able to change the serfs of Vicos because it was in a position of power over them. This is true in a limited sense, but there is another sense in which the power wielded by the Cornell Peru Project has been even more important.

Allow us to distinguish here between those forms of power that are backed up by severe deprivations and those that consist of some type of influencing [Lasswell and Kaplan, 1950, pp. 55–74]. The manor management always enjoys the right to employ severe sanctions: Andean manors operate with private jails, whipping posts, forceable seizure of person and property of serfs, and the national police at the beck and call of the management, plus the national court system cooperating with it as well.

The Cornell Peru Project as the management of the Vicos manor could indeed have exercised severe sanctions in order to force the serfs to change. It did not in fact do so. The Project chose to persuade the serfs to change by a process of explanation and enlightenment that exposed serfs to new experiences and afforded them new knowledge on which to build new perceived needs and desires and with which to structure novel ways to satisfy needs and desires.

The Cornell Peru Project promptly abolished a number of forms of extra unrecompensed services that the Vicos serfs regarded as most irksome, such as stableboy, houseboy, nursemaid, and cook. Yet serfs were required to continue working the obligatory three days a week, to which they did not especially object, in order to carry out a gradual transition and to provide a demonstration and training experience in new agricultural and social practices; and to produce a new investment capital [Holmberg, 1965].

Thus, when innovations in agricultural technology were introduced on the manor's commercial fields, the serfs had to adjust to them. The Cornell Peru Project resorted to persuasion to insure that these innovations would be applied by the serfs to their own fields, and not simply be ignored as things the rich and slightly crazy gringos understood and could afford to do but that poor, ignorant Indian serfs could not. The Cornell Peru Project offered to make improved seed, fungicides, insecticides, fertilizer, and the like, available to those serfs who wanted to try them on their own subsistence plots, through a sharecropping arrangement [Vazquez, 1962]. The serfs, subject to repeated crop failures, were accustomed to obtaining new seed from local merchants upon fairly disadvantageous terms. The Cornell Peru Project offer permitted them to keep a considerably large share of the harvest but charged them enough to convince them the Project was making a serious offer and was not foolish. A member of the Project staff devoted nearly full time for several months to daily visits to 17 cooperating serf farmers during the first season's agricultural extension activities under the sharecropping program. This procedure was repeated during four agricultural seasons.

Enlightenment has continued after the first five years of direct Cornell Peru Project instruction in modern agriculture through the supervised credit program of the Peruvian Ministry of Agriculture and Agricultural Development Bank, which lends Vicos money for crop production each year. Efficiency has reached the point where today knowledge of modern potato production techniques is generalized in Vicos among its new peasants, who are now purchasing their own lands.

The increase in agricultural productivity in Vicos can be measured in rough socioeconomic terms. We noted early in this discussion that in 1952 7.7 per cent of the serf families at Vicos owned 11 or more head of livestock—that is, a sufficient number to enjoy significant economic freedom of decision, and power over less well-to-do serf families. In a recent crop year, some 22.3 per cent (103 of 461 families) sold potatoes from their former subsistence fields on the national wholesale market through the community farm enterprise. These families averaged a cash income of S/.961. These families sold other potatoes, and other families sold additional tubers on the local and regional markets. Thus agricultural produce has become, in addition to livestock, a major source of cash income for many more Indians. Thus Vicos mountain peasant agriculture has moved, not only toward commercialization, but also toward that type of crop specialization characteristic of the relatively well-developed coastal valleys. The coastal Ica Valley provides one model, with 81.8 per cent of its cultivated area planted to cotton in 1956, 6 per cent to grapes, and the rest to a wide range of food and forage crops [Smith, 1960].

Although the Cornell Peru Project did not choose to wield power backed by severe deprivations toward its serfs in Vicos, the fact that the Project occupied such a potentially powerful position is of fundamental importance in another way. It excluded other would-be wielders of power from Vicos for a period of time sufficient to permit the former Indian serfs to achieve sufficient social and economic power and enlightenment to be able to defend their own interests. By establishing its power domain over Vicos, the Cornell Peru Project thereby excluded other power domains that had traditionally borne down upon the manor serfs. Only by firmly establishing its legitimate power over the Vicos serfs could the Cornell Peru Project open up for them the degrees of freedom of choice and action necessary if they were to achieve meaningful liberty [Holmberg, Dobyns, and Vazquez, 1961].

The Cornell Peru Project power domain excluded from Vicos the traditional type of management—a leasor who had submitted the highest bid at a public auction for the right of exploiting the Vicos lands and serfs for a period of years. Traditional managements were concerned with obtaining the greatest possible short-term profit, and not with the conservation of either the human or natural resources of the manor. The Cornell Peru Project power domain permitted a conservation-minded scientific management to introduce forestation as well as to teach the serfs how to augment their agricultural productivity. The Cornell Peru Project power domain also excluded in large measure literate non-Indian mercantile exploiters of rural Indians.

This approach has allowed the former serfs of Vicos to develop through gradual en-

lightenment and the experience of democratic management of their own community farm enterprise and affairs into a technologically efficient peasantry contributing significantly to Peruvian national productivity. They have also gradually established relationships with national institutions, such as ministries and courts that are direct and like those of other citizens of the country, in place of manorial control of nearly all aspects of life save market activities.

The Vicos community farm enterprise operates with crop loans from the Peruvian National Agricultural Development Bank, much like any good plantation owner. It contracted for independent truckers to haul its produce to market from 1957 to 1962; and it purchased its own heavy-duty truck to insure shipment to the wholesale market when price quotations are highest.

Over 100 peasants annually market their own personal potatoes through the community farm enterprise, obtaining a cash income per farmer of nearly $40 from this source alone. These potatoes are grown on fields that could not support the serfs of 1951. The Vicos peasants today subsist on their own third-grade potatoes, and the third-grade potatoes harvested from the community farm enterprise fields, which are divided among the workers. Only first- and second-grade tubers are marketed. The community farm enterprise also grows sufficient grain to meet the local demand, selling at nearly token prices, thus destroying a large part of the market for grains formerly enjoyed by town merchants, who charged high prices to the impoverished serfs.

Many Vicos serfs sell their produce on the regional market, catching tramp trucks on the highway to carry their products to the departmental capital city of Huaraz, thereby keeping a social anchor out against adverse occurrences and maintaining the extant fictive kinship ties with local dominant group merchants. The notable aspect of this continued web of social relations is that the Vicos peasants produce enough, not only to supply this demand, but also for the regional and national markets.

The Vicos peasants today sell agricultural produce for cash and purchase commodities for cash. Thus they have escaped from the traditional subservience of interpersonal dependence. Subservience in the Andean region has been expressed in terms of personal service. Cash permits the serf or peasant to commute personal services into money. Thus the poorer serfs of Vicos have increasingly won their freedom from the few well-to-do serf cattle owners, as they have earned cash from their own fields. Now the Vicos peasant can pay cash for fertilizer, without supplicating the cattle owner to stake his animals in the poor man's fields. The Vicos peasant can hire plow oxen when needed (and sometimes obtain the aid of the tractor donated to the community by members of the National Farmers Union), instead of begging for them at the owner's convenience [Vazquez, 1965a]. After the Cornell Peru Project initiated sewing instruction on machines in 1960 [Dobyns, 1965a], the increasing purchasing power of Indian hands permitted the acquisition of over 20 brand new Singer machines by Vicos families, and direct purchases of yard goods in the city of Huaraz, sometimes at wholesale prices. Thus one more traditional aspect of Indian subservience—dependence upon mestizo seamstresses and tailors—steadily diminishes along with the necessity for seeking menial wage labor, so as to earn cash to buy clothing.

The shift from serfdom to peasant status has been a salutory one in interpersonal relations within Vicos. At the same time, this shift has won the formerly impoverished individual, not only greater equality among his fellows, but also more respect from the mestizo population outside [Dobyns, Monge, and Vazquez, 1962].

If such a social and economic transition could occur widely in the Andean region, its serious agricultural problems might be solved. If the agrarian problems of the Andean republics would be effectively solved, then the entire population of the region could move ahead more rapidly into the industrial, more affluent, and in many respects more egalitarian society emerging on the coast and in some jungle-colony areas [Martinez, 1963, p. 142] than has heretofore been possible. The Vicos case, although it is only one optimistic drop in the Andean bucket of agrarian despond, is significant because it demonstrates that a head-on, scientifically planned and executed strategic attack on the problem of

less-than-subsistence production by serf and peasant can succeed. The transition from less-than-subsistence to surplus production for the commercial market can be made within a few years by enlightening the farmers themselves, by providing serfs with increased incentives to produce in their own interest, and by land tenure reforms that convert them into peasants. This transaction can be accomplished without venturing into expensive irrigation projects that accommodate a few score farmers at best, nor problematic resettlement ventures, nor assuming (unrealistically) that extension inputs on plantations automatically trickle out to Indian serfs and peasants across rigid ethnic, social, and even linguistic, barriers: nor forcing great numbers of farmers off the land before they are educated for industrial employment and urban life.

The Vicos case holds regional significance because this experience has proved that sociopolitical techniques are already at hand to solve many of the socioeconomic problems most characteristic of the Andean area, through the application of modern technological knowledge [Holmberg, 1960, pp. 97-100, 106-107]. The Vicos case appears significant outside the Andean region to the extent that less-than-subsistence production constitutes a national development problem in other countries plagued by food deficits arising from social structures of gross inequality, with peasants or serfs in subordinate positions with little motivation to produce and minimal access to modern technological skills.

References

ADAMS, 1959. Richard N. Adams, *A Community in the Andes: Problems and Progress in Muquiyauyo* (Seattle: American Ethnological Society, 1959).

AGUILAR DÁVILA, 1963. Víctor M. Aguilar Dávila, "Crisis Agrícola en la Sierra de Ancash y Huánuco," *Mensajero Agrícola*, No. 158 (May 1963).

ALENCASTRE MONTÚFAR, 1960. Gustavo Alencastre Montúfar, *Informe Sobre los Estudios Preliminares de Antropología Social en Huayre* (Lima: Plan Nacional de Integración de la Población Aborigen, Ministerio de Trabajo y Asuntos Indígenas, 1960).

ALERS, 1964. J. Oscar Alers, *Population and*

Development in a Peruvian Community (Ithaca, N.Y.: Cornell University, Department of Anthropology, Comparative Studies of Cultural Change, 1964). (Mimeographed.)

ALERS, 1965. J. Oscar Alers, "The Quest for Well-Being," *American Behavioral Scientist*, Vol. 8, No. 7 (March 1965), 18–22.

ALERS MONTALVO, 1960. Manuel Alers Montalvo, "Social Systems Analysis of Supervised Agricultural Credit in an Andean Community," *Rural Sociology*, Vol. 25, No. 1 (March 1960), 51–64.

ALLRED, et al., 1959. Wells M. Allred, et al., *Funciones y Medios de Gobierno Local* (Lima: Plan Regional para el Desarrollo del Sur del Peru, Vol. XXIII, PS/F/52, 1959).

ANDREWS, 1963. David H. Andrews, "Migración e Integración en Paucartambo, Pasco, Perú," in H. F. Dobyns and M. C. Vázquez, eds., *Migración e Integración en el Perú* (Lima: Editorial Estudios Andinos, Monografía Andina No. 2, 1963), 143–51.

ARGUEDAS, 1956. José María Arguedas, "Puquio, una cultura en proceso de cambio," *Revista del Museo Nacional*, T. 25 (1956), 184–232.

BAZANTE M., 1963. Carlos Bazante M., "Economía," *Cuadernos Monográficos de Chimbo* (Quito: Editorial Casa de la Cultura Ecuatoriana, 1963), 93–142.

BEALS, 1952. Ralph L. Beals, "Acculturation, Economics, and Social Change in an Ecuadorean Village," in Sol Tax, ed., *Acculturation in the Americas*, Proceedings and Selected Papers of the 29th International Congress of Americanists (1952), 67–73.

BIRD, 1951. Junius B. Bird, "South American Radiocarbon Dates," in Frederick Johnson, ed., *Radiocarbon Dating*, Society for American Archaeology, Memoir 8 (1951), 37–49.

BOLUARTE, 1959. Francisco Boluarte, "Comunidad de Santiago de Anchucaya," in Jose Matos Mar, ed., *Las Actuales Comunidades de Indigenas: Huarochirí en 1955* (Lima: Universidad Nacional Mayor de San Marcos, Instituto de Etnologia, 1959).

BUITRÓN, 1947. Aníbal Buitrón, "Situación económica y social del Indio Otavaleño," *América Indígena*, Vol. 7, No. 1 (Enero 1947), 45–62.

CASALS M., et al., 1964. Juan F. Casals M., et al., *Informe del Instituto Nacional de Colonización 1963-1964* (Quito: Ministerio de Fomento, 1964).

CASTILLO, CASTILLO and REVILLA, 1964a. Hernán Castillo, Teresa Castillo and Arcenio Revilla, *Carcas: The Forgotten Community*, Translated and edited by Eileen Maynard (Ithaca, N.Y.: Cornell University, Department of Anthropology, Socio-Economic Development of Andean Communities, No. 1, 1964).

CASTILLO, CASTILLO and REVILLA, 1964b. Hernán Castillo, Teresa Castillo and Arcenio Revilla, *Accopata: The Reluctant Recipient of Technological Change*, Translated and edited by Eileen Maynard (Ithaca, N.Y.: Cornell University, Department of Anthropology, Socio-Economic Development of Andean Communities, No. 2, 1964).

CASTILLO, et al., 1964a. Hernán Castillo, et al., *Mito: The Orphan of Its Illustrious Children*, Translated and edited by Eileen Maynard (Ithaca, N.Y.: Cornell University, Department of Anthropology, Socio-Economic Development of Andean Communities, No. 4, 1964).

CASTILLO, et al., 1964b. Hernán Castillo, et al., *Chaquicocha: Community in Progress*, Translated by Patricia Deustua and edited by Eileen A. Maynard (Ithaca, N.Y.: Cornell University, Department of Anthropology, Socio-Economic Development of Andean Communities, No. 5, 1964).

CASTRO POZO, 1946. Hildebrando Castro Pozo, "Social and Economico-Political Evolution of the Communities of Central Peru," in Julian H. Steward, ed., *Handbook of South American Indians, Vol. II. Andean Civilizations*, Bureau of American Ethnology, Bulletin 143 (1946), 483–99.

CHENG and PORTUGAL, 1963. Alberto Cheng and José Portugal, "Migración en el Valle de Lurín," in H. F. Dobyns and M. C. Vázquez, eds., *Migración e Integración en el Perú* (Lima: Editorial Estudios Andinos, Monografía, No. 2, 1963).

CISNEROS CISNEROS, 1949. César Cisneros Cisneros, "Comunidades Indígenas del Ecuador," *América Indígena*, Vol. 9, No. 1 (Enero, 1949), 37–55.

COLLIER and BUITRÓN, 1949. John Collier, Jr. and Aníbal Buitrón, *The Awakening Valley* (Chicago: University of Chicago Press, 1949).

COMISIÓN, 1961. Comisión para la Reforma Agraria y la Vivienda, *La Reforma Agraria en el Peru. Documentos—I.* (Lima: Imprenta Casa Nacional de Moneda, 1961).

COTLER, 1959. Julio Cotler, *Los Cambios en la Propiedad, la Comunidad, y la Familia en San Lorenzo de Quinti* (Lima: Instituto de Etnología y Arqueología, Universidad National Mayor de San Marcos, 1959).

COTLER, 1961. Julio Cotler, "Las Comunidades de San Lorenzo de Quinti," in *Las Actuales Comunidades de Indígenas Huarochirí en 1955* (Lima: Instituto de Etnología, Universidad Nacional Mayor de San Marcos, 1961), 113–66.

DÍAZ B. and CORDOVA, n.d. Gustavo Díaz B. and Nelly Cordova, *Estudio de Algunas Comunidades de Cotopaxi* (Quito: Misión Andina del Ecuador, no date). (Mimeographed.)

DÍAZ MARTÍNEZ, 1962. Antonio Díaz Martínez, "Regimen de Tenencia de la Sierra: Ayacucho," *Mensajero Agrícola*, No. 152 (Jul.-Ago. 1962), 14–16.

DOBYNS, 1963. Henry F. Dobyns, "Migración e Integración," in H. F. Dobyns and M. C. Vázquez, eds., *Migración e Integración en el Perú* (Lima: Editorial Estudios Andinos, Monografía Andina, No. 2, 1963).

DOBYNS, 1965a. Henry F. Dobyns, "The Strategic Importance of Enlightenment and Skill for Power," *American Behavioral Scientist*, Vol. 8, No. 7 (March 1965), 23–27.

DOBYNS, 1965b. Henry F. Dobyns, *Agrarian Reform in Ecuador* (Ithaca, N.Y.: Seminar in Applied Anthropology, Cornell University, April 12, 1965 assignment).

DOBYNS, MONGE M. and VÁZQUEZ, 1962. Henry F. Dobyns, Carlos Monge M. and Mario C. Vázquez, "Summary of Technical-Organizational Progress and Reactions to It," *Human Organization*, Vol. 21, No. 2 (Summer 1962), 109–15.

DOUGHTY, 1963a. Paul L. Doughty, "El Caso de Huaylas: Un Distrito en la Perspectiva Nacional," in H. F. Dobyns and M. C. Vázquez, eds., *Migración e Integración en el Perú* (Lima: Editorial Estudios Andinos, Monografía Andina, No. 2, 1963).

DOUGHTY, 1963b. Paul L. Doughty, *Peruvian Highlanders in a Changing World: Social Integration and Culture Change in an Andean District* (Ph.D. Thesis, Cornell University, 1963).

DOUGHTY and NEGRÓN, 1964. Paul L. Doughty and Luís Negrón, *Pararín: A Break with the Past* (Ithaca, N.Y.: Cornell University, Department of Anthropology Socio-Economic Development of Andean Communities, No. 6, 1964).

ESPINOSA ZEVALLOS, 1965. Javier Espinosa Zevallos, "Aculturación de Indígenas en Guayaquil," *Procesos de Integración, V Congreso Indigenista Interamericano* (Quito: Talleres Gráficos Nacionales, 1965).

FARON, 1960. Louis C. Faron, "The Formation of Two Indigenous Communities in Peru," *American Anthropologist*, Vol. 62, No. 3 (June 1960), 437–53.

FORD, 1955. Thomas R. Ford, *Man and Land in Peru* (Gainesville: University of Florida Press, 1955).

GARAYAR PACHECO, 1961. Gregorio Garayar Pacheco, *Boletín de Estadística Peruana (Año IV, No. 5)* (Lima: Ministerio de Hacienda y Comercio, Dirección Nacional de Estadística y Censos, 1961).

GARAYAR PACHECO, 1962. Gregorio Garayar Pacheco, *Boletín de Estadística Peruana (Año V, No. 6)* (Lima: Dirección Nacional de Estadística y Censos, Instituto Nacional de Planificación, 1962).

GENERAL ENGINEERING LABORATORY, 1962. *Preliminary Report of Field Survey Teams on the Generation and Utilization of Power in Rural Areas of Developing Countries* (Schenectady, N.Y.: General Electric Company, 1962).

GHERSI BARRERA, 1963. Humberto Ghersi Barrera, "Características de la Migración en el distrito de Marcará," in H. F. Dobyns and M. C. Vázquez, eds., *Migración e Integración en el Perú* (Lima: Editorial Estudios Andinos, Monografía Andina, No. 2, 1963), 128–34.

GHERSI BARRERA and DOBYNS, 1963. Humberto Ghersi Barrera and Henry F. Dobyns, "Migración por Etapas: El Caso del Valle de Virú," in H. F. Dobyns and M. C. Vázquez, eds., *Migración e Integración en el Perú* (Lima: Editorial Estudios Andinos, Monografía Andina, No. 2, 1963).

GILLIN, 1947. John Gillin, *Moche: A Peruvian Coastal Community* (Washington, D.C.: Smithsonian Institution, Institute of Social Anthropology, Pub. 3, 1947).

GUILLÉN ARAOZ, 1961. Teresa Guillén Araoz, "Las Comunidades de Huarochirí," in *Las Actuales Comunidades de Indígenas Huarochirí en 1955* (Lima: Instituto de Etnología, Universidad Nacional Mayor de San Marcos, 1961), 47–110.

HEARN, 1950. Lea T. Hearn, "A Geographic Study of the Village of Cotocollao, Ecuador," *Journal of Geography*, Vol. XLIX (1950), 225–231.

HEATH, 1959. Dwight B. Heath, "Land Reform in Bolivia," *Inter-American Economic Affairs*, Vol. 12, No. 4 (Spring 1959), 3–27.

HEATH, 1960. Dwight B. Heath, "Land Tenure and Social Organization: An Ethnohistorical Study from the Bolivian Oriente," *Inter-American Economic Affairs*, Vol. 13, No. 4 (Spring 1960), 46–66.

HICKMAN, 1963. John M. Hickman, *The Aymara of Chinchera, Peru: Persistence and Change in a Bi-Cultural Context*, Ph.D. dissertation (Ithaca, N.Y.: Cornell University, 1963).

HOLMBERG, 1950. Allan R. Holmberg, "Viru: Remnant of an Exalted People," *Patterns for Modern Living*, Vol. II (Chicago: Delphian Society, 1950), 365–416.

HOLMBERG, 1960. Allan R. Holmberg, "Changing Community Attitudes and Values in Peru: A Case Study in Guided Change," *Social Change in Latin America Today* (New York: Harper for the Council on Foreign Relations, 1960), 63–107.

HOLMBERG, 1965. Allan R. Holmberg, "The Changing Values and Institutions of Vicos in the Context of National Development," *The American Behavioral Scientist*, Vol. 8, No. 7 (March 1965), 3–8.

HOLMBERG, DOBYNS and VÁZQUEZ, 1961. Allan R. Holmberg, Henry F. Dobyns and Mario C. Vázquez, "Methods for the Analysis of Cultural Change," *Anthropological Quarterly*, Vol. 34, No. 2 (April 1961), 37–46.

HOLMBERG and MONGE M., 1952. Allan R. Holmberg and Carlos Monge M., "Acuerdo celebrado entre la Universidad de Cornell y el Instituto Indigenista Peruano para el Desarrollo de un Plan de Antropología y Ciencias Sociales Aplicadas en la Zona de Vicos, Dpto. de Ancash," *Perú Indígena*, Vol. 2, No. 4 (Enero 1952), 85–86.

HOLMBERG and VÁZQUEZ, 1951. Allan R. Holmberg and Mario C. Vázquez, "Un Proyecto de antropología aplicada en el Perú," *Revista del Museo Nacional*, Vols. 19 and 20 (1951), 311–20.

JUNTA INTERMINISTERIAL DIRECTIVA, 1963. *Plan Nacional del Desarrollo Rural* (La Paz: Dirección Nacional del Desarrollo Rural, 1963).

KANTOR, 1961. Harry Kantor, "Agrarismo y tierra en Latinoamérica," *Combate*, No. 14 (Enero 1961), 9–14.

KEENLEYSIDE, et al., 1951. H. L. Keenleyside, et al., *Report of the United Nations Mission of Technical Assistance to Bolivia* (New York: United Nations, 1951).

KUCZYNSKI-GODARD, 1944. Maxine Kuczynski-Godard, *La Pampa de Ilave y Su Hinterland* (Lima: Ministerio de Salúd Pública y Asistencia Social, 1944).

KUCZYNSKI-GODARD, 1945. Maxine Kuczynski-Godard, *Estudie Familiar, Demográfico-Ecologico, en Estancias Indias de la Altaplanicie del Titicaca (Ichupampa)* (Lima: Ministerio de Salúd Pública y Asistencia Social, Asesoria Técnica para Encuestas Médico-Sociales de Sierra y Montaña, 1945).

LASSWELL and KAPLAN, 1950. Harold D. Lasswell and Abraham Kaplan, *Power and Society: A Framework for Political Inquiry* (New Haven, Conn.: Yale University Press, 1950).

LLOSA LARRABURE, 1962. Jaime Llosa Larrabure, "Carquin, Comunidad Agrícola Ayer; Hoy, Olor y Pesca y . . . Esperanza Detenida en el Tiempo," *Mensajero Agrícola*, No. 150 (Mayo 1962), 34–40.

McWILLIAMS, 1939. Carey McWilliams, *Factories in the Field: The Story of Migratory Farm Labor in California* (Boston, Mass.: Little, Brown, 1939).

MALPICA, 1964. Carlos Malpica, *Los Dueños del Perú* (Lima: Fondo de Cultura Popular, 1964).

MARTÍNEZ, 1961. Héctor Martínez, *Las Migraciones Altiplanicas y la Colonización del Tambopata* (Lima: Plan Nacional de Integración de la Población Aborigen, Serie Monográfica, No. 1, 1961).

MARTÍNEZ, 1962. Héctor Martínez, *Enfermedad y Medicina en Pillapi, Bolivia* (Lima: Plan Nacional de Integración de la Población Aborigen, Serie Monografíca, No. 10, 1962).

MARTÍNEZ, 1963. Héctor Martínez, "La Migración Puno-Tambopata," in H. F. Dobyns and M. C. Vázquez, eds., *Migración e Integración en el Perú* (Lima: Editorial Estudios Andinos, Monografía Andina, No. 2, 1963).

MARUS and RADA, 1962. John S. Marus and José Monje Rada, *Estudios de Colonización en Bolivia. II. Análisis de las Características Socio-Económicas de las Colonias* (La Paz: Ministerio de Economía

Nacional y Asuntos Campesinos, Agencia de los Estados Unidos para el Desarrollo Interamericano y las Naciones Unidas, 1962).

MATOS MAR, 1951. José Matos Mar, *La Ganadería en la Comunidad de Tupe* (Lima: Instituto de Etnología, Universidad Nacional Mayor de San Marcos, Pub. No. 2, 1951).

MATOS MAR, 1953. José Matos Mar, "El Proyecto Yauyos-Huarochirí," *Revista del Museo Nacional*, Vol. XXII (1953), 179–90.

MATOS MAR, 1957. José Matos Mar, "La propiedad en la Isla de Taquile (Lago Titi-caca)," *Revista del Museo Nacional*, Vol. XXVI (1957), 211–71.

MILLER, 1959. E. V. Miller, "Agricultural Ecuador," *Geographical Review*, Vol. XLIX (1959), 183–207.

MINISTERIO, 1962. Ministerio de Agricultura, *La Actividad Cafetalera en Tingo María* (Lima: Ministerio de Agricultura, Servicio de Investigación y Promoción Agraria, 1962).

MONTALVO V., 1958. Abner Montalvo V., *Exploraciones Antropologicas en Ilave. Qamicachi (Parcialidad)* (Lima: Instituto Indigenista Peruano, Programa Puno-Tambopata. Serie de Monografías, No. 1, 1958).

MONTALVO VIDAL and GALDO PAGAZA, 1960. Abner Montalvo Vidal and Raúl Galdo Pagaza, *Las Artesanías Tradicionales y Sus Posibilidades de Desarrollo. La Sombrerería en Chinchera, Una Comunidad Indígena del Departamento de Puno* (Lima: Plan Nacional de Integracíon de la Población Aborigen, Programa Puno-Tambopata, Sección de Investigación Antropologica, Serie de Monografías, No. 3, 1960).

MORRIS, 1964. Earl W. Morris, ed., *Etapas para el desarrollo socio-económico de Mayobamba* (Lima: Folletos del Proyecto Perú-Cornell, No. 3, 1964).

NUÑEZ DEL PRADO, 1949. Oscar Nuñez del Prado, *Chinchero, un Pueblo Andino del Sur (Algunos Aspectos)* (Cuzco: Universidad Nacional del Cuzco, 1949).

NUÑEZ DEL PRADO, 1951. Oscar Nuñez del Prado, *Aspecto Económico de Virú, Una Comunidad de la Costa Norte del Perú* (Cuzco: Editorial H. G. Rozas, S. A., 1951).

NUÑEZ DEL PRADO, 1960. Oscar Nuñez del Prado, *El Proyecto de Antropología Aplicada del Cuzco, Informe Anual 1960* (Kuyo Chico: Proyecto 1960). (Mimeographed.)

NUÑEZ DEL PRADO, 1959. Wilfredo Nuñez del Prado, *Andarapa: Problemas Medico-Antropológicos* (Lima: Plan Regional para el Desarrollo del Sur del Peru, Vol. VI, PS/B/12, 1959).

OBANDO, 1961. Eduardo Obando, "Acueducto de 4 Kilometros Inaugura Comunidad Cajacay," *La Tribuna* (Lima, Peru: 8 de Febrero, 1961).

ORTIZ VERGARA and GALDO PAGAZA, 1958a. Pedro Ortiz Vergara and Raúl Galdo Pagaza,

Informe Amantaní (Lima: Instituto Indigenista Peruano, Programa Puno-Tambopata, 1958).

ORTIZ VERGARA and GALDO PAGAZA, 1958b. Pedro Ortiz Vergara and Raúl Galdo Pagaza, *Reconocimiento de la Provincia de Chucuito* (Lima: Instituto Indigenista Peruano, Programa Puno-Tambopata, Serie de Monografías, No. 2, 1958).

PARSONS, 1945. Elsie Clews Parsons, *Peguche, Canton of Otavalo, Province of Imbabura, Ecuador: A Study of Andean Indians* (Chicago, Ill.: University of Chicago Press, 1945).

PATCH, 1958. Richard W. Patch, *The Indian Emergence in Cuzco*, American Universities Field Staff Letter, Peru, RWP-8, 1958.

PATCH, 1959a. Richard W. Patch, *The Role of a Coastal Hacienda in the Hispanization of Andean Indians*, American Universities Field Staff, Latin America (Peru), RWP-2, 1959.

PATCH, 1959b. Richard W. Patch, *How Communal Are the Communities?*, American Universities Field Staff, Latin America (Peru), RWP-5, 1959.

PRESTON, 1963. David A. Preston, "Weavers and Butchers: A Note on the Otavalo Indians of Ecuador," *Man*, Vol. 176 (September 1963), 146-48.

PULGAR VIDAL, 1945. Carmela Pulgar Vidal, "Los indios operarios de Huánuco—Los indígenas de Muquiyauyo y los Clientes del Dispensario de San Sebastián," *Boletín de la Sociedad Geográfica de Lima*, T. LXII (1945), 24-53.

REVILLA CORRALES and RAMÓN CORDÓVA, 1964. Arcenio Revilla Corrales and César Rámon Córdova, "Características Generales de la Irrigación La Esperanza," *Cuadernos de Antropología*, Vol. 2, No. 3 (Junio 1964), 78-82.

RUBIO ORBE, 1956. Gonzalo Rubio Orbe, *Punyaro: Estudio de Antropología Social y Cultural de una Comunidad Indígena y Mestiza* (Quito: Casa de la Cultura Ecuatoriana, 1956).

SABOGAL W., 1962. José R. Sabogal W., "Pucará, Bastión Huanca en el Valle de 'Xauxa'," *Mensajero Agrícola*, No. 149 (April 1962), 22-25.

SAINTE MARIE S., 1945. Darío Sante Marie S., ed., *Perú en Cifras 1944-1945* (Lima: Ediciones Internacionales, 1945).

SAUNDERS, 1961. J. V. D. Saunders, "Man-Land Relations in Ecuador," *Rural Sociology*, Vol. 26, No. 1 (March 1961), 57-69.

SEOANE, 1963. Edgardo Seoane, *Surcos de Paz* (Lima: Industrialgrafica S. A., 1963).

SHERMAN, 1963. Brian Sherman, *Santa Clara* (Ithaca, N.Y.: Cornell University, Department of Anthropology, Comparative Studies of Cultural Change, 1963).

SMITH, 1960. C. T. Smith, "Aspects of Agriculture and Settlement in Peru," *Geographical Journal*, Vol. CXXVI, pt. 4 (December 1960), 397-412.

SOLER BUSTAMANTE, 1954. Eduardo Soler Bustamante, "La Agricultura en la Comunidad de San Pedro de Huancaire," *Revista del Museo Nacional*, Vol XXIII, Publ. No. 9, Instituto de Etnología, Universidad Nacional Mayor de San Marcos (1954), 1-52.

SOLER BUSTAMANTE, 1963. Eduardo Soler Bustamante, "Fuentes de Migración al complejo Agrícola Industrial de Paramonga," in H. F. Dobyns and M. C. Vázquez, eds., *Migración e Integración en el Perú* (Lima: Editorial Estudios Andinos, Monografía Andina, No. 2, 1963), 82-87.

STEIN, 1961. William W. Stein, *Hualcan: Life in the Highlands of Peru* (Ithaca, N.Y.: Cornell University Press, 1961).

SUAREZ ARNEZ, 1958. Faustino Suarez Arnez, *Monografía Historica, Geográfica, Cultural y Folklorica de la Provincia Campero, Capital Aiquile* (La Paz: Talleres Gráficos Bolivianos, 1958).

TSCHOPIK, 1947. Harry Tschopik, Jr., *Highland Communities of Central Peru* (Washington, D. C.: Smithsonian Institution, Institute of Social Anthropology, Pub. 5, 1947).

VÁZQUEZ, 1952. Mario C. Vázquez, "La Antropología Cultural y Nuestro Problema del Indio: Vicos, un Caso de Antropología Aplicada, *Perú Indígena*, Vol. II, Nos. 5-6 (Junio 1952), 7-157.

VÁZQUEZ, 1961. Mario C. Vázquez, *Hacienda, Peonaje y Servidumbre en los Andes Peruanos* (Lima: Editorial Estudios Andinos, Monografía Andina, No. 1, 1961).

VÁZQUEZ, 1962. Mario C. Vázquez, "Cambios Socio-Económicos en una Hacienda Andina del Perú," *América Indígena*, Vol. 22, No. 4 (October 1962), 297-312.

VÁZQUEZ, 1965a. Mario C. Vázquez, "The Interplay Between Power and Wealth," *The American Behavioral Scientist*, Vol. 8, No. 7 (March 1965), 9-12.

VÁZQUEZ, 1965b. Mario C. Vázquez, "Campesinos Andinos en un Valle Costeño del Perú," *Procesos de Integración, V Congreso Indigenista Interamericano* (Quito: Talleres Gráficos Nacionales, 1965), 131-40.

VÁZQUEZ, 1965c. Mario C. Vázquez, "Viru: Land and Society," Department of Anthropology, Cornell University, Ithaca, N.Y., 1965. (Mimeographed.)

WEEKS, 1946. David Weeks, "Bolivia's Agricultural Frontier," *Geographical Review*, Vol. XXXVI, No. 4 (1946), 546-67.

CASE STUDY

The Comilla Program in East Pakistan

SYED A. RAHIM

TWO HUNDRED YEARS AGO farming in the Bengal Delta was a profitable business. We find evidence of this in the writings of famous travelers. In Bengali folklore we find farming described as a source of wealth and prosperity followed over generations and earning plenty of food and a good wife. A good farmer possessed several pairs of bullocks, which were his source of power for all kinds of farming activities.

The situation today is totally different. The Bengali farmer has lost everything. He has not followed the path of progress. He is bound by the old traditions. To earn a minimum amount of food for subsistence is his biggest problem in life. His fellow farmers in the West have learned how to earn more from farming. The farmer of the West maintains a high standard of living because he uses tractors and pumps and many other inventions of science in his farming operations.

From bullock to tractor is a long struggle with nature. In the West the transformation has taken place gradually over a long period of time. The progress has gone hand in hand with the development of science and technology.

How to modernize traditional farming? How to do it quickly? These are the questions that are foremost in the minds of the planners and administrators of most of the developing nations of the world. They want a strategy and tactic for rural agricultural development. They are willing to borrow methods and techniques from anywhere, provided they fit into the social, political, and administrative structure of their country. The problem of modernization of traditional farming is an extremely complex one, and therefore scientific analysis of the problems, experimentation, testing of theories under local conditions, pilot programs, and their continuous evaluation are needed to arrive at a satisfactory solution. In the past the social scientists, especially the economists and sociologists in

the developing countries, have shown little interest in studying traditional farming and developing techniques for modernization.

It is encouraging to note today that at several places around the world pilot experiments for the development of subsistence agriculture are being made. At Comilla, East Pakistan, one such experiment was started by the Pakistan Academy for Rural Development in 1960.[1] A group of social scientists started their experiment under the able leadership of Dr. Akhter Hameed Khan.

In this paper I propose to give a brief description of subsistence farming at Comilla and then discuss three major aspects of the "Comilla Experiment" in rural development.

SUBSISTENCE FARMING IN COMILLA THANA

GENERAL CHARACTERISTICS OF THE AREA

Comilla Kotwali Thana is one of the 413 *thanas* of East Pakistan. It has an area of 107 square miles with a population of 217,297 persons, a density of 2,031 persons per square mile [Census, 1961]. There are 246 villages in the Thana. The greater portion of the Thana is a rice-growing plain. The inundation level is about 26 feet above the mean sea level; most of the countryside is inundated during the rainy season to a depth of a few feet. In the southern part of the Thana extends the Lalmai Hill range, covering an area of about 17 square miles, with an average elevation of 90 feet above the sea level.

There are a number of hill streams flowing

1. There are actually two academies, one in East Pakistan and another in West Pakistan. Both were set up by the government of Pakistan, with assistance from the Ford Foundation and Michigan State University. For further information on the Academy, see its various annual reports and PARD [1963b]. Two recent case studies are Stevens [1967] and Luykx [1968]. Professor Arthur F. Raper of Michigan State University is preparing a book on the Comilla experience.

through the Thana, of which the most important is the Gumti. The Gumti river originates in the hilly areas of Tripura State, India. It carries a huge quantity of silt-laden water during monsoon and frequently causes heavy flood damage when the protecting earthen embankment gives way. Comilla has a moderately hot and humid climate. The temperature varies from 90° F in the dry summer (March to May) through 82° F in monsoon (June to October) to 57° F in the winter (November to February). The average annual rainfall is about 90 inches. Over two-thirds of the total rainfall occurs during the months of June, July, and August. Rainfall during winter is negligible. The geological formation of the Thana is alluvial. The soil texture is clay to clayloam in the plains and sandy loam along the course of the rivers. The soil is moderately fertile, deficient in nitrogen and organic matters.

The district town of Comilla, located at the center of the Thana, has a population of 54,000 persons. The town is the center of administration, business, education, and professional activities. Most of the villages in the Thana are accessible from the town during dry seasons.

Over 80 per cent of the population in Comilla Thana is Muslim. During the period 1951–1961, the population has increased by 26 per cent in the town and 12 per cent in the rural area. The percentage of literates is 27 per cent [Census, 1961].

THE FARMING SYSTEM

In Comilla Thana 30,000 farm families operate 50,000 acres of cultivated land. An average farm of 1.7 acres supports a family of six persons. Over 75 per cent of the farms are owner-operated farms. The rest are owner-cum-tenant farms. About 95 per cent of the farms are five acres or less in area. Comilla has a rice-growing agriculture largely dominated by the monsoon. Rice is grown in 80 per cent of the total cropped area. The principal rice crop seasons are Aus (April to August) and Amon (August to December). The Amon crop is grown in 80 per cent and the Aus crop in 50 per cent of the total cultivated area. There is a third rice crop, Boro, which is grown in small patches of low-lying areas (about 5 per cent of the total area) from December through April. The other minor crops grown in the area are jute, sugar cane, vegetables, pulses, and oil seeds. The bullock is the only source of farm power. About half of the farm families own bullocks. A pair of bullocks is available, on an average, for 3.8 acres of cultivated land. Two-thirds of the total bullock population is owned by farm families owning over two acres of land [PARD, 1963b]. Land is cultivated by bullocks owned or hired. The usual labor requirements for farming operations are met by the family, but at peak seasons additional hands are hired on a wage or exchange basis. Seed and manure requirements are generally met by the family's own resources. Two-thirds of the total agricultural produce is consumed at home. The surplus is sold at local markets in cash to meet other necessities of life.

The traditional methods of agriculture employed produce low crop yields. The average yield of Amon paddy is 1,500 pounds per acre. This figure is about one-third of the average yield in Japan.

THE MAJOR FEATURES AND PROBLEMS

In Comilla all the cultivable land has been brought under cultivation. However, the intensity of cultivation is low. In the dry winter season over 80 per cent of the land remains fallow. Water for irrigation is not generally available in the present state of farming. Water from rivers and underground resources is available; use of this water, however, requires organization, new skills, and capital investment. During the peak monsoon season a large part of the relatively low-level land is not cultivated because of the risk of crop damage by floods. Again, the farmer is very reluctant to increase intensity of cultivation for fear of destroying the fertility of the land.

The holdings are small and fragmented. The farmers are very attached to their land. There is a lot of variation in the level and fertility of land. Consolidation of holdings is an extremely difficult proposition. Small and fragmented holdings present special difficulties in introducing mechanized cultivation and planned irrigation.

There is no shortage of labor. But the highly seasonal nature of employment puts a heavy demand on labor during the short land preparation, sowing, and harvesting seasons. Bullocks are used for land preparation, thrashing of paddy, and transportation. The bullocks are usually undersized, often sickly.

The farmers are constantly in need of credit. A relatively well-to-do farmer who has saved some money finds it is a very good investment to lend out money at 50 to 100 per cent rate of interest. The poorer farmers are constantly exploited by their well-off neighbors. The average per capita indebtedness is about Rs.100, whereas the per capita income is Rs.250. Most farmers sell their produce at harvest time. A total lack of organized marketing and processing industries compels the farmers to sell their raw materials at the year's lowest prices in the local markets. The undeveloped marketing and processing system has given rise to a group of middlemen traders. They avail themselves of every opportunity to deprive farmers of their rightful profits.

The more prosperous farmers and traders invest money in the education of their children. The educated persons move to the cities and towns. By this process the village loses its enlightened and enterprising individuals. The modernization of subsistence farming in Comilla is an extremely difficult task. The primary need is to increase the productivity of the land. Priority should be given to intensive cultivation. This requires the development of an infrastructure of flood control, drainage, irrigation, and a road system. A beginning in this direction has been made under a national public works program [PARD, 1963a]. Development of a suitable irrigation system is most vital, because cultivation during the dry season is impossible without irrigation water. Improved practices—such as heavier fertilization, better varieties of plants, and plant protection measures—are needed. Only a good extension program can delay the operation of the law of diminishing returns. Mechanization should be introduced selectively. With proper organization at the village level and adequate servicing arrangements, tractors can be used for plowing and hauling purposes. The most important mechanization needs are pumps and tube wells for irrigation. Comilla is fortunate in having the Karnafuli hydro-electric power line passing through it. Electric power from this source is available at reasonable cost. The development of processing units and storage facilities in the town of Comilla is essential. Without this, a marketing system cannot be developed.

Development of a sound credit system is an immediate need. The progress in the villages will be slow until and unless the farmers are saved from the local moneylenders and traders.

It appears that a system of organization based on cooperative principles is most suitable for the people in Comilla Thana. It is quite clear that a sound program of development requires a large amount of capital, skill, concentration, and pioneering work. It is unrealistic to expect that the farmers can meet these demands. A directed program must come from outside.

THE COMILLA EXPERIMENT

The Government of Pakistan turned over the Comilla Thana to the Pakistan Academy for Rural Development as an "experimental laboratory" where the Academy could develop and test patterns and procedures that might be suitable for developing East Pakistan's agriculture. The "Comilla experiment" consisted of a number of integrated pilot projects aimed at the comprehensive development of the *thana*, both to modernize its agriculture and to improve the rural life of its inhabitants. Each project developed out of initial studies of the area made by the Academy staff before action programs were launched.

The central and initial project was the "cooperative experiment," started in 1960, which developed into an integrated system of primary and central cooperatives. The other projects that followed were rural administration, irrigation and rural electrification, education, women's education, and family planning. Reports on each of these projects have been published by the Academy.

The key project revolves around the central cooperative association, the Kotwali Thana Central Cooperative Association, Ltd., inaugurated in 1962. This cooperative experiment has been amply documented in the annual reports published by the Academy, but a brief review is necessary. The project is a system of primary cooperative societies federated into a central cooperative at the *thana* level. The primary societies are each composed of from 20 to 75 persons, with an average membership of 38. They have a program of small savings, weekly meetings, and joint planning for production purposes. Each society has an elected chairman and an elected manager. The managers meet once a week, and chairmen meet once a month at the office of the Central Association to attend meetings and training classes. The Central Association is run by a board of directors that is composed of members elected by the primary associations and members nominated by the government. The Central Association has a staff of directing, supervising, and inspecting personnel.

An important feature of the Comilla experiment is the extent to which all the agencies involved in the development of the *thana* have been located at a single physical location and have had their activities coordinated. A commercial bank has opened a branch on the premises of the Central Association, which manages all financial transactions for the association and maintains saving accounts for the primary societies. The *thana*-level officers of the various nation-building departments of the government— such as agriculture, education, health, and the like—and the Thana Council of the local self-government system are also located in the premises of the Central Association. These offices assist the Central Association in its training and extension program. The work of the various departmental offices are coordinated by the Thana Council, which operates in close collaboration with the Central Association.

The pilot scheme is sponsored officially by the Agriculture Department, Government of East Pakistan, through the director of the Academy for Rural Development at Comilla. The scheme has a five years' total budget of Rs.4.9 million, about Rs.1 million of which is a grant for organizational, educational, and training purposes. The remaining Rs.3.9 million is a loan, of which the working capital of Rs.800,000 is repayable in eight equal installments, beginning with the sixth year, and the remaining amount is repayable in 20 instalments, beginning with the fourth year. The loan was provided by the Ford Foundation.

The Central Association furnishes loans to the primary societies, organizes training and extension services; maintains a mechanized unit of tractors, power pumps, and other implements that are hired out; and organizes joint marketing for the primary societies. Recently it has undertaken the work of building up processing units and storage units to service the primary societies.

The status of the cooperative project as of June 1964 is as follows. There are 122 village-level cooperative societies, with a total membership of 3,833 persons. These are farmers' cooperatives. There are 45 special cooperative societies, with a total membership of 2,425 persons. These societies are formed by various occupational groups, such as carpenters, masons, butchers, printing press workers, weavers, rickshaw pullers, and so on. Most of these societies are located in or near the town. There is a newly established dairy society, which has members from all over the Thana. The primary societies have accumulated cash savings of Rs.430,000, purchased shares worth Rs.63,000, and built up a reserve fund of Rs.24,000. A total of Rs.1,301,000, has been issued as loans of various kinds to these societies, of which Rs.761,000 has already been repaid. The loan repayment rate is over 99 per cent.

The Central Association has organized a large number of demonstration and training classes. Selected members of the societies have been trained as accountants, tractor drivers, mechanics, and the like. Considerable amounts of seeds, fetilizers, and insecticides have been supplied.

The mechanized unit has 25 medium-sized tractors, a few Japanese hand tractors, and 113 irrigation pumps. The maintenance section has been properly developed with mechanics and stores. Under the irrigation scheme 40 deep wells have been sunk in the villages. The Central Association has established a small rice-processing unit and a dairy and is building up a cold storage unit.

In the following pages, three major aspects of the program—namely credit, extension, and irrigation—will be discussed in some detail.[2]

2. The other pilot projects—such as rural administration, women's education, and family planning—work closely with the cooperative project but will not be discussed in this paper.

CREDIT

The credit system of the project is designed with two purposes in mind. The first purpose is to replace the local credit institution of moneylenders with a less costly (for the borrower) and equally efficient and safe system. The second purpose is to guide the loans into productive channels by proper supervision. Even a superficial investigation of indebtedness of the farmers in the area indicated that a considerable amount of capital is passed on to the moneylenders as interest. A check on this flow would enable the farmers to accumulate some capital.

A liberal loan policy has been adopted by the Central Association. Loans are issued in such a manner that at least a part of the loan can be used in repaying old debts, releasing mortgaged land, or purchasing cattle. Loans are issued on the basis of a production plan submitted by a cooperative society. This plan contains the names of the candidates with their loan requirements for each specific purpose. Necessary documentation on security (land or stocks of produce) are included in the plan. The primary society prepares its own plan, sometimes assisted by the inspecting staff of the Central Association. The method of utilization of the loans, the expected benefits, and the time and mode of repayment are also described in the production plan. After proper scrutiny and, if necessary, field checks, the amount of the loan granted is transferred to the bank account of the village cooperative society within a week of the submission of the production plan. Loans are issued to societies, and not to individuals. The society remains responsible for proper utilization and for repayments. The Central Association charges interest at the rate of 6 per cent on a loan. In addition, another 5 per cent is charged for supervision expenses and payment of allowances and bonuses to the managers of the societies.

The credit system operates on a "no saving no credit" policy: "There can be no credit system without deposits; therefore every cooperative society and every member of a society should save regularly and deposit with the Central Association. Members should not only make cash deposits; they should also deposit as much of their produce as possible in the godown of their village

cooperative" [Khan and Hussain, 1963]. A society is granted a loan only if it has accumulated some capital through small weekly savings of the members. The members of a society place deposits (very small amounts) with the society in the weekly meetings. Savings books are maintained. Each week the manager of the society collects the deposits and puts the money in the bank account of the society. If a member fails to deposit for four consecutive weeks and cannot explain the failure satisfactorily, his membership is rescinded. The savings deposits of a society serve as a collateral against loans.

The credit system of the project has successfully removed the monopoly of the moneylenders in villages with cooperatives. The results of a recent survey[3] furnish evidence of this. This survey found that about half of the total outstanding debts of the members of the cooperative societies are owed to moneylenders, while in a neighboring *thana* almost the total outstanding debts are owed to the moneylenders. It is also interesting to note that the existing government credit agencies, the Central Co-operative Bank and the Agricultural Development Bank, have been able to serve only a very small number of persons. The total amount of credit from these sources does not exceed 10 per cent of the total outstanding debt. The government agencies have not succeeded in increasing their credit operations very fast, even though their interest rates are low.

The supervision of credit is accomplished through the mechanism of the production plan and periodic visits by the inspectors. The seed and fertilizer needs cited in the plans are met, and adequate training courses are organized to insure their proper use. A survey of loan utilization by the members of the cooperative societies shows the following: of total amount spent, the repayment of outstanding debts is 20 per cent; fertilizers 16 per cent; purchase of bullocks 15 per cent; labor charges 25 per cent; seed 3 per cent; housing 12 per cent; domestic expenses 4 per cent; and payment of land revenue 3 per cent [Ahsan, 1964].

The repayment of loans has been highly satisfactory—over 99 per cent. Repayments have been made in cash and also in kind, by

3. Unpublished material. The survey was conducted by the Academy in 1964.

depositing crops valued at the market rates. More than 50 per cent of the total repayments have been made in kind. The repayment situation is satisfactory mainly on account of the close contacts with the societies and occasional campaigns during harvesting periods. A defaulting member is placed under the constant pressure of criticism by fellow members.

Several problems are associated with the credit system of the cooperative project. Cost of supervision is high, and the members are reluctant to pay the 5 per cent service charges. It is expected that with more experience, better management, and a growing sense of responsibility of the members of the societies, less vigilance in supervision will be needed. So far the production plans of the societies have been only partial production plans. Much of the loan amount has been used to release land or repay old debts. This, however, was inevitable. As the farmers consolidate their position, more investment will be made for productive purposes. Another problem has arisen out of the farmers' hunger for land, a problem that has to be tackled carefully.

The most serious problem at present is the farmers' lack of enthusiasm for investment in modern methods of agriculture. Many farmers are unwilling to take a loan for drilling a deep well for irrigation water. They are doubtful about the wisdom of making such a joint investment. Some farmers have put a large part of their savings in separate private accounts in the bank. They do not trust the joint account of the society.

THE EXTENSION EDUCATION SYSTEM

The extension system of the Comilla Project is developed on the experiences of the Village-AID community development program in East Pakistan, on field research on diffusion and communication patterns in Comilla villages [Rahim, 1961b], and on the "Volkschule" concept. Earlier experiences with village-level workers were disappointing. People in the villages looked upon them with distrust and suspicion. In most cases the village-level worker, who was an educated and trained person, found life in the villages difficult. He could not hire a house and bring his family; there were no educational or medical facilities. Field research conducted by the Academy revealed that in a village certain persons occupy "strategic positions" in the communication network, and to these persons other villagers went for information and advice. These "central persons" or "opinion leaders" have one characteristic in common: they maintain regular contacts with sources of information and influence in the town and other places outside the village.

The intensive nature of the supervision required by the credit program and the concentration on developing the village-level cooperative institutions made it necessary that a regular communication channel between the Central Association and the village-level societies be established. This has been achieved through the practice of regular weekly village meetings of the cooperative members and the meetings of the managers at the Central Association. The extension education program has been fitted into this system of communication.

Every week, on a fixed day, the managers of the cooperative societies come to the office of the Central Association. Special training classes are arranged for them. They learn about the use of fertilizers, new methods of cultivation, use of insecticides, and the like. They ask questions and present their problems to the experts. They are given instruction sheets, picture stories, and so forth. They see demonstrations arranged at the five-acre farm near the Central Association's office. The managers go back, and in their own village meetings they pass on the information to other members. They read out the instruction sheets, answer the questions raised. If there is any special problem, they bring it back to the experts the next week. The training goes on continuously. Special care is taken in preparing training material on the basis of seasonal requirements. As all the *thana*-level government officers of various departments are located in the training center, an integrated training program is prepared without extra cost. Besides the managers, other groups of leaders—teachers, model farmers, weavers, and so on—come for such one-day-a-week training courses. The extension program is further strengthened by the demonstrations in the villages organized by a Japanese team of rice experts stationed at Comilla [PARD, 1962].

It is too early to assess correctly the

effectiveness of the extension program in terms of tangible results. Survey results show that a large proportion of the members of the cooperatives have adopted certain recommended improved practices. Adoption of certain other practices has been slow [Rahim, 1964a]. Crop-cutting estimates show that the average yield of rice obtained by society members is 25 per cent higher than the average yield in the whole Thana [Rahim, 1964b]. There have also been significant increases in the acreage of Boro rice, potato and other vegetables.

The biggest problem confronting the extension program is that many of the improved practices have not been properly adjusted and adapted to local conditions. New practices suitable for the local conditions have not yet been developed. This problem is likely to become more serious in the future unless the quality of the technical research on agriculture at the government experimental stations and farms is improved and the scope enlarged. The team of Japanese experts stationed at Comilla has done some good work in rice cultivation [PARD, 1962]. But more extensive experimentation is needed.

A second problem for the extension program is the farmers' lack of interest in investment in agriculture on account of high rates of interest on loans from the moneylenders. This is being tackled by the credit program.

A third problem is the illiteracy, ignorance, and fatalistic attitude of the farmers. A solution to this will come gradually through the intensive training and discussion program.

In the Comilla extension program the emphasis has been rightly placed on education, training, and group action. But the effectiveness of such a program is likely to encounter diminishing returns or may even produce negative results unless the "contents" of the communications are improved. The extension agent must have a better product to promote. There is a great need for an improved Indica variety of rice; more information is needed on better fertilization techniques, on pest and disease control, and on many other matters. This is a problem for the technical research specialists. So far very little has been achieved in this regard by the research institutions in East Pakistan.

IRRIGATION

The Comilla Pilot Project in Irrigation, developed in 1963,[4] consists of three complementary projects utilizing three different methods [PARD, 1964]. In the Sonaichari Project, water from the Gumti river will be taken through pipe sluices into the Sonaichahi Khal. Water from this main channel will be lifted by pumps to cover 6,000 acres. The second project is designed to lift water from the Gumti river by placing low-lift pumps, floated on rafts placed in the river. This will irrigate about 960 acres of land in the vicinity of the river. The third and the most important project is the tube-well project. Two hundred tube wells of 1.5 cusec capacity will be sunk over a period of four years. This will irrigate 12,000 acres. It is estimated that the irrigation project will raise the cropping intensity from 1.6 to 2.5. A detailed discussion on all the three projects is not possible; I shall take only the tube-well project.

Installation of the tube wells is made through the cooperative organization. The Central Association encourages the village cooperatives to accept tube wells in their villages. The Central Association has a few drilling rigs and a group of workers trained for drilling purposes. When a village society agrees to have a tube well, the drilling team starts working. A simple labor-intensive method is used in the drilling operation. A 300-foot-deep six-inch-diameter tube well with a centrifugal pump and a small pumphouse costs about Rs.21,000. The tube well operates on diesel electric power derived from power lines installed under separate electrification program. So far, 40 tube wells have been installed in 40 village cooperatives, of which 11 tube wells operated during the 1963–1964 winter crop season. Boro rice crop was grown in over 400 acres of land. Potato and other vegetable crops were grown at a few places in small areas. It is estimated that in the winter 1964–1965 all the 40 tube wells will be used in growing Boro and other vegetable crops. The acreage per tube well is likely to reach about 80 acres. The extension section of the Central Association has taken up a special program in the tube-well villages.

It is too early to evaluate the tube-well

4. For the Academy's earlier work with irrigation, see Rahim [1961a] and Stevens [1957, 42–49].

irrigation project. Facts are now being collected so that a proper economic analysis can be made and improved organizational arrangements can be developed. The up-to-date number of installations and the cost figures have been within the target set in the plan. The figures of acreage irrigated was low in the first year. But this is likely to increase as the villagers gather experience.

In the tube-well irrigation project several local adjustments have been made, and a number of problems are still unsolved. In choosing a suitable site for the tube wells, opinions of the local people have been sought. Usually a tube well is placed near a tank, so that water can be stored in the tank. The pump can then operate at night, when the electric charges are lower than in the daytime. Water from the tank is led as needed by field channels to the areas to be irrigated. The village cooperative organizes proper distribution of water and keeps the necessary records on water use. The Central Association organizes training courses for pump operators and pump maintenance workers.

It has not yet been possible to decide the mode of payment and ownership questions. One proposal is that the total cost of the tube-well installation should be treated as a long-term loan against the village society. The society would operate and maintain the installation; the loan would be repaid in installments. The transfer of ownership to the village society would insure better maintenance and intensive utilization. The reaction of the primary societies to this proposal has not been favorable. They are not sure this heavy investment will be a paying one. They are inclined to gather more experience before making a decision. An alternative procedure for the Central Association is to retain ownership and charge the societies on a per-acre-irrigated basis. Last year 11 societies were charged at the rate of Rs.35 per acre. The rate was too low. The societies are reluctant to pay at higher rates. It is estimated that the average cost of irrigation by tube well would be about Rs.53 per acre (calculated on the basis of 60 acres irrigated per tube well) [PARD, 1964]. To cover this cost, maximum utilization of water and improved cultivation is required.

Experience of the use of eleven tube wells in 1963–1964 shows that the water available from the tube well can irrigate about 100 acres of land. A substantial increase in the acreage of crops other than paddy is likely to take place in a few years' time. In fact, increase in the acreage of these crops is possible only when irrigation water is available. Water is a prerequisite for launching an extension program for cultivation of crops in the dry winter season. With the increase in the acreage irrigated per tube well, the cost will come down. The farmers will gradually learn the best uses of the water for which they are paying money. It is also hoped that the tube wells will be used to irrigate Aus and Amon crops when necessary. The sowing of Aus paddy can be started without waiting for rains. An early sowing may save the crop from floods, which generally occurs during the end of the growing season of the Aus crop. In the case of the Amon crop, occasional irrigation during the dry spell will insure a higher yield of crop.

The problem before the Central Association is clear. The Central Association should intensify extension education in the tube-well villages. It may become necessary to run the program at a subsidized rate for a year or two. But the program cannot be stopped or slowed down because intensive cultivation is not possible without water. Increase in production cannot take place without irrigation. Experience of Boro crop cultivation in 1964 in two villages and estimates of crop acreages given in the 1965 production plans indicate that in the future the average acreage that a pump can irrigate will be higher than 60 acres. Boro cultivation in experimental fields has given yields 100 per cent higher than the *thana* average. It is possible that the cost of tube-well installation will come down with large-scale operation. Therefore the expectation is that the tube-well irrigation program will succeed and have a major impact on local agriculture.

CONCLUSION

In his third annual report, Dr. Akhter Hameed Khan, the architect of the Comilla Experiment and Chairman of the Central Co-operative Association wrote: "The experimental projects are of crucial importance. If they fail it is like salt losing its savour. If they succeed a trail is blazed." In the short years of life of the experiment at Comilla there have been failures and successes. Solutions to some problems have been found. But many problems are still unsolved and need further study. We have come to certain general conclusions that indicate broad directions in which the project should move. But many of the details of different programs are yet to be determined.

Experiences at Comilla tell us that, within the limitations of the traditional technology and a given value system, the farmers over generations of trial and error have learned to make good use of their limited resources. Rural reconstruction programs of the past advocated "hard work," "thrift," and "village self-sufficiency." These are obsolete ideas. The problems of village development are far more complex. A great deal of experimentation, coordinated and integrated work is called for.

The Comilla experiment is based on three principles:[5] (1) to supply farmers with new material, new knowledge, and new skills; (2) to train farmers in using these factors; and (3) to insure profit by their use. The tactic is to work with groups of farmers through an organization of their own. Hence we have the village cooperatives supported by a central autonomous organization.

The village cooperative promotes group action, joint planning, and saving. The Central Association lends credit, arranges continuous training, services, and supplies, and processing and marketing of product. The whole program depends heavily on the government and research institutions. Control of water (flood and irrigation), supply of power, availability and low prices for inputs are things that the government should arrange under national programs. There is the need of developing and adapting new materials and practices under local conditions. This is the function of research institutions.

The government of Pakistan is giving considerable emphasis to rural and agricultural development in its developmental plans. The pilot experiment at Comilla has resulted in a nationwide Public Works Program of building roads, canals, embankments, and so on. Fertilizers are being sold at highly subsidized rates. Irrigation facilities are being

developed. The Comilla results are being used in making policy decisions. The Comilla experiment has aroused interest in the minds of many people working on similar problems in other countries.

But there are limitations and problems too. The village cooperatives have covered only about one-third of landowning farmers in the area. Membership in the cooperative societies is growing at a slow rate. It has not been possible to devise a permanent program for the landless laborers, 20 per cent of the total population. A substantial number of cooperative members are still skeptical of the new practices and are bound by strong traditional values. A good system of marketing is yet to be developed. There is an acute shortage of skilled workers. The sense of urgency is lacking in most of the government officers. They are unwilling to take on the role of teacher. The training programs need refinement and more substance. Better management skill is required to maintain the growing sections of the Central Association, especially the storage and processing units. It is hoped that these problems will be solved gradually. But then there will be more problems. The experiment will have to continue for a long time if rapid, sound progress is to be made.

---

5. Professor Schultz has derived similar principles in his recent book [1964].

References

AHSAN, 1964. Nasmul Ahsan, *Loan Utilization by the Co-operative Members of Comilla*, Research and Survey Bulletin No. 3 (Comilla: PARD, 1964).

CENSUS, 1961. *Census of Pakistan 1961*, "District Census Report, Comilla" (Karachi: Ministry of Home Affairs, Government of Pakistan, 1961).

KHAN and HUSSAIN, 1963. Akhter Hameed Khan and M. Zakir Hussain, *A New Rural Co-operative System for Comilla Thana* (Comilla: PARD, 1963).

LUYKX, 1968. Nicolaas M. Luykx, "The Comilla Project, East Pakistan," Paper prepared for International Seminar on Change in Agriculture, University of Reading, September 2–14, 1968.

PARD, 1962. Pakistan Academy for Rural Development, *Annual Report of the Japanese Experts, 1962* (Comilla: PARD, 1962).

PARD, 1963a. Pakistan Academy for Rural Development, *An Evaluation of Rural Public*

Works Programme, East Pakistan, 1962–63 (Comilla: PARD, October 1963).

PARD, 1963b. Pakistan Academy for Rural Development, *Livestock population in Comilla*, Survey and Research Bulletin No. 1 (Comilla: PARD, 1963). (Mimeographed.)

PARD, 1963c. Pakistan Academy for Rural Development, *The Academy at Comilla–an Introduction* (Comilla: PARD, 1963).

PARD, 1964. Pakistan Academy for Rural Development, *The Comilla Pilot Project in Irrigation and Rural Electrification* (Revised edition), (Comilla: PARD, 1964).

RAHIM, 1961a. S. A. Rahim, *Voluntary Group Adoption of Power Pump Irrigation in Five East Pakistan Villages*, Technical Publication No. 12 (Comilla: PARD, 1961).

RAHIM, 1961b. S. A. Rahim, *Diffusion and Adoption of Agricultural Practices: A Study in a Village in East Pakistan*, Technical Publication No. 7 (Comilla: PARD, 1961).

RAHIM, 1964a. S. A. Rahim, *Partial and Full Adoption of Improved Practices in Comilla Co-operatives*, Research and Survey Bulletin No. 8 (Comilla: PARD, 1964).

RAHIM, 1964b. S. A. Rahim, *Yield of Aus Paddy in Comilla Thana*, Survey and Research Bulletin No. 9 (Comilla: PARD, 1964). (Mimeographed.)

SCHULTZ, 1964. Theodore W. Schultz, *Transforming Traditional Agriculture* (New Haven, Conn.: Yale University Press, 1964).

STEVENS, 1967. Robert D. Stevens, "Institutional Change and Agricultural Development—Some Evidence from Comilla, East Pakistan," Agricultural Economics Report No. 64 (East Lansing, Mich.: Department of Agricultural Economics, Michigan State University, April 1967).

CASE STUDY

The ACAR Program in Minas Gerais, Brazil

JOSÉ PAULO RIBEIRO and CLIFTON R. WHARTON, JR.

IN 1948 THE American International Association for Economic and Social Development,[1] at the invitation of the state government of Minas Gerais, Brazil, organized a rural-development program called the Associacao de Credito e Assistencia Rural, usually called ACAR. ACAR was organized as a nonprofit civil society to give assistance to the farm families of the state, mainly through supervised credit and extension-education activities.

The first agreement was for three years, but after the initial period was renewed several times, giving continuity to the organization for the next twelve years. In 1960 AIA and the state government of Minas Gerais decided that the organization was ready to continue on its own, without AIA support.

Five years after its establishment the ACAR program had become recognized as an important example of a successful approach to the problems of rural development [Mosher, 1955, 1957; Brossard, 1955; Wharton, 1958]. The ACAR idea began to be widely copied by several states in Brazil. The first similar organization elsewhere in Brazil was a regional organization, ANCAR, set up in the drought area of northeastern Brazil in 1954. A national organization, ABCAR (Associacao Brasileira de Credito e Assistencia Rural), was set up in 1956 by AIA and the Brazilian national government patterned on the ACAR approach and designed to promote and to service such programs in other states. Many other states developed similar organizations until today there are 15.[2]

The 16-year experience of the ACAR program in Minas Gerais offers a useful case

---

1. The American International Association (AIA) is a nonprofit corporation which was founded in 1946 by Mr. Nelson A. Rockefeller to plan, organize and operate self-help programs in underdeveloped areas [Wharton, 1954]. The ACAR program was only one of AIA's activities in Brazil. AIA also began a similar rural-development program in Venezuela in 1947 [Wharton, 1950].

2. ASCAR (state of Rio Grande do Sul); ACARESC (Santa Caterina state); ACARPA (Paraná state); ACAR-RJ (Rio de Janeiro state); ACARES (Espirito Santo state); ACAR-GO (Goiás state); ANCARBA (Bahia state); ANCARPE (Pernambuco); ANCARAL (Alagoas); ANCARSE (Sergipe); ANCARPA (Paraiba); ANCARRN (Rio Grande do Norte); ANCARCE (Ceará); ACARMA (Maranhão); ACARMAT (Mato Gross). Only the states of Acre, Amazonas, Pará, Piauí, and São Paulo do not have this type of service and are now asking ABCAR to help them to establish it.

study of methods and techniques of planned change for farmers under conditions of semi-subsistence agriculture.

THE AGRICULTURE OF MINAS GERAIS

The state of Minas Gerais is located in south-eastern Brazil between parallels 14 and 23 and had a 1960 population of 9.8 million persons. With an area of about 224,000 square miles, the state is slightly larger than Kenya or France or Thailand.

The altitude varies from 77 meters above sea level up to 2,000 meters. There is similar variation in topography and climate, ranging from high and relatively dry plateaus to hot, humid river valleys. Most of the yearly rainfall is concentrated in the months between November and March, but the state has had sustained droughts since 1949.

Although the state has considerable mineral wealth (hence its name), agriculture is still the largest sector of the state economy and constituted 47 per cent of the revenue of the state in 1960. Despite gradual reduction in the percentage of its population that is rural, over the past 20 years, 60 per cent of its people still live from the land, while the absolute number of rural people has actually increased (Table 13.9).

The total area suitable for agriculture was estimated in 1960 to be 120,000 square kilometers, of which only one-third was under cultivation. Thus the total cultivated area of the state was 39.4 million hectares (hectare = 2.45 acres), located in 372,000 farms, 80 per cent of the farms are less than 100 hectares in size, and slightly over one-fourth are less than ten hectares (Table 13.10).

Table 13.9. Population of Minas Gerais, Brazil.

	Urban	%	Rural	%	Total
1940	1,693,040	25	5,043,376	75	6,736,416
1950	2,320,054	30	5,397,738	70	7,717,792
1960	3,940,557	40	5,858,323	60	9,798,880

The major crops measured by cultivated area in 1962 are corn (1.4 million hectares), coffee (0.8 million), rice (0.6 million), and beans (0.4 million). These four are also the most important crops by value totalling Cr$88.4 billion. However, the most important agricultural product by value is milk, totaling Cr$40.4 billion. In 1962, the state had some 17.2 million head of cattle, 9.3 million head of hogs, and 0.9 million chickens.

Like several other Brazilian states, Minas Gerais has semifrontier and frontier areas that have been gradually moving westward and where farm production is predominantly subsistence. Except in those regions devoted to livestock, the main goal of production is family consumption. This frontier has been moving westward but in the process has left behind areas where the productive capacity of the land has been impaired by unskilled methods of cultivation.

Ten years ago, one could observe:

Many hilly areas, previously forested, have been cut bare and cultivated without contouring, resulting in serious problems of erosion. In other areas, brush is burned off prior to planting, producing added problems of sheet erosion and humus destruction. ... Like the rest of Brazil, Minas Gerais faces the dual problem of exploiting the potential of its undeveloped regions and of adjusting and redeveloping areas that have been badly depleted by previous use. [Wharton, 1958, pp. 29–30]

Table 13.10. Number of Farms and Total Area in Minas Gerais, Brazil by Farm Size in 1950 and 1960 Census

	NUMBER OF FARMS		TOTAL HECTARES	
FARM SIZE (*Ha.*)	*1950*	*1960*	*1950*	*1960*
Less than 10	51,641	100,880	279,852	544,439
Over 10 but less than 100	149,030	199,405	5,908,937	7,513,155
Over 100 but less than 1,000	59,776	66,574	16,378,508	17,933,538
Over 1,000 but less than 10,000	4,989	4,751	10,896,681	10,108,031
10,000 and over	120	106	3,168,543	3,272,750
Area not specified	3	117	—	—
Total	265,559	371,833	36,632,521	39,371,913

The situation is much the same today, and the general process of agricultural development has been further aggravated by the sustained droughts that have become increasingly severe, with only occasional interruption.

In Minas Gerais, as in any other developing area, there are the expected factors inhibiting the more rapid growth of agriculture. There are the usual obstacles in the cultural, institutional, and community conditions of rural areas. The very nature of a technologically stagnant and socially isolated life is a major force creating social inertia and attitudes that are unreceptive to the changes implied by new technology.

The agrarian structure imposes problems along two lines: the large number of farm units that are too small to provide adequate family living; and the number of large farms that are unproductive owing to absentee ownership or defective managerial skill. The problems of low levels of general education are created by a lack of both schools and teachers. Access to educational opportunities is limited, and where available, farm youth rarely continue beyond the third grade or attend classes regularly because of the labor demands on the farm. There are also problems of health. Inadequate sanitary conditions and nutritional deficiencies frequently lead to health conditions below the minimum desirable levels. Endemic diseases, such as worm infestations, are prevalent in the rural areas, and there is a high rate of infant mortality. Lack of knowledge of the most simple principles of hygiene further aggravate the situation. Such are the conditions of life facing the typical small farmer in Minas Gerais.[3]

The agricultural practices of small farmers in Minas Gerais are essentially primitive. Slash-and-burn agriculture is common. Even on a single farmstead, only a fraction of the total land will be cultivated in any year, while the rest recuperates prior to being burned over for use once again. Draft animals are still the main source of farm power. Simple hand tools, such as hoes and sickles, pre-

dominate. Fertilizer is rarely used or, if so, inadequately. The introduction and utilization of new technology is fundamental if the *mineiro* farmer is to raise his productivity and his income.

Credit is another major problem. For most farms, all types of capital are in short supply, and what little credit is available generally goes to the larger farms. The bulk of credit for small farmers flows through private channels[4]—merchants, warehousemen, and affluent neighbors. Credit is usually short term, not exceeding two years, and is used for operational or consumption needs. Credit from such sources is rarely available for long-term investment purchases or used for inputs reflecting improved technology.

Projects in these two areas—technology and credit—formed the basic, initial core of the ACAR program, though its activities quickly broadened into other areas of need.

THE ACAR PROGRAM

OBJECTIVES AND ORGANIZATION

ACAR began in 1948 as a joint cooperative venture of the state government of Minas Gerais and a private nonprofit agency, the American International Association for Economic and Social Development from the United States. Although ACAR became an independent, solely Brazilian agency in 1960, its general objectives have remained virtually unchanged since its inception. The agreement that gave permanence to ACAR, signed in February 1960, says:

In order to second the purposes and efforts of the State Government to pursue the economic and social progress of Minas Gerais and Brazil, and due to the common plans of the Government and of the institutions that are willing to cooperate in the development of its assistance program to the Minas rural population, ACAR will proceed, having as its main objective to intensify agricultural production and to improve the economic and social conditions of rural life. This objective will be accomplished through the continuation of its linked system of:

(a) *Rural Extension* to take to rural families, through direct educational action, the necessary knowledge for the betterment of

---

3. It should be emphasized that there are two other groups of farmers in the state: medium-sized and big farmers, and the large cattle ranchers who, while small numerically, control the sizable land resources, have access to government services, are eligible for credit, and sometimes reach out for new technology [Mosher, 1957, p. 138].

4. An earlier study of a sample of ACAR farms [Wharton, 1958, p. 38] revealed that prior to joining the program, over 60 per cent of indebtedness was to private sources at rates ranging from 22 to 40 per cent per year.

their agricultural and home economics practices, as well as to promote changes in their habits and attitudes as a means to attain better economic, social and cultural levels;

(b) *Rural Supervised Credit* aiming to habilitate technically, economically and socially, small and medium farm families and to better their living conditions through the use of credit based upon farm and home management plans and the techniques imparted during the subsequent supervision.

ACAR's policy and programs are determined by a Board of Directors (see Figure 13.1). The board is made up of two repre-

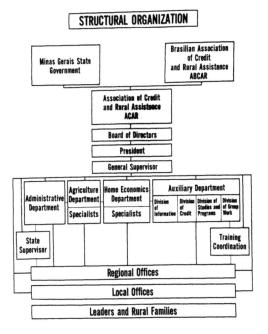

STRUCTURAL ORGANIZATION

Figure 13.1.

sentatives of the state government, one being the President of ACAR; one representative of ABCAR; one representative from the Rural University; and two representatives of the Federal Department of Agriculture (Minas branch).[5] The board responsibilities include approval of the plans of work, the selection of counties where the local offices will be installed, approval of the annual budget, authorization of agreements, and election of the agency's executive officers— president, secretary, and general supervisor.

5. From 1948 until 1960 AIA had representatives on the Board.

The president presides at the board meetings and carries out the board's decisions. The general supervisor executes the ACAR plans, receives funds, prepares and submits to the board the annual budget, prepares the annual plan of work, appoints administrative and technical personnel, and fixes salaries, expenses, and conditions of work. He is also responsible for all preservice and in-service training activities.[6]

The central office is located in Belo Horizonte, the state capital, with a staff organized around four departments:

a. Administrative Department, responsible for personnel, material, accounting, maintenance, purchases, and the like.

b. Department of Agriculture, responsible for the technical part of the program concerning agriculture. It has a staff of subject-matter specialists.

c. Department of Home Economics, responsible for the technical part of the program concerning home economics. It is made up of subject-matter specialists.

d. Auxiliary Department, responsible for program planning, extension methods, evaluation, economics, statistics, information, group work, leadership, educational credit. It is divided into divisions, with specialists in the fields mentioned.

Field activities are carried out by state, regional, and local offices. Under the general supervisor there are state supervisors, with general responsibility for the direction of regional supervisors.

The fourteen regional offices are responsible for the execution of the program in a given region of the state. Each takes care of an average of eight local offices. Every regional office is made up of a regional agricultural supervisor, a regional home supervisor, and a clerk.

Local offices are responsible for the exe-

6. Lack of trained personnel has always been a limiting factor in the expansion of the ACAR program and in the development of similar programs in other states. Since few Brazilian schools of agriculture teach farm management, agricultural economics, sociology, credit, and expansion, ACAR has to do it. The types of training provided are: "pre-service" for those entering the organization, "in-service" for those already in the organization, and postgraduate training for those serving at the Central Office level.

cution of the program working directly with farm families and communities. There are 120 local offices, each staffed by an agricultural supervisor, a home supervisor, and a clerk.

The general policy of ACAR is established in the Central Office, in accordance with federal and state agricultural policies. The program and annual plans of work are developed at the county level by the people served and by the supervisors. The total of local programs furnishes the regional programs that, put together, provide the state program.

In the early days ACAR's finances were provided by contributions from both AIA and the state government. According to AIA philosophy, its contributions diminished progressively while the states increased progressively. Most of the AIA contributions were made in dollars, in equipment, and in technical assistance personnel;[7] while the state contributed in Cruzeiros. When the ABCAR (Brazilian Association of Credit and Rural Assistance) was created in 1956, with the responsibility of preserving on a national scale the work started by ACAR, substantial funds from the federal government were channeled to ACAR. More recently there have been funds from U.S. Agency for International Development.

In 1964 ACAR had a staff of about 550, operating through 14 regional offices and 120 local offices, reaching more than three million people a year through its various activities and projects (see Figure 13.2). The brief history of ACAR's expansion, from a modest beginning with its first three local offices in 1949 to the stage where it effectively serves 180 municipios (counties) out of the state's 722 and 30 per cent of the state population, is a fascinating case study of the evolution of a rural-development project.

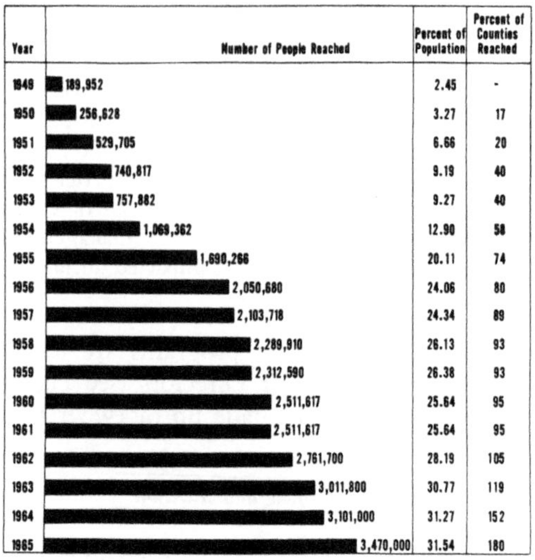

THE PROGRAM

Under its first objective of "rural extension," the ACAR program has developed and operated a fairly wide range of activities: meetings and demonstrations for farmers; 4-S youth clubs; women's clubs; extension county committees; and leadership training projects. All of these educational activities

7. At no period in ACAR's history were there more than three technicians from the United States.

Year	Number of People Reached	Percent of Population	Percent of Counties Reached
1949	189,952	2.45	-
1950	256,628	3.27	17
1951	529,705	6.66	20
1952	740,817	9.19	40
1953	757,882	9.27	40
1954	1,069,362	12.90	58
1955	1,690,266	20.11	74
1956	2,050,680	24.06	80
1957	2,103,718	24.34	89
1958	2,289,910	26.13	93
1959	2,312,590	26.38	93
1960	2,511,617	25.64	95
1961	2,511,617	25.64	95
1962	2,761,700	28.19	105
1963	3,011,800	30.77	119
1964	3,101,000	31.27	152
1965	3,470,000	31.54	180

Figure 13.2. ACAR expansion

were considered by ACAR as tools to promote the dissemination of knowledge and to assist farm people to raise their productivity and improve their life. General extension service is provided to all farmers, regardless of size of farm, financial or social status, or political affiliation. For the large or commercial farmers ACAR provides information and training in farm management practices, new technology, and related matters.

For the small farmer whose capital is insufficient, whose access to credit is difficult, and whose educational level is low, more than extension education is required. ACAR provides "supervised credit," which is considered a tool to accelerate the educational function of extension. The basic philosophy underlying the ACAR approach in supervised credit is the belief that the small farmer, who is numerically the largest, can be helped by the threefold combined provision of credit, supervision in loan fund use, and instruction in improved farming methods, so that he will eventually reach a level where he can continue to increase his productivity on a sustained basis and where he has sufficient internal capital to become more eligible for credit from standard sources.

Extension Education

The number of ACAR activities conducted under "extension education" and the number of persons contacted have grown through the years, until today such activities are reaching a sizable fraction of farm people. For example, in 1964 there were more than 50,000 meetings and demonstrations held on a variety of topics, attended by some 750,000 people.

Throughout its history ACAR has employed most known extension methods— youth clubs, nutrition and health projects, community exhibits or demonstrations, technical bulletins, and radio programs for diffusing innovations, new farm and home practices. Some approaches, such as demonstrations and group work, have been successful; others, like radio and the press, were attempted but did not produce the results expected. Group work with adults through the men's and women's clubs has developed slowly. In the early years it was fairly easy to get women together but not the men; today the picture is changing. Group work with youth through the 4-S clubs, similar to 4-H in the United States, has proven spectacularly successful from the beginning. An example of how newer agricultural inputs are introduced through youth is the corn project. The average production of corn per hectare in Minas Gerais is around 1,300 kilograms, but the youths in the clubs are obtaining yields that are much higher. A state corn contest for youth clubs was begun in 1960. The following are the winning counties for each year and the record yields achieved by the 4-S club members:

1960/1961 Raul Soares County 8,276 kg/ha
1961/1962 Formiga County   11,262 kg/ha
1962/1963 S. João Nepomuceno 9,460 kg/ha
1963/1964 Três Pontas County 8,540 kg/ha

The relative importance of extension education in the ACAR program has grown through the years. Actually, there was an extension component from the very beginning, even though at the outset greatest emphasis was given to the supervised-credit program. Today, however, ACAR tends to function far more as a state "extension service" with a broad role to play and where the agency embraces a wide range of activities. In addition, all activities in any given area are coordinated rather than kept separate [Alves, 1968, p. 89]. But activities are under-

taken only in selected areas within *municipios* (counties), rather than throughout the area. Individual and group activities are concentrated among those farmers and in those areas that seem to provide better prospects for developmental takeoff and that may also serve as points within the *municipios* from which new practices, ideas, and technologies may spread to nonparticipating farmers.

With the advent of the rural extension committees in 1961, the overall ACAR extension approach at the local level became directed in a coordinated fashion upon the predetermined program goals. The committees offered an opportunity for persons participating in various aspects of the ACAR program in each community to offer suggestions regarding community problems and to participate in the determination of programs to help resolve the problems. Such committees, plus participation in leadership groups and adult groups, contributed considerably to the greater involvement of rural people and to their greater experience with community organization for the consideration of community problems.

Supervised Credit

The ACAR program of supervised credit has moved through three phases. In the earliest days the program involved the more traditional approaches of detailed farm and home planning for each farm. As the number of farm families increased, a form of "oriented" credit was inaugurated that did not involve such detailed planning and supervision. Today major reliance is upon the provision of credit to farm families identified as "early adopters."

The traditional supervised credit approach is one where selected farm families receive short-term farm-operating or production loans, combined with individual farm and home planning and supervision of their farm operation during the year.

The typical procedure is as follows: a farmer hears of or becomes interested in the ACAR supervised credit program and requests a visit from the ACAR technicians. The technicians in the local office visit his farm; if the borrower is considered an eligible candidate for this type of ACAR assistance, the technician and the farmer together prepare a farm plan for the coming crop year. This form includes the farmer's assets, his liabilities, last year's production and expenses, the new practices to be followed, crops to be grown, projected expenditures (and the use of the loan funds in this projection), the proposed loan repayment schedule, and expected production and income. This form becomes the basis for the ACAR recommendation of the loan to the bank. If the loan applicant is successful, he then receives, in addition to the loan, visits from the ACAR technicians during the crop year or years of participation.

Supervision and guidance to each borrower family covers general farm and home problems as well as adherence to the planned improvements and to the planned use of the loan funds. The farmer thus receives personal instruction on how to improve his farming practices while the family is taught how to make improvements in the home and family life by a woman technician trained in home management. This dual approach reflects ACAR's underlying philosophy that the factors affecting the human agent such as nutrition, sanitation, and housing are equally important; and that it is not sufficient merely to increase income, but that farm people should be educated in ways of achieving improved levels of living.

Borrowers obtain credit to purchase seeds, fungicides, equipment, and livestock with which to improve their farming operations. These families may also participate in other ACAR projects such as classes, demonstrations, group meetings, and similar educational services. These services, available to borrower and non-borrower alike, include such topics as: advice on trench silos; improved seed; ant-control; cattle spraying and feeding; soil preparation, contouring; food preparation, protection and storage; child and home care; carpentry; and sewing.

The ACAR "supervised credit families" have therefore received three main types of aid from ACAR: (1) farm and home planning; (2) educational visits; and (3) loans. [Wharton, 1958, pp. 49–50]

Over the years ACAR has developed a classification of farm families into three groups which facilitates the work of the supervisor in determining the likely eligibility of a family for supervised credit. One group are farmers who are large, managerially sophisticated, technologically modern, and usually have adequate access to credit. At the other extreme is a second group whose farms are too small to produce minimum subsistence living or to provide a modest base for capital formation, who practice traditional techniques, and who are too deficient in all respects to be able to

take advantage of the program.[8] Most ACAR credit has gone to farmers in the middle between these two groups. Naturally this classification is not rigidly followed, but it does assist the local supervisors in the pre-selection process. (It is also useful in determining the intensity of educational supervision that should be given.) Many other factors are taken into consideration for the selection of families and the approval of loans. Ultimately the loan is approved by a county committee appointed jointly by ACAR and the Caixa Economica (see below). Since available resources and time do not permit assistance to all needy farmers, ACAR has also developed a selection pattern based on the adoption of new practice curves, selecting for credit the families in the group called "early adopters."

After working about 12 years with supervised credit, ACAR also found that many farm families who left the program needed an intermediate type of credit between supervised and commercial. For this reason ACAR established four types of credit, all educational:

a. Supervised credit—intensive action, with families selected among those who have subsistence problems. They must have some potential to respond to credit and preferably be among the early adopters or leaders. The loans are based on farm and home management plans and cover all needs of the farm and the home except purchase of land.

b. Oriented credit—with the objective of the improvement of levels of production, productivity, and income. The loans are made based upon farm management plans, directed to a given crop or livestock operation. The home is not financed. Generally this type of credit is given to families that have left the supervised credit.

c. Housing credit—with the objective of house improvement. The loans are primarily for families who have already increased their income, but families

8. In the earliest phase of the ACAR program the intention had been to include these small, most poverty-stricken farmers. One of the most significant findings of ACAR's first program efforts was that there were farmers too poor to benefit from the ACAR type approach [Mosher, 1955, 55].

with supervised or oriented credit are also eligible.

d. Credit for youth (4-S)—for boy and girl members of 4-S clubs. It is also educational, since supervision is involved.

ACAR does not make the actual supervised credit loans from its own funds but through the Caixa Economica do Estado de Minas Gerais, a state bank, and the Bank of Brazil. ACAR does the planning and educational work. While the bank is responsible for the banking functions, ACAR "recommends" the loans to the bank for approval, and in the early days loans were limited to a maximum of Cr$50,000, though actual amounts in each case are decided on the basis of careful study by the technician and the farmer. Duration is for one to three years, depending on loan use. Today the maximum amount per supervised credit loan is Cr$700,000. The interest rate charged is 6 to 8 per cent per year.

Availability of funds in the Caixa for this program have always been a problem, and the funds available for the program have gradually increased over the years from Cr$1.5 million in 1949 to Cr$25 million in 1955 and Cr$120 million in 1960. In 1964 the situation was alleviated somewhat by a loan from the Inter-American Development Bank to the Caixa of $6.4 million to be used exclusively for the ACAR program and raising the level of available funds to Cr$3 billion.

Until the 1963–1964 crop year, when "oriented" and "housing credit" were introduced, the average number of loans awarded in any year were around 1,300 (see Table 13.11). The loan repayment records of the borrower families has been extremely good. Through November 30, 1964, there had been a 99.95 per cent repayment on Cr$563,275, 830.40 that had matured (see Tables 13.12 and 13.13).

Table 13.11. Number, Amount and Average Size of ACAR Loans Made by Crop Year & Type

Type and Crop Year	Number	Amount	Average	Maximum amount per loan
1. Supervised Credit				
1949/50	118	1,780,295	15,087	50,000
1950/51	318	5,326,295	16,750	50,000
1951/52	371	6,865,900	18,506	50,000
1952/53	322	6,363,000	19,760	50,000
1953/54	355	6,330,100	18,895	50,000
1954/55	645	12,186,450	18,893	50,000
1955/56	1,107	24,113,520	21,782	50,000
1956/57	1,467	32,996,000	22,492	50,000
1957/58	1,284	29,147,675	22,700	50,000
1958/59	1,321	41,304,700	31,262	100,000
1959/60	1,317	61,469,550	48,673	100,000
1960/61	1,204	115,637,740	96,044	200,000
1961/62	1,734	220,801,200	127,336	200,000
1962/63	1,184	202,230,500	170,794	300,000
1963/64	1,508	324,338,100	215,078	500,000
1964/65[a]	815	462,924,500	568,005	700,000
2. Oriented Credit				
1963/64	1,551	1,031,097,000	677,690	1,200,000
1964/65[a]	1,892	1,714,223,135	906,037	1,200,000
3. Housing Credit				
1963/64	44	26,047,000	591,977	750,000
1964/65[a]	83	52,170,000	628,559	1,500,000
4. Youth Credit				
1960/61	23	172,000	7,478	30,000
1961/62	78	831,590	10,661	50,000
1962/63	46	1,058,600	23,013	70,000
1963/64	159	5,141,440	32,336	100,000
1964/65[a]	145	8,637,100	59,566	100,000

[a] Up to December 1964.

Table 13.12. Repayment of ACAR Loans, by Year Through November 30, 1964

Years	Maturity	Payments	Uncollected	Lost	%
1949	—	—	—	—	—
1950	963,050.00	963,050.00	—	—	100.00
1951	4,059,445.00	4,059,445.00	—	—	100.00
1952	5,861,800.00	5,851,300.00	—	10,500.00	99.82
1953	6,697,900.00	6,695,900.00	—	2,000.00	99.97
1954	6,091,800.00	6,091,800.00	—	—	100.00
1955	9,978,650.00	9,976,150.00	—	2,500.00	99.97
1956	19,431,040.00	19,428,540.00	—	2,500.00	99.98
1957	31,891,670.00	31,856,461.40	34,208.60	1,000.00	99.88
1958	33,002,955.00	32,987,955.00	15,000.00	—	99.83
1959	34,611,680.00	34,601,680.00	10,000.00	—	99.97
1960	47,437,450.00	47,437,450.00	—	—	100.00
1961	70,899,510.30	70,899,510.30	—	—	100.00
1962	122,076,670.10	122,016,670.10	60,000.00	—	99.95
1963	170,272,210.00	170,137,210.00	135,000.00	—	99.92
Total	563,275,830.40	563,003,121.80	254,208.60	18,500.00	99.95

THE RESULTS AND ISSUES

From the very beginning the ACAR program included provision for a statistics and research unit that was the basis for on-going study and evaluation of the program. Therefore there is a wealth of data on the ACAR experience, and several detailed studies of the activities of ACAR and of its impact have been made. As would be expected, the credit program has received the greatest attention.

Since greatest research and analysis have been made of the ACAR credit program, the critical review will be limited to this dimension. However, it must be reemphasized that ACAR is much more than solely a credit program and that today it would more properly be viewed as a rural development service within which credit is an important, but not dominant, part.

Three criticisms have perennially plagued the ACAR credit program: the "subsidy" rates of interest; the cost of the program; and the actual impact of the program on farmer and state production and productivity.

The Interest Rate "Subsidy" Issue

The interest rate charged on ACAR loans range from 6 to 8 per cent, and there is a legal ceiling on loans of 12 per cent per year. Since Brazil has had a chronic inflation for an extended period, these rates constitute a significant "subsidy." For example, from 1939 through 1953 the general price index for Brazil proceeded at the rate of 12 per cent per year. During the 1950's the rate of inflation fluctuated between 15 and 25 per cent, but by 1964 it had reached a peak of 120 per cent per year. At such rates of inflation, persons securing ACAR loans were in effect securing credit subsidies in real terms [Wharton, 1958, 34, 39–41]. Interestingly, when the ACAR program was first set up, one of the arguments for such credit programs for small farmers was their exclusion from normal banking system, whose rates of 8 per cent were equally negative in real terms and whose loan funds were consequently totally monopolized by larger commercial farmers. There is evidence that prior to the ACAR program the larger farmers were securing their loan funds through organized formal money markets and banks at subsidy rates, while the small farmers were securing their credit from informal and unorganized sources at rates that were 10 to 28 interest points higher. Provision of loans to ACAR farmers, therefore, had some merit in providing them with a "share of the pie" also at subsidy rates. Another justification for these subsidy rates in the case of the smaller farmers served by ACAR related to their risk sensitivity, because many are so close to subsistence levels of living. The loan enables the farmer to adopt a new practice or technology that involves an additional cost, the subsidy rate encourages him to try it, and the supervision provided gives him added technical backstopping with the new practice.

Table 13.13. Repayment Record of ACAR Borrowers, by Income Classes

BY GROSS INCOME	REPAYMENT RECORD AS OF			
	END OF 1ST YEAR		END OF 2ND YEAR	
	No.	%	No.	%
I. Under Cr$20,000:				
No delay in payment	37	82.2	33	73.4
Up to 1 month delay	5	11.1	10	22.2
More than 1 up to 2	1	2.2	1	2.2
More than 2 up to 3	2	4.5	1	2.2
Total	45	100.0	45	100.0
II. Cr$20,000 to Cr$40,000:				
No delay in payment	34	85.0	30	75.0
Up to 1 month delay	3	7.5	5	12.5
More than 1 up to 2	1	2.5	1	2.5
More than 2 up to 3	1	2.5	4	10.0
More than 3 up to 4	1	2.5	—	—
Total	40	100.0	40	100.0
III. Over Cr$40,000:				
No delay in payment	38	76.0	39	78.0
Up to 1 month delay	7	14.0	10	20.0
More than 1 up to 2	5	10.0	1	2.0
Total	50	100.0	50	100.0
IV. All Classes:				
No delay in payment	109		102	
Up to 1 month delay	15		25	
More than 1 up to 2	7		3	
More than 2 up to 3	3		5	
More than 3 up to 4	1		—	
Total	135		135	

But subsidy rates had two other implications: they probably accounted for the continued upward pressure on available loan funds and chronic "credit squeezes," since the rate of interest charged was below the equilibrium level; and they undoubtedly had effects upon the allocation of resources within the farms securing the loans (see below and Alves [1968, 76–78].

The Issue of Program Costs

A second major criticism of the ACAR credit program has been its cost on one of three grounds: (1) the *total* cost of the program divided by the number of supervised credit program families; or (2) the total value of the loans outstanding compared with the *total* cost of the ACAR program (credit plus extension); or (3) the cost per family served under a supervised credit program, compared with the cost per family served solely

by an extension program. The first criticisms are obviously fallacious, since ACAR was never solely a credit program and as costs include noncredit activities as well. If only the true costs of the credit program are measured, then a valid query could be raised regarding the return derived from such an expenditure upon credit, as opposed to extension activities without credit.

In an effort to analyze these criticisms, a careful detailed cost study was made of the ACAR program for the year 1953 [Wharton, 1958, Appendix C]. The regular monthly reports of ACAR technicians on their actual work time spent in each ACAR activity were used to determine the percentage of time devoted to credit. These percentages were then applied to actual total costs for the calendar year 1953, covering central, regional and local offices. The study revealed that such costs represented between 7 and 11 per cent of the value of the loan.

This amount could be viewed as the cost for the "supervision" component in a loan (assuming that the interest rate charges covered the costs of loan administration and collection). If one compares this cost with the value of the total change in annual output per farm not accounted for by changes in factor inputs, and if one views such a cost as an investment in human capital, then one finds that the rate of return on such an investment is 6.5 times (see Table 13.14).

Table 13.14. Cost and Returns of ACAR Supervised Credit Program in Curvelo, Minas Gerais, Brazil.

Proportion of Change in Output:	
Accounted for by change in input	44%
Not accounted for by change in input	56%
Value of total change in annual output per farm not accounted for by change in inputs	Cr$7,800
Average annual costs of assistance program per family	Cr$1,200
Return in increased output per Cr$1 of investment in new knowledge	Cr$6.5

SOURCE: Wharton [1965, p. 226].

NOTE: Curvelo is a semisubsistence frontier area; all costs and returns are deflated and output/input figures are corrected ones; loan funds for the program resulted in purchases of new factor inputs and are reflected by changes in the level of the input index. Changes in output not accounted for by changes in inputs have been ascribed to the new knowledge or practices (technology) that was introduced simultaneously with the loan via farm and home planning and extension education (farm visits) received by farmers during participation in the program.

We have no study on the rate of return for a comparable expenditure for extension alone, as a basis for evaluating the two approaches. However, even with such data, there would be a strong presumption that any analysis would involve nonhomogenous groups, since the credit program and the extension program tend to serve different types of farm families.

The Issue of Program Impact

Has the ACAR program had a significant, visible impact on agricultural production and productivity? Among the farmers served? In the state as a whole? Assessing such impact is difficult enough under the best of circumstances, but particularly complicated in the present case, where the state has suffered chronic droughts. For example, from 1958 to 1962 average yields in the state for rice, corn, and beans showed virtually no change. Does this mean that ACAR had no effect or that it did by offsetting the effect of the drought?

A more meaningful and somewhat easier method of assessing the impact of the program is to study the effect of the program upon the participating farmers.

The first study of ACAR was made by Mosher [1955, pp. 38–47], who employed a number of productivity measures, such as net income and production per hectare secured from the record of borrower families. Since most farmers had participated for only a few years, the results tended to be mixed. But his study of 81 borrowers who had received three or more loans showed a general upward trend in their net worth, especially among subsistence farms.

A second more detailed study was made in 1958 [Wharton, 1958; 1960] of 126 selected borrower families covering the period 1949 to 1954. The study was an attempt to measure rigorously the impact of the supervised credit program (i.e. credit plus extension) over a five-year period, based upon the individual farm family records; 77 of the 126 sampled were semisubsistence-type farmers in an area called Curvelo; the other 49 were in the commercial agricultural area of Uba. Two measures were used to evaluate the impact of the program among the farmers, in the two offices: the changes in their agricultural output through time, and the changes in their output/input ratios through time. The latter was considered a measure of productive efficiency or technological progress. Both of these measures were tested against similar ones for the state of Minas Gerais as a whole and for Brazil as a whole. The index of aggregate output for the ACAR borrowers in Curvelo revealed a growth rate between 21 and 32 per cent per year and a growth rate in productive efficiency between 7 and 16 per cent per year. In Uba, however, the combined growth rate in aggregate output lay between 7 and 11 per cent per year, while productive efficiency decreased at a rate between 3 and 7 per cent per year. When the Curvelo output trends were compared against the state trends or those for Brazilian agriculture as a whole, the results for the semisubsistence area of Curvelo were significantly different. In Uba, however, only one group of farmers proved to be significantly different from the state and national trends. In the case of the efficiency measure of output/input, the differences were more mixed. On the whole, the Curvelo area continued to be significantly different from the state and the national trends, though not as dramatically as in the case of output; while Uba showed little difference. One of the more significant findings of the study was that the technological changes resulting from the introduction via a combination of credit plus extension (i.e. supervision and planning) yielded a return of more than sixfold (see Table 13.14).

Professor Erly Dias Brandao conducted a third major study involving ACAR "cooperators" and "noncooperators" in seven local offices covering the crop year 1956–1957 [Brandao, 1958]. Comparison of various productivity indices showed considerable variability between the two groups as well as between the local offices. However, Brandao's analysis of practice adoption showed that ACAR involvement was significantly related to the adoption of new practices.

Two internal studies of supervised credit families were subsequently undertaken. In 1958 a study was made of 135 borrower families, covering the period 1955 to 1958; and in 1965 a survey was made of 1,727 borrower families. All these studies revealed a consistent pattern of positive change by the borrower families in their productivity, farm income, and net worth, as well as in their levels of living. The improvements that these farm families were able to make on the consumption/social side attest to the effect of the increased income upon the quality of farm living (see Table 13.15).

Table 13.15. Social Improvements among Sample of 123 ACAR Farm Families, Selected Family Living Items.

Improvements	Year before Joining Program	Two years after Joining Program
Number of Farmers	123	123
Privy	23	53
Treated Water	18	65
Well Construction	2	6
Water Inside House	4	12
Construction or Repair of Stove	8	41
Kitchen Improvement	8	37
House Repair	10	36
House Construction	6	5
Sewing Machine Available	36	51
Purchase of Furniture	9	47
Provision of Electricity	7	11
Better Laundry Methods	1	43
Soap Making	17	67
Improved Nutrition	9	50
Food Preservation	—	12

The most recent study of ACAR has been made by Eliseu Alves [1968]. Alves used a measure of economic efficiency comprised of two elements—price efficiency (the relative ability of the firm to maximize profit) and technical efficiency (the relative ability to select the most appropriate technology). These measures were determined from a sample of 60 farmers who worked with ACAR in an area called Senador Firmino and another sample of 60 farmers not assisted by ACAR from the municipio of Presidente Bernardes. His study found that the non-ACAR farmers had a higher level of technical efficiency and a lower level of price efficiency than the ACAR farmers, a result exactly opposite to what one would expect. Alves advances a number of possible reasons for the contrary result, such as noncomparability, memory and enumeration errors, and difficulties in measuring differences in managerial abilities. Of the possible explanations, the one that has the greatest logical and intuitive appeal is the probable impact of the

subsidy rates of interest with ACAR loans in the context of general inflation. At the time of the Alves study the rate of inflation was around 80 per cent. Under these conditions farmers who borrow may be using a goal of asset rather than income maximization [Alves, 1968, pp. 66, 76–78].

In an inflationary environment, the maximization of profits on current account may not be an appropriate optimizing criterion for firms. The point is that firms have both an asset account and a flow account. From the standpoint of the welfare of the individual, what he does on his asset account may be much more important than what he does on his flow account. . . .

In an inflationary situation such as in Brazil, larger gains and losses are to be had by the appropriate or inappropriate investments in assets. The purchase of land as a hedge against inflation is much more important than its use as a factor of production.

The consequence of this to the present study is that technical efficiency may be a relatively unimportant goal of farm people. The capital gains that they obtain from their asset account may dwarf the increases in income obtained from a higher level of technical efficiency. Moreover, if farmers are sufficiently sophisticated to recognize this, the "better" farmers may have very low levels of efficiency, simply because they are concerned only with the accumulation of assets [Alves, 1968, 76–77].

Despite the positive and negative findings of the various studies made, any overall assessment of the ACAR program would conclude that it has been quite successful in a number of ways and in a number of areas. Besides the tangible evidence on the successful impact of the ACAR program, there has been the rapid extension of the program within the state and the adoption of similar programs in other states in Brazil.

SUMMARY EVALUATION

The accomplishments of ACAR did not come easily. As with any program of change, there were problems and difficulties. There were times when the program was hampered by a lack of technicians or insufficient loan funds or half-hearted cooperation from other allied institutions. Nevertheless, the program has proven successful in several respects.[9]

What are some of the factors which contributed to this record and what are some of the lessons that may be gleaned?

First, ACAR approached its task with three critical ingredients—*experimentation*, *adaption*, and *flexibility*. This was true from the very beginning.

ACAR conceived of its job as seeking to promote increased agricultural production and improved levels of living among the farmers served. The ACAR program thus had within its focus both farm production and family welfare goals: it sought to increase the agricultural production and efficiency of participating farmers and to improve their general levels of living.

A general sense of experimentation in approach was introduced at the outset. For example, when the first local offices were opened, they were frequently referred to as "pilot projects" or areas to "demonstrate." the usefulness of the supervised credit approach. Interestingly, this experimental attitude, which was imbued in the Brazilian technicians from the very beginning, continued for quite some time despite the gradual expansion of ACAR into other activities and probably accounts for a great deal of the early success of the program. The technicians in each local office saw themselves as participating in and contributing to an experiment in the dynamics of economic and social change that imbued a strong esprit de corps, a missionary dynamism and a willingness to adapt activities to local needs. (See also Mosher [1967]).

Although the original conception of the program was to transfer the basic approach of the Farm Security Administration (FSA), which had proved so successful in the United States with low-income farmers, ACAR from the outset saw the need to adapt this approach to local Brazilian conditions. Moreover, it was quickly realized that accomplishing the stated goals involved more activities than just supervised credit. Admittedly, supervised credit (and later variations) were always a major activity in the ACAR program. But throughout its life ACAR has always utilized a wider range of change devices than credit—general farm and home extension education, medical care and health education, youth groups, and farm leadership projects. Hence the common image of ACAR as solely a "supervised credit" approach is mistaken and could be misleading in drawing insights regarding its success in coping with the problems of low-income farmers in a developing area. Credit was an important element in the ACAR program, but only one item in its arsenal for promoting development. In fact, a major cause of ACAR's success has been the flexibility employed in selecting the more useful armaments from the available arsenal which might meet the needs and requirements of each specific situation in all its uniqueness. Each approach was initiated with a spirit of experimentation aimed at determining its potential usefulness and at making whatever adaptations seemed necessary to suit local conditions.

Within the limits of its financial and personnel resources ACAR tailors its activities to meet the specific conditions encountered in each of its areas of operation. In an area where farmers are hampered by inadequate credit facilities and inefficient techniques, ACAR places heavier emphasis on its educational and supervised credit programs. Where disease or poor management have reduced livestock herds, ACAR emphasizes the extension type services of vaccination, spraying, and artificial insemination. ACAR intentionally operates in localities whose problems are representative of larger areas. This aspect of ACAR's approach to rural development makes each operational area a pilot demonstration. When successful educational and development methods are devised for several such representative areas, the way has been prepared for a larger-scale operation with proven programs and techniques. This is the feature which makes ACAR an experimental program which attempts to find new methods for the international transfer of techniques capable of stimulating more rapid economic growth. [Wharton, 1958, pp. 45–46]

This lack of rigidity and willingness to experiment in large measure accounts for

---

9. Elsewhere an attempt has been made to set forth certain basic propositions on the critical elements for success in the execution of development efforts at the "village level" [Wharton, 1966]. Interestingly, the ACAR program demonstrates two of them: "(a) that an 'experimental and innovative spirit' be encouraged and maintained at all levels among the individuals involved in the developmental process in recognition of the uniqueness of agriculture's special characteristics; (b) that the organization or institution for change be as insulated as possible from the political process in its early stages" [Wharton, 1966, p. 13].

much of the early success of ACAR. Another interesting flexibility in the program was its gradual recognition that different farmers required different activity approaches. Fairly early in the supervised credit program, for example, it was learned that there was a group of extremely small, low-asset farmers who could not benefit from the program. But such farmers were provided other forms of assistance through the ACAR extension activities.

Second, there was notable *administrative and financial continuity to the program with insulation from the political process.* For example, there has been no change in the two representatives of the state government on the ACAR board since 1951. Yet during that same period Minas Gerais has had four governors of three different political parties. Part of the continuity and stability of the program was due to the assured financial support of an external agency, AIA. In addition, ACAR as a private entity, although operating with federal and state government funds, was viewed as a private entity and experienced little political interference. Outstanding government officials were involved from the beginning and quickly established the status of ACAR as being outside the political sphere. The apolitical nature of ACAR, led to growing confidence in the organization not only among government officials, and legislators but also among farmers. Once the tradition was established, it became reinforcing.

Third, from the very beginning the program *used and trained Brazilian technicians* almost exclusively. As pointed out previously, ACAR never had more than three U.S. technicians at any stage. Utilizing Brazilian technicians, many of whom had no previous experience with credit or extension, meant a slow beginning, perhaps much slower than if greater reliance had been placed upon U.S. technicians. But every effort was made (a) to provide the Brazilian technicians with the necessary in-service training to provide each with the necessary technical skills; (b) to give them the necessary technical backstopping and especially the transport facilities to enable them to reach farm people; and (c) to move them up into supervisory positions as rapidly as possible. This reliance upon Brazilian expertise brought with it its own problems

for over the years ACAR has had great difficulty in keeping its technicians. Other change agencies, both in the state of Minas Gerais and elsewhere, are anxious to hire ACAR technicians because they have received such valuable training and experience. While from the standpoint of national agricultural development such transfers are good, from the standpoint of the organization they contribute to personnel and program instabilities.

Fourth, ACAR has *allowed for organizational and program evolution.* The ACAR program began small and grew slowly. Not only did it work within the limitations imposed by its finances and personnel, but, more important, within the competencies acquired through its cumulative experience. Mistakes were made, but they became lessons. A great deal was learned about what would work and what would not in serving *mineiro* farmers. The role of the research unit, which provided continuing review and evaluation of the program, was most significant. Out of this highly pragmatic approach the history of the ACAR program can be seen to trace an interesting evolutionary path such that the program today in 1968 is quite different from the program and activities of 1948. Some of the change is due to the changing circumstances of the agriculture of the state, but a great deal is due to the lessons learned along the way and the willingness of the organization to make such changes. This capacity for change in response to the lesson from experience and to changing needs may well be a most significant characteristic of successful institutionalized programs of change —change agencies must be willing and able to change themselves.

References

ALVES, 1968. Eliseu Roberto de Andrade Alves, "An Economic Evaluation of an Extension Program, Minas Gerais, Brazil," Unpublished Master's thesis, Department of Agricultural Economics, Purdue University (January 1968).

BRANDAO, 1958. Erly Dias Brandao, "Principios de Administracao Rural que Interessam a um Programa de Extensao e Credito Supervisado," Tese de concurso para provimento efetivo de catedra de Contabilidade e Administracao Rural, Escola Superior de Agricultura da

Universidade Rural do Estado de Minas Gerais, Unpublished thesis, UREMG, Vicosa, Minas Gerais, 1958.

BROSSARD, 1955. Bario Brossard, *Manual of Supervised Credit in Latin America* (Rome: Food and Agriculture Organization, October, 1955).

MOSHER, 1955. Arthur T. Mosher, *Case Study of the Agricultural Program of ACAR in Brazil* (Washington, D.C.: National Planning Association, December 1955).

MOSHER, 1957. Arthur T. Mosher, *Technical Cooperation in Latin-American Agriculture* (Chicago: University of Chicago Press, 1957).

MOSHER, 1967. Arthur T. Mosher, "Administration Experimentation as a 'Way of Life' for Development Projects," *International Development Review*, Vol. IX, No. 2 (June 1967), 38–41.

WHARTON, 1950. Clifton R. Wharton, Jr., "CBR in Venezuela," *Inter-American Economic Affairs*, Vol. IV, No. 3 (Winter 1950), 3–15.

WHARTON, 1954. Clifton R. Wharton, Jr., "Aiding the Community: A New Philosophy for Foreign Operations," *Harvard Business Review*, Vol. XXXII, No. 2 (March–April 1954), 64–72.

WHARTON, 1958. Clifton R. Wharton, Jr., "A Case Study of the Economic Impact of Technical Assistance," Ph.D. dissertation (Chicago: Department of Economics, University of Chicago, 1958).

WHARTON, 1960. Clifton R. Wharton, Jr., "The Economic Impact of Technical Assistance: A Brazilian Case Study," *Journal of Farm Economics*, Vol. XLII, No. 2 (May 1960), 252–67.

WHARTON, 1965. Clifton R. Wharton, Jr., "Education and Agricultural Growth: The Role of Education in Early-Stage Agriculture," in Mary Jean Bowman and C. Arnold Anderson, eds., *Education and Economic Development* (Chicago: Aldine, 1965).

WHARTON, 1966. Clifton R. Wharton, Jr., "Strategies for Rural Development: Selected Propositions on the Planning and Execution of Agricultural Development in Southeast Asia," Revision of paper presented to Southeast Asian Development Advisory Group, Agency for International Development, December 1, 1966. (Mimeographed.)

CASE STUDY

The Rockefeller Foundation Program in Corn and Wheat in Mexico

DELBERT T. MYREN[1]

THE COOPERATIVE PROGRAM[2] between the Mexican Ministry of Agriculture and the Rockefeller Foundation has been hailed as an exemplary case of collaborative effort in agricultural research [Mosher, 1957, pp. 100–126; Schultz, 1964; pp. 148–149; Stakman et al., 1967]. The two crops that received major attention from the very beginning were corn and wheat—two of Mexico's basic food crops. A similar investment has been made during the past 20 years in each crop—

in salaries of research workers, in equipment, in scholarships for advanced training of junior scientists, in extension effort. Yet if the results of work with these crops are measured in terms of the change in yield per unit area on a national scale, one finds a sharp contrast between the two. Average corn yields in 1940 were 626 kilograms per hectare; in 1960 they were 839 kg/ha.[3] Average wheat yields in 1940 were 763 kg/ha; in 1960 they were 1,341 kg/ha. Thus, over the 20-year period corn yields increased 34 per cent, while wheat yields went up 76 per cent— more than twice as fast. The difference

1. I am grateful to Dr. Edwin J. Wellhausen and Dr. Norman E. Borlaug, the scientists who initiated and have guided for two decades the corn and wheat research referred to, as well as to Dr. Elmer Johnson, corn geneticist of the International Center for Corn and Wheat Improvement, for their critical reading and comments on the manuscript. The interpretation of the available evidence is the author's own.

2. Established in 1943 and operated through an Office of Special Studies from 1945 through 1960. Cooperation continues at present through the International Food Crop Improvement Program.

3. The metric system is used throughout this article. For a quick conversion of yield figures, the shelled corn yields in kg/ha can be multiplied by 0.01593 to obtain bushels (55 lbs.) per acre. Use 0.01487 for converting wheat kilos to bushel (60 lbs.) yields. For example, one metric ton (1,000 kgs) per hectare of corn is equivalent to 15.93 bushels per acre.

accentuated from 1960 to 1963, with wheat showing a yield per unit area gain of 54 per cent while corn yields remained about constant.[4] Preliminary figures for 1967 show corn yields well above one ton (1204 kg/ha) —a 44 per cent gain over 1960. Wheat, however, gained substantially more, putting the average 1967 yields for the entire country at 2,800 kg/ha, or 109 per cent above those of 1960 and 267 per cent above those of 1940.

Total production of both crops has also advanced because of an expansion in area. However, the main concern of this paper is with the introduction of improved technology and therefore yield per unit area will be the most relevant measure.

We have in wheat and corn two parts of a single program of directed change which show quite different results. It should be productive to attempt to isolate the components of the why?

Developing The Package of New Technology

EARLY HISTORY OF CORN AND WHEAT

The plant scientists who initiated the cooperative corn and wheat improvement programs in 1943 were dealing with crops that had been grown in Mexico for a long time. Wheat was brought by the Spaniards soon after the conquest and found to be well adapted to the soil and climate of Mexico. Corn is indigenous to Mexico, and evidence has been found of its cultivation prior to 5000 B.C. Natural selection occurred over the years in both crops, resulting in better adaptation of the existing varieties. In all likelihood ample crossing also took place, especially in the case of corn, between local varieties and new ones brought in by traders and other travelers.

From such selection the lines would have been preserved that yielded seed to reproduce themselves and, insofar as man intervened, those that produced the greatest amount of seed for human food. In this way the most productive varieties were developed for the conditions under which corn and wheat were grown. The kind of selection that took place in corn is evident in present-day varieties still grown in various parts of Mexico. Obviously this selection was not directed toward obtaining the highest possible yield under optimum conditions, but rather toward the selection of lines that would yield something even under the worst conditions. The severity of drought and other conditions for which natural selection took place varied greatly from one area to another and consequently led to enormous variety in the native germ plasm found in Mexico.

Assuredly yields must have moved up as the early cultivators of corn, and later those who introduced wheat, learned better cultivation practices through experience. However, as we move into the second quarter of the present century and are able to trace what is happening through statistics collected annually by a government agency, we find both corn and wheat yields nearly static for the two decades from 1925 to 1945. The lowest and highest annual corn yield for 1925–1929 was 513 and 698 kg/ha, and the corresponding figures for wheat were 646 and 729 kg/ha. These moved along together with a slow rate of increase, perhaps owing principally to new fertile land being brought into production, until the mid-1950's, when wheat yields began to move sharply ahead of corn, as can be seen in Table 13.16.

Table 13.16. *Highest and Lowest Annual Average Yields of Corn and Wheat in Mexico by 5-Year Periods, 1925–1964*

	CORN		WHEAT	
	Lowest	*Highest*	*Lowest*	*Highest*
1925–29	513	698	646	729
1930–34	448	633	703	869
1935–39	545	605	708	864
1940–44	491	690	710	815
1945–49	634	761	740	941
1950–54	721	854	863	1,098
1955–59	803	880	1,063	1,592
1960–64	946	1,133	1,471	2,056
1965–67	1,090	1,204	2,400	2,800

SOURCE: Direccion General de Economia Agricola; the 1965–1967 data are still considered preliminary.

4. The first figures are based on census data; the other are data of the Direccion General de Economia Agricola, Mexico. The reporting year for the 1960 census was May 1, 1959, to April 30, 1960, thereby including the principal irrigated wheat harvest of May and June 1959 but not that of 1960. The figures of Economia Agricola cover the calendar year. Therefore, in speaking of yield gains for the most recent four years, the Economia Agricola figures are also used for the base. Wheat yields in kg/ha or 1960–1963 were respectively: 1,417; 1,676; 1,946; 2,187. Corn yields in kg/ha for 1960–1963 were respectively: 975, 993, 995, 946.

It was during this period that the plant scientists who formed the cooperative corn-and-wheat-improvement programs entered the picture. Starting with a one-man Rockefeller Foundation task force in 1943, by the mid-1950's the group had grown to 18 Foundation staff and about 100 fulltime Mexican associates, many of whom had received advanced training abroad under Foundation scholarships. The results of the program are amply documented in annual reports, books, and published papers [Harrar, 1963; Stakman et al., 1967], so I shall not go into a general description of the program. What interests us here is how new knowledge was brought to bear on problems of wheat and corn production and whether there were any important differences between the approaches used on the two crops.

THE RESEARCH APPROACHES ON CORN AND WHEAT

There was actually considerable similarity in the broad outline of attack.

1. A team of outside scientists—made up of a plant pathologist, a geneticist, and a soil scientist—traveled through more than 5000 miles of Mexico's agricultural areas and recommended the approach and general lines of research that appeared to offer most promise.

2. This scientific observation tour led to the selection of certain types of individuals for the research posts. The most serious limitation to wheat production appeared to be stem rust, and recent experience in the United States had suggested that important progress could be made through incorporating genetic resistance. A plant pathologist with a strong genetic background was chosen to lead the wheat-improvement work. For the corn program, where no single disease limitation was evident, a geneticist well versed in the production of the new hybrids that were revolutionizing yield expectations in the corn belt was obtained for the research post. A soil scientist and an entomologist were added to study what appeared to be other serious yield limitations.

3. These specialists had several characteristics in common. They were relatively young. They had top scientific preparation in a field that was judged to have real potential for solving an applied problem. They had previous practical experience, and they were looking for a challenge. Within their persons they were carriers of the best knowhow that had been developed in other areas. Equally important, they knew the main sources from which additional information could be quickly obtained.

4. Young graduates of local agricultural colleges were given specialized in-service training with both the wheat and corn research programs, and the most promising were sent abroad for advanced study, first at the Master's and then at the Ph.D. level. These young local scientists provided additional information links with specialized research programs under way in the United States. As they completed their specialized training, they also perfected their knowledge of English and specialized vocabulary, making the major scientific journals of the world readily accessible to them.

5. Simultaneously a well-organized technical library was established, to assist scientists in keeping contact with latest research methods and theory from other parts of the world.

6. A policy of prompt release of research results was established from the beginning and applied equally to corn and wheat.

There were also differences. As the work progressed and new varieties were ready for release, corn and wheat took slightly different tacks. In the case of the corn hybrids, a governmental organization, the National Corn Commission, was set up in 1946 under the Ministry of Agriculture to handle seed multiplication and distribution. In the case of wheat, where the genotype perpetuates itself unchanged and the only possible problem is mechanical mixing of the seed, multiplication and distribution has been handled mostly by private farmers. The ministry has limited its intervention to the first increase and to a voluntary seed certification program.

The nature of the product was also different. As corn is an open pollinated plant, new seed of the hybrids had to be purchased each year in order to get full benefit of the hybrid vigor. The self-pollination of wheat meant that a farmer could buy a small amount of the new seed, multiply it himself, and then grow it as many years as he wished. But in both cases an effort was made to assure that all interested farmers should receive seed. In relation to this, Dr. Sterling Wortman comments as follows:

I think that there was one additional difference between the wheat and corn programs in Mexico, at least as I recall the situation when I was in charge of corn from 1951–1954. As I look back I realize that in the corn program we primarily had a plant breeding effort under way, not a comprehensive production program of which plant breeding was a necessary part. We were concerned very much with the problem of developing the many varieties of hybrids needed for the great number of ecological situations in Mexico and we carried this program to the point of producing foundation seed for the National Corn Commission. We did not, unfortunately, measure our own progress by what happened to the national average yields of corn in Mexico. Rather we worried about getting enough foundation seed to the Corn Commission to allow it to plant the projected acreage of single crosses for the production of doubles. The wheat program on the other hand was concerned not only with development of rust resistant, high yielding varieties but with seed production, the use of higher amounts of fertilizer, and adoption by farmers. [Personal communication]

In summary, the way of bringing knowledge to bear was on the whole similar for both crops. Has equal research progress been made?

RESEARCH RESULTS: EXPERIMENTAL
AND FARMERS FIELDS

The highest possible yields are a good reflection of the level of technology currently available. In both corn and wheat, not only the research workers, but also farmers have made efforts at different times to obtain maximum yields. Other progressive farmers are using modern technology to obtain a lower level of yields that they consider optimum. If the distance between the two is great, it may be possible to change procedures or costs to raise the optimum level of production without a change in the basic technological components.

Interestingly, the highest-recorded corn yields are well above those of wheat, both on individual experimental plots and where farmers have tried for maximum yields without considering cost. In fact, experience with yield contests has shown that a farmer may give the same care on a larger area that the scientist gives on small plots and obtain similar results. In the case of corn this means special attention to: (1) selecting a fertile piece of land that is level, of uniform quality, and has good drainage; (2) overplant and then thin out by hand in order to obtain an optimum number of plants, uniformly distributed; (3) irrigate with sufficient frequency, so that the plants have an optimum water supply available at all times; (4) use proper fertilizer in excess of usual needs and apply it at intervals, to assure an optimum supply available to the plant at all times; (5) cultivate by hand as needed, to avoid any detriment from weeds.

Providing this kind of care, in 1957 one farmer in the valley of Mexico obtained a yield of 15 ton/ha of dry shelled corn (15.5 per cent moisture content) on 1.7 hectares with the hybrid H-125 [Itie, 1957]. Earlier, in 1950 and 1951, two farmers in the Valley of Mexico had obtained yields of 12.96 tons and 12.20 tons per hectare of dry shelled corn (15.5 per cent moisture) on 1 hectare and 20 hectare lots, respectively, with the hybrid H-1. In 1954 another farmer in the Valley of Mexico, an *ejidatario*, obtained 12 ton/ha on a 4-hectare plot of H-1 (Diaz del Pino, 1957].

An optimum population of corn is crucial for obtaining high yields. In fact, as fertilization is increased, plant population must also be increased in order to get maximum yields [Dag, 1964, p. 95]. For wheat, on the other hand, although much of the same special care is essential, the heavy labor investment in overplanting and hand thinning is not needed because of the plant's tillering ability. For example, in one wheat experiment with 25 varieties, including all of the commercial ones and using recommended fertilization rates, there was no statistically significant difference in yield between seeding rates of 60, 80, 100, and 120 kilos per hectare [Rockefeller, 1958, p. 120].

A top wheat yield in 1957 was about 6.5 tons. The best farmers were getting at the most 6 tons/ha in commercial production. Today the best farmers are getting 8 ton/ha on acreages of 50 hectares and over.[5] The wheat

5. This yield information was provided by Dr. Ignacio Narvaez, wheat specialist of Mexico's National Institute for Agricultural Research; that on corn, which follows, is from Dr. Elmer Johnson, Rockefeller Foundation corn geneticist.

breeders credit the higher level of the top yields to a continuous improvement of yield potential of the new varieties and to the fact that farmers have simultaneously learned to manage more precisely the key factors of production, such as land leveling—which permits more accurate water management—density of planting, timing, and amount of fertilizer application and insect control. However, they estimate that the varieties grown in 1950 would not yield over 3.5 ton/ha today under the very best care. Thus, under optimum conditions the increment attributable to variety changes alone is calculated at 4.5 ton/ha. In addition, the new varieties are an insurance policy against a complete loss from stem rust, such as sometimes occurred with the old varieties.

In corn, the increment in yield because of varietal changes alone is estimated in more modest terms. Where original varieties have been compared in recent years with the best hybrids for a region, the gain averaged about 35 per cent. Interestingly, the evidence indicates that the best obtainable yields with the varieties that existed 20 years ago were substantially higher for corn than for wheat. Even with present varieties and technology for the two crops, it appears that the top level of corn yields is well above that for wheat and probably has been at all times during the past two decades. In other words, it is not the yield ceiling that has kept down average yields in the case of corn relative to wheat.

POSSIBLE EXPLANATIONS FOR YIELD DIFFERENCES BETWEEN CORN AND WHEAT

Based upon experience to date, there are four areas that may offer possible explanations for the differences in yields between corn and wheat.

LOCATIONAL DIFFERENCES AND QUALITY OF LAND

Both corn and wheat are grown on substantial land areas, but the acreage is greater in the case of corn. In 1960 the harvested area of wheat was 846,162 hectares, while that of corn was 6,802,491, or eight times as much.

Much more relevant is the quality of land involved, and here we see an important difference that has resulted from shifts in the predominant locations where the crop is grown. There has been a substantial geographical shift in wheat production. In 1940 the main wheat-producing area, accounting for 43 per cent of the harvest, was the central part of Mexico, especially the Bajio region. The northwest produced 17 per cent. By 1950 the northwest had 30 per cent of the wheat acreage and 38 per cent of the harvest. In 1960 this had grown to 38.5 per cent of the acreage and 46.5 per cent of the harvest. By 1964 the northwest accounted for 54.5 per cent of the wheat area and 71.5 per cent of the harvest.

Because of the expansion in the total area planted to wheat, up to 1960 the percentage reduction of area in the other production regions took place without reducing total area planted. In fact, in Guanajuato of the center and in Zacatecas, Nuevo Leon, Chihuahua and Coahuila in the north there were substantial increases in area planted. By 1964, however, the area planted had dropped off again sharply in the north, especially in the states of Coahuila, Durango, and Zacatecas, as well as in the states of Guanajuato and Puebla in the center region.

A geographical shift in production area might account for an increase in yields if the shift was to better land or from poor rainfall to good rainfall or irrigated areas. There was no indication of such change in the data of the past three censuses, which show 73.4 per cent of the wheat land under irrigation in 1940, 72.3 per cent in 1950, and 68.3 per cent in 1960. However, yearly data since then show a growing predominance of irrigated production. There is a problem in making comparisons here because of a substantial discrepancy between the census data and those of the Direccion General de Economia Agricola. There is reason to believe that the data of the DGEA are more accurate in this case. Theirs show 82.4 per cent of the harvested wheat area under irrigation in 1959, 84.3 per cent in 1960, 87.8 per cent in 1961, 87.4 per cent in 1962, and 89.0 per cent in 1963. According to these same figures, 93.7 per cent of the total wheat harvest was produced under irrigation in 1962 and 95.2 per cent in 1963.

The geographical shift in corn production has been relatively minor, and because of the vagaries of natural rainfall, cultivation, a

Table 13.17 Geographical Distribution of Corn Production Percentage of Area and of Production, by Region for 1940, 1950, 1960, 1964, 1967.

	1940		1950		1960		1964	
	Area	Prod.	Area	Prod.	Area	Prod.	Area	Prod.
Region	%	%	%	%	%	%	%	%
North	23.91	19.77	25.24	21.79	23.70	20.71	19.31	15.57
Gulf of Mexico	9.07	14.24	9.03	11.51	11.22	12.63	15.30	18.32
Pacific North	4.88	6.78	4.84	6.39	5.17	7.74	3.50	4.23
Pacific South	12.80	13.56	16.92	18.10	18.88	18.72	13.51	12.44
Center-High Valleys	20.56	21.13	18.03	17.40	17.19	17.80	16.93	13.13
Center-Bajio	28.78	24.52	25.94	24.81	23.84	22.40	31.45	36.31
	100.00	100.00	100.00	100.00	100.00	100.00	100.00	100.00

The 1940, 1950, 1960 data are from the national census. Those for 1964 and 1967 are preliminary estimates of the Direccion General de Economia Agricola.

larger sampling of years than available at present should be analyzed. There does, however, appear to be a definite increase in both percentage of area and percentage of production in the gulf states and in the Bajio, while the states of the central high valleys have decreased on both counts. There may also have been some decrease in the north (see Table 13.17).

As in wheat, part of the shift has been from low-yield areas to new lands, in this case the gulf states. In addition, the amount of land planted to corn appears to be increasing again in the Bajio, where yields had stagnated at a low level but in the past few years have increased notably (see Table 13.18). In spite of this, the geographical shift in corn production has been of minor proportions compared to that for wheat.

The census figures on crop area lost provide a further indication of the better quality of land used in wheat production. The 1940, 1950, and 1960 data show that the planted corn area that was not harvested varied from 16.1 to 18.0 per cent, while that for wheat

varied from 12.0 to 13.1 per cent. The majority of corn crop failures were due to drought, varying from 9.1 to 14.2 per cent. In wheat, drought was also the leading cause (up to 6.6 per cent) but was followed closely by frost and, in descending order, insects and diseases, flooding, hail, and others.

The tabulation of corn acreage according to natural rainfall or irrigated production is available only from 1959 through 1962. However, during that four-year period there was no obvious shift from one to the other, the percentage of irrigated area being respectively 9.53, 9.17, 9.23, and 9.91, accounting for 17.38, 9.98, 14.74, and 14.95 per cent of the total production. The extent of advantage that could be gained from this kind of shift is evident in Table 13.19.

Clearly, natural-rainfall yields of wheat have not moved ahead of corn. In fact, the yields of corn grown on residual moisture are ahead of wheat. Only in the irrigated area does the scale tip heavily in favor of wheat. This, added to the fact that most of the wheat acreage is now on irrigated land, explains

Table 13.18. Corn Yields by Regions (in Kilograms per Hectare), 1940–1964

Region	1940	1950	1960	1959	1960	1961	1962	1963	1964	1965	1966	1967
North	518	683	733	655	745	734	750	621	914	794	755	631
Gulf of Mexico	983	1,008	944	1,097	1,161	1,059	1,052	1,443	1,357	1,471	1,650	1,650
Pacific North	870	1,044	1,257	1,386	1,282	1,523	1,522	1,324	1,372	1,799	1,217	1,634
Pacific South	664	846	832	939	972	960	964	1,018	1,043	989	917	898
Center-High Valleys	644	763	869	781	764	751	763	629	879	979	934	949
Center-Bajio	534	757	788	884	1,067	1,144	1,140	969	1,308	1,223	1,377	1,664
Mexico as a whole	626	836	839	880	975	993	995	946	1,133	1,124	1,090	1,204

The first three columns are Agricultural Census data, and the others are from the Direccion General de Economia Agricola of the Mexican Ministry of Agriculture.

Table 13.19. Average Corn and Wheat Yields (in Kilograms per Hectare) on Three Types of Plantings Over a Four-Year Period, 1959–1962

	CORN		WHEAT	
	Lowest	Highest	Lowest	Highest
Natural rainfall	772	962	860	972
Residual moisture	1,043	1,463	881	1,002
Irrigated	1,062	1,587	1,447	2,086

SOURCE: Direccion General de Economia Agricola.

much of the difference in average yields per hectare. It does not explain, however, why more of the yield potential of corn is not being realized in its irrigated areas.

THE PRODUCERS OF CORN AND
WHEAT: SUBSISTENCE VERSUS
COMMERCIAL ORIENTATION

Another possible explanation for the failure to exploit the yield potential of corn in irrigated areas might be found by taking a closer look at the people who decide which crops to grow, which seeds to plant, and on what land to plant them—the individual farm operators. Their decisions may be affected by a number of factors—by past experience, by access to new information, by access to markets, by price expectations (which may in turn be stabilized by government), by availability of resources for purchasing new inputs, and by many other factors. But in the final analysis it is the sum of their individual decisions on the adoption of new practices that determines the level of technology used on a national scale in corn and wheat cultivation.

Are there any differences in the kind of decision-makers who grow corn and wheat?

In spite of the fact that numerous farmers grow both crops, the average wheat producer and the average corn producer are indeed quite different. The wheat farmer tends to be the operator of a commercial farming enterprise; he grows his crop under irrigation and sells it, either directly or indirectly, to the millers for processing. Considerable corn is also produced for sale, but the vast majority of farmers who grow corn do so first of all to provide food for the family (often interplanted with beans, in an attempt to assure some production of the two most basic subsistence

crops) and secondly to produce a marketable surplus.

Although we have no accurate figures on the number of farmers who grow wheat and corn, one indication is provided by the 1960 census in a classification of farms by predominant crop. Corn predominates on 748,378, or 54.8 per cent, of the farm units,[6] while wheat predominates on only 28,388, or 2.1 per cent. It is probable that corn is grown on at least two-thirds of the farms by some two million farm families, while wheat is grown by less than 50,000. If so, there are 40 times more corn farmers than wheat farmers, and consequently 40 times as many decision-makers to be reached with information about new production practices. If this is true, it also indicates something about problems of mechanization of the two crops, as the average wheat land per farmer would be about 17 hectares, while the average for corn would be about 3 hectares. These, of course, are rough estimates at best.

The census data, as presented, offer only one clue as to the type of farmers who grow wheat and corn. Acreage data for the two crops is given under a three-way tenancy classification of *larger than five hectares, five hectares or less,* and *ejido.* The percentage of wheat land is least on the small private farms and has tended to drop off from 1940 through 1960. These same farms have more than 80 per cent of their harvested area in corn, and this has tended to move up slightly during the same period. In contrast, the percentage of area in corn among the larger farms dropped off from 71.2 in 1940 to 64.1 in 1950 and 61.4 in 1960. In the *ejido* sector there appears to be a slight percentage drop in both crops from 1940 to 1950 and then a slight rise again in 1960 as shown in Table 13.20.

The corn/subsistence and wheat/commercial distinction, though not wholly appropriate in all cases, does highlight the importance of the shift in emphasis from security to profitability as a farmer moves from subsistence toward greater commercial production or, conversely, in areas of growing rural

6. In this case the census considers each *ejido* a farm unit, even though, as is now usually the case, the land area has been officially parceled and most farming decisions are made by the individual *ejidatarios.* In 1960 there were 18,699 *ejidos,* with 1,597,691 *ejidatarios.* In addition there are 1,346,442 private operators.

Table 13.20. Percentage of Total Farming Area in Corn and Wheat by Farm Class for 1940, 1950, 1960

	1940		1950		1960	
	% in corn	% in wheat	% in corn	% in wheat	% in corn	% in wheat
More than 5 ha.	71.2	7.8	64.1	7.3	61.5	10.7
5 ha. or less	83.6	4.2	86.2	3.5	86.2	3.2
Ejido	67.7	9.6	65.2	6.0	66.3	6.5
Average	70.9	8.3	66.8	6.3	65.6	8.2

SOURCE: National Census data.

population and static technology, a shift to corn in order to have the security of an adequate harvest of the basic food crop. It is evident that whoever grows a crop—an *ejidatario*, a small or a large private operator—does so for economic reasons. As soon as he is in a position to produce something beyond what his family consumes, he becomes concerned with profitability [Myren, 1964]. In this case the relative profitability of the two crops is especially pertinent because corn can be grown successfully wherever wheat is currently produced, although in most places not during the same growing period.

The main problem in getting a fair comparison of relative profitability of corn and wheat under field conditions is the great variation of managerial ability among the farmers who grow the two crops. For this kind of comparison we have to go to the Bajio region, where many farmers grow both crops under irrigation. Data for 1960 from 16 of these farmers show the following average results:[7]

	Corn	Wheat
Total area (ha)	464.00	774.00
Yield (kg/ha)	2,477.74	2,576.87
Value of production (pesos/ha)	2,146.19	2,413.31
Cost (pesos/ha)	2,066.51	2,071.67
Net return (pesos/ha)	79.68	341.64

Twelve had higher returns with wheat and four with corn. On the average, and in spite of the demonstrated higher yield potential of corn, these farmers achieved greater average profits from wheat than from corn. Costs were nearly identical, and the difference in profit was due principally to yields and the higher support price for wheat.

7. Based on data provided by the Departamento de Economia Agricola, Instituto Nacional de Investigaciones Agricolas, Mexico.

Since then, however, two important changes have taken place. On the one hand the corn guarantee price has been raised from 800 to 940 pesos per ton, while wheat has remained at 913 in the Bajio, drastically changing the relative profitability of the two. (During the past four years the guarantee price for wheat in the northwest has been adjusted downward to permit sales on the world market at a relatively small loss for the price-support agency.)

Another interesting and closely related factor has been the influence of commercialism when linked with a technology that required continual change. In the case of wheat, initial success coupled with an ever-changing technology contributed to the development of farmer entrepreneurs who began to look to agricultural science as a handmaiden in their mastery of nature.

Undoubtedly the precondition for the takeoff in wheat yields was the water-resources policy of the Mexican government, which was responsible for constructing the dams and canals for irrigating the desert valleys of the northwest coast. The initial breakthrough in wheat improvement was made by the scientists who found that they could produce varieties resistant to steam rust, thereby providing insurance against the heavy losses that sometimes occurred with existing susceptible varieties. This stimulated the farmers to make heavier investments in fertilizer and in equipment for better land preparation, as well as to give greater care to the crop, especially in applying irrigation. It also stimulated public and commercial investment in farm credit, machinery, and fertilizer distribution. With readily available inputs and assurance of higher yields, the irrigated area planted to wheat expanded rapidly.

It turned out, however, that the production

of improved varieties was to be a continuing battle. The races of stem rust have shown remarkable talent at hybridization and mutation, producing new races that again and again have threatened wheat harvests, especially in the northwest, where production was expanded most rapidly. Fortunately the research program has anticipated this eventuality and has been able to quickly offer new varieties.

As farmers continued to increase fertilization rates, another problem appeared—serious yield limitations because of lodging. To contend with this, dwarf varieties incorporating the Japanese Norin strain were developed.

In the process of fighting stem rust and lodging, farmers have changed varieties at least a half a dozen times. In one case a single new variety came to dominate more than 90 per cent of the total area planted to wheat within three years after its introduction. Other varietal changes have been as rapid but have been distributed among several varieties with similar yield potential. Over the years farmers have profited by, and then discarded, the Kentanas, the Chapingos, the Gabos, the Yaquis, the Tolucas, the Lermas, the Lerma Rojos, and the Nainaris. More recently there has been a rapid shift to the dwarfs and semi-dwarfs—first the Pitics, Penjamos, Mayos, Sonoras, Nadadores, and Lerma Rojo 64, and now the 66's Tobaris, Jaral, INIA, Noroeste, Siete Cerros, Norteño, CIANO, Azteca, and Bajio—which today account for most of Mexico's wheat acreage.

Through the necessity of rapid change (where a new race of rust would cause disastrous results) farmers have learned much about wheat genetics. More important, they have developed an acute awareness of the possibilities of agricultural science for producing useful results and have come to view change as an expected and normal thing in their operations. In much the same way that North American farmers compare new models of automobiles, those of northwestern Mexico talk about the relative merits of the new wheat varieties. The experiment station has replaced tradition as the source of guidelines for agriculture. Now technology has helped to develop a "new breed" of farmer in the case of wheat. Corn was not so fortunate.

THE TECHNICAL DIFFERENCES BETWEEN CORN AND WHEAT

Perhaps the most important explanations for the differential success of corn and wheat lie in the technical differences between the two crops.

First is the fact, already mentioned, that in the case of wheat there was a serious yield limiting factor, in the form of stem rust, that could be effectively removed by plant breeding, thereby offering a dramatic yield increase at practically no cost to the farmer through the use of new seed. A single yield-limiting factor of this type was not present in corn.

Second is the lesser geographic and ecologic adaptabilities of hybrid corn, versus the improved wheat varieties. While the same varieties of wheat have given excellent results throughout the country, and in fact also in Pakistan, India, Egypt, and other countries [Borlaug et al., 1964; CIMMYT, 1967], the corn hybrids have had a more limited area of adaptation. Part of this is related to temperature. In Mexico wheat is grown in the high valleys in the summertime and in the other principal producing regions—El Bajio, La Laguna and the northwest coastal plain—in the winter, so that the temperature is somewhat similar in all cases. However, breeding methods have also influenced the development of varieties with very wide adaptation. Mexican wheat varieties have been among the highest yielding at locations from 0 degrees to 50 degrees latitude, over a wide range of longitudes, and under both irrigated and natural rainfall conditions. This is due in part to their insensitivity to changes in day length and date of planting and is in sharp contrast to the Canadian and northern United States spring-wheat varieties, which are all very sensitive to changes in day length [Borlaug, 1965].

The Mexican wheat varieties also differ from the corn hybrids in this sense. Although the best corn hybrid developed for natural rainfall plantings at sea level on the Gulf Coast is also the best one available for irrigated production at sea level on the northwest coast 3,000 kilometers away, this breadth of adaptation is not common. In order to obtain hybrids that yield better than local native varieties, it has generally been necessary to develop them for specific climatic conditions.

In most of Mexico corn is produced under natural rainfall and is grown during the June-to-October rainy season. The temperature during this period is much lower on the mountain slopes and in the high valleys than it is in the coastal areas. As the corn hybrids are very sensitive to temperature, this means that many different varieties or hybrids are needed in order to have one with optimum production potential for each situation. At the cool temperatures of high altitudes the best tropical variety develops extreme vegetative growth and takes nearly 12 months to mature, extending well beyond the frost-free period and the normal rainy season. As a result, there are still many areas of Mexico for which improved varieties or hybrids have not been developed. The present situation on hybrid corn use is reflected in the national census data (Table 13.21).

Table 13.21. Selected Measures on Use of Improved Corn Varieties on a National Scale, 1940, 1950, 1960

	1940	1950	1960
Average yield (kg/ha)			
Common variety alone	664	812	841
Common varieties inter-planted with beans	486	666	636
Improved or Hybrid	a	1,621	1,471
Over-all average	626	791	839
Proportion of area in improved or hybrid corn	a	0.64%[b]	4.54%
Proportion of harvest from improved or hybrid corn	a	1.34%[b]	7.96%

[a] Not available for planting in 1940.
[b] Based on only the *ejido* and larger than 5-ha farms. The subdivision by kind of corn planted was not included for farms of 5 ha and under in the 1950 Census.

On the irrigated corn land a much higher percentage is planted to improved varieties and hybrids, as shown in Table 13.22. Less than 8 per cent of the land planted to native varieties is irrigated, in contrast to 32 per cent

13.22. Irrigated Land as Percentage of Total for Three Types of Corn Plantings

Common varieties alone	8.43
Common varieties interplanted with beans	6.15
Improved or hybrid	31.83
Average, all corn	9.14

SOURCE: 1960 Census Data.

for improved corn. The corn hybrids have made an impact under good rainfall as well as irrigated conditions, but they have received by far the greatest acceptance for planting under irrigation.

Incidentally, the census comparison of the average yield of the improved varieties or hybrids with that of the native varieties may give a misleading impression of their relative merits. Hybrids show a distinct advantage, but not of the magnitude suggested by the census data, which does not show the higher percentage of irrigated land among hybrid plantings. This is pointed out, perhaps a bit too strikingly, in the data (Table 13.23) from a marginal rainfall area in the Bajio region, collected from farm operators in four municipios near Celaya, Guanajuato, and covering the period from November 1, 1959, to October 31, 1960.

We can move another step closer to seeing the actual benefits from improved corns under field conditions by comparing fertilized-irrigated hybrid with fertilized-irrigated native corn. Although we are dealing with small numbers here, Table 13.24 is at least suggestive of what happens.

Using these same figures as a basis for calculation, it appears that the cash return, after subtracting the cost of fertilizer, is nearly twice as great for fertilizer applied to hybrid as to the native varieties. On the average, the 9 native plantings received more fertilizer per unit area than the 15 hybrid plantings, but the hybrids yielded 450 kg/ha more, suggesting that where an adapted hybrid is available, it offers important yield potential.

So in corn growing we begin to see three basic systems of production, two of which overlap to some extent. At the one extreme we have typical subsistence farming, with native varieties interplanted with beans. At the other extreme we have the hybrids, seldom interplanted, frequently grown under irrigation, and usually fertilized. In between is the large number of farmers who still grow native varieties without interplanting and in many cases attain considerable success on irrigated land through adequate fertilization. A few others may plant hybrids for certain purposes and native varieties for others.

In the main producing areas, the recommended corn varieties have changed three or four times during the past two decades, and a

Table 13.23. Comparative Data on Corn Production Under Natural Rainfall and Irrigation for Selected Farmers in Bajio Region[a]

| | NATURAL RAINFALL | | | | IRRIGATED | | | |
	No. of cases	Area harvested (ha)	Production (kg)	Yield (kg/ha)	No. of cases	Area harvested (ha)	Production (kg)	Yield (kg/ha)
Native corn interplanted	47	489.0	135,795	278	1	3.0	1,000	333
Native corn alone	24	496.5	180,072	363	16	480.5	1,144,700	2,382
Improved corn or hybrid[a]	7	235.5	98,750	419	18	385.0	1,158,970	3,010
	78	1,221.0	414,617	340	35	868.5	2,304,670	2,654
Improved corn or hybrid as % of total		19.29	23.82			44.33	50.29	

[a] This covers all plantings that farmers indicated as hybrid, including those from seed saved from previous hybrid plantings. In this area of low precipitation, only 8 9% of the natural rainfall plantings were entirely or partly hybrid, in contrast to 51.4% for the irrigated plantings.

number of progressive farmers have promptly followed the recommendations. Other farmers have benefited indirectly from new germ plasm introduced to an area through hybrid plantings and distributed by natural crossing with native varieties. The majority, however, have still to plant their first hybrid.

A third major technical factor favoring the rapid adoption of the new wheats has been the ready availability of good seed. When necessary, phenomenal increases have been obtained from small initial quantities of seed. On a trial basis Dr. Norman E. Borlaug, wheat scientist of the Rockefeller Foundation, has shown that it is possible to start with as little as 200 grams of seed and increase it to 150 tons within one year by using adequate fertilization, watering, spacing, and care. The 200 grams were seeded on October 5 and yielded 19 kilos in late February. Six kilos of this were set aside and the remaining 13 seeded at a rate of 8 kg/ha in the first days of March. A total of 3.8 tons were harvested on

June 15 and immediately transported from the northwest to the Bajio, where 3.5 tons were seeded on June 18. This was seeded at a rate of 100 kg/ha on 35 hectares, and 150 tons were harvested in October, in good time for winter plantings. In going from 200 grams to 150 tons, the seed supply is increased 740,000 times in one year. Two additional increases would provide more than all of the 80,000 tons of seed wheat used annually in Mexico.

The improved wheat varieties also have the advantage that the genotype maintains itself for an indefinite period. This means that if wheat seed is made available to 20 farmers, from the following harvest they can in turn distribute to 20 or 30 more, until all have seed. Each farmer in effect becomes a secondary distribution center. Open pollinated corn varieties can be increased even more rapidly. But with the hybrid corns the farmers must go back each year to the original source to obtain seed possessing the hybrid vigor (see Figure 13.3). As a result, the adequacy of

Table 13.24. Comparative Data For Different Methods of Irrigated Corn Production. Bajio Region, 1960

	Fertilized-irrigated native (9)	Fertilized-irrigated hybrid (15)	Nonfertilized-irrigated native (8)	Nonfertilized irrigated hybrid (3)
Harvested area (ha)	386.5	366.5	97.0	18.5
Production (kg)	998,500.0	1,111,170.0	147,200.0	48,800.0
Yield (kg/ha)	2,583.4	3,031.8	1,517.5	1,688.3
Fert. Cost pesos/ha	438.68	296.27	—	—
Fert. Cost pesos/ton corn	169.80	104.40	—	—

Based on data of the Departamento de Economia Agricola, Instituto Nacional de Investigaciones Agricolas, Mexico.

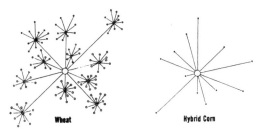

Wheat   Hybrid Corn

Figure 13.3. Seed distribution patterns

distribution depends heavily, in the case of Mexico, on a single seed multiplication agency.

The advantages of hybrid corn are based upon the hybrid vigor of specific crosses between selected genotypes. If the farmer replants this seed, he can expect a 15 to 20 per cent reduction in yield, giving a result only slightly better than that from an unimproved variety. This means that the double-cross hybrids needed to cover the different climates of Mexico must be produced anew each year, requiring an enormous seed multiplication and distribution network. Whether this network is made up of many private firms or is government-operated, as in Mexico, it must function at a high level of efficiency. It has basically two responsibilities: maintaining consistent high quality in the seed produced, and assuring that sufficient seed is readily available to all interested farmers.

On the first score, the task is to deliver to the farmer seed of the same quality and with identical yield potential as that produced originally by the plant breeder. This is not an easy task because of the complex seed-increase process involved in hybrid production.

The second problem is to make seed available to farmers in all parts of Mexico. Availability in this case must include price, location, timing—everything that makes the seed readily accessible to the farmer. The fact that a hybrid is available at certain times and places does not necessarily make it accessible to a small farmer without a vehicle who lives far removed from the seed outlets.

A more ample distribution network, combined with greater seed production, would undoubtedly result in greater use of hybrids. Yet if distribution has been a limitation on the benefits that Mexican farmers have realized from the corn hybrids, there are many extenuating circumstances. In fact, precisely because of this difficult distribution problem, the corn breeders are today working seriously toward the development of improved open-pollinated varieties with equivalent production potential. They feel now that in many of the developing countries it will be easier to change the breeding procedures than to attempt to surmount the difficult problems of multiplying and distributing hybrids. At some later time, when the greater development of various aspects of national economies permits adequate organization of hybrid seed increase and distribution, the gains obtained through varietal selection may serve as a basis for even more productive hybrids.

THE ROLE OF INFORMATION AND EXTENSION: ILLITERACY AND UNCERTAINTY

Even if measures are developed to cope with or to offset the important technical differences, there still remain the important problems of communication and extension of the new knowledge. What special information or extension activity is necessary to convince farm operators to make the desired changes? Obviously, in the first place the farmer must know of the existence of the new variety or new practice. He also needs other kinds of knowledge. He needs to know if the new varieties are adapted to his locality and his farm, and where he can buy seed and under what conditions. Beyond that, he needs specific instructions on cultivation practices in order to get the maximum good out of the new varieties.

In the case of wheat, where the growers were concentrated in a few rather well-defined areas, an important part of this work was undertaken by the research scientists. When a new variety was ready for increase, the breeders gave small quantities to both *ejidatarios* and private operators, but only under the condition that they would follow a strict set of cultural practices to guarantee a maximum increase and at the same time make a convincing demonstration for their neighbors. In this way the new wheat varieties served as a wedge to introduce a whole package of new practices, the most important of which were adequate fertilization and water management. The experiment station personnel have also taken the initiative to reach farmers through well-organized field days and through yearly publication of four regional bulletins, giving specific recommendations on varieties and cultural practices. These, in turn, have usually been reprinted in full in regional newspapers. In addition, the dramatic increases in yield which were obtained caused the message to spread by word-of-mouth. No large-scale extension effort was needed to bring about the yield increases that we have seen in wheat.

In the case of corn, the research workers have also participated in experiment-station field days, published regional farmers' bulletins, and collaborated closely in training extension agents. The Mexican government set up an emergency plan in 1954 to stimulate corn production in the Bajio, and this was expanded into a national extension program in 1955. Within recent years this national extension program has taken the initiative in promoting corn production campaigns in the major corn-producing states of Jalisco and Veracruz. This initiative, tying together technical assistance with credit and easier availability of new inputs, such as improved seed and fertilizer, is generally considered to

have had creditable results. However, because of the variability of natural rainfall the impact is hard to measure, as can be seen in Table 13.25. If we take 1964 as our basis of comparison, Jalisco looks especially good; if we take 1963, Veracruz looks much better. When compared to 1957, both gained more than the national average in 1963, but Veracruz gained less in 1964. Tentative data for the past three years appear to indicate greater gains in Jalisco.

If we look specifically at the corn hybrids, we must conclude that they have not played the same key role as the improved wheat varieties, which were essential as insurance against the attack of stem rust. The corn hybrids have performed an important supporting role in attaining the maximum return from relatively heavy investment in fertilizer.

Whatever the progress up to now, it is clear that the problem of communicating with the numerous decision-makers who grow corn is much greater than for wheat. Although in certain irrigated areas many of the same farmers grow both corn and wheat, on the average the corn producer is a quite different person than the wheat producer. A general indication of this can be obtained from the 1960 population census. In the state of Sonora, which produces very little corn

Table 13.25. Comparison of Corn Yields for Jalisco, Veracruz, and Mexico for Selected Years 1940–1964[a] (in kilograms per hectare)

	Jalisco	Veracruz	Mexico as a whole
1940	549	1,050	626
1950	731	1,069	791
1957	1,052	1,085	835
1958	916	958	828
1959	1,250	1,158	880
1960	1,378	1,214	975
1961	1,464	1,085	993
1962	1,450	1,086	997
1963	1,340	1,590	946
1964	1,683	1,432	1,113
1965	1,679	1,600[b]	1,124
1966	1,828	1,650[b]	1,090
1967	2,046	1,650[b]	1,204
Percent Increase			
1957 to 1963	127	147	113
1957 to 1964	160	132	136
1950 to 1964	230	134	143
1940 to 1964	307	136	181

[a] The 1940 and 1950 data are from the National Census. Yearly data are from the Direccion General de Economia Agricola.
[b] Preliminary data, Direccion General de Economia Agricola.

and nearly three-quarters of the wheat, 66.5 per cent of the rural adult population (20 years and over) is literate. By contrast, in the two main corn producing states, Jalisco and Veracruz, literacy among the rural adult population is only 36.0 and 43.4 per cent, respectively.

In other areas where the rainfall varies around the bare minimum needed to produce a crop, the corn producers have a similar level of education. The data for the farmers without irrigation in Table 13.26 is indicative. Whereas there is no illiteracy among the farmers who operate more than 10 hectares of irrigated land, 44 per cent of those who operate only under natural rainfall conditions can neither read nor write. Incidentally, all of the farmers in this sample grow corn, and 86 of the 103 grew it every year during the 1950–1960 decade.

In spite of these deficiencies in formal schooling, all but nine of the farmers knew about hybrid corn. Nevertheless, of the 94 who were aware of hybrid corn, only 41 had planted it. At first glance this looks promising, as we know that farmers usually go through several steps in the adoption process, including: (1) initial knowledge of the practice; (2) acceptance of the practice as a good idea; (3) testing of the practice on their own land; and (4) full adoption of the practice once they are convinced of its usefulness. It appears that we have a large group in steps 1 and 2 who may soon become adopters. In fact, there is some support for this interpretation in the following chart (Figure 13.4) showing the number of persons who planted hybrid in each of the past ten years [Reding, 1963].

In spite of the slow increase, this does look like the beginning of a typical S-shaped

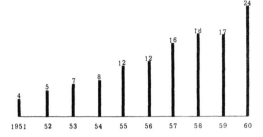

Figure 13.4. Number of farmers who planted hybrid corn from 1951 to 1960. Sample of 103 private operators in four municipios near Celaya, Gto.

adoption curve. Some doubt, however, is cast by the large number of persons who have planted hybrid on their own land and then discontinued its use after supposedly forming an opinion on its adaptability to their particular farms. In 1960 this group represented 41.5 per cent of all who had planted hybrid. This group will probably also have its influence on those who have not as yet tried hybrids.

Those who have used hybrids continuously since the first time they tried them are also frank in listing disadvantages, such as complaints about the condition of the seed that they purchase; however, they insist that the advantages more than compensate. The principal advantage that they list is higher yield, followed by others, such as that it matures more evenly and has more uniform plant and ears, better drought resistance and better tolerance of excess water, has a better market, heavier grain, commonly produces two ears per stalk, does not lodge, has less plants with no ears, and so forth.

There is no strong indication here that illiteracy or other impediments to the flow of

Table 13.26. Comparison of Educational Levels of a Sample of Farm Operators According to Size of Acreage Irrigated

| | | (ACREAGE IRRIGATED) | | |
EDUCATION OF FARM OPERATOR	*None*	*10 ha or less*	*10.1 to 50.0 ha*	*50.1 ha or more*	*Total*
Illiterate	22	4	0	0	26
Learned by himself or only a few months in school	11	8	3	4	26
1 to 4 years schooling	11	5	7	4	27
5 years or more	6	1	6	11	24
Total	50	18	16	19	103[a]

[a] Sample of private farm operators in four municipios near Celaya, Gto.

knowledge are holding back corn yields. The most basic limitation is the uncertainty of both the quantity and the distribution of the rainfall.

In the earlier Table 13.23 we saw that 78 natural rainfall plantings with 1,221 hectares of corn produced less than one-fifth as much as the 868.5 hectares in 35 irrigated plantings. In this type of area with serious rainfall limitations, it is doubtful that corn production will ever be a profitable enterprise, even with the best foreseeable drought-resistant varieties. Yet farmers continue to plow and plant each year, with no investment except their own labor and seed, in the hope that this year will bring good rainfall and a good harvest. Obviously this is not where the yield increases are going to be made; but until these farmers find better alternatives for their labor, they will continue to plant corn. For this group, cultivation practices and yields will not be greatly influenced by whether or not there is good communication of information.

Even in the areas with more adequate rainfall, it is likely that the slow adoption of improved practices is related more to the uncertainty and risks involved than to lack of information about existence of new practices. The success of extension programs will likely depend heavily on the degree to which they help the farmer reduce the risk which he faces in trying something new [Myren, 1964].

An attempt has been made to evaluate the impact of new technology on corn and wheat yields in Mexico over the past two decades. In comparing the many aspects that have influenced yields at the farm level, it has been possible to focus on a number of factors that have determined relative success at different points. It is hoped that this type of comparison may begin to lay the groundwork for a set of more general guidelines or principles for future programs aimed at raising the levels of crop production.

References

BORLAUG, 1965. Norman E. Borlaug, "Wheat, Rust and People," *Phytopathology*, Vol. 55, No. 10 (October 1965), 1088–98.

BORLAUG, et al., 1964. Norman E. Borlaug, et al., Reports of the Near East-American Spring Wheat Yield Nurseries. Miscellaneous reports 4 and 5 of The International Center for Maize and Wheat Improvement (Mexico: 1964).

CIMMYT, 1967. Centro Internacional de Mejoramiento de Miaz y Trigo (International Maize and Wheat Improvement Center), *1966–67 Report* (Mexico City: CIMMYT, 1967).

DAG, 1964. Direccion de Agricultura y Ganaderia del Estado de Mexico, Campo Agricola Experimental Santa Elena, "Informe de Labores, 1958–63," Instituto Nacional de Investigaciones Agricolas, SAG, Toluca, 1964.

DIAZ DEL PINO, 1957. Alfonso Diaz del Pino, "Como Obtener Doce Toneladas de Maiz por Hectarea," *Tierra*, Vol. XII, No. 9 (1957).

HARRAR, 1963. J. G. Harrar, *Strategy for Conquest of Hunger* (New York: The Rockefeller Foundation, 1963).

ITIE, 1957. C. Gabriel Itie, "Quince Toneladas de Maiz por Hectarea," *Tierra*, Vol. XII, No. 12 (1967), 1053–55.

MOSHER, 1957. Arthur T. Mosher, *Technical Cooperation in Latin American Agriculture*, (Chicago: University of Chicago Press, 1957).

MYREN, 1964. Delbert T. Myren, "The Role of Information in Farm Decisions under Conditions of High Risk and Uncertainty," in Delbert T. Myren, ed., *Proceedings of First Inter-American Research Symposium on Role of Communications in Agricultural Development*, Mexico City, Mexico, October 5–13, 1964 (Mexico City: Imprenta Venecia for the Rockefeller Foundation, 1965).

REDING, 1963. Jesus Martinez Reding, "La Difusion y Adopcion del Maiz Hibrido en Cuatro Municipios del Edo. de GTo," Professional thesis (Mexico: Escuela Nacional de Agricultura, 1963).

ROCKEFELLER, 1958. Rockefeller Foundation, Director's Annual Report, Mexican Agricultural Program, September 1, 1957–August 31, 1958, (New York; Rockefeller Foundation, 1958).

SCHULTZ, 1964. T. W. Schultz, *Transforming Traditional Agriculture* (New Haven, Conn.: Yale University Press, 1964).

STAKMAN, et al., 1967. E. C. Stakman, et al., *Campaigns against Hunger* (Cambridge, Mass.: The Belknap Press of Harvard University Press, 1967).

V

Research Priorities
on Subsistence Agriculture

CHAPTER

14

The Issues and a Research Agenda

CLIFTON R. WHARTON, Jr.

THE MAJOR PURPOSE of the conference was to provide an opportunity for interdisciplinary exchanges in order to determine the major issues and to arrive at some general consensus on the priorities for research that might help attack the problems of developing subsistence agriculture. Although the exchanges were at times difficult, a number of issues did emerge on a wide range of topics. Some of the issues that arose are contained and reflected in the various papers, comments, and case studies. However, in an effort to pull together the various issues and research priorities, a few of the major ones have been selected that deserve major emphasis.

Not all areas of knowledge and current concern on subsistence agriculture that might have been on the agenda were included in the conference. In the brief space of a week it was not possible to have presentations on each and every aspect of peasant economics and agrarian societies. The conference was weighted in favor of economists and was meant for them to focus upon the economic aspects of subsistence and peasant agriculture. At the same time it was felt that to a considerable extent economists and agricultural economists should be made aware, if they were not so already, of the considerable body of research and analysis pioneered by the sister disciplines of anthropology, sociology, political science, and social psychology.

Here as well not all could be represented.

The second goal was to select those aspects within economics where future research seemed likely to provide major returns. Careful perusal of the literature on subsistence and peasant economics indicated that there were a number of areas where a general consensus or a majority opinion prevailed. Such areas were by and large omitted, though it was expected that these topics might well come up for discussion if, in fact, the consensus was an illusion.

Out of these exchanges it was hoped that the group would arrive at some idea of the major areas of interdisciplinary agreement and disagreement, interdisciplinary research priorities, and intradisciplinary priorities.

THE ISSUES

Alternative Analytical and Research Approaches

Given the wide range of disciplines represented in the group, there was an equally wide range of preferred analytical and research approaches. A few felt that descriptive research, coupled with conceptual clarification that gave valid characterization to the dimensions of the problem, was a basic precondition for all subsequent analysis. While most agreed, there were those who felt that such an approach sometimes led to the development of a purely taxonomic approach, which some considered sterile. The usefulness of research on the past rather than the present, and whether historical evidence is really applicable today, had its partisans on both sides.

Another difference in approach reflected a split in preferences between abstraction and specificity or between generalization and the idiosyncratic (individuation). Some argued that general principles are futile, since each situation is unique and aggregation may hide important variation. Much of the issue centered on the possibility and desirability of developing a fully generalized social-sciences model applicable to subsistence agriculture. Some held that a general model that took account of the diversity embraced by the terms "subsistence agriculture" and "peasant farmer" could in fact be developed that would prove valid and useful. Others felt that any such model, if developed, would prove so general and abstract as to be virtually meaningless in any particular problem situation. A third group believed that the most that could be hoped for was a diagnostic approach to each particular problem situation. This particularistic procedure was seen as necessary to provide meaningful policy and program prescriptions. Reservations were expressed about the possibility and validity of many theoretical models that failed to capture the interactions and complexities involved because they are too great and too numerous. There was, however, a willingness to accept some degree of generalization and abstraction, provided the assumptions are valid and provided that the theories and principles are not used mechanically. Several pleas were made for selective intensive analysis in a search for key facilitators and inhibitors of change.

The difficulties of cross-cultural generalization came in for a good deal of comment, as did the extent to which our theories and even tools of analysis may reflect unwitting ethnocentric biases. This led to frequent stress of the need for empirical tests of theory and a recognition of the interrelationship between theory and empirical analysis.

Few disagreed as to the importance of greater multidisciplinary attacks upon the problem of developing subsistence agriculture, though there was no agreement on

the appropriate interdisciplinary approach. The question of disciplinary integration in the mind or in a team—interdisciplinary versus multidisciplinary—was not resolved. The value of the exchanges between the disciplines was unquestioned, though there were some who held that each discipline should not attempt to master the skills of the other but merely call upon colleagues in areas of their special competence.

Thus, although there was no total synthesis or no fully generalized social-sciences model, there was a heightened recognition of the interactions between the foci of concern in the relevant disciplines and of the important variables in the interaction.

A Fundamental Issue: Dominance of "Economic" or "Noneconomic" Forces

Throughout the meeting a fundamental issue repeatedly raised concerned the dominance of economic versus noneconomic forces upon the economic behavior of subsistence farmers. For some participants the general conditions of subsistence agriculture automatically de-delimit an area where, on net balance, the noneconomic frequently outweighs the purely economic, leading to behavior that goes against the postulated behavior of economics. For others, the economic forces dominate the noneconomic, and the observed behavior patterns are considered quite consistent with the postulates of economics. The disagreements involved concepts, principles, theories, and empirical evidence.

The subsistence farmer was recognized as a key factor in the transformation of traditional agriculture because his day-to-day actions determine in large measure the direction and pace of development. But these actions are also influenced both by his internal nature as well as by the setting within which his actions take place. Economizing behavior takes place within an economizing setting. But despite the dichotomization, there are recognized interactive influences between the subsistence farmer and his setting.

For those who see the economic behavior of subsistence and peasant farmers as deviant, three categories of factors are commonly used as explanations: the motives, values, and attitudes of the farmers themselves are negative forces that inhibit or prevent "rational" economic behavior and hence development; the institutional matrix within which the subsistence farmers operate involves forces that influence the economic behavior of subsistence farmers in a fashion that hinders economic change; and there are social and cultural factors that characterize the societies associated with traditional and subsistence agriculture that dominate human behavior so as to dilute or overwhelm its economic dimension.

The most massive empirical evidence on the influence of sociocultural and institutional factors upon economic behavior has been accumulated by the anthropologists. Over the years their intensive studies of nonliterate, primitive communities have broadened to include those societies further along the modernization spectrum. Although each study has involved the intensive study of a small, local social unit on a limited cross-sectional basis, the number of such studies is considerable, and their accumulation now offers splendid opportunities for delineating a wide variety of cross-cultural comparisons on the variations in sociocultural forms and their influence on economic behavior at the microlevel. A selective summary of this evidence and the issues are presented in Chapter 3.

The second major body of empirical and analytical literature on the influence of sociocultural and institutional factors upon economic behavior revolves around the traditional "peasantry" of Europe. Much of this literature was written by economic historians and until recently rarely received attention by today's neoclassical economists. This area is the focus of Chapter 4.

A third body of relevant knowledge on the motivations, values and attitudes of peasant and subsistence farmers is beginning to emerge. Conducted largely by social psychologists and sociologists, this literature is still in its infancy, and the number of studies touching upon this dimension of the problem is still quite meager. Yet what it reveals is proving to be helpful in determining the influence of these factors upon the economic goals and economic behavior of subsistence farmers. Chapter 5 attempts to summarize the evidence in this area.

As has been seen, much of this evidence seems to indicate that farmers in traditional agriculture are indifferent to economic influences and, because of sociocultural and/or institutional and/or motivational factors, do not respond to changes in product and factor prices or to changes in the profitability of investment. Long-standing cultural institutions such as land tenure, caste, and extended family are judged to be more important in determining how resources are allocated and how the product is distributed. These views have in turn led to a variety of positions regarding the adequacy of received economic theory for explaining the economic behavior of peasant farmers and the extent to which subsistence farmers behave "economically" or "rationally." Three main groups could be distinguished.

The first group were those who accept the noneconomic dominance of economic behavior and therefore argued for a total recasting of economic theory to handle the economics of subsistence agriculture.

A second group were those who hold to the middle ground and who believe that traditional farmers are "partial economic men." Their economic behavior can not wholly be classified in accordance with received economic theory. For example, when prices of their product increase, not all peasant farmers increase their offerings on the market—some do and some don't, depending on a range of other noneconomic influences. According to this view, because they are peasants or subsistence farmers, their economic behavior is such that accepted economic analysis is unable to cope with it entirely. Their behavior is rational and economic, though it may appear deviant until one takes account of the sociocultural forces that are at work on the values held by the farmers. Thus, the generally accepted parts of economic theory require modifications and extensions before they can fully explain the behavior of peasant farmers.

A third group were those who maintain that, despite the influence of such factors, subsistence and peasant farmers are highly rational and economic in their behavior, surmounting all such negative forces whenever the economic gains and returns outweighed the losses and costs. According to this view, leisure, work, thrift, and wealth with an eye to the marginal calculus are significant and are identical with, or not too dissimilar from, that which can be observed in modern societies.

Much of what is ultimately prescribed in the way of programs and policies for the development of subsistence agriculture depends upon which of these three positions one takes. The fact that disagreements could extend from theories to the empirical evidence on this issue is an excellent indication of the need for research to secure a better resolution.

A Research Agenda[1]

The first step in any research is the clarification of the problem. Without precision in the formulation of the problem, analysis will suffer if not be totally misguided. A second step is to decide upon the criteria that must be used to evaluate the state of knowledge—facts, generalizations, propositions, principles, hypotheses, theories, and models—which we have regarding the phenomenon in question.

Hopefully, the papers in this volume have helped with the first task of problem clarification associated with the goal of how to promote the more rapid development of subsistence agriculture. On the second step, the criteria that received the greatest emphasis throughout the papers and the discussions advocated were operational significance and policy implication or significance. The group was especially concerned that research be directed toward those areas where additional insights might help to accelerate the modernization of subsistence agriculture. Therefore, most of the items included in the agenda are those that seem to offer this promise of identifying those problems that are critical.

Since the primary focus of the conference was upon economic behavior, it was the economic dimension that received the greatest attention. The basic objective throughout was how the process of change and development should be analyzed if we wish to

1. During the conference, I was assisted in drawing up a preliminary set of research priorities by a selected group of conferees: Dean J. Norman Efferson, Louisiana State University; Dr. A. T. Mosher, Agricultural Development Council, Inc.; Prof. William H. Nicholls, Vanderbilt University; Prof. Emilio Quintana, University of the Philippines; Prof. William H. Sewell, University of Wisconsin; and Dr. Edward W. Weidner, East-West Center, University of Hawaii. In addition, several participants submitted specific research suggestions during the conference and after. These suggestions have been included where deemed relevant.

accelerate it. While many of the factors associated with subsistence farming were considered of interest, there was a strong feeling that a catalog of these factors was not as useful as distinguishing those characteristics that are crucial in a causative sense—in the move toward greater productivity and commercialization of farm inputs and products. The search, therefore, was for more effective policy and operational tools.

The research priorities have been grouped under four major headings. The priorities and suggestions have not been attributed to individuals, mainly because the ideas were very often suggested by more than one person or constitute the product of an exchange among several persons. Thus, the ideas are in most cases direct products of the papers and discussions, but their selection and priority emphasis are largely mine.

THE NATURE OF SUBSISTENCE FARMERS

As was explained in Chapter 2, one of the major issues at the conference concerned the concept of a "subsistence farmer" or "peasant". But underlying and closely related to the conceptual dispute was a fundamental question: Are subsistence farmers basically different from nonsubsistence farmers? If so, in what way? Or are the differences merely a matter of degree?

The conference sought to examine the premise that there is something special about subsistence farmers and subsistence agricultural sectors. The procedure employed was to define ex ante the characteristics that were expected to segregate those farmers and that economic sector where "different" economic behavior was believed to exist. Hence the conceptual and definitional issue is inextricably linked with the issue of presumed behavioral differentiation.

Some felt that "subsistence farmers" and "peasants" are in fact significantly different; others emphasized that they are not. Most agreed that "subsistence farmers" do maximize a bundle of wants, subject to the restraints as they see them, but the basic problem is that their wants or goals are a reflection of both economic and noneconomic factors, with differing weights assigned to each. A majority agreed that both economic and noneconomic goals are involved. The source of disagreement was rooted in the relative importance of the economic versus the noneconomic in arriving at some "net" resultant effect upon economic behavior. Depending upon the relative weights assigned, subsistence farmers may or may not be judged as responsive as purely economically rational individuals.

There is still considerable need for conceptual clarification in the use of these terms. In fact, one could argue that greater damage has been done as a result of imprecision in specifying the particular content of the terms used than from any attempts at securing common agreement upon a single definition or concept.

Rationality

Another cause of disagreement revolved around the conceptual difficulties in the differing disciplinary definitions of "rational" and "rationality." Economists use the terms most frequently, and to them the terms refer to behavior that seeks to maximize economic returns or income. To sociologists and anthropologists, however, the terms have the more general meaning, associated with behavior in conformity with one's own values after having consciously considered alternative courses of action. Thus, to an economist it would be rational for a farmer to shift from growing wheat to growing vegetables if by so doing he could increase his income, whereas to an anthropologist the same action might be irrational if it resulted in the farmer's having to break a strongly entrenched social value holding that the growing of vegetables is the prerogative of persons of a different family or clan.

Interestingly, both groups tended to argue in the conference that subsistence farmers are "rational," each using its own definition of the term. But this did not deter the noneconomists from pointing out deficiencies in the data presented by economists to bolster their position.

Confusion over the use of the terms is understandable for several reasons:

1. Much of economics deals with quantitative data consisting mainly of prices and monetary values, leaving an impression of materialistic determinism, reinforced by the greater attention in economics to free competitive theories.

2. The individual objective functions or goals used by economists are summarized in the preference function or map, but economists rarely examine this map.

3. "Maximization" can be applied to any single valued goal, both economic and noneconomic, but economists tend to concentrate upon its economic use.

Several questions that deserve research attention were raised:

1. Do subsistence farmers want more rather than less of "something" that perhaps should be called the "good things of life"? If so, do they behave accordingly?

2. What goes into the bundle of "good things"? How is it determined? Is it predominantly economic? Is the desire for "gain" exclusively economic? How strong? How strong are other forces, such as familial obligations? What are subsistence farmers in fact maximizing—profit, income, welfare, prestige, power? If all of these, how do they rank them?

3. Are subsistence farmers capable of discerning their best interests and of thinking logically regarding the means to achieve them?

4. Will any change in the circumstances facing subsistence farmers produce a "rational" reaction by them in line with their best interests and desire for more of the "good things"?

5. What are the critical differences in the range of opportunities available to subsistence farmers? How are these affected by their perception of the real world?

Values, Motives, Attitudes, and Aspirations

The basic question raised in this area was to what extent is it true that the motivations, values, and attitudes of subsistence farmers relevant for economic progress are different. Do these affect human economic behavior in such a way as to have a negative effect in production and organization that is detrimental to rapid economic growth?

Rogers in Chapter 5 attempted to assemble the available evidence on the motivations, values, and attitudes of subsistence farmers. The evidence has been arranged around ten central elements that he feels make up a subculture of peasantry: mutual distrust, lack of innovativeness, fatalism, low aspirational levels, lack of deferred gratification, limited time perspective, familism, dependency upon government authority, localiteness, and lack of empathy. Doob attempted to test the ten elements, using empirical data from some of his own previous research in Africa, Jamaica, and the Tyrol. The majority of Rogers' elements were confirmed. The elements of time perspective and localiteness proved to be somewhat ambiguous, and only the element of mutual distrust was not verified.

But the research effort in this field is still deficient; a great deal more needs to be known. A special need would involve comparative studies of the ten elements cross-culturally—a geographic and cultural extension of the Doob tests—that might include the developed as well as the underdeveloped world.

Eight major areas of needed inquiry were delimited:

1. What are the aspirations of subsistence farmers? Research is needed to determine the specific components of aspiration among subsistence farms in different sociocultural settings (ethnic groups, institutional settings), ecological conditions, and economic levels. Correlatively, research is needed to determine the relative strengths of the components and their interrelationships as they relate to economic behavior. The evidence that we have is seriously deficient.

2. What specific components in any "aspirational bundle" are relevant for economic development? Admittedly not all of them are, but we really do not know which ones are significant from a policy or operational standpoint. Not all elements and components in aspirations are equally relevant for the process of development. Indeed, scattered evidence indicates that we may have had strong aspirational levels along different nondevelopmental lines. Research is required to determine the components of the "aspirational bundle" that are relevant for the process of development.

3. Another important area are studies that can determine the role of availability of incentive goods in regard to aspirational levels. A recurring disagreement throughout the conference concerned the importance of the availability of new consumer goods in economic behavior. Some considered that the absence of such goods set a significant ceiling upon the goals and aspirations of subsistence farmers.

4. What relevant components in the "aspirational bundle" are the most manipulable and which ones the most resistant? A good deal of evidence from the developed nations indicates that there is a lag in aspirations change. Comparable evidence is not available on subsistence agriculture and subsistence farmers on the relative sensitiveness and elasticities in aspirations and lags. Research is also needed to determine the key independent and manipulable variables that affect aspirational levels of subsistence farmers. For some, the issue was not the need to stimulate particular aspirations, but choices among competing aspirations and how these were affected by the network of socioculturally determined obligations in which the individual is immersed.

5. Greater attention needs to be placed upon the distinction between "expectional variables" and "aspirational variables." The divergence between the two may be great and often gives the impression of fatalism among peasant farmers. How large is the gap between aspirational and expectational levels among subsistence farmers? What are the factors that affect the divergence? What are the independent and manipulable variables which affect expectations? Research on these points might prove extremely rewarding.

6. What is the nature of the time preference of subsistence farmers? There is a good deal of conflicting evidence on deferred gratification in consumption and in production among subsistence and peasant farmers. Variations seem to be related to security, asset structure, kinship, and similar variables, but research is needed to delineate rigorously the nature of time preference of subsistence farmers and the independent variables that affect their time preference.

7. An occasional query raised at the meeting was whether there is a psychology of the hungry or the poor. There was a feeling among some that the mere fact of closeness to critical minima for physical survival could result in a significant difference in attitudes, values, and motivations. Moreover, there were a few who believed that there was also

an effect upon those who are not hungry but live with others who are poor, such that the limited choices of one group affected the choices of the others.

8. Finally, a great deal of research is needed that focuses upon the positive aspects of the motivational, attitudinal, and goals structure of peasant and subsistence farmers—those elements that could be successfully utilized and exploited for the more rapid development of subsistence agriculture. For whatever reason, prior work in this area seems to have concentrated almost exclusively upon the negative features of the motivations, values, and attitudes of subsistence farmers rather than the positive features. Yet there are positive features that could be effectively utilized. Research in this area offers considerable promise.

THE ECONOMIC BEHAVIOR OF
SUBSISTENCE FARMERS

The primary focus of research requirements in this area concerns the issue of whether "subsistence man" is also "economic man" and whether the economic behavior of subsistence farmers has any basic general properties.

A great deal more knowledge is required on exactly how peasant and subsistence economic systems operate and change. The evidence presented in the case studies constituted an insignificant fraction of the available evidence. A great deal more is needed on the exact course and direction of change as well as the forces that influenced the changes and that inhibited them.

The "Dual" Peasant

Although there was predictable disagreement, many participants believed that the pure theory of the firm and the pure theory of the household were not exactly appropriate for the subsistence farm family because of the duality involved; i.e. the entire operation is a dual entity—farm firm plus household—where product, consumption, labor use and decision-making are intertwined. A critical research need in this area is how to get a greater degree of integration between the economists and noneconomists in a rigorous analysis of this dualism.

Among the questions that require study are:

1. Do subsistence farmers really have consumption ceilings, as some have argued? What is their content and what affects them?

2. How do levels of consumption out of farm production affect labor use? To what extent is consumption influenced by sociocultural variables?

3. What are the patterns of consumption and savings among subsistence farmers, and how do these relate to such variables as time preferences and cropping complexes?

Another important dimension where work is required concerns the handling of the psychosociocultural dimensions of economic analysis. Research is needed on how sociocultural factors are reflected in such areas as producer-consumer preferences and sale ratio.

Resource Efficiency

1. As indicated by Mellor in Chapter 7, many studies of subsistence farmers have been directed at the issue of efficiency in resource allocation. As was repeatedly pointed out in the papers and during the conference, the aggregation involved in most studies has tended to mask inefficiencies within the sample. There is considerable possibility of interfarm variation in allocative efficiency on an individual farm basis. Studies that open up the variations that may exist regarding inefficiency are desparately needed. These studies should seek to examine the variations in levels of efficiency among farms and the associated characteristics, plus the lengths of time required to arrive at these levels of efficiency.

2. Another issue of considerable relevance is the extent to which variations in performance are a reflection of the environment faced by such farmers, rather than the "goodness" of their individual economic decisions and performance. Studies are needed to determine exactly what the environment is that faces different groups of subsistence farmers and its dimensions.

3. A final question is whether there is any possibility for economic growth from raising the levels of allocative efficiency in traditional agriculture. Do noneconomic cultural components impose limits that are too severe? If not, how much room is there for economic

progress within the cultural framework and technology that characterizes subsistence agriculture?

Labor Use

The importance of labor and labor inputs in subsistence agriculture was discussed several times during the meeting.

1. Surprisingly, the whole topic of disguised unemployment or underemployment or zero marginal productivity of labor did not result in serious areas of disagreement. There were some issues with regard to the relevance of this particular problem in developing countries, but the existence of certain degrees of unemployment/underemployment were not causes of basic contention. Part of the reason is that the analytical apparatus for the study of this particular problem and the available empirical evidence have considerably strengthened of late.

One aspect that did emerge arises from the fact that most of the empirical evidence is of a cross-section type, covering labor input for a full calendar year. Where cropping involves annuals maturing in three to eight months and only one harvest a year, these studies fail to catch the evidence of seasonal unemployment or underemployment. These facts suggest several areas of needed research.

a. Studies of the labor-use cycle during the crop year for a variety of cropping situations and a variety of crops are required, in order to assess the cyclical fluctuations in the demand for family and hired labor under different conditions. This problem is of considerable importance in view of its relationship to the needs for mechanization at particular stages in the cropping cycle, as well as to the involvement of farm families in off-farm employment.

b. Work is needed on the question of year-to-year fluctuations in labor use; how does the labor requirement fluctuate between years of bumper crops and those of drought? We have very limited evidence of a micro type on this topic.

c. Another area that has been neglected is the influence and interaction of farm production labor requirements with family size. This variable is of special significance, because there may be a causal relationship with desired family size, a variable of considerable

significance in the current problem of population.

2. Another critically important research area concerns the nature and functioning of rural labor markets in traditional agriculture. Several dimensions of this problem have been neglected and require exploration: the extent to which the functioning of labor market is influenced by payment in cash as opposed to payment in kind; the degree to which custom may tend to prevent or slow down adjustment in the share wage; the extent to which increasing population pressure forces adjustment through reduced land allotments per sharecropper family or by reducing the cropper family's share. Such situations could conceivably foster conditions where land is "rationed" at a subcompetitive price at the expense of total farm employment.

3. What happens as soon as any part of family labor is made marketable? Does it satisfy the marginality conditions, such that its marginal subjective valuation equals its wage?

4. There is need for additional work on leisure, especially its conceptual specification. This is a point that has been stressed by Jones both in the present volume and in some of his subsequent work. The whole concept and the dimensions of leisure require rigorous study, especially cross-culturally. Caution should, of course, be exercised to assure that the conceptions of labor and leisure are those of the sampled population, not ours; but information is needed on the extent to which these vary, if at all, across cultural boundaries.

5. An interesting question raised at the meeting was whether output was indeed the dependent variable for subsistence farmers. Do they select output on the basis of maximizing the use of available labor? Or does the typical subsistence farmer choose a crop mix and then let the available technology dictate the labor input, making the labor input a derived or implicitly derived variable rather than a decision variable?

6. Investigations are needed on the importance of peasant labor in the formation of capital at the farm and village level. The historical evidence from today's advanced nations indicates the considerable importance of such labor in developing additions to infrastructure.

7. Several persons commented on the

importance of investigating the relationships that might exist between levels of nutrition and labor use. The impact of nutrition and general health was seen as possibly having an important effect upon labor use—both physical and mental efficiencies.

8. Other studies of labor suggested were: the significance of rural-to-rural migration as well as rural-to-urban migration; the productive efficiency of labor under different forms of tenure systems; the use and returns to farm labor during the off seasons in those areas where there is a definite cropping cycle for a single crop.

Economic Responsiveness

There seemed to be no tendency among the conference participants to blame the subsistence farmer or to categorize him as being lazy; on the contrary, there is extensive empirical evidence of economic influences having a measurable response among subsistence farmers. A good deal of the theory and empirical evidence on this area was presented in Part Two. Unfortunately most of the recent work has dealt with questions or resource allocation or with the economic responsiveness with a single crop or with shifts between crops in response to changes in relative price.

Despite the excellent work that has been done on the economics of marketed surplus and marketable surplus, an area of greatest relevance to subsistence agriculture, there are a number of additional research topics that require attention:

1. There are cases where there has not been response to an obvious change in economic incentives. It would be extremely valuable to have studies made of these situations.

2. A good deal of additional work is needed on the responsiveness of agriculture as a whole to economic incentives, especially the influences of the terms of trade between agriculture and nonagriculture.

3. Despite the available evidence on the extent to which economic forces do play a significant role, the subsistence farmer groups that have been studied have not been totally homogeneous. There has been indication of sizable variance with regard to the level of response within a given sample. Therefore additional work is needed that will segregate out those farmers who have not been responsive, in order to delineate the relative influence of other economic and noneconomic forces upon their behavior.

4. Historical studies are needed on the forces that led to the several crop explosions that took place during the colonial era in developing countries in the sixteenth, seventeenth and eighteenth centuries in Asia, Latin America, and Africa. The available historical data might very well prove to be of significant value if made using recently developed techniques of analysis. Examining the role of infrastructure in historical studies of crop explosions might be especially rewarding.

5. A great deal more effort is needed on dissecting the incentive framework. Thus far much of the work has involved the use of price as a surrogate for economic profit or gain. Improved specification is needed on what constitutes "profitability" as seen by peasant farmers. Research should be directed at determining the constituent parts of economic incentives and what affects them.

6. The responsiveness of subsistence farmers to investment opportunities is another area where further research should prove worthwhile. What are the rates of return on particular investment opportunities in traditional agriculture? How have such farmers been able at times to display considerable investment acumen regarding new high-potential inputs?

7. The economic aspects of innovation among subsistence farmers have been neglected, especially as it relates to risk and uncertainty. What is the relationship between risk resistances and such variables as minimal levels of living, asset patterns, and the availability of alternative economic opportunities? Do subsistence farmers look upon subsistence crops differently from commercial crops?

8. The influence of demand on subsistence agriculture requires investigation. This is especially true with regard to the export sector. There is a good deal of evidence that demand factors often play an important role in the expansion of particular crops. For some students, deficiencies in demand or its absence are even more important in stimulating or retarding agricultural development.

THE INFLUENCE AND SIGNIFICANCE
OF NON-ECONOMIC FACTORS

Sociocultural and Institutional Forces

As described above, a critical issue at the conference concerned the relative weights assigned to economic versus institutional forces. For some, the general condition of subsistence agriculture is one where institutional variables dominate the economic, and therefore change requires a rearrangement of this hierarchy. There is difficulty in ascertaining just how this hierarchy affects decision-making patterns and particular aspects of economic behavior in fashions that are detrimental to development.

There was only minor discussion of the impact of development upon the social structure and its possible adverse effects. A few arguments were made that change and monetization bring about social disintegration, making development costly in human terms. There is a psychological backwash comparable to that which occurs under rural-urban migration, when the recent migrant to an urban area becomes the victim of a causality that he does not understand and must work out an inner transition of values. Increased linkage with the outside world through commercialization and monetization has a similar effect of exposing the subsistence farmer to forces external to his control and often his comprehension. Change frequently leads to a breakdown in the traditional village power structure that affects previous patterns of status and inter-personal relations. But though the movement toward greater commercialization may or may not mean an improvement in the welfare sense, it was recognized that some progress and change are inevitable in today's world. Hence minimizing the negative features of change while maximizing the positive is mandatory.

What are the strengths of the existing economic, institutional, and cultural organizations of subsistence farmers that can be used to promote change, and which ones can be left alone without hindering the process of growth? How can elements of social structure be used to promote social change and which ones? How can we promote change without destroying the useful elements in the social structure or adversely affecting social institutions? Can sociocultural variables be identified that do not require change and can be used to promote economic, social, and political stability, while other disruptive but necessary changes are taking place? To answer these questions, research is needed that relates particular social institutions to particular patterns of economic behavior. We need to know how peasant institutions came to be and to discern their influence upon the functioning of the economic mechanism. A great deal more research needs to be done on the relation of social structures to specific economic processes linked with sequential studies through time.

The institutional cultural matrix within which peasant economic decisions take place were seen as functioning in an interactive two-way causation with the economic dimension (Firth in Chapter 3). Systematic study of the two-way causation of each set of variables is in order, hopefully to clarify issues of socioeconomic change. A promising area of research on this topic would be a careful examination of the introduction of new and alien legal and political institutions during the colonial era and the way in which these affected economic institutions and economic activities. Comparisons between the precolonial, colonial, and postcolonial periods would be highly instructive on the two-way causation between these sets of variables.

The role of land and its associated institutions was frequently mentioned as primary in its relationship to economic activity and the development process. The rights in land and in its product were seen as only one facet of institutions that can fundamentally affect the development process. A number of different features were stressed—communal vs. individual ownership, transferability, usufruct, inheritance, tenure. A systematic summary of the various institutions associated with agricultural land in agrarian socieities and how they relate to economic process in subsistence economies would be extremely valuable.

Several other questions were raised and specific research suggestions made.

1. To what extent do the sociocultural matrices at the village level vary from village to village around the world? How are these

variations associated with particular levels of economic efficiency?

2. Is it possible to identify those new products or factors of production that are "culturally neutral" or "not taboo," such as bicycles?

3. How are institutional and cultural variables built into the indifference maps used by economists?

4. Do peasants rank institutional variables higher than the usual economic ones because their economic base is more limited?

5. How useful is it to view the extended family as an efficient and rational way of handling poverty? How is this social institution affected by changes in income and by sources of income?

6. What is the relationship between the opportunity structure of a peasant society and the position of the individual in the social structure? Does his position in society influence significantly the subsistance farmer's perception of economic opportunities?

7. What is the best method to effectuate— required changes in specific elements of the social structure—through a direct attack or through the support of the innovators in a community?

8. Which forces historically have caused or been associated with the elimination or reduction in the sociocultural variables impeding change—monetization? communication? transport? education? technology?

Agricultural Technology

There was general agreement among the participants that the state of the arts in subsistence agriculture is low and that it is fairly constant or changes rather slowly through time. However, the evidence was more inferential than rigorous. The "efficient but poor" hypothesis examined in Chapter 12 is based upon a somewhat limited number of studies.

A good deal more investigation is called for in several areas.

1. More evidence is needed on the variation in technological levels and economic performance among the subsistence farmers and the factors influencing these variations.

2. The majority of the work on diffusion and adoption of new technology has been undertaken by sociologists with very limited

participation by economists. This is particularly strange in view of the emphasis most economists place on new technology as being a primary force for the acceleration of the development of subsistence agriculture.

3. A great deal more analysis needs to be done on research itself; that is, there was a feeling that we know very little about the role of research in development, especially in the physical and biological sciences.

4. To what extent are the new technologies geared too much to the requirements of commercial farmers and not sufficiently to the needs of subsistence farmers?

Closely related were questions of the possible interrelationships between technology and institutions. What are the interrelationships? In what fashion does specific technology determine and affect the character of social institutions? Correspondingly, how do institutions affect the choice of technologies? How does this interrelationship, if true, affect the general validity of models of economic behavior and change?

Other Factors

Two other areas received frequent comment: population and the political process.

The role of population and its significance were the special focus of Nicholls and Dandekar in Chapters 10 and 12. More analysis of the population variable in a historical context was felt to be required, especially at levels below national aggregates focused on subsistence agriculture. Why did much of traditional agricultural lose its race with population? What are the critically different features of those that did not? How was population growth affected by patterns of agrarian structure?

One of the major gaps in the conference presentations and discussions concerned the role of political structures in the development of subsistence agriculture. To what extent do particular political forms promote or retard the process of modernization of subsistence societies? We need to understand how the strategic factor of law and order operates in subsistence societies in providing stability and a reduction in risk. The analysis of cultural differences in the sources of political power are especially required at village levels, so as to understand how these impinge upon the process of change. Also, research is needed at the micro level on the distribution of political power.

A Digression on Interdisciplinary Research and Exchanges

The conference's multidisciplinary confrontation, focused upon the problem of analyzing the development process in subsistence agriculture, inevitably led to a number of suggestions regarding the conduct of interdisciplinary research and the need for interdisciplinary exchanges.

There was occasional questioning of research methodologies employed to study peasant farmers. Each approach was seen to have its strengths and weaknesses, from the participant-observation technique of the anthropologists to the one-shot survey interviews of the economist. Are the field-survey techniques commonly employed by economists securing valid information? Are we asking the right questions? What do we really know about the dynamics of interviewing among peasant farmers? Do we know the range and degrees of sensitivity in field research? How much of the similarities in what we observe is due to the fact that the majority of interviewers are "modern" men and women?

Several participants emphasized the need for greater exchange of information among the disciplines. Such exchanges were seen as strengthening current research, helping to avoid past mistakes, and permitting the systematic collection of required information. Greater attempts should be made to assemble all the available information from the different disciplines related to a particular, carefully delimited problem area. For example, some of the possibilities suggested in this connection were: the determinants of aspiration levels, the forces affecting levels of deferred gratification, and the differing dimensions of decision-making regarding a particular form of economic behavior such as saving or hoarding.

Another possibility suggested was the greater use of the data generated in one discipline to test basic developmental hypotheses in another, such as was done by Doob in Chapter 5. Needless to say, there were occasional queries about how much inter-disciplinary research is useful or possible or even desirable, but there was little question that greater efforts should be made to communicate relevant findings on the same basic behavioral phenomena to each other.

THE DEVELOPMENT OF SUBSISTENCE AGRICULTURE

There was general agreement on the importance of agriculture and the relationship between agricultural development and economic development. The analytical underpinning on the point seems to be in better shape than the empirical evidence, but some question remains whether the subsistence sector does in fact offer opportunities for significant growth.

On the empirical side, much more work is needed, especially on the interrelationships between the relative rates of growth in the two sectors. There is a great deal of theoretical evidence that the relative rates of growth in the two sectors are linked, but we have very limited evidence as to the tolerances in divergence between the two rates of growth as well as what the past evidence has been with regard to the influence of relative rates of growth between the two sectors.

Predictably, there were some who argued that greater attention is required on the dynamics of the process of development, since much of current analytical work deals with statics. In today's world we are basically trying to cope with a group who are in a transitional situation. The rapidity of change may not be at a rate we deem desirable, but change is taking place, and not all of it is positive. Some things lead and some lag. What are they? Which ones are important in hindering the process? Which ones in accelerating it? Which ones are unnecessarily being adversely affected by the changes? Is there any discernible pattern of cumulative causation?

Despite the attention given to theoretical and empirical aspects of subsistence agriculture during the meeting, the majority of the participants had a strong policy and program orientation. Repeatedly during the conference attempts were made to isolate the critical variables that would effect the more rapid transformation of agriculture and that were subject to significant external control. As would be expected, there was no unanimity as to the critical variables, but there were several areas of general agreement. Many found Mosher's five essentials and five accelerators a useful set of variables (see Chapter 1 and Editor's Introduction to Chapter 12). The importance of transport, communications, and education were frequently mentioned as being of utmost importance. The role of incentive goods and the importance of land tenure were also offered but with less unanimity.

When discussing the execution of planned programs of change for subsistence agriculture, two issues emerged as echoes of previous discussions.

The first issue concerned the extent to which most models of change are too general to be useful in program and policy specification for the widely varying types of subsistence farmers and subsistence economies. One group believed that such generalizations were useful in providing guides to action provided the appropriate adaptations were made. Others felt that separate diagnosis of each specific problem area is required.

The second issue reflected a division between those who felt that the main problem was a lack of economic opportunities and those who believed that the major cause was a lack of aspiration. This division was also another facet of the economic-vs-institutionalist differences referred to above. For many, the problem was not either/or but both—and how much of each. The choice of policy and program emphasis also reflected these positions. Those who favored activities and projects affecting economic opportunities believed that these would overcome and force

changes in the institutional dimension; others argued that the institutional factors severely limit response to economic factors and therefore require change. Others believed that the most efficient strategy was to focus on both the economic and social changes required simultaneously.

One of the more surprising things about the conference was that there were certain areas that did not elicit serious disagreements or bases for contention. These were issues that would probably have arisen ten or twenty years ago in a conference of a similar group of social scientists. There was also considerable agreement on several of the variables that are considered to be important. Hence some progress has been made in resolving certain issues and in acquiring a better understanding of how to foster and to promote the more rapid modernization of subsistence agriculture.

A great deal still remains to be done. We hope that the publication of this volume and the research priorities will serve as a stimulus to heightened activity in this vitally important area. The participants, as leaders in their respective fields, will undoubtedly maintain a continuing interest as well as stimulate their students and colleagues to undertake further work on the topic. In turn we hope that this work will eventually be reflected in the kinds of national development plans and action programs undertaken in the developing countries. Hopefully, subsistence man will be the eventual beneficiary and be transformed into a modern, commercial farmer, making his contribution to overall economic development.

Index

ACAR program in Brazil, 391, 424–38
Africa, 6–7
Africa
 aspirations, 145, 146
 chiefs, 34, 148
 communal ownership and land use, 29–30
 disguised unemployment, 339*ff.*
 empathy, 149, 150
 familism, 147
 fatalism, 145
 government, attitudes toward, 147–48
 gratification patterns, 145–47
 innovativeness, 144–45
 interpersonal relations, 144
 land holding and use, 29–32
 localiteness, 148
 peasant subculture, 143*ff.*
 product allocation and status, 33–34
 status structure and land holding, 28
 traditional agriculture, 209–26, 227–28
 women's rights, 31, 32
 see also specific countries
Agrarianism, 66, 72, 73–74, 77, 82–82, 98
 sociological approach to peasantry, 64, 81
American Indians, land holding and use, 30
Analytic methodology, 9, 12–13, 95–96, 455–58, 466
 classical economics, 61–63, 320*ff.*
 diffusion simulation, 130–31
 field experiments, 130
 growth models, classical vs. neoclassical, 320–58
 institutionalization, 223, 228
 linear programming, 380–81
 models, 24, 100, 165–96, 247–53, 320–58
 policy formulation and, 353*ff.*
 quantitative vs. qualitative, 62–63, 81, 85–86, 98
 relevance, 100
 sampling, national, 130
 semisubsistence farming and, 207–8
 social anthropology and economics, interaction of,
  23–24, 37–41
 social research worker training, 129–30
 subjective equilibrium models, 165–96
 supply models for tree crops, 247–53
 see also Research
Andalusia
 inheritance system and land fragmentation, 32
 wage labor, 33
Andean agriculture, 392*ff.*

Anthropology
 analytical tool, 8–9
 economic, 63–64
 economics, interaction of, 23–24, 37–41
Asia, 6
 disguised unemployment, 340*ff.*
 product allocation and status, 33–34
 traditional agriculture, 209–26, 227
 see also specific countries, subjects
Aspirations, 119–21, 139, 145, 146, 459–61
 achievement motivation, 120
 consumption and, 120–21
 economic opportunity and, 23–24, 45–46, 47, 101
 educational, 23–24, 47, 119, 139, 159, 226
 labor investment and, 277–79
 living, level of, 120
 material welfare, 211–13, 222–23, 227, 277–79
 resource availability, 188
 savings and investment, 215–16
Austria, localiteness, 148–49

Baganda, land use and status, 33–34
Bananas, 393
Barley, 196
Barnett, Milton L., 284–95
Bateman, Merrill J., 243–53
Behrman, Jere R., 232–42
Bolivia, 392*ff.*
 land ownership, 401*ff.*
 product consumption and sale, 398, 399, 401
 wheat, 395
Brazil, 7
 ACAR program, 391, 424–38
 cocoa, 251, 252
 coffee, 245–46, 251, 313*n.*
 credit, 429–35
 economic development, 313*n.*
 extension, 428–29, 433*ff.*
 internal migration, 100
 sugar, 313*n.*
British colonialism, 47–48, 49
 sociological approach to peasantry, 64–65
Buddhism
 economic growth and values of, 59
 monks, and change, 59, 129
Burma
 credit structure, 53–54, 56–58
 immigration, 48

income and expenditure, 54–56, 58
Indian control of agriculture, 48–49
land ownership and tenancy, 48–49, 58, 101
semisubsistence economy, 47–60, 101

California, lemons, 245–251
Cameroons
    land holding and use, 31–32
    cocoa, 251, 252
Capital and capital investment
    agricultural surplus and, 301–4, 309–11, 317n.
    cash cropping stimulation, 267–69
    decision making regarding, 218–18
    dual economy models, 324ff., 348ff., 354, 356ff.
    external, and production improvement, 261, 317–18
    foreign, 268–69, 311, 312, 318
    gross, as function of price, and supply model, 247–48
    human resources, 364, 369–71
    improvements, agricultural, 303, 304, 309–11, 356–57
    innovation and, 225, 228, 268
    penny capitalism, 118
    population growth and, 371–75
    resource expansion, 273–74
    rice growing, 53
    technology and labor, 321ff.
    traditional agriculture, 210, 215–16, 218–19, 369ff.
    see also Credit
Cassava, 234, 237, 239
Castillo, Gelia, 136–42
Cattle
    communal pasture, 73n., 75–76
    forest fodder, 74
    range management, 394, 406
    rice variety choice and, 278, 289
    see also Livestock
Ceremony and ritual, 78–79
    crop decisions and, 288
    economic effects of, 34–35, 58–59, 292–93
Change
    attitudes toward, 79, 101–2, 105–7, 112ff., 156,
        214–15, 376ff.
    contact, 112–13
    decision-making and, 217–18
    diffusion simulation, 130–31
    directed, see also specific names, subjects, 112–13,
        387–452
    economic-mindedness, growth of, 152–61
    familism, 123, 137
    imminent, 112
    innovativeness and, see Innovativeness
    interpersonal communication and use of mass media,
        127–28
    mass media exposure, 125–26
    religious institutions, 59, 129, 288, 292–93
    security vs., 214–15, 228, 377–78
    selective contact, 112
    social organizations, use of, 128–29
    social, types of, 112–13
    systems problem, 388–89
    time preferences, 377, 378, 460
    see also Development, agricultural; specific subject
Chettyars, 48–49, 58
Chiefs
    administrative services, 34
    land tenure and, 33–34
China
    disguised unemployment, 340ff.
    politicolegal structure and peasants, 25–26
    population growth and subsistence farming, 19
    productivity and population, 314–15
Clothing
    expenditures, 55, 121, 198
    incentive, 276
    serfs, Andean, 407, 410
Clubs and organizations, 10, 428, 429

Cocoa, 243–44, 250–52
Coffee, 158, 160, 313n., 393, 403, 404
    supply relations, 245–47, 251, 252
Colombia
    aspirations, 119, 120
    coffee, 246, 251, 252
    empathy, 126
    fatalism, 118, 119n.
    government, reliance on, 124
    innovativeness, 117
    interpersonal relations, 115–16
    land clearing and ownership, 75n.
    living, levels of, 120
    mass media exposure, 125–26
    mobility, geographical, 124
    radio programs, educational, 128
    religious institutions, and change, 129
    time perspective, 122
Colonialism
    agricultural development and, 158–59
    crop introduction, 44, 158
    land ownership and production control, 44
    nationalism and, 47, 49
    sociological approach to peasantry, 64–65
Comilla program in East Pakistan, 390, 415–24
Commercialization and commercial farmers, 13, 14–15
    aspirations, 119, 120, 159
    Andean, 393ff., 408–10
    asset income change, 170–71, 187
    cash receipts and expenditures, 197–99
    colonialism and, 44, 158
    crop choice and growth of, 160
    development and, 206
    economic-mindedness, growth of, 152–61
    evolution and subsistence to, 257–95
    extension, response to, 157–58
    family size, 173–75, 187, 192
    farm size and, 7, 173, 187, 201–4
    full-time farming, 166n.
    home-consumption ratios, 186
    incentives, 262ff.
    innovativeness, 117
    Korea 196–208
    labor productivity, 205–6
    land productivity, 201–5
    marketed production and total product value,
        199–201
    market economy, 156
    medium farmers, Andean, 393, 401–2
    multiple products, 181–83, 188–89
    nationalization, 317n., 29
    part-time farming, 166n., 188, 193
    plantations, 393, 403–4
    poverty, 177–79, 188
    price changes, 171–73, 188, 192, 194–95, 219–21
    productivity, 201–6
    purchased inputs, 156–57
    pure commercial with competitive labor market,
        subjective equilibrium model, 179–82, 188–89,
        193
    pure commercial without labor market, subjective
        equilibrium model, 166–79, 186–88
    ranches, 393
    seasonality, 176, 188, 193
    semicommercial, subjective equilibrium models,
        182–83, 186, 188–89
    serfs, 408–10
    shifting agriculture concurrent with, 227
    specialization, 99, 271–73, 281–82
    subjective equilibrium models, 165–96
    subsistence production and living and, 13, 14–15,
        262ff.
    supply response and modernization, 232–53
    technological innovations, 175–76, 187–88, 192
    tenure and innovation, 225

two-sector economy, 306, 311–13
  see also specific subjects
Communication
  geography and, 42
  incentive lack, 42
  interpersonal, and mass media, 127–28
  mass media exposure, 125–26
  peasant economy, creation of, and, 41–42
  planning, 151–52
  social and economic change and, 41
  transportation and, 42
  understanding of audience, 111–12
  yield differences and, 449–52
Communities
  evolution and mutation, 65–67
  history, reconstruction of, 67, 72
  Middle Ages, 66, 68
  products, *see* Community projects
  see also Villages
Community projects
  development acceleration and, 10
  incentive, 33
  interpersonal relations, distrust in, 116
  labor, communal, 33
  obligations, traditional, 43–44
  religious institutions and, 59, 129
Conformity
  status and, 45–46
  village, 80–81, 121
Congo, land resources, 227
Conservatism, 17, 101–3
  conformity pressures and, 45
  financial, 214–15, 218–19
  risks and, 214–15, 218–19
  security, 214–15
  traditions and, 79, 288, 292–93
Consumer goods and services
  cash production and, 264*ff.*
  felt poverty and, 178
  material welfare aspirations, 222–23, 277–79
  savings and availability, 215
Consumption
  ceiling and wealth, 42
  ceremony and ritual and, 34–35
  crop introduction and, 106
  demand and supply, 191
  expenditures, 55–56, 121–22, 198–99
  income allocation, 55–56, 121–22, 198–99
  living, levels of, and aspirations, 120–21
  subsistence production and living, 13, 262*ff.*, 275*ff.*,
    395*ff.*
  see also Consumer goods and services
Cooperatives
  Comilla experiment, 417–20
  credit, 418, 419–20
  development acceleration and, 10, 417*ff.*
Cornell program in Vicos, Peru, 389–90, 392–414
Corn, 107*n.*, 234, 237–40
  Rockefeller Foundation program in Mexico, 391–92,
    438–52
Costs
  credit, 53–54, 56–57
  crop introduction and, 105–7, 138
  equipment and supplies, 53
  labor, 53, 57
  returns, and innovations, 377
  rice growing, 52–53
  technological changes, 377
Cottage industries, 394
Cotton, 313*n.*, 393, 403
Credit
  ACAR program in Minas Gerais, 429–35
  collateral, 53, 54
  cooperatives, 418, 419–20
  costs, 53–54, 56–57, 432–33

crop loans, 384–85
  decision-making regarding, 218–19
  economic progress and, 160, 408–10
  government, 54, 58, 419
  housing improvement, 430–31
  innovation and, 225
  land ownership and, 48–49
  moneylenders, 48–49, 58, 160, 417, 419
  production, 384–85, 388, 430, 431
  productivity and, 10, 54, 57
  reform, India, 384–85
  repayment with product, 54, 58
  rice growing and, 53–54, 56–58
  risks and conservatism, 218–19
  supervised, 429–30
  see also Capital
Crops
  bananas, 393
  barley, 196
  cassava, 234, 237–40
  cocoa, 243–44, 250–52
  coffee, 158, 160, 245–47, 251, 252, 313*n.*, 393, 403,
    404
  colonialism and, 44, 158
  commercial, *see also* Commercialization and
    commercial farmers, 15, 99, 138
  corn, 107*n.*, 234, 237–40, 391–92
  cotton, 313*n.*, 393, 403
  double-cropping, 50, 51, 287–89
  equatorial regions, 158
  family ownership, 44
  flax, 107
  food grains, *see also* specific names, 196
  fodder, and variety choice, 287, 289
  groundnuts, 50, 51, 377
  inedible, and home foodstuff production, 15
  introduction of new, 101–2, 105–7, 124, 138, 156,
    158, 240
  kenaf, 234, 237–40
  lemons, 245, 251
  madder, 107
  maize, *see also* corn, 107*n.*
  markets, and supply response, 51, 105–7, 237–40
  noneconomic factors in choice, 16, 287, 288, 289
  palm oil, 243, 244
  potatoes, 105–6. 124, 395, 408, 409
  price response, 221, 229, 235*ff.*, 243*ff.*
  rice, 47–60, 157, 196, 200, 201–3, 233–37, 285–92,
    356, 385, 393, 416
  rotation, 77–78
  rubber, 156–57, 158, 160, 244–45, 251
  specialization, commercial, 99
  sugar, 313*n.*, 317*n.*, 29, 393, 403
  sugar beets, 106
  tea, 403
  tobacco, 138
  tree, supply and relations, 243–53
  vegetable, 200–1, 203–4, 395, 396*ff.*, 408–9
  wheat, 391–92, 395, 438–52
  women's ownership and management, 31–32
Cuba, nationalization, 317*n.*
Cyprus, fragmentation, 32*n.*

Dandekar, V. M., 366–75
Dantwala, M. L., 382–86
Decision-making
  additional resources, command of, 218–19
  allocation of existing resources, 216–18, 228
  dynamic environment, 217–18, 228
  economic-mindedness and, 156–57
  empirical studies of, 217, 228
  noneconomic factors in, 16, 24, 84–86, 123, 287,
    288, 456–58
  peasant, 84–86, 118, 210
  price responses, 219–21, 228

social systems and, 159–60
subjective equilibrium model, 184
subsistence farming criterion, 16
supply models, tree crops, 247–53
technological change response, 221–26, 228, 408–10
traditional economies, 210, 216–26, 228
yield differences and, 444–46
Deferred gratification, 121–22, 138–39, 142, 145, 146, 377, 378, 460
Demand and supply, law of, 191
Demonstrations, 113, 420, 429
Development, agricultural
  apolitical programs, 437
  associations, voluntary, 10
  capital, *see also* Capital and capital investment, 210, 215–16, 357–58
  case studies, 387–452
  collectivization, 317
  colonialism, *see* Colonialism
  commercialization and, 206
  cultural impact, 281–82
  directed social change, 112–13
  dualism, growth models, 320–58
  equilibrium trap, low-level, 193–95
  factors affecting, classification of, 389
  freeholder system, 300–4, 305*ff*., 314–16
  growth and acceleration, essentials for, 9–10, 388
  industrial interrelationship of, 8
  institutional and ideological factors, 24
  landlord-tenant system, 304–11, 316–17
  models, classical vs. neoclassical, 320–46
  nationalism, 47, 49, 159
  nationalization, 317*n*., 29
  one-sector economy, 299–311
  pilot projects, 388, 417*ff*.
  planned change and, 388
  program costs and returns, ACAR, 433–35
  social considerations, 8, 365, 378–79, 383–84
  stimulation, external, 261, 267–69, 281–83, 357–58
  subsistence agriculture, 362*ff*.
  supply response and modernization, 232–53
  surpluses and, 279*ff*., 296*ff*.
  systems problem, 388–89
  technology as factor of, *see also* Technology, 364, 365, 369, 371
  two-sector economy, 306, 311–13; 320*ff*., 348*ff*., 353–58
  values and objectives, 210–16
Diet, *see* Nutrition
Dobyns, Henry F., 392–414
Dominican Republic, cocoa, 251, 252
Doob, Leonard W., 142–52
Dutch colonialism, 44, 153, 158, 159*n*.

East Africa, 376*n*.
East Pakistan, Comilla program, 390, 415–24
Economic anthropology, 63–64
Economic opportunity and aspirations, 23–24
Economics
  anthropology interaction with, 23–24, 37–41
  classical, 61–64, 97
  development, 354
  Marxian, 61, 63, 66, 67, 73*n*.
  opportunism, 62–63
  Methodenstreit, 62
  Ricardian, 62–63, 97
  categorization, 17–18
  ceremonial and ritual institutions, 34–35, 58–59, 288
  dualism, and growth models, 320–58
  equilibrium, and traditional agriculture, 363, 366–75
  equilibrium trap, low-level, 193–96, 322, 332, 354
  exchange, stimulation of participation in, *see* Commercialization and commercial farmers, 261, 267–69
  farmer vs. peasant, 64

growth of, *see also* Development, agricultural, 7–10, 38–41, 232–33
  ideological and social factors, 24
  marketless, and allocation of resources, 26
  peasant, 24, 25–36, 38, 41–47, 71, 94–104
  primitive, evolution to trade and specialization, 257–95
  social structure, 26–36, 37–41
  subsistence, and subsistence agriculture, 17–19
  traditional, and subsistence farmer, 209–26, 227–28
  values and, 38
Ecuador, 392*ff*.
  cocoa, 251, 252
  land ownership, 400, 401*ff*.
  livestock, 394
  product consumption and sale, 398, 399
  wheat, 395
Electrification, 417
Environmental factors
  planned change, 387–88
  yield differences, 442–44
Education
  alienation and, 293
  aspirations regarding, 23–24, 47, 119, 139, 159, 226
  development and, 10, 364, 388, 408, 420–21
  extension, *see also* Extension, 420–21, 428–29
  mass media and interpersonal communication, 127–28, 429
  restriction, 226
  status, 159
  youth, and planned development, 47
Egypt, disguised unemployment, 339*ff*.
Eicher, Carl K., 227–28
El Salvador radio programs, educational, 128
Empathy, 126–27, 139, 149, 150
Employment
  income relationship, and development, 322–24
  India, 382, 383
  opportunity, 81–82
England
  expansion and contraction of agriculture, 108–10
  pasture, open field, 75–76
Entrepreneurship
  peasant cut off from, 42
  penny capitalism, 118
  sex division of, 31
  see also Commercialization and commercial farmers
Equipment and tools
  coaration, 83
  introduction of new, 106–7
  labor-saving, 192, 224, 259–61, 270–71
  mechanization, 90–91, 375
  plowing, and crop rotation, 78*n*.
  productivity and, 9, 192, 259–61
  rice growing, 53
  sickles and scythes, 106–7
  subsistence farming criterion, 16
Eritrea, land holding and status structure, 28
Europe
  crop rotation, plowing and, 78*n*.
  disguised unemployment, 339*ff*.
  land clearing, 74
  land redistribution, 77
  see also specific regions, countries
Exports, economic development and, 301–4, 312–13, 318
Extension
  economic-mindedness and response to, 157–58
  exchange economy stimulation, 267–68, 294–95
  committees, 429
  costs and returns, ACAR, 433–35
  native technicians, use and training, 437
  relevance and suitability, 221, 228
  traditional agriculture response, 221–22, 420–21, 428–29

yield differences and, 449–52

Familism, 122–23, 137, 147
Family
  crop ownership, 44
  familism, 122–23, 137, 147
  labor, 25, 32–33, 52, 53, 165*ff.*
  organization, 25
  passivity and fatalism, 119
  practices and beliefs, lag in, 149–51
  size, 86–87, 173–75, 187
  supply response and size of, 235, 236–37
  women's dominance in, 44
  see also Kinship structure
Family farms
  part-time, 166*n.*, 188, 193
  subsective equilibrium models, 165–96
  subsistence production, 166
  theory, nature and purpose of, 185–86
  see also specific types
Farmer economy, 64
Farms
  classification, 165–66, 186
  see also specific types, subjects
Fatalism, 118–19, 122, 145
  savings and investment, 215, 216
Fertilizers, 78
  expenditures, 199, 202–4
  rice production, 202, 289–90
Feudalism, peasants and, 25
Field experiments, as analytic tool, 130
Films, exposure to, 125–26
Firth, Raymond, 23–37
Fisheries, Peruvian, 403–4
Fisk, E. K., 257–74
Flax, 107
Food
  expenditures, 55, 121–22, 198
  exports, and goods imports, 301–4, 312–13, 318
  output and labor input relationship, 257–61, 275–77, 279*ff.*
  population growth and, 88–91, 299*ff.*
  production. *see* Subsistence farmers and farming; Commercialization and commercial farming; Crops; specific subjects
  surpluses, 279*ff.*, 296*ff.*
  tenure systems, and production of, 300*ff.*
  two-sector economy, 306, 311–13, 349
  see also Nutrition; specific foods
Food grains, *see also* names, 196
Forests
  cattle fodder, 74
  clearing, 14, 47–48, 74–77
4-H and 4-S clubs, 10, 428, 429
France
  expansion and contraction of agriculture, 108–10
  land clearing, 74
  pasture, communal, 75–76
  redistribution of land, 77
  sugar beets, 106
Frontier, American, as model, 100

Gambling, 117
Ganda, 143–50
Georgescu-Roegen, Nicholas, 61–93
Germany, communal pasture, 75–76
Ghana
  cocoa, 250–52
  status and product allocation, 34
Good, belief in limited, 116–17, 222
Government
  attitudes, peasant, 123–24, 139, 147–48
  credit, 54, 58, 419
  dependence on, 124
  exchange economy stimulation, 267–69

planning and development, 388
price support and stabilization, 138, 240
research, 240
tenure systems, and role of, 301, 306, 308–11, 317
Gratification patterns, 121–22, 138–39, 142, 145, 146, 377, 378, 460
Greece, disguised unemployment, 340*ff.*
Group action and development, *see also* types of groups, 388
Groundnuts, 50, 51, 377
Guatemala
  penny capitalism, 118
  subsistence agriculture, 364

Harvest share incentive, 10
Head tax, 46
Health, *see* Medicine and health
Holmberg, Allan R., 392–414
Honduras, educational radio programs, 128
Households, 32–33
Households,
  expenditures, 55–56, 121–22, 198–99
  India, 382–83
  size, and supply response, 235, 236–37
Housing
  expenditures 55, 121, 198
  improvement credit, 430–31
  serf, Andean, 406, 407
Hungary, land ownership, 73
Hunters and fishers, 14

Ibaloi, agricultural development among, 284–95
Illiterates
  interpersonal communication and mass media for education of, 128
  mass media exposure, 126
Immigration and immigrants
  Burma, 48
  internal, and labor, 101
  labor, 101, 308
  land grants, 66*n.*
  technological introductions, 158
  urbanization, 46, 101
  village formation, 71
Implements, *see* Equipment and tools
Imports
  agricultural surpluses and, 301–4, 312–13, 318
  food, 395
Improvements, investment in, and agricultural surpluses, 303, 304, 309–11
Incentives
  acceptance of change and, 105–10
  accustomed living standards and, 42
  achievement motivation, 120
  ceremony and ritual, 34
  community pride, 33
  conformity pressures and, 45–46
  consumption, 121, 262*ff.*, 276*ff.*
  economic, 25, 100–4, 105–10, 138, 221–26. 229*ff.*, 262*ff.*, 276*ff.*, 364, 385–86
  harvest share, 10
  land tenure, 10, 29, 101
  productivity, 9–10, 101, 102–3, 388
  price relationships, 9–10, 377, 385–86
  psychological bent, 16
  resource availability, 188
  savings and investment, 215–16
  status, 159
  tax, lump-sum, and price adjustment, 195
  urbanization, 46, 101
  see also Aspirations
Income
  achievement standard of, 177–79, 188, 193
  administrative services and, 34
  allocation, 55–56, 58, 121–22, 198–99, 277–79

asset, and subjective equilibrium, 170–71, 187
Burma and disposition, 54–55, 56, 58–59
cash, 197–98
commercial farm family with labor market, 179–82
commercial family without labor market, 166–79, 186–88
demand and supply, 191
diversification and individual rights, 32
double-cropping, 51, 59
elasticity of product demand, 355
equilibrium trap, low-level, 193–96, 322, 332, 354
labor, and sharing, 73–78, 81–83, 102
labor input and, 166*ff*., 186*ff*., 191*ff*.
nonfarm activities, 42, 166*n*., 197, 198, 293–94, 336, 394
per head, employment, and development, 322–24, 330*ff*.
poverty, 177–79
present vs. future, 215–16
productivity and, 55
risks and innovation, 214–15, 228
semicommercial family farms, 182–83
status structure and land holding, 28
subjective equilibriam models, 166*ff*., 187*ff*.
subsistence farming criterion, 16
supplementary cash production, 262*ff*.
supply response, risk and, 235, 236
tax, 46
technological changes and, 223–24
village control of land, 71
world subsistence farming, 19
India, 7, 356
    communal land use, 75
    disguised unemployment, 339*ff*.
    emigration, 48
    empathy, 126
    interpersonal relations, 116
    land resources, 227
    land clearing and use, 75
    land ownership, 66*n*.
    living, level of, and aspiration, 121
    legal structure and peasants, 25
    population growth and subsistence farming, 19
    radio programs, educational, 128
    rice, 385
    subsistence agriculture, 364–66, 382–86
    tobbaco, 138
Individualism, peasant, 83, 122–23, 147
Indonesia
    disguised unemployment, 340
    economic-mindedness, growth of, 152–61
    land holding and use, 29–30, 42, 43
    peasant social structure and economy, 41–47
    population growth and subsistence farming, 19
Industrialization
    agricultural development and, 8, 104, 357–58
    agricultural labor force and, 342*ff*., 350–51, 354–55
    agriculture, 90–91
    cottage industries, 394
    dual economy models, 320–58
    familism, 123
    investment in, and agricultural surplus, 301–4, 309–11, 317*n*.
    labor, 90
    rice milling, 48
    trade movement, 355
    youth, 46
Inheritance
    land use and rights, 29–30, 31, 32, 44
    labor supply and systems of, 32
    primogeniture, 32
    women's rights, 31, 32, 44
Initiative, kinship land rights and, 29, 30
Innovativeness, 117–18, 137–38, 144–45
    capital and, 225

Cornell Vicos Project, 407–10
costs and returns, 377
    familism, 123
    marketing and, 225
    restrictions by power agents, 225–26
    risks and, 214–15, 223, 377–78
    skills and education, 224
    tenure, 224–25
    social costs, 378–79
    status, 378, 379
    time preference, 377, 378
    traditional agriculture, 214–15, 221–26, 228, 379
    see also Change
Insecticides, expenditures, 202, 204
Intelligentsia, sociological interests and, 64
Interdisciplinary approach to analysis, 9, 12–13, 95–96, 456, 466
    social anthropology and economy, interaction of, 23–24, 37–41
Interpersonal relationships
    distrust in, 115–17, 144
    subsistence farming criterion, 16
Investment, *see* Capital and capital investment
Involvement, external
    conformism and, 81
    definition of subsistence farmer, 15–17
    development and, 260*ff*.
    peasants, *see also* Towns, 25, 96–97
    social structure and economic change, 40–41
Ireland, family size and land, 86*n*.
Iroquois, land ownership, 65–67
Irrigation, 78, 417
    cooperative, 421–22
    land use patterns and, 44
Italy
    disguised unemployment, 340*ff*.
    fatalism, 118
    government, attitude toward, 123
    localiteness, 148–49
    interpersonal relations, 115, 116
    short view, 122
Ivory Coast, cocoa, 251

Jamaica
    disguised unemployment, 339
    time perspective, 146, 147
Japan, 317*n*., 356
    agriculture, and industrial investment, 317*n*.
    commercial farming and farm size, 7
    economic development, 342*ff*., 352, 354*n*.
    familism, 137
    farm categories and percentages, 166*n*.
    legal structure and peasants, 25
    part-time farming, 166*n*., 188
    technology transfer and modification, 137
Java, 72*n*.
    communication, production and market, 41–42
    conformity pressures, 44–46
    land holding and use, 43–44
    peasant social structure and economy, 41–47
    tax structure, 47
    younger generation values, 46–47
    women, freedom of movement, 31*n*.
Johnston, Bruce F., 348–53
Jones, William O., 275–83
Jorgenson, Dale W., 320–48
Joy, J. Leonard, 376–81

Kenaf, 234, 237–40
Kinship structure
    land holding and, 26–32
    social status, hereditary, 28
    transmission rights, 29, 31, 32
    village unity and, 68–69
    see also Family

Korea, commercialization and resource use, 196–208
Krishna, Raj, 185–90

Labor
    alienation, and non-farm, 293
    Andean, 393–94, 404*ff.*
    attitude, peasant, 84, 101, 211–14
    availability and poverty, 177
    capital relationships, technology and, 321*ff.*, 354*ff.*
    cash productive, 262*ff.*, 279*ff.*, 393–94
    cheap, agricultural surplus and, 308
    commercialization, and productivity, 205–6
    communal, 33
    costs, 7, 53, 56, 57
    cottage industries, 394
    crop introduction and, 107
    demand and supply, 191
    disguised unemployment, 101, 321*ff.*
    division of, 31
    dual economy models, 320*ff.*
    equilibrium trap, low-level, 193–95
    exchange basis, 53
    expenditures, 179–81, 199
    family, 25, 31, 52, 53, 165*ff.*
    food output relationship, 257–61, 275–77, 279*ff.*
    growth rate and population, 356
    hired/total ratio, 15–16, 165
    household unit, 32–33
    immigrant, 48, 308
    income sharing and, 73–78, 81–83, 102
    India, 382, 383
    industrialization, 90
    inheritance systems and supply of, 32
    innovations and input of, 223–24
    internal migration, 101
    leisure, and hired labor costs, 214
    marginal productivity, 81–82, 102, 169, 181, 193, 368, 373
    money utility and, 262*ff.*
    opportunity, 73–74, 77, 81–82, 102
    overpopulated subsistence agriculture, 193–95
    payment, 52, 53
    peonage, 308
    preferable to produce sale, 42
    price response, 219–21
    resources, subsistence economy, 259*ff.*, 269*ff.*, 279*ff.*
    rice growing, Burma, 52–53, 56, 290–92
    seasonal, 52–53, 176, 188, 193, 340
    serf, 393, 394–95, 404*ff.*, 408*ff.*
    sex division of, 31, 406–7
    slave, 308
    status, 33, 52, 293
    subjective equilibrium models, 165–96
    surplus, 90, 259*ff.*, 281, 296, 320*ff.*
    traditional agriculture, 210, 227, 370, 373–75
    urbanization, 81–82, 293, 355, 394
    use research agenda, 462–63
    value theory, 73
    village formation and control of, 66
    wages, *see* Wages
    women, 31, 52–53, 406–7
Lag in beliefs and practices, 149–51
Land
    allocation and use, kin ownership and, 29–30
    clearing, 14, 47–48, 74–77
    communal use, 73*n.*, 75–76
    crop rotation, 77–78
    development and settlement assistance, 268–69
    fertility, 78
    improvement, 78, 388
    as input, 356
    irrigation, and use patterns, 44, 78
    price, and status structure, 28
    production factor, 364–65
    productivity and commercialization, 201–5

reallocation, 74, 76–77
reclamation and prices, 109–10
resources, 227
strip cultivation, 76, 77
use, and modernization, 233*ff.*
see also Land holding; Land ownership
Land holdings
    Andean, 393–95, 400–4
    chiefs, administration and allocation by, 33–34
    clearing and, 74–75
    fragmentation, 32, 393, 405
    innovations and, 224–25
    kinship structure and, 26–27
    improvements and, 78
    nomadism, 72
    rights based on, 28
    serf, 72, 73, 405
    sharecropping, 43, 373, 394
    size and productivity, 7, 201–4, 205–6, 227, 372
    status structure and, 28, 46
    strips, 76, 77
    technological limits to, 43
    traditional agriculture, production and, 210, 224–25
    see also Land; Land ownership
Land ownership
    agrarian reforms, 50–51, 73, 75
    Andean, 400–4
    collective, 66, 71–73, 94–95
    collectivization and productivity, 317
    colonialism and, 44
    communal, 29–30, 44, 66, 69, 71–73, 94–95, 393
    corporations, tribal, 30
    credit operations and, 48–49
    evolution of, 65–67, 71–73
    family size and, 86*n.*
    hereditary, 29–30, 31, 32
    incentive, 10, 29
    India, 382–83, 384
    Indigenous Communities, 393
    individual, 29–30, 44, 66, 69, 94–95
    latifundia, 308, 394–95, 400, 402–4
    manors, Andean, 403
    minifundia, 392*n.*, 400
    nationalization, 50–51, 53
    landlordism growth and population, 305–11
    legal restrictions, 30, 42, 43
    markets, productivity and, 29, 30
    nonagriculturalists, 49
    plantations, Andean, 402*ff.*
    production and, 300–18, 316–17
    reform, 384, 400
    serfdom, 72, 73
    tribal, 30
    village classification according to, 66–67
    vivification and, 75*n.*
    women, 30–32, 44
    see also Land; Land holding
Laos, Buddhist monks, and community projects, 129
Latifundia, 308, 394–95, 400, 402–4
Latin America
    aspirations, 119
    disguised unemployment, 339*ff.*
    fatalism, 119
    frontiers, 100
    land resources, 227
    religious institutions, and change, 129
    traditional agriculture, 209–26, 227–28
    see also specific countries
Leaders
    communication programs, 127–28
    mass media exposure, 126
    religious institutions, 129
Legal structure
    common law and village tradition, 80
    land ownership, 30, 42, 43

peasants, 25–26, 80
Leisure
  as economic activity, 278
  economic opportunity and, 101
  income-leisure model, 186–87, 191, 192
  labor cost and, 214, 227
  material goods vs., 211–13, 227
  productivity and, 194, 213, 278
Lemons, 245, 251
Limited good, belief in, 116–17, 222
Liquor consumption, 121–22
Literacy, mass media exposure, 125–26
Livestock
  communal pasture, 73n., 75–76
  consumption and sale, Andean, 395ff.
  expenditures, 199
  feeds, 74, 199
  income from, 197, 198, 395ff.
  manors, 394, 406
  marketed production and total product value, 200–1
  production, Andean, 404
  productivity and commercialization, 204–5
  ranches, 393
  range management, 394, 406
  rice variety choice and, 287, 289
  serfs, Andean, 395, 406
  see also specific subject
Living, levels of
  achievement standard, 177n., 178
  aspirations and, 120–21
  conformity, 42, 45, 121
  economic growth and, 8
  marginal productivity, 367–68
  poverty and, 177
  subsistence, definition, 12, 13–14, 16
Localiteness, 124–26, 148–49
  interpersonal communication and mass media, use for planned change, 127–28
Lower Burma, semisubsistence economy, 47–60
Luo, 143–50
Luzon, 284–95

Madder, 107
Maize, see also Corn, 107n.
Malaria control, supply response and, 238, 239
Malaya
  ceremony and ritual, 35
  communal labor, 33
  land holding and use, 29–30, 31
  rubber, 245, 251
  sex division of labor, 31
Management, women's role in, 30–32
Manors, Andean, 394–95, 404–10
Maori
  chiefs, roles of, 34
  land holding and use, 29, 30, 32n.
Markets and marketing
  commercialization and, 156
  crop innovations and, 51, 105–7, 237–40
  innovations and, 225
  labor urbanization and, 355
  land ownership and, 29, 30
  marginal profits and, 42
  monopolies, and economic progress, 160
  nationalization, 51
  peasant economy, 96–97
  price elasticity and, 235–36
  production, 41–42, 260–61
  productivity and, 9, 29, 388
  resource allocation and, 26
  specialization and, 273
  supplementary cash production and, 262ff.
Marx and Marxism
  economics, 63, 67, 97
  peasant policies and attitudes, 61, 66, 81, 82, 97, 102

value theory, 73n.
Mass media
  exposure to, 125–26, 127
  interpersonal communication and, use for planned change, 127–28, 429
Mayin Village (Burma), 50–60
Mechanization, 90–91, 375
Medicine and health
  epidemics and productivity, 341
  expenditures, 55
  malaria control and supply response, 238, 239
  subsistence living, 14
Mellor, John W., 209–27
Menomini, land holding and use, 30
Mexico
  aspirations, 119
  ceremony and ritual, 35
  collectivization, 317
  corn, 391–92, 438–52
  decision making, 118
  familism, 122–23
  household unit and labor resources, 33
  interpersonal relations, 115, 117
  peonage, 308
  Rockefeller Foundation program, 391–92, 438–52
  wheat, 391–92, 438–52
Middle Ages
  communities, 66, 68
  expansion and contraction of agriculture, 107–10
Middle East, see specific countries
Midwest (U.S.), economic development, 313n.
Minangkabau, land holding and use, 29
Minas Gerais, 7
  ACAR program in, 391, 424–38
Minifundia, 394n., 400
Mir, 66, 68, 77
Mobility, geographical, 124–25
Models
  analysis of, 24
  growth, classical vs. neoclassical, 320–58
  subjective equilibrium, 165–96
  supply, tree crops, 247–53
Monetization
  peasant economy, 99–100
  social and economic change and, 41
  utility of money and, 262ff.
Moneylenders, 48–49, 58, 160, 417, 419
Monopolies, economic progress and, 160
Monte Carlo diffusion simulation, 130–31
Mosher, A. T., 6–11
Motivations, values and attitudes, 114–15, 457, 459–61
  see also Aspirations; Incentives
Muslims, ideological factors and economic decisions, 24
Myint, H., 99–104
Myren, Delbert T., 438–52

Nakajima, Chihiro, 165–85
Narodniki, 64, 66, 81, 82, 98
Nationalism
  agricultural development and, 159, 312
  colonialism and, 47, 49
Navaho land holding and use, 30
Ndesa, 72n.
Negri Sembilan
  communal labor, 33
  entrepreneurship, 31
  land holding and use, 29, 31
Netherlands, sugar beets, 106
New England, economic development, 313n.
New Guinea, 7, 257ff., 276ff.
  ceremony and ritual, 35
New Zealand, see Maori
Newspapers
  educational use, 429
  exposure to, 125–26

Nicholls, William H., 296–318
Nigeria
  cocoa, 244, 251
  communal labor, 33
  palm oil, 244
Noneconomic influences, 16, 24, 84–86, 123, 287, 288,
    456–58, 464–66
North (U.S.), economic development, 313n.
North Sumatra, growth of economic-mindedness,
    152–61
North Tyrol, localiteness, 148–49
Northeast (U.S.), economic development, 313n.
Nsaw, land holding and use, 31–32
Nutrition
  labor input and food output relationship, 258,
    275–77, 279ff.
  serf, Peruvian, 395
  subsistence living, 14

Occupations
  household heads, Burma, 52
  see also Labor
Office holding, economic effects, 35
Opportunity
  aspirations and, 23–24, 101, 119, 120
  equality of, 73–74, 77, 81–82, 102
Oral tradition, 71, 79
Orient, *see* Asia; specific areas

Pakistan
  Comilla program, 390, 415–24
  empathy, 126
  population growth and subsistence farming, 19
Palm oil, 243, 244
Papua, 257ff.
Park, Jin H., 196–208
Pasture
  Andean, 394, 406
  communal, 73n., 75–76
Peasants and peasant economy
  agrarian communism, 66, 72, 73–74, 77
  Andean, 393–401
  Bolivia, 393–94
  Burma, 47–60
  classical economists' attitude toward, 61–63
  culture and subculture of, 113ff., 136ff., 142ff.
  definition, 24, 25, 38, 94–98
  disintegration, 99–100, 186, 293
  diversity, 99–100, 113
  Ecuador, 393–94
  expansion, 71, 100–101
  family size, 86–87
  governments, attitudes toward, 123–24, 139, 147–48
  households, 32–33
  Java, 41–47
  labor resources, 25, 32–33
  lag in beliefs and practices, 149–51
  legal structure, 25–26, 80
  nonagricultural sector, 27–28
  Peru, 393–401
  political structure and, 25–26, 50
  population and agricultural surplus, 314–16
  towns, relationship with, 25, 81–82, 84, 87–88, 90–91,
    96–97
  transitional, 99–100, 186
  villages, *see* Villages
  see also Subsistence farmers and farming; specific
    subjects
Penny capitalism, 118
Penny, D. H., 152–61
Peonage, 308
Peru
  coffee, 393, 403
  Cornell program, 389–90, 392–414
  exports, 403–4
  imports, 395
  land ownership and production, 400–4, 405
  manors, 394–95, 404–10
  peonage, 308
  plantations, 393, 403–4
  product consumption and sale, 395–99, 406, 407
  production, 404
Pfanner, David E., 47–60
Philippines, 7, 284–95
  aspirations, 139
  ceremony and ritual, 288, 292–93
  familism, 137
  government, dependence on, 139
  rice, 285–92
  technology adaptability, 137–38
  supplies and technology, 138
  tobacco, 138
Pilot projects, 388, 417ff.
Plantations, Andean, 393, 402ff.
Plowing
  coaration, 83
  crop rotation, 78n.
Poland, 317n.
Political structure
  agricultural development and, 301ff.
  peasants and, 25, 50
  product allocation and, 33–34
Polygyny, 66
Population
  agricultural surplus and, 299ff., 313ff.
  capital formation and, 371–75
  equilibrium trap, low-level, 193–96, 322
  expansion and contraction of agriculture, 107–8
  farm population and growth of, 7, 19
  growth and economic development, 322, 325ff.,
    349ff., 354ff.
  fertility, peasant, 86–87
  food supply and, 88–91, 299ff.
  India, 382
  landlordism growth and, 305–11
  productivity and, 193–95, 261, 275, 371ff.
  subsistence agriculture and, 365, 371–75
  subsistence farmers, 7, 18–19
  two-sector economy and, 311, 322
  urbanization, 46, 101
  villages, 69–71
  wages and, 305–6, 322
Populism, Russia, 98
Potatoes, 105–6, 124, 395, 408, 409
Poultry and poultry products, 395ff.
Poverty
  aspirations and, 120
  causes, 177, 188
  culture, 114
  felt, 178–79, 188
  subsistence living and, 13–14
Prices
  crop introduction and, 138
  decision making response, 219–21, 228
  elasticity, and availability of alternative economic
    opportunities, 235–36
  expansion and contraction of agriculture, 108–10
  investment as function of, 247–48
  land, and status structure, 28
  need for nonagricultural commodities, 42
  poverty and, 177, 188
  product, and subjective equilibrium, 171–73, 192,
    194–95
  production response, 219–21, 228, 229ff.
  relationships of, as incentives, 9–10
  risks, and credit decisions, 219
  seasonality, and production, 221
  stabilization, and supply response, 240
  supply response, 229, 235ff., 243ff., 364
  support programs, 138, 195

tree crops, and supply models, 247*ff*.
Primitive cultivators, definition, 14
Primogeniture, 32
Print media, exposure to and educational use of, 125–26, 429
Production
  cassava, 234, 237–40
  ceremony and ritual and, 34–35
  communications and, 41–42, 260–61
  consumer goods introduction and, 178
  corn, 237–40
  costs, *see* Costs
  expenditures, *see also* specific subjects, 198, 199
  hired/total labor ratio, 15
  income elasticity of demand, 355
  kenaf, 234, 237–40
  labor input and food output relationship, 257–61, 275–77, 279*ff*.
  land inputs and increased, 356–57
  marketed, and total product value, 199–201
  methods, *see* Technology; specific subjects
  price response, 219–21, 228, 229*ff*., 364
  purchased factor inputs ratio, 15–16
  resource availability, 270
  rice, 47, 49–52, 233–37
  seasonality, 176, 188
  specialization, 271–73, 281–82
  subsistence, definitions, 12, 13, 14–15
  supplementary cash, primitive economy, 262*ff*.
  supplies, *see* Supplies; specific subjects
  surplus, 279*ff*., 296*ff*., 313*ff*., 355
  tenancy and, 304–11, 316–17
  tenure and, 300*ff*.
  traditional agriculture, 210, 227
  tree crops, 243–53
  see also Productivity; Supply; Yields; specific subjects
Productivity
  collectivization and, 317
  commercialization and, 201–6
  credit and, 10, 54, 57
  dual economy models, 324*ff*., 349–50
  health and, 238, 239, 341
  incentives, 9–10, 101, 102–3, 388
  income and, 55
  labor, and commercialization, 205–6
  labor-intensive subsidiary enterprises and, 194
  labor-saving innovations and, 192, 224, 259–61, 270–71
  land and commercialization, 201–5
  land ownership and, 29, 30
  leisure and, 194, 213, 278
  marginal, 81–82, 102, 169, 181, 192, 368, 373
  markets and marketing, 9, 29, 388
  nationalization, 317*n*.
  population pressure and, 193–95, 261, 275, 371*ff*.
  serfs, 395, 405–6, 408–10
  size of farm and, 7, 201–4, 227, 372
  supplies and equipment and, 9, 388
  technology and, 9, 42, 74, 89–91, 137, 388, 408–10
  transportation, 9, 388
  see also Production
Profits
  marginal, and marketing, 42
  peasant attitude toward, 25
Psychological characteristics, subsistence farmers, 16, 458–16
Purchased inputs, ratio of and involvement, 15–16

Radio
  exposure to, 125–26
  planned change use, 128, 429
Rahim, Syed A., 415–24
Ranches, Andean, 393
Religious institutions
  change and, 59, 129, 288, 292–93

crop decisions and, 288
  fatalism and, 118
  support of, 43, 55–56, 58–59
Rent, population levels and, 305–8, 316–17
Research
  areas and priorities, 130, 140–41, 190, 216, 232, 380–81, 455–67
  corn and wheat, 440–42
  development of subsistence agriculture and, 364, 365
  government, 240
  relevance and adaptability, 100, 124, 137–38, 232, 377, 421
  see also Analytic methodology
Resources
  additional, command of, 218–21, 228
  allocation, 216–18, 228, 229, 364–66, 367*ff*., 461–62
  aspirations and availability of, 188
  commercialization, and use of, 196–208, 228
  expansion of, 273–74
  labor, subsistence economy, 259*ff*., 269*ff*., 279*ff*.
  land, 227, 271–73
  nonsubsistence, 356
  poverty and, 177
  specialization and, 271–73
Resti, 28
Ribeiro, Jose Paulo, 424–38
Rice
  Burma, 47–60
  East Pakistan, 416*ff*.
  Ecuador, 393
  fertilizers, 202, 289–90
  India, 385
  Korea, 196, 200, 201–3
  labor, 52–53, 56, 290–92
  land inputs and production, 356
  North Sumatra, 157
  Peru, 393
  Philippines, 285–92, 356
  Thailand, 233–37
  variety evaluation, 286–90
Risks
  innovation and, 214–15, 219, 228
  specialization and, 273
  supply response and, 235, 236
Roads
  change and, 158
  see also Transportation
Rockefeller Foundation program in Mexico, 391–92, 438–52
Rockefeller, John D., 3rd, 3–5
Rogers, Everett M., 111–35
Role, social change and, 112
Roman Empire, land ownership and community development, 66–67
Rubber, 156–57, 158, 160
  supply relations, 244–45, 251
Rumania
  communal land use, 75
  land clearing, 74
  land distribution *per stirpes*, 77
Russia
  communal land use, 75
  immigrants, land grants to, 66*n*.
  mir, 66, 68, 77
  Narodniki, 64, 66, 81, 82, 98
  peasant economy, sociological studies of, 64
  Populism, 98
  village evolution, 66
  see also Soviet Union
Ruttan, Vernon W., 353–60
Ryotwari, 25

Savings, 122, 215–16
  ceremony and ritual and, 58–59, 292–93
  decision-making regarding, 218–19

dual economy models, 339
noncash, 53
see also Capital and capital investment
Schultz, T. W., 105–10
Scotland, land redistribution, 77
Scythes and sickles, 106–7
Seasonality
labor, 52–53, 176, 188, 193, 340
prices, and production, 221
rice growing, 52–53
subjective equilibrium and, 176, 188, 193
Security
change vs., 214–15, 228
savings and investment, 215–16, 228
Self-help, fatalism and, 119
Semicommercial family farms, subjective equilibrium
models, 182–83, 186, 188–89
Serfdom
Andean, 393, 394–95, 404*ff.*
Cornell Peru Project, 407–10
farm produce consumption and sale, 395–99, 406,
407, 408, 409
land communalism and, 72, 73
shelter and clothing, 406, 407, 410
thievery, 406–7
Shand, R. T., 257–74
Sharecropping
Andean, 394
social characteristics, 43
surplus production and population, 373
Shifting agriculture, 14, 227
Sickles and scythes, 106–7
Silesia, sugar beets, 106
Slash and burn agriculture, 14
Slave labor, 308
Social anthropology, interaction with economics,
23–24, 37–41
Social change
types of, 112–13
see also Change
Socialism, Burma, 50
Social structure
ceremony and ritual, 34–35, 58–59, 78–79, 292–93
change introduction through, 128–29
economic development and, 8, 32, 40–41, 159–60,
383–84, 408–10
innovation and, 379, 408–10
peasant economy and, 24, 25–60
sharecropping, 43
taxation and, 46
youth, 46–47
Social welfare, economic growth and, 8, 365, 378–79,
383–84
Sociology
analytical tool, 8–9
peasant economy, development of interest in, 62–65
Soemardjian, Selo, 41–47
South (U. S.), economic development, 313*n.*
South America, 7
see also specific countries
South Korea, commercialization and resource use,
196–208
South Tyrol, localiteness, 148–49
South Vietnam
fatalism, 118*n.*
interpersonal relations, 116
Southeast Asia, export explosion, 100–1
Soviet Union
politicolegal structure and peasants, 25–26
productivity and collectivization, 317*n.*
towns, peasants and, 25
see also Russia
Specialization, 99, 271–73, 281–82
Statistics as analytical tool, 8–9
Status

conformity and, 45–46, 378, 379
education, 159
hereditary and income, 28
land holding and use, 28, 45–46
production allocation, 33–34
religious roles, and economic development, 59
social change and, 112
wage labor and, 33, 52, 293
Strip systems, 76, 77
Subjective equilibrium models, 165–96
Subsistence agriculture
and subsistence economy, 18
developing, 363*ff.*
planned change, 112–13, 387–452
pure, typical and expanded, 154
resource allocation, 364–66, 367*ff.*
see also Peasants and peasant economy; Subsistence
farmers and farming; specific subjects
Subsistence farmers and farming
commercialization, *see* Commercialization and
commercial farmers
definitions, 6–7, 12–19, 38
developmental criteria, 17
dual agriculture, 186
economic behavior research, 461–63
economic criteria, 15–16
economic-mindedness, growth of, 152–61
evolution to trade and specialization, 257–95
"expanded," 154
income, as criterion, 16
proportion of, 7, 18–19, 186
production/consumption ratio, 15
psychological characteristics, 16, 458–61
purchased factor inputs ratio, 15–16
pure, 154
rationality, 459
semisubsistence, subjective equilibrium models,
182–83
sociocultural criteria, 16
subjective equilibrium models, 190–96
technological level, 16
traditional economies, 209–26, 227–28
typical, 154
values and program objectives, 210–16
world income percentage, 19
see also Peasants and peasant economy; specific
subjects
Sudan, land resources, 227
Sugar, 313*n.*, 317*n.*, 403
Sugar beets, 106
Sumatra
economic-mindedness, growth of, 152–61
production and market communication, 42
Supplies
commercialization and, 156–57
crop introduction and, 106, 138
expenditures, 198, 199, 201–4
productivity and, 9, 388
rice growing, 53
see also specific subjects
Supply
economic incentives and, 229–53
elasticity, critical distinctions and economic
incentives, 230
models, for tree crops, 247–53
tree crops, 243–53
see also Production
Surpluses, 279*ff.*, 296*ff.*
Swidden agriculture, 14
Switzerland
fragmentation, 32*n.*
mowing, and communal pasture, 73*n.*

Taiwan
commercial farming and farm size, 7

rice production, 356
Tallensi kinship structure and land holding, 26–27
Tang, Anthony M., 190–96
Tanganyika, 377
Taxation
   agricultural surpluses and, 301, 303, 313*n.*
   community formation and, 66
   expenditures for, 199
   lump-sum, and price adjustment, as incentive, 193
   social values and, 46
Taxonomic classification of villages, 65
Tea, 403
Techniques
   development acceleration and, 9
   primitive cultivators, 14
Technology
   changes, attitudes toward, 17, 45, 101–2, 105–7,
      113*ff.*, 156, 221–26, 376*ff.*
   costs and returns, 377
   crop introduction and, 101–2
   decision making response, 221–26, 228
   directed change in, 112–13
   immigrant introduction, 158
   labor/capital relationships, 321*ff.*, 349, 354*ff.*
   land holdings and, 43
   low level of and poverty, 177
   ownership systems affected by, 32
   productivity and, 9, 74, 89–91, 137, 259–61, 270–71,
      388, 408–10
   risks and innovation, 214–15, 219, 228
   serfs, Peruvian, 405*ff.*, 408–10
   subjective equilibrium and, 175–76, 187–88, 192
   subsistence farming criterion, 16
   supply response and modernization, 232–53, 364
   traditional agriculture, 210, 364, 365, 369, 371
   transfer, 124, 137
Television
   exposure to, 125–26
   planned change use, 128
Tenancy
   agricultural development and, 304–11, 316–17
   Burma, 49, 101
   incentives and, 10, 101
   innovation and, 224–25
   poverty and, 177, 188
   sharecropping, 43
Tepoztlan, 115, 122–23
Thailand
   cassava, corn and kenaf, 234, 237–40
   rice, 233–37
Thorner, Daniel, 94–99
Thrift, 119, 122
Time perspective, 122, 146, 147
Tobacco, 138
Tools, *see* Equipment and tools
Topography
   factors affecting village formation, 70–71
   classification criterion for villages, 65
Towns, peasant relationships with, 25, 81–82, 84,
      87–88, 90–91, 96–97
Tradition
   common law and, 79
   decision-making and, 84–86, 288, 289
   economic-mindedness, growth of, and, 159–61
   innovativeness and, 117–18, 379
   oral, 71, 79
   resiliency and power, 79–81
   see also specific subjects
Traditional agriculture
   definition, 363
   production process in, 210
   see also Peasants and peasant economy; Subsistence
      agriculture; Subsistence farmers and farming;
      specific subjects
Transportation

change and, 158–59
communication and, 42
crop innovations and, 51, 106, 107
productivity and, 9, 388
social and economic change and, 41
specialization and, 273
village location and size, 70
Tree crops, supply relations, 243–53
   see also specific crops
Turkey
   empathy, 126–27
   government, attitude toward, 123, 124
   hunger, 122
   mass media exposure, 125
   mobility, geographical, 124–25
   time perspective, 122
Tyrol, localiteness, 148–49

Unemployment, disguised, 101, 321
   famines and epidemics and, 341
   seasonality and, 340
   withdrawal of labor and, 341*ff.*
Uganda, 6–7, 379
Ultimogeniture, 32
United States
   agricultural economics, classical, 63–64
   economic development, 309*n.*, 313*n.*
   frontier, as model, 100
   tariff policies, 303*n.*
Urbanization
   achievement motivation, 120
   alienation and, 293
   employment, 81–82, 293, 355, 394
   familism, 123
   incentives, 46, 101
   youth, 46
U.S.S.R., *see* Soviet Union

Vegetable crops
   marketed production and total product value, 200–1
   Peruvian consumption and sale, 395–99
   productivity and commercialization, 203–5
Venezuela
   cocoa, 251, 252
   mass media exposure, 125
Vicos (Peru), Cornell project, 389–90, 395, 404–10
Vietnam
   fatalism, 118*n.*
   interpersonal relations, 116
Villages
   activity and size, 70*n.*
   agrarianism, 66, 72, 73–74, 77, 82–83, 98
   "aristocracies," 82
   class antagonisms, 97
   classification, 65–66
   communalism, 82–83
   conformity, 80–81
   definition, 67–68
   economic-mindedness, growth of, 152–61
   evolution and mutation, 65–67
   gregariousness, 69, 97
   history, reconstruction of, 67
   individualism, 83
   kinship, 68–69
   labor, and income sharing, 73–78
   land clearing and use, 74–77
   land ownership and use, 66–67, 69, 71–73, 94–95
   leader, and settlement of, 66–67
   markets, 96–97
   migration, 71
   needy and indigent, care of, 84, 85
   oral tradition, 71, 79
   population, 69–71
   size, 69–71
   tenancy and, 101

traditions, *see also* specific subjects, 71, 78–81
transportation, 70
topography, 65, 70–71
unity, 68–69, 97
see also Communities; Peasants and peasant economy;
   specific subjects

Wages
   dual economy models, 326*ff.*, 352–53, 354–55
   expansion and contraction of agriculture, 108–10
   population and, 305–6, 322
   rice growing, 52, 53, 290–91
   unemployment and, 322
Wealth
   consumption ceiling and lack of marketing, 42
   redistribution, 116–17, 222
   social mechanisms for leveling, 35, 43–44
   technology and production of, 223
Weisblat, Abraham M., 37–41
West Africa
   cocoa, 244, 252
   export explosion, 100–1, 117
   technology, conservatism in, 101–2
Western Europe, expansion and contraction of
   agriculture, 107–10
Wharton, Clifton R., Jr., 12–20, 424–38, 455–67

Wheat
   Bolivia, 395
   Ecuador, 395
   Rockefeller Foundation program in Mexico, 391–92,
      438–52
Women
   community obligations, 44
   entrepreneurship, 31
   family economy control, 44
   labor role, 31, 52–53, 406–7
   land ownership and use, 30–32, 44

Yields
   differences, factors affecting, 442–52
   expected, and supply response, 235, 236, 238, 239,
      250
   land inputs and, 356
   specialization and, 273
   technology and, 439–44
   see also Production; Productivity; specific subjects
Youth
   clubs, 10, 428, 429
   progressivism, 46–47

Zamindars, 25
   Zulu, 143–50

For Product Safety Concerns and Information please contact our EU
representative GPSR@taylorandfrancis.com
Taylor & Francis Verlag GmbH, Kaufingerstraße 24, 80331 München, Germany